# Female Psychology:
## An Annotated
## Psychoanalytic
## Bibliography

# Female Psychology: An Annotated Psychoanalytic Bibliography

edited by

Eleanor Schuker

Nadine A. Levinson

 THE ANALYTIC PRESS

1991 Hillsdale, NJ London

Published by The Analytic Press.
365 Broadway
Hillsdale, NJ 07642

Set in Baskerville and Optima type by
Sally Ann Zegarelli, Long Branch, NJ 07740

Library of Congress Cataloging-in-Publication Data

Female psychology : an annotated psychoanalytic bibliography / edited
    by Eleanor Schuker, Nadine A. Levinson.
          p.   cm.
       ISBN 0-88163-087-X
       1. Women—Mental health—Abstracts.    2. Women—Psychology-
-Abstracts.  3. Psychoanalysis—Abstracts.    I. Schuker, Eleanor,
1941-   . II. Levinson, Nadine A., 1945-   .
       [DNLM: 1. Mental Disorders—abstracts.    2. Psychoanalytic Theory-
-abstracts.  3. Women—psychology—abstracts.    ZWM 460.5.W6 F329]
RC451.4.W6F45    1991
155.6'33—dc20
DLC
for Library of Congress                                                91-4562
                                                                            CIP

Printed in the United States of America
10  9  8  7  6  5  4  3  2  1

*This book is dedicated to our wonderful families:*
*our husbands, Drs. Alan Melowsky and Gerald Levinson,*
*and our children, Julie Melowsky, and Samantha and Jordan Levinson.*
*Without their patience, love, support, and sacrifice,*
*this book would not have been remotely possible.*

# About the Editors

**Eleanor Schuker, M.D.**, is a Training and Supervising Analyst at the Columbia University Center for Psychoanalytic Training and Research, where she teaches a course for candidates on Gender and Sexuality and leads a seminar for graduate analysts on the Psychology of Women. She is an Associate Clinical Professor of Psychiatry at the Columbia University College of Physicians and Surgeons. Dr. Schuker founded the St. Luke's Hospital Rape Intervention Program in 1977 and was the psychiatric consultant to the Women's Counseling Project at Columbia from 1974 to 1989. She has been a member of the American Psychoanalytic Association's Workshop on Issues for Women in Psychoanalytic Training since 1981. Dr. Schuker has written and lectured on gender-related issues and on female psychology.

**Nadine A. Levinson, D.D.S., F.A.C.D.**, is a member of the San Diego Psychoanalytic Society and Institute and Associate Clinical Professor of Psychiatry and Human Behavior, University of California, Irvine. Dr. Levinson combines the private practice of psychoanalysis and psychotherapy with consultative work as a liaison to dentistry. She has lectured widely on the psychological manifestations of dental disorders, TMJ and facial pain, and cosmetic dentistry and has organized many dental and medical seminars addressing dual-career conflicts in female and male professionals. A past member of the American Association of Women Dentists' Task Force on Women in Dentistry, she was the American Dental Associations's National spokesperson in 1986. Dr. Levinson currently gives psychoanalytic workshops on various aspects of female development, including eating disorders, pregnancy, and gender issues in treatment. She has been a member of the American Psychoanalytic Association's Workshop on Issues for Women in Psychoanalytic Training since 1986.

# Contents

## SECTION IV: CLINICAL CONCEPTS

## SECTION V: READING LISTS

# Acknowledgments

Like the beautiful early American patchwork quilts, sewn by many people working together, this book is the result of the labor of many individuals. Some analysts furnished just a few annotations; others prepared annotations of their own work; and still others worked on major portions of chapters or on complete chapters of their own. In all, more than 60 psychoanalysts from the COPE Workshop on Issues for Women in Psychoanalytic Education and from psychoanalytic institutes in the United States and elsewhere have contributed. Both women and men were invited to join this effort in their areas of competence, and the professional community responded with enthusiasm in order to further research on gender-related issues in psychoanalytic theory and practice. The initial phases of the project received financial assistance from the American Psychoanalytic Association. Helen Meyers and Barbara Deutsch, who chaired the COPE Workshop, graciously permitted us to use Workshop time to organize assignments and solicit editorial suggestions.

The chapters as initially projected have been condensed, expanded, and altered to reflect the evolution of our thinking about how best to organize such a vast amount of information and maintain consistency of style. Contributors who originally prepared a block of annotations scheduled for one section will often find these annotations revised in emphasis and placed in different sections; such rearrangement reflected ongoing changes in the format of the book. Obviously, these modifications have complicated attribution. The authors listed in the chapter headings exercised major responsibility for chapter format, composed many annotations, or contributed to the introductions. These primary authors may have also contributed minor portions of other chapters, although they are not specifically credited. The term "additional contributions" credits those people who provided more than eight annotations for the chapter. Those who prepared fewer than eight, who contributed their own annotations or bibliographic suggestions, or who did not have major responsibility for the introduction or editorial organization of a chapter can be found in the list of contributors. Also included among these contributors are those leading researchers in the area of female psychology who graciously took time to annotate their own work. Without the collaborative efforts so generously proffered by all, we would not have mustered the courage to undertake such a massive work. We have tried to credit accurately, but sincerely apologize for misattributions or errors of omission.

Our original reference lists were enhanced by a number of people who shared their personal bibliographical materials. We thank Judith Alpert, Virginia Davidson, Ruth Fischer, Marianne Goldberger, Martha Kirkpatrick, Muriel Laskin, Ruth F. Lax, Doryann Lebe, Helen Meyers, Frances Millican, Ruth Moulton, Carol Nadelson, Ethel Person, Lynn Whisnant Reiser, Miriam Tasini, and Elisabeth Young-Bruehl. Paul Mosher generously put at our disposal his own computer searches on specific topics as well as furnished materials from his book, *Title Key Word and Author Index to Psychoanalytic Journals, 1920-1986* (The American Psychoanalytic Association, 1987). Editorial suggestions at the Workshop came from numerous colleagues; in this connection we offer special thanks to Janine Chasseguet-Smirgel, Judith Chertoff, Virginia Clower, Mary Anne Delaney, Barbara Deutsch, Nancy Kulish, Lynn Whisnant Reiser, Barbara Rosenfeld, Brenda Solomon, Phyllis Tyson, and Joan J. Zilbach.

We have also benefited from editorial consultations on segments of the book from a number of colleagues. We especially appreciate the advice of Stanley Coen, Judith Chertoff, Kirsten Dahl, Gerald Fogel, Ruth Imber, Muriel Laskin, Ethel Person, Ellen Roundtree, and Elisabeth Young-Bruehl. A number of European analysts contributed annotations that we were unfortunately unable to utilize because of the ultimate decision to restrict the scope of the book. Janine Chasseguet-Smirgel and Madeleine Aderhold, librarian for the Societé Psychanalytique de Paris, solicited and compiled this material. Patricia Klein Frithiof collected annotations from the Swedish Psychoanalytic Society.

Alice Brand Bartlett and the Menninger Library staff helped with various tasks. Those included transcribing and scanning annotations not submitted on disk, conducting a supplementary literature search, and checking numerous references. We could FAX an obscure reference question to Ms. Bartlett and the correct answer would appear as if by magic the same day—instant technological gratification. Doris Parker, the librarian at the Columbia University Psychoanalytic Center for Training and Research, and Joyce Harding at the San Diego Psychoanalytic Society and Institute also helped in locating papers and providing some computer assistance in the initial stages of the project; Eva Quintero and Lesley Spencer provided reliable and loyal assistance.

Our special thanks to Stephen Schuker, who read each of the introductions, offered insightful comments, taught us about editorial scholarship, and provided encouragement for our labors. Eleanor Starke Kobrin and Paul Stepansky from The Analytic Press deserve our deep thanks. They welcomed our project from the beginning and made innumerable suggestions about form and content as we proceeded. Lastly, we warmly thank our families. They relinquished us with equanimity beyond the call of duty on many late nights and working weekends.

*Eleanor Schuker, M.D.*
*Nadine Levinson, D.D.S.*

# Contributors

**Anna Balas, M.D.**, Affiliated Staff, The New York Psychoanalytic Institute; Assistant Attending Psychiatrist, The New York Hospital-Cornell Medical Center.

**Samoan R. Barish, D.S.W.**, Faculty, California Institute for Clinical Social Work; Clinical Associate, Southern California Psychoanalytic Institute.

**Alice Brand Bartlett, M.L.S.**, Associate Dean, Karl Menninger School of Psychiatry and Mental Health Sciences, Menninger Clinic.

**Estelle P. Bender, M.D.**, Lecturer in Psychiatry and Staff Psychoanalyst, Columbia University Center for Psychoanalytic Training and Research.

**Jessica Benjamin, Ph.D.**, Faculty, New York University Postdoctoral Program in Psychotherapy and Psychoanalysis; Co-Founder, The New York Center for the Study of Psychoanalysis and Gender.

**Anni Bergman, Ph.D.**, Professor of Clinical Psychiatry, The City University of New York; Training and Supervising Analyst, The New York Freudian Society.

**Anne Bernstein, M.D.**, Clinical Professor of Psychiatry, Columbia University; Attending Psychiatrist, Presbyterian Hospital.

**Isidor Bernstein, M.D.**, Associate Clinical Professor of Psychiatry, New York University College of Medicine; Instructor, The New York Psychoanalytic Institute.

**Lesley K. Braasch, M.D.**, Training and Supervising Analyst, University of North Carolina-Duke University Psychoanalytic Education Program; Private Practice, Psychiatry and Psychoanalysis.

**Ada Burris, M.D.**, Senior Instructor, San Diego Psychoanalytic Society and Institute; Associate Clinical Professor of Psychiatry, School of Medicine, University of California at San Diego.

**Eve Caligor, M.D.**, Assistant Clinical Professor of Psychiatry, Columbia University; Faculty, Columbia University Center for Psychoanalytic Training and Research.

**Diane Hoye Campbell, M.D.**, Advanced Clinical Associate, San Diego Psychoanalytic Society and Institute; Assistant Clinical Professor of Psychiatry, School of Medicine, University of California at San Diego.

**Janine Chasseguet-Smirgel, Ph.D.**, Training Analyst, Paris Psychoanalytic Society; Professor, University College, London—Freud Memorial Chair, 1982-1983.

**Judith M. Chertoff, M.D.**, Teaching Analyst, Baltimore-Washington Institute for Psychoanalysis; Clinical Associate Professor of Psychiatry and Behavioral Sciences, George Washington University Medical Center.

**Nancy Chodorow, Ph.D.**, Professor of Sociology, University of California, Berkeley; Author, *The Reproduction of Mothering* and *Feminism and Psychoanalytic Theory*.

**Virginia L. Clower, M.D.**, Formerly Training and Supervising Analyst, Adult and Child Psychoanalysis, Washington Psychoanalytic Institute and New Orleans Psychoanalytic Institute; Clinical Professor of Psychiatry, Medical College of Virginia, Richmond.

**Sandra Kopit Cohen, M.D.**, Member, The New York Psychoanalytic Society; Clinical Instructor in Psychiatry, Cornell University Medical College.

**Calvin Colarusso, M.D.**, Clinical Professor of Psychiatry, School of Medicine, University of California at San Diego; Training and Supervising Analyst and Child Supervising Analyst, San Diego Psychoanalytic Society and Institute.

**Sally Comer, M.A., M.S.W.**, Raleigh, North Carolina.

**Virginia Davidson, M.D.**, Faculty, Houston-Galveston Psychoanalytic Institute; Clinical Associate Professor of Psychiatry, Baylor College of Medicine, Houston.

**Mary Anne Delaney, M.D.**, Faculty, Philadelphia Psychoanalytic Institute; Vice Chair, Department of Mental Health Sciences, Hahnemann University.

**Barbara Deutsch, M.D.**, Faculty, The Psychoanalytic Institute at New York University; Assistant Clinical Professor of Psychiatry at New York University.

**Denise Dorsey, M.D.**, Training and Supervising Analyst, New Orleans Psychoanalytic Institute; Clinical Associate Professor of Psychiatry, Louisiana State University Medical Center.

**Irene Fast, Ph.D.**, Professor of Psychology at the University of Michigan, Ann Arbor.

**Ruth S. Fischer, M.D.**, Training and Supervising Analyst, Philadelphia Psychoanalytic Institute; Faculty, University of Pennsylvania, School of Medicine.

**Jules Glenn, M.D.**, Clinical Professor of Psychiatry, New York University Medical Center; Training and Supervising Analyst, The New York Psychoanalytic Institute.

**Marianne Goldberger, M.D.**, Training and Supervising Analyst, The Psychoanalytic Institute at the New York University Medical Center; Clinical Assistant Professor of Psychiatry, Cornell University Medical College.

**Henry Haberfeld, M.D.**, Collaborating Psychoanalyst, Columbia University Center for Psychoanalytic Training and Research.

**Deena R. Harris, M.D.**, Assistant Clinical Professor of Psychiatry, Columbia University; Faculty, Columbia University Center for Psychoanalytic Training and Research.

**Thomas A. Hessling, M.D.**, Faculty, San Diego Psychoanalytic Society and Institute; Clinical Instructor of Psychiatry, School of Medicine, University of California at San Diego.

**Deanna Holtzman, Ph.D.**, Training and Supervising Analyst, Michigan Psychoanalytic Institute; Assistant Professor, Department of Psychiatry, Wayne State University.

**Ruth R. Imber, Ph.D.**, Training and Supervising Analyst, William Alanson White Psychoanalytic Institute.

**Lida Jeck, M.D.**, Consulting Associate, Department of Psychiatry, Duke University.

**Louise J. Kaplan, Ph.D.**, Co-editor, *American Imago*. Author, *Female Perversions: The Temptations of Emma Bovary*.

**Bonnie S. Kaufman, M.D.**, Assistant Clinical Professor of Psychiatry, Columbia University; Faculty, Columbia University Center for Psychoanalytic Training and Research.

**Judith S. Kestenberg, M.D.**, Clinical Professor of Psychiatry, New York University; Co-Project Director, International Study of Organized Persecution of Children.

**James A. Kleeman, M.D.**, Associate Clinical Professor of Psychiatry, Yale University.

**Cassandra M. Klyman, M.D.**, Assistant Clinical Professor of Psychiatry, Wayne State University College of Medicine, Michigan; Faculty, Michigan Psychoanalytic Institute.

**Nancy Kulish, Ph.D.**, Director of Psychology, Detroit Psychiatric Institute; Adjunct Clinical Professor, Department of Psychiatry, Wayne State Medical School.

**Susan Lazar, M.D.**, Clinical Professor of Psychiatry, George Washington University School of Medicine; Teaching Analyst, Washington Psychoanalytic Institute.

**Eva P. Lester, M.D.**, Professor of Psychiatry, McGill University Medical Center; Training and Supervising Analyst, Canadian Institute of Psychoanalysis.

**Howard Levine, M.D.**, Faculty, Boston Psychoanalytic Society and Institute; Private Practice, Psychoanalysis.

**Nadine A. Levinson, D.D.S.**, Faculty, San Diego Psychoanalytic Society and Institute. Associate Clinical Professor, Department of Psychiatry and Human Behavior, School of Medicine, University of California at Irvine.

**Nancy Livingston, M.D.**, Faculty, University of North Carolina-Duke University Psychoanalytic Education Program; Consulting Associate, Department of Psychiatry, Duke University Medical Center.

**Mary Ann Levy, M.D.**, Training and Supervising Analyst, Denver Institute for Psychoanalysis; Associate Clinical Professor of Psychiatry-Department of Psychiatry, University of Colorado Health Sciences Center.

**Diane Martinez, M.D.**, Clinical Assistant Professor, Department of Psychiatry, The University of Texas Health Science Center at San Antonio; Faculty, Houston-Galveston Psychoanalytic Institute.

**Joyce McDougall, D.Ed.**, Training Analyst, Paris Psychoanalytic Society; Member, Association for Psychoanalytic Medicine and The New York Freudian Society.

**Edith McNutt, M.D.**, Faculty, New York Psychoanalytic Institute; Clinical Assistant Professor of Psychiatry, The New York Hospital-Cornell Medical Center.

**Alan Melowsky, Ph.D.**, Adult Psychoanalytic Training Program, Postgraduate Center for Mental Health, New York City.

**Monica Michell, M.D.**, Clinical Instructor in Psychiatry, New York University School of Medicine; Candidate, The Psychoanalytic Institute at New York University.

**Ylana Miller, Ph.D., C.C.S.W.**, Instructor, Division of Social Work, Department of Psychiatry, Duke University; Adjunct Assistant Professor, Department of History, Duke University.

**Howard Millman, M.D.**, Assistant Clinical Professor of Psychiatry, Columbia University. Collaborating Psychoanalyst, Columbia University Center for Psychoanalytic Training and Research.

**Michael G. Moran, M.D.**, Associate Professor of Psychiatry, University of Colorado School of Medicine; Head, Adult Psychiatry, National Jewish Center for Immunology and Respiratory Medicine.

**Muriel Gold Morris, M.D.**, Clinical Associate Professor, New York University Post-Doctoral Program in Psychoanalysis; Faculty, Columbia University Center for Psychoanalytic Training and Research.

**Kathryn Ney, M.D., Ph.D.**, Clinical Assistant Professor of Psychiatry, University of North Carolina.

**Malkah T. Notman, M.D.**, Training and Supervising Psychoanalyst, Boston Psychoanalytic Institute; Clinical Professor of Psychiatry, Harvard Medical School.

**Wendy Olesker, Ph.D.**, Associate Clinical Professor, New York University Post-Doctoral Program in Psychoanalytic Psychotherapy; Assistant Clinical Professor of Psychiatry, Albert Einstein College of Medicine.

**Anna Ornstein, M.D.**, Professor of Child Psychiatry, Department of Child Psychiatry, University of Cincinnati.

**Nancy Perault, M.S.W., C.C.S.W.**, Chapel Hill, North Carolina.

**Ethel S. Person, M.D.**, Training and Supervising Analyst, Columbia University Center for Psychoanalytic Training and Research; Professor of Clinical Psychiatry, Columbia University.

**Henri Parens, M.D.**, Professor of Psychiatry, Jefferson Medical College; Training and Supervising Analyst, Philadelphia Psychoanalytic Institute.

**Dr. Dinora Pines**, Training Analyst, British Psychoanalytic Society; Editorial Board, *International Journal and Review of Psychoanalysis*.

**Ingrid Buhler Pisetsky, M.D.**, Instructor, University of North Carolina-Duke University Psychoanalytic Education Program; Associate Clinical Professor of Psychiatry, University of North Carolina, School of Medicine.

**Lynn Whisnant Reiser, M.D.**, Faculty, Western New England Psychoanalytic Institute; Director of Medical Studies, Associate Clinical Professor, Department of Psychiatry, Yale School of Medicine.

**Owen Renik, M.D.**, Training and Supervising Analyst, San Francisco Psychoanalytic Institute.

**Joyce L. Root, M.D.**, Assistant Clinical Professor of Psychiatry, Tufts University School of Medicine.

**Barbara R. Rosenfeld, M.D.**, Faculty, Columbia University Center for Psychoanalytic Training and Research; Assistant Clinical Professor of Psychiatry, Columbia University.

**Guy R. Russell, M.D.**, Clinical Associate, San Diego Psychoanalytic Society and Institute, Child and Adult Psychoanalytic Programs; Private Practice in Child Psychiatry.

**Eleanor Schuker, M.D.**, Training and Supervising Analyst, Columbia University Center for Psychoanalytic Training and Research; Associate Clinical Professor of Psychiatry, Columbia University.

**Sally Severino, M.D.**, Associate Professor Clinical Psychiatry, New York Hospital-Cornell Medical Center, Westchester Division; Collaborating Psychoanalyst, Columbia University Center for Psychoanalytic Training and Research.

**Mary H. Shwetz, M.D.**, Faculty, Seattle Institute for Psychoanalysis; Clinical Assistant Professor of Psychiatry and Behavioral Sciences, University of Washington.

**Donald Silver, M.D.**, Editor, *Psychoanalytic Inquiry*. Lecturer, Michigan Psychoanalytic Institute.

**Martin A. Silverman, M.D.**, Clinical Professor of Psychiatry, Training and Supervising Analyst, The Psychoanalytic Institute at New York University Medical Center; Associate Editor, *The Psychoanalytic Quarterly*.

**Brenda Clorfene Solomon, M.D.**, Faculty, Chicago Institute for Psychoanalysis; Clinical Assistant Professor or Psychiatry, Abraham Lincoln School of Medicine, University of Illinois.

**William G. Sommer, M.D.**, Director of Mental Health Division, Columbia University Health Service; Faculty, Columbia University Center for Psychoanalytic Training and Research.

**Michele Stewart, M.D.**, Senior Faculty, San Diego Psychoanalytic Society and Institute; Assistant Clinical Professor of Psychiatry, School of Medicine, University of California at San Diego.

**Alan Sugarman, Ph.D.**, Faculty, San Diego Psychoanalytic Society and Institute; Associate Clinical Professor of Psychiatry, School of Medicine, University of California at San Diego.

**Bluma Swerdloff, D.S.W.**, Special Lecturer in Psychiatry, Columbia University Center for Psychoanalytic Training and Research.

**Nettie Terestman, D.S.W.**, Assistant Clinical Professor, Columbia University Center for Psychoanalytic Training and Research.

**Phyllis Tyson, Ph.D.**, Training and Supervising Analyst and Child Supervising Analyst, San Diego Psychoanalytic Society and Institute; Associate Clinical Professor of Psychiatry, School of Medicine, University of California at San Diego.

**Sara A. Vogel, M.D.**, Training and Supervising Analyst, The Psychoanalytic Institute at New York University Medical Center; Assistant Clinical Professor of Psychiatry, New York University Medical Center.

**Priscilla Wald, Ph.D.**, Assistant Professor of English, Columbia University; Mellon Fellow, Stanford University.

**Sharon R. Weinstein, M.D.**, Instructor of Psychiatry, Harvard Medical School; Candidate, Boston Psychoanalytic Society and Institute.

**C. Philip Wilson, M.D.**, Senior Attending Psychiatrist, St. Luke's-Roosevelt Hospital Center, New York City; Assistant Clinical Professor of Psychiatry, Columbia University.

**Elisabeth Young-Bruehl, Ph.D.**, Professor of Letters, Wesleyan College; Author, *Anna Freud: A Biography* and *Freud on Women*.

**Joan J. Zilbach, M.D.**, Training and Supervising Analyst, Faculty, Boston Psychoanalytic Institute; Senior Faculty, Fielding Institute, Santa Barbara, California.

# Editors' Introduction

Until recently, few psychoanalytic institutes in the United States had developed specialized courses on female psychology. This lacuna became a matter of discussion in the mid-1980s at the COPE Workshop on Issues for Women in Psychoanalytic Education of the American Psychoanalytic Association. Some Workshop members reported the view of their curriculum committees that the psychoanalytic literature was insufficient to justify extensive exploration of this area.

One editor of this volume, Eleanor Schuker, expressed surprise and described her own course on Gender and Sexuality at the Columbia University Center for Psychoanalytic Training and Research. She offered to supply the group with sample reading lists, based on material she had collected over the years, and proposed to divide the papers into categories in order to demonstrate the richness of the existing literature and to help guide curriculum planning. Other members of the Workshop, which was chaired by Helen Meyers and Barbara Deutsch, suggested that we annotate these articles to provide more specific guidance. The other editor of this *Bibliography*, Nadine Levinson, promoted the use of computer technology and contributed her expertise in that field to search the literature systematically and to keep track of the resultant data. Without computer technology, the task of writing and organizing this book would have been impossible. A number of Workshop members generously agreed to annotate the initial list of books and articles. The list of entries expanded as we worked on each topic in depth. From these beginnings, *Female Psychology: An Annotated Psychoanalytic Bibliography* evolved.

The *Bibliography* in its final form provides annotations of more than 2,000 psychoanalytic books and articles, as well as books and articles from allied disciplines. It has developed into an encyclopedic text outlining psychoanalytic views of female psychology from Freud to the present and is designed to serve as a compendium for psychoanalytic researchers and students of female psychology. The *Bibliography* should prove useful for curriculum planning at psychoanalytic institutes, psychiatric residencies, and psychology and women's studies programs. Over 60 psychoanalysts, primarily from the COPE Workshop, have contributed to the book over the past five years. Letters from the American Psychoanalytic Association invited well-known psychoanalytic writers in the field to annotate their own work.

The book comprises four major sections. Section I, Historical Perspective, includes early psychoanalytic views and review commentaries and modern overviews. Section II, Developmental Perspective, considers vicissitudes of preoedipal and oedipal development, superego development, latency, adolescence, adulthood, and influences on gender differences. Specific adult developmental issues and challenges, such as menstruation, love, pregnancy, mothering, menopause, and achievement conflicts, are also reviewed. Other aspects of development, such as the influence of fathers and siblings are included here as well. Section III, Adult Female Sexuality, Character, and Psychopathology, covers normal and pathological aspects of female sexuality, disorders of gender identity, ego-dystonic homosexualities, paraphilias, consequences of sexual abuse, and issues in female character and character pathology, including writings on narcissism, masochism, and other character traits sometimes considered common to women. Section IV, Clinical Concepts, addresses issues involving transference and countertransference in the four patient-analyst gender combinations. A separate chapter assesses clinical issues and the pregnant analyst. Finally, Section V offers Suggested Reading Lists for various levels of academic and clinical study as well as a reading list of feminist/academic writings.

This volume provides a psychoanalytic perspective on female psychology and is designed to be comprehensive rather than exclusionary. Thus, articles with divergent theoretical viewpoints are included. The final date for incorporating the current literature was December 1, 1990, although we were fortunate enough to acquire advance copies of some additional papers in press. *Chicago Psychoanalytic Literature Index, Jourlit, Index to Psychoanalytic Study of the Child (Vol. 1-25), Index Medicus, Psychological Abstracts,* and Mosher's *Title Key Word and Author Index to Psychoanalytic Journals, 1920-1986* figured as our basic bibliographical sources. We did not include biographical material about early psychoanalysts, nor did we attempt a systematic coverage of the European psychoanalytic literature. The task of soliciting, selecting, translating, and evaluating literature written in other languages might have delayed publication until the Greek calends. With some exceptions, we therefore narrowed our purview to contributions in English, with a primary focus on contemporary American literature. In any comprehensive undertaking such as this, some valuable works are bound to be inadvertently omitted. We aimed toward exhaustive coverage, but accepted this as an ideal rather than as an achievable goal. We sincerely regret omissions and apologize to those authors whose contributions we overlooked. We have noted in the acknowledgments the many individuals who have contributed their time and effort to this compilation.

In each chapter of the *Bibliography* the annotations are arranged in chronological order, so that users can develop a frame of reference in relation to the ideas within that topic. The editors hope that the individual annotations will clarify the key concepts in each book, paper, or article. Papers that relate to more than one area are cross-referenced to facilitate scholarly review. In addition to the psychoanalytic literature itself, contributions from other fields that expand psychoanalytic thinking on particular subjects are included. Each chapter is introduced by a brief commentary. These introductions provide an overview of the chapter contents, note trends in the development of key ideas, and suggest areas where psychoanalytic thought remains incomplete.

In writing portions of the book and in coordinating the work of others, the editors have experienced the satisfaction of exploring a fascinating area. The editors hope that *Female Psychology: An Annotated Psychoanalytic Bibliography* will prove useful for both research and clinical study and will serve to highlight areas in need of future exploration. The book may also provide a bridge to scholars, teachers, and clinicians outside of psychoanalysis itself.

# Section I

# Historical Views

# Chapter 1

# Sigmund Freud and the Psychology of Women

Nadine Levinson, Eleanor Schuker,
Phyllis Tyson, Ruth Fischer

Freud's ideas on female psychology figure among his most controversial writings. Freud repeatedly expressed dissatisfaction with the speculative nature of his investigations in this domain. Yet, despite his unease, Freud never systematically reformulated his theories on female psychology as he did in other areas of psychoanalysis. He clung instead to early assumptions that emphasized psychosexuality and phallic monism. This tenacity probably stemmed from his wish to maintain internal coherence in his theory rather than from any sort of misogyny (Young-Bruehl, 1990).

Several writers (e.g., Gay, 1988) have also noted that Freud's work reflected patriarchal, culturally bound ideas commonly held about women in the Victorian era. Although Freud embraced women as equal colleagues in the psychoanalytic movement, and indeed saw female analysts as having strengths lacking in male analysts (Gay, 1988), his theories about women remained contradictory and at times may offend women with a modern sensibility. These theories reflected what Freud considered the immutable nature of women's psychic life, as it evolved developmentally from their reaction to discovery of the anatomical differences. Despite his cultural limitations, Freud's writings on female psychology illustrate the profundity of his clinical observations, the sophistication of his theoretical formulations, and the magnitude of his achievements.

This chapter surveys Freud's major contributions to the area of female psychology. It begins with this Introduction to provide a brief overview of the progression of some of Freud's ideas on female psychology. The chapter further comprises specific annotations of Freud's writings that are most relevant to female psychology. Many of Freud's basic psychoanalytic concepts are considered here as well, including his theories of sex differences, drive progression, infantile sexuality, the castration complex, the Oedipus complex, bisexuality, superego formation, and female character traits. Other concepts in the corpus of Freud's writings such as his emphasis on psychic structure and an inner representational world; his observations about the functions of affects, fantasy, and symbols; his views about the centrality of conflict; and his concept of developmental processes also bear on the study of female psychology. These broader concepts cannot all be surveyed here.

Female psychology was not a central focus for Freud. His ideas about female development are fragmentary and scattered throughout his works. He specifically addressed female psychology in only two papers, "Female Sexuality" (1931a), and "Femininity" (1933), and he composed these late in his career. In addition, several early books and papers, including *Studies on Hysteria* (1893), and "Fragments of An Analysis of Hysteria" (The Dora Case, 1905a), use clinical material about women patients serendipitously to illustrate general clinical and metapsychological points. Freud's subsequent major case histories mostly concern men. After the Dora Case (1905a), no female case reports appeared until 1915, when Freud published a case about a paranoid woman, followed by another report about a homosexual woman (1920).

In *Three Essays on the Theory of Sexuality*, Freud (1905b) proposed a comprehensive psychoanalytic theory on sexuality to serve as the theoretical and clinical basis for the development of both males and females. Freud viewed neurosis as originating from infantile sexuality. He developed a psychological theory of the mind to explain clinical phenomena, yet remained preoccupied with the biological underpinnings of the mind-body relationship. In contrast to the prevailing beliefs of his era, Freud asserted that strong psychological factors could influence the development of a sense of masculinity and femininity. He perceived that behavioral differences between the sexes did not correspond directly to biological (sexual) differences. But strangely, Freud concluded that masculinity was "natural" for both boys and girls, whereas femininity for girls was an acquired and purely psychological product. Freud held that girls and boys had parallel development from early childhood until puberty, when girls became aware of their vagina, and thus, their femininity. He maintained that masturbation for girls in early childhood involved only the clitoris, which he equated with a little penis and hence with masculinity.

Over the years, in each succeeding edition of the *Three Essays*, Freud made important changes pertaining to female psychology. Thus, he addressed the topics of penis envy (1915), pregenital infantile sexuality and libido theory (1915), the castration complex in women (1915, 1924), and masochism (1920, 1924). Freud first recognized different lines of development in boys and girls from his observations of the dissimilar forms taken by their beating fantasies (1919). From that point onward, Freud struggled openly with biological and psychological explanations in order to understand bisexuality and the contrasting developmental experiences of boys and girls.

In "The Dissolution of the Oedipus Complex," Freud (1924b) explicitly acknowledged that the course of sexual development differed for boys and for girls, and concluded that this difference was triggered by the recognition of anatomical sexual differences at about three years of age. In that paper, as well as in "Some Psychical Consequences of the Anatomical Distinction between the Sexes," Freud (1925) identified the recognition of anatomical differences by girls as a pivotal point in their development of femininity. He maintained that this recognition causes a sense of castration that leads to penis envy. The development of femininity then depended on girls' turning away from early masculinity and "masculine," clitoral masturbation. For boys, the fear of castration became the primary motive for dissolving the Oedipus complex, whereas for girls the castration complex initiated the Oedipus complex. The discovery of castration explained the shift in object from mother to father in girls. Freud emphasized the completeness of girls' turning to their fathers and the depth of hostility toward and rejection of their mothers. The original wish for a penis in girls became transformed into the wish for a baby from the father.

Freud's only two papers devoted exclusively to the topic of women, "Female Sexuality" (1931a) and "Femininity" (1933), largely extend the basic ideas contained within the (1924b) and (1925) papers and also respond to criticism of these earlier papers. Freud further attempted to explain girls' more difficult developmental pathway to femininity by the need to change both erotogenic zone and object. He proposed three lines of development that can proceed from the female castration complex: sexual inhibition/neurosis; the masculinity complex; and normal femininity. Importantly, Freud now acknowledged the significance for women of the preoedipal attachment to their mothers, which was exclusive, strong, and durable. He even reconsidered, if only briefly, the centrality of the Oedipus complex by suggesting the etiological significance of the preoedipal mother-daughter relationship as the nucleus of the female neuroses. He explained that the intense oedipal attachment to the father only replicated an earlier close tie to the mother. Both papers (1931a, 1933) struggle unsuccessfully to clarify why girls give up such a strong preoedipal attachment in order to become feminine. Freud concluded that hostility toward the mother is not a consequence of oedipal rivalry alone but also originates in the preceding preoedipal stages. He contended that the hostility and disappointment derived primarily from the mother's failure to give her daughter a penis. Later, in the "Outline," Freud (1940a) added another motivation to that of penis envy—early jealousy (or envy) of the mother linked to early identification with her—which guides the girl's entry into the oedipal phase and leads her to abandon her intensely loved mother. He explained that the consolation for the loss of an object may come from identification with that object. Thus, the daughter identifies with her mother, puts herself in her mother's place, and tries to take her mother's place with her father. The wish to have a baby from the father and also, perhaps, the wish for a penis, grow out of identification with the mother, who has both the baby and father's penis.

Freud also elaborated on the topic of bisexuality (1925, 1931a, 1933, 1940). He felt that girls' original masculinity could be explained by the assumption of universal innate bisexuality (1905b). Curiously, however, Freud could not bring himself to invoke the principle of bisexuality and concede primary femininity as a part of bisexuality in females. Rather, he viewed libido as masculine; therefore, femininity had to be derived from the discovery of anatomical differences, an identification with the mother, and a shift in libidinal object. Thus, in addition to contending that bisexuality for girls had a biological underpinning, Freud also perceived bisexuality as related to oscillations in girls' libidinal object-choice between father and mother and to the respective identifications made with each parent (1923a). He observed the complexity of the Oedipus complex with its positive and negative counterparts and thought that the positive oedipal phase in girls followed the so-called negative oedipal phase (1931a). These views contrasted with the approaches taken by Horney (1924) and Jones (1927), who contended that the phallic phase constituted a regression from oedipal disappointments and fears.

Freud's comments about superego formation and functioning in women (1923a, 1923b, 1924b, 1925, 1931a, 1933) have evoked strong criticism. Freud maintained that because women are more emotional and personal in their sense of justice, their superego structure must therefore be inferior. He asserted that girls must accept "castration" in order to develop an Oedipus complex and thus that they do not have sufficient motivation for giving up oedipal attachments or for identifying with authority and developing a strong superego. He concluded that girls are more dependent on external constructs like fear of loss of love.

Freud took into consideration different polarities of female character such as activity/passivity and masochism/sadism. In retrospect, his theories of activity and passivity appear forced; he has drawn particular criticism for his tendency to equate masculinity with activity and femininity with passivity. However, early in his writings, in "The Claims of Psychoanalysis to Scientific Interest" (1913), as well as in a significant (1915) footnote added to *Three Essays*, Freud emphasized that "an instinct is always active, even when it has a passive aim in view" (p. 219, 1905b). In 1933, Freud observed that passive sexual aims consistent with femininity are not the equivalent of passivity since the achievement of a passive aim can involve a good deal of activity. He felt, however, that early doll play in girls represented the wish to be active rather than the wish for a baby in identification with the mother.

Critics have also castigated Freud for his tendency to equate femininity with masochism (or pleasure in pain). Feminine masochism, in Freud's view, included the wish to be treated like a small, naughty child, with masochistic fantasies signifying castration, copulation, and giving birth. Later, Freud noted that the cultural suppression of women's aggression favored the development of masochism. Yet Freud was never satisfied with his formulations on the problems of masochism and, in his final observations on the subject, cautioned against equating masochism with femininity (1933).

Had Freud concluded what he had to say about "the riddle of femininity" by stressing the importance of girls' preoedipal tie to their mothers, in addition to the castration complex, fewer polemics would probably have arisen both within the psychoanalytic movement and outside of it. However, in "Analysis Terminable and Interminable," Freud (1937) reiterated his early view that women's castration complex was central to feminine personality development. It was unanalyzable, he claimed, and thus was the biological bedrock of women's sexuality. In short, almost to the end, Freud remained caught up with 19th-century biological theorizing. His view that "anatomy is destiny," belied his own clinical contributions, in particular his exploration of the meanings of developmental data such as penis envy and its functioning as a screen for early losses and deprivations. Finally, in "An Outline of Psychoanalysis," Freud (1940a) again expressed his bewilderment about the "riddle of femininity." That posthumously published essay serves as an example of both his tenacity and his flexibility. He held strongly to his early convictions about female psychology, while he also wrestled with and revised areas that remained unclear within his theoretical constructs, such as girls' preoedipal ties to their mothers.

In summary, Freud's ideas about female development were drawn primarily from transferences and reconstructions made in the course of the analyses of adults. Freud made few systematic developmental observations of children. He frequently confessed that he remained perplexed about female development. Judged from our current vantage point, his perplexity seems to be based more on intrapsychic conflicts, cultural blind spots, and prejudices than on lack of developmental information. According to Thompson (1942), Gay (1988), and Young-Bruehl (1990), Freud's views were largely determined by his Victorian background and by his personal relationships with Victorian and post-Victorian women, among them his mother, sisters, wife, sister-in-law, daughter, and female colleagues. Although Freud had no difficulty recognizing that women were sexual and sensual like men, he shared the unspoken assumptions of his era about women, which limited his clinical and theoretical framework.

In addition to cultural factors, what other considerations might account for Freud's limited interest in modifying his theories about the psychology and development of women? While we may not be able to answer this question definitively, we observe that Freud based his theory of female sexuality on a misunderstanding of female infantile masturbation. As noted earlier, Freud believed that all libido is masculine and therefore that infantile female masturbation must be masculine. He then erroneously generalized his theories of female sexuality and female masturbation to the entirety of female psychology and character. Although Freud's (1905b) illumination of the importance of infantile masturbation and infantile sexuality to personality development was significant, his understanding of female masturbation was flawed and led to false conclusions about female sexuality and development.

Undoubtedly, Freud's reluctance to modify his theories about women also reflected a desire for theoretical consistency and a wish to maintain some basic assumptions of libido theory in the context of dissension within the psychoanalytic movement (see Fliegel 1973, 1986 for a summary). Finally, Freud felt under pressure to publish quickly because of the life-threatening nature of his oral cancer. Nevertheless, Freud felt dissatisfied with his knowledge of female development and admitted that his understanding of the sexual life of women remained incomplete. He anticipated further collaboration by his colleagues and called upon them to confirm or refute his hypotheses on the mysteries of early feminine development and adult female sexuality—in his own words, the "dark continent (1925)." He stated (1931a) that knowledge of female psychology must await the findings of female analysts who had first-hand experience with maternal transferences. This statement implies an unstated hypothesis about cross-gender transferences and the nature of the maternal transference with a male analyst, yet it may also reflect an aging Freud whose interest had become more theoretical than clinical.

One of Freud's final statements on the subject of female psychology contains both an apology and a challenge to future researchers. "That is all I have to say to you about femininity. It is certainly incomplete and fragmentary and does not always sound friendly. . . . If you want to know more about femininity, inquire from your own experiences of life, or turn to the poets, or wait until science can give you deeper and more coherent information" (1933, p. 135). *Female Psychology: An Annotated Psychoanalytic*

*Bibliography* hopes to illustrate how psychoanalytic researchers, both past and present, have drawn on their clinical and personal experiences to shed light on the psychology of women, following profoundly in the spirit of Freud. (N.L., P.T., and E.S.)

Freud, Sigmund (1893-1895). Studies on hysteria II. Case Histories. *Standard Edition*, 2:19-181. London: Hogarth Press, 1953.

Freud presents and discusses the case histories of four female patients, Frau Emmy von N., Miss Lucy R., Katharina, and Fraulein Elizabeth von R. These cases demonstrate the origin and dynamics of hysteria which results from conflicts over sexuality. [See also Chapter 24.]

Freud, Sigmund (1894). The neuro-psychoses of defense. *Standard Edition*, 3:43-61. London: Hogarth Press, 1953.

[See Chapter 20 for annotation.]

Freud, Sigmund (1896a). Further remarks on the neuro-psychoses of defense. *Standard Edition*, 3:159-185. London: Hogarth Press, 1953.

[See Chapters 20 and 24 for annotations.]

Freud, Sigmund (1896b). The aetiology of hysteria. *Standard Edition*, 3:189-221. London: Hogarth Press, 1953.

[See Chapter 20 for annotation.]

Freud, Sigmund (1899). Extracts from the Fliess papers, Letter 105. *Standard Edition*, 1:278. London: Hogarth Press, 1953.

[See Chapter 23 for annotation.]

Freud, Sigmund (1900). Interpretation of dreams. *Standard Edition*, 4:250-255. London: Hogarth Press, 1953.

[See Chapter 17 for annotation.]

Freud, Sigmund (1905a). Fragment of an analysis of a case of hysteria. *Standard Edition*, 7:3-122. London: Hogarth Press, 1953.

This case of Dora, an adolescent girl, is presented by Freud primarily for the purpose of further illustrating his dream theory and methodology. The case study also illuminates the universality of homosexual masculine trends in female hysterics, inasmuch as Dora unconsciously desired her father's mistress. Freud states that Frau K. may have been a stand-in for her governess. In a postscript, Freud notes that the case ended because he had neglected to explore the transference; he alludes to the role of the maternal transference.

**Freud, Sigmund (1905b). Three essays on the theory of sexuality. *Standard Edition*, 7:125-243. London: Hogarth Press, 1953.**

Among the most influential of Freud's contributions, this paper serves as a theoretical and clinical basis for his later theories of female sexuality and character development. Modifications added in 1910, 1915, 1920, and 1924 reflect his changing views about infantile sexuality and its impact on female development. The concepts presented in these pivotal emendations include the instinct for knowledge (1915), penis envy (1915), pregenital infantile sexuality and libido theory (1915), the castration complex (1915, 1924), and masochism (1920, 1924). In the "Three Essays," Freud postulates infantile sexuality as the centerpiece in the etiology of the psychoneuroses and in normal human development. The paper is divided into three sections: 1) sexual aberrations, 2) infantile sexuality, and 3) the transformation of puberty.

In section 1, Freud discusses the perversions and deviations in aim and object. Sexual instinct, the component instincts, and erotogenic zones are described. Psychical hermaphroditism and bisexuality are proposed as a partial explanatory principle for perversion and inversion. Normal childhood and its polymorphously perverse character are described.

In section 2, Freud discusses various aspects of infantile sexuality, including childhood amnesia, sexual latency, and the progression of infantile sexuality from the oral to the anal to the genital erotogenic zones. Freud defines the characteristics of the instinctual drive as having an origin from a body source, having an object, and having an aim. In a prototypic example of the instinctual drives, he describes the oral instinctual drive as originating from a vital somatic organ, the mouth; as having no sexual object (autoerotic); and as having a sexual aim that derives pleasure from stimulation of the mouth through sucking. Freud notes three stages of masturbation for boys and girls: early infancy, childhood (from two to four years), and puberty. Usually during the second stage children are confronted by the riddle of where babies come from and recognize the anatomical sexual differences. In this section, in a 1915 addition, Freud notes the idea that the male sexual organ is the only one recognized by children of either sex. Accordingly, boys fear castration, which Freud labels the castration complex. Boys resort to denial and eventually resolve these fantasies after severe internal struggle. Girls do not deny the anatomical differences but feel that something is missing, that they are castrated, and they wish they were boys (penis envy). Later, in a 1920 footnote, Freud identifies the castration complex in girls as well, although first discussing the castration complex only in relation to boys in "The Sexual Theories of Children" (1908). Finally, in an important 1924 addition to the "Three Essays," he proposes a third phase of pregenital organization, the phallic phase. He asserts that the existence of the vagina and femininity are virtually unknown until puberty.

In the third section, Freud outlines as a primary task of puberty the transformation of the sexual instinct from one that is predominantly autoerotic to one that requires a sexual object. The new sexual aim subsumes all the component instincts and subordinates them to the primacy of the genital. According to his libido theory, all libido is "invariably and necessarily of a masculine nature, whether it occurs in men or in women . . ." (p. 219). The instinct is always active, although its aim can be passive. Freud asserts that the difference between male and female development commences after puberty and that development is more difficult for girls. Clitoral (masculine) sexuality in girls must be repressed and shifted to the vagina. Hence, the necessary zone change and wave of repression predispose women to neurosis. Frigidity reflects an infantile fixation of libido. [See also Chapters 20 and 24.]

Freud, Sigmund (1908a). Hysterical fantasies and their relation to bisexuality. *Standard Edition*, 9:157-166. London: Hogarth Press, 1953.

The relationship between unconscious fantasies and hysterical symptoms are furthered discussed in this article. Freud observes that hysterical symptoms reflect a bisexual nature that express both a masculine sexual fantasy and a feminine sexual fantasy. This observation in the analyses of neurotics confirms his view of the postulated existence of innate bisexuality. [See also Chapter 20.]

Freud, Sigmund (1908b). Character and anal erotism. *Standard Edition*, 9:169-175. London: Hogarth Press, 1953.

[See Chapter 20 for annotation.]

Freud, Sigmund (1908c). Civilized sexual morality and modern nervousness. *Standard Edition*, 9:179-204. London: Hogarth Press, 1953.

[See Chapters 13 and 20 for annotations.]

Freud, Sigmund (1908d). On the sexual theories of children. *Standard Edition*, 9:207-226. London: Hogarth Press, 1953.

Freud elaborates on the sexual theories of children having to do with the riddle of where babies come from and which are often prompted by the birth of a younger sibling. Male children's sexual theories are based on defensive fantasy formations, including theories of oral impregnation, anal birth, sadistic coitus, and the fantasy of the woman with a penis. This is the first time that Freud mentions the importance of possession of the penis to both boys and girls. Penis envy emerges in girls who want the penis they do not have. Girls feel unfairly treated and deficient and wish they had a penis. The castration complex in boys, with accompanying castration anxiety, results in the fantasy of the woman with a penis. Both boys and girls are ignorant of the existence of the vagina and thus think that the baby is evacuated like a stool. According to Freud, even though boys experience impulses to penetrate, their need for denial obscures any such natural conclusion.

Freud, Sigmund (1912a). Contributions to a discussion of masturbation. *Standard Edition*, 12:241-254. London: Hogarth Press, 1953.

Freud reviews what was known at the time about masturbation and emphasizes the developmental stages of masturbation, the return of masturbation during therapy, and the role of fantasy and unconscious guilt. He questions the potentially injurious consequences of masturbation and describes the etiologic relationship of masturbation to actual neurosis and psychoneurosis. Freud notes that it is regrettable that little is known about female masturbation and calls for further study of it.

Freud, Sigmund (1912b). On the universal tendency to debasement in the sphere of love. *Standard Edition*, 11:178-190. London: Hogarth Press, 1953.

[See Chapter 13 for annotation.]

Freud, Sigmund (1913). The disposition to obsessional neurosis: A contribution to the problem of choice of neurosis. *Standard Edition*, 12:313-326. London: Hogarth Press, 1953.

[See Chapter 20 for annotation.]

Freud, Sigmund (1914). On narcissism: An introduction. *Standard Edition*, 14:69-102. London: Hogarth Press, 1959.

Although he does not discuss female psychology specifically, Freud introduces the concept of narcissism and how it brings a deeper understanding of psychosis, love relationships, and the relationship of penis envy to narcissistic vulnerability and feminine identity. [See also Chapters 13 and 22.]

Freud, Sigmund (1915a). A case of paranoia running counter to the psychoanalytic theory of the disease. *Standard Edition*, 14:262-272. London: Hogarth Press, 1953.

This case history of a woman illustrates Freud's thesis about the relationship between paranoia and homosexuality by tracing the various defenses of displacement, projection, and identification the woman uses both to protect against and to express her strong attachment to her mother. Freud emphasizes that the object attachment is not to the real mother, but to the earliest image of her. Thus he highlights the importance of object relations (and the tie to the mother), neurotic conflict, and homosexuality.

Freud, Sigmund (1915b). Instincts and their vicissitudes. *Standard Edition*, 14:111-140. London: Hogarth Press, 1953.

[See Chapter 13 for annotation.]

Freud, Sigmund (1915c) Observations on transference-love. *Standard Edition*, 12:158-171. London: Hogarth Press, 1953.

[See Chapter 25 for annotation.]

Freud, Sigmund (1916). Some character types met with in psychoanalytic work. *Standard Edition*, 14:310-333. London: Hogarth Press, 1953.

This paper is an early reference to a woman's need to be special or an exception because narcissistic injury has led to resentment toward her mother for having damaged her by not giving her a penis. Success neuroses in women are also described. [See also Chapter 12.]

Freud, Sigmund (1916-1917). Introductory lectures. *Standard Edition*, 16:333-334. London: Hogarth Press, 1953.

[See Chapter 17 for annotation.]

Freud, Sigmund (1917). On transformation of instinct as exemplified in anal eroticism. *Standard Edition*, 17:126-133. London: Hogarth Press, 1953.

Freud first postulates that the wish for a baby is a secondary compromise formation. He reiterates that fantasies about feces, penis, and baby are all interchangeable in the unconscious. Freud asserts that for girls the discovery of the penis is accompanied by envy and a transformation of anal instinctual interests. The wish to have a baby is a symbolic substitute for the wish for a penis or for a man, who possesses a penis. In addition, the baby represents early anal interests.

Freud, Sigmund (1918a). An infantile neurosis. *Standard Edition*, 17:106. London: Hogarth Press, 1953.

[See Chapter 23 for annotation.]

Freud, Sigmund (1918b). The taboo of virginity. *Standard Edition*, 11:192-208. London: Hogarth Press, 1953.

The primitive motives for the taboo of virginity and defloration that persist in female frigidity are explored. Freud observes that in primitive societies defloration may be performed outside marriage and before the first marital sexual experience, whereas in modern civilization first coitus is encouraged within the marriage in order to increase the likelihood of sexual attachment of the woman to her first lover. Freud explains the taboo of virginity as related to men's fear of blood, fear of any new first experience (including the first act of intercourse), a generalized dread of women and all aspects of their sexuality, and fear of castration by the woman, now hostile as a result of being deflowered by him. Women's hostility stems from their pain, penis envy and the castration complex, and narcissistic injury because the loss of virginity produces a feeling of sexual devaluation and causes dissatisfaction and disappointment. This hostility is frequently manifested by sexual inhibition or frigidity. Freud postulates that frigidity also may be caused by fixation to the father. Freud concludes that defloration not only causes sexual bondage of women, but also unleashes archaic hostility, which can be manifested by erotic inhibition. The taboo of virginity protects men from women's hostility.

Freud, Sigmund (1919). A child is being beaten. *Standard Edition*, 17:177-204. London: Hogarth Press, 1953.

This paper is important historically as Freud now proposes that masochism, derived from sexual excitation that is expressed in a beating fantasy, provides a way for both boys and girls to remain guilt free by disguising incestuous wishes for the father. In contradiction to his previous idea, he notes that these fantasies take a different form in males and females. [See also Chapter 21.]

Freud, Sigmund (1920). The psychogenesis of a case of homosexuality in a woman. *Standard Edition*, 18:146-172. London: Hogarth Press, 1953.

Female homosexuality is explored in the analysis of an 18-year-old woman. The importance of the little girl's preoedipal attachment to her mother and the mother's influence on the girl's erotic life, gender identity, and object choice is demonstrated. Freud states that constitutional and environmental factors alike are important in determining homosexual object choice. He suggests that a female therapist might have had better access to the maternal transference. [See also Chapter 19.]

Freud, Sigmund (1923a). The ego and the id. *Standard Edition*, 19:3-66. London: Hogarth Press, 1953.

In the third section of the text, Freud struggles with his concept of infantile bisexuality and its impact on the formation, resolution, and subsequent outcome of the Oedipus complex. He views both sexes as developing analogously. The Oedipus complex consists of two valences, one positive (made up of love of the opposite-sex parent and identification with the same-sex parent) and the other negative (made up of love of the same-sex parent and identification with the opposite-sex parent). The dissolution of the Oedipus complex consolidates a girl's femininity through identification with her mother. Freud observed that in some cases, after abandoning her father as a love-object, a girl identifies with him instead. The relative strength of the masculine and feminine sexual positions ultimately determine the final maternal or paternal identification.

Freud, Sigmund (1923b). The infantile genital organization: An interpolation into the theory of sexuality. *Standard Edition*, 19:140-153. London: Hogarth Press, 1953.

The infantile genital phase of development is elaborated by Freud in this paper which amends his 1905 work, "Three Essays on The Theory of Sexuality." He views infantile genital organization and adult genital organization as similar in object choice. The main difference is that pregenital sexual organization is phallic and male, whereas adult sexuality is both male and female. Freud proposes that in infancy, neither boys nor girls believe there are two organs, although in this paper he freely admits that he knows very little about the female developmental process. He continues, however, to emphasize that pregenital sexual development for girls is active, male, and phallic. The castration complex in boys leads to the belief that the mother possesses a penis. The idea of the castrated woman results in depreciation and horror of women or a disposition to homosexuality. Boys only gradually accept that all women are without a penis. At

puberty, the male and female polarity is completed with the discovery of
the vagina. The wish for a baby is substituted for the wish for a penis,
passivity replaces activity; and femininity is finally established. At the genital
phase, three antithetic male-female transformations arise concerning choice
of object, activity and passivity, and having a male phallus or being
castrated. The remainder of the paper describes early sexual development
for little boys, with interspersed but important remarks about female
development that serve as a basis for his subsequent papers on femininity.

Freud, Sigmund (1924a). The economic problem of masochism. *Standard
Edition*, 19:157-172. London: Hogarth Press, 1961.

Freud describes three types of masochism, one being feminine
masochism, which he equates with a passive feminine wish. [See also
Chapter 21.]

Freud, Sigmund (1924b). The dissolution of the Oedipus complex.
*Standard Edition*, 19:172-179. London: Hogarth Press, 1953.

This is the first paper in which Freud notes that the course of the
development of sexuality is different for boys and for girls. The different
developmental sequences in boys and girls from the phallic phase to the
oedipal complex, castration anxiety, superego formation, and latency are
discussed. Freud regards pregenital sexual organization as male for boys
and girls alike. He contends that girls are not aware of the vagina and thus
are not aware of their femininity until puberty. Although admitting his
knowledge is fragmentary and full of gaps, he considers the castration
complex to be of central importance to girls and their phallic organization.
Girls recognize that they have an inferior penis (the clitoris) or that they
have been castrated (castration complex). Little girls accept castration,
whereas boys fear it. Thus, for girls, there is less motivation for developing
a superego and for giving up their infantile sexual organization. Freud
states that girls are more dependent than boys on such external controls as
fear of loss of love, intimidation, and education. Girls develop a feminine
attitude and turn to father; they wish for his penis and a baby as compensation for their inferior genital.

Freud, Sigmund (1925). Some psychical consequences of the anatomical
distinction between the sexes. *Standard Edition*, 19:243-258. London:
Hogarth Press, 1953.

Freud reviews his earlier findings about the differences in development
between girls and boys. Again, Freud elaborates the role of the castration
complex as a motive in the dissolution of the Oedipus complex for the boy
and its part in the initiation of the Oedipus complex for the girl. During

the preoedipal period, little girls and little boys alike are attached to the mother. At the phallic phase, little girls have one extra task: they must shift libidinal objects from mother to father. Freud postulates that recognition of the anatomical differences accounts for the shift and ushers in the castration complex and anger for not having a penis. Freud proposes several psychic consequences of penis envy, which include: 1) narcissistic vulnerability and a compensatory masculine identification to offset the state of inferiority; 2) displacement of envy to the character trait of jealousy, which is a relic of phallic masturbation; 3) loosening of the object tie to the mother; and 4) massive repression of the girls' masculine sexuality. Girls can accept their state of castration, but, longing to have a penis, they take the father as the new love object. The wish for a baby replaces the wish for a penis. The Oedipus complex is primary in boys and secondary in girls, because the attachment to the father is only the consequence of penis envy. Freud emphasizes the significance of repression of the girl's masculine sexuality as an important mechanism in the development of her femininity. This developmental difference, based on the observation of the anatomical differences, results in a weaker formation of the superego because girls have no threat of castration. This paper is the first one in which Freud alludes to the centrality of girls' preoedipal attachment to mother. Freud reiterates the tentativeness of his findings and the need for verification. The editor's note contains a useful survey of Freud's previous statements about female psychology.

Freud, Sigmund (1926). Inhibitions, symptoms and anxiety. *Standard Edition*, 20:77-174. London: Hogarth Press, 1953.

In Freud's new theory of signal anxiety, he proposes a developmental schema for internal dangers or fears that change with each period of life. Freud notes that castration anxiety is the primary motivating force for signal anxiety and defense which leads to neuroses in men. In women, the danger situation of loss of love of the object plays the important role in neurosogenesis. [See also Chapter 20.]

Freud, Sigmund (1931a). Female sexuality. *Standard Edition*, 21:223-243. London: Hogarth Press, 1953.

Freud elaborates on his 1925 paper, discussing the two extra tasks that girls have: changing libidinal objects from mother to father and changing their sexual zone and aim. However, he emphasizes and details the importance of the intensity or long duration of a girl's preoedipal relationship with her mother. He feels that an intense father attachment only reflects an earlier exclusive phase of attachment to the mother. Freud momentarily reconsiders the centrality of the oedipal phase by remarking, "it would seem as though we must retract the universality of the thesis that the Oedipus complex is the nucleus of the neuroses" (p. 226). He postulates a negative oedipal phase that precedes the positive oedipal phase for girls as representative of girls' bisexuality. Paranoia and hysteria are proposed to result from fixations at this early phase of development.

Freud repeats many of his statements about girls' sexual life, which begins with a masculine phase and then shifts to a feminine one. As a consequence of the castration complex, three lines of development are possible for women: 1) sexual repulsion, repression, and inhibition, 2) a clinging to the masculinity complex; and 3) normal femininity, taking father as their libidinal object. He elaborates on the many preoedipal factors to account for girls' hostility towards mother and their turning to father. Among these factors are sibling rivalry; infantile love, which is eventually disappointed and unsatisfied; and hostility derived from the phallic phase and the castration complex. The girl is angry at her mother, who fails to give her daughter a penis, who forbids masturbation, and who thus impedes the girl's masturbatory pleasures. However, Freud states that a girl's attachment to her mother is also strongly ambivalent. Finally, new and important ideas are presented in this paper on active and passive sexual aims for girls. The wishes are at first passive and then become active as a way of achieving mastery of the external world. Freud proposes that active sexual wishes of the phallic stage are the same for boys and girls. The phallic stage, with the change in object, encompasses a cessation of clitoral masturbatory activity, a decrease in active sexual trends, a repression of previous masculinity, and a rise of passive aims, opening the developmental path to femininity. The final section of this paper surveys and critiques findings by other psychoanalysts such as Abraham, Lampl-de Groot, Deutsch, Horney, Jones, and Klein.

Freud, Sigmund (1931b). Libidinal types. *Standard Edition*, 21:216-220. London: Hogarth Press, 1953.

[See Chapter 20 for annotation.]

Freud, Sigmund (1933). Femininity. *Standard Edition*, 22:112-135. London: Hogarth Press, 1953.

Freud's previous work on femininity is reviewed in this paper, with further emphasis on the importance of a girl's preoedipal affectionate attachment to her mother and its decisive effect on subsequent development. Freud begins by highlighting the importance of bisexuality as characteristic of both men and women. He struggles with definitions for masculine and feminine, noting that the qualities of masculine/aggressive and feminine/passive are not always congruent. Importantly, Freud observes that passive sexual aims consistent with femininity are not the same thing as passivity per se, since "to achieve a passive aim may call for a large amount of activity" (p. 115). He believes that the suppression of women's aggression favors masochism in women.

In trying to solve the riddle of femininity, Freud repeats his early formulations that femininity develops from a pregenital masculine phase. During the phallic phase, girls must go through two separate steps and change both their libidinal object from mother to father as well as their erotogenic zone from clitoris to vagina. The last task cannot be completed until puberty. Freud refers to the girl's strong pregenital attachment to her mother, which culminates at the phallic phase with the bisexual wish to both bear mother's child and give mother a child. The fear of seduction by the father originates from this early relationship with the seductive, powerful mother. Freud raises the question "What brings this to an end?" and proposes that the discovery of the anatomical differences between men and women and the sight of the male genital instigates the castration complex and penis envy. The girl's future development can follow any of three possible pathways: 1) sexual inhibition/neurosis, 2) masculinity complex, or 3) normal femininity.

In the development of normal femininity, having discovered that they do not possess a penis, girls give up clitoral masturbation and phallic activity, suffer narcissistic injury, and finally repudiate their love for mother. Out of disappointment, they become feminine by turning to father for the penis. The wish for a baby is a substitute for the lost penis. Freud emphasizes that early doll play does not represent the wish for a baby, but rather, the wish to be active. For boys, the castration complex ends the oedipal complex, whereas for girls, there is no motive for its resolution. Freud concludes that the female superego never attains the strength or independence of the male's.

Finally, Freud considers such aspects of feminine character as narcissism, vanity, sense of justice, lack of capacity for sublimation, predominance of envy, and psychical rigidity. He again reiterates the fragmentary nature of his work.

**Freud, Sigmund (1937). Analysis terminable and interminable. *Standard Edition*, 23:211-253. London: Hogarth Press, 1953.**

In Section VIII of this paper, Freud discusses the two most difficult themes to analyze: penis envy in women and passive/feminine attitude in men. Freud emphasizes the "repudiation of femininity" as central in both sexes through the phallic phase. A girl's masculinity complex and the wish for a penis must then be repressed and converted into the wish for a baby, or there will be a constriction of her femininity. Freud seems to disregard his previous emphasis on the importance of the maternal attachment during the preoedipal phase. He contends that the woman's castration complex is the unanalyzable and biological bedrock of her sexuality. [See also Chapter 20.]

Freud, Sigmund (1940a). An outline of psycho-analysis. *Standard Edition*, 23:141-207. London: Hogarth Press, 1953.

Freud outlines and reviews his previous theoretical and clinical principles of psychoanalysis. Section III, "The Development of the Sexual Function," and Section VII, "The Psychoanalytic Work," clearly state his view of libidinal development and its impact on male and female sexuality. In the preoedipal period, development in the oral, anal, and phallic phases is similar. Both sexes universally accept a penis in both sexes until the phallic phase. The first divergence is marked by the entry into, and dissolution of the oedipal phase. Freud emphasizes the role of the castration complex in girls' sexual life, character, and superego formation. It is not until the fourth phase that genital sexual organization is completed. In Section VII, Freud elaborates on the difference in development between males and females at the time of the oedipal phase, yet struggles to explain psychic bisexuality as derived from biology. He notes that equating active with masculine and passive with feminine is inadequate. In describing the child's early development, Freud traces libidinal development for each sex, again noting the castration complex as central to the development of masculine and feminine sexuality. In contrast to boys, girls do not fear the loss of the penis, but react with envy for not having received one. During the phallic phase they masturbate like boys, but feel inferior for having a "stunted penis" and renounce their sexuality. Freud reiterates his previous papers on the three outcomes to the girl's penis envy: 1) homosexuality with marked masculine traits, 2) abandonment of the mother and the substitute of the father as an object of love, or 3) sexual inhibition. In discussing the abandonment of mother, Freud delineates identification as the mechanism by which girls replace their attachment to mother. Resenting mother for not giving them a penis, girls turn to father and identify with mother to ward off the loss. Their wishes for a baby from father replaces the wish for a penis. For boys, the threat of loss of the penis ends the Oedipus complex, whereas for girls it is the lack of a penis or the castration complex that leads to the Oedipus complex. Freud again states that the mental structure least accessible to influence in women is the wish for a penis, whereas in men it is their feminine attitude toward their own sex.

Freud, Sigmund (1940b). Splitting of the ego in the process of defense. *Standard Edition*, 23:273-278. London: Hogarth Press, 1953.

[See Chapter 19 for annotation.]

# Chapter 2

# Early Psychoanalytic Views

Lynn Whisnant Reiser, with Nadine Levinson

This chapter includes papers by early psychoanalysts other than Freud. It does not aim to be exhaustive, nor does it select papers on the basis of merit in the light of current views of the psychology of women. Rather, it includes the early papers on this subject that continue to be cited often, whether with praise or as the subject of controversy, and that have provided the basis for more recent work on this topic. Only articles that directly address the psychology of women are listed.

The reader should keep in mind that many of these papers were presented at meetings several years before they were published. Because the psychoanalytic community at that time was so small and oral presentations and personal correspondence among analysts were the prevailing means of communication, an unpublished paper could have significant impact. These papers are listed chronologically by date published, even though they may have been presented earlier. They constitute a developing dialogue (and debate) that is best comprehended when the articles are placed in context. Freud's articles on the psychology of women, which have been included separately in chapter 1 for the convenience of the reader, form an integral part of this series. With some exceptions, papers through 1940 are included here. The articles are cited in English except when the complete text is not available in translation. (L.W.R.)

Abraham, Karl (1916). The first pregenital stage of the libido. In: *Selected Papers*. New York: Brunner/Mazel, 1979, pp. 248-279.

[See Chapter 23 for annotation.]

Andreas-Salomé, Lou (1916). "Anal" und "Sexual." *Imago*, 4:429-473.

Freud cites this article first in 1917 and then again, in a 1920 footnote in "The Three Essays" (1905) as important to his understanding of the psychology of women and the wish for a baby.

Sachs, Hanns (1920). The wish to be a man. *Int. J. Psycho-Anal.*, 6:262-267.

This is a case report of a young woman with the symptoms of handbiting and a fear of kissing. At adolescence, upon viewing her own menstrual blood, expressed the primitive fantasy that her penis had been bitten off. Sachs links the patient's terror of her menarche to her earliest experiences of penis envy and the wish to be a man, and connects this with her need for punishment and masturbatory guilt. He discusses these conflicts in relation to symptoms, character traits, and layers of defense.

Andreas-Salomé, Lou (1921). The dual orientation of narcissism. *Psychoanal. Q.*, 1962, 31:1-30. (Translated from *Narzissmus als Doppelrichtung. Imago*, 7:361-386, by Stanley Leavy.)

Andreas-Salomé emphasizes that the concept of primary narcissism includes not only self-love, but also the persistent feeling of identification with the totality. She applies this concept of a movement toward fusion to three issues: object love, values, and transformations of narcissism to creativity. She describes "libido with a feminine trend," which does not deplete primary narcissism, in contrast to Freud's masculine object-libido. Feminine sexual expression is not simply masochistic suffering via a thrust to passivity, but also involves the ego side of narcissism, in which tenderness and infantile erogeneity are maintained, culminating in the birth of a child. The activity of bearing and raising a child not only fulfills women's bisexuality, but also keeps them grounded in primary narcissism. This primary narcissism can be seen in the image of the mother who procreates herself and holds herself at the breast. The wish of men to give birth to themselves parallels penis envy in women.

Hug-Hellmuth, Hermine von (1921). *A Young Girl's Diary*, New York: Thomas Selzer.

With a preface by Sigmund Freud, this is a vivid diary of a young adolescent girl. Controversy about the authorship has resulted in its current obscurity.

Abraham, Karl (1922). Manifestations of the female castration complex. *Int. J. Psycho-Anal.*, 3:1-29. Also in: *Selected Papers*. New York: Brunner/Mazel, 1979, pp. 338-369.

Originally presented in 1920, this paper was a major contribution, frequently cited by contemporaries. It is organized into theoretical and clinical sections. Parts I and II review early female development, focusing on women's castration complex and penis envy. He briefly summarizes his view of the normal outcome of feminine development: women who identify with their mother replace their original penis envy with the wish for a child and as adults become reconciled to their feminine role and desire passive gratification. In Part III, Abraham describes perverse resolutions, such as homosexuality, the fantasy of having a penis, and the conscious wish to castrate the man. Parts IV, V, VI, and VII address neurotic outcomes. Case examples illustrate symbolic equivalents and neurotic transformations. Finally, in Part VIII, Abraham discusses the effects that mothers with these problems have upon their children.

Jones, Ernest (1922). Notes on Dr. Abraham's article on the female castration complex. *Int. J. Psycho-Anal.*, 3:327-328.

Jones briefly discusses case material and an example from the literature to confirm Abraham's observations on manifestations of the female castration complex. Although not explicitly disagreeing with Abraham, Jones' case example supports another origin for the castration complex in women by implying that their masculine position reflects a retreat from disappointment with the father and that femininity is innate.

Abraham, Karl (1923). An infantile theory of the origin of the female sex. In: *Selected Papers of Karl Abraham, M.D.* New York: Brunner/Mazel, 1979, p. 333.

Through the reconstruction of a dream, Abraham briefly formulates one woman's infantile theory of her femininity—that she had become a female because her penis was bitten off by the father while she was a baby in utero.

Abraham, Karl (1924). A short study of the development of the libido, viewed in the light of mental disorders. In: *Selected Papers of Karl Abraham, M.D.* New York: Brunner/Mazel, 1979, pp. 418-501.

In Part II of this paper, Abraham discusses the vicissitudes of object love in relation to sexual aims and provides a table with six developmental stages. He proposes that object love begins with an autoerotic stage where there is no object, and is followed by a narcissistic stage (total incorporation of the object), a partial-love-with-incorporation stage, a partial-love stage, an object-love-with exclusion-of-the-genitals stage, and, finally, object love. Two hysterical female patients whose primary symptoms of frigidity derive from their female castration complex illustrate the consequent fixations and regressions in aim and object. Inhibition of libido in both sexes proceeds from the castration complex. Women's anxiety results from being deprived of the penis and from their castration desires directed against men. Abraham concludes that the highest level of psychosexual development must parallel the final step in object love. [See also Chapter 23.]

**Harnik, Jeno (1924). The various changes undergone by narcissism in men and women. *Int. J. Psycho-Anal.*, 5:66-83.**

This article, which draws on Freud's early models of development, is most often cited for Harnik's proposal that girls substitute whole body narcissism for the "loss" of the penis at puberty.

**Horney, Karen (1924). On the genesis of the castration complex in women. *Int. J. Psycho-Anal.*, 5:50-65. Also in: *Feminine Psychology*, ed. H. Kelman. New York: Norton, 1967, pp. 37-53.**

This paper is of major importance in the history of views on the psychology of women. Horney wrote it as a response to Abraham's paper "Manifestations of the Female Castration Complex," which he presented in 1920. Her paper was first delivered in 1921 to the Berlin Society. Freud cited this paper and reacted to it in "The Dissolution of the Oedipus Complex" (1924b).

Horney describes the impact of sociocultural factors in early penis envy and then emphasizes the secondary nature of the neurotic castration complex. "Primary penis envy," an inevitable early reaction, is usually mild and transient. "Secondary penis envy," which she asserts is the result of oedipal disappointment, is the clinically significant form of penis envy, which, operating as a defensive reaction, gives rise to some of the pathological clinical manifestations of the castration complex described by Abraham. One source of the castration complex is a regressive identification with father and return to pregenital conflicts following the father's rejection of the girl's positive oedipal impulses. The second source of the castration complex derives from the girl's guilt about her own wishes, so that she fantasizes having a penis to defend against her fantasy of having been castrated in a love relationship with the father. "Secondary penis envy" is discussed as a symptomatic aspect on a continuum from normal development through the "castration complex" to homosexuality.

**Van Ophuijsen, Johan (1924). Contributions to the masculinity complex in women. *Int. J. Psycho-Anal.*, 5:39-49.**

In this paper, first delivered in 1917, Van Ophuijsen refers to Freud's assertion in "Some Character Types Met with in Psychoanalysis" (1916) that all women feel they were injured in infancy by not having a penis and that

they reproach their mothers for this absence. Based on his analysis of five
women with obsessional neuroses, he asserts that the "masculinity complex"
in women is founded on a belief in the possibility of possessing a male
genital organ, and this conviction wards off guilt from the "castration
complex." He traces the origin of the "masculinity complex" to the sight of
the male organ and a desire to urinate like a boy. In extended clinical
material he focuses on urethral eroticism and its connection with bedwet-
ting, weeping, and sublimation in music. He concludes by interrelating
concepts about the masculinity complex, infantile masturbation of the
clitoris, and urethral eroticism.

Deutsch, Helene (1925a). The psychology of women in relation to the
function of reproduction. *Int. J. Psycho-Anal.*, 6:405-418. Also in: *The
Psychoanalytic Reader*, ed. R. Fliess. New York: International Universities
Press, 1948, pp. 165-179.

This is a key theoretical paper in which Deutsch introduces ideas first
presented at the Salzburg Congress in 1924, which she draws upon in her
later essays and books. She outlines normal female libidinal development
throughout the life cycle. Deutsch asserts that girls have two sexual zones
and that their task is to renounce the masculinity attached to the clitoris
and discover a "new organ," the vagina, within their own bodies. In doing
so, little girls are guided by "masochistic subjugation to the penis." Deutsch
believes that coitus, parturition, and motherhood have dynamic importance
in both the mastery of castration trauma and the earlier traumas of birth
and weaning, through reparative identifications. Accepting Freud's
formulation that the wish for a child is secondary, she feels that women
find in reproduction what men have in sublimation.

Deutsch, Helene (1925b). The menopause: Psychoanalysis of the sexual
functions of women. *Int. J. Psycho-Anal.*, 65:55-62, 1984.

This paper is taken from a section of Deutsch's book, *Psychoanalyse der
Weiblichen Sexualfunktionen* presented at Wurzberg in 1924 and published
in 1925. Deutsch bases her discussion of menopause on Freud's libido
theory. She asserts that women's loss of reproductive capacity is accompanied by a decathexis of the vagina as somatic changes necessitate libidinal
shifts. This loss is a severe narcissistic blow, which is initially defended
against by a reinforcement of genital trends. Deutsch views menopause as
puberty in reverse with a shift to a regressive libidinal recathexis of the
clitoris. With this shift, oedipal and castration conflicts reemerge. After
menopause, there is further libidinal regression to pregenital stages.
Deutsch illustrates her formulations with clinical examples.

Horney, Karen (1926). The flight from womanhood. *Int. J. Psycho-Anal.*, 12:360-374. Also in: *Feminine Psychology*, ed. H. Kelman. New York: Norton, 1967, pp. 54-70.

In this well-known paper, which was first presented in 1925, Horney attempts to refute Freud's 1925 paper "Some Psychical Consequences of the Anatomical Distinctions Between the Sexes." Horney begins by commenting that many studies of female sexuality were biased by the sex of the observer, and she states that views expressed by her male analyst contemporaries about the value of the penis parallel the views of little boys. She describes the importance of early vaginal awareness and feminine libidinal wishes in girls and asserts that penis envy is secondary to fear of internal injury; thus, the girl's wish to be a man is a defensive flight that wards off oedipal fantasies of fear of vaginal injury from the father's large penis. Penis envy is conceptualized as the first expression of attraction between the sexes, part admiring envy, part longing for the penis of a true love object—first the father, and then other men. Horney declares that girls' actual anatomical disadvantage (see Horney, 1924) is only pregenital. She stresses both boys' envy of motherhood and her view that the wish for motherhood is primary for girls. The wish for motherhood is associated with early awareness of vaginal sensations and innate attraction to the opposite sex. She argues against the idea of "transfer" of sensation from clitoris to vagina, seeing both organs as part of the same female genital apparatus. She adds that the flight from womanhood is supported by a cultural "actual disadvantage" of women's role in a culture with a masculine orientation.

Muller-Braunschweig, Carl (1926). Genesis of the feminine superego. *Int. J. Psycho-Anal.*, 8:359-362.

[See Chapter 7 for annotation.]

Jones, Ernest (1927). The early development of female sexuality. *Int. J. Psycho-Anal.*, 8:459-472. Also in *Papers on Psychoanaysis*. Baltimore, MD: Williams and Wilkins, 1948, pp. 438-451.

Jones refers to data from the analyses of five homosexual women. He acknowledges the work of both Horney and Freud but differs from both. He asks, "What in women corresponds to fear of castration in men?" and "What differentiates the development of homosexual from that of heterosexual women?" Jones defines castration as loss of the penis and postulates the fear of "aphanisis" (the complete extinction of the capacity for sexual enjoyment) as central in both sexes. In women "aphanisis" is conceived of in terms of separation; in men, in terms of castration. Jones maintains that

privation of early receptive feminine vaginal sexual wishes—to share a penis
with father in intercourse and get a baby—lead to fear of "aphanisis" and
subsequently to guilt (and to formation of the superego) as a defense
against ungratified wishes. He stresses intrapsychic factors but appreciates
the reinforcing effects of social prohibitions. A complex schema for
libidinal development for both sexes is elaborated with an emphasis on the
importance of oral eroticism and sadism. Jones regards girls' femininity as
primary and accepts the importance of early receptive wishes based on
awareness of early vaginal sensations. Opposing Freud, he thinks the
"phallic stage" in girls is a secondary defense and elaborates on Horney's
postulate of primary and secondary penis envy. He bases his understanding
of homosexuality on the premise that children must give up either their
own sex or the incestuous love object. For girls, this refusal to give up the
incestuous object results in two kinds of homosexuality. In the first type,
the girl identifies with the father and seeks acceptance as a man from men.
The other type is characterized by dependence on another woman, whom
the girl gratifies "as a man." Ideas from this early paper are later considerably expanded and modified as Jones incorporated Melanie Klein's concepts
into his thinking. [See also Chapters 7 and 19.]

Lampl-de Groot, Jeanne (1927). The evolution of the Oedipus complex in
women. *Int. J. Psycho-Anal.* 9:332-345. Also in: *The Psychoanalytic Reader,*
ed. R. Fliess. New York: International Universities Press, 1948, pp. 180-194.

---

Lampl-de Groot responds to Freud's 1924 request for more empirical
data for his theories about the psychology of women. Citing her analytic
work with homosexual women, she agrees with Freud that the girl's
pregenital development is like that of the boy, "a little man," as to her love
aim and object choice. Stating that fears of castration cause girls to give up
their mother as love object, Lampl-de Groot stresses the importance of the
negative oedipal phase. The positive oedipal phase for girls follows. Thus,
women's jealousy is stronger than men's, not only because of penis envy,
but because women cannot have the mother. She concludes that truly
feminine women can only form a narcissistic object choice based on the
need to be loved. Two clinical examples illustrate this view and emphasize
the importance of the female analyst in understanding a girl's early
attachment to her mother. Freud adopted Lampl-de Groot's views on the
preoedipal phase in girls, though he felt that Lampl-de Groot had not put
enough emphasis on girls' hostility to their mother.

Horney, Karen (1928). The problem of the monogamous ideal. *Int. J. Psycho-Anal.*, 9:318-331. Also in *Feminine Psychology*, ed. H. Kelman. New York: Norton, 1965, pp. 84-98.

In this article, Horney looks at the diverse unconscious motivations concerning marriage, the wish for a monogamous ideal, and the ubiquity of marital conflicts. Horney proposes that marriage promises fulfillment of early wishes from the oedipal phase and the desire to have exclusive possession of the spouse. These wishes from the id are never fulfilled, for the spouse is only a substitute for the parent and thus disillusionment inevitably results. Horney discusses the role of the superego in this conflict and details the instinctual contribution from the different developmental levels to the wish for a monogamous ideal. Gratification of oedipal wishes through marriage threatens the superego and incest-prohibitions. Hostility, as manifested in frigidity and impotence, often is a consequence of denial of the marriage and a need to drive the spouse away. The outcome is a reinstitution of the Oedipus complex where the alienated spouse ends up in the role of child in the mother/father/child triad. She proposes that the difference in outcome of the Oedipus complex for boys and girls has a distinct psychical representation that affects future sexual role and genital inhibition.

Klein, Melanie (1928). Early stages of the Oedipus conflict. In: *Love, Guilt and Reparation and Other Works: The Writings of Melanie Klein*, Vol. 1. London: Hogarth Press, 1975, pp. 186-198.

[See Chapter 7 for annotation.]

Riviere, Joan (1929). Womanliness as a masquerade. *Int. J. Psycho-Anal.*, 10:303-313. Also in: *Psychoanalysis and Female Sexuality*, ed. H. Ruitenbeek. New Haven, CT: College and University Press, 1966, pp. 209-220.

Riviere presents a clinical case of a female patient who excelled as wife, mother, and career woman and who used womanliness as a defense against the wish to rob the man of his penis and secretly own it herself. Riviere clinically illustrates the theories proposed by Deutsch (1925), Jones (1927), and Klein (1928). Oscillations between a masculine identification and a pseudo-feminine identification to protect against the emergence of a genuine feminine identity are stressed. Riviere emphasizes the woman's need for reparation to the mother to compensate for her own aggression. She concludes with a discussion of the essential nature of fully developed femininity and cites Deutsch's "ultra womanly woman" as founded on the "oral-sucking stage," gratified by receiving the (nipple, milk) penis, semen, child from the father.

Sachs, Hanns (1929). One of the motive factors in the formation of the super-ego in women. *Int. J. Psycho-Anal.*, 10:39-50.

This paper was first presented in 1927. Sachs describes cases of mainly professional women with well-developed superegos who have normal affective reactions in their love life. He states that the development of an independent superego is based on renunciation of the father. [See also Chapter 7.]

Deutsch, Helene (1930). The significance of masochism in the mental life of women. *Int. J. Psycho-Anal.*, 11:48-60. Also in: *The Psychoanalytic Reader*, ed. R. Fliess. New York: International Universities Press, 1948, pp. 195-207.

Deutsch discusses the origin of femininity, the central importance of masochism to feminine psychology, and the nature of frigidity. She equates femininity with the "feminine passive-masochistic disposition" in women. She believes that masochism is an elemental force in feminine life that finds its ultimate gratification in motherhood. Developmentally, with the discovery of the anatomical difference and with the recognition of the lack of the penis, girls cease to value the clitoris and "the hitherto active-sadistic libido attached to the clitoris" becomes deflected in a regressive direction toward masochism. Thus, the first libidinal relation with the father is masochistic, with the earliest feminine wish being, "I want to be castrated by my father." Deutsch denies the importance of early vaginal sensations. Frigidity is related to the repression of normal feminine masochistic wishes, to the masculinity complex, or to a normal sublimation of masochism into maternity. [See also Chapter 21.]

Fenichel, Otto (1930). The pregenital antecedents of the Oedipus Complex. *Int. J. Psycho-Anal.*, 12:141-166, 1931. Also in: *The Collected Papers of Otto Fenichel* (First Series), ed. H. Fenichel and D. Rapaport. New York: Norton and Co., 1953, pp. 181-203.

This paper was written in the midst of the early controversy about the development of female sexuality. Fenichel attempts to integrate the ideas of M. Klein, Horney, and Jones, as well as Freud. He substantially agrees with Freud, but disagrees with Lampl-de Groot in her formulation of the role of the girl's negative oedipal complex. He explores the relationship of preoedipal sexuality to the development and characteristics of the oedipal conflict and presents material from three cases (one man and two women). He concludes that girls redirect their love to the father because of disappointment in their pregenital attachment to the mother; the disappointment includes components from all pregenital levels, but the decisive disappointment is the mother's failure to provide the girl a penis. Conflicts from preoedipal phases color the form of the oedipal fantasies. Fenichel questions, but does not answer, how much regressive distortion versus real pregenital experience influences the pregenital aspects of oedipal fantasies.

Lewin, Bertram (1930). Smearing of feces, menstruation, and the female superego. In: *Selected Writings of Betram D. Lewin*, ed. J. Arlow. New York: Psychoanalytic Quarterly Press, 1973.

[See Chapter 7 for annotation.]

Brierley, Marjorie (1932). Some problems of integration in women. *Int. J. Psycho-Anal.*, 13:433-448.

In the first part of this paper Brierley reviews the literature on controversial aspects of female development. She discusses the development of the Oedipus complex in girls, the relation between the positive and negative oedipal positions, and the resolution or nonresolution of the complex. Brierley examines and compares the findings and theories of Freud, Jones, Deutsch, Mueller-Braunschweig, Sachs, Payne, and Klein. Citing the need for more investigation, she then presents findings from two groups of patients. One group had suppressed all manifest sexuality in relationships, and the other consisted of married women with inhibited sexuality. On the basis of material from both groups, she concludes 1) that violation and revenge fantasies provide a strong motivation for dissolution of the female Oedipus complex; 2) that oral problems are significant in the etiology of later genital difficulties; 3) that masculinity in women is both primary and defensive; 4) that female superego development is often arrested at a pregenital stage; and 5) that women may have a greater degree of oral cathexis than men. [See also Chapter 19.]

Deutsch, Helene (1932). On female homosexuality. *Psychoanal. Q.*, 1:484-510. Also renamed: Homosexuality in women. *Int. J. Psycho-Anal.*, 14:34-56, 1933.

These two papers have the same contents but are slightly different translations. The formulations are based on transference manifestations from the analyses of 11 women with overt, acted-out, and latent homosexual conflicts. From this material Deutsch makes observations and draws conclusions about the genetics and dynamics of female homosexuality. She finds oedipal material in all these cases and sees the homosexuality as based on regression from the positive oedipal position to the preoedipal relationship with mother. In addition, the manifest symptom—homosexuality—in several of her cases serves to undo an intense anger at the mother while simultaneously reversing some of the deprivations that initially instigated the anger. [See also Chapter 19.]

Horney, Karen (1932a). The dread of women. *Int. J. Psycho-Anal.*, 13:348-360. Also in: *Feminine Psychology*, ed. H. Kelman. New York: Norton, 1967, pp. 133-146.

Horney points out that in many cultures and throughout history men have feared women. She argues that castration anxiety is an insufficient explanation and that men have a fear of the vagina as devouring. She contends that the presence of the vagina is known in early childhood by both girls and boys and that boys feel that their penis is too small for their mother's vagina. It is this blow to male narcissism, rather than fear of castration, that results in dread of women. Finally, she examines character and men's need to prove their masculinity to women. This paper is a complement to "The Denial of the Vagina," by Horney (1933a), which also focuses on fantasies about the vagina.

Klein, Melanie (1932). *The Psychoanalysis of Children*. New York: Norton.

Klein first presented these ideas at a meeting in Salzburg in 1924 and in London in 1925. She emphasizes the importance of the preoedipal period, the early oral phase, and early superego development. She believes that girls have a dominant feminine instinctual disposition and that penis envy originates secondarily from oral envy of the maternal breast and the mother's body and contents. Children of both sexes wish to push their way into the mother to obtain the incorporated penis and babies. Oral desires for the paternal penis precede vaginal desires for the penis, and fears of a sadistic "bad" penis are derived from earlier maternal relations. Oedipal conflict begins very early, motivated by oral frustrations, and is acute because the small girl is still bound to her mother by powerful oral fixations and helplessness. Copulation may be imagined as a sadistic act. Girls have both unconscious and conscious knowledge of their vaginas. Since they do not possess a visible genital, they have difficulty reassuring themselves that they have not been damaged by maternal retaliation for their sadistic impulses. [See also Chapters 6, 16, and 19.]

Mueller, Josine (1932). A contribution to the problem of libidinal development of the genital phase in girls. *Int. J. Psycho-Anal.*, 13:362-368.

This paper was first delivered in 1925 to the Berlin Society. Mueller, a pediatrician and analyst, describes medical evidence of early vaginal awareness in little girls long before puberty. She supports Horney's views and speculates that the awareness of early vaginal sensations contributes to anxiety, which focuses on fantasies of being wounded and castrated. This anxiety secondarily leads girls away from identification with the mother (with a wish for a baby from father) to focus defensively on the exterior of their bodies and to regress to "primary penis envy," which then results in "secondary penis envy," identification with her father, and vaginal frigidity in later life. Mueller asserts that the earlier the interest in the vagina, the more anxiety there will be about the internal genital and the greater the likelihood of later repression of vaginal awareness.

Horney, Karen (1933a). The denial of the vagina. *Int. J. Psycho-Anal.*, 14:57-70. Also in: *Feminine Psychology*, ed. H. Kelman. New York: Norton, 1967, pp. 147-161.

Horney addresses woman's anxieties about the vagina. She traces little girls' development and how their instinctive knowledge of the vagina results in specific anxieties about penetration and injury from father's large penis. Later, reinforcing fears about menstruation and masturbation lead to repression of knowledge of the vagina. Social disadvantages add to unconscious processes beginning in early childhood. This paper complements "The Dread of Women," by Horney (1932), which also focuses on fantasies about the vagina.

Horney, Karen (1933b). Psychogenic factors in functional disorders. *Amer. J. Ob. Gyn.*, 25:694-704. Also in: *Feminine Psychology*, ed. H. Kelman. New York: Norton, 1967, pp. 162-174.

[See Chapter 18 for annotation.]

Jones, Ernest (1933). The phallic phase. *Int. J. Psycho-Anal.*, 14:1-13. Also in: *Papers on Psychoanalysis*. Baltimore, MD: Williams and Wilkins, 1948, pp. 452-484.

In this article, presented at Weisbaden in 1932, Jones presents an elaborate developmental schema and introduces new terms such as the "protophallic stage," (when the child is consciously ignorant of the difference between the sexes) and the "deuterophallic stage," (when the child is enlightened about the anatomical difference and tries to cope with it.) Jones first addresses two pairs of problems—in boys, the fear of castration and the dread of the vulva; in girls, the desire to own a penis and the hate directed at the mother. In the second part of the paper, Jones sets forth a schematic division of writers about female sexuality; first, those who agree with "Position A" (particularly, Freud and Deutsch), that girls' sexuality is essentially male to start with, and that girls are driven into femaleness by failure of the male attitude (disappointment with the clitoris);

and then those who agree with "Position B" (Horney, Klein, and Jones), that girls' sexuality is essentially female to start with, and that they are driven into phallic maleness by failure of the female attitude. (In making this rhetorical division, Jones disregards fundamental agreements and disagreements among the two groups of analysts.) Jones supports "Position B" and concludes that in both boys and girls the typical (deutero) phallic phase is defensive—a neurotic compromise that serves to avoid the fear of mutilation (girls) and castration (boys) by the parent of the same sex. Thus he postulates a symmetrical oedipal complex for both sexes.

Lampl-de Groot, Jeanne (1933). Problems of femininity. *Psychoanal. Q.*, 489-518. Also in: *Man and Mind-Collected Papers of Jeanne Lampl-de Groot*. New York: International Universities Press, 1965, pp. 12-31.

Lampl-de Groot develops the idea of "active" and "passive" as equivalent to masculine and feminine. She affirms that early development is the same for both sexes and that there is only a masculine libido. She examines vicissitudes of the psychic differences between the two sexes and explains the shift of object in girls from mother to father as being a result of narcissistic disappointment because of failure of the mother to provide the penis. The normal course of development for girls is to desire to be passively loved by their father and to turn their active aggressive instincts inward, resulting in a masochistic tendency. Following this theoretical path, Lampl-de Groot arrived at a series of surprising and often quoted conclusions: "The feminine woman does not love, she lets herself be loved"; "Both maternal love and woman's love for man are 'masculine'"; "Good mothers are frigid wives"; and, finally, "There is no way to account for the presence of a superego in purely feminine women." In the 1965 introduction to this paper, Lampl-de Groot emphasizes the paper's "purely speculative" nature and states that it may even represent "a youthful sin."

Rado, Sandor (1933). Fear of castration in women. *Psychoanal. Q.*, 2:425-475.

The ideas in this paper were first presented in 1931. Rado reiterates the importance of castration fantasies for women. He does not acknowledge awareness of early vaginal sensations nor contend with its significance. Emphasis is placed on the moment girls first catch sight of a penis. He asserts the following sequence: the wish "I want it," the fantasy "I have it," and the realization "But I haven't." This chain of events produces a traumatic "paralysis of feeling," which results in a variety of forms of "genital masochism." [See also Chapter 18.]

Fenichel, Otto (1934). Further light upon the preoedipal phase in girls. In: *The Collected Papers of Otto Fenichel*. New York: Norton, 1953, pp. 241-288. First published in *Int. Z. Psa.*, 20:151-190, 1934.

While Fenichel agrees with Freud's formulations of penis envy and the resolution of the Oedipus complex, he stresses the importance of preoedipal antecedents in female development. Fenichel emphasizes girls' pregenital love and attachment to the mother as pivotal for entry into the oedipal phase. He describes various paths for entry into the oedipal period. Fenichel disagrees with Freud about the essentially masculine nature of preoedipal girls and the phallic nature of clitoral masturbation. His rich and extensive case material includes early reconstructions from analytic material.

Bonaparte, Marie (1935). Passivity, masochism and femininity. *Int. J. Psycho-Anal.*, 16:325-333.

Bonaparte bases her theory on the now discredited work of Mararon, a biologist who postulated that a woman is biologically a man, but with arrested development. Bonaparte describes biological bisexuality by stating that women's sexual pleasure is derived from their virility. Women's "masculinity complex" is primary and is based on the anatomical existence of a "mutilated" organ, the clitoris, which is regarded as phallic, masculine, and sadistic. Bonaparte asserts that women must give up their masculinity complex to attain a passive masochistic position. She stresses the importance for girls of a "sadistic cloacal" phase with an early awareness of a cavity and anxiety about invasion from without. Later there is a fear of penetration, with intercourse imagined to be a sadistic attack on the woman. This fear can lead to the confusion of passivity with masochism and a rejection of the passive role. Bonaparte differs with Freud in emphasizing the pleasure differs with women receive from their whole body and the need for a harmonious collaboration between clitoris and vagina; from Deutsch in arguing against the centrality of female masochism; and from Jones and Klein in her belief that the fear of penetration is biological and self-preservative.

Bunker, Henry (1935) Three brief notations relative to the castration complex. *Psychoanal. Q.*, 4:341-343.

This brief paper illustrates the presence of the female castration complex by describing it in two female patients and the Greek mythological character Kaineus.

Horney, Karen (1935b). The problem of feminine masochism. *Psychoanal. Rev.*, 22:241-257. Also in: *Feminine Psychology*. New York: Norton, 1967, pp. 214-233.

[See Chapter 21 for annotation.]

Jones, Ernest (1935). Early female sexuality. *Int. J. Psycho-Anal.*, 16:263-273. Also in: *Papers on Psychoanalysis*. Baltimore, MD: Williams and Willkins, 1948, pp. 485-495.

In this historically important paper presented to the Vienna Society in 1935, Jones attempts to summarize the views of the London group for the Vienna Society. He makes a complex theoretical presentation with both disagreement and attempts at concordance with Freud's position on female sexuality. Basic points of contention are Jones's assertions that girls' oedipal attachment develops out of their innate femininity's undergoing its own maturational processes and that oedipal feelings arise spontaneously, although girls may temporarily take flight in a phallic position.

Payne, Sylvia (1935). A concept of femininity. *Br. J. Med. Psychol.*, 15:18-33.

This paper was first presented in 1934. Noting that previous efforts to discuss femininity focused on an active/passive dichotomy and on questions of biological bisexuality, Payne concentrates instead on the reproductive function and the psychological characteristics in genitally mature women: 1) Oral and vaginal erotism are linked and integrated with receptivity. Oral sadism is not so intense as to contaminate this linkage and interfere with genitality. 2) The female ego is able to sustain periodic large fluctuations in narcissistic libido, as these are inevitably encountered in intercourse, pregnancy, parturition, and lactation. 3) Women must be able to sublimate masculine tendencies. 4) Using their most essential feminine capacity, women must coordinate smoothly between wishes to receive and retain and wishes to give out. Adult femininity requires women to tolerate and adapt to changes of mind and body and to coordinate conflicting male and female tendencies.

Brierley, Marjorie (1936). Specific determinants in feminine development. *Int. J. Psycho-Anal.*, 17:163-180.

In an attempt to understand specific factors affecting adult female heterosexuality, Brierley targets the earliest phases of ego integration and tries to link oral pathology with sexual symptoms and development. She refers to several frames of reference including Glover's theories of ego-nuclei; Klein's concepts of "good" and "bad" breast, part objects, and object representations; and Freud's instincts and aims. She emphasizes the importance of ego development and object relations. The paper is a creative attempt to synthesize many complex theories and frames of reference on preoedipal development.

Fenichel, Otto (1936). The symbolic equation: Girl=phallus. *Int. Z. Psa.*, 22:299-314. Also in: *The Collected Papers of Otto Fenichel: Second Series.* New York: Norton, 1953, pp. 3-18.

Fenichel discusses the multidetermined origin and function of girls' identifying themselves with a penis in their unconscious fantasies. He notes that the phallic wish "I also want the penis" shifts to the oral wish "I want to incorporate the penis. . . and now myself become a penis" (pp. 4-5). This shift reflects early pregenital antecedents, particularly oral fixations, when oral sadistic wishes in relation to the mother are in the foreground. The penis is a later symbolic introject equivalent to baby, feces, and milk. The fantasy of being the penis and within the mother's body is a way to disavow the wish to appropriate something from the mother's body or to express the wish to return to the state of symbiotic union in the mother's body. Several analytic cases and examples from literature are presented.

Jacobson, Edith (1936). On the development of a girl's wish for a child. *Psychoanal. Q.*, 37:523-538, 1968.

In this paper, first presented in 1933, Jacobson discusses the analysis of a little girl who had a strong preoedipal fixation to her mother. The case illustrates Freud's description of girls' resolution of penis envy by wishing for a child. Jacobson adds the importance of the wish for a child from the ambivalently regarded preoedipal mother in order to cope with envy of the father and future siblings. The development of the girl's wish for a child is seen as the product of oral sadistic impulses, phallic strivings, and castration anxiety as the girl traverses the psychosexual stages. Finally, Jacobson demonstrates this developmental progression in a short vignette about an adult female analysand.

Jacobson, Edith (1937). Ways of superego formation and the female castration complex. *Psychoanal. Q.*, 45:525-538, 1976.

Jacobson delineates an alternate route for female development in response to the discovery of the sexual differences. In contrast to the view that girls, beset with object loss, find a narcissistic compensation for castration in submission to the father (and having his penis), Jacobson proposes that girls may fantasize an internal penis, accompanied by an active erotization of the vagina, which is valued in and of itself.

Implications of these two routes for superego development are then explored. Although a fear of bodily injury is present along both paths, in Jacobson's new route, the formation of ego ideal and restrictions are not as inexorably linked to "the other" (the father) in a "projective dependent," masochistic manner. Instead, superego formation is based on greater female self-esteem and autonomy. In a 1976 note, Jacobson suggests labeling this ever-increasing group of women not as "masculine women," but rather as "female 'vaginal' characters." [See also Chapters 7, 18, and 20.]

Klein, Melanie (1937). Love, guilt and reparation. In: *Love, Guilt and Reparation*. London: Virago Press, pp. 306-343, 1988.

[See Chapter 13 for annotation.]

Lampl-de Groot, Jeanne (1937). Masochism and narcissism. In: *The Development of the Mind*. New York: International Universities Press, 1965, pp. 82-92.

[See Chapter 21 for annotation.]

Dooley, Lucile (1938). The genesis of psychological sex differences. *Psychiat.*, 1:181-195.

This article begins with a survey of the historical psychoanalytic debates about women. Dooley asserts that there is a primary femininity, that the repudiation of femininity in women is not necessarily biologically based, and (with Horney) that penis envy is defensive. Dooley states that girls wish for a penis as a way of winning their mothers' love, and their primary desire during the phallic phase is for the person, not the organ. Dooley presents case illustrations from two female and two male analytic patients.

Searl, Nina (1938). A note on the relation between physical and psychical differences in boys and girls. *Int. J. Psycho-Anal.*, 19:50-62.

This article asserts three major points, taking into account the complex mutual interaction of psychological and cognitive factors. Searl observes that there are multiple meanings of the recognition of the anatomical differences. She discusses the limited cognitive development of boys and girls at two or three years of age, a limitation that has an impact on the meaning and comprehension of the concepts of masculinity and femininity. Finally, she considers the interaction of the physical and psychical that results in an overdetermined view and different reactions to girls' discovering that they do not have a penis.

Eissler, Kurt (1939). On certain problems of female sexual development. *Psychoanal. Q.*, 8:191-210.

Eissler presents reports of cases from the nonanalytic literature about vaginal sensations in young girls to shed light on the controversy about early female sexual development and Freud's theory of the double shift of girls with regard to sexual object, activity and passivity, and change of erotogenic zone. Eissler explains that this shift takes place because of the neurotic fantasy that the mother has taken the girl's penis away, not because of the reality of the discovery of the anatomical differences. Eissler proposes that the discovery of a hollow organ, the vagina, is responsible for girls' new oedipal position and passive libidinal attachment to the father since he has the organ of penetration.

Brunswick, Ruth Mack (1940). The preoedipal phase of the libido development. *Psychoanal. Q.*, 9:293-319. Also in: *The Psychoanalytic Reader*, ed. R. Fliess. New York: International Universities Press, 1948, pp. 261-284.

In this frequently cited article, Mack Brunswick outlines a schema of development that emphasizes the preoedipal phase of development. She draws upon Freud's earlier papers, referring to him as her collaborator, and summarizes Freud's views on libido development, but does not acknowledge clearly where her views differ. This paper was written after a 1935 summary paper by Jones (see annotation in this chapter), and some of the emphasis can be viewed as responding to points raised by Jones.

Mack Brunswick presents an elaborate "diagram" of early development, setting up three antithetical pairs: active-passive, phallic-castrated, and masculine-feminine. She introduces the terms "active and passive oedipal." Following Freud and Lampl-de Groot, she asserts that "at the beginning of her sexual life the little girl is to all intents and purposes a little boy," but acknowledges early anally-derived vaginal sensations and the connection between clitoral and vaginal sensations. Mack Brunswick emphasizes the importance of the regressive preoedipal fantasy of the all-powerful phallic mother and of primal scene memories, and traces the wish for a penis in girls and the wish for a baby in both sexes.

Deutsch, Helene (1944 and 1945). *The Psychology of Women: A Psychoanalytic Interpretation*, Vol. 1 and 2. New York: Grune and Stratton.

These two volumes are classic studies of female development from mid-childhood (prepuberty), through adolescence, adulthood, pregnancy, motherhood, the climacteric, and grandmotherhood. Deutsch presents a systematic view of female psychosexual development and reproductive functioning in order to explain normal female psychic life and conflicts. She uses data from psychoanalytic practice, psychotherapy, and the observations of others. Her emphasis is on the biological underpinnings of libidinal development. Three themes evolve: a discussion of the psychological life of women that begins with the onset of menstruation in the young girl and the formation of the feminine core; the analysis of the feminine core, which contains three essential traits of femininity—narcissism, passivity, and masochism; and the analysis of the nonfeminine aspects of femininity, or what compels women to be masculine. The first volume includes chapters on "Prepuberty," "Early Puberty," "Puberty and Adolescence," "Menstruation," "Eroticism," "Feminine Passivity," "Feminine Masochism," "Masculinity Complex," "Homosexuality," and "The Environment." The second volume, subtitled "Motherhood," covers "Social and Biological Aspects," "Motherhood, Motherliness and Sexuality," "Preliminary Phases," "Psychology of the Sexual Act," "Problems of Conception," "Pregnancy, Delivery, Confinement and Lactation," "Mother-Child Relation," "Unmarried Mothers," "Adoptive Mothers," "Stepmothers," and finally "The Climacteric." The books are rich in interesting case material. [See also Chapters 9, 10, 14, 18, 19, 21, 22.]

Bonaparte, Marie (1953). *Female Sexuality*. New York: International Universities Press.

This book contains Bonaparte's writings about the psychology of women, including the paper "Passivity, Masochism and Femininity," as well as a longer section on development in both sexes and bisexuality. There is a final anthropological section on excision, or female circumcision. She emphasizes the role of biology, particularly anatomy, and the struggle to cope with bisexuality. [See also Chapter 18.]

# Chapter 3

# Modern Commentaries on Historical Writings from 1900–1940

Lynn Whisnant Reiser, with
Nadine Levinson and Eleanor Schuker

---

Commentaries on the early psychoanalytic writings on the psychology of women through 1940 are annotated in this chapter. Articles that review, provide a critique, and expand the ideas of the early writers are covered; biographies are not. Articles that emphasize new formulations and major revisions have been placed in Chapter 4, *Modern Theoretical Formulations*, which can be read as a companion to this chapter. Because some articles in this chapter contain elements of new formulations as well as critiques of early formulations, there is an inevitable overlap with Chapter 4; this overlap is indicated by cross-referencing between the two chapters. Some papers are cross-referenced as well in other chapters, where they indicate the historical beginnings of particular clinical concepts that are discussed in those chapters. [For the original writings prior to 1940, see Chapters 1 and 2.]

This chapter is divided into Section A—Modern Commentaries on Early Historical Writings: Overviews; Section B—Modern Commentaries on Ideas of Specific Authors, including Marie Bonaparte, Helene Deutsch, Sigmund Freud, Karen Horney, Melanie Klein, Sylvia Payne, and Joan Riviere; and Section C—Collections of Papers and Books. (E.S. and N.L.)

## SECTION A—MODERN COMMENTARIES ON EARLY HISTORICAL WRITINGS: OVERVIEWS

Thompson, Clara (1941). The role of women of this culture. *Psychiat.*, 4:1-8. Also in: *Women and Analysis*, ed. J. Strouse. New York: Grossman/Viking Press, 1974, pp. 265-277.

[See Chapter 4 for annotation.]

Thompson, Clara (1942). Cultural pressures on the psychology of women. *Psychiat.*, 5:331-339. Also in: *Psychoanalysis and Women*, ed. J. B. Miller. New York: Brunner/Mazel, 1973, pp.49-64.

[See Chapter 4 for annotation.]

Zilboorg, Gregory (1944). Masculine and feminine. *Psychiat.*, 7:257-296. Also in: *Psychoanalysis and Women*, ed. J. B. Miller. New York: Brunner/Mazel, 1973, pp. 96-131.

[See Chapters 4 and 17 for annotations.]

Chasseguet-Smirgel, Janine (1970a). Introduction. In: *Female Sexuality: New Psychoanalytic Views*, ed. J. Chasseguet-Smirgel. Ann Arbor, MI: University of Michigan Press, pp. 1-46.

Chasseguet-Smirgel briefly reviews Freud's main studies and divides other historic papers into Freud's disciples and Freud's opponents; she then summarizes papers that present significant and controversial positions. She includes a precis of Freud's major papers: *Three Essays*, 1905; "Infantile Genital Organization of the Libido," 1923; "Dissolution of the Oedipal Complex," 1924; "Some Psychical Consequences," 1925; "Female Sexuality," 1931a; "Femininity," 1933. The group of papers with similar views includes Lampl-de Groot (1927, 1933); Deutsch (1925a, 1930, 1960); Mack Brunswick (1940); Bonaparte (1951). The papers with opposing views include Mueller (1924); Horney (1932); Klein (1932); Jones (1927, 1932, 1935). There are detailed expositions of the papers, with emphasis on theoretical positions, rather than on the clinical or historical context. Chasseguet-Smirgel points out that the debates about the psychology of women never took into account the potential positive contributions of either side. This chapter may be difficult to read for the beginner, but it is a useful resource.

Fliegel, Zenia (1973). Feminine psychosexual development in Freudian theory. *Psychoanal. Q.*, 42:385-409.

In a scholarly review, Fliegel examines why early criticisms of Freud's theory on female psychosexual development met with so little serious consideration. She reconstructs the sequence of events in the early debate on female psychology. She begins by discussing two major points in Horney's 1924 paper "On the Genesis of the Castration Complex in Women": primary and secondary penis envy and different origins for the female Oedipus complex. Fliegel asserts that Freud's 1925 paper was a response to Horney's 1924 article, but also reflected a pressure he felt to publish because of his limited life expectancy and the availability of analyst collaborators who could confirm or refute his tentative formulations. Freud differed from Horney by asserting that girls develop their feminine oedipal wishes out of frustrated phallic jealousy. Horney argued that girls' phallic position is a defensive retreat from their oedipal wishes. According to Fliegel, Jones, Fenichel, and Klein continued to question various points raised by Freud until 1931, when the debate essentially closed and remained uncontested until several decades later. Fliegel contends that Freud was reacting to dissenting ideas as threats to the cohesion of his theory at a vulnerable time in his life and in the midst of tension in the psychoanalytic movement.

Miller, Jean Baker (1973). *Psychoanalysis and Women.* New York: Brunner/Mazel.

[See Chapter 4 for annotation.]

Kleeman, James (1976). Freud's view on early female sexuality in the light of direct child observation. *J. Amer. Psychoanal Assn.* (Suppl.), 24:3-27.

[See Chapter 19 for annotation.]

Fliegel, Zenia (1982). Half a century later: Current status of Freud's controversial views on women. *Psychoanal. Rev.*, 69:7-28.

[See Chapter 4 for annotation.]

Lampl-de Groot, Jeanne (1982). Thoughts on psychoanalytic views of female psychology 1927-1977. *Psychoanal. Q.*, 51:1-18. Also in: *Man and Mind-Collected Papers of Jeanne Lampl de Groot, M.D.* New York: International Universities Press, 1985, pp. 408-417.

This paper surveys psychoanalytic concepts of female development from the 1920s to 1977. The author solidly agrees with Freud about the important role of penis envy and the castration complex in female development. She reasserts the thesis from her 1927 paper on the importance of the negative oedipal configuration as a part of the developmental process. Lampl-de Groot reviews and reaffirms her earlier opinions but also acknowledges some new theoretical developments, without elaborating on the impact of this knowledge on the theory of female psychology. Finally, she defends Freud's view of women as unbiased and attacks those who have disagreed with his views.

Fliegel, Zenia (1986). Women's development in analytic theory: Six decades of controversy. In: *Psychoanalysis and Women: Contemporary Reappraisals*, ed. J. Alpert. Hillsdale, NJ: The Analytic Press, pp. 3-31.

[See Chapter 4 for annotation.]

## SECTION B—MODERN COMMENTARIES ON IDEAS OF SPECIFIC AUTHORS

### Marie Bonaparte

Person, Ethel (1974). Some new observations on the origins of femininity. In: *Women and Analysis*, ed. J. Strouse. New York: Grossman, pp. 250-261.

This paper reevaluates the conclusions about female development in the early psychoanalytic literature. Contrasting the work of Marie Bonaparte with recent work in the area of core gender identity. Person tracks the shift from the old idea that "anatomy is destiny" to the current view that the characteristics of gender are more strongly influenced by sociocultural expectations than by biology. Hence, feminine masochism would be viewed not as the biological bedrock of female development, but as a consequence of the perception by both sexes of the degraded status of women in our culture. The specific attributes of femininity are not inevitable concomitants of femaleness, but rather are subject to modifications in response to child-rearing practices and changes in social role. This shift in thinking focuses attention on early psychosexual development and the importance of primary identifications with the mother. Boys' need to change this identification, which is vulnerable to interference from separation or early trauma, is a reason for the greater prevalence of gender disorders in males. The paper contains a focused bibliography on female psychology.

[See also Chapter 21.]

### Helene Deutsch

Wimpfheimer, Muriel and Schafer, Roy (1977). Psychoanalytic methodology in Helene Deutsch's *The Psychology of Women*. *Psychoanal. Q.*, 46:287-318.

The authors assert that Deutsch's general theories about feminine development and character are based on a deterministic biologic approach that neglects psychologic and social factors. They argue that Deutsch's behavioral observations of biologic suffering do not consider the meaning or context of individual experiences. The importance of object relations and ego functioning as applied to Schafer's "action language" is suggested as an alternative to Deutsch's explanatory model.

Thompson, Nellie (1987). Helene Deutsch: A life in theory. *Psychoanal. Q.*, 56:317-353.

Reviewing Deutsch's work in the context of her personal life, Thompson suggests that Deutsch's repeated reliance on personal experience both helped and hindered her theoretical work. She argues for the importance of identification in Deutsch's work, especially reparative identifications which allow reexperiencing of the bliss of the early mother-child relationship and those which enable women to deal with the traumas of female development.

### Sigmund Freud

Mitchell, Juliet (1974a). On Freud and the distinction between the sexes. In: *Women and Analysis*, ed. J. Strouse. New York: Grossman/Viking Press, pp. 27-36.

Mitchell discusses and assesses Freud's 1925 paper, "Some Psychical Consequences of the Anatomical Distinction between the Sexes." She proposes that Freud's paper had two primary themes: the nature of female sexuality and the larger question about female psychology. She argues that Freud's theories are about sexism, which he himself promulgated by equating masculine with active and feminine with passive and by overemphasizing the role of the powerful father in feminine development. Mitchell focuses on Freud's description of the asymmetrical Oedipus complex in girls and boys alike. She asserts that his propositions are a reflection of psychological formations produced within patriarchal societies. Mitchell's ideas have influenced feminist writers.

Schafer, Roy (1974). Problems in Freud's psychology of women. *J. Amer. Psychoanal. Assn.*, 22:459-485. Also in: *J. Amer. Psychoanal. Assn.* (Suppl.), 24:331-360, 1976.

[See Chapter 7 for annotation.]

Stoller, Robert (1974). Facts and fancies: An examination of Freud's concept of bisexuality (1973). In: *Women and Analysis*, ed. J. Strouse. New York: Grossman/Viking Press, pp. 391-415.

[See Chapters 18 and 19 for annotations.]

Chassequet-Smirgel, Janine (1976). Freud and female sexuality: Some consideration of the blind spots in the exploration of the "dark continent." *Int. J. Psycho-Anal.*, 57:275-286.

Chasseguet-Smirgel challenges Freud's concepts of sexual phallic monism (the idea of a single genital) and the child's supposed ignorance of the vagina. Children break away from the omnipotent mother by denying the vagina and projecting maternal power onto the father and his penis. [See Chapter 18 for annotation.]

Grossman, William (1976). Discussion of "Freud and Female Sexuality." *Int. J. Psycho-Anal.*, 57:301-305.

Grossman asserts that Freud's theories are an attempt to explain children's misunderstandings of the experience of recognition of the sexual differences, i.e., children's perceptions of how biology affects experience. He notes that theorists have sometimes confused children's interpretations with those of the analyst. Are children's minds phallocentric or is the theory? Grossman outlines his understanding of development; he views genital difference as an important organizer of experience at every level of psychic differentiation. The psychological tasks required by development are the same for both sexes, but the content is not. Early genital recognition has ego-psychological consequences, and children's early aggression toward the mother gives a narcissistic warp to castration anxiety and penis envy.

Meluk, Tufik (1976). Discussion of "Freud and Female Sexuality." *Int. J. Psycho-Anal.*, 57:307-310.

Meluk highlights the difference between direct observation and psychoanalytic observation. The mother-father couple functions in relation to the vicissitudes of instinct in the child, first as the mother-infant dyad and later as the mother-father-infant triangle. Psychoanalytic observation, not direct observation of children, gives meaning to these interrelated structures. She reviews the bedrock of psychoanalytic theory—Freud's ideas about instinct and sexuality, as rooted in biology. Meluk stresses the role of adequate parenting in healthy gender development for both sexes, but also believes that the penis, which can be clearly seen and easily manipulated, may lead to earlier integration of certain aspects of gender identity in boys and contribute to some aspects of penis envy in girls.

**Moore, Burness (1976). Freud and female sexuality: A current view.** *Int. J. Psycho-Anal.*, 57:287-300.

This extensive overview contrasts Freud's theories with modern, conservative analytic views. Moore reevaluates and modifies Freudian theory of female psychology in the light of recent findings. [See Chapter 18 for annotation.]

**Serebriany, Robert (1976). Dialogue on "Freud and Female Sexuality."** Panel report. *Int. J. Psycho-Anal.*, 57: 311-313.

This article summarizes the important points of the four papers by Meluk, Grossman, Moore, and Chasseguet-Smirgel on the subject of "Freud and Female Sexuality." It is organized according to the topics covered and the theoretical framework informing the theories of the participants. The topics that involve discussion of Freud's theories include bisexuality, the Oedipus complex, the idea that "anatomy is destiny," and the significance of anatomy in the development of specific fantasies. Chasseguet-Smirgel's concepts encompass the archaic mother image, the defensive function of penis envy, and the debate about whether psychosexual development is easier for girls or for boys. Other topics include transference and counter-transference issues related to the analyst's gender.

**Meissner, William (1979a). A study on hysteria: Anna O.** *The Annual of Psychoanalysis*, 7:17-52. New York: International Universities Press.

Meissner reviews data on the Anna O case (Breuer and Freud, 1893) and the biography of Bertha Pappenheim to argue that a diagnosis of borderline psychopathology with hysterical features was most likely. Prior to Anna O's acute illness, hysterical features defended against an underlying depressive core. After recovery from her acute hysterical symptoms, she achieved a "paranoid resolution," with an integrated paranoid construction of her beliefs. This paranoid resolution of sexual and aggressive conflicts allowed her to channel her energies constructively and gain stability for an uncertain sense of self, but nevertheless also directly expressed her paranoid views and sexual conflicts. This patient's projective system was based on seeing herself as victimized and narcisstically injured and stemmed from early traumatic object relations, including preoedipal traumatic separation, a depressed mother, sibling rivalry with a favored brother, and oedipal disappointment. She hated men, repressed her sexual impulses, and showed single-minded zeal in her work. Meissner notes that one cannot postulate repression of sexual impulses without finding a meaningful context within which such conflict takes place. For this patient, repressed sexual and aggressive impulses were tied to introjective formations that underlay a sense of rejection and victimization. Core introjects were projected to provide a new paranoid construction and coherent projective system.

Meissner, William (1979b). Studies on hysteria—Katarina. *Psychoanal. Q.*, 48:587-618.

Meissner offers a reinterpretation of Freud's short case history of Katarina. He uses his economic notion of repression of sexual tensions to show how a modern analytic perspective emphasizing developmental vicissitudes, developing ego strengths, internalizations, qualitative aspects of object relations, self-integration, and mastery of affects can be employed for a deep understanding of the consequences of this incestuous father-daughter relationship and the dynamics of hysteria. He vividly demonstrates how sexual conflicts and primal-scene memories are embedded in a much more complex matrix than can be understood by a drive/defense model. Introjective processes relevant to the pathogenic organization of an internal sense of self as victim are discussed. Projection and externalization of aggressive introjects creating phobic anxiety are closely related to paranoid projections and hallucinations.

Glenn, Jules (1980). Freud's adolescent patients: Katharina, Dora and the "Homosexual Woman." In: *Freud and His Patients*. New York: Aronson, pp. 23-47.

[See Chapter 9 for annotation.]

Jayne, Cynthia (1980). The dark continent revisited: An examination of the Freudian view of the female orgasm. *Psychoanalysis and Contemporary Thought*, 3:545-568

[See Chapter 18 for annotation.]

Kofman, Sarah (1980). *The Enigma of Woman—Woman in Freud's Writings*. Trans. Catherine Porter. Ithaca, NY: Cornell University Press, 1985.

This scholarly but acerbic book, translated from French by Catherine Porter, is in two parts, "The Enigma and the Veil" and "Freud Investigates." In the first part, Kofman proposes some explanations and interpretations of what Freud meant at various times in his papers either about femininity or about the women with whom he worked. Various theoretical points are addressed, such as bisexuality, narcissistic women, sublimation by mothers, and Freud's own multiple and intrapsychic motivations for writing about women. In the second part, Kofman offers a scholarly investigation of Freud's papers about women. She systematically details, examines, and critiques his paper "Femininity" (1933) and compares it with his previous papers about female development.

Kohon, Gerald (1984). Reflections on Dora: The case of hysteria. *Int. J. Psycho-Anal.*, 65:73-84.

[See Chapter 20 for annotation.]

Krohn, Alan and Krohn, Janis (1982). The nature of the Oedipus complex and the Dora Case. *J. Amer. Psychoanal. Assn.*, 30:555-578.

[See Chapter 7 for annotation.]

Mitchell, Juliet (1984). The question of femininity and the theory of psychoanalysis. In: *The British School of Psychoanalysis: The Independent Tradition*, ed. G. Kohon. New Haven, CT: Yale University Press, 1986, pp. 381-398. Also in: *Women: The Longest Revolution*. London: Virago Press, 1984, pp. 295-315.

Mitchell analyzes the connection between femininity and the construction of psychoanalytic theory. She suggests that "for Freud, 'femininity' sets the limits—the starting and the endpoints—of his theory, just as its repudiation marked the limits of the possibility of psychotherapeutic cure" (p. 381). Mitchell discusses Freud's theory of the mind as it arose out of his work with hysteria. She also discusses the castration complex, which Freud felt explained the inextricable connection between the formation of the human psyche and sexual differences. Contrasting Freud's theories with those of M. Klein, Mitchell believes Klein's formulations are less intimately bound than Freud's to the problem of femininity.

Bernheimer, Charles and Kahane, Claire (ed.)(1985). *In Dora's Case: Freud-Hysteria-Feminism*. New York: Columbia University Press.

This anthology includes chapters by F. Deutsch, who evaluated Dora several years later; by Marcus, who views the case as a great work of literature, but one in which Freud, not Dora, was the central actor; and by Lacan, who sees Freud as the paternal metaphor and also asserts that the sexual difference reflects a construction of culture, not biology. The rest of the 12 chapters are by literary critics, a historian, and some contemporary French feminist theorists. They discuss the role of sexual differences in development, the oedipal paternal transference, the preoedipal desire for the mother and her body, homosexuality, sadomasochism, and gender issues in transference and countertransference.

Chodorow, Nancy (1986a). Feminism, femininity, and Freud. In: *Advances in Psychoanalytic Sociology*, ed. J. Rabow, G. Platt, and M. Goldman. Malabar, FL: Robert E. Krieger. Also in: *Feminism and Psychoanalytic Theory*, ed. N. Chodorow. New Haven, CT: Yale University Press, 1989a, pp. 166-177.

Chodorow offers a theoretical discussion of psychoanalytic and feminist contributions to theories of femininity. Social and cultural realities in relation to gender and sex are experienced intrapsychically, while intrapsychic conflict can lead to conformity to or deviation from societal norms. Psychoanalysis and Freudian theory offer models for the development of masculinity and femininity and for heterosexual roles in the family; these serve as internal mechanisms for sociocultural organization. Chodorow proposes that psychoanalysis and feminism are as intrinsically linked as sexuality and gender. Just as sexuality and gender are both central to personality and identity development, so are psychoanalytic and feminist theories crucial for understanding social and political organization and sexual inequality. Human development, including gender development, occurs in a social setting where there is an asymmetry of power, control, dependency, and love with important objects. By observing individual and universal responses and the intrapsychic representations that are derived from this early social context, psychoanalysis explains women's need for relationships and men's need for power and dominance.

Gillespie, William (1986). Woman and her discontents: A reassessment of Freud's views on female sexuality. In: *The British School of Psychoanalysis: The Independent Tradition*, ed. G. Kohon. New Haven, CT: Yale University Press, pp. 344-361.

Gillespie attempts to reassess Freud's views on female sexuality in the light of recent developments in the study of sexual behavior. In addition to reviewing Freud's theories, Gillespie refers to other major psychoanalytic contributions on female sexuality, focusing on the question of primary versus secondary femininity and emphasizing the work of M. Klein. He discusses Masters and Johnson's findings on female orgasm as they relate to Freud's views on clitoral sexuality. Starting from a description of the sexual behavior of fish (Freud started with eels), Gillespie conjectures that the internalization of female sexuality through the course of evolution has had far-reaching psychological consequences. He concludes that although Freud seems to have overestimated the psychological importance of the penis, the penis retains its powerful psychological impact as the outward representation of the differences in reproductive roles allotted to men and women.

Lewis, Helen Block (1986). Is Freud an enemy of women's liberation? In: *The Psychology of Today's Woman: New Psychoanalytic Visions*, ed. T. Bernay and D. Cantor. Hillsdale, NJ: The Analytic Press, pp. 7-36.

Lewis traces the multiple themes of interest to feminists, such as morality, androcentrism, sexism based on biology, gender identity, cognitive style, and the relationship of feminism to psychoanalysis, that are intrinsic in Freud's work. Lewis feels that one of Freud's significant contributions was his opening of morality to scientific investigation, resulting in research hypotheses related to sex differences and early caretaking experiences. She proposes that Freud's discoveries of the unconscious and primary process offers insights into conflicts about gender identity and cognitive style. She also notes, however, that gender identity, with sexism as its byproduct, is the result of primary-process transformations of conflicted emotions and self-images. The affects of shame and guilt in relation to superego, narcissistic regulation, and affectional ties to others (field dependency) are explored in Freud's work and compared with Lewis's own research. Many examples illustrate Freud's androcentrism and misogynist statements. Lewis concludes with a summary of Lacan and Mitchell as they have attempted to effect a rapprochement between psychoanalysis and feminism.

Schimek, Jean (1987). Fact and fantasy in the seduction theory: A historical review. *J. Amer. Psychoanal. Assn.*, 35:937-966.

[See Chapter 24 for annotation.]

Gay, Peter (1988). Woman, the dark continent. In: *Freud: A Life for Our Time*. New York: Norton, pp. 501-522.

This chapter in Gay's biography of Freud is devoted to the cultural, political, and personal context surrounding Freud's views on femininity. The term 'dark continent' was Freud's reference to his own puzzlement and fragmentary knowledge about female sexuality and early feminine development. The debate about female psychology took place between 1924 and 1933 and included Abraham, Deutsch, Fenichel, Lampl-de Groot, Jones, and Horney. Gay suggests that Freud's view of women was inextricably overdetermined by Freud's unconscious fantasies, cultural commitments, and psychoanalytical theorizing. Gay traces Freud's relationships with women in his personal and professional life. He describes how those affiliations may have influenced Freud's views on female psychology, including his ideas on superego formation, penis envy and the castration complex, female sexuality, and the early preoedipal relationship with the mother. Freud's major papers on femininity are concisely reviewed and reassessed.

Grossman, William and Kaplan, Donald (1989). **Three commentaries on gender in Freud's thought: A prologue on the psychoanalytic theory of sexuality.** In: *Fantasy, Myth, and Reality: Essays in Honor of Jacob A. Arlow*, ed. H. Blum, Y. Kramer, A. K. Richards, and A. D. Richards. Madison, CT: International Universities Press, pp. 339-370.

Three lines of thought ("commentaries") are distinguishable in Freud's writings on female sexuality and gender differences. The first focuses on alleged feminine traits, a line of thought to which Freud held despite his own reservations. The prescribed feminine traits (e.g., passivity, masochism, narcissism) are static, fixed, and conventional. This line of thought, based on assumptions about gender meanings and conformity, was not formulated through the psychoanalytic method and hence is "nontechnical." Freud's second commentary addresses gender in terms of developmental lines or narratives. Here Freud's problem is that the discovery of significant nodal points and conflicts in development becomes equated with a discovery of how these points were inevitably traversed. This view contrasts with the technically psychoanalytic approach that addresses how an individual's fantasies develop in relation to developmental crises, and what are the diverse ways of reckoning psychologically with issues of sex and gender. The third commentary in Freud's writing is more technically psychoanalytic. It understands the complexity of issues of development and outcome that allow for variability, overdetermination, and multiple function. No single developmental outcome is fixed, no single event (such as the discovery of anatomical differences) is isolated, abstract, or absolute. In this technical approach, interest in female sexuality and femininity merge with the general theory of neurosis and psychoanalytic process.

Decker, Hannah (1990). *Freud, Dora and Vienna 1900*. New York: Free Press.

Decker reexamines Freud's psychoanalytic encounter with Dora in the wider historical and cultural context of turn-of-the-century Vienna.

Young-Bruehl, Elisabeth (1990). *Freud on Women*. New York: W.W. Norton.

[See Chapter 4 for annotation.]

Chodorow, Nancy (1991). Freud on women. In: *Cambridge Companion to Freud*, ed. J. Neu. New York: Cambridge University Press.

Chodorow considers several types of women presented by Freud: theoretical woman in the developmental theory; clinical women; women's intrapsychic representations of women; women in social and historical contexts; women as creators of psychoanalytic technique and understanding; and women as explicit or implicit objects to the male psyche. This brief but encyclopedic survey is an excellent guide to the many dimensions of Freud's views on women and to the major lacunae in those views.

Silver, Donald (1991). Freud, Gisela, Silberstein, the Academia Castellana and the repudiation of femininity. *Psychoanal. Inq.*, 11(4).

Freud's adolescent letters reveal a passionate triangular relationship between Gisela, a girl from his hometown of Freiberg, and Eduard Silberstein, his intimate correspondent. Silver argues that this triangle became so intense that Freud took refuge in the pursuit of learning and the repudiation of women. Throughout this correspondence with Silberstein, Freud's self-examination and self-revelations can be seen to presage his subsequent self analysis and intimate correspondence with Wilhelm Fliess.

Young-Bruehl, Elisabeth (1991). Rereading Freud on female development. *Psychoanal. Inq.*, 11(4).

Young-Bruehl shows how Freud's later revisions, including the dual instinct theory (1920), structural theory (1923), and theory of anxiety (1926), introduced contradictions into his views on female development and obscured contradictions already existing in his views based on *Three Essays on the Theory of Sexuality*. She notes that Freud did not illustrate his new theories with fully developed male or female cases as he did prior to the development of his new metapsychology after 1920. She suggests that his work on masochism, narcissism, and superego development would have been better informed by such a revision and reassessment and even further integrated by an understanding of the impact of the girl's preoedipal relationship to her mother.

### Karen Horney

Moulton, Ruth (1975). Early papers on women: Horney to Thompson. *Amer. J. Psychoanal.*, 35:207-223.

Setting Horney's work in a historical context, this article reviews Horney's contributions to understanding the psychology of women. Moulton stresses Horney's challenge to Freud. She traces the transition between Horney's nine papers written between 1922 and 1932. She then gives an overview of the history of the psychology of women. Particularly highlighting and summarizing the work of Clara Thompson, Moulton briefly describes several papers that contributed to later ideas. Freud's views and his personal history are presented in a very simplified form. More historical information about the psychoanalysts Moulton described has since become available.

Garrison, Dee (1981). Karen Horney and feminism. *Signs*, 6:672-691.

This article is an introduction to Horney's work from a feminist viewpoint. Tracing Horney's career as a psychoanalyst, Garrison focuses on Horney's contributions to the psychology of women. She emphasizes both Horney's view of a biological basis for female psychology and the importance of the interaction between the individual and the culture. Garrison notes Horney's apolitical stance and her lack of emphasis on political and social factors. Garrison speculates about how factors in Horney's personal and professional life may have affected her choice of topics and theoretical stance, particularly in her ceasing to write about the psychology of women after 1933.

Kerr, Norine (1989). Wounded womanhood: An analysis of Karen Horney's theory of feminine psychology. *Perspect. Psych. Care*, 24:132-141.

Karen Horney's life is overviewed, focusing on her theories of feminine psychology and particularly, her disagreement with Freud about penis envy as a primary phenomenon in females.

### Melanie Klein

Elmhirst, Susanna Isaacs (1980). The early stages of female psychosexual development: A Kleinian view. In: *Women's Sexual Development: Explorations of Inner Space*, ed. M. Kirkpatrick. New York: Plenum Press, pp. 109-125.

The author laments that misunderstandings and prejudices have obscured the scientific basis for disagreement between Kleinians and Freudians. Klein asserted that babies and young children have intense, violently aggressive feelings and fantasies. Because of inevitable frustrations, the breast is rendered bad in the imagination and the external object (mother) is responded to as an attacker. Elmhirst argues that Winnicott simplistically implied that mothers can satisfy their infant's emotional needs. Instead she conjectures that mothers are felt to contain satisfactions, including penis and baby, that are envied. Clear sex differences in development are manifest in the last quarter of the first year, when the genital phase is incipient. Girls are more absorbed with the insides of toys and their contents. Girls' wishes for a penis are partly infantile wishes to have every object possessed by those they admire, a way of getting gratification from mother, and a source of rivalry with father. The wish to be orally gratified by mother through eating and sucking is transferred to the vagina. Anal fantasies can involve taking over both parental roles, with feces representing penis and babies, as well as the greedy and spoiling parts of the infant.

Silverman, Doris (1987a). Female bonding: Some supportive findings for Melanie Klein's views. *The Psychoanal. Rev.*, 74:201-215.

Silverman asserts that certain aspects of Klein's views about early infant female experience are confirmed by recent research, and Klein's views are more accurate than some ideas proposed by Freud. Klein emphasized as prominent in females the immediate recognition and connection to objects and the development of depressive anxieties with reparative fantasies. Silverman reviews infant observation studies whose findings sustain many of Klein's views, including the immediacy of mother-infant synchronicity, a differential early strong attachment of mother and female infant, and an increased potential for connectedness to the caregiver. Reparation fantasies discussed by Klein are also supported by data showing that female infants have greater fears of loss, anger at brief separations, and sensitivity to the emotional state of others, particularly their mothers.

Sayers, Janet (1989). Melanie Klein and mothering: A feminist perspective. *Int. Rev. Psychoanal.*, 16:363-376.

The author argues that women's primary role as mother and their actual experience of mothering provide them a unique point of view, as exemplified in the work of Melanie Klein. Klein's work is reviewed, including her views of maternal transferences and female development and sexuality.

### Sylvia Payne

Arden, Margaret (1987). "A concept of femininity": Sylvia Payne's 1935 paper reassessed. *Int. Rev. Psycho-Anal.*, 14:237-244.

Arden reviews Payne's requirements for femininity and adds her own emphasis on viewing femininity as the result of the integration of bisexuality, or male/female complementarity. Arden postulates that primary-process thinking is feminine and secondary-process thinking is masculine and that the two together represent an integrated human mind. An analytic case illuminates Payne's bisexual theory that the organization of femininity must include a phallic symbol and that this symbol is not necessarily pathological.

### Joan Riviere

Heath, Stephen (1986). Joan Riviere and the masquerade. In: *Formations of Fantasy*, ed. V. Burgin, J. D. Kaplan, and L. Kaplan. New York: Methuen, pp. 45-61.

This chapter offers an analysis of Riviere's 1929 paper, "Womanliness as a Masquerade." Heath reviews the main points of the paper and speculates on the personal dilemmas this topic posed for the author in the light of her relationships to her own male analysts, Jones and Freud. He believes that the central question in Riviere's paper concerns feminine identity, with womanliness and the masquerade paradoxically being the same thing in the end. Heath analyzes this question from a Lacanian perspective; he focuses on the meaning of the phallus as signifier and on sexual identity as something that is precariously constructed from symbolic division. Heath attempts to elucidate Lacanian concepts pertinent to his argument for readers not intimately familiar with them.

## SECTION C—COLLECTIONS OF PAPERS AND BOOKS

Ruitenbeek, Henrik (1966). *Psychoanalysis and Female Sexuality*, New Haven, CT: College and University Press.

This collection of classic and contemporary psychoanalytic and nonanalytic essays about female sexuality emphasizes developmental factors and special sociocultural conditions. Selected papers by Jones, Lampl-de Groot, Thompson, Horney, Bonaparte and Deutsch are presented but not discussed. Freud's paper on "Female Sexuality" (1931a) is included because of his emphasis on the preoedipal stage of development and its salience for female sexuality. Three papers, by Greenacre, Marmor, and Lorand, address clitoral and vaginal sensitivity and orgasm. The volume concludes with chapters by Maslow, Freedman, Riviere, and Thompson. This is an idiosyncratic collection.

Horney, Karen (1967). *Feminine Psychology*, ed. H. Kelman. New York: Norton.

Kelman begins this collection of Horney's papers about feminine psychology with an introduction tracing the biographical, theoretical, and clinical parallels and divergencies between Horney and Freud. He summarizes each of Horney's papers. Horney's essays include "On the Genesis of the Castration Complex in Women" (1924), "The Flight from Womanhood" (1926), "Inhibited Femininity: Psychoanalytic Contribution to the Problem of Frigidity" (1927), "Premenstrual Tension" (1931), The Dread of Women (1932), "The Denial of the Vagina" (1933), and other selections. [Many of these papers have been individually annotated in other chapters.]

**Strouse, Jean (1974). *Women and Analysis*. New York: Grossman/Viking Press.**

This book, a series of dialogues about female psychology, takes as its starting point 10 historic psychoanalytic papers written by Freud, Horney, Abraham, Erikson, Bonaparte, Deutsch, Jung, Thompson, and Erikson. Contemporary authors from a variety of disciplines respond to the original papers. Several of Freud's papers (1925, 1931a, 1933) are discussed by Janeway, Mead, Mitchell, and Stoller. Erikson criticizes his own paper, "Womanhood and the Inner Space." The various chapters represent a wide range of historic psychoanalytic views and modern counterpoint ideas about female development on many topics, including masochism, biological determinism, bisexuality, gender identity, penis envy, the female castration complex, childbearing, social and cultural roles, and the development of sexual identity.

# Chapter 4

# *Modern Theoretical Formulations*

Nadine Levinson, Lynn Whisnant Reiser, Eleanor Schuker
Additional contributions by Joyce L. Root

The articles and books listed in this chapter provide modern comprehensive perspectives or overviews of female psychology. They include papers and books written since 1940 that elaborate, revise, or dissent from classical psychoanalytic views. These writings include both new formulations and concepts that are within the evolving psychoanalytic mainstream and other formulations that offer alternative or reactive perspectives. Some of these writings have been central to modern psychoanalytic revisions of female psychology, while others represent the work of theorists who have developed in more radical directions. Papers pertinent to topics covered in other chapters are cross-referenced. (E.S.)

Thompson, Clara (1941). The role of women of this culture. *Psychiat.*, 4:1-8. Also in: *Women and Analysis*, ed. J. Strouse. New York: Grossman/Viking Press, 1974, pp. 265-277.

Thompson's work is a reaction against the biologism and inevitability of the Freudian schema of female development. Thompson presages later contributions from object relations theorists with her emphasis on the importance of cultural influences. She contrasts Freud's view of women as biologically destined with her own view of women as responding to culturally determined challenges that affect women's character development, attitudes toward themselves, and societal roles. Thompson views culture as an essential ingredient in personality. Vignettes illustrate cultural influences on women's attitudes toward marriage, childbearing, genitals, and sexuality. Thompson describes her women contemporaries as being in a period of transition, and she delineates both healthy and pathological responses to cultural pressures.

Thompson, Clara (1942). Cultural pressures on the psychology of women. *Psychiat.*, 5:331-339. Also in: *Psychoanalysis and Women*, ed. J. B. Miller. New York: Brunner/Mazel, 1973, pp. 49-64.

Thompson assumes that in both sexes certain neurotic trends are found, such as masochism, the neurotic need to be loved, strivings for power, and insatiable ambition. Women have their own specific biological experiences, including menstruation, pregnancy, and menopause, which can be experienced positively or negatively, depending on the culture. Thompson contends that Freud's concept of feminine masochism, based on these biological experiences, is erroneous and was influenced by his Victorian background and male bias. Thompson describes cultural inequities that can distort women's development and produce neurotic characteristics. To the extent that women are biologically fulfilled, they have no tendency to envy men's biology or to feel inferior. Thompson concludes that the basic nature of women is still unknown. This work was not appreciated by mainstream psychoanalysts of the time partly because it eschewed technical language and a developmental approach. [See also Chapter 12.]

Zilboorg, Gregory (1944). Masculine and feminine. *Psychiat.*, 7:257-296. Also in: *Psychoanalysis and Women*, ed. J. B. Miller. Baltimore, MD: Penguin, 1973, pp. 96-131.

Zilboorg's work is an early challenge to classical views. He reconstructs a primitive human history, contrasting with Freud's primal horde myth. In Zilboorg's view, women are the primary life force and power. Males play a secondary role, for they are chosen by women for preferred traits (natural selection), including physical strength and size. Men then use this physical advantage to overthrow the matrilineal tradition, because of their envy of its power, their frustrated dependency yearnings, and, most important, their phallic sadistic/sexual drive. This "male efflorescence" produces "the primal rape." Militating against men's hostility both toward women and toward intrusive children is their identification with the still envied mother/woman, the beginning of psychological fatherhood. Zilboorg posits that the evolution of the psychoanalytic concept of women's penis envy is both a projection of the men's envious hostility onto women and also women's desire to regain their lost power via identification with the male. [See also Chapter 13.]

Thompson, Clara (1950). Some effects of the derogatory attitudes toward female sexuality. *Psychiat.*, 13:349-354. Also in: *Psychoanalysis and Women*, ed. J. B. Miller. New York: Brunner/Mazel, 1973, pp. 65-74.

[See Chapters 13 and 18 for annotations.]

Stoller, Robert (1968a). *Sex and Gender: On the Development of Masculinity and Femininity.* New York: Science House.

[See Chapter 5 for annotation.]

Chasseguet-Smirgel, Janine (1970). *Female Sexuality: New Psychoanalytic Views,* ed. J. Chasseguet-Smirgel. Ann Arbor: University of Michigan Press.

The contributions to this collection of original articles present theoretical and clinical material that both reviews and revises Freud's psychology of female sexuality. Using both Kleinian and Freudian approaches, the authors emphasize the overwhelming importance of the mother for the development of the little girl, linking early preoedipal fantasies to later sexual adjustment. Chasseguet-Smirgel offers an introduction that scrutinizes the range of disparate early theories on female sexuality. Luquet-Parat proposes that feminine masochism plays a dynamic role in influencing the change from maternal object to paternal object. Female narcissism and its origins are discussed by Grunberger. McDougall discusses female homosexuality, Torok considers penis envy, and Chasseguet-Smirgel explores the role of the father in relation to the female superego and the Oedipus complex. [Most of these papers are individually annotated.]

Miller, Jean Baker and Mothres, Ira (1971). Psychological consequences of sexual inequality. *Amer. J. Orthopsychiat.,* 41:767-775.

This article discusses psychopathology from a sociological perspective. The psychological attributes of less powerful groups are characterized. The authors address social inequality and its influence on women by postulating that women often respond to social inequities by interacting with their families in ways that generate a "dominant mother-ineffectual father" pattern. A clinical illustration explores the authors' views.

Miller, Jean Baker (1973). *Psychoanalysis and Women.* New York: Brunner/Mazel.

Miller's book is one of the first collections of old and new psychoanalytically relevant papers on the psychology of women. Several chapters are highly critical of early psychoanalytic models or eschew a psychoanalytic approach. Many chapters emphasize a new model based on the positive aspects of femininity. The first section reviews early papers from the 1920s to 1950s by Horney, Thompson, and Zilboorg. These papers emphasize that many traits relevant to female development and ascribed to biology are artifacts of social conditions. The second section reviews the emergence of new evidence, criticism, and observations about femininity and female sexuality. It includes papers by Sherfey, Stoller, Marmor and M.B. Cohen. The personality of women is viewed by several authors as being primarily the outcome of strong social, cultural, political and historical forces. Intrapsychic factors are minimized. [See also Chapter 11.]

Mitchell, Juliet (1974a). On Freud and the distinction between the sexes. In: *Women and Analysis*, ed. J. Strouse. New York: Grossman/Viking Press, pp. 27-36.

[See Chapter 3 for annotation.]

Mitchell, Juliet (1974b). *Psychoanalysis and Feminism*. New York: Pantheon.

Mitchell offers a reading of Freud based on the work of Lacan and supporting a feminist approach. This book attempts to integrate Freud's work on female development with feminist concerns. Mitchell argues the Lacanian position that the unconscious is structured like a language. Thus, she suggests that the unconscious is the vehicle for the transmission of social and cultural laws. These laws stem from the ideology that women are inferior. The asymmetrical sociological dynamics involved in the mother-infant-father relationship are proposed as the mechanism for the transmission of these laws. The father intervenes in the mother-infant relationship and is the main representative of a patriarchal culture and society. This society, with the father as its representative, neither recognizes nor values the distinctively different attitudes of femininity.

Schafer, Roy (1974). Problems in Freud's psychology of women. *J. Amer. Psychoanal. Assn.*, 22:459-485. Also in: *J. Amer. Psychoanal. Assn.* (Suppl.), 24:331-360, 1976.

[See Chapter 7 for annotation.]

Strouse, Jean (1974). *Women and Analysis*, New York: Grossman/Viking Press.

[See Chapter 3 for annotation]

Barglow, Peter and Schaefer, Margret (1976). A new female psychology? *J. Amer. Psychoanal. Assn.* (Suppl.), 24:305-350.

Barglow and Schaefer review and comment on five books: *Psychology of Women* (1971) by J. Bardwick; *Female Sexuality* (1970) edited by J. Chasse-guet-Smirgel; *Man's World, Women's Place* (1971) by E. Janeway; *Feminine Psychology* (1967) by K. Horney, and *Psychoanalysis and Women* (1973), edited by J. Baker Miller. The authors chose books that criticize aspects of psychoanalytic theory, and they have grouped these books according to three major theoretical approaches to female psychology. The Miller, Horney, and Janeway books emphasize social, cultural, and historical factors. The Bardwick book emphasizes biological influences and the Chasseguet-Smirgel book looks at intrapsychic dimensions. The article both clarifies the predominant points of view in these works and suggests biases and limitations. The books in the first group follow Horney's early lead in rejecting Freud's central theories about female psychology. Many of these authors view the ideas of penis envy and female masochism not only as reflections of what Victorian society allowed women, but also as expressions of male fantasies and fears of women. Barglow and Schaefer assert that parts of Horney's critique of Freud's attitudes are persuasive. Nevertheless, they end their review of that first group of articles by commenting on the obvious shortcoming of theories that deny biological or unconscious determinants and view women as a tabula rasa for the culture rather than acknowledging the importance of internal reality. They comment that a psychoanalytic ideology puts the analyst at risk for transference and countertransference distortions. [See Fliegel, 1982, in this chapter for a critique of that view].

In discussing the book edited by Chasseguet-Smirgel, Barglow and Schaefer begin by clarifying the Kleinian point of view that little girls endure early narcissistic injury because they somehow understand that mother is not an adequate sexual object; the authors then describe the resulting breast and penis envy and narcissistic vulnerability. They comment that the idea that women have lower self-esteem than men is widespread but difficult to demonstrate, citing Maccoby and Jacklin's (1975) findings of no difference in self-esteem between boys and girls. Barglow and Schaefer suggest a different timetable for narcissistic disequilibrium in boys and girls and present an extensive discussion of the separation-individuation processes in the two sexes. They elaborate their own view that girls' feminine self-image is both biologically based and facilitated or inhibited by parental mirroring responses.

Blum, Harold (ed.)(1976). Female Psychology: Contemporary Psychoanalytic Issues, *J. Amer. Psychoanal. Assn.* (Suppl.), Vol. 24. New York: International Universities Press.

This anthology, reissued in 1977, has become a classic in psychoanalytic inquiry into female psychology, covering a variety of topics by a number of authors. The purpose of the book is to clarify, correct, and stimulate further investigation of theoretical assumptions and propositions pertinent to female development. In doing so, each of the contributors has taken a fresh look at definitions, origins, and developmental transformations in exploration of feminine traits and tendencies. The book begins with a paper by Kleeman that reconsiders Freud's views of female sexuality through the lens of direct child observation. Galenson and Roiphe, Parens et al., Lerner, Clower, and Stoller each add their own revisions based on clinical and child observational studies and, through clinical reports or child observation, provide a developmental look at women from birth through adulthood. Finally, in addition to viewing gender identity and sexual identity, the book surveys special issues in female psychology such as female values, maternal attitudes, masturbation, and creative interests. This book is essential for any course about female development. [All the individual articles are annotated in this bibliography.]

Clower, Virginia (1976). Theoretical implications in current views of masturbation in latency girls. *J. Amer. Psychoanal Assn.* (Suppl.), 24:109-125.

[See Chapter 18 for annotation.]

Dinnerstein, Dorothy (1976). *The Mermaid and the Minotaur.* New York: Harper.

[See Chapters 5 and 13 for annotations.]

Galenson, Eleanor and Roiphe, Herman (1976). Some suggested revisions concerning early female development. *J. Amer. Psychoanal. Assn.* (Suppl.), 24:29-57.

[See Chapter 18 for annotation.]

Kleeman, James (1976). Freud's views on early female sexuality in the light of direct child observation. *J. Amer. Psychoanal. Assn.* (Suppl.), 24:3-27.

[See Chapter 18 for annotation.]

Lewis, Helen Block (1976). *Psychic War in Men and Women.* New York: New York University Press. Also published as: *Sex and the Superego: Psychic War in Men and Women.* Hillsdale, NJ: Lawrence Erlbaum Associates, 1987.

This book emphasizes the importance of society and its influence on psychic development. The author asserts that the exploitative social and economic institutions of developed cultures foster relations between the sexes that are based on aggression, dominance, and subjugation. Citing literature from physiology, genetics, and experimental psychology to illustrate the innate differences between the sexes, Lewis theorizes that it is not these, but acculturation, that leads to the development of the oppression of women by men. Lewis views women as more vulnerable to shame and men as more vulnerable to guilt, because of differing object relations.

Miller, Jean Baker (1976). *Toward A New Psychology of Women*. Boston, MA: Beacon Press, 1986.

This book focuses on gender and personhood in contemporary society. The chapter on "The Makings of the Mind—So Far" discusses the structured inequality in personal relationships; "Looking in Both Directions" asserts that some psychological qualities are more highly developed in women than men, including vulnerability, emotionality, participation in the growth of others, cooperation, and creativity, and explores the reasons why these feminine characteristics should be seen as strengths and as the foundation for positive changes needed in society as a whole. "Notes in a Future Key" discusses topics that women must confront in order to develop greater equality in relationships including, authenticity through cooperation, creativity, power, self-determination, and the necessity for engaging in conflict.

Moore, Burness (1976). Freud and female sexuality: A current view. *Int. J. Psycho-Anal.*, 57:287-300.

[See Chapters 3 and 18 for annotations.]

Stoller, Robert (1976). Primary femininity. *J. Amer Psychoanal. Assn.* (Suppl.), 24:59-78.

[See Chapter 6 for annotation.]

Chodorow, Nancy (1978). *The Reproduction of Mothering: Psychoanalysis and the Sociology of Gender*. Berkeley, CA: University of California Press.

This influential book contends that the role of mothering is central to social organization and the reproduction of gender. In Part I, Chodorow looks at why women mother and how women's mothering affects society by its influence on personality structure. In Part II, highlighting the various asymmetries in the mother-child internal object relationship, she proposes a reinterpretation of feminine and masculine personality development. Preoedipal, oedipal and postoedipal development are emphasized. In Part III, Chodorow elaborates on how the mother-child relationship affects future parenting for men and women. [See Chapters 5, 6, 7, 11, and 14 for individually annotated chapters.]

Flax, Jane (1980). Mother-daughter relationships: Psychodynamics politics and philosophy. In: *The Future of Difference*, ed. H. Eisenstein and A. Jardine. Boston, MA: G. K. Hall, pp. 20-40.

Flax criticizes Freud from a feminist perspective, for neglecting a full account of the preoedipal period and early mother-daughter relationships. Similarly, she illuminates the repression of this period in the philosophy and political theory of Descartes, Hobbes, and Locke. Through the analysis of a patient's dream, Flax illustrates typically female psychodynamics: 1) ego boundary confusion between mother and daughter; 2) rage at the mother, covered by conscious desire to protect mother; 3) penis envy symbolically reflecting preoedipal roots, including wishes for symbiotic unity, access to mother, and resentment of mother; 4) separation of nurturance and autonomy within the family, reinforced by patriarchal control of both social relations and economic and political structures, creating a psychological equation of separation with abandonment by and of mother. Flax argues that differentiation is at the core of women's psychological problems. She disagrees with Chodorow about the meaning of the preoedipal ambivalent mother-daughter tie.

Kirkpatrick, Martha (1980). *Women's Sexual Development; Explorations of Inner Space*. New York: Plenum Press.

This collection of papers on issues about female sexuality includes contributions by authors from psychoanalytic, feminist, academic, medical, and sex education backgrounds. Chapters cover physiological aspects of sexual development, psychoanalytic views of female psychosexual development, masturbation, lesbianism, father-daughter relationships, history of sexuality, and sex education and gynecological self-help issues.

Person, Ethel (1980). Sexuality as the mainstay of identity: Psychoanalytic perspectives. *Signs*, 5:605-630. Also in: *Women: Sex and Sexuality*, ed. C. Stimpson and E. Person. Chicago, IL: University of Chicago Press, 1980, pp 31-61.

[See Chapter 18 for annotation.]

Fliegel, Zenia (1982). Half a century later: Current status of Freud's controversial views on women. *Psychoanal. Rev.*, 69:7-28.

This article contains a look backward at earlier controversies about female psychology existing in the 1920s and critiques Freud's views on women in the light of modern evidence. The author notes that Freud's ideas, including those thought to be untenable, cannot simply be discarded, but must be addressed. Early dissenters like Horney and Jones have still not been sufficiently acknowledged, though many of their views are now incorporated into some modern formulations. Moreover, new evidence from child observation has not been adequately integrated into contemporary theory. Freud's developmental sequence has been postulated as normative but needs further testing. Fliegel reviews the newer, but also controversial, evidence from direct child observation that seems to challenge the central role of the castration complex and penis envy. Formulations by Galenson and Roiphe, Kleeman, Kestenberg, Edgcumbe et al., and other authors are discussed, critiqued, and compared with the work of the early analytic theorists. The historic controversy between Horney and Freud and their ideas about female development is examined.

Gilligan, Carol (1982a). *In A Different Voice: Psychological Theory and Women's Development.* Cambridge, MA: Harvard University Press.

This creative book evaluates different modes of thinking of men and women and proposes that women value attachment and connectedness to others, whereas men value individuation and separateness from others. Care and concern are more fundamental to women, whereas justice and fairness are more central to men. Three previous research studies provide the data to explore the issues of identity, relationships, morality, rights, and responsibilities. In the chapter, "Concepts of Self and Morality," Gilligan postulates that women view moral problems in terms of conflicting responsibilities between self and others. Three sequentially complicated perspectives of morality, with each perspective representing a more complex relationship between self and other are proposed. In the sequence, there is an initial concern with survival, then a focus on goodness, and finally a reflective understanding of care as the central guide to resolving conflicts in relationships. Gilligan calls for an expanded developmental theory of women to explain the precursors of these distinctive moral conceptions. [See also Chapter 7.]

Kirkpatrick, Martha (ed.)(1982). *Women's Sexual Experience: Explorations of the Dark Continent.* New York: Plenum Press.

Kirkpatrick presents a collection of diverse essays on female sexuality, emphasizing gaps in research. [See Chapter 18 for annotation.]

Lacan, Jacques and the École Freudienne (1982). *Feminine Sexuality*, ed. J. Mitchell and J. Rose (Trans. J. Rose). New York: Norton, 1985.

This collection of essays by Jacques Lacan and the members of the Ecole Freudienne sets forth Lacan's reexamination and revision of Freud's theories of female sexuality. Lacan's theories of female sexuality are based on his general formulations about the human subject and language within what he calls the symbolic realm. The essays examine such linguistic terms as castration complex, desire, and the phallus in the context of the social dimensions of sexual identity. They situate the construction of sexual difference within the symbolic realm. Lacan feels that because of historical circumstances Freud was prevented from fully articulating the importance of his discoveries about the role of language and social symbolism in the creation of sexual identity. This collection reopens questions about the analytic and social constitution of (female) sexuality and identity, and it revises the task of psychoanalysis through Lacan's resistance to the analytic and social fictions of a coherent self.

Mendell, Dale (ed.)(1982). *Early Female Development: Current Psychoanalytic Views*. New York: S.P. Medical and Scientific Books.

This book is a collection of ongoing contemporary formulations of various aspects of female development, including the development of identifications, narcissism, and separation-individuation. An explanation of how these developmental lines interface with the attainment of gender identity is proposed. Ego development, object relations, and narcissistic vicissitudes are highlighted, in contrast to more traditional formulations about female psychosexual development. Divergent views of the same chronological period from infancy through latency are presented. (Each of the chapters is individually annotated elsewhere.)

Tyson, Phyllis (1982). A developmental line of gender identity, gender role, and choice of love object. *J. Amer. Psychoanal. Assn.*, 30:61-86.

Tyson views gender identity in a broad sense as composed of three interacting aspects: core gender identity, gender role identity, and sexual partner orientation. [See Chapter 6 for annotation.]

Person, Ethel (1983). The influence of values in psychoanalysis: The case of female psychology. *Psychiatry Update*, ed. L. Grinspoon. Washington, DC: American Psychiatric Press, Vol. 2, pp. 36-50.

In this historical review, Person traces the changes in our understanding of female psychology. She summarizes early Freudian theory and its patriarchal biases and describes changes the theory has undergone since the 1970s. She demonstrates how these changes have resulted from new data, both from psychoanalysis and from related disciplines; examines why it took so long for the changes to occur; and then notes how underlying, unexamined cultural assumptions and values prevented the integration of data that was available earlier. Changes in theories of female sexuality, gender identity, and the centrality of penis envy are delineated. Person believes that a shift in the scientific paradigms of psychoanalysis to include underlying cultural assumptions and values, by way of internalization and object relations as psychic organizers, now allows for a more complete integration of the data.

Bernstein, Anne and Warner, Gloria (1984). *Women Treating Women.* New York: International Universities Press.

Theoretical aspects of female psychology are investigated and critically reviewed, beginning with the propositions of Freud and other early analysts. Contributions from direct child observation and research are offered to explore contemporary metapsychological considerations of feminine development. The question "What does a woman want?" is examined throughout the different developmental phases of the life cycle from the preoedipal phase through adulthood. The authors stress the importance of the preoedipal mother-daughter relationship, which they feel shapes the future of the daughter's self-regard, oedipal complex, and sexuality. Case material from the psychoanalyses of women illuminates the relationship of separation/individuation to a variety of clinical phenomena and developmental experiences such as sexual fantasies, perversion, masochism, narcissism, anorexia; experiences connected to reproduction; and gender issues and transference and countertransference.

Alpert, Judith (ed.)(1986). *Psychoanalysis and Women: Contemporary Reappraisals.* Hillsdale, NJ: The Analytic Press.

In a dozen chapters subsumed in four sections—an Overview, Freudian Theory and Beyond, Female Patient (conflicts in work and love), and Female Analyst (gender issues in treatment and the pregnant analyst) —contributors discuss controversies concerning female psychology. In the larger framework, these chapters also represent disputes about some fundamental premises of psychoanalysis itself. The drive-defense, ego-psychological model is less prominent than are object relations and self psychology approaches. Alpert's book features an interpersonal emphasis on the effects of social reality factors on the psychotherapeutic situation. [Several chapters are individually annotated.]

Alpert, Judith and Spencer, Jody (1986). Morality, gender, and analysis. In: *Psychoanalysis and Women: Contemporary Reappraisals*, ed. J. Alpert. Hillsdale, NJ: The Analytic Press, pp. 83-111.

Freud, Horney, Kohlberg, and Gilligan's contrasting theories of moral development in relation to gender differences are considered. The authors begin by reviewing Freud's views on superego development in women, views contending that women have weaker superegos as a result of their acceptance of castration and lack of castration anxiety. According to the authors, Freud confuses values with observation. Kohlberg's work on cognitive development and his measurement of moral values in males are reviewed and criticized for being applied to women and thus creating the impression that women are deficient in moral reasoning. On the other hand, the authors cite Gilligan's work, which focuses on women's orientation toward attachment and connectedness to others and men's orientation toward autonomy and separateness from others. They discuss Gilligan's proposal that men and women have distinctively different values and moral development. Justice, equity, and fairness are more salient issues for men; care and concern are more central concepts for women. The authors conclude by considering the similarities and differences among the theorists about the development and conceptualization of moral behavior in the different genders. The different theoretical perspectives are shown to have implications for clinical work.

Bernay, Toni and Cantor, Dorothy (ed.)(1986). *The Psychology of Today's Woman: New Psychoanalytic Visions.* Hillsdale, NJ: The Analytic Press.

This book is thought provoking, though not comprehensive nor reflective of a consolidated psychoanalytic understanding of female psychology. The four sections in the book are Traditional Visions of Femininity Reassessed, New Visions of Femininity, Today's Woman (a section dealing with life cycle issues), and Issues in the Therapeutic Relationship. Sociocultural, interpersonal, and feminist perspectives are emphasized. Contributors include Lewis, Galenson, Person, Herman, Applegarth, and Eisenbud. Among several interesting articles are those on reproductive motivations, childless women, and working mothers and can be found in the Developmental Perspective Section.

Chehrazi, Shalah (1986). Female psychology: A review. *J. Amer. Psychoanal. Assn.*, 34:141-162.

This article gives a comprehensive overview of current psychoanalytic theory of female development and its influence on clinical work. [See Chapter 6 for annotation.]

Fliegel, Zenia (1986). Women's development in analytic theory: Six decades of controversy. In: *Psychoanalysis and Women: Contemporary Reappraisals*, ed. J. Alpert. Hillsdale, NJ: The Analytic Press, pp. 3-31.

This extensive overview updates Fliegel's 1982 paper summarizing the history of the development of ideas about the psychology of women. Contemporary research is placed in relationship to historical formulations of Freud, Horney, Lampl-de Groot, Deutsch, Fenichel, and M. Klein. Fliegel points out that Horney's idea that primary and secondary penis envy have separate psychic components is echoed by Edgcumbe and Burgner and others. The concept of an innate, pleasure-oriented, nondefensive feminine libido is traced. Fliegel closely follows the arguments against Freud's position that masturbation, excitability, and libido are all quintessentially masculine. She asserts that despite the struggle for neutrality, analysts' traditional convictions guide both infant observation and clinical interventions. She disagrees with the concept of a universal, negative oedipal phase in girls. She feels that Freud's principle of complementarity would probably be useful in integrating the theories of drive/instinct and object relations. Fliegel emphasizes the importance of the historical context of the early papers, highlights major issues in the early controversies, points out how positions became codified into doctrines, and samples later research studies in relation to the early views to offer a perspective on later literature.

Gillespie, William (1986). Woman and her discontents: A reassessment of Freud's views on female sexuality. In: *The British School of Psychoanalysis: The Independent Tradition*, ed. G. Kohon. New Haven, CT: Yale University Press, pp. 344-361.

[See Chapter 3 for annotation.]

Tyson, Phyllis (1986). Female psychological development. *The Annual of Psychoanalysis*, 4:357-373. New York: International Universities Press.

[See Chapter 6 for annotation.]

Walsh, Mary (1987). *The Psychology of Women: Ongoing Debates*. New Haven, CT: Yale University Press.

Walsh has arranged a medley of diverse viewpoints from previously published feminist and psychological papers, but without any historical context. Fourteen controversial issues about female psychology are represented from two opposing points of view. In one section, pro- and antianalytic authors deal with the relevance of psychoanalytic theory to understanding female psychology. Other sections include Femaleness and Psychological Health; New Theories and Evidence in the Psychology of Women (fear of success, gender issues, children, mothering and devaluation of women); and Social Issues Affecting Women. This collection emphasizes a polemical and heterogeneous feminist perspective but does not similarly address current and controversial psychoanalytic issues.

Benjamin, Jessica (1988). *The Bonds of Love: Psychoanalysis, Feminism, and the Problem of Domination.* New York: Pantheon.

This book addresses the psychoanalytic theory of gender development in the broader context of psychoanalytic metapsychology and social theory. It contends that a revision of Freudian metapsychology to integrate infant and gender development is crucial to understanding the dynamics of women's subjugation. Using data from infancy research, the first chapter presents a reformulation of infant development. The second chapter offers an analysis of the dynamics of submission and domination, with a reinterpretation of Freud's views on masochism, aggression, and the death instinct. The third chapter discusses the controversy around female psychology and penis envy, with special emphasis on the father-daughter relationship. A critique of the Oedipus complex and its emphasis on separation from the archaic mother is presented in the fourth chapter. Finally, the fifth chapter explores the implications of this psychoanalytic critique for understanding the social forms of gender domination.

Lerner, Harriet (1988). *Women in Therapy.* Northvale, NJ: Aronson.

This compilation of articles written by Lerner over a 15-year period carefully critiques and challenges both psychoanalytic and feminist theories of female psychology. The first four chapters review the early years of female development. Penis envy is not seen as biological bedrock but as derived from an early envy of the omnipotent mother. Parental mislabeling of female genitals and conflicts with aggression are reviewed. Part II reviews special problems of diagnosis; "female" clinical syndromes such as depression, dependency, and hysteria; and, finally, discusses psychotherapy with women. Extensive case material with samples of treatment interactions are presented. The book argues for a systems approach to female development wherein the final outcome of female development is seen as a circular and reciprocal interaction of intrapsychic, cultural, and familial patterns. [Many chapters are individually annotated.]

Mendell, Dale (1988). Early female development: From birth through latency. In: *Critical Psychophysical Passages in the Life of a Women*, ed. J. Offerman-Zuckerberg. New York: Plenum, pp. 17-36.

[See Chapter 6 for annotation.]

Small, Fern (1989). The psychology of women: A psychoanalytic review. *Can. J. Psychiat.*, 34:872-878.

Early classical Freudian psychoanalytic theories of female psychology are succinctly reviewed and revised by presenting modern psychoanalytic views organized around recent contributions to the knowledge of female psychosexual development and clinical applications. Preoedipal development of feminine gender identity, female body and genital representation, penis envy, the Oedipus complex, superego development, and conflicts over aggression and the avoidance of success are discussed.

Tyson, Phyllis (1989). Infantile sexuality, gender identity, and obstacles to oedipal progression. *J. Amer. Psychoanal. Assn.*,37:1051-1069.

Tyson presents clinical material from the analyses of four children to discuss their divergent progression from preoedipal through oedipal development. [See Chapter 6 for annotation.]

Chodorow, Nancy (1989). *Feminism and Psychoanalytic Theory*. New Haven, CT: Yale University Press.

This book collects most of Chodorow's essays from 1972 to the present and shows the development of her thoughts as she integrates psychoanalysis and feminism. Writing from an object relations perspective, in Part I, The Significance of Women's Mothering for Gender Personality and Gender Relations, Chodorow reviews her previous work on the centrality of the preoedipal mother to the construction of femininity and masculinity. In Part II, Gender, Self and Social Theory, she discusses a wide range of topics including differentiation, gender differences, beyond drive theory, and intersubjectivity. Finally, in Part III, Feminism, Femininity, and Freud, she delineates the asymmetric approaches to the issues of gender and sexuality taken by psychoanalytic feminists and psychoanalysts. She suggests that a continuing dialogue between psychoanalysts and feminists in the area of object relations theory can be mutually beneficial. The last chapter reports her research on gender consciousness in the female analysts trained in the 1920s, 1930s, and 1940s. [Several chapters are individually annotated.]

Chodorow, Nancy (1989b). Psychoanalytic feminism and the psycho-analytic psychology of women. In: *Feminism and Psychoanalytic Theory,* New Haven, CT: Yale University Press, pp. 178-198. Also published as: What is the relation between the psychoanalytic psychology of women and psychoanalytic feminism? *The Annual of Psychoanalysis,* 17:215-261. Hillsdale, NJ: The Analytic Press.

This essay reviews dominant trends in the psychoanalytic literature on gender: new attention to genital awareness in the second year; arguments for primary feminine genital awareness; attention to the development of gender identity; and concern with cross-gender transference. It then surveys dominant perspectives in psychoanalytic feminism: object-relations feminism; cultural school feminism; and Lacanian feminism. Chodorow argues that there are complex divisions among all of these approaches that make communication and dialogue difficult. The problem cannot be solved, as psychoanalysts might assume, by waiting for new evidence to emerge, because the divisions are epistemological, theoretical, and pretheoretical. Gender and sexuality gain meaning only in the context of a gendered and sexualized social and cultural world, and our theoretical and epistemological assumptions always affect and shape our evidential understandings.

Kaplan, Donald (1990). Some theoretical and technical aspects of gender and social reality in clinical psychoanalysis. *The Psychoanalytic Study of the Child,* 45:3-24. New Haven, CT: Yale University Press.

Kaplan argues that from a narrow psychoanalytic vantage point, emanating from the psychoanalytic method itself, gender is the result of processes of maturation, conflict, and conflict resolution. Gender develops similarly to character, symptoms, and neurosis and is subject to the same principles of pathogenesis. Kaplan proposes that aspects of social reality are what constitute optimal, normal, or ideal femininity. For Kaplan, what is important in the clinical situation is how social reality and gender issues, including stereotypes, roles, and ideals, can be used defensively by the ego. Thus, conformity to social role may be used as a defense, which needs to be analyzed as resistance. In the psychoanalytic situation, conformity to gender stereotypes or to what is socially normative constitutes psychopathol-ogy of conformity, as conformity and normality are employed for neurotic purposes. Kaplan presents the case of a woman whose superficially uninhibited affairs masked unconscious homosexual longings. Kaplan argues that the analyst's gender is not inherently predictive of the course of an analysis. To the extent that the analyst agrees with notions of "ideal sex-gender concordance" and specificity of gender traits, the analyst has relinquished an analytic viewpoint.

Tyson, Phyllis and Tyson, Robert (1990). *Psychoanalytic Theories of Development: An Integration*. New Haven, CT: Yale University Press.

An integrated developmental view of psychoanalytic theories and the developmental process is presented in this book and serves as a conceptual, theoretical, and clinical basis for understanding female development. The book is organized into eight interrelated sections which focus on intrapsychic processes, including Developmental Process, Psychosexuality, Object Relations, Affect, Cognition, Superego Development, Gender Development, and Ego Development. A wide variety of theoretical assumptions, clinical findings and experimental data are examined. Separate developmental lines for female and male development are traced throughout the book. Two chapters, "Gender Differences in Superego Development," and "Gender Development-Girls," are of particular interest and use. [See Chapters 6 and 7 for annotations.]

Young-Bruehl, Elisabeth (1990). *Freud on Women*. New Haven, CT: Yale University Press.

This anthology of Freud's writings about women traces chronologically the origin and subsequent revisions of Freud's views of female psychology. Young-Bruehl asserts that Freud's theories were not merely a reflection of patriarchal or misogynous prejudices, but rather, reflected his need for verifiability and internal coherence of his science. The introduction, illuminating the main elements of Freud's views on female psychology, is comprehensive and defines three main periods: the work prior to the 1905 *Three Essays on the Theory of Sexuality*; the work from 1905 to 1924, when Freud repeatedly revised the *Three Essays* to reflect his modification of other aspects of his general theory; and works after 1924, when Freud wrote a series of separate essays on female sexuality. Young-Bruehl offers a commentary for each selected annotation. One theory that stayed constant and that is emphasized by the Young-Bruehl as a governing concept is Freud's notion of bisexuality. The last part of the book provides an annotated bibliography to indicate how the criticisms made by Freud's contemporaries have been reiterated since 1939.

Zanardi, Claudia (ed.)(1990). *Essential Papers on Psychology of Women*. New York: New York University Press.

This anthology on female psychology provides multiple classical and feminist psychoanalytic perspectives, emphasizing the scientific differences in the context of a historical and cultural continuity. The papers address the evolution of thought on female sexuality on the following topics: castration, penis envy, wish for a child, homosexuality, masochism, and superego formation. The cultural context and the diverse formulations on female sexuality into the 1980s are presented with commentary reviewing the controversies and agreement between psychoanalysis and feminism, between a biological and a psychological approach, and within England, France, and the United States. In her introduction, Zanardi provides a broad and in-depth summary and interpretation of the papers included in the anthology, as well as a presentation of the history of the theoretical concepts and dissenting views about female psychology that are not included in the anthology. She notes the importance of psychoanalysis in providing the only instrument of research for the study of the unconscious, including those social values which have been repressed. The book begins with an exploration of psychoanalytic views on female sexuality in Europe and by Mack Brunswick, M. Klein, Chasseguet-Smirgel, Winnicott, Moustafa, Lacan, and McDougall. In addition to clinical tradition, the European literature also reflects humanist and philosophical attitudes. Contributors from the United States—Jacobson, A. Reich, Thompson, Menaker, Kestenberg, Stoller, Grossman and Stewart, and Person —represent two opposite tendencies: one group is tied to classical analysis, firmly grounded in medical practices and scientific research and emphasizing the unconscious, ego development, and psychosexuality; the other group emphasizes the influence of culture and society. The last section, Feminism and Psychoanalysis, contains European and American contributions that aim to widen psychoanalytic thought about female psychology to include a symbolic approach to understand the repression of femininity. Essays by Mitchell, Irigaray, Montrelay, Kristeva, Dinnerstein, Chodorow, J. B. Miller, J. Benjamin, and Gilligan are included.

Person, Ethel (1991). The "construction" of femininity: Its influence throughout the life cycle. In: *The Course of Life*, Vol. 4, ed. S. Greenspan and G. Pollock. Madison, CT: International Universities Press.

[See Chapter 18 for annotation.]

Tyson, Phyllis (1991). Some nuclear conflicts of the infantile neurosis in female development. *Psychoanal. Inq*, 11(4).

Integrating Freud's later work in metapsychology, including his formulations about the structural model and signal anxiety, Tyson proposes some salient preoedipal conflicts in women. Many divergent pathways of development are possible for each individual girl. [See Chapter 6 for annotation.]

# Section II

# Developmental Perspective

_____ Chapter 5 _____

# Influences on Gender Differences

Mary Anne Delaney and Malkah Notman

Since Freud first wrote about gender differences, psychoanalytic understanding of this area has been revised significantly. Gender and sexual identity have been defined and the conflictual and nonconflictual components of each have been delineated. In the past two decades, psychoanalysts have attempted to integrate findings from research on the differences between boys and girls and men and women from such diverse fields as anthropology, embryology, genetics, endocrinology, and general psychology. This chapter highlights the large body of literature from other disciplines that has influenced current psychoanalytic thought. The chapter samples key papers that have stimulated psychoanalytic writings and also lists and cross-references key papers by psychoanalysts themselves. This chapter is integrally related to Chapters 6 and 18. (M.A.D.)

Freud, Sigmund (1905b). Three essays on the theory of sexuality. *Standard Edition*, 7:125-243. London: Hogarth Press, 1953.

In the third section, Freud discusses the differences between male and female development. He views sexual development as parallel until puberty. [See Chapter 1 for annotation.]

Dooley, Lucile (1938). The genesis of psychological sex differences. *Psychiat.*, 1:181-195.

[See Chapter 2 for annotation.]

Searl, Nina (1938). A note on the relation between physical and psychical differences in boys and girls. *Int. J. Psycho-Anal.*, 19:50-62.

[See Chapter 2 for annotation.]

Kohlberg, Lawrence (1966). A cognitive-developmental analysis of children's sex-role concepts and attitudes. In: *The Development of Sex Differences*, ed. E. Maccoby. Stanford, CA: Stanford University Press, pp. 82-172.

The development of sex-role concepts is addressed in this comprehensive book on sexual differences. Concepts and attitudes in boys and girls from a cognitive and developmental standpoint are discussed. Kohlberg provides an extensive review of research from various disciplines while presenting his own research in this area. Kohlberg asserts that the development of sex roles is influenced by both environmental and cognitive factors. He focuses on the primary significance of the cognitive task of self-categorization, which together with the influence of cognitive maturation and the adaptation to physical and social reality, serves as the most salient organizer of sex-role attitudes. He disagrees with Freudian theory that sexual attitudes are basically instinctual and then channelled by socio-cultural forces.

Maccoby, Eleanor (1966). *The Development of Sex Differences*. Stanford, CA: Stanford University Press.

Diverse psychobiological, hormonal, cultural, social-learning, and cognitive developmental theories on the development of sex differences are presented. This book is not psychoanalytically informed.

Erikson, Erik (1968). Womanhood and the inner space. In: *Identity: Youth and Crisis*. New York: Norton, pp. 261-294. Also in: *Women and Analysis*, ed. J. Strouse. New York: Grossman, 1974, pp. 291-319.

This essay draws on direct observations of play activity of boys and girls ages ten through twelve. Erikson characterizes the play of girls and boys as paralleling the genital anatomical differences between boys and girls. "Inner" space typifies girls, who usually develop scenes of the interior of houses. Boys' play emphasizes "outer" space such as street scenes. He feels that these phenomena cannot be explained by socialization alone, but also must be understood by the contribution of intrapsychic factors. Erikson postulates that girls have a considerable attachment to their "inner potential," which arises from "solidarity" with their womanliness. He rejects the hypothesis that girls accept their femininity only after resolving their feelings of anger at their mother for being narcissistically damaged by lacking a penis.

Stoller, Robert (1968a). *Sex and Gender.* New York: Science House, 1968.

This book primarily elucidates the mechanisms involved in gender-identity development. The author postulates that the establishment of gender identity results from a variety of psychological, cultural, and biological forces. Stoller studies the development of gender identity by examining cases in which acts of nature, impaired genetic and developmental experiences, or both, have resulted in aberrant gender-identity formation. He finds that sex assignment at birth and parental attitudes are crucial to the child's core gender identity. Although much of this book is devoted to the discussion of male gender-identity development, the author provides valuable clinical data supporting the hypothesis of a core female gender identity existing well before the discovery of anatomical differences.

Broverman, Inge, Broverman, Donald, Clarkson, Frank, Rosenkrantz, Paul, and Vogel, Susan. (1970). Sex-role stereotypes and clinical judgements of mental health. *J. Consult. Clin. Psychol.,* 32:1-7.

This classic article demonstrates that sex-role stereotypic beliefs among clinicians about differing character traits of men and women have led to an adherence to a double standard of mental health. Psychiatrists, psychologists, and social workers of both sexes indicated by questionnaire the healthy psychological attributes characterizing adult male, adult female, or adult persons. The clinicians' concept of a healthy mature man was similar to their concept of a healthy adult person. Their concept of a healthy mature woman included a powerful negative assessment, including more submissiveness, dependency, easily influenced, excitable, easily hurt, emotional, and less adventurous, competitive, and science minded. It is suggested that these sex-role biases affect clinical work and research about gender characteristics.

Kleeman, James (1971a). The establishment of core gender identity in normal girls. Part I. Introduction: Development of the ego capacity to differentiate. *Arch. Sex. Behav.,* 1:103-117.

[See Chapter 6 for annotation.]

Kleeman, James (1971b). The establishment of core gender identity in normal girls. Part II. How meanings are conveyed between parent and child in the first three years. *Arch. Sex. Behav.,* 1:117-129.

[See Chapter 6 for annotation.]

Money, John and Ehrhardt, Anke (1972). *Man and Woman, Boy and Girl.*
Baltimore, MD: Johns Hopkins University Press.

The authors integrate a vast amount of experimental and clinical data
on the differentiation and dimorphism of gender identity. Drawing on
concepts, and reviewing relevant literature, from the fields of genetics,
embryology, endocrinology, neurosurgery, social anthropology and social,
medical, and clinical psychology, they organize the available information
into a theoretical formulation of gender-identity formation that emphasizes
the interaction between prenatal and postnatal factors. As one moves up the
phylogenetic scale, prenatally determined, stereotypic behaviors become
increasingly subject to the influence of postnatal biographical history. This
is especially true in the higher primates and man. Of particular interest is
the authors' discussion of work with hermaphroditic children that indicates
that sex assignment is the single most important factor in determining
gender identity.

Sherfey, Mary Jane (1972). On the nature and evolution of female
sexuality. In: *Psychoanalysis and Women*, ed. J. B. Miller. New York:
Brunner/Mazel, 1973, pp. 115-129.

In addition to reviewing the work of Masters and Johnson and its
relevance to psychoanalytic theory, the author advances the hypothesis that
women possess a "biologically determined" heightened sexual drive that has
had to be suppressed by societal pressures in order to insure that stable
child-rearing practices and family stability will be maintained. If this
premise is substantiated by further research and study, it will have
important implications for the study of the development of gender identity
in girls. No mechanism for the maintenance of drive suppression is
proposed.

Chodorow, Nancy (1974). Family structure and feminine personality. In:
*Women, Culture and Society*, ed. M. Rosaldo and L. Lamphere. Stanford,
CA: Stanford University Press, pp. 43-65. Also in: *Feminism and Psychoan-
alytic Theory*. New Haven, CT: Yale University Press, 1989a, pp. 45-65.

Chodorow describes differences in gender-identity development in
relation to interpersonal relationships, child care experiences, and female
socialization. A crucial differentiating experience in male and female
development arises out of the fact that women, universally, are responsible
for child care and female socialization. Chodorow argues for the central
importance of the mother-daughter relationship to women and presents her
first account of how, as a result of this relationship, women develop a self
in relation to a complex inner object world and to an outer world. By

contrast, men develop a self that denies relatedness. The male is self based on a more fixed, firmly split, and repressed inner self-object world. A psychoanalytic and anthropological framework is used to trace the differences in development between girls and boys, particularly in relationship to the mother, who has greater identification with her daughter. Concepts using object relations and separation-individuation theories are emphasized.

Friedman, Richard, Richart, Ralph, and Vande Wiele, Raymond (ed.) (1974). *Sex Differences in Behavior.* New York: Wiley.

This book consists of the papers from a conference on sex differences in psychological functioning and discusses several major topics, including effects of prenatal hormones on development of behavior; effects of stress and early life experience in nonhuman populations; studies of early mother-child interaction in humans; development of sex differences in behavioral functioning; gender identity development; sex differences in aggression and its possible relation to evolution and adaptation; psycho-endocrine differences and their relation to behavior in human and animal populations. Of special interest are papers by Ehrhardt and Baker on fetal androgens and behavioral differences; Moss on early sex differences in mother-child interaction; Lewis and Weinraub on behavioral effects of the sex of the parent interacting with the sex of the child; Korner on sex differences in newborns; Kohlberg on stages in the development of psychosexual concepts; Galenson and Roiphe on emergence of genital awareness; Stern and Bender on sex differences in children's approaching a stranger; and Coates on sex differences in field independence.

Green, Richard (1974). *Sexual Identity Conflict in Children and Adults.* New York: Basic Books.

[See Chapter 19 for annotation.]

Lerner, Harriet (1974). Early origins of envy and devaluation of women: Implications for sex-role stereotypes. *Bull. Menn. Clin.*, 38:538-553. Also in: *Women in Therapy.* Northvale, NJ: Aronson, pp. 5-24.

Lerner examines the development of female and male gender roles in relationship to the role of the preoedipal mother. Males tend to seek a position of power and dominance in relationships. Lerner postulates that this behavior is a defensive maneuver against acknowledging their dependence on and envy of the omnipotent maternal imago of pregenital development. Women adopt a more dependent, passive posture so as not to challenge men, and to replay also their early submission to their omnipotent mother. Women who are more aggressive or competitive are devalued. Lerner asserts that the influence of the imagoes of the preoedipal mother is as powerful in determining gender roles as the recognition of anatomical differences and the resolution of the oedipal conflict.

Maccoby, Eleanor and Jacklin, Carol (1974). *The Psychology of Sex Differences*. Stanford, CA: Stanford University Press.

This book summarizes and systematically analyzes reports from an extensive number of research studies about the existence of sex differences and changes in these differences at successive stages of development in several areas of functioning, including self-concept, cognition, aggression, activity, sociability, and dominance. Well-established differences include girls' greater verbal ability, boys' visual-spatial and mathematical abilities and greater male aggressivity. The authors argue that male aggressiveness has a significant biological component, although they also assert the importance of socialization. Methodological difficulties in research of sexual differences are discussed. There is also a comprehensive annotated bibliography of the more than 1,400 studies summarized in the book. Although the authors rely heavily on studies that use ratings and self-reports, the scope of this book makes it valuable for psychoanalytic research.

Mead, Margaret (1974). On Freud's view of female psychology. In: *Women and Analysis*, ed. J. Strouse. New York: Viking, pp. 95-106.

Mead discusses Freud's assertion that "anatomy is destiny." While acknowledging that in certain societies men's or women's gender roles may be overvalued, Mead states that the reproductive roles of both males and females have influenced the nature of gender-specific behaviors in all societies. Childbearing is exclusively feminine, and, until recently, the feeding of newborns was also. Therefore, women's anatomical capacity for reproduction and nurturance defines their importance to and their participation in any society. Mead emphasizes the central role of the females' and males' body experience of their own reproductive capacities, rather than castration fears, in children's gender development.

Rosaldo, Michelle (1974). Theoretical overview. In: *Women, Culture and Society*, ed. M. Rosaldo and L. Lamphere. Stanford, CA: Stanford University Press, pp. 17-42.

Rosaldo, an anthropologist, reviews the social relations between the sexes. She states that there is a universal asymmetry in the cultural evaluation of the sexes. Although women may be inherently as important and powerful as men, they are neither as recognized as men nor as culturally valued for their authority because women's authority roles have been in the domestic sphere and men's roles have been in the public sphere. Until men are more involved in the domestic sphere, there will be no political equivalence. This paper stresses social roles rather than intrapsychic phenomena.

Stoller, Robert (1975b). *Sex and Gender: The Transsexual Experiment*, Vol. 2. London: Hogarth Press, 1976; and New York: Aronson.

[See Chapter 19 for annotation.]

Dinnerstein, Dorothy (1976). *The Mermaid and the Minotaur*. New York: Harper and Row, 1977.

Dinnerstein investigates those factors which influence the gender roles that men and women assume as adults. While the author's observations draw from several theoretical perspectives, her understanding and use of psychoanalytic concepts is well informed and creative. Dinnerstein proposes that the early relationship of both boys and girls with the mother has a profound effect on the subsequent development of a sense of ownership in sexual relationships that characterizes men but not women. For girls, the mother remains the primary internal object; thus women's heterosexual relationships are based on the model of a nonexclusive second relationship. A rich and varied understanding of gender arrangements and stereotypes is elaborated.
[See also Chapter 13.]

Kleeman, James (1976) Freud's views on early female sexuality in the light of direct child observation. *J. Amer. Psychoanal. Assn.* (Suppl.), 24:3-27.

[See Chapter 18 for annotation.]

Lee, Patrick and Stewart, Robert (ed.)(1976). *Sex Differences: Cultural and Developmental Dimensions*. New York: Urizen Books.

By providing a multidisciplinary approach from varying viewpoints and methodologies, this anthology discusses how sex differences are rooted in development and culture. Genetic, sociocultural, and psychological perspectives and research are emphasized. Of particular interest to psychoanalysts is the first section, "The Psychoanalytic Dimension of Sex Differences," which considers both old and recent psychoanalytic controversies about sex differences. A selection of papers by Freud, Horney, Deutsch, and Erikson is presented, with a reassessment of Freud's view by Gillespie. The second and third sections focus on anthropology and ethology, with classic papers by Mead, Money, Birdwhistle, and Lorenz, which discuss cross-cultural and cross-species dimensions. The fourth section, "The Psychological Dimension," samples the salient literature on sex-role development. Kohlberg and Maccoby are among the writers presented. Commentaries for each section and chapter crystallize the major issues and controversies.

Stoller, Robert (1976). Primary femininity. *J. Amer Psychoanal. Assn.* (Suppl.), 24:59-78.

[See Chapter 6 for annotation.]

Chodorow, Nancy (1978a). Gender differences in the preoedipal period. In: *The Reproduction of Mothering: Psychoanalysis and the Sociology of Gender.* Berkeley: University of California Press, pp. 92-111.

[See Chapter 6 for annotation.]

Chodorow, Nancy (1978). *The Reproduction of Mothering: Psychoanalysis and the Sociology of Gender.* Berkeley: University of California Press.

This book, written at the height of feminist concerns about gender and equality, describes the development of mothering as derived from the close preoedipal mother-daughter relationship and the mutual identifications of the girl and her mother, which is reinforced by role training and socialization. Gender differences in relation to independence, nurturance and affiliation are examined. Chodorow also discusses the importance of social and experiential contexts for psychological development. Several controversial hypotheses are proposed to explain the greater relational needs of women. [See also Chapters 4, 6, 7, 11, and 14.]

Lerner, Harriet (1978). Adaptive and pathogenic aspects of sex-role stereotypes. *Amer. J. Psychiat.*, 1:48-52. Also in: *Women in Therapy.* Northvale, NJ: Aronson, 1988, pp. 79-92.

Lerner discusses the difficulties inherent in acceptance or rejection of stereotypic notions of appropriate male and female sex roles. Younger children may find clear dichotomies useful in establishing their gender identities and, in fact, may feel considerable discomfort if their behaviors are judged to be gender inappropriate; she argues that sex-role stereotypes do not need to be so dichotomous if young children are being raised in families where the adults have firmly established and comfortable gender identities.

[See also Chapter 13.]

Frankel, Steven and Sherick, Ivan (1979). Observations of the emerging sexual identity of three- and four-year-old children: With emphasis on female sexual identity. *Int. Rev. Psycho-Anal.*, 6: 297-310.

[See Chapter 6 for annotation.]

Kestenberg, Judith with Marcus, Hershey (1979). Hypothetical monosex and bisexuality: A psychoanalytic interpretation of sex differences as they reveal themselves in movement patterns of men and women. In: *Psychosexual Imperatives: The Self-in-Process Series*, ed. M. Nelson and J. Ikenberry. New York: Human Sciences Press, pp. 146-181.

Male and female movement patterns are observed and used to describe psychological traits and to construct monosexual models as well as to understand bisexual conflicts. Aggression, action, control of motility, shunning of contact, and self-destructive behavior are seen in males. Sexuality, passivity, lack of inhibition, and opening up the outside and inside of the body to objects are observed in females. Kestenberg proposes that the female components in men decrease their self-destructive impulses by turning aggression outward. The male components in women are the basis for females' restraint of sexuality, which makes monogamy and child survival possible.

Baker, Susan (1980). Biological influences in human sex and gender. *Signs*, 6:80-96.

This article summarizes the evidence for the overriding influence of cultural/rearing practices over biological/hormonal influences on gender-role behavior. Six populations of biologically aberrant patients are examined. The author concludes that the prenatal environment is not responsible for sexual object choice in adolescence and that gender identity is overwhelmingly determined by rearing practices, as determined by sex assignment at birth, and not by chromosomal, gonadal, or prenatal hormonal influences. Prenatal hormonal environment, however, can affect some behavioral or temperament proclivities. One exception (the Imperato-McGinley Study) is evaluated.

Chodorow, Nancy (1980). Difference, relation and gender in psychoanalytic perspective. In: *The Future of Difference*, ed. H. Eisenstein and A. Jardine. Boston, MA: G. K. Hall, pp. 3-19. Also in: *Feminism and Psychoanalytic Theory*. New Haven, CT: Yale University Press, 1989, pp. 99-113.

This theoretical essay argues that traditional psychoanalytic theories, written from the developmental viewpoint, conceptualize the mother (other) as someone from whom to be separated; the mother is not recognized as a self. Chodorow also suggests that separation-individuation theory and psychoanalytic theory more generally have emphasized the goal of separateness and autonomy over the goal of a differentiated form of relating to the other as a self. These traditional approaches both reflect and contribute to problematic attitudes toward mothers in particular and toward women in general. Adequate differentiation should be seen not as separation from the other, but relationally; thus, development of self involves recognition of and connection to the mother as a subject. Because of the intertwining of gender-identity development with differences in forms of relating, issues of separateness are more salient psychologically for males than for females and more entangled with male-female differences. Males are more invested in seeing themselves as different from females than the reverse.

Gadpaille, William (1980). Biological factors in the development of human sexuality. *Psychiat. Cl. N. Amer.*, 3:3-20.

The author reviews some of the studies that have contributed to the elucidation of the relative influence of genetic and prenatal hormonal factors in the development of gender identity and gender-specific behaviors. Current data indicate that postnatal psychosocial factors probably have a greater impact on gender identity than do biological factors. The author suggests that these findings reemphasize the need for careful examination of the parenting process so that children can achieve a healthy gender identity. From the perspective of female psychology, this article also provides evidence that inborn male/female differences do exist.

Stone, Michael (1980). Traditional psychoanalytic characterology reexamined in the light of constitutional and cognitive differences between the sexes. *J. Amer. Acad. Psychoanal.*, 8:381-401.

Stone reviews the traditional concept of the pathogenesis of obsessional and hysterical character pathology as arising from fixation at the anal or genital stages of psychosexual development. After evaluating a number of studies of primate and human hormonal abnormalities, brain lateralization, and cognitive development, the author concludes that gender differences in cognitive and constitutional capacities occur. He suggests that character pathology might be better viewed as manifestations of normal gender differences exaggerated to the point of being dysfunctional. In addition to presenting an important and necessary revision of clinical theory, this article provides a review of the research supporting the existence of biologically-based gender differences.

[See also Chapter 20.]

Weissman, Stephen and Barglow, Peter (1980). Recent contributions to the theory of female adolescent psychological development. *Adolescent Psychiatry: Development and Clinical Studies*, Vol. 8, ed. S. Feinstein, P. Giovacchini, J. Looney, A. Schwartzenberg, and A. Sorosky. Chicago, IL: University of Chicago Press, pp. 214-230.

[See Chapter 9 for annotation.]

Formanek, Ruth (1982). On the origins of gender identity. In: *Early Female Development*, ed. D. Mendell. New York: S.P. Medical and Scientific Books, pp. 1-24.

[See Chapter 6 for annotation.]

Meyer, Jon (1982). The theory of gender identity disorders. *J. Amer. Psychoanal. Assn.*, 30:381-413.

[See Chapter 6 and 19 for annotations.]

Wisdom, John (1982). Male and female. *Int. J. Psycho-Anal.*, 64:159-168.

Wisdom asserts that men and women have both male and female characteristics, but biology does not completely account for commonality. Societal norms determine what constitutes a healthy gender identity. He describes a "new primary process," which he calls personality exchange, where mothers and children exchange personality characteristics. A boy with a large complement of feminine characteristics may become neurotic out of his need to deny his femininity. Homosexuality would serve as a defense against femininity and thereby avoid castration anxiety stimulated by sex with a penisless female.

Gadpaille, William (1983). Innate masculine/feminine traits: Their contributions to conflict. *J. Amer. Acad. Psychoanal.*, 11:401-424.

Gadpaille asserts that men and women differ in ways that reflect rearing, cultural influences, and innate differences resulting from biological realities and evolutionary pressures. These different traits contribute to conflict, both intrapsychically and interpersonally. Data is cited from evolutionary, cross-cultural, brain lateralization, physiological, fetal-hormonal, and clinical studies. Men and women are seen as having evolved different reproductive strategies, patterns of sexual interest and behavior, traits, and identification patterns. There are differential readinesses to learn certain kinds of behavior. Females are inwardly attentive and aware and thus show a greater acceptance of internal genitality and qualities of mind and emotion. Feminine identity is more primary because of maternal rearing. Four clinical vignettes include those of two women who were helped to accept patterns of sexual attraction and longings for maternity. Sex-related conflict sources can be intrapsychic, engendered whenever sex differences are perceived as threatening or guilt- or anxiety-producing. This threat can arise when normal innate traits are seen as ominous, are unacceptable because of impaired identifications, or are contrary to beliefs or goals. Interpersonal conflict occurs when differences are not credited as valid and understood, are misused in conflict, or are seen as hurtful.

Person, Ethel and Ovesey, Lionel (1983). Psychoanalytic theories of gender identity. *J. Amer. Acad. Psychoanal.*, 11:203-226.

[See Chapters 6 and 19.]

Olesker, Wendy (1984). Sex differences in 2- and 3-Year olds: Mother-child relations, peer relations, and peer play. *Psychoanal. Psych.*, 4: 269-288.

The results of a study of preschool children using direct observational methods are discussed. Boys and girls differed in the level of involvement with their mothers, in the quantity and quality of their peer interactions, and in the level of development of their play activities. The author postulates that these differences result from girls' acknowledging their separateness from their mothers at an earlier age than boys. The girls' capacity to perceive separateness depends on their relatively more advanced cognitive capacities. [See also Chapter 6.]

Silverman, Doris (1987b). What are little girls made of? *Psychoanal. Psychol.*, 4:315-334.

[See Chapter 6 for annotation.]

Levenson, Ricki. (1988) Boundaries, autonomy and aggression: An exploration of women's difficulty with logical, abstract thinking. *J. Amer. Acad. Psychoanal.*, 16:189-208.

[See Chapter 12 for annotation.]

Fuerstein, Laura (1989). Some hypotheses about gender differences in coping with oral dependency conflicts. *Psychoanal. Rev.*, 76:163-184.

[See Chapter 23 for annotation.]

Kaplan, Donald (1990). Some theoretical and technical aspects of gender and social reality in clinical psychoanalysis. *The Psychoanalytic Study of the Child*, 45:3-24. New Haven, CT: Yale University Press.

[See Chapter 4 for annotation.]

Olesker, Wendy (1990). Sex differences during the early separation-individuation process: Implications for gender identity formation. *J. Amer. Psychoanal. Assn.*, 38:325-346.

[See Chapter 6 for annotation.]

Tyson, Phyllis and Tyson, Robert (1990). Gender Development: Girls. In: *Psychoanalytic Theories of Development: An Integration*. New Haven, CT: Yale University Press, pp. 258-276.

[See Chapter 6 for annotation.]

Notman, Malkah (1991). Gender development. In: *Women and Men: New Perspectives on Gender Differences*, ed. M. Notman and C. Nadelson. Washington, DC: American Psychiatric Press, pp. 117-127.

This chapter reviews literature on biological, psychological, and cultural influences contributing to gender differences. Socialization processes are seen as augmenting factors described in early psychoanalytic views about gender development. Recent psychoanalytic views about the multiple sources for gender identity are summarized for a psychiatric audience.

Notman, Malkah and Nadelson, Carol (ed.)(1991a). *Women and Men: New Perspectives on Gender Differences*. Washington, DC: American Psychiatric Press.

This book includes papers presented at a 1985 American Psychiatric Association meeting, which featured multidisciplinary perspectives on gender differences. Research from anthropology, endocrinology, neurophysiology, sociology, and economics are integrated within a biopsychosocial approach. The volume also includes a review of gender differences in brain function and behavior and two psychoanalytic papers by Notman and Clower [See Chapter 11] that emphasize different developmental lines for men and for women.

Notman, Malkah and Nadelson, Carol (1991b). A review of gender differences in brain and behavior. In: *Women and Men: New Perspectives on Gender Differences*, ed. M. Notman and C. Nadelson. Washington, DC: American Psychiatric Press, pp. 23-34.

The authors review the current knowledge about gender differences and the brain. Although innate biological differences occur, their impact on human behavior is difficult to study scientifically because of the reciprocity between biology and experience. Methodological difficulties are evaluated for the studies on hemispheric lateralization, electroencephalography, language, and cognitive development. The impact of differential development on sensation, learning, perception, and other brain functions is discussed. The early neurologic maturity of girls leads to a different relationship between mothers and female infants as compared to male infants, which is characterized by a more stable state system. The role of psychological processes, such as identification, has not yet been integrated into theories about brain influences on behavior.

Mayer, Elizabeth (1991). Towers and enclosed spaces: A preliminary report on a study of children's associations to block structures and gender. *Psychoanaly. Inq.*

Mayer presents data from a study that extends Erikson's (1968) work on boys' and girls' preferences for constructing certain structures with blocks during free play. Mayer presented school-age children with block structures preconstructed to represent the "towers" and "enclosed spaces" described by Erikson. A third structure, the cross, represented a blend of features of the tower and enclosed space. Younger boys tended to choose the "tower" figure, whereas girls of all ages chose the "enclosed space" figure. The girls' associations to their choice of the "enclosed space" were characterized by positive statements rather than narcissistically devalued ones. Some older boys chose the "cross" and indicated that they would have chosen the "tower" when younger. Mayer's findings of a gender-specific pattern of choice were convincing. However, Mayer cautions against interpreting differences in genital morphology as the cause of these findings.

# Chapter 6

# Preoedipal Development in Girls

Eleanor Schuker, with Virginia Clower and Joan J. Zilbach.
Additional contributions by Anni Bergman, Nadine Levinson,
Sara Vogel

Although the psychoanalytic literature on preoedipal development is extensive, this chapter focuses specifically on issues pertinent to preoedipal development in girls. Included are writings on primary femininity, female gender identity, and gender differentiation; gender-specific aspects of separation-individuation and preoedipal object relations; early feminine genital awareness and body-image development, including divergent views on the role of penis envy, castration anxiety, and vulval and vaginal sensations; gender-related vicissitudes of drive development; and particular conflicts in the preoedipal period that may influence progression to later stages.

Early psychoanalytic writers wrote from various perspectives about early feminine sexual development. Horney and Jones proposed the concept of primary and innate femininity and viewed the phallic phase as a defensive compromise-formation. Abraham (1922), Freud (1931a, 1933), Lampl-de Groot (1927), Deutsch (1925a), and Mack Brunswick (1940) emphasized the importance of penis envy and the castration complex in girls' acquisition of femininity. Freud's later papers, "Female Sexuality" (1931a) and "Femininity" (1933), focused on the endurance and intensity of a girl's preoedipal tie to her mother but stressed the core significance of the castration complex. Klein (1932) emphasized preoedipal vicissitudes, and with others like Deutsch, confirmed a mother's central impact on her daughter's development. These early analysts advanced diverging opinions about the presence and implication of early vaginal sensations and the relative significance of the preoedipal or oedipal phases for personality organization, gender formation, and consequent psychopathology.

In the 1950s, Greenacre and Kestenberg wrote extensively about pregenital sexual development in girls. With great clarity and originality, Greenacre (1950, 1952a, 1952b) discussed the specific advantages and problems accompanying early female sexual development; she emphasizes particularly the importance of narcissistic issues and self-object differentiation in relation to the recognition of anatomical differences. Psychoanalytic interest in gender-specific aspects of early development has burgeoned since the early 1970s, stimulated by the infant observation studies of Mahler and her colleagues, and by the contributions of Stoller to the concept of gender identity. Over the years, the developmental line of gender taking place after infancy and before the phallic-oedipal phase has been characterized by many names and overlapping subphases, including the early genital phase, the infantile genital phase, and the phallic-dyadic, phallic-narcissistic, preoedipal maternal, protogenital, and preoedipal genital phases.

Papers in this chapter take varying approaches and reflect multiple perspectives and substantial revisions of early theories about preoedipal development. They emphasize drive psychology, ego psychology, self psychology, object relations, and cultural influences. The current literature incorporates a number of ongoing debates about preoedipal development. Controversies include the nature of early genital awareness, the centrality of such awareness to feminine gender identity, the meanings of penis-envy phenomena, the relative importance of preoedipal and oedipal factors in later pathology, the usefulness of differentiating genital, oedipal (triadic) features from pregenital, preoedipal (dyadic) features, the role of object relations, and the antecedents of superego and feminine ego-ideal development. Some writers caution that analytic data from preoedipal transferences should not be equated with phenomena reflective of primitive or arrested development, but rather may reflect deep levels of psychoanalytic exploration and regression in the service of the ego and the superego, stemming from this early period. In order to maintain conceptual continuity with related and overlapping ideas, the reader should also consult Chapters 5, 7, 14, 16, and 18. (E.S.)

Abraham, Karl (1922). Manifestations of the female castration complex. *Int. J. Psycho-Anal.*, 3:1-29. Also in: *Selected Papers*. New York: Brunner/Mazel, 1979, pp. 338-369.

Abraham focuses on the female castration complex and penis envy. [See Chapter 2 for annotation.]

Horney, Karen (1924). On the genesis of the castration complex in women. *Int. J. Psycho-Anal.*, 5:50-65. Also in: *Feminine Psychology*, ed. H. Kelman. New York: Norton, 1967, pp. 37-53.

Two stages of penis envy are described: an initial transient stage, as a result of the recognition of sexual differences, and a second stage, as the result of oedipal disappointment. [See Chapter 2 for annotation.]

Deutsch, Helene (1925a). The psychology of women in relation to the function of reproduction. *Int. J. Psycho-Anal.*, 6:405-418. Also in: *The Psychoanalytic Reader*, ed. R. Fliess. New York: International Universities Press, 1948, pp. 165-179.

Deutsch asserts that girls have two sexual zones and that their task is to renounce the masculinity attached to the clitoris and discover a "new organ," the vagina, within their own bodies. [See Chapter 2 for annotation.]

Freud, Sigmund (1925). Some psychical consequences of the anatomical distinction between the sexes. *Standard Edition*, 19:243-258. London: Hogarth Press, 1953.

Until recognition of the anatomical differences, boys and girls have parallel, masculine development. Freud proposes for girls several psychic consequences of penis envy in girls. [See Chapter 1 for annotation.]

Horney, Karen (1926). The flight from womanhood. *Int. J. Psycho-Anal.*, 12:360-374. Also in: *Feminine Psychology*, ed. H. Kelman. New York: Norton, 1967, pp. 54-70.

Horney emphasizes early vaginal awareness and penis envy as representing an oedipal fear of penetration by the father. [See Chapter 2 for annotation.]

Jones, Ernest (1927). The early development of female sexuality. *Int. J. Psycho-Anal.*, 8:459-472.

Jones presents a complex schema for libidinal development for both sexes with an emphasis on the importance of oral eroticism and sadism. [See Chapters 2 and 7 for annotations.]

Lampl-de Groot, Jeanne (1927). The evolution of the Oedipus complex in women. *Int. J. Psycho-Anal.*, 9:332-345. Also in: *The Psychoanalytic Reader*, ed. R. Fliess. New York: International Universities Press, 1948, pp. 180-194.

Lampl-de Groot asserts that the girl's pregenital development is like that of the boy, "a little man," as to her love aim and object choice. She proposes that the negative oedipal phase precedes the positive oedipal phase in girls. [See Chapter 2 for annotation.]

Fenichel, Otto (1930). The pregenital antecedents of the Oedipus Complex. *Int. J. Psycho-Anal.*, 11:141-166.

Fenichel explores the relationship of preoedipal sexuality to the development and characteristics of the oedipal conflict. [See Chapter 2 for annotation.]

Freud, Sigmund (1931a). Female sexuality. *Standard Edition*, 21:223-243. London: Hogarth Press, 1953.

Freud emphasizes and details the importance of the intensity or long duration of the girl's preoedipal relationship with the mother. [See Chapter 1 for annotation.]

Brierley, Marjorie (1932). Some problems of integration in women. *Int. J. Psycho-Anal.*, 13:433-448.

Brierley discusses pregenital conflicts and their relation to oedipal development and superego formation. [See Chapters 2 and 18 for annotations.]

Klein, Melanie (1932a). The effects of early anxiety-situations on the sexual development of the girl. In: *The Psychoanalysis of Children*. New York: Norton, pp. 194-239.

Klein elaborates and refines the ideas she introduced in "The Early Stages of the Oedipus Complex" (1927). She stresses the importance of early fantasies stemming from an innate awareness of the vagina, the penis, and copulation—particularly fantasies of the parents united in intercourse—and discusses girls' anxiety about destruction of the interior of their bodies. Klein contends that the wish for a baby occurs very early but that it is preceded by oral incorporative wishes for the father's penis. Preoedipal sexuality, early superego formation, and the importance of identifications in ego formation are proposed. Klein emphasizes the importance of attachment to the mother and girls' oral relationship with the breast, which later shifts to a fantasized oral relation with the penis (nipple=penis). Girls' turning from mother to father is a result of being weaned by their mother as well as being deprived in the toileting experience. Thus, penis envy is influenced by girls' attitudes and experiences with the breast as a part of their mother's body. [See also Chapters 2 and 16.]

Freud, Sigmund (1933). Femininity. *Standard Edition*, 22:112-135. London: Hogarth Press, 1953.

Freud further emphasizes the importance of the girl's preoedipal affectionate attachment to her mother and its decisive effect on subsequent development. [See Chapter 1 for annotation.]

Jones, Ernest (1933). The phallic phase. *Int. J. Psycho-Anal.*, 14:1-13.

Jones presents an elaborate developmental schema, differentiating two substages (pregenital and oedipal aspects) of the phallic phase. [See Chapter 2 for annotation.]

Lampl-de Groot, Jeanne (1933). Problems of femininity. *Psychoanal. Q.*, 489-518. Also in: *Man and Mind: Collected Papers of Jeanne Lampl-de Groot.* New York: International Universities Press, 1965, pp. 12-31.

Lampl-de Groot affirms that early development is the same for both sexes and that there is only a masculine libido. [See Chapter 2 for annotation.]

Fenichel, Otto (1934). Further light upon the preoedipal phase in girls. In: *The Collected Papers of Otto Fenichel.* New York: Norton, 1953, pp. 241-288. First published in *Int. Z. Psa.*, 20:151-190, 1934.

While Fenichel agrees with Freud's formulations of penis envy and the resolution of the Oedipus complex, he stresses the importance of pre-oedipal antecedents in female development. [See Chapter 2 for annotation.]

Jacobson, Edith (1936). On the development of a girl's wish for a child. *Psychoanal. Q.*, 37:523-538, 1968.

Jacobson discusses the analysis of a little girl who had a strong preoedipal fixation to her mother. [See Chapter 2 for annotation.]

Jacobson, Edith (1937). Ways of superego formation and the female castration complex. *Psychoanal. Q.*, 45:525-538, 1976.

Jacobson proposes that girls may fantasize an internal penis, erotize their vagina, and then value the vagina itself. [See Chapters 2, 7, and 18 for annotations.]

Barrett, William (1939). Penis envy, urinary control, pregnancy fantasies, constipation. *Psychoanal. Q.*, 8:211-218.

Incidents occurring in the life of a little girl from the time she was two-and-a-half until she was four-and-a-half years-old describe her efforts first to deny her lack of a penis and then to compensate for this lack by achieving an identification with her mother. Denial of the brother's penis, insistence she had one like Daddy's, and attempts to urinate standing up were accompanied by urinary dyscontrol following an earlier period of training. As mother encouraged her, she became pleased with elements of her femininity and wetting diminished. Episodes of fecal retention began at age four, shortly after her mother became pregnant, and were associated with fantasies of gestation.

Eissler, Kurt (1939). On certain problems of female sexual development. *Psychoanal. Q.*, 8:191-210.

Eissler reviews the nonanalytic literature that provides evidence for the existence of early vaginal sensations and discusses Freud's theory of female development. [See Chapter 2 for annotation.]

Brunswick, Ruth Mack (1940). The preoedipal phase of the libido development. *Psychoanal. Q.*, 9:293-319. Also in: *Psychoanalytic Reader*, ed. R. Fliess. New York: International Universities Press, 1948, pp. 261-284.

Mack Brunswick presents an elaborate "diagram" of early development, setting up three antithetical pairs: active-passive, phallic-castrated, and masculine-feminine. She discusses the preoedipal fantasy of the all-powerful phallic mother. [See Chapter 2 for annotation.]

Hayward, Emeline (1943). Types of female castration reaction. *Psychoanal. Q.*, 12:45-66.

Hayward discusses two types of adult women who orient their lives around penis envy. [See Chapter 18 for annotation.]

Deutsch, Helene (1944, 1945). *The Psychology of Women: A Psychoanalytic Interpretation*, (Vol. 1 and 2). New York: Grune and Stratton.

Deutsch presents a systematic view of female psychosexual development and reproductive functioning in order to explain normal female psychic life and conflicts. [See Chapters 2, 9, 18, and 23 for annotations.]

Greenacre, Phyllis (1945). Urination and weeping. *Amer. J. Orthopsychia.*, 15:81-88. Also in *Trauma, Growth and Personality*, New York: Norton, 1952, pp. 106-119.

Urination and weeping are linked to penis envy. [See Chapter 18 for annotation.]

Spitz, Rene and Wolf, Katherine (1949). Autoerotism. *The Psychoanalytic Study of the Child*, 3/4: 85-120. New York: International Universities Press.

This classic paper describes observations on three autoerotic activities—genital play, rocking, and fecal play—in a group of 170 children in the first year of life. [See Chapter 18 for annotation.]

Greenacre, Phyllis (1950a). Special problems of early female sexual development. *The Psychoanalytic Study of the Child*, 5:122-138, New York: International Universities Press. Also in: *Trauma, Growth and Personality*. New York: Norton, 1952, pp. 237-258.

Greenacre discusses vaginal and clitoral sensations through all phases of development, including their development and interaction in the preoedipal phase. [See Chapter 18 for annotation.]

De Monchy, Rene (1952). Oral components of the castration complex. *Int. J. Psycho-Anal.*, 33:450-453.

The author argues that oral experiences do not merely color the castration complex, but rather have a primary influence. [See Chapter 18 for annotation.]

Greenacre, Phyllis (1952a). Pregenital patterning. *Int. J. Psycho-Anal.*, 33: 410-415.

Drawing on her analytic work with large numbers of severely neurotic and borderline patients in whom pregenital development has been disordered, Greenacre discusses certain conditions that influence and distort the regular development of the libidinal phases. She finds that the Oedipus complex sometimes develops prematurely or intensely when there are preoedipal problems. Possible sequelae of varying combinations of interphasal stimulations occurring in the pregenital era are traced and divided into four main observations: 1) very early stimulation increases the somatic components of memories and resultant symptoms; 2) massive or severe stimulation suffuses an infant with excitement, so that the infant then uses all possible channels of discharge; 3) overstimulation arouses drives prematurely from phases that are not yet mature; and 4) genital arousal and primitive erotization occur from early states of frustration or overstimulation, and the extent of premature genital arousal affects the nature of genitality later. Illustrative clinical vignettes are presented.

Greenacre, Phyllis (1952b). Some factors producing different types of genital and pregenital organization. In: *Trauma, Growth and Personality*. New York: Norton, pp. 293-302.

This chapter is closely adapted from "Pregenital Patterning" (1952a). Here, Greenacre adds an emphasis on biological maturation in evaluating the effect of excessive stimulation or trauma. The maturational phase at which the trauma occurs and the specific nature of the trauma is important, as it may reinforce libidinization of the dominant phase or reinstate an antecedent phase either by direct stimulation or by encouraging regression.

Greenacre, Phyllis (1953). Penis awe and its relation to penis envy. In: *Emotional Growth*, Vol. 1, New York: International Universities Press, 1971, pp. 31-49.

In this classic paper, Greenacre defines and differentiates penis awe and penis envy. Three cases illustrate the interrelationship between these two concepts. Envy involves covetousness and resentment based on comparisons of anatomical differences with a male peer. Awe involves intense admiration; feelings of strangeness, with little sense of possible possession; and sometimes fearfulness. Penis awe is based on observations by the small girl of the flaccid or erect penis of an adult man. The strong, aggressive feelings that are aroused in penis awe are suspended and diffuse and may be converted into submission, quasi-religious feelings, or states of excitement. The three cases are rich and contain particularly useful dream examples.

Kramer, Paul (1954). Early capacity for orgastic discharge and character formation. *The Psychoanalytic Study of the Child*, 9:128-141. New York: International Universities Press.

[See Chapter 18 for annotation.]

Kestenberg, Judith (1956a). On the development of maternal feelings in early childhood: Observations and reflections. *The Psychoanalytic Study of the Child*, 11:257-291. New York: International Universities Press.

[See Chapter 14 for annotation.]

Kestenberg, Judith (1956b). Vicissitudes of female sexuality. *J. Amer. Psychoanal. Assn.*, 4:453-476.

The role of the vagina in early female development is explored. An excellent discussion of activity and passivity precedes a review of psychosexual stages of female development, case examples, and early observations of girls. An early preoedipal maternal phase is detailed. [See also Chapter 18.]

Ovesey, Lionel (1956). Masculine aspirations in women. *Psychiat.*, 19:341-351.

Penis envy may represent wishes for magical repair and adaptation to social privileges for males. [See Chapter 20 for annotation.]

Lichtenstein, Heinz (1961). Identity and sexuality: A study of their interrelationship in man. *J. Amer. Psychoanal. Assn.*, 9:197-268.

Lichtenstein asserts that the main function of nonprocreative sexuality is to maintain identity, which was originally and unconsciously imprinted on the infant by the sensual ministrations of the mother during the early symbiotic relationship. [See Chapter 18 for annotation.]

Sprince, Marjorie (1962). The development of a preoedipal partnership between an adolescent girl and her mother. *The Psychoanalytic Study of the Child*, 17:418-450. New York: International Universities Press.

[See Chapter 9 for annotation.]

Barnett, Marjorie (1966) Vaginal awareness in the infancy and childhood of girls. *J. Amer. Psychoanal. Assn.*, 14:129-140.

[See Chapter 18 for annotation.]

Greenson, Ralph (1968). Disidentifying from mother: its special importance for the boy. *Int. J. Psycho-Anal.*, 49:370-376. Also in: *Explorations in Psychoanalysis: Collected Papers*, ed. R. Greenson, New York: International Universities Press, pp. 305-312.

In this historically important paper, disidentification is defined as the male child's replacement of his original identification with the mother by an identification with his father. Greenson adds that girls must also disidentify from the mother in order to achieve their own unique identity, but the identification with mother "helps" them to establish their femininity. A case of a boy and his disidentification from his mother is presented. Greenson defines four factors contributing to gender identity: 1) an awareness of anatomical and physiological structures in oneself (particularly the face and genitals), 2) assignment of gender by parents and others, 3) a biological force present at birth, and 4) disidentification from mother and the development of a new identification with the father (in boys).

Roiphe, Herman (1968). On an early genital phase. *The Psychoanalytic Study of the Child*, 23:348-365. New York: International Universities Press.

Roiphe proposes a normal genital phase between 18 and 24 months of age. The dynamic content of this phase concerns self- and object representations without oedipal resonance. Roiphe infers that there is a spread of excitation to genital organs as sphincter control becomes neurophysiologically possible. Vaginal sensitivity is associated with anal stimulation, and in some girls there is a strong oral-vaginal response to primal scene observation. Maturation of the genitals so that they are a channel for tension release and pleasure establishes their high narcissistic cathexis. The differentiation of self from object and the internalization of object representations proceeds, concurrently. During this early genital phase, observation of sexual anatomical differences provokes severe anxiety if previous experiences created a disturbance in the sense of body self, for example because of illness or maternal deficits. Since genital awareness and the sense of self are coextensive, castration anxiety, fears of object loss, and annihilation anxiety are indissoluble. Early genital-phase anxiety is a frequent etiological element in the psychopathology of adult men and women. Anxiety characterized by a combination of castration anxiety and separation reactions with threats of object loss can commonly be observed in certain adult neurotic women. Their histories reveal major disturbances in the first 18 months of life, resulting in an unstable body image and strong fears of dissolution. Their subsequent experience of phallic-phase anxieties was overly strong, resonating with the earlier fears of dissolution and instability in the genital outline of the body.

Stoller, Robert (1968b). The sense of femaleness. *Psychoanal. Q.*, 37:42-55. Also in: *Psychoanalysis and Women*, ed. J. B. Miller. New York: Brunner/Mazel, 1973, 231-244.

[See Chapter 18 for annotation.]

Clower, Virginia (1970). Reporter, Panel: The development of the child's sense of his sexual identity. *J. Amer. Psychoanal. Assn.*, 18:165-176.

This panel report reviews current concepts of gender identity in 1970 as presented by Settlage, Stoller, Bell, and Kleeman. In the introduction, Settlage discusses a 1957 panel on identity, which emphasized the resolution of bisexual identity as essential to the development of a sense of identity. The panelists agree to focus more specifically by using the term gender identity as proposed by Stoller and reserving the word sexual to reflect biological factors. Stoller describes how several factors converge to produce a male transsexual: a bisexual mother, a sustained symbiosis between mother and son, and an absent father. Bell's paper concerns testicular movement and castration anxiety. Kleeman proposes that gender identity begins with a mother's expectations about her unborn child and is established by 18 months. By 22 months, a girl he studied became aware of male genitalia. Kleeman notes the importance of identification with the mother and speculates that penis envy and castration anxiety are not the sole determinants of female gender identity. Several audience participants comment on the early awareness of sexual differences and question whether penis envy and the castration complex are major organizers of normal feminine development.

Moulton, Ruth (1970a). A survey and reevaluation of penis envy. *Contemporary Psychoanalysis, 7*:84-104. Also in: *Psychoanalysis and Women*, ed. J. B. Miller. New York: Brunner/Mazel, pp. 207-230, 1973.

Discussing theoretical and clinical issues relevant to penis envy, Moulton asserts that this phenomenon in female development is frequent but neither primary nor universal. An evanescent primary penis envy may occur at the time of the recognition of the anatomical differences. Secondary reinforcement of penis envy can eventuate from multiple factors at each stage of development, including sibling rivalry, envy based on oral needs, dependent wishes for the mother, envy of a male's position with the mother, a disappointing or remote father in the oedipal phase or adolescence, dread of femininity, and persistent conflicts about dependency. Moulton also discusses misconceptions about female sexuality and orgasm in relation to masochism, passivity, and the castration complex. Three case reports illustrate the author's view that penis envy should not be taken literally but must be studied in terms of its preoedipal basis and reinforcing cultural and developmental influences.

Torok, Maria (1970). The significance of penis envy in women. In: *Female Sexuality*, ed. J. Chasseguet-Smirgel, Ann Arbor: University of Michigan Press, pp. 135-170.

Torok suggests that the penis as a concrete object must be left aside if penis envy is to be understood. Penis envy is a disguise or a camouflage for girls' deeper attempts to take an unconscious "oath of fidelity" to a maternal imago and not achieve genital fulfillment. This hypothesis is amplified by case vignettes, including one with extensive sequential material from 20 analytic sessions.

Abelin, Ernest (1971). The role of the father in the separation-individuation process. In: *Separation-Individuation*, ed. J. McDevitt and C. Settlage. New York: International Universities Press, pp. 229-252.

Abelin proposes that the specific relationship between infants and fathers begin with a smiling response in the symbiotic phase. Infants seldom show stranger anxiety towards their father, and during the practicing subphase there is conspicuous turning towards him, wherein the father represents a "nonmother" space for the elated exploration of reality.

Triangulation, consisting of an "identification with the rival" for the mother is the "third organizer," which leads to the formation of a first self-image. Infants may have an inner readiness to respond to certain primordial differences between men and women, and this readiness may differ between boys and girls. Girls tend to attach themselves to their fathers earlier than boys do but are more wary of unfamiliar persons in general, including strange men. Abelin speculates about the symbiotic roots of girls' early ties to mothers and fathers. Mother are experienced as similar to the girl, and thus less fascinating. The father, although within the symbiotic orbit, is different. Abelin suggests that the world of the father and the animate world in general differs for boys and for girls because the dichotomy between the symbiotic and the nonmaternal world is less clear cut for girls. [See also Chapter 16.]

Galenson, Eleanor and Roiphe, Herman (1971). The impact of early sexual discovery on mood, defensive organization, and symbolization. *The Psychoanalytic Study of the Child*, 26:195-216. New York: Quadrangle Books.

This paper reports extensively on a case from Galenson and Roiphe's original study of a little girl with an early somatic problem—a congenital defect that required wearing a corrective device in the perineal area. They describe the onset of her genital curiosity, subsequent mutilation reactions, loss of self-esteem, and a depressive reaction that continued throughout later development. Her early difficulties were still in evidence in the oedipal period, and castration anxiety had not disappeared. This case is one of the deviations included to delineate the impact of the discovery of the sexual differences on development.

Kleeman, James (1971a). The establishment of core gender identity in normal girls. Part I. Introduction: The development of the ego capacity to differentiate. *Arch. Sex. Behav.*, 1:103-116.

Kleeman delineates observable differences between boys and girls in the preoedipal period. The girl's sense of femaleness or core gender identity is described, and Freud's view that femininity emerges in the phallic phase is modified. Core gender identity is normally established and irreversible by age three and more firmly secured by age four or five. The development of the ego's capacity to differentiate is stressed as a necessary, pivotal precondition to the establishment of core gender identity. Kleeman cites multiple contributions to core gender identity, including biology, genetics, experiential factors, and the psychological attainment of body- and self-images. Psychoanalytic and other literature is reviewed to support the view that cognitive functions play a more significant and universal role in core gender identity formation before age three than do identification, envy of the male genitals, or castration anxiety. Ascription of gender at birth and environmental confirmation normally impinge on maturing cognitive capacities as the normal organizers of gender identity, although not as the sole factors. [See also Chapter 18.]

Kleeman, James (1971b). The establishment of core gender identity in normal girls. Part II. How meanings are conveyed between parent and child in the first three years. *Arch. Sex. Behav.*, 1:117-129.

This article sets forth longitudinal observations of a girl from birth through her third year to study the establishment of core gender identity in normal girls. A healthy girl of three is feminine and knows it. Freud's contention that the first definitive femininity appears in the phallic phase is refuted. A series of observations illustrates how early gender identity is established before the phallic phase, and before penis envy, castration anxiety, and the Oedipus complex contribute their main influences. Kleeman's observations include the child's response to her mother's pregnancy, observations of her brother's genitals, interest in identification with mother and a special relationship with father, and categorizations of gender attributes with increasing complexity. Four areas are illuminated by the data: 1) fluctuations in and progression of self-stimulation occur from infancy onward; 2) early experience of the self develops with reference to body image, tactile exploration of one's own and the mother's body, and visual stimulation through mirroring by the mother's facial responses and the sighting of the self in mirrors; 3) direct observation, as contrasted with that from psychoanalytic reconstruction, elevates the relative importance of identifications and meanings conveyed by parents and lessens the importance of penis envy and castration anxiety in the early development of gender identity; and 4) direct observation confirms pregnancy and breast-feeding fantasies in both girls and boys, and indicates gender differences in their manifestations and in the ways in which mothers respond to them.

Novick, Kerry (1974). Issues in the analysis of a preschool girl. *The Psychoanalytic Study of the Child*, 29:319-340. New Haven, CT: Yale University Press.

The analysis of a four-year-old girl traces the interaction between her developing sense of separateness and autonomy and the development of her inner controls over her impulses. The child's symptoms included anxious clinging and tantrums at times of separation, angry behavior toward her younger siblings and parents, soiling, and wetting. The child had well-developed ego functions, yet few defenses. Several theoretical and clinical issues are discussed, including the unconscious equivalence of feces and baby, wishes for a baby, differentiation between inhibitions and ego restrictions, and conflicts surrounding separation-individuation and aggression. Examples of clinical interpretations are provided. The author concludes that this child perceived independent functioning as a threat to her relationship with her mother. Giving up her instinctual wishes and her omnipotence meant giving up her mother, who also had conflicts regarding aggression and separation.

**Edgcumbe, Rose and Burgner, Marion (1975). The phallic-narcissistic phase: A differentiation between preoedipal and oedipal aspects of phallic development. *The Psychoanalytic Study of the Child*, 30:161-180. New Haven, CT: Yale University Press.**

The authors differentiate between two different levels of object related-ness and ego development within the phallic phase of drive organization. They assert that a dyadic phallic-narcissistic phase should be differentiated from a triadic phallic-oedipal phase. In the preoedipal phallic-narcissistic phase, girls consolidate their body and self representations and begin the acquisition of sexual identity. The genital is used primarily for exhibitionistic and narcissistic purposes, to gain admiration of the object. One-to-one relationships dominate, and triangular oedipal rivalry has not developed. Children in the phallic-narcissistic phase face the tasks of recognizing anatomical differences and accepting genital immaturity. A sexually differentiated body image becomes consolidated, and there is gradual divergence of fantasies, identifications, and modes of relating. Penis envy occurs in the phallic-narcissistic phase, but may reflect wishes for an object not possessed, dissatisfaction with the body image, or prephallic oral or maternal deprivation. The case material distinguishes between feminine exhibitionism that represents the wish to be loved on a preoedipal level, and exhibitionism on an oedipal level, which involves envy of the mother with competition and positive identifications. The authors suggest that many adult patients had strong phallic-narcissistic fixations and then failed to resolve oedipal conflicts.

**Kleeman, James (1975). Genital self-stimulation in infant and toddler girls. In: *Masturbation: From Infancy to Senescence*, ed. L. Marcus and J. Francis. New York: International Universities Press, pp. 77-106.**

This paper reviews current psychoanalytic knowledge about genital self-stimulation in infant and toddler females. Observations of five girls in different families, with a detailed description of one child, are presented along with a review of the psychoanalytic and developmental literature. The developmental line from earliest genital discovery to genital play and subsequently to behavior that can justly be termed masturbation is traced, and the role of this activity in the emergence of female gender identity is discussed. Comparisons with male development are included.

Kohut, Heinz (1975). A note on female sexuality. In: *The Search for the Self*, Vol. 2, ed. P. Ornstein. New York: International Universities Press, 1978, pp. 783-792.

Kohut initially states a classical position: "I have no doubt that the sight of the male genital will inevitably make a very strong impression on the little girl, that it will become a crystallization point for her envy. . . .it will leave a distinct imprint on the personality of women" (p. 783). Then, he reviews his own theories and discusses women's wish for a child as a manifestation of their nuclear self, including their central ambitions and ideals, rather than as a wish for a penis. Wishes for a baby or a penis may also reflect narcissistic disturbances and attempts to heal that pathology or a neurotic conflict. [See also Chapter 22.]

Mahler, Margaret, Pine, Fred, and Bergman, Anni (1975). *The Psychological Birth of the Human Infant*. New York: Basic Books, (esp. pp. 104-106, 109-116, 210-224).

Mahler et al.'s important work on separation-individuation has provided a conceptual framework for later studies of early gender identity and sexual development. In the first of the three sections highlighted here (pp. 104-106), the authors discuss the beginnings of gender identity. The effect of the child's discovery of anatomical differences, between 16 and 17 months and more often at 20 or 21 months, is accorded a central role. According to the authors, girls are confronted with something they lack, and the consequent anxiety, rage, and defiance reflect early penis envy. Cathy, a 14-month-old, is described as searching for her mother's "hidden penis." In the next section (pp. 109-116), the authors discuss the fourth subphase, the consolidation of identity and the beginning of emotional object constancy. They feel that in this subphase the early consolidation of gender identity takes place. The case examples emphasize the development of object constancy. In the last section (pp. 210-224), the authors discuss the development of basic moods and gender identity. They contrast the reactions of toddler boys and girls, as they repeatedly experience helplessness as they discover their separateness from mother. Girls are more prone to depressed moods, which are attributed to lessened motor activity and an awareness of "anatomical shortcomings." Satisfactory resolution of penis envy takes place in the latter part of the third year in favorable cases.

Edgcumbe, Rose, Lunberg, Sara, Markowitz, Randi, and Salo, Frances (1976). Some comments on the concept of the negative oedipal phase in girls. *The Psychoanalytic Study of the Child*, 31:35-61. New Haven, CT: Yale University Press.

[See Chapter 7 for annotation.]

Galenson, Eleanor (1976a). Reporter, Panel: Psychology of women (1) infancy and early childhood. *J. Amer. Psychoanal. Assn.*, 24:141-150.

This panel presentation is devoted to an appraisal of current analytic concepts about the psychology of women, which include new developments from biological and psychological studies. Stoller's introduction emphasizes the importance of the earliest periods of development and the development of the body ego in the earliest stage of core gender identity. Women develop a primary, unquestioned, and conflict-free sense of femaleness in this stage. Wolff continues the theme of equal but different development of boys and girls. He discusses some suggestive evidence of early differences in cerebral lateralization and visual and auditory acuity that may be significant in understanding sexual dimorphism. Kleeman's longitudinal observational study of normal development also considers the vicissitudes of gender identity. There is evidence of genital sensations from birth, whereas focused awareness of the genitals and self-stimulation occurs between 15 and 24 months without climax or emotional excitement. He disagrees with Roiphe and Galenson and feels that penis envy and castration anxiety are not primary organizers of the early development of femininity. Glenn presents the case of a three-and-a-half-year-old girl to illustrate the presence of early structuralization and conflict in the preoedipal years. The clinical material is consistent with concepts proposed by Stoller and Kleeman. All panelists agree on the central importance of the developmental events of the latter part of the second year for feminine gender development. [See also Chapter 9.]

Galenson, Eleanor and Roiphe, Herman (1976). Some suggested revisions concerning early female development. *J. Amer. Psychoanal. Assn.* (Suppl.), 24:29-58.

[See Chapter 18 for annotation.]

Grossman, William and Stewart, Walter (1976). Penis envy: From childhood wish to developmental metaphor. *J. Amer. Psychoanal. Assn.* (Suppl.), 24:193-213.

This article discusses the need to understand the origins and many unconscious meanings and functions of penis envy rather than view it as a "bedrock" explanatory concept. The reanalyses of two women patients are described. In each of their first analyses, unconscious penis envy was interpreted and had an organizing, but not a therapeutic, effect. In the second analyses, a conscious wish for a missing organ, anger, and a sense of inferiority at not having the penis were seen to reflect other, more global aspects of envy, identity conflicts, narcissistic sensitivity, and conflicts about aggression. The inexact or incomplete interpretation only reinforced their sense of being damaged or deprived. The cases illustrate the effect of inexact and explanatory use of the concept of penis envy, and the necessity to analyze penis envy rather than consider it "bedrock." Two developmental phases of penis envy are described, first, a narcissistic injury that can be resolved, and, second, a regressive effort to resolve oedipal conflict.

Kleeman, James (1976). Freud's views on early female sexuality in the light of direct child observation. *J. Amer. Psychoanal. Assn.* (Suppl.), 24:2-29.

[See Chapter 18 for annotation.]

Lerner, Harriet (1976). Parental mislabeling of female genitals as a determinant of penis envy and learning inhibitions in women. *J. Amer Psychoanal. Assn.* (Suppl.), 24:269-283. Also in: *Women in Therapy.* Northvale, NJ: Aronson, 1988, pp. 25-41.

The title of this interesting article, though technically accurate, is misleading. Instead of discussing *mis*labeling, Lerner documents the *non*labeling of important parts of female genitalia by parents and others. The clitoris, labia, and vulva are seldom designated by parents or when they are, it is in a vague or confused manner. Using case material, Lerner suggests that the failure to label the genitals was a factor in the penis envy and "castration complex" of a female patient, since what the little girl did have was not acknowledged or valued. This nonlabeling may lead to sexual inhibition and other difficulties.

Lester, Eva (1976). On the psychosexual development of the female child. *J. Amer. Acad. Psychoanal.*, 4:515-527.

This article questions the centrality of the discovery of anatomical differences for the development of female gender identity and challenges Freud's formulations of the female Oedipus complex. Sex assignment at birth is seen as the primary factor for the development of gender identity; whereas the discovery of anatomical differences, occurring usually after a ceiling for core gender identity has been established, has no effect on this identity. Lester questions the reversal in object ties in the oedipal phase (turning away from the mother as the primary love object), postulated by

Freud to follow the girl's mortification at the discovery by age three or four that she lacks a penis. The author notes that such reversal is not observed at this age; in addition, male or female children already have a preoedipal attachment to their father.

Moore, Burness (1976). Freud and female sexuality: A current view. *Int. J. Psycho-Anal.*, 57:287-300.

[See Chapter 18 for annotation.]

Parens, Henri, Pollock, Leafy, Stern, Joan, and Kramer, Selma (1976). On the girl's entry into the Oedipus complex. *J. Amer Psychoanal. Assn.* (Suppl.), 24:79-108.

Parens's research group designates three major elements in the girl's Oedipus complex: evidence of a castration complex; development of triadic object relationships, with rivalrous behavior toward the mother and heterosexual attitudes toward the father; and the manifest wish to have her own baby. Using detailed child observation, the authors deduce variable pathways by means which girls enter the Oedipus complex. Data from three normal girls are used to refute Freud's 1925 postulate that every girl takes this step by way of her castration complex. The authors conclude that girls, as well as boys, given a favorable environment, move into the Oedipus complex from age two-and-a-half on, compelled by psychobiologically determined, gender-related changes in the libido and inherited ego dispositions. The authors observe no single pattern for the chronology or the sequence of appearance of the three characteristics identifying oedipal conflict. [See also Chapter 7.]

Stoller, Robert (1976). Primary femininity. *J. Amer Psychoanal. Assn.* (Suppl.), 24:59-78.

Stoller rejects the classical Freudian theory of development, which views normal femininity as derivative of restitutive defensive operations against the castration complex. He conceptualizes a primary femininity based on core gender identity and distinguishes between the terms "male and female," meaning biological sexual identity, and gender identity, meaning psychological aspects of the conviction that one belongs to one sex. Core gender identity is composed of several elements including genetically ordained biological forces establishing neurophysiological organization of the fetal brain; sex assignment at birth; attitudes of the mother about the sex of the infant and that infant's constructing interactions with the mother into experience; early postnatal imprinting and other learning that modifies infantile brain function and perception; and developing body ego, especially from genital sensations. Stoller concludes that healthy femininity is the product of a solid core gender identity, permanent and nonconflictual identifications with feminine women, and mastery of oedipal conflict. He notes that theoretical views of femininity determine attitudes toward women and influence therapeutic goals and analytic technique.

Glenn, Jules (1977). Psychoanalysis of a constipated girl: Clinical observations during the fourth and fifth Years. *J. Amer. Psychoanal. Assn.*, 25:141-161.

[See Chapter 7 for annotation.]

Chodorow, Nancy (1978a). Gender differences in the preoedipal period. In: *The Reproduction of Mothering: Psychoanalysis and the Sociology of Gender,* Berkeley: University of California Press, pp. 92-111.

Chodorow emphasizes the special importance of the prolonged preoedipal mother-daughter relationship as the first stage of a general process in which separation and individuation remain particular female developmental issues. Extended symbiosis, narcissistic overidentification, and ambivalent feelings characterize preoedipal mother-daughter relationships. Female personality is seen as defining itself in relation to and connection with other people. There is a tendency toward boundary confusion, lack of sense of separateness, and primary identification, even though most women do develop ego boundaries and a sense of a separate self.

Fast, Irene (1978). Developments in gender identity: The original matrix. *Int. Rev. Psycho-Anal.*, 5:265-273.

Fast conceptualizes an original matrix from which the development of gender identity proceeds. Rather than this matrix being male and masculine, as Freud proposed, children are overinclusive in their earliest experience of gender and are not attuned to sex differences nor aware of the limitations inherent in belonging to one sex. Interest in sex difference begins with the recognition of limits—the boy's awareness of the mother's role in the origin of babies and the girl's recognition that she has no penis. Boys and girls envy the sex and gender attributes of the other sex and perceive the lack of those attributes as a loss or incompleteness. Girls enter the oedipal phase knowing their specifically female genitals rather than experiencing themselves as partly male and partly unknown. Recognition that they have no penis confronts them with limits rather than with the loss of the only known genital. Envy of the penis is responsive to this recognition and is resolved in a change of focus from deficiency to feminine characteristics objectively and experientially present. The relationship to the mother is, then, a specifically feminine identification, and the wish for a baby from father involves identification with maternal childbearing capacities.

Brenner, Charles (1979). Depressive affect, anxiety and psychic conflict in the phallic-oedipal phase. *Psychoanal. Q.*, 48:177-197.

[See Chapters 7 and 20 for annotations.]

Fast, Irene (1979). Developments in gender identity: Gender differentiation in girls. *Int. J. Psycho-Anal.*, 60:443-453.

Fast clarifies the next step in her theory of gender development based on differentiation. Her 1978 article defined an early, overinclusive, and undifferentiated stage as the matrix for development. Differentiation follows, in which experience is recategorized in gender terms, either as part of the self or independent of it. Female genitality is integrated with the girl's body image, male genitality is attributed to boys, and parental relations are appreciated in gender terms. Fast discusses feelings of loss and wishes for a male genital organ as part of the differentiation process and the necessary loss of narcissism. [See also annotation of Fast's (1984) book *Gender Identity: A Differentiation Model* in this chapter.]

Frankel, Steven and Sherick, Ivan (1979). Observations of the emerging sexual identity of three and four year old children: With emphasis on female sexual identity. *Int. Rev. Psycho-Anal.*, 6:297-310.

Observations of a group of normal nursery school children are used to examine the development of sexual identity; the authors assert that analytic theory and clinical data must be linked with observations of normal behavior. Groups of children, ages two to six, were observed at play. Girls at age three, before the appearance of oedipal phase behaviors, spontaneously chose female companions and formed groups for the sustained playing of house and doll care; their play was distinctly different from the less intimate play of boys of this age, which involved individual active play and sporadic groupings. Girls showed great confidence and used the groups to consolidate feminine identity. The findings are consistent with Edgcumbe and Burgner's (1975) hypothesis of a preoedipal phallic-narcissistic phase and Parens's (1976) protogenital phase, in which girls manifest a dominantly feminine disposition. Friendships between girls at this age are frequently exclusive, with elements of exhibitionism, consolidation of feminine identity, and resolution of ambivalence toward the mother by dividing love and hate among female playmates. By age four, girls show elaborate domestic play, take superhero roles, and forcefully (defensively) exclude boys from their groups. These observations are consistent with penis envy, in the sense of feeling inadequate and wishing to be a boy, notwithstanding a continued commitment to being a girl. Girls between four and five demonstrate sophisticated gender role identity, cooperative play, and emergence of oedipal themes.

Galenson, Eleanor and Roiphe, Herman (1979). The development of sexual identity: Discoveries and implications. In: *On Sexuality, Psychoanalytic Observations*, ed. T. Karasu and C. Socarides. New York: International Universities Press, pp. 1-18.

This paper is a concise summary of the authors' research, which is also detailed in their book *Infantile Origins of Sexual Identity* (1981). [See Chapter 18.] Here they review findings from a 10-year project that studied 60 normally developing infants and 10 infants selected for potential deviations because of threats of object loss and the undermining of body- and self-representations. An early genital phase, consolidated at about 18 months, was verified by their observations. Disturbances following the discovery of genital differences occurred in all the girls. Children with untoward early experiences developed severe castration reactions, to which girls were more vulnerable. Girls showed disturbances in genital derivative behavior, mood, and symbolic functioning, as well as renewed oral- and anal-phase anxieties. Fears of object loss and self-dissolution were connected with preoedipal castration reactions.

Abelin, Ernest (1980). Triangulation, the role of the father, and the origins of core gender identity during the rapprochement subphase. In: *Rapprochement*, ed. R. Lax, S. Bach, and A. Burland. New York: Aronson, pp. 151-179.

[See Chapter 16 for annotation.]

Greenspan, Stanley (1980). Analysis of a five-and-a-half-year-old girl: Indications for a dyadic-phallic phase of development. *J. Amer. Psychoanal. Assn.*, 28:575-604.

The analysis of a five-and-a-half-year-old girl illustrates the concept of a dyadic-phallic phase, which is considered as a pivotal transitional stage between the dyadic and triadic and the preoedipal and oedipal levels of development. Stage-specific character traits, transference configurations, and technical problems in the analysis are discussed. While phallic drive organization is on the ascendancy, object constancy is not yet sufficiently consolidated to permit triadic patterns and differentiated ego and superego functions. The patient's early phallic stage symptoms included impulsivity, exhibitionism, unstable self-esteem, impersonal ways of relating to objects with lack of full object constancy, entitlement, intense neediness, rage, stubbornness, fear of brief separations, and intense sexual curiosity. Analytic themes included fears of oral aggression, separation, and castration; ambivalence about sexual identification; difficulty regulating pregenital impulses; envy of body parts; wishes to be admired and other preoedipal narcissistic issues; wishes for control; primal-scene fears; and oedipal wishes. Analytic work on her sense of entitlement, wishes for control, sibling jealousy, and sense of badness allowed a shift to the triangular oedipal level as well as more differentiated ego functioning and self- and object representations. She then could work through earlier issues around separation and loss. Transference issues and implications are described.

Kestenberg, Judith (1980c). The three faces of femininity. *Psychoanal. Rev.*, 67:313-335.

Kestenberg emphasizes that an early maternal phase precedes a later phallic-oedipal phase. [See Chapter 18 for annotation.]

Lerner, Harriet (1980a). Penis envy: Alternatives in conceptualization. *Bull. Menn. Cl.*, 44:39-48. Also in: *Women in Therapy*, Northvale, NJ: Aronson, 1988, pp. 43-56.

Symptomatic penis envy is understood as a common clinical symptom. However, penis envy as a reflection of anatomical realities is reformulated as anxiety, vagueness, and confusion about girls' own genitalia. Girls may feel their genitals would be more manageable if they possessed male genitals. Thus penis envy is secondary to girls' anxiety about their own genitals. A second category of penis envy is also discussed, in which narcissistic injury, deprivation, and a disturbance in object relations, particularly with the mother, are underlying factors. The theoretical formulations in this brief article are clear, but clinical material is limited.

Karme, Laila (1981). A clinical report of penis envy: Its multiple meanings and defensive functions. *J. Amer. Psychoanal. Assn.*, 29:427-446.

Karme reports the analysis of a woman for whom "penis envy" had many determinants and unconscious meanings that are richly illustrated in dreams and analytic material. Wishes for a penis reflected the penis as symbolizing an umbilical cord, baby, womb, breast, defense against rage, weapon of preoedipal and oedipal competition, defense against feminine competition, and generalized envy.

Mahler, Margaret (1981). Aggression in the service of separation-individuation: Case study of a mother-daughter relationship. *Psychoanal. Q.,* 50:625-638.

The case study of a girl, Cathy, illuminates how aggression is utilized in the service of disengagement and distancing for successful separation-individuation and then for the maintenance of individual identity later on. Girls are seen as having to go through a "tortuous and complicated" process of splitting, repression, and reintegration to separate from their postsymbiotic mothers and to attain self- and gender identity. Mahler traces the normal development of aggression.

Cathy experienced conflict between the aggressive impetus to extricate herself from symbiotic bondage to her mother and the equally impelling regressive pull to undo the acknowledged separateness by coercively negating the distance. The loss of her father at 15 months, and exposure to showering with her mother and to viewing a boy's penis sometime between 16 and 19 months, preceded an intense rapprochement crisis at 19 months. Aggressive provocativeness was understood as representing a defense against closeness and merger and a demand for amends for anatomical shortcomings. Threatening regressions were warded off by defensively aggressive, sometimes rageful distancing behaviors and ridding mechanisms. Distancing from mother was understood as a defense against the regressive pull of symbiotic fusion and closeness, made more dangerous because of the father's absence, resulting in a lack of opportunity for early (preoedipal) triangulation. Cathy developed a fixation to ambivalent dyadic relationships that were sadomasochistically tinged. Selective identifications with mother and father occurred, and later "bad" mother part-representations became split off, introjected, and repressed. Separation from the postsymbiotic mother involves disidentifying from part-object representations of the mother. Mahler feels this task is difficult for girls; boys can identify with "uncontaminated" personality traits of the father, which better fit their gender identity needs.

Roiphe, Herman and Galenson, Eleanor (1981). *Infantile Origins of Sexual Identity,* New York: International Universities Press.

[See Chapter 18 for annotation.]

Silverman, Martin (1981). Cognitive development and female psychology. *J. Amer. Psychoanal. Assn.,* 29:581-606.

Silverman proposes that core feminine gender identity, which may be irreversible by the middle of the second year, is mediated more by cognitive development and learning than by the observation of genital differences. [See Chapter 18 for annotation.]

Bergman, Anni (1982). Considerations about the development of the girl during the separation-individuation process. In: *Early Female Development*, ed. D. Mendell. New York: S.P. Medical and Scientific Books, pp. 61-80.

Bergman uses the concepts of Mahler, Pine, and Bergman (1975) and of Abelin (1975, 1980) to focus on female development in the subphases of practicing through rapprochement during the second year of life. She outlines four factors shaping female separation-individuation, which then are expressed in the identity formation in girls: 1) the discovery of sexual differences, 2) the resolution of the rapprochement crisis, 3) identification versus disidentification, and 4) the mother's attitude toward her own and her daughter's femininity. Two evocative case examples emphasize the role of a mother's attitudes toward her daughter's femininity and how this influences the girl's sense of herself. Bergman suggests that giving birth to a girl may fulfill a mother's rapprochement wish for generational identity, which is the double wish to be a baby and to have a baby. A daughter's separation-individuation may involve a double loss for a mother, with this mother's idiosyncratic reactions being connected to her own previous separation-individuation process.

Formanek, Ruth (1982). On the origins of gender identity. In: *Early Female Development*, ed. D. Mendell. New York: S.P. Medical and Scientific Books, pp. 1-24.

Gender identity is viewed as an epigenetic developmental phenomenon resulting from the integration of many confluent factors continuing beyond childhood. Sex, gender, and core gender identity are defined, and the physical contributions to gender identity are reviewed, including a critical assessment of studies of hormones and behavior. Infant research on sex differences is evaluated in detail. Formanek criticizes Freud and considers divergent views and recent literature in a section on psychoanalytic views of gender. The methodologies of Mahler and of Galenson and Roiphe are examined. Formanek suggests that gender identity is an aspect of the self and is subject to developmental influences, including externally furnished organizers, growth of cognitive structures, differentiation of affects, and the progressive internalization of experiences. Gender identity differentiates simultaneously on both the primary-process and secondary-process levels, with new maturational factors influencing both. A series of gender identities progresses over time, with primitive, self-centered categorizations and primary-process ideas simultaneously held yet overlaid by increasing reality oriented functioning and self-images on the secondary-process level.

Glover, Laurice and Mendell, Dale (1982). A suggested developmental sequence for a preoedipal genital phase. In: *Early Female Development*, ed. D. Mendell. New York: S.P. Medical and Scientific Books, pp. 127-174.

On the basis of the analysis of dreams of six adult females, the authors propose a preoedipal developmental phase occurring between the anal and the oedipal periods in which the dominant zone is genital and the dominant task is the defining of self as female. The authors prefer the term preoedipal genital phase for this period rather than the less appropriate term phallic phase. They propose and define four sequential developmental subphases which include a focus on: 1) inner bodily sensations and a beginning awareness of the female sexual apparatus, 2) the father in specifically gender terms, with an awareness of femaleness in relation to his maleness, 3) identification with the mother's genitality, within the context of sexual differentiation from her, and 4) "the total genital self": comparisons with others in order to obtain narcissistic gratification and evaluation; organization of component instincts into an increasingly mature genital drive; formation of a consolidated sexual identity. The fourth subphase is similar to Edgcumbe and Burgner's (1975) phallic-narcissistic phase. Dream analyses are used as evidence for the subphases. This paper is interesting and provocative, although the sequences of developmental subphases as reconstructed from adult analyses are not convincing.

Kestenberg, Judith (1982). The inner-genital phase: Prephallic and preoedipal. In: *Early Female Development*, ed. D. Mendell. New York: S.P. Medical and Scientific Books, pp. 71-126.

Kestenberg reviews her theories of female development and an inner genital phase. She postulates a period between anal and phallic phases called the early maternal or inner genital phase, in which there is a triangular-maternal attitude and projection of inner genital tensions onto representations of the baby. Her data are extrapolated from analyses, longitudinal studies, and movement analyses. The paper also includes several children's drawings that elucidate her findings. The inner genital phase is part of the developmental line of maternality. In addition, the author postulates three basic feminine attitudes: the tender-maternal, the efficient-competitive, and the enticing-sensuous. These attitudes are repeated in adolescence and become the basis of motherhood/creativity, competence in the outside world and home, and fulfillment in a constant heterosexual relationship.

Meyer, Jon (1982). The theory of gender identity disorders. *J. Amer. Psychoanal. Assn.*, 30:381-413.

This article reviews the development of gender identity, which is consolidated during separation-individuation, and discusses hypotheses about the preoedipal origins of transsexualism and its link to perversions. [See Chapter 19 for annotation.]

Oliner, Marion (1982). The anal phase. In: *Early Female Development: Current Psychoanalytic Views*, ed. D. Mendell. New York: S.P. Medical and Scientific Books, pp. 25-60.

The author highlights anal-phase developmental conflicts in girls that interfere with later libidinal strivings and sublimations, such as mastery and achievement. In this phase, love for the mother is in conflict with wishes to control anal productivity, and aggressive aims dominate. The literature is reviewed and the contributions of French Kleinian analysts are summarized. Developmental issues in the anal phase include separation from the mother, mastery of the body, deaggressivizing of receptivity, progressing from narcissistic to full object relations, and turning to the father. Since mothers often feel less differentiated from, more possessive of, and more identified with daughters, mothers' own anal-sadistic elements are more likely to enter the relationship. Girls often become submissive and inhibited to close off the mother, turn inward, and control their impulses by introjective and identificatory mechanisms. Mastery and control of the inside of the body paves the way for feminine receptivity. Many adult women are inhibited in accepting a reliable love object because they have difficulties in integrating anal (intrusive, aggressive, sadistic) impulses into genitality, because of the greater identification between mothers and daughters. Further development hinges on realizing that objects can be mastered and can gratify needs without becoming destroyed or fused.

Slap, Joseph (1982). Unusual infantile theory of the origin of the female sex. *Psychoanal. Q.*, 51:428-420.

This article describes a female patient's fantasy that a father created the female sex by biting off a baby's penis in utero. Abraham (1923) described a dream and a similar interpretation in his early paper, "An Infantile Theory of the Origin of the Female Sex" [see Chapter 2].

Tyson, Phyllis (1982). A developmental line of gender identity, gender role, and choice of love object. *J. Amer. Psychoanal. Assn.*, 30:61-86.

This important article proposes a developmental line for the establishment of gender identity. Tyson views gender identity in a broad sense as composed of three interacting aspects: core gender identity, gender role identity, and sexual partner orientation. She reviews the acquisition of feminine core gender identity, beginning with sex assignment at birth, progressing through development of the body image, the impact of the discovery of anatomical differences, and the vicissitudes of penis envy. The wish for a baby, appearing as early as age one, may represent gender role identification with the mother. This identification is reworked during the oedipal phase, latency, and adolescence. By late adolescence girls have a fairly clear idea of the role they play with love objects, and sexual partner orientation is established. Tyson stresses the need to look at early identifications with the idealized mother/ego ideal in order to understand feminine personality organization. Feminine identity, the sense of being feminine, and gender role identity based on observed behavior must each be differentiated. Several refinements of classical theory are offered and include 1) emphasis on the quality of the mother-daughter relationship as affecting the girl's reaction to the anatomical differences between the sexes; 2) penis envy as a developmental stage with multiple meanings and as evidence of girls' core gender identity, 3) pervasive lowered self-esteem as reflecting prephallic problems in object relations; and 4) an apparent negative oedipal constellation as actually representing a dyadic fixation on the mother. There is an extensive bibliography and review of the literature.

Wagonfeld, Samuel (1982). Reporter, Panel: Gender and gender role. *J. Amer. Psychoanal. Assn.*, 30:185-196.

The papers in this panel present clinical data and systematic longitudinal observations of children that challenge earlier formulations and pose new questions about gender identity. Tyson's paper studies male and female development and the separate but interrelated strands constituting gender identity, which she traces developmentally and documents with clinical examples. Parens's paper reports direct child observations of the origins of wishes for a baby. He proposes that the wish for a baby results from a psychobiological drive that has both an instinctual drive and an ego-dispositional component. The wish for a baby is therefore primary and not a substitute for the wish for a penis. Galenson summarizes her research on preoedipal development and reiterates that girls develop castration anxiety with the discovery of anatomical sexual differences and that this anxiety affects the relationship with the mother by increasing hostility during the rapprochement crisis. There is a lively audience discussion.

Dahl, Kirsten (1983). First class or nothing at all? Aspects of early feminine development. *The Psychoanalytic Study of the Child*, 38:405-428. New Haven, CT: Yale University Press.

The treatment of a four-and-a-half-year-old girl illustrates the vicissitudes of female preoedipal development. Vivid clinical material demonstrates that penis envy is a complex fantasy configuration used in coming to terms with genital differences. Dahl takes a classical point of view, following Freud and Nagera, and emphasizes the phallic-narcissistic dyadic phase (Edgcumbe and Burgner, 1975). She stresses the problems of a prolonged preoedipal attachment to the mother as well as the rage and blame directed at mother for their lack of a penis.

Montgrain, Noel (1983). On the vicissitudes of female sexuality: The difficult path from "anatomical destiny" to psychic representation. *Int. J. Psycho-Anal.*, 64:169-186.

[See Chapter 18 for annotation.]

Person, Ethel and Ovesey, Lionel (1983). Psychoanalytic theories of gender identity. *J. Amer. Acad. Psychoanal.*, 11:203-226.

This article evaluates Freud's theory of gender identity and the theories of his early critics, Horney and Jones; reviews Greenson's (1968) concept of disidentification and Stoller's (1968, 1976) hypothesis of protofemininity; and presents a new theory of gender identity based on ego psychology and object relations theory. The authors conclude that there is no evidence that the original gender state is masculine, as Freud asserted; feminine, as suggested by Stoller; or innate, as argued by Horney and Jones. Person and Ovesey believe that normal core gender identity arises from sex assignment and rearing, is nonconflictual, and is cognitively and experientially constructed. Gender role identity, both normal and aberrant, evolves from body ego with socialization and sex-discrepant object relations; it is fraught with psychological conflict. Gender precedes sexuality in development and organizes sexuality, not the reverse. Thus, children are launched into the oedipal period only by learning their gender and identifying with the appropriate parent. [See also Chapter 19.]

Fast, Irene (1984). *Gender Identity: A Differentiation Model*. Hillsdale, NJ: The Analytic Press.

Expanding on her previous work (1978, 1979), Fast proposes that the child's earliest gender experience is undifferentiated rather than male or female. She traces the developmental implications of the recategorization that occurs during the process of differentiation. Female genitality is integrated into girls' body image, and object relations replace narcissistic elaboration; the recognition of limits leads to a recategorization into self and other in productive relationship, including the bodily and social definitions of femininity and masculinity in the oedipal phase. Fast asserts that her differentiation model casts new light on clinical observations of gender-related conflicts, explains differences in gender-related imagery in a research study, and illuminates a reanalysis of the Wolf Man case. Gender differentiation is seen in the larger context of identity development.

Olesker, Wendy (1984). Sex differences in 2- and 3-year olds: Mother-child relations, peer relations, and peer play. *Psychoanal. Psychol.*, 4:269-288.

This article examines behavioral differences in 20 boys and girls between two and three years of age in a nursery setting, including elements of peer play, relationships with mother, and mothers' reactions to boys and girls. Girls showed more intense involvement with their mothers, engaged in less peer play, and showed lower mood, lower levels of active play, less direct aggression, and more controlling peer play than did boys. In a second pilot study of eight infants in their first year, girls showed a higher level of object permanence. The author concludes that girls have an earlier awareness of psychological separateness than boys. She emphasizes that girls' more rapid cognitive development may lead to an early awareness of separateness and more intense rapprochement conflicts. This article is also useful in providing descriptive and behavioral data about girls in the preoedipal period.

Mayer, Elizabeth (1985). Everybody must be just like me: Observations on female castration anxiety. *Int. J. Psycho-Anal.*, 66:331-348.

Mayer proposes a particular form of female castration anxiety that is different in form from the familiar phallic castration complex, characteristically involving anxiety over the possible loss of a penis. Mayer presents toddler observations and clinical data from adult analyses to demonstrate that this different form of female castration anxiety involves fantasies of loss of the female genitals or of the capacity to be genitally open. Girl toddlers expect that "everybody must be just like me": they cannot conceive of anyone without a genital that opens toward an inner space. The early genital awareness of girls includes an opening with a potential space inside, as well as the outside external genitalia. Three interesting clinical cases share uniquely feminine fears of genital damage and a self-punitive (masochistic oedipal) fantasy of genital loss, in which they imagine they could be genitally closed over as they suppose men to be.

Silverman, Martin (1985). Sudden onset of anti-Chinese prejudice in a four-year-old girl. *Psychoanal. Q.*, 54:615-619.

This brief article describes the sudden appearance of an intense anti-Chinese attitude in a four-year-old girl. A seductive older brother was rejecting of her and teased her about not having a penis, while the father was planning to leave the home. Her anti-Chinese attitude appeared immediately after a little boy said to her, "I'll show you my penis, and you show me your china [sic]." In the course of treatment, her mother discussed sexual anatomical differences with her and protected her better against her brother, while her father reassured her about his love. The anti-Chinese sentiment promptly vanished.

Chehrazi, Shalah (1986). Female psychology: A review. *J. Amer. Psychoanal. Assn.*, 34:141-162.

Summarizing and integrating the contributions from preoedipal infant observation, Chehrazi details the ways that current theories and their clinical applications differ from the early psychoanalytic views. Early preoedipal female genital awareness and body schematization in little girls contribute to an early sense of femaleness (core gender identity). Chehrazi observes that recognition of anatomical differences occurs when the girl already sees herself as female. Penis envy in women is now viewed as a developmental phenomenon, as well as a complex and symptomatic attitude with multiple defensive functions derived from different developmental levels and expressing unique self- and object representations.

This view differs from the idea that penis envy is bedrock and intractable. Instead, penis envy, as a phase-specific developmental phenomenon, can be reworked and resolved. The wish for a penis may reflect the wish to have an organ in addition to what girls already have. Idealization of the man or the penis can have many defensive functions. A current view emphasizes factors responsible for an erroneous fantasy of being damaged that may derive from object relations, cultural influences, developmental factors, cognitive development, and difficulties in resolution of oedipal conflict or in identification with the mother. Chehrazi also discusses structuralization of the female superego, entry into the oedipal phase, the wish for a baby, and female genital anxieties in the light of current understanding of female development. Three case examples illustrate how a revised understanding of manifest penis envy and genital anxieties is utilized for more meaningful and facilitative interpretive work.

Galenson, Eleanor (1986a). Some thoughts about infant psychopathology and aggressive development. *Int. Rev. Psycho-Anal.*, 13:349-354.

Galenson describes five infant syndromes that involve disturbances in aggression. On the basis of observations made in research nursery settings, she attempts to identify particular environmental stimuli that contribute to these disturbances. One syndrome constitutes "female infants who show deviant patterns of early sexual development" during their second year. These infant girls were tenderly and effectively nurtured by their mothers during their first year but were emotionally abandoned and verbally and physically abused by their mothers once autonomous strivings and independent ambulation appeared. The emergence of genital arousal and awareness of genital differences during the early genital phase (16-19 months) was accompanied in these girls by teasing and flirtatious and markedly attacking behavior with men, whereas overly aggressive behavior characterized their interactions with their mothers.

Laufer, M. Egle (1986). The female Oedipus complex and the relationship to the body. *The Psychoanalytic Study of the Child*, 41:259-276. New Haven, CT: Yale University Press.

[See Chapter 7 for annotation.]

Spieler, Susan (1986). The gendered self: A lost maternal legacy. In: *Psychoanalysis and Women: Contemporary Reappraisals*, ed. J. Alpert. Hillsdale, NJ: The Analytic Press, pp. 33-56.

Spieler asserts that an idealization of the masculine values of separation and autonomy may be used defensively by both men and women to provide an illusion of closeness to an elusive father who may be unconsciously imagined as protective. As long as mother is the primary caretaker, she will eventually be experienced as the source of greatest disappointment. Her lack of a penis and her empathic failures dissipate the early maternal idealization, and the child turns to her father for suitable compensation. Cultural factors etch this hope into the child's representational world. Many analysands are unable to pardon their mothers for fallibilities that have interfered with their development of self-cohesion and self-esteem.

Tyson, Phyllis (1986). Female psychological development. *The Annual of Psychoanalysis*, 4:357-373. New York: International Universities Press.

Tyson uses the organizational framework of gender identity to provide a schema for understanding female development, constructing a three-strand developmental line differentiating core gender identity, gender role identity, and love object choice. Clinical vignettes and a literature review demonstrate the multiple issues and viewpoints, tracing aspects of libidinal progression, ego and superego structuralization, and the development of object relations. Tyson describes the establishment of primary femininity and female gender role, wishes to create and nurture babies, early steps in superego formation, and conflicts between wishes to be "at one with" an ideally viewed mother and, at the same time, be autonomous from her. The clinical examples stress that unresolved anal/rapprochement conflicts may jeopardize development. Resolution of rapprochement conflicts leads to confidence in mother's continuing emotional availability and support for independent and feminine exhibitionistic strivings and selective feminine identifications. Examples are given of girls who achieve libidinal object constancy and of those who must abandon oedipal strivings because of unresolved aggression and an ambivalent maternal tie. Tyson emphasizes that the level of object relations, dyadic/preoedipal or triadic/oedipal, must be differentiated. Although the Oedipus complex is central to development, the resolution of antecedent separation-individuation conflicts is necessary for confident feminine identifications, gender role development, oedipal resolution, and feminine choice of love object.

Bergman, Anni (1987). On the development of female identity: Issues of mother-daughter interaction during the separation-individuation process. *Psychoanal. Inq.*, 7:381-396.

On the basis of nursery observations, the author explores the development of girls during separation-individuation. Special emphasis is given to the effect of mothers' feelings about their daughter as female, and thus like themselves, and to girls' difficulties in identifying with the same mother from whom they have to separate. Bergman feels that the period of early rapprochement is one of special pleasure for girls in the relationship with their mothers, just as boys take special pleasure in the practicing subphase. Clinical vignettes from child cases and applications to adult analyses are given.

Silverman, Doris (1987a). Female bonding: Some supportive findings for Melanie Klein's views. *Psychoanal. Rev.*, 74:201-215.

[See Chapter 3 for annotation.]

Silverman, Doris (1987b). What are little girls made of? *Psychoanal. Psychol.*, 4:315-334.

Silverman reviews research suggesting that female infants demonstrate earlier and more intense attachments. Several characteristics of female neonates facilitate bonding: a more stable state system, earlier responsiveness in several sensory modalities, and a greater readiness to initiate and maintain gazing and vocalizing. Silverman suggests modifications in the Freudian theory of female psychology based on these findings. Bonding is felt to have special salience for female infants, and females develop powerful bonding proclivities. Object attachment (bonding need) is felt to be more essential for development than drive gratification, although sexual and aggressive wishes and conflicts may also motivate behavior. Thus, penis envy and female oedipal dynamics also need to be understood as including a central object relations cast. Sex differences in depression may be primarily related to differing object relations rather than to phallic issues. Autonomy has been overemphasized as an achievement by psychoanalytic theorists, while attachment has been devalued.

Kestenberg, Judith (1988). Der komplexe charakter weiblicher identitat. Betrachtungen zum entwicklungsverlauf. [The complex character of feminine identity: Observations on the developmental process.] *Psyche*, 42:349-364.

This article discusses the relationship between female psychosexual development and women's role in society. The author describes three developmental phases of feminine identity that must be integrated in adulthood: the maternal phase, the phase of phallic achievement strivings, and the sensual-oedipal phase. Their integration makes possible the coexistence or the alternation of contradictory female character traits. Kestenberg asserts that gender differentiation occurs early in girls, and she downplays the role of the masculinity complex.

Mendell, Dale (1988). Early female development: From birth through latency. In: *Critical Psychophysical Passages in the Life of a Woman*, ed. J. Offerman-Zuckerberg. New York: Plenum, pp. 17-36.

This excellent review discusses early female development and considers the integrative capacities that allow girls and women to encompass uniquely female physiological maturational steps throughout the life cycle. Little girls' developing relation to their body and the meanings that body assumes, from birth through latency, are discussed along with an extensive review of past and current psychoanalytic literature. Psychosexual phases, changes in self-representations and object relations, and specific issues related to body image are delineated. Developmental themes mentioned include close early bonding with the maternal representation; earlier capacity for self-control; sameness and diffusivity between mother and daughter making more essential, yet difficult, the establishment of separateness in the anal-rapprochement phase; gender differentiation; entwining of anal and genital concerns with separation-individuation; a sensual diffusion of female anatomical structures creating specific female genital anxieties; cavity erotism and an inward focus that creates interest in a procreative inside; genital comparisons with males and females; an oedipal relation as triadic rather than as a change in love object; superego consolidation involving further separation-individuation; maternal identifications and emphasis on maintaining of relationships in female superego development; and latency consolidation of maternal ego ideal and identifications.

Pines, Dinora (1988). Wozu Frauen ihren Korper unbewisst benutzen: Eine psychoanalytishe Betrachtung. [A woman's unconscious use of her body: A psychoanalytic discussion.] *Zeitschr. f. psychoanal. Theorie und Praxis*, 3:94-112.

Women are confronted throughout their lives with conflicting tasks: to identify with the inner representation of the mother and to separate and individuate from her, with the assumption of responsibility for one's own body and sexuality. When the preoedipal relationship between mother and daughter is difficult, problems reemerge in every phase of the life cycle, especially during adolescence and the childbearing years. Three cases illustrate treatment issues.

Tyson, Phyllis (1989). Infantile sexuality, gender identity, and obstacles to oedipal progression. *J. Amer. Psychoanal. Assn.*, 37:1051-1069.

Infantile sexuality is considered as one of several variables in the broader perspective of gender identity. Many developmental lines, including object relations, ego and superego functioning, aggression, and conflict resolution, also contribute to gender identity and the sense of self. The Oedipus complex is viewed as a normal developmental conflict providing a nexus for the convergence of evolving developmental currents. Tyson delineates obstacles to oedipal progression in two boys and two girls who were treated in analysis. For girls, a feminine sense of self (primary femininity) is facilitated by identification with the mother and experiencing genital sensations. A girl's narcissistic investment in her femininity is vulnerable if she experiences excessive hostility toward her mother, especially related to rapprochement conflict. Penis envy may occur but is not a necessary part of normal development. Masochistic fantasies, rather than serving to master castration, often result from hostility toward the mother and from helplessness accompanying the sense of separateness. Other obstacles to oedipal progression and positive self-esteem for girls include breast envy and fear of loss of love of the mother. Tyson emphasizes that separation anxiety, not castration anxiety, is central. Failure to resolve rapprochement crisis impedes oedipal progression and may jeopardize future object choice.

Bernstein, Doris (1990). Female genital anxieties, conflicts, and typical mastery modes. *Int. J. Psycho-Anal.*, 71:151-165.

According to Bernstein, females' experience of their own bodies include specific anxieties, which have unique influences on psychic structure. [See Chapter 18 for annotation.]

Fast, Irene (1990). Aspects of early gender development: Toward a reformulation. *Psychoanal. Psychol.* (Suppl.), 7:105-118.

Fast argues that Freud's strongly phallocentric perspective distorts his conceptions of both female and male gender development; he fails to explain bisexual themes in both sexes and gives no positive status to the mother, nor to feminine identifications. Fast reviews her differentiation paradigm for understanding three major phases of gender development: 1) the period before recognition of sex differences (undifferentiated) in which all sex and gender possibilities seem open, 2) the period of awareness of sex differences, and 3) the subsequent (oedipal) period in which sex and gender orientations are consolidated. In the second phase, both sexes experience wishes for opposite-sex characteristics in addition to their own. Girls' fantasy that the clitoris is a male organ is seen as a normal variation in the second phase and as a developmental failure later on. Parents are seen as the central reality figures in the differentiation process, against whom children test their developing notions of what it is to be a boy or a girl.

Kestenberg, Judith (1990). Two-and-a-half to four years: From disequilibrium to integration. In: *The Course of Life*, Vol. 3, ed. S. Greenspan and G. Pollock. New York: International Universities Press, pp. 25-51.

Kestenberg's work on the inner-genital phase and its relationship to maternal behavior in girls and boys between two and four years of age is reviewed. This phase ends with denial of the inside genital and turning to the outer genital, a move which ushers in the phallic phase in both sexes.

Olesker, Wendy (1990). Sex differences during the early separation-individuation process: Implications for gender identity formation. *J. Amer. Psychoanal. Assn.*, 38:325-346.

Observations of 22 infants from 9 to 12 months of age in a nursery setting suggest that girls become aware of psychological separateness earlier than boys do. Girls show a more intense focus on their mother, seek her out without seeing her (a beginning form of evocative memory), insist on tactile contact, initiate contact more often, and stay involved with her for longer periods of time. More girls reach higher stages of object permanence than boys do. The nature of infant girls' means of coping, and their relationship to their mother and to play objects are reported. Sex differences in the expression of aggression and in maternal handling of aggression are also discussed. Female tendencies toward depression (autoplastic defenses) and turning toward others, in contrast to male tendencies to use activity to change the external world (alloplastic defenses), may have their origins during this period. Implications for gender identity formation are described.

Parens, Henri (1990). On the girl's psychosexual development: Reconsiderations suggested from direct observation. *J. Amer. Psychoanal. Assn.*, 39:743-772.

Two decades of child observation suggest revisions of Freudian psychosexual theory. The concept of the "phallic phase" is not representative of the first genital phase in girls and should be discarded. Freud's (1925) hypotheses about how girls enter the oedipal phase and the nature of their wishes to have babies are challenged. In this sample, phallic aggression was also less manifest in girls than in boys in the two to four-year-old period. Parens proposes that we should attend to early experiences of ambivalence in girls in formulating dynamics. This ambivalence also lies at the heart of the Oedipus complex, so that formulations of superego development can be made compatible with clinical findings.

Schmukler, Anita and Garcia, Emanuel (1990). Special symbols in early female oedipal development: Fantasies of folds and spaces, protuberances and cavities. *Int. J. Psycho-Anal.*, 71:297-307.

Using child observation, the authors present three prelatency girls who displaced their penis envy and castration anxiety onto other anatomic regions of the body. In two of the cases, the first interdigital fold was employed as the locus of concern; and in the third case, the laryngeal prominence and jugular notch were the areas of the body for the locus of displacement.

Tyson, Phyllis and Tyson, Robert (1990). Gender development: Girls. In: *Psychoanalytic Theories of Development: An Integration.* New Haven, CT: Yale University Press, pp. 258-276.

Core gender identity (primary femininity), gender role identity, and sexual partner orientation are traced from infancy through adolescence, with an elaboration on how object relations, ego development, and superego formation contribute to the broader aspects of gender identity. The authors emphasize that core gender identity includes contributions from early identifications with the mother and from mental representations of a female body image, in addition to being influenced by hormones, sex assignment, and parental handling. Narcissistic investment in a feminine body representation develops early. Female genital awareness includes the vagina as well as pleasurable sensations arising from the external genitals which are easily located. Pride or shame about one's female body and the impact of the recognition of the anatomical differences are viewed in relation to 1) the role of the father in affirming the daughter's narcissistic investment in her body, 2) the resolution of anger towards the mother during the rapprochement subphase, resulting in an ability to selectively identify with a female ego ideal, 3) the early steps in superego formation, and 4) drive progression. The authors suggest a separate developmental line for female genital anxieties and they question whether penis envy and castration anxiety are central features of female development. Penis envy is considered an ubiquitous phase-specific phenomenon with multiple meanings and functions. Phallic castration anxiety should be differentiated from fears of object loss and from other uniquely female genital concerns. The preoedipal infantile genital phase (rather than the misnamed phallic phase) is differentiated from the later triadic oedipal phase. In this preoedipal genital phase, feminine gender role identity and a narcissistically valued feminine body image are consolidated.

A separate developmental line for gender role identity is proposed which includes mannerisms, interactions, and wishes to have breasts and babies in identification with the mother. These identifications and "role-relationship" identifications are reworked and revised throughout the life cycle. Sexual partner orientation is viewed as a separate developmental line, with early foundations in the establishment of triadic oedipal object relations. The authors differentiate negative oedipal manifestations from more common failures to resolve dyadic pregenital struggles with the mother. A negative oedipal phase is not obligatory, and when it occurs, it follows after a positive oedipal phase. Although oedipal resolution may not have the same urgency as for the boy, motivation for the resolution of libidinal wishes for father comes from fear of narcissistic mortification, fear of loss of mother's love, and guilt from an earlier, more developed superego originating from rapprochement resolution.

Gender identity development in latency is reworked and consolidated by expanding social relations. Masturbation is present, although sometimes disguised. In adolescence, sexual partner orientation is finally consolidated. Contributions to gender identity from the ego, drives, and object relations, and each of the separate developmental lines of gender identity are elaborated and revised during adolescence. Resolution of conflicts over object choice comes from a revision and deidealization of the ego ideal and the infantile self- and object representations.

Clower, Virginia (1991). The acquisition of mature femininity. In: *Women and Men: New Perspectives on Gender Differences*, ed. M. Notman and C. Nadelson. Washington, DC: American Psychiatric Press, Inc., pp. 75-88.

The analyses of two girls in rapprochement and the quality of their close relationship to their mothers are discussed. [See Chapter 11 for annotation.]

Person, Ethel (1991). The "construction" of femininity, its influence throughout the life cycle. In: *The Course of Life: Adolescence*, Vol. 4, ed. S. Greenspan and G. Pollock. Madison, CT: International Universities Press.

[See Chapter 18 for annotation.]

Tyson, Phyllis (1991). Some nuclear conflicts of the infantile neurosis in female development. *Psychoanal. Inq*, 11(4).

Tyson integrates insights from Freud's later work that were never included in his theory of female psychology, including his formulations about signal anxiety, superego formation, and the structural model. She uses this integration to reevaluate the nuclear conflicts in the female infantile neurosis. Tyson suggests that many divergent perspectives and intertwining themes can be integrated into every clinical picture. There are also many possible developmental narratives, partly representing several mythical stories, rather than one superordinate theory of female development.

Tyson proposes that rather than castration anxiety, the fear of loss of love, with the wish to retain the love of the idealized same-sex object, is a central motivator for superego development in girls. A girl's negative feelings toward her mother can threaten her with fears of loss of this idealized relationship. In addition to penis envy, other sources of a girl's aggression toward her mother can come from struggles with ambivalence from the rapprochement subphase over issues related to willfulness and control, separation, independence, and the establishment of a separate identity. Rapprochement fears contribute to early, but harsh, superego formation. Tyson emphasizes that since this need for closeness and intimacy with the idealized mother may be central, issues of gender identity, narcissism, and self-esteem will be bound up with superego development. A narcissistically valued femininity relies on selective identification made with an ideally viewed mother and requiring resolution of ambivalence.

Superego development in girls is necessary for oedipal progression and oedipal resolution. Resolution and internalization of rapprochement conflicts can also imply a shift in the ego and development of the capacity for affective control, using signal anxiety. In lieu of the phallic phase, Tyson proposes the infantile genital phase, which includes a narcissistically valued sense of femininity and a consolidated gender role identity. Mother and father are both important for different developmental tasks and identifications. Triadic object relations form the second half of the infantile genital phase. Tyson offers segments from the analysis of an adult woman that simultaneously illustrate her infantile neurosis, her adult neurosis, the transference neurosis and the confluent applicability of theories of anxiety, the structural model, the concept of gender identity, and superego formation.

# Chapter 7

# Superego and the Oedipus Complex
### Phyllis Tyson

Freud's views have had an enormous impact on theories of the Oedipus complex and the development of the superego in women. Freud thought that early childhood masturbation for girls involved only the clitoris, which he equated with a little penis; thus he thought that female development was identical to that of males until the infantile genital phase. He explained oedipal progression as being based on girls' acknowledging castration and inferiority, turning angrily from mother, and taking father as a libidinal object. Consequently, because there was no further fear of castration, formation of the superego in females was insufficiently motivated.

Not all analysts share Freud's views of oedipal and superego development in women, nor did all his contemporaries agree with him. From the papers reviewed in this section it is apparent that analysts vary in the extent to which they base their thinking on Freud's ideas, accept some aspects of his theory while rejecting others, or forge new theories. Some current formulations of the female Oedipus complex emphasize the convergence of object relations, ego and superego development, and drive progression. Therefore, on closer scrutiny, progression to the phase Freud originally termed the "infantile genital phase" (later called the phallic phase) cannot automatically be considered as synonymous with entering oedipal phase as Freud assumed; rather, preoedipal, dyadic object relations may still persist. [The reader is also referred to Chapter 21 for papers on beating fantasies and the superego.]

Freud, Sigmund (1924b). The dissolution of the Oedipus complex. *Standard Edition*, 19:172-179. London: Hogarth Press, 1953.

Freud considers the castration complex of central importance for oedipal progression and superego formation. He asserts that girls are more dependent on external controls such as loss of love. [See Chapter 1 for annotation.]

Freud, Sigmund (1925). Some psychical consequences of the anatomical distinction between the sexes. *Standard Edition*, 19:243-258. London: Hogarth Press, 1953.

Freud elaborates on the role of the castration complex as a motive in the dissolution of the Oedipus complex for the boy and its part in the initiation of the Oedipus complex for the girl. [See Chapter 1 for annotation.]

Horney, Karen (1926). The flight from womanhood. *Int. J. Psycho-Anal.*, 12:360-374. Also in: *Feminine Psychology*, ed. H. Kelman. New York: Norton, pp. 54-70, 1967.

Horney protests against comparing female development with that of the male, as if the latter were somehow the normal and objective standard. She assumes that both clitoral and vaginal sensations are present in early childhood and that these lead to masturbation and to the familiar associated fantasies of the Oedipus complex and eventually to superego formation. She asserts that oedipal wishes develop in parallel (with different contents) to those of males for their mother. Little girls, on observing the disproportionate size between father and child, fear vaginal injury as they entertain fantasies of intercourse associated with their oedipal wishes. Therefore, girls give up oedipal wishes and their feminine position and instead take a male role and wish for a penis. Penis envy is thus a regressive solution to the Oedipus complex, as girls assume that castration (womanliness) is evidence of guilt; possessing a penis would prove girls to be guiltless. While Horney's views that girls may fear genital damage can be corroborated clinically, these fears derive more from masturbation guilt than from fantasies of intercourse in normally developing, unmolested girls. [See also Chapter 2.]

Muller-Braunschweig, Carl (1926). Genesis of the feminine superego. *Int. J. Psycho-Anal.*, 8:359-362.

In an early and virtually unknown article, this author assumes equivalent superego functioning in males and females. He proposes motivations responsible for superego formation in girls. Muller-Braunschweig argues that female sexuality emerges early and is based on an unconscious knowledge of the passive role played by the vagina. The feminine id strives for the fulfillment of a passive masochistic wish to be violated. Fulfillment of incestuous impulses, which express a wish to be violated by the father, would lead to fear of loss of father's and mother's love; since the father also represents a judge, such fulfillment would overwhelm the ego. To guard against such a danger, girls develop penis envy or fantasize possessing a penis. Penis envy is seen as a defensive reaction formation against the masochistic wish to be violated by the father. The penis ideal then becomes the foundation for the ego ideal and superego. This imagined penis represents the superego's power over the demands of the id. The author proposes that the anxiety connected with the possible loss of the fantasized penis is at least as great for women as is castration anxiety in men; it is this anxiety that leads girls to relinquish their oedipal wishes and form a superego.

Jones, Ernest (1927). The early development of female sexuality. *Int. J. Psycho-Anal.*, 8:459-472.

Jones comments on the male bias in psychoanalytic theory and disagrees with Freud's speculations about inadequate superego functioning in women. He suggests that the concept of castration limits understanding of those fundamental conflicts in the female which lead to superego formation. Jones proposes that women's primary fears are of separation and rejection and that they develop a superego to avoid them. Criticizing Freud's oedipal bias, he points to the importance of women's preoedipal tie to the mother. Fears of rejection and separation related to the mother are transferred to the father in the oedipal phase. Then, in an effort to win father's approval and avoid rejection and abandonment, girls identify with father's moral ideals. Jones suggests that penis envy may be prominent in women because they often develop the idea that men (i.e., father) are strongly opposed to feminine wishes and disapprove of femininity. Identification with father in an attempt to ward off separation and rejection involves adopting male ideals and disparaging feminine wishes and ideals. Jones's ideas find sympathy in the context of modern psychoanalytic thinking, but historically they had surprisingly little influence. [See also Chapters 2 and 19.]

Lampl-de Groot, Jeanne (1927). The evolution of the Oedipus complex in women. *Int. J. Psycho-Anal.*, 9:332-345. Also in: *The Psychoanalytic Reader*, ed. R. Fliess. New York: International Universities Press, 1948, pp. 180-194.

Lampl-de Groot asserts that the girl's pregenital development is like that of the boy, "a little man," as to her love aim and object choice. She proposes that the negative oedipal phase precedes the positive oedipal phase in girls. [See Chapter 2 for annotation.]

Klein, Melanie (1928). Early stages of the Oedipus conflict. In: *Love, Guilt and Reparation and Other Works: The Writings of Melanie Klein*, Vol. 1. London: Hogarth Press, 1975, pp. 186-198.

Klein postulates that the superego both in boys and in girls functions much earlier in life than Freud proposed. She maintains that oedipal tendencies and the superego arise as a consequence of deprivation of the breast and the frustration of weaning at the end of the first or the beginning of the second year of life. The superego thus arises in connection with the oral sadistic phase, and with wishes to bite and destroy the libidinal object, and with the dread of being devoured. In addition, she believes that girls fear that their mother will destroy their capacity for motherhood and so fear that the contents of their body will be robbed, destroyed, or mutilated. These fears arise because of the girls' destructive fantasies toward the mother's body and toward the children in the womb of the mother's body. This archaic superego is characterized by extremes of goodness and severity because of very early identifications. Klein notes that if identification with mother takes place predominantly at this early oral and anal-sadistic stage, dread of a primitive maternal superego leads to repression and fixation and may interfere with further genital development. Dread of the mother impels little girls to give up identification with her, and identification with the father begins.

Sachs, Hanns (1929). One of the motive factors in the formation of the superego in women. *Int. J. Psycho-Anal.*, 10:39-50.

Contrary to Freud, Sachs believes that women can develop an independent superego. This development is possible to the extent that women are able to give up oedipal strivings and tolerate the frustration inherent in the final renunciation of their father. Sachs traces a line of superego development for women. The little girl, in accepting castration, finds clitoral masturbation unsatisfactory. She is then frustrated in her genital desires for father and transfers to him "with passionate intensity" oral wishes originally associated with oral frustration and the mother. The oral wishes toward the father determine the final form of the superego. If the oral wishes cannot be relinquished, the girl remains fixated to the father and simply identifies, in a dependent manner, with his (or his substitute's) ideals and moral values. If the frustration can be tolerated, the father is introjected, and the girl detaches herself from him and develops an independent superego. This is a well written paper, the thesis is clear, and it is illustrated with a clinical example and dream material.

Fenichel, Otto (1930). The pregenital antecedents of the Oedipus complex. *Int. J. Psycho-Anal.*, 11:141-166.

[See Chapter 2 for annotation.]

Lewin, Bertram (1930). Smearing of feces, menstruation, and the female superego. (Kotschmieren, Menses und Weibliches Uber-ich.) *Int. Ztschr. f. Psa.* 16:43-56, 1930. Also in: *Selected Writings of Betram D. Lewin*, ed. J. Arlow. New York: Psychoanalytic Quarterly Press, 1973.

Lewin discusses the role of the compensatory impulse to smear, which is displaced to the skin of the body and its relationship to early superego formation. He agrees with Sachs (1928) that oral wishes toward the father must be renounced in order for (oral) introjection and superego formation to take place. In cases where libido has been displaced to the body surfaces, there will be less oral libido for introjection and thus a second cause for incomplete superego formation. [See also Chapter 10.]

Freud, Sigmund (1931a). Female sexuality. *Standard Edition*, 21:223-243. London: Hogarth Press, 1953.

Freud momentarily reconsiders the centrality of the oedipal phase in the context of acknowledging the importance of the preoedipal mother-daughter relationship. [See Chapter 1 for annotation.]

Jacobson, Edith (1937). Ways of female superego formation and the female castration conflict. *Psychoanal. Q.*, 45:525-538, 1976.

This article is an example of the pervasiveness of Freud's idea that the superego is a consequence of castration anxiety. Jacobson, observing women's tendency to devalue their femininity and to defer to the opinions of men, agrees with Freud that the female superego is weak and unstable; but she is puzzled by women's suffering from cruel superego demands. This suffering leads her to suspect that superego formation in females is more complicated than Freud assumed. She suggests that the superego in women has its origin in early castration conflicts that are preoedipal, not oedipal, and are related to the mother. Jacobson asserts that girls, on discovering they are "castrated" cultivate the idea that there is a penis hidden inside their body. Fear of castration then becomes fear of destruction of this internal genital. A derivative of this fear is seen later in fantasies and fears of pregnancy. The narcissistic wound of "castration" may be healed by libidinal displacements to other body parts or to the body as a whole. Then narcissistic compensations are initiated, such as emphasizing feminine virtue, in which an ego ideal of a modest, gentle, obedient, clean little girl develops, or overvaluing feminine beauty, while the genital is devalued.

What is decisive for the sexual vicissitudes, Jacobson notes, is how successfully the love relationship to the father develops. At first, the narcissistic compensation for the devalued genital is the paternal penis. Then fear of loss of the penis is replaced by fear of loss of the phallic love object. From then on, female "anxiety of conscience" becomes secondary to "social anxiety," and the opinions and judgments of the love object become decisive. The early harsh female superego is warded off by a dependency on the superego of the father, which, however, mitigates further development of an independent female superego. The formation of an independent female superego, but one qualitatively different from that of the male, depends on the extent to which the vagina can be accepted as a valued genital. [See also Chapters 2 and 18.]

Greenacre, Phyllis (1948). Anatomical structure and superego development. *Amer. J. Orthopsychiat.*, 18:636-648. Also in: *Trauma, Growth, and Personality*, New York: Norton, 1952, pp. 149-164.

Greenacre proposes that children's character and superego may be influenced by the reaction to the physical body. While girls must accept not having a penis, they nevertheless assume this lack to be a punishment for past masturbation inasmuch as it is often masturbatory arousal that brings girls' attention to their penisless state. The hypothetical sin for which they have already been punished appears to provide a fund of guilt, which contributes to later guilt feelings in situations of conflict. Greenacre suggests that this fund of guilt contributes to some of the high ideals and the tendency toward marked, although rather diffuse and aimless, conscientiousness and worrying. Although not all modern authors would agree that the lack of a penis is universally experienced as punishment, the diffuse and aimless conscientiousness that Greenacre observed in some women deserves serious study and further thought.

Keiser, Sylvan (1953). A manifest Oedipus complex in an adolescent girl. *The Psychoanalytic Study of the Child*, 8:99-107. New York: International Universities Press.

[See Chapter 9 for annotation.]

Reich, Annie (1953). Narcissistic object choice in women. *J. Amer. Psycho-anal. Assn.*, 1:22-44. Also in: *Annie Reich: Psychoanalytic Contributions.* New York: International Universities Press, 1973, pp. 179-208.

Reich distinguishes between the superego as a later, more reality-syntonic structure, and the ego ideal as an earlier, more narcissistic structure, composed of grandiose images and functioning to maintain self-esteem. These distinctions facilitate an understanding of the dynamic configurations of those women who make narcissistic object choices. She describes two types of women who make pathological narcissistic object choices. The first group of women are highly submissive to men to whom they feel deeply attached. These women suffer intense inferiority feelings and are overly critical of themselves. Their identifications are with idealized males. As children, these women idealized their fathers. As adults, they long to share the parental greatness to undo their sense of weakness and inability to obtain idealized masculine values and ambitions for themselves. Women in the second group, classified as "as if" personalities, demonstrate greater attachment to a grandiose, unrealizable ego ideal than to an external object. They manifest continuous cycles of overidealization and denigration of male objects. The object, to whom they relate in a primitive and transitory manner, represents a personification of the phallic ego ideal in attempts to undo narcissistic want and the fear of castration. This object is often given up because of criticism from a third person, as these women have immature superego development in that external judgment overpowers internal judgment. Reich remains loyal to Freud's notion that superego maturation is judged as the ability to maintain values and morals independently of environmental influence. Although this idea has been recently reevaluated, this is nevertheless a worthwhile article in the history of the theory of the superego of women. Clinical manifestations are vividly described, including an attempt to understand preoedipal roots of the female superego.

Jacobson, Edith (1964). *The Self and the Object World.* New York: International Universities Press.

In contrast to her earlier view (1937), Jacobson discards the idea that the female superego is weak and unstable. She also discards her idea about fears of inner body destruction. Most of her thesis, however, remains identical to her earlier one about the early and different pathway for the female superego as compared with that of the male. The female superego has its origin in early castration reactions, where devaluation of the female genital leads to depression, angry turning away from and devaluing of mother, and an intensely ambivalent approach to the father. An early maternal ego ideal, grounded in anal reaction formations, is established to cope with the dangers and conflicts associated with devaluation of the mother. With oedipal attachment to the father, the narcissism the daughter previously invested in her own genitals is displaced to the love object; and fear of loss of the phallic love object leads the girl to become subservient to the father's ideas and values, delaying the establishment of an independent ego and independent ethical codes. The basis for an eventually self-reliant ego, and of a mature ego ideal and autonomous superego in women, Jacobson believes, "is all the more successful the better the little girl learns to accept her femininity and thus can find her way back to maternal ego and superego identifications" (pp. 114-115). Jacobson's ideas, especially her stress on early formation and the role of early introjects, have had an important influence on subsequent thinking about the early roots of the superego in women.

Barnett, Marjorie (1968). I can't versus he won't. *J. Amer. Psychoanal. Assn.*, 16:588-600.

This article reconsiders positive oedipal development in the light of new anatomic and physiological information regarding differences between the sexes. [See Chapter 18 for annotation.]

Chasseguet-Smirgel, Janine (1970b). Feminine guilt and the Oedipus complex. In: *Female Sexuality: New Psychoanalytic Views*, ed. J. Chasseguet Smirgel. Ann Arbor: University of Michigan Press, pp. 94-134.

Chasseguet-Smirgel asserts that the wish to incorporate the paternal penis and to depose the omnipotent mother is the source of female oedipal guilt. She contends that children of both sexes see the mother as powerful and omnipotent and feel helpless and incomplete in comparison. Whereas boys feel narcissistically satisfied that they have something mother does not have, girls must turn to father to free themselves from mother. Girls do not envy the penis for its own sake, but as a revolt against the omnipotent mother who caused the narcissistic wound. To defend against rivalry with the mother, fear of identifying with the castrating mother, and fear of castrating the father, girls may choose to remain in the role of the dependent caretaker of the father. The author includes a number of clinical examples that have in common a sadistic and castrating mother, and a good but vulnerable father.

Luquet-Parat, Catherine (1970). The change of object. In: *Female Sexuality: New Psychoanalytic Views*, ed. J. Chasseguet-Smirgel. Ann Arbor: University of Michigan Press, pp. 84-93.

This article examines the complex and interwoven factors involved in girls' change of love object from mother to father. The author emphasizes that this change coexists with changes in drive, erogenous zones, and the structuralization of the ego. Combining Kleinian and Freudian ideas, this article presents a unique and original approach. [See also Chapter 21.]

Muslin, Hyman (1972). The superego in women. In: *Moral Values and the Superego Concept in Psychoanalysis*, ed. S. Post. New York: International Universities Press, pp. 101-125.

Focusing on Freud's use of superego signals of shame and guilt to reflect an autonomous superego, Muslin begins with a summary of Freud's views. Muslin maintains that the wish for love and approval from parental/environmental objects continues in women and that loss of love or esteem is as important a set of signals in regulating psychic economy as is fear of superego punishment. He concludes that the superego in women is unique in its contents but not in the function it serves. Specific contents include prohibition against aggressive activity; censorship surrounding sexual activity; restriction against instinctuality; and an ideal of "sweet, kind, shy" or "unaggressive, clean, neat"; and an ideal to be mother to her own mother. The chapter contains a comprehensive review of the early and later psychoanalytic literature.

Schafer, Roy (1974). Problems in Freud's psychology of women. *J. Amer. Psychoanal. Assn.*, 22:459-486. Also in: *J. Amer. Psychoanal. Assn.* (Suppl.), 24:331-360, 1976.

Schafer maintains that Freud's ideas on the development and psychological characteristics of girls and women, though rich in clinical and theoretical discoveries, are significantly flawed by the influence of traditional patriarchal and evolutionary values. This influence leads to questionable presuppositions, logical errors and inconsistencies, under-emphasis on certain developmental variables, and confusion between observation, definition and value preference.

Under three headings—1) the problem of women's morality and objectivity, 2) the problem of neglected prephallic development, and 3) the problem of naming—Schafer first discusses Freud's generalizations concerning ego and superego development in boys and girls. He observes, for instance, that Freud's observation of a quality of moral rigidity in men's superego was in fact related to a greater capacity for isolation of affect and obsessionality and had little to do with morals and values. Whereas a fear of disapproval may overrule whatever independent sense women may have of what is right, men's castration anxiety frequently remains so unresolved and so intense that it continuously incites them to violate conventional morality.

Schafer considers Freud's neglect of prephallic development, questions why penis envy may be so central, and suggests that Freud did not ask the questions about the relationship of girls to the mother. He suggests that Freud's schema maintains an evolutionary value system based on overvaluation of procreativity with an accompanying overvaluation of the phallic or genital phase. Finally, he discusses the consequences of Freud's linkages of such terms as male-masculine-active-aggressive-dominant and female-feminine-passive-masochistic-submissive. Schafer concludes that Freud's generalizations about girls and women do injustice both to Freud's clinical findings and to his psychoanalytic method, as he fails to consider the maternal transference and his own countertransference. [See also Chapter 21.]

Nagera, Humberto (1975). *Female Sexuality and the Oedipus Complex.* New York: Aronson.

Using the idea that development involves several simultaneously evolving developmental lines, Nagera seeks a reevaluation of the female Oedipus complex. He suggests that behavioral manifestations be considered along four different developmental lines: object chosen, erotogenic zone, sexual position (masculine, feminine, bisexual), and active-passive position. He then discusses the interaction of these with three other influences that simultaneously shape the person's sex life: the innate variations in the strength of the different component instincts; the rate of progress on the line of ego development; and environmental circumstances and experiences that either favor or interfere with normal developmental progress.

He proposes two distinct stages of the female Oedipus complex. In the first stage, which Nagera calls the phallic-oedipal (instead of the more traditional negative oedipal), girls' dominant libidinal position is active and the mother is the primary libidinal object. The second is the oedipal phase proper, wherein girls assume a receptive position, with the father as the primary object.

During the first stage, the sexuality of girls is essentially masculine, and girls believe that everyone possesses a phallus. A move to the second stage involves several changes: change of object from mother to father; suppression or abandonment of the clitoris as the essential erotogenic zone; change from a masculine position to a feminine one; change from activity to passivity; and abandonment of the belief in the universal existence of the penis. This transition involves girls' accepting the absence of a penis in women, and in themselves in particular; accepting that babies can be substitutes; a concomitant reduction of penis envy; finding suitable feminine identifications, and changing fantasies and ideas about intercourse. Nagera perceives girls' sexual life until and beyond puberty as one deprived of an executive organ, since he considers the contribution of the vagina to be minimal, even with physical maturity. He thus struggles to understand the significance of the absence of a leading erotogenic zone during the positive Oedipus complex. This void, he maintains, is filled by means of such mechanisms as identifications, desexualization, and sublimation.

Applegarth, Adrienne (1976). Some observations on work inhibitions in women. *J. Amer. Psychoanal. Assn.* (Suppl.), 24:251-268.

Gender specific aspects of superego contents are discussed. [See Chapter 12 for annotation.]

Blum, Harold (1976). Masochism, the ego ideal and the psychology of women. *J. Amer. Psychoanal. Assn.*, (Suppl.), 24:157-192.

This article considers masochism and the female ego ideal. The author notes that Freud continually emphasized girls' disappointments, deprivations, inferiority, feelings of damage, and defeat by their oedipal rival. Freud saw girls as identified with a devalued and castrated mother and with a masochistic biological role (anticipation of, as well as the experience of, menstruation, defloration, penetration, and parturition). This identification stimulates masochistic fantasies. Believing that masochism was an important part of the female ego ideal, Freud (1924a; 1933) categorized masochism as erotogenic, feminine, and moral. Blum points out that masochism is a residue of unresolved infantile conflicts and is neither essentially feminine nor a valuable component of the female character. An intense masochistic ego ideal is usually associated with impaired object relations and reflects preoedipal and oedipal pathology. He also argues that it is impossible to derive mature maternal devotion from masochism, narcissism, or penis envy. This article contests the view that masochism is a normal, expectable character trait of the well-adjusted woman. In challenging the coupling of masochism and motherhood, Blum proposes a further examination of the important ingredients for mature mothering. [See also Chapter 21.]

Edgcumbe, Rose, Lunberg, Sara, Markowitz, Randi, and Salo, Frances (1976). Some comments on the concept of the negative oedipal phase in girls. *The Psychoanalytic Study of the Child*, 31:35-61. New Haven, CT: Yale University Press.

After examining the analytic material of several young girls, these authors question whether a negative oedipal phase is a necessary step in normal female development. They observe that what is often described as a negative oedipal constellation, wherein the mother appears to be the preferred love object and the father is seen as a rival in a triangular situation, is actually a regression to, or an arrest at, the preoedipal phallic narcissistic level in which dyadic object relationships persist. The authors think that normal penis envy, which is ubiquitous in girls during the phallic phase, is more related to girls' narcissistic evaluation of themselves than to their attempts to gain the mother as love object. Therefore, the appearance of penis envy should indicate progression in drive development but not necessarily in object relations. Determining whether the mother-daughter relationship is preoedipal or negative oedipal requires making a distinction between dyadic and triadic object relationships. The nature of the drives and aims directed toward those objects are seen to provide valuable clues to whether object relationships are dyadic or triadic. Several case examples illustrate the points made.

Gray, Sheila (1976). The resolution of the Oedipus complex in women. *J. Phila. Assn. Psychoanal.*, 3:103-111.

Gray develops the thesis that a woman who is unable to utilize her intellectual skills has not resolved the Oedipus complex. Freud's ideas about the wish for a baby are reviewed. Gray employs the concept of "genitality" (Reich, 1929), the genital character being a person who has reached the postambivalent genital stage where aggression is sublimated in social achievement and genital libido is freely available for gratification, i.e., cathexis of the vagina. Gray postulates that women who remain fixed on the wish for a penis, or see a baby as a substitute, have not progressed from the phallic to the feminine oedipal stage. This progression is facilitated by girls' experiencing themselves as attractive to father, who refrains from exploitation and who encourages desexualization and inhibition of sexual aim. With the resolution of the Oedipus complex, the vagina can be cathected as an organ of pleasure beyond its function for reproduction. The onset of puberty and the cathexis of inner space heightens vaginal pleasure. Oedipal resolution is accompanied by a concomitant sense of oneself as a complete, functioning person, and the neutralization of sexual and aggressive drive energies permits the full realization of intellectual capacities as well as a mature capacity to undertake the task of motherhood.

Parens, Henri, Pollock, Leafy, Stern, Joan, and Kramer, Selma (1976). On the girl's entry into the Oedipus complex. *J. Amer Psychoanal. Assn.* (Suppl.), 24:79-108.

Reporting on detailed observations of three normal girls who were studied since birth, Parens and his colleagues suggest that the data do not support the generalizability of Freud's (1925) hypothesis that girls enter the Oedipus complex by way of the castration complex. The authors use as criteria for the Oedipus complex 1) evidence of a castration complex; 2) triadic object relations and heterosexual attitude toward father; and 3) the manifest wish to have their own baby. The three girls studied entered their respective Oedipus complexes by somewhat different pathways. One showed evidence of a castration complex before she demonstrated a wish for a baby or a heterosexual attitude toward father; another exhibited a castration complex several months after the manifestation of a wish for a baby. The third child showed all three attitudes simultaneously.

The authors observe that entry into the Oedipus complex by way of the castration complex is not universal; nor does interest in babies depend on the wish to have a penis, but may appear as early as 12 to 14 months associated with an identification with the mother. Once girls enter the first genital phase, or what the authors term protogenital phase (the female equivalent of the phallic phase), the wish for a baby acquires a driven, pressured quality that they postulate has biological roots.

Ticho, Gertrude (1976). Female autonomy and young adult women. *J. Amer. Psychoanal. Assn.* (Suppl.), 24:139-155.

Ticho argues that superego identifications with both parents play a significant role in women's sense of autonomy. [See Chapter 12 for annotation.]

Glenn, Jules (1977). Psychoanalysis of a constipated girl: Clinical observations during the fourth and fifth years. *J. Amer. Psychoanal. Assn.*, 25:141-161.

Using the data from the analysis of a prelatency girl, Glenn evaluates controversial issues in female development. These include issues of core gender identity, the role of male and female identifications as well as cognition and body image in the formation of a sense of femininity, and the female superego. Glenn reports that the key determinants in his patient's bowel movement retention symptom, which began at 2 years 9 months, were a wish to have a baby in identification with the mother, envy of male genitals and of a male's role and privileges, and a wish for control in conflict with mother.

Contrary to Freud's suggestion that women do not develop strong superegos, Glenn's patient, Betty, conspicuously demonstrated preoedipal superego precursors. Glenn attributes these precursors to the fear of bodily damage, including genital damage. He notes that Betty imagined that she had a penis (equating her BM with penis and baby) and feared losing it. Early anal determinants were also apparent in a distorted "sphincter morality" as Betty tried to control herself in accordance with her mother's wishes. She defended against anal aggression and the wish to soil and mess by being good, affectionate, friendly, neat, and clean, reaction formations that formed the basis of her superego. Also contrary to Freud's theory, Glenn concludes that the analysis of Betty demonstrates that the sense of femininity and the wish for a baby emerge prior to the phallic (infantile genital) phase and the Oedipus complex. While the case supports Freud's contention that penis envy plays an important role in female development, it also shows that Freud underestimated the significance of early maternal identifications in girls' establishment of a sense of femininity.

Gilligan, Carol (1977). In a different voice: Women's concepts of self and morality. *Harvard Educational Review*, 47:481-517.

[See Gilligan, 1982, this chapter.]

Chodorow, Nancy (1978b). Object relations and the female oedipal configuration. In: *The Reproduction of Mothering*. Berkeley: University of California Press, pp. 111-129.

[See Chodorow (1978c), this chapter.]

Chodorow, Nancy (1978c). Oedipal resolution and adolescent replay. In: *The Reproduction of Mothering*. Berkeley: University of California Press, pp. 130-140.

Writing against the masculine bias of psychoanalytic theory, Chodorow argues that in the classical formulation of the female Oedipus complex the emphasis on the difficult libidinal path to heterosexuality fails to give due recognition to the role of object-related wishes and conflicts. Chodorow maintains that psychoanalytic theories about the female Oedipus must include considerations about the relationship to each object. The shift to the father is also based on girls' love and their need to defend against a primary identification with their mother. Girls want love from their father and also his penis in order to win their mother's love. Girls want both mother and father. Because of the depth of their maternal attachment and because of the emotional and physical distance of the father, the "turn" is never absolute. Oedipal girls thus oscillate between attachment to their mother and to their father. Because girls have a longer preoedipal period of development than boys do and because they have a different oedipal configuration, Chodorow also argues that boys and girls differ in their manner of resolving the Oedipus complex. She maintains that the attachment of girls to their father is less intense than boys' to their mother. Given this less charged attachment, and given their ongoing close relationship to mother, girls are less likely to fear maternal retaliation and so do not feel as much pressure to repress their oedipal longings, which can remain for an indeterminant length of time. Chodorow goes on to describe the painful adolescent struggle to resolve the renewed preoedipal and oedipal conflicts. Among the most painful of these is the task of finding a way to identify with, yet find psychological separation from, the mother. Chodorow's views would find favor among many current psychoanalytic writers. She includes a review of the historical literature.

Bernstein, Doris (1979). Female identity synthesis. In: *Career and Motherhood: Struggles For A New Society*, ed. A. Roland and B. Harris. New York: Human Science Press, pp. 103-123.

Bernstein emphasizes differences in superego contents between the sexes, rather than differences in structure. [See Chapter 12 for annotation.]

Brenner, Charles (1979). Depressive affect, anxiety, and psychic conflict in the phallic-oedipal phase. *Psychoanal. Q.*, 48:177-197.

In this theoretical article, three "calamities" of psychic life are postulated as occurring in the phallic-oedipal phase: object loss, loss of love, and castration. Depressive affect and anxiety play important roles in triggering psychic conflict related to all three calamities. Depressive affect and anxiety play an equal role in boys and girls with respect to object loss and loss of love. With respect to castration, depressive affect is more significant than anxiety in phallic-oedipal girls. Brenner asserts that the loss of the fantasied penis is universal in girls' development in the phallic-oedipal phase. Clinical material is not presented. [See also Chapter 20.]

Muslin, Hyman (1979). The superego in the adolescent female. In: *Female Adolescent Development*, ed. M. Sugar. New York: Brunner/Mazel, pp. 296-309.

[See Chapter 9 for annotation.]

Blos, Peter (1980). Modification in the traditional theory of female adolescent development. In: *Adolescent Psychiatry: Developmental and Clinical Studies*, Vol. 8, ed. S. Feinstein, P. Giovacchini, J. Looney, A. Swartzberg, and A. Sorosky. Chicago, IL: University of Chicago Press, pp. 8-24.

Blos understands female superego development in relation to the preoedipal tie to the mother. [See Chapter 9 for annotation.]

Bergmann, Maria (1982). The female Oedipus complex. In: *Early Female Development*, ed. D. Mendell. New York: S. P. Medical and Scientific Books, pp. 175-202.

This article traces the evolution of girls' feminine identity and their Oedipus complex from "primary femininity," body-image formation, the phases of separation-individuation, the various oscillations in the expression of sexual and aggressive drive impulses, and the oscillations from dyadic to triadic object relations within the phallic phase. In what the author describes as a contemporary view of the female Oedipus complex, she stresses that oedipal object relations are simultaneous identifications directed toward either parent, with both dyadic and triadic pressures determining oedipal object relationships. She maintains that identification with the mother is the most important influence on the development of psychic structure and on girls' experience of themselves first as girls and later as mothers.

Gilligan, Carol (1982a). *In A Different Voice*. Cambridge, MA: Harvard University Press.

This book and Gilligan (1977) contain the same points about female superego and morality. Observing with others that women follow a different line of moral development than men do, Gilligan, in this nonanalytic study, highlights the issues and complements psychoanalytic contributions since Horney and Jones. Her work shows that superego contents differ in men and women, that women have different ideals and prohibitions, and that women tend to value relationships. Using Kohlberg's (1966) [see Chapter 5] stages of moral development, she points out a paradox: the traits traditionally associated with the "goodness" of women, their caring and sensitivity to others, are the same characteristics that are rated as inferior to men's concern with law and justice on moral judgment scales. Building on Chodorow's (1978) attention to sex differences in personality formation, Gilligan notes that relationships and issues of dependency are experienced differently by women and men. Masculinity is defined through separation, whereas femininity is defined through attachment; hence, men tend to have difficulty with relationships while women have more difficulty with individuation. Gilligan gives ample evidence that women develop well-functioning superegos. Her study is well documented, and the book includes many interview dialogues that make her hypothesis convincing. [See also Chapter 4.]

Krohn, Alan and Krohn, Janis (1982). The nature of the Oedipus complex and the Dora Case. *J. Amer. Psychoanal. Assn.*, 30:555-578.

The authors reexamine Freud's case of Dora and contend that Freud neglected the implication of Dora's regression to a phallic-oedipal, or negative oedipal position, which led to her eventual premature termination. The so-called phallic-oedipal position to which the authors refer is a concept postulated by Nagera (1975), in which two substages of the oedipal phase are assumed. In elaborating their thesis, the authors suggest that Dora's regression and her unconscious identification with her father were either a defense against her hostility and rivalry with him or an expression of an unconscious wish to love a woman as a man, that is, from a phallic active position. Freud viewed Dora's homosexual trend as a regression to an undefined longing for the mother rather than as an identification with the father. The authors think that Dora's phallic wishes were manifested in the transference with her first acting to engage Freud's interest and then thwarting his interpretive efforts, ultimately leaving the treatment altogether.

Bernstein, Doris (1983). The female superego: A different perspective. *Int. J. Psycho-Anal.*, 64:187-202.

Bernstein views Freud's concept of the female superego as problematic because he assumed identical chronology in the formation of the superego at the time of dissolution of the Oedipus complex, because he felt that the only motivation for oedipal renunciation was castration anxiety, and because he took male characteristics as universal standards for adequate superego development. Paying particular attention to superego contents (admonitions and prohibitions), to the strength or efficiency with which the contents are regulated or enforced, and to the structure or the interrelationship of the superego contents, Bernstein examines and compares superego development in boys and in girls. She concludes that the superego in women is no less effective than that in men, but that the constraints imposed by women's superego are derived from sources other than castration anxiety. These sources are fears of the grandiose, narcissistic mother of infancy; the spread of anal prohibitions to genital impulses because of confusion and diffusion between genital and anal body zones; and fears of bodily harm such as from sexual penetration or childbirth. This article is well written and clinically based and makes a valuable contribution to understanding the superego in women.

Alpert, Judith and Spencer, Jody (1986). Morality, gender, and analysis. In: *Psychoanalysis and Women: Contemporary Reappraisals*, ed. J. Alpert, Hillsdale, NJ: The Analytic Press, pp. 83-111.

[See Chapter 4 for annotation.]

Laufer, M. Egle (1986). Female Oedipus complex and the relationship to the body. *The Psychoanalytic Study of the Child*, 41:259-276. New Haven, CT: Yale University Press.

Laufer examines the so-called castration complex in female development and proposes that the significance of early masturbatory activities lies in the relationship that these activities establish between girls and their own bodies and the extent to which this relationship then facilitates or hinders girls' ability to detach themselves from their dependence on the mother. During the preodipal period, girls' relationship to their own bodies becomes established. How girls manage the perception of their body as "castrated" (that is, "not having a body that enables them to become a man") is central and determines their future sexual development. Laufer maintains that the competitive and triangular meanings of the Oedipus complex aids its dissolution. Relying heavily on the ideas of Freud and M. Klein about female sexuality, Laufer attempts to understand her clinical observations of disturbed adolescent girls who attempt suicide and of women who experience a psychotic or depressive breakdown following the birth of their first child. She then applies her understanding to normal development.

Lebe, Doryann (1986). Female ego ideal and conflicts in adulthood. *Amer. J. Psychoanal.*, 46:22-32.

Lebe explores the development of the female ego ideal from childhood through middle age. [See Chapter 12 for annotation.]

Plaut, Eric and Hutchinson, Foster (1986). The role of puberty in female psychosexual development. *Int. Rev. Psycho-Anal.*, 13:417-432.

The authors maintain that the events of puberty are more important than the oedipal phase for girls' psychosexual development because of the anxiety and body concerns aroused in puberty. They consider that before puberty the female body image lacks the coherent organization that is provided to the male by the visible penis. The combination of parental mislabeling of genitals, the inability to distinguish between clitoral and vaginal sensations, and the inability to surpass concrete and rigid preoperational thinking, all limit the extent to which girls can satisfactorily experience their vaginas as a physical organizer of gender identity. The lack of visibility of the vagina causes a sense of mystery, incompleteness, anxiety, and inferiority. With the onset of menarche and the vaginal awareness that comes with menstrual function, vaginal sensations become palpable, clearly located, and so can be integrated into the body image. Basing their argument on Jacobson's (1937) idea that the formation of the superego in females is more successful when the vagina is accepted as a fully valued genital, and their own claim that this cannot happen until puberty, the authors maintain that puberty is also the most important time for superego formation for the girl. This structuralization is analogous to that process occurring in boys at the time of the Oedipus complex. They reverse Freud's original judgments and suggest that the female superego is more realistic and adaptive because so much of it is shaped at a time during puberty when it can be tempered by reality. Though the authors are critical of certain psychoanalytic ideas, they use false assumptions about early female development to buttress unsupported and unconvincing conclusions about the importance of puberty for the female.

Silverman, Martin (1986). The male superego. *Psychoanal. Rev.*, 73:427-444.

This is one of a series of papers in which male and female superego differences are examined developmentally. Differences in aggressivity and self-control, deriving from innate and cultural-parental factors, influence the introjective-projective identification process. The narcissistic deflation of separation-individuation in boys and girls alike leads to a compensatory identification with the preoedipal mother. When boys become aware of genital differences and are thrust into oedipal conflicts and castration anxiety, they are impelled to disidentify with the mother and her attributes. Boys' complex, ambivalent relationship with the oedipal father lead them to identify with the imperiously strict and impersonal, harshly punitive moral attitude they perceive in, or attribute to, him. Boys' capacity to mitigate this identification by incorporating the softer, gentler, more empathic and compassionate moral attitude they perceive in the mother is limited by their need to disidentify with her. Girls are directed away from mother to father by multiple developmental factors. They are able, to varying degrees, to derive identificatory "strength" and toughness from father. In normal circumstances, however, girls tend to identify with the maternal moral and ethical values from which boys have to distance themselves. These identifications lead to a superego that is not "weaker" than that of boys but is more flexible, reflective, and humane.

Benjamin, Jessica (1987). The decline of the Oedipus complex. In: *Critical Theories of Psychological Development*, ed. J. Broughton. New York: Plenum, pp. 211-244.

[See Chapter 22 for annotation.]

Ogden, Thomas (1987). The transitional oedipal relationship in female development. *Int. J. Psycho-Anal.*, 68:485-498

Difficulties in Freud's female oedipal narrative are cited as a backdrop for the author's rather unusual thesis about the early phase of the female Oedipus complex. Ogden is influenced particularly by the ideas of Winnicott, but also of others from the English object relations school. He maintains that infant girls develop a form of transitional relationship to the mother that mediates their entry into oedipal object love. That is, a subjective sense of the mother is experienced as if it were "created" according to the infant's needs, just as the infant creates a transitional object. Ogden suggests that the transition from preoedipal to oedipal object relations entails a transition not from one object to another, but from a relationship to this subjective, internal object to one with an external object. Thus, the first triadic object relationship occurs in the context of this two-person transitional relationship. Since the relationship with the mother embodies, among other things, the mother's identifications with her own father, the father as libidinal object is first discovered in the mother. Hence, the little girl falls in love with the mother-as-father and with the father-as-mother. An intense, triangulated set of whole-object relationships follows, in which the father is taken as love object while the mother is established as an ambivalently loved rival, but this reorganization is not traumatic, because it is mediated by the transitional relationship with the mother.

A case example illustrates the thesis, and aspects of pathology are discussed in relation to it. Ogden's ideas have certain merit, but care should be taken not to confuse conflictual triadic object relations with concepts about triangulation.

Rees, Katherine (1987). "I want to be a daddy!": Meaning of masculine identifications in girls. *Psychoanal. Q.*, 56:497-522.

This article takes issue with a unicausal meaning of the negative oedipal phase, "castration shock," primary femininity, and masculine identification and proposes a more complex approach. [See Chapter 16 for annotation.]

Roth, Sheldon (1988). A woman's homosexual transference with a male analyst. *Psychoanal. Q.*, 57:28-55.

This article presents clinical material from the case of an adult female analysand that differentiates a preoedipal from a negative oedipal transference to an opposite-sex analyst. [See Chapter 25 for annotation.]

Dahl, Kirsten (1989.) Daughters and mothers: Oedipal aspects of the witch-mother. *The Psychoanalytic Study of the Child*, 44:267-280. New Haven, CT: Yale University Press.

Using primary analytic data from several adult women, an adolescent girl, and a prepubertal girl, Dahl describes common fantasies of a fascinating and terrifying witch-mother. She feels these fantasies are oedipal in origin, although they are often misunderstood as preodipal. Elements of the fantasies include projection onto the mother of a daughter's envious and jealous feelings; a secret excitement over the mother's body, causing the daughter to fear being taken over by her mother for mother's pleasure; the mother is experienced as hostile and aggressive toward the daughter's search for genital pleasure; the daughter oscillates between homosexual and heterosexual desires, including wishes to be mother's erotic partner while also being erotically tied to father. Analysis of secrets and silences in the transference revealed the oedipal meaning of the fear that the mother would know about and destroy the daughter's erotic tie to the father. The reworking of these fantasies in an oedipal context revealed defensive efforts to deny oedipal reality and postpone grief about anatomical and generational differences.

Tyson, Phyllis (1989). Infantile sexuality, gender identity, and obstacles to oedipal progression. *J. Amer. Psychoanal. Assn.*, 37:1051-1069.

[See Chapter 6 for annotation.]

Gillman, Robert (1990). The oedipal organization of shame: The analysis of a phobia. *The Psychoanalytic Study of the Child*, 45:357-376. New Haven, CT: Yale University Press.

[See Chapter 20 for annotation.]

Tyson, Phyllis and Tyson, Robert (1990). Gender differences in superego development. In: *Psychoanalytic Theories of Development: An Integration.* New Haven, CT: Yale University Press, pp. 228-245.

The authors assert that Freud erred in thinking that superego development and functioning in women are inferior to that of men. They propose that superego development is infinitely complex, as it must take into account a myriad of factors, including sexuality, aggression, the mother-daughter and father-daughter relationships, gender-identity formation, narcissistic regulation, and contributions from other preoedipal and oedipal developmental stages. Intrasystemic conflicts concerning conflicting goals, ideals, and introjects should not be mistaken for a weaker superego structure. A developmental timetable and a review of important motivators are discussed with vivid clinical illustrations. The authors emphasize that the wish for love of the idealized maternal object and the fear of loss of love are of central importance for superego development in girls and are closely intertwined with character development, issues of gender identity, narcissism, and self-esteem. The wish for love of the idealized mother can be interfered with by rapprochement conflicts and by struggles over control, which can lead to feelings of loss of love. Resolution of conflicting feelings about the mother must take place prior to oedipal progression. A comprehensive literature review and clinical discussions are provided.

Bernstein, Doris (1991a). The female Oedipal complex. In: *The Personal Myth and Psychoanalytic Theory*, ed. I. Graham and P. Hartocollis. Madison, CT: International Universities Press.

Despite descriptions of the different oedipal experiences of girls and boys, Bernstein claims that in maintaining the term Oedipus, analogous development is assumed. She proposes that the Electra myth better describes the prototypical theme of female development. Quoting from the plays of Aeschylus, Sophocles, and Euripides, Bernstein describes the anger, envy, outrage, masochism, and helplessness of Electra, the abandoned daughter of Agamemnon. The absent father leaves Electra frustrated in her need to identify with her father. She is also left unaided in her struggle with erotic and preerotic ties to her mother. She does not regress, but because she is unable to relinquish her rage for her mother, her development comes to a standstill—she cannot go forward or back. Electra is a picture of lonely helplessness in whom rage and sexuality merge into masochism and suffering is idealized and eroticized. Paying special attention to the role of the father, Bernstein discusses with insight the gender-related issues of female development. Bernstein does not always, however, clearly demarcate normality from pathology. She seems to portray girls' "normal" oedipal experience as similar to Electra's, as lonely helplessness accompanied by rage and sexuality that merge into masochism. Though Bernstein is in tune with the problems inherent with absent fathers, the Electra myth should not be generalized to describe the psychology of the normally developing, competent female.

Chasseguet-Smirgel, Janine (1991). Altglas, altpapier (empty bottles, waste paper): Reflections on certain disorders of the superego in relation to houseproud mothers. *Psychoanal. Inq*, 11(4).

Chasseguet-Smirgel offers a brief review of the psychoanalytic literature on superego precursors. She presents her own conception of the early anal-sadistic superego system, which she distinguishes from the ego and the fully developed superego. Children of both sexes face the quandary of how to preserve a primary maternal fusion with mother without total loss of identity. Toilet training and sphincter morality play an important role in early superego formation and in the archaic matrix of the Oedipus complex. Chasseguet-Smirgel argues that the Oedipus complex is rooted in the wish to become one with the mother (the archaic matrix), and all obstacles to this wish—the father, his children, and his penis—are objects to be hated and eliminated. Love and admiration for the father, for his penis, and for his children develop later, with the hate being replaced by ambivalence. If the mother's superego has anal-sadistic dimensions, the child identifies with her and devalues everything related to feces, as well as everything that is alien to the mother-child symbiosis. This anal-phase fusion with the mother through the formation of an early superego can drastically affect mental functioning by causing impoverishment of thought and judgment processes and recurrent use of projection. A binary clean/dirty system of values is established, and there is a return of repressed anal erotism and an ideology of cleanliness. Chasseguet-Smirgel speculates that penis envy may stem from viewing the penis as a symbol of something that would help the girl be autonomous and have a separate identity from her mother.

Tyson, Phyllis (1991). Some nuclear conflicts of the infantile neurosis in female development. *Psychoanal. Inq*, 11(4).

Tyson integrates insights from Freud's later work that were never included in his theory of female psychology, including his formulations about signal anxiety, superego formation, and structural model. [See Chapter 6 for annotation.]

Lax, Ruth (1992). A variation on Freud's theme in "A Child is Being Beaten": Mother's role—Some implications for superego development. *J. Amer. Psychoanal. Assn.*

The mother's role in superego development is discussed. [See Chapter 21 for annotation.]

# Chapter 8

# *Latency*

Nadine Levinson and Guy Russell
Additional contributions by Michael Moran

Latency is usually thought of as a time of lessened drive activity and expanding ego and superego development. Most of the early papers discussed in this chapter are clinical, theoretical, and technical papers about latency, whose themes include cognitive development, defense formation, family romance, and the relation of pregenital psychosexuality and oedipal trauma to psychopathology and neurosis. The more contemporary papers focus on the interplay of aggression, narcissism, character traits, and sexual and gender identity. Papers on latency-age girls also provide rich clinical psychoanalytic data, although they do not explicitly discuss female psychology.

Many early psychoanalytic writers assumed that repression of sexual drives and of masturbation during latency was a prerequisite for normal feminine development. This view contrasts with contemporary ones. Recent authors have used child observation and developmental data to complement analytic material and provide insights about male-female differences in latency. They have made several salient points about latency-age girls: 1) development for boys and girls is not symmetric during latency; 2) so-called (sexual) latency is only a relative term in comparison with the enormous growth taking place in the ego and superego; and 3) masturbation is present but often hidden and does not necessarily indicate psychopathology or unfeminine behavior. Body exploration, including masturbation, can consolidate self-regard and identity in relation to a more complex sexual anatomy. A contemporary psychoanalytic view also emphasizes the importance of pregenital antecedents to ongoing psychic structure formation in latency. Annotations on prepuberty, preadolescence, and masturbation can be found in chapters 9 and 18. (N.L.)

Freud, Sigmund (1905b). Three essays on the theory of sexuality. *Standard Edition*, 7:125-243. London: Hogarth Press, 1953.

In the second section, Freud talks about latency and the interruption of sexual development. Choice of an object is diphasic, retreating at latency. [See Chapter 1 for annotation.]

Klein, Melanie (1932a). An obsessional neurosis in a six-year-old girl. *The Psychoanalysis of Children*, New York: Norton, pp. 65-93.

[See Chapter 19 for annotation.]

Deutsch, Helene (1944). *The Psychology of Women*, Vol. 1, pp. 1-23. New York: Grune and Stratton.

[See Chapter 9 for annotation.]

Bornstein, Berta (1946). Hysterical twilight states in an eight- year-old child. *The Psychoanalytic Study of the Child*, 2:229-240. New York: International Universities Press.

[See Chapter 24 for annotation.]

Lampl-de Groot, Jeanne (1950). On masturbation and its influence on general development. *The Psychoanalytic Study of the Child*, 5:153-174. New York: International Universities Press.

Lampl-de Groot contends that the gradual renunciation of masturbation is necessary during latency for sound feminine development to occur. [See also Chapter 18.]

Bornstein, Berta (1951). On latency. *The Psychoanalytic Study of the Child*, 6:279-285. New York: International Universities Press.

In this classic paper, Bornstein conceptualizes important developmental aspects of latency, although she does not specifically discuss female development. In early latency, between five and eight years of age, the child must deal with both pregenital and genital impulses. A pregenital regression can defend against genitality (incestuous wishes and masturbatory temptations), followed by reaction formations against pregenital impulses. Ambivalence is often observed to be followed by self-reproach. In the second period between eight and ten years of age, there is less drive pressure and consequently the ego can cope better with reality. Defenses against masturbation are not as intense. Both phases are characterized by "strictness" of the superego, particularly in an attempt to control incestuous wishes. Despite recent structuralization of the personality, the latency child is still vulnerable to the eruption of drive derivatives.

Bonaparte, Marie (1952). Masturbation and death or a compulsive confession of masturbation. *The Psychoanalytic Study of the Child,* 7:170-172. New York: International Universities Press.

This brief article describes the characteristics and determinants of a symptomatic neurosis in a nine-year-old girl with a masturbatory conflict. Obsessional symptoms of persistent question-asking replace masturbation and are tied to the effects of the child's witnessing adult sexual intercourse.

Bornstein, Berta (1953). Masturbation in the latency period. *The Psychoanalytic Study of the Child,* 8:65-78. New York: International Universities Press.

Bornstein agrees with and reiterates Freud's view on female masturbation during the pregenital and phallic psychosexual stages of development. On the basis of her extensive analytic experience with latency-age children, Bornstein describes masturbation in latency-age boys and girls. She asserts that there is a strong repression of sexuality and an intense masturbatory struggle at the end of the oedipal phase, a struggle that leads to latency and to strictness of the superego. She observes a normal, occasionally orgastic gratification in girls during the latency period. In three cases where masturbation was intense and compulsive, the girls had similar masturbatory techniques, fantasies, and defenses. They achieved orgasm through thigh pressure, rather than manually, had vaginal sensations, were fearful of death, and were ashamed. She notes that little is known about the course and rhythm of masturbation in late-latency children; they resist discussing such matters, have better channels for sublimation, and with a less rigid superego are less conflicted. Masturbatory equivalents such as nail biting, head banging, and scratching are linked to sadomasochistic component drives. Many clinical examples are given.

Peller, Lilli (1958). Reading and daydreams in latency, boy-girl differences. *J. Amer. Psychoanal. Assn.,* 6:57-70.

This article clarifies important differences in latency-age boys' and girls' use of reading and daydreams. Family romance themes are preferred by girls as an attempted resolution of oedipal conflict. Regression to the pregenital level is more characteristic of boys than of girls. Girls in latency read literature that help them deal with their penis envy.

Novick, Jack (1970). Vicissitudes of the "working alliance" in the analysis of a latency girl. *The Psychoanalytic Study of the Child*, 25:231-256. New York: International Universities Press.

This paper does not specifically focus on female development during latency but presents the core conflicts of an eight-year-old girl in a three-year analysis. One of her primary conflicts was her phallic competitiveness and wish to possess a penis. The patient's ego-syntonic solution to feelings of loss, damage, and castration was the fantasy that she had a penis. Working through the fantasied wish for a penis allowed the emergence of oedipal wishes toward her father.

Fraiberg, Selma (1972). Some characteristics of genital arousal and discharge in latency girls. *The Psychoanalytic Study of the Child*, 27:439-475. New York: Quadrangle.

[See Chapter 18 for annotation.]

Becker, Ted (1974). On latency. *The Psychoanalytic Study of the Child*, 29:3-11. New Haven, CT: Yale University Press.

The author reviews Berta Bornstein's ideas on latency with a focus on female children's temporary regression to pregenital impulses and their typical defenses against these impulses. Becker elaborates on the specific dynamics in latency. He has observed the same basic problems in males.

Goldings, Herbert (1974). Jump-rope rhymes and the rhythm of latency. *The Psychoanalytic Study of the Child*, 29:431-448. New Haven, CT: Yale University Press.

This paper briefly reviews psychoanalytic theories about children's play and then focuses on a study of the jump-rope rhymes of latency-age girls. The multiple functions of this form of play are noted, including the expression of numerous prelatency issues and the anticipation and practice of adult roles and heterosexuality. The author observes developmental instability and vulnerability to regression in latency-age girls. He speculates that rhythmic psychomotor play activities such as jumping rope may provide a stabilizing influence.

Evans, Robert (1975). Hysterical materialization in the analysis of a latency girl. *The Psychoanalytic Study of the Child*, 30:307-340. New Haven, CT: Yale University Press.

Extensive clinical material is presented from the analysis of a latency-age girl who had severe emotional lability, hysterical phenomena, and numerous somatic expressions. The author traces the developmental aspects of hysterical organization and character formation.

Bernstein, Isidor (1976). Masochistic reactions in a latency-age girl. *J. Amer. Psychoanal. Assn.*, 24:589-607.

[See Chapter 21 for annotation.]

Clower, Virginia (1976). Theoretical implications in current views of masturbation in latency girls. *J. Amer. Psychoanal. Assn.* (Suppl.), 24:109-125.

Clower discusses current views of masturbation in latency-age girls based on child observation and adult female patients' memories. She cogently argues that masturbation is normal in latency-age girls and that penis envy and cessation of clitoral masturbation are not obligatory steps for mature feminine development. [See also Chapter 18.]

Galenson, Eleanor (1976a). Reporter, Panel: Psychology of women: (1) infancy and early childhood. (2) latency and early adolescence. *J. Amer. Psychoanal. Assn.*, 24:141-160.

[See Chapter 9 for annotation.]

Kaplan, Elizabeth (1976). Manifestations of aggression in latency and preadolescent girls. *The Psychoanalytic Study of the Child*, 31:63-78. New Haven: Yale University Press.

[See Chapter 9 for annotation.]

Levinson, Laurie (1979). The world of disguises: Unusual defenses in a latency girl. *The Psychoanalytic Study of the Child*, 34:273-306. New Haven, CT: Yale University Press.

This case report of a six-year-old girl describes a type of character pathology that uses "disguises." The "disguise" is a compromise formation comparable to Winnicott's "false self" and Deutsch's "as if" personality. Amy's personality, developed around a suppression of affects and a need to pretend or disguise how she felt, resulted from an insecure infant-mother relationship.

Kestenberg, Judith (1981a). Eleven, twelve, thirteen: Years of transition from the barrenness of childhood to the fertility of adolescence. In: *The Course of Life: Latency, Adolescence and Youth,* Vol. 2, ed. S. Greenspan and G. Pollock. Adelphi, MD: NIMH, pp. 229-263.

Using endocrinological findings, psychoanalytic insights, and developmental data, Kestenberg attempts to correlate psychic and hormonal organization during puberty. The central theme during prepuberty is a revival of childhood inner genital feelings and representations, built on a solid acknowledgment of a reproductive core and culminating in the consolidation of a new body image.

Sherick, Ivan (1981). The significance of pets for children. *The Psychoanalytic Study of the Child,* 36:193-216. New Haven, CT: Yale University Press.

Using analytic case material, Sherick discusses the multiple defensive and adaptive functions of pets in latency. Taking care of a pet as an expression of the wish to nurture (in identification with the mother) and the use of the pet as a symbolic substitute for the ideal self are illustrated.

Silverman, Martin (1982). The latency period. In: *Early Female Development, Current Psychoanalytic Views,* ed. D. Mendell. Jamaica, NY: S. P. Medical and Scientific Books, pp. 203-226.

Silverman compares latency development in boys and girls. He observes that the so-called latency period is only a relatively quiet time in the developmental process. Actually, it is a time of vigorous ego growth and superego development, during which drive satisfaction is disguised and diverted away from primary objects into the realm of fantasy expression. Comparing girls and boys, Silverman finds that there is less pressure for girls to repress positive oedipal strivings, more struggle with negative oedipal longings, more ease in disguising masturbatory activities, less difficulty in self-control, and more self-esteem vulnerability. Bodily exploration is necessary for girls to clarify their complex genital anatomy. A central task of female latency is the overcoming of feelings of rejection, humiliation, and inferiority related to preoedipal and oedipal losses and defeat. Aggressive impulses tend to be more successfully controlled and suppressed in girls than in boys. The superego tends to be less rigid, less harsh, and less moralistic in girls and to function with more sensitivity in an interpersonal context.

Novick, Kerry (1983). Communication in the analysis of a latency girl. *The Psychoanalytic Study of the Child*, 38:481-500. New Haven, CT: Yale University Press.

Novick focuses on the differences between adult and child analysis. Although special issues concerning female latency development are not discussed, there is detailed case material about a seven-year-old girl and her forms of communication.

Friedman, Lester (1985). Beating fantasies in a latency girl: Their role in female sexual development. *Psychoanal. Q.*, 54:569-596.

[See Chapter 21 for annotation.]

Winestine, Muriel (1985a). Weeping during the analysis of a latency-age girl. *The Psychoanalytic Study of the Child*, 40:297-318. New Haven, CT: Yale University Press.

Winestine describes a latency-age girl who displayed weeping, as compared with crying, as an overdetermined symptom during her analysis. The weeping was understood both as an attempt to relieve affective tension and as a form of communication. Meanings from the oral, anal, and phallic levels of organization are illustrated. Greenacre's (1945) findings [see Chapter 18 for annotation] that weeping in adult women is a substitute for urination and represents both a narcissistic injury for not having a penis and an aggressive wish to have a penis are substantiated in latency girls. Phallic-narcissistic traumas and their connection to drive and ego formation in girls are illustrated.

Palmer, Allen (1988). Heidi's metaphoric appeal to latency. *The Psychoanalytic Study of the Child*, 43:387-398. New Haven, CT: Yale University Press.

Palmer uses Spyri's story of *Heidi* to illustrate the salient developmental themes of loss, separation, reunion, and the family romance fantasy in latency-age girls. These themes reflect derivative expressions of preoedipal regressive trends and oedipal incestuous wishes. Latency-age girls develop an affective resonance with the core themes in *Heidi*. Palmer argues that girls' identification with the main character has an ego-building effect.

Tyson, Phyllis and Tyson, Robert (1990). *Psychoanalytic Theories of Development: An Integration*. New Haven, CT: Yale University Press.

Latency-age development in girls is discussed in the chapter "Gender Development—Girls." [See Chapter 6 for annotation.]

# Chapter 9

# Adolescence

Ingrid Pisetsky, Barbara Deutsch, Nadine Levinson
Additional contributions by
Deanna Holtzman and Michael Moran

Contemporary psychoanalytic theories about female adolescence examine many areas of development not extensively explored in the early formulations of Freud and his contemporaries. The concepts of preoedipal feminine gender identity and the infantile awareness of the vagina are now widely accepted, so that adolescence is no longer viewed as the time when the vagina is "discovered" by girls. The negative and positive Oedipus complex and girls' preoedipal relationship to their mothers are now thought to be substantially reworked during early adolescence, and several papers in this chapter discuss these topics. During adolescence girls' body image and sexual identity become consonant with the physical sexual maturation of puberty. Superego and ego ideal undergo maturation and revision as ties to infantile objects are loosened and new forms of object relations are established. The papers in this chapter examine the normal processes of adolescent development as well as clinically observed disturbances of this period. [See also Chapter 23.] (I.P.)

Horney, Karen (1935a). Personality changes in female adolescents. *Amer. J. Orthopsychiat.*, 5:19-26. Also in: *Feminine Psychology*, ed. H. Kelman. New York: Norton, 1967, pp. 234-244.

In this early article, Horney describes the conflicts underlying four patterns of character change occurring in girls at the onset of adolescence. Although the defensive, characterologic styles are different in the four groups she observed, all the girls have a defensive attitude toward masturbation, with fear of their unconscious masturbatory fantasies. From an early background of strong jealousy and rivalry toward their mother or an older sister, the girls develop intense hostility toward women, accompanied by guilt and fear of punishment. This hostility is readily observed in the transference during analysis with a female analyst. Horney discusses the defensive constellations in the four groups.

Deutsch, Helene (1944/1945). *The Psychology of Women*, Vol. 1 and 2. New York: Grune and Stratton.

Developmental aspects of prepuberty, puberty, and adolescence and the outcome of normal femininity are discussed in the first few chapters of Volume I. Deutsch also considers pubertal and adolescent aspects of several specific topics, such as menstruation, homosexuality, masochism, narcissism, and reproductive functioning throughout Volumes I and II. Prepuberty, occurring between 8 and 10 years of age, is characterized by a thrust toward activity in order to break the bonds of dependency on the mother. Stronger ego functions facilitate the drive of the ego toward independence and adaptation toward reality. Tomboyish behavior is evident and intense libidinal wishes for the mother are displaced onto a best friend or older woman mentor. Clinical examples of prepuberty girls illustrate various themes, such as narcissistic vulnerability, acting out, sibling relationships, secrets, new identificatory objects, sexuality, and defensive operations. The hallmark of girls' early puberty is sexual maturation, with a shift toward increased interest in the body and its development and functioning. Reactivated interest in the genitals and masturbation, with menstruation further effecting interest, can be observed. Boyfriends often end the strong dyadic friendships with other girls, echoing oedipal betrayals of the past. [See also Chapters 2, 14, 19, and 22.]

Greenacre, Phyllis (1950b). The prepuberty trauma in girls. *Psychoanal. Q.*, 19:298-317. Also in: *Trauma, Growth and Personality*. New York: Norton, 1952, pp. 204-223.

Using case material from four adult women, Greenacre examines fateful traumata occurring in the prepuberty period that appear as memories of the event with little apparent distortion, that are part of the presenting picture of the neuroses, and that are extremely resistant to analysis. These traumata are provoked by the victims and are compulsive repetitions of preoedipal conflicts that influence the oedipal phase and subsequent severity and deformation of the superego. Prepubertal conditions favoring the occurrence of such traumata are heightened curiosity, physiological thrust of activity, increased sadomasochism, and a strong masculine identity during latency. The use of the trauma as a masochistic justification for a defense against sexuality and for subsequent masochistic gratification is demonstrated.

Brenman, Margaret (1952). On teasing and being teased: And the problem of "moral masochism." *The Psychoanalytic Study of the Child*, 7:264-285. New York: International Universities Press.

Moral masochism is discussed in the treatment of a 15-year-old adolescent girl. [See Chapter 21 for annotation.]

Keiser, Sylvan (1953). A manifest Oedipus complex in an adolescent girl. *The Psychoanalytic Study of the Child*, 8:99-107. New York: International Universities Press.

Using case material from the analysis of a neurotic adolescent girl who develops an intensely sexualized transference, the author elucidates defects in superego organization that allow incestuous fantasies to become conscious. A review of theories on the development and function of the ego and superego with particular reference to adolescence is presented. Failure of the superego's repressive function is related to the special relationship with the two parents that includes teasing, erratic absences, and perpetuating of infantile sexual attachments to the original objects. Because of the physical separation and seductiveness, there is no fulfillment or resolution.

Blos, Peter (1957). Preoedipal factors in the etiology of female delinquency. *The Psychoanalytic Study of the Child*, 12:229-249. New York: International Universities Press. Also in: *On Adolescence: A Psychoanalytic Interpretation*. New York: Free Press, 1962, pp. 230-244.

In contrast to the delinquency of boys, which often is manifested as destructive action or imposterlike adventuring, delinquency in girls is related to the perversions in that it is a form of sexual acting out. A regressive pull toward the preoedipal mother is resisted by the adolescent girl, who may show excessive independence, hyperactivity, and a frantic attachment to boys. Blos distinguishes two types of female delinquents, one who regresses to the preoedipal mother and the other who clings defensively to an oedipal struggle. In the first type, a pseudoheterosexuality serves as a defense against the regressive pull to the preoedipal mother and to homosexuality. In the second type, the girl forms a hostile identification with mother based on a shared disappointment with the father. The girl fantasizes that father would be transformed if only mother and daughter could change places. A case illustrates the former type of delinquency.

Levy, Kata (1960). Simultaneous analysis of a mother and her adolescent daughter: The mother's contribution to the loosening of the infantile object tie. *The Psychoanalytic Study of the Child*, 15:378-391. New York: International Universities Press.

Preoedipal and oedipal factors in both mother and daughter are vividly described in this short case presentation. The daughter, strangely, showed no urge to detach herself from her parents, and this peculiarity was understood as reflecting an insecure mother who indulged in an exclusive body-related and sadomasochistic relationship with her daughter. Because of her guilt, the mother could not stand up to the daughter's excessive demands, thus intensifying the clinging.

Harley, Marjorie (1961). Masturbation conflicts. In: *Adolescents: Psychoanalytic Approach to Problems in Therapy*, ed. S. Lorand and H. Schneer. New York: Hoeber, pp. 51-77.

The author contends that disturbances originating in the pregenital era in connection with premature genital stimulation can be reflected in masturbation conflicts at adolescence. She traces impairments in egolibidinal development that result from stimulation throughout the psychosexual stages. These impairments leave a vulnerability to the pressures of puberty, making integration of genitality at adolescence difficult. The effects of too early and excessive genital stimulation are evidenced in 1) quality and patterning of the later genital strivings, 2) feelings of uncontrollability and helplessness that genital strivings threaten to reawaken, and 3) an excess of destructive aggression, resulting in increased sadomasochism. A discussion of the bizonal factor in girls' psychosexual development is presented. Special problems in adolescent girls, intensified by the factor of premature genital stimulation are 1) an enhanced defensive need to preserve the illusory phallus, 2) dichotomization of clitoris and vagina into active sadistic and passive masochistic, and 3) suppression of vaginal sexuality. Analysis at adolescence is strongly indicated. Technical interventions are discussed.

Kestenberg, Judith (1961). Menarche. In: *Adolescents: Psychoanalytic Approach to Problems and Therapy*, ed. S. Loran and H. Schneer. New York: Hoeber Press, pp. 19-50.

Menarche is presented as a major organizer in feminine development. Diffuse prepubertal behavior is contrasted with the more sharply delineated pubertal organization. The author describes "feminine masochism" as becoming intense after menarche. She considers this masochism normal, as it leads to tolerance for, and appreciation of, the relief qualities of sharp sensations. Attitudes toward menarche are described as determined by earlier infantile solutions, including identification with mother. Kestenberg stresses that the mother acts throughout development as the organizer from the outside, providing a model for organization of stimuli stemming from the inside.

Blos, Peter (1962). *On Adolescence: A Psychoanalytic Interpretation*. New York: Free Press.

Genetic and dynamic considerations of adolescence are systematically elucidated and documented with a case history, case vignettes, and literary examples; and vicissitudes of early female development are briefly summarized. The unfolding of the major events previously described in the theoretical chapter is illustrated by the case of Judy to show how early significant emotional patterns determined her adolescent development.

Blos introduces the concept of five developmental phases of adolescence: preadolescence, early adolescence, adolescence proper, late adolescence and postadolescence. In each of these phases, the development of males and females is differentiated in terms of central conflicts, defenses, superego and ego development, and object relations. In preadolescence, girls defend themselves against the regressive pull to the preoedipal mother, often by turning to manifest heterosexuality. Early adolescence is characterized by a bisexual position. There is an idealization or erotization (a crush) that can extend to men and women alike as a wish for attention or affection. The decline of bisexuality marks the entrance of girls into adolescence proper. Heterosexual object finding, the elaboration of femininity, and a disengagement from early object ties prevail. Late adolescence is marked by a consolidation in the areas of ego interests and functions, sexual-partner orientation, genital primacy, and stable self- and object representations. In postadolescence, which is midway between adolescence and adulthood, instinctual interests recede and ego integrative interests become prominent. Other chapters are devoted to masturbation in adolescence, ego development, and the case illustration of a delinquent female adolescent whose pseudoheterosexuality defended against a regressive pull to the preoedipal mother.

Sprince, Marjorie (1962). The development of a preoedipal partnership between an adolescent girl and her mother. *The Psychoanalytic Study of the Child*, 17:418-450. New York: International Universities Press.

Sprince presents the analysis of a girl from age 12 to 17 whose mother was in a concurrent analysis with the author. Sprince justifies simultaneous analyses when there is an intractable resistance for forward movement developmentally. The developmental arrest was found to be related to an inability to sever ties to the preoedipal mother because of an early and prolonged infantile trauma associated with excessive bodily stimulation. Ego distortion in these cases may thus lead to permanent damage; thus, analyses should be undertaken with a limited aim. A detailed, lucid account of the case from beginning to termination, with reconstruction of psychosexual development, is included.

Jacobson, Edith (1964). *The Self and the Object World*. New York: International Universities Press.

[See Chapters 7 and 22 for annotations.]

Leonard, Marjorie (1966). Fathers and daughters: The significance of fathering in the psychosexual development of the girl. *Int. J. Psycho-Anal.*, 47:325-334.

[See Chapter 16 for annotation.]

Spiegel, Rose (1966). The role of father-daughter relationships in depressive women. In: *Science and Psychoanalysis*, ed. J. Masserman. New York: Grune and Stratton, pp. 105-120.

The traumatizing role of the unavailable father during adolescence is discussed. [See Chapter 16 for annotation.]

Deutsch, Helene (1967). *Selected Problems of Adolescence: With Special Emphasis on Group Formation*. New York: International Universities Press.

This book consists of four chapters reflecting on the author's experiences with normal contemporary (1960s) adolescents. Deutsch focuses on the degree to which social conditions influence adolescents, particularly in the formation of their social groups. Chapters 1 and 3 concern both boys and girls and cover such topics as sublimation, narcissism, empathy, reactions to sexual maturity, postadolescence, identity in boys and girls, and bisexual fantasy. Whereas Chapter 2 concerns object relations in adolescent boys, Chapter 4 is devoted entirely to the subject of adolescent girls and includes the following topics: Group Formation in Adolescent Girls (oriented around the phenomenon of Beatles fans); Sexual Freedom; Illegitimate Motherhood; Infantilism; Other Typical Problems, and Late Adolescence.

Laufer, Moses (1968). The body image, the function of masturbation, and adolescence. *The Psychoanalytic Study of the Child*, 23:114-137. New York: International Universities Press.

Laufer examines the role of adolescent masturbation and masturbation fantasies in establishing genital primacy and an integrated body image that includes mature genitals. He briefly reviews the literature on body image and on masturbation in adolescence. Four adolescent patients who were unable to reach genitality, and in whom preoedipal fixations led to distorted relationships to their own bodies, are presented and discussed. He concludes that in these cases puberty endangers the earlier defenses against aggression toward the mother. He postulates that for girls, menstruation brings about a collapse of the identification with the phallic mother and confirms the fact of being damaged. He speculates about possible etiologies for this pathology in the early parent-child relationship.

Hart, Marion and Sarnoff, Charles (1971). The impact of the menarche: A study of the stages of organization. *J. Amer. Acad. Child Psychiat.*, 10: 257-271.

[See Chapter 10 for annotation.]

Clower, Virginia (1975). Significance of masturbation in female sexual development and function. In: *Masturbation: From Infancy to Senescence*, ed. M. Marcus and J. Francis. New York: International Universities Press, pp. 107-144.

[See Chapter 18 for annotation.]

Kestenberg, Judith (1975). Phases of adolescence, with suggestions for a correlation of psychic and hormonal organizations. I: Antecedents of adolescent organizations in childhood. II: Prepuberty diffusion and reintegration. III: Puberty growth, differentiation, and consolidation. In: *Children and Parents: Psychoanalytic Studies in Development*. New York: Aronson, pp. 313-377.

The emphasis in these chapters is on the correlation between behavior, sex organs, and the activities of sex hormones. A section is devoted to menarche, and examples are cited to illustrate the differences in the concept of an "inner genital" between a three-year-old and a prepuberty girl. The three-year-old feels internal sensations, which she fantasizes is an illusory baby. The prepuberty girl is also aware of her inner genital, but fears pregnancy. Kestenberg suggests that stages of cortical-hypothalamic-pituitary maturation influence psychic and hormonal constellations during development by creating an imbalance in the total psychosomatic economy of the young adolescent.

Feigelson, Charles (1976). Reconstruction of adolescence (and early latency) in analysis of an adult woman. *The Psychoanalytic Study of the Child*, 31:225-236. New Haven, CT: Yale University Press.

Feigelson asserts that reconstruction of adolescent experience is necessary for successful outcome in the analyses of adults. During the adolescent phase of development, new editions of the infantile neurosis are worked through and serve as a bridge to the earlier period. A case of a female patient with agoraphobia is presented. She had been overstimulated by her father as a child, and relived this experience as she attempted to master the trauma with her adolescent masturbation. The analysis of her experiences during adolescence was a bridge to understanding the repressed events of her childhood and her adult symptoms. The case also illustrates the management of typical female conflicts around sexuality.

Galenson, Eleanor (1976a). Reporter, Panel: Report on the psychology of women. (1) Infancy and Early Childhood. *J. Amer. Psychoanal. Assn.*, 24:141-160.

This panel, the first of two panels on feminine psychology, focuses on the early origins of feminine identity. In the first part of the article, contributions toward the formation of feminine identity from the "conflict-free sphere" are reviewed. A developmental view is proposed utilizing infant observational studies and clinical cases. Presentations by each of the panelists, Stoller, Wolff, Kleeman, and Glenn, are reviewed. Stoller contends that women's femininity is primary. Wolff and Stoller observe that many developmental determinants never manifest in intrapsychic conflict but may contribute to character formation. Although castration anxiety may be observed in the child, Kleeman doubts that it plays a significant role as a primary organizer of femininity. A case by Glenn is presented to highlight the following points: conscious identification as a girl does not preclude unconscious fantasies of being a boy; there is evidence of intrapsychic structuralization in girls younger than age three; and early vaginal sensation exists and is important in the formation of girls' body image. Differences in the maternal handling of boys and girls and its impact on adolescence are noted to result in "mother fixation" and aggressive drive conflicts. [See also Chapter 6.]

Galenson, Eleanor (1976b). Reporter, Panel: Report on the psychology of women. (2) Late adolescence and early adulthood. *J. Amer. Psychoanal. Assn.*, 24:631-645.

This second panel on late adolescence included Settlage, Easser, and Ritvo as participants. Discussing Freud's views on 19th-century Viennese women, Settlage reviews female psychological development. Two developmental issues—preoedipal development (and separation individuation) and recapitulation of the oedipal conflict and genital anxieties—are highlighted. Settlage views early adolescence as a time for recapitulation of infancy and for an initial confrontation with the changes of puberty, and late adolescence as a time for experimentation and mastery of the drives, resulting in new adult capabilities. He suggests that an adult sense of female gender identity does not require, but is augmented by, the experiences of childbearing and motherhood. Noting that females are complete beings and that heterosexuality and procreation are not necessary for a full sense of femininity, Easser emphasizes the developmental task of integrating feminine body sensations and identifications. She notes that many analysts erroneously overemphasize women's capacity for orgasm as a measure of their psychological maturity and neglect other aspects of female identity and body-image development. Ritvo presents analytic cases of adolescent girls illustrating the following issues: the upsurge of instinctual pressure during preadolescence; menarche as a normal developmental crisis; and the universally female attitude of concealment that is derived from the pronounced repression of pregenital and genital strivings that is present in all aspects of their life. Sociocultural and psychological contributions to the uniqueness of women's experiences are discussed by other panelists.

Kaplan, Elizabeth (1976). Manifestations of aggression in latency and preadolescent girls. *The Psychoanalytic Study of the Child*, 31:63-78. New Haven, CT: Yale University Press.

Emphasizing the interplay of aggression and narcissism with the castration complex and penis envy, the author examines manifestations of normal and pathological aggression in latency and preadolescent girls. She uses brief clinical and observational vignettes to support her ideas. Aggression is seen as a drive, regardless of its origin, that can be deployed constructively or destructively. Normal aggression in girls is described and contrasted with that of boys. Abnormal manifestations in girls include 1) pathological stealing; 2) obscene language as an externalization of feelings of dirtiness, damage, and worthlessness; 3) running away and accident-proneness; and 4) psychosomatic disorders. Kaplan differentiates between receptivity (directing aggression inward) and masochism (directing aggression against the self). She also suggests renaming the castration complex and penis envy to mitigate the derogatory defensiveness and aggressive reactions that are aroused.

**Ritvo, Samuel (1976). Adolescent to woman. *J. Amer. Psychoanal. Assn.* (Suppl.), 24:127-137.**

Ritvo traces the changes of puberty that lead to psychological maturity in women. He emphasizes the changes of menarche and its regressive and progressive effects on body image. The universal issue of concealment of menarche in women is connected to girls' more powerful repression of pregenital, particularly anal, strivings. He asserts that mature sexuality results from the successful resolution of adolescent conflicts concerning body image and menarche. The need to loosen the infantile tie to mother often is manifested by defensive heterosexual behavior. Ritvo also discusses whether actualization of the wish to have a baby is necessary for normal adult female development.

**Ticho, Gertrude (1976). Female autonomy and young adult women. *J. Amer. Psychoanal. Assn.* (Suppl.), 24:139-155.**

The author examines both intrapsychic and external/social psychological stresses that result from the developmental step of an adolescent's moving out of the parental home to live on her own. A brief summary of female development and a clinical case are provided. Ticho asserts that reactivation of the Oedipus complex can either facilitate further growth and transformation to autonomy or result in a pathologically irreversible regression with permanent inability to develop further. Examples of pathological solutions are explored. The motivations for seeking female therapists are discussed.

**Barglow, Peter and Schaefer, Margret (1979). The fate of the feminine self in normative adolescent regression. In: *Female Adolescent Development*, ed. M. Sugar. New York: Brunner/Mazel, pp. 201-213.**

The authors reexamine female adolescent development and its regressive revival of early childhood dynamics in the light of recent reformulations of early development and narcissism. For each subphase of adolescence, they identify questionable constructs and assumptions from early theoretical models. The centrality of penis envy in preadolescence is questioned. The authors reconsider the "U-shaped tube model" of self- and object representations in early adolescence and the prevailing emphasis on feminine masochism and passivity. They challenge the prototype of massive regression to primitive functioning in mid-adolescence. The significance of cultural factors in feminine self-definition in late adolescence is discussed. For each adolescent subphase, research data and alternative models are presented.

Benedek, Elissa, Poznanski, Elva, and Mason, Sheila (1979). A note on the female adolescent's psychological reactions to breast development. *J. Amer. Acad. Child Psychiat.*, 18:537-545.

This article includes a review of the literature on adolescent breast development, including the physiological sequence of normal female adolescent breast development, and the psychological responses to this development by the adolescent, her family, and her peers. The authors regard reactions to breast development as a neglected line of developmental growth.

Dalsimer, Katherine (1979). From preadolescent tomboy to early adolescent girl: An analysis of Carson McCullers's "The Member of the Wedding." *The Psychoanalytic Study of the Child*, 34:445-461. New Haven, CT: Yale University Press. Also in: *Female Adolescence: Psychoanalytic Reflections on Literature*, New Haven, CT: Yale University Press, 1986, pp. 13-26.

Using the central figure in Carson McCullers' "A Member of the Wedding" as an illustration, Dalsimer discusses how Frankie's development demonstrates important preadolescent issues conceptualized by Mahler and Blos. These include separation-individuation, bisexuality, the defensive use of regression and fantasy, and the restitutive meaning of friendship.

Esman, Aaron (1979). Adolescence and the "new sexuality." In: *On Sexuality: Psychoanalytic Observations*, ed. B. Karasu and C. Socarides. New York: International Universities Press, pp. 19-28.

Esman reviews findings from several studies of the behavior and attitudes of adolescents. He describes a "new morality" condoning serial monogamy among unmarried, uncommitted adolescents. The shift is largely the result of changes in the values and behavior of adolescent girls. As a result of the feminist movement, girls now feel permitted to do what earlier had been forbidden. There is no evidence that perverse sexual behavior, promiscuity, or weakening of the incest taboo have resulted from the new sexual climate, or that the greater sexual freedom has interfered with the adaptive successes of contemporary adolescents. Vignettes about one female and one male case are presented.

Giovacchini, Peter (1979). The dilemma of becoming a woman. In: *Female Adolescent Development*, ed. M. Sugar. New York: Brunner/Mazel, pp. 253-273.

Giovacchini examines the adolescent task of consolidating a sexual identity in contemporary culture. He questions whether the current trend toward role equalization of the sexes is compatible with the psyche's inner structure. The culture either overtly or covertly urges girls to deny their biological heritage. He concludes with an analysis of the developmental lag in psychical maturity during adolescence in both sexes that necessitates a period of psychological integration before heterosexual activity can be meaningfully assimilated into the personality. The sexual adjustment of contemporary adolescent girls tends to be characterized by dissociative elements formerly more common among males. Giovacchini also develops ideas about biologically and culturally ordained feminine traits and the "natural destiny" of the female self-representation that are not apparently substantiated by clinical observations.

Muslin, Hyman (1979). The superego in the adolescent female. In: *Female Adolescent Development*, ed. M. Sugar. New York: Brunner/Mazel, pp. 296-309.

Muslin expands on his earlier work on the female superego. He reiterates that the specific content of the superego of women reflects contemporary cultural values and that these contents must never be confused with some abstract "psychologic destiny" of women. The literature on women that describes an eternal feminine or mothering core as the so-called maternal ideal reflects the ubiquitous childhood fantasy of a "Great Mother." In adolescence there is a disequilibrium between the superego of latency and the pubertal upsurge of drives. Adolescents then seek identifications and new moral codes and values that will be internalized as the voices of conscience. Of particular importance in adolescence is the establishment of reliable ego ideals that are determined primarily by the culture.

Rosenbaum, Maj-Britt (1979). The changing body image of the adolescent girl. In: *Female Adolescent Development*, ed. M. Sugar. New York: Brunner/Mazel, pp. 234-251.

Using anecdotal material from interviews with 30 "normal" early and middle adolescent girls, the author traces the meaning of the physical changes in the body of the developing adolescent girl, including menstruation, breast development, and loss of virginity, and their impact on the internal development of the adolescent's body image.

Rothchild, Ellen (1979). Female power: Lines to development of autonomy in adolescent girls. In: *Female Adolescent Development*, ed. M. Sugar. New York: Brunner/Mazel, pp. 274-295.

Using case vignettes and concepts from other authors, Rothchild reviews the developmental vicissitudes of autonomy in adolescent girls. She evaluates the impact of the women's movement on concepts of female autonomy and girls' development. She discusses the defensive use of feminist concepts by some girls to avoid full development of their autonomy.

Shopper, Moisy (1979). The (re)discovery of the vagina and the importance of the menstrual tampon. In: *Female Adolescent Development*, ed. M. Sugar. New York: Brunner/Mazel, pp. 214-233.

The author contends that the intrapsychic as well as external events surrounding the use of an internal tampon are crucial to vaginal (re)discovery and (re)cathexis in menarcheal girls. A brief historical account of the theories of vaginal repression in infancy are offered. The regressive meanings of menses to girls are reviewed and include its association with toilet training, in that menstrual flow is regarded as dirty, messy, and unsanitary like feces and urine. The sanitary napkin emphasizes the outside of the body, not the inside. Three case histories are included.

Spruiell, Vann (1979). Alterations in the ego-ideal in girls in mid-adolescence. In: *Female Adolescent Development*, ed. M. Sugar. New York: Brunner/Mazel, pp. 310-329.

This paper focuses on changes in the ego ideal as a crucial part of the maturation process of adolescence. Girls' conscious and unconscious perceptions of physical parity with adults and of inner bodily changes serve as organizers for their psychological progression from early to late adolescence. Separation from the parents is accompanied by the acquisition of a new internal structure based on selective identifications with new models from the environment. Concomitantly, the prohibitory functions of the superego become more flexible and reasonable. The new system of regulators helps girls begin to think, feel, and act like adults. There is both opportunity and risk for girls during this developmental period, as there are at other life stages of great internal change. Spruiell presents a case illustrating both normal and neurotic changes in the ego ideal during adolescence.

Sugar, Max (1979a). Developmental issues in adolescent motherhood. In: *Female Adolescent Development*, ed. M. Sugar. New York: Brunner/Mazel, pp. 330-343.

Sugar reviews demographic and psychological features of teenage pregnancy. He describes his own study, in which he found that adolescent mothers had over one-and-a-half times more crises than did adult mothers and were more than twice as likely to understimulate their infants than were adult mothers. For most adolescent girls, motherhood prolongs dependency on their own mothers, thus delaying separation-individuation. Unconsciously the adolescent pregnancy may be an effort to effect separation from mother, an attempt to make up for loss of the infantile objects, a substitution for and avoidance of early separation-individuation conflicts, or an accident to avoid aggression.

Sugar, Max (ed.)(1979b). *Female Adolescent Development*. New York: Brunner/Mazel.

This book covers many areas within the broad topic of female adolescence. There are short sections on Research and Biological Issues, including chapters on the problems of research, female pubertal development, and cognitive development. The two longer sections are devoted to Societal Issues and to Psychodynamics. Of particular interest to psychoanalysts are the chapters in the Psychodynamics section, including "The Fate of the Feminine Self in Normative Adolescent Regression," by Barglow and Schaefer; "(Re)Discovery of the Vagina and the Importance of the Menstrual Tampon," by Shopper; "The Changing Body Image of the Adolescent Girl," by Rosenbaum; "The Dilemma of Becoming a Woman," by Giovacchini; "Female Power: Lines to Development of Autonomy," by Rothchild; "The Superego in the Adolescent Female," by Muslin; "Alterations in the Ego-Ideal in Girls in Mid-Adolescence," by Spruiell; and "Developmental Issues in Adolescent Motherhood," by Sugar. [Many of these chapters are annotated here.]

Blos, Peter (1980). Modification in the traditional theory of female adolescent development. In: *Adolescent Psychiatry: Developmental and Clinical Studies*, Vol. 8, ed. S. Feinstein, P. Giovacchini, and A. Miller. Chicago: University of Chicago Press, pp. 8-24.

This chapter proposes the need for revision of the theory of female development, particularly as it pertains to female adolescents. Reviewing

some salient features of classical Freudian theories about female development, Blos notes the controversies over the concept of primary feminine
identity in girls and the question of timing of girls' awareness of the vagina.
He compares adolescent conflicts around resolution of the negative
Oedipus complex in boys and girls. Femininity and mature object relationships cannot be established until adolescent girls have thoroughly reworked
their relationship to their preoedipal mother. He contends that early
heterosexual activity may frequently constitute an oedipal defense or a
retreat from early maternal conflicts. Blos understands female superego
development in relation to women's need to maintain some aspects of the
preoedipal tie to the mother. Women maintain a broader range of empathy
and more fluid potential for identification primarily because they repress
the negative Oedipus less rigorously than men.

Glenn, Jules (1980). Freud's adolescent patients: Katharina, Dora and the
"Homosexual Woman." In: *Freud and His Patients*. New York: Aronson,
pp. 23-47.

Glenn discusses the adolescent status of Freud's three female patients,
Katharina, Dora, and "the homosexual woman." He asserts that Freud's
therapeutic failure and technical errors reflected his lack of adequate
knowledge and sophistication about adolescent drive and defense organization. Glenn suggests that treatment of adolescents is difficult because of
drive-dominated and at times unmanageable sexual interest, narcissistic
vulnerability, dependency conflicts with parents, and typical adolescent
defenses and adaptations, such as intellectualization and isolation. Glenn
notes that countertransference is particularly intense in a male analyst
because of the adolescent's seductiveness.

Weissman, Stephen and Barglow, Peter (1980). Recent contributions to the
theory of female adolescent psychological development. *Adolescent
Psychiatry: Developmental and Clinical Studies*, Vol. 8, ed. S. Feinstein,
P. Giovacchini, and A. Miller. Chicago: University of Chicago Press, pp.
214-230.

The classical psychoanalytic theory of female adolescent development
is reviewed and reexamined in the light of new knowledge from the
behavioral sciences. Neurophysiology suggests new ways of looking at
libido. Cerebral cortical differences between girls and boys may partially
explain gender differences in behavior previously attributed to superego
differences, to an innate "passivity" in girls, and to children's fantasies
about genital differences. Cognitive development may contribute to the
ability to form more complex relationships with others in adolescence, to

disengage from the parents, and to establish more mature ideals and values. Finally, the findings of self psychology may contribute to an understanding of self-esteem regulation in adolescence.

Dalsimer, Katherine (1982). Female adolescent development: A study of "The Diary of Anne Frank." *The Psychoanalytic Study of the Child*, 37:487-522. New Haven, CT: Yale University Press. Also in: *Female Adolescence: Psychoanalytic Reflections on Literature*. New Haven, CT: Yale University Press, 1986, pp. 44-76.

The author uses *The Diary of Anne Frank* to illustrate aspects of middle adolescence when childhood ties to parents are given up. Anne's psychological separation occurred under circumstances where physical separation was impossible, but her psychological separation was facilitated and documented by her diary writing. The central unconscious theme of middle adolescence, having to do with the resurgence and beginning resolution of the Oedipus complex, is charted. At the same time, there is a continuing struggle in relation to the powerful preoedipal bond with the mother. Self-awareness of Anne's own sexuality and falling in love modulates the intensity of her close ties with her parents.

Laufer, M. Egle (1982). Female masturbation in adolescence and the development of the relationship to the body. *Int. J. Psycho-Anal.*, 63:295-302.

The unique role of masturbation in female development and the avoidance of the use of the hands, which other authors have linked to penis envy, are explored. [See Chapter 18 for annotation.]

Kaplan, Louise (1984). *Adolescence: The Farewell to Childhood.* New York: Simon and Schuster.

Countering the tendency to reduce adult gender-identity solutions to early infantile development, Kaplan stresses the importance of the transition phase of adolescence and the reasons for its neglect in the psychoanalytic considerations of gender identity. Changing drive organization, object relations, and narcissistic structures of adolescence are traced, illustrating their contributions to feminine and masculine identifications. The differing courses of female and male gender identity solutions, as they are influenced by biological, social, and family structures, are also discussed.

Laufer, Moses and Laufer, M. Egle (1984). *Adolescence and Developmental Breakdown*. New Haven, CT: Yale University Press.

This book examines the developmental functions of adolescence and their relation to psychopathology in adolescence. The integration of body image and psychic restructuralization are emphasized. The authors assert that adolescents are particularly vulnerable to a break with reality, which need not be a sign of early psychosis. Instead, it may be the adolescent's reaction to overwhelming sexual and aggressive fantasies that are contrary to the idealized body image; the break with reality serves to maintain the original distortions of the past. Central masturbation fantasies and their impact on gender identity are explored. The book contains four principal sections. Part I, Adolescent Development, Pathology, and Breakdown, discusses sexual organization, developmental breakdown, body image and masturbation, the female adolescent, and the superego and the idealized body image. Part II, Breakdown and the Treatment Process, has chapters on transference and reconstruction, object relationships, use of the body and transference, and attempted suicide. Part III, Clinical Issues, covers compulsive behavior and the central masturbation fantasy, developmental foreclosure, and countertransference and sexual development. The final section covers assessment of adolescence. "The Female Adolescent, the Relationship to the Body, and Masturbation," appears in this book as a rewritten version of the M.E. Laufer (1982) article. [See also Chapter 18.]

Ritvo, Samuel (1984). The image and uses of the body in psychic conflict: With special reference to eating disorders. *The Psychoanalytic Study of the Child*, 39:449-469. New Haven, CT: Yale University Press.

Several analyses of adolescent women with eating disorders illustrate the multiple functions of using the body for externalization of psychic conflict. In his analytic work with college students, Ritvo finds that girls' wanton eating, which they describe as "pigging out," is an early adolescent group phenomenon and a regressive, peer-sanctioned, homosexual mode of expressing and discharging heightened sexual tension which cannot attain adequate genital discharge. [See also Chapter 23.]

Klyman, Cassandra (1985). Community parental-surrogates and their role for the adolescent. *Adolescence*, 20:397-404.

The role of community parental-surrogates for the adolescent is explored against the backdrop of classical psychoanalytic theory, self psychology, and the sociological prevalence of one-parent families. Surrogates, including clergy, tutors, coaches, and umpires, help resolve oedipal issues and promote the establishment of a cohesive self for both male and female teenagers. Clinical vignettes illustrate how deidealization by proxy may aid detachment from childhood love-objects and allow health and partial identification with the same-sex parent.

Person, Ethel (1985). Female sexual identity: The impact of the adolescent experience. In: *Sexuality: New Perspectives*, ed. Z. DeFries, R. Friedman, and R. Corn. Westport, CT: Greenwood Press, pp. 71-88.

Person identifies orgasmic sexual gratification in an interpersonal relationship as an indicator of a fully consolidated sexual identity. Although acknowledging contributions from individual intrapsychic disturbances, she emphasizes the impact of socialization differences between boys and girls in the construction and consolidation of sexual identity. Young women have normative problems in consolidating sexual identity by achieving a gratifying interpersonal sexual life (qua sex) because of the nature of heterosexual practice; intercourse is not the preferential route of orgasmic satisfaction in many normal women. Young women are deferential sexually because of the need to preserve the relationship as a confirmation of their femininity. Adolescence is viewed as a crucial phase in the consolidation of a sense of femininity and is linked to differential social acceptance of sexual behavior.

Dalsimer, Katherine (1986a). Early adolescence: *The Prime of Miss Jean Brodie*. In: *Female Adolescence: Psychoanalytic Reflections on Literature*. New Haven, CT: Yale University Press, pp. 27-43.

Dalsimer uses this novel to illustrate the vicissitudes of intense adolescent friendship and the passionate attachment of the adolescent to an older girl or woman. These attachments help the girl relinquish her ties to the parents and her powerful bond to her mother, as she longs to return to the protective mother of early childhood. The new relationships also represent regression, however, and are accompanied by fears of reengulfment that threaten the teenage girl's sense of self. Jean Brodie, the older woman, is a displaced object for the mother, but in a safer, more distant form.

Dalsimer, Katherine (1986b). *Female Adolescence: Psychoanalytic Reflections on Literature*, New Haven, CT: Yale University Press.

This study of the psychoanalytic theories of female adolescent development utilizes literary works of authors who have been able to communicate about the inner and outer worlds of the adolescent. Dalsimer follows Blos's outline of the successive phases of adolescence (Blos, 1962) to illustrate the normal tasks of adolescence with works of literature. [Several papers are individually annotated in this chapter.]

Dalsimer, Katherine (1986c). Late adolescence: *Persuasion*. In: *Female Adolescence: Psychoanalytic Reflections on Literature*. New Haven, CT: Yale University Press, pp. 113-138.

The author uses this Austen novel to illuminate that the dissolution of the strong tie to the maternal object is necessary for adolescent development and for heterosexual love and mature independent behavior.

Dalsimer, Katherine (1986d). Middle adolescence: Romeo and Juliet. In: *FemaleAdolescence: PsychoanalyticReflections on Literature*. New Haven, CT: Yale University Press, pp. 77-112.

Dalsimer demonstrates how heterosexual love, as represented by Romeo and Juliet, facilitates the separation-individuation process in adolescence with the necessary concomitant loosening of ties to the mother and family.

Pines, Dinora (1986). Working with women survivors of the Holocaust: Affective experiences in transference and countertransference. *Int. J. Psycho-Anal.*, 67:295-307.

This article describes and discusses some late effects of massive traumatization of two women survivors of the Holocaust. The normal transitional crises of adolescence in their children, when children emotionally separate from their parents, led to severe breakdown in both these patients. Analysis showed that denial, repression, and splitting enabled them to distance themselves from the overwhelming horror of the past, but it also led to concrete as opposed to metaphorical thinking, including lack of differentiation between psychic and somatic pain.

Plaut, Eric and Hutchinson, Foster (1986). The role of puberty in female psychosexual development. *Int. Rev. Psycho-Anal.*, 13:417-432.

[See Chapter 7 for annotation.]

O'Brien, John (1987). The effects of incest on female adolescent development. *J. Amer. Acad. Psychoanal.*, 15:83-92.

[See Chapter 24 for annotation.]

Balsam, Rosemary (1989). The paternal possibility: The father's contribution to the adolescent daughter when the mother is disturbed and a
denigrated figure. In: *Fathers and Their Families*, ed. S. Cath, A. Gurwitt,
and L. Gunsburg. Hillsdale, NJ: The Analytic Press, pp. 245-263.

[See Chapter 16 for annotation.]

Meyers, Helen (1989). The impact of teenaged children on parents. In:
*The Middle Years: New Psychoanalytic Perspectives*, ed. J. Oldham and R.
Liebert. New Haven, CT: Yale University Press, pp. 75-88.

[See Chapter 15 for annotation.]

Tyson, Phyllis and Tyson, Robert (1990). Gender Development: Girls. In:
*Psychoanalytic Theories of Development: An Integration*. New Haven, CT:
Yale University Press, pp. 258-276.

[See Chapter 6 for annotation.]

Fischer, Ruth (1991). Pubescence: A psychoanalytic study of one girl's
experience of puberty. *Psych. Inq.*, 11(4).

Using psychoanalytic material, Fischer reports on a female patient's
experience as she progresses through puberty, focusing on her sense of
herself as female (primary femininity). Three developmental issues are
examined: 1) prepubertal ambiguity about gender role, 2) the role of the
best friend, and 3) the impact of menarche. Pubertal girls need to integrate
urgent inner genital sensations with changing feminine outer body
contours, which include breasts, vulva, and vagina, as well as to accept the
absence of a penis. Fischer finds that a sense of joy frequently accompanies
menarche and other bodily changes; prolonged penis envy is not the norm.

# Chapter 10

# Menstrual Cycle Experience

Sally Severino

The abstracts in this chapter delineate an evolving understanding of female psychology in the area of menstrual cycle experience. Psychoanalysts in the beginning of the 20th century viewed women as innately frail and vulnerable at the time of menstruation. Women were "defective men," and disturbances of menstruation were used to illustrate the effect of a physical condition on ego functioning. It was thought that the ego was weakened by menstrual disturbance and thus was vulnerable to neurosis. Menstruation in symptomatic adult women, then, could trigger unresolved conflicts about castration and penis envy. The early abstracts reflect variations on this theme.

The ensuing decades saw a growth of psychosocial theories about women's functioning that paralleled an expansion of knowledge in the biological sciences. The creation and refinement of hormone assay techniques in the 1930s furthered progress in the study of hormone metabolism, endocrine regulation, and body tissue responses. Numerous hormones were studied in relation to the psychological functioning of women. No one-to-one, cause-and-effect relationship between hormones and women's psychology was found in any of these studies.

Accumulating data suggest that estrogen and progesterone may directly affect nerve cell functions and thus may profoundly influence behavior, mood, and the processing of sensory information. In addition, these hormones modulate many central neurotransmitters. The more recent literature emphasizes the interaction of psychobiological, developmental, and sociocultural factors and their effect on menstrual cycle functioning. Furthermore, systematic exploration of psychopathology in relation to psychobiological interactions is considered. Future investigations must try to understand women's unconscious mental life, fantasies, dreams, and inner representational object worlds, as these aspects affect and are affected by each woman's monthly biological rhythm, the menstrual cycle. Menopause is discussed in Chapter 15. [See Chapters 12, 14, and 18 for related information.]

Lewin, Bertram (1930). Smearing of feces, menstruation, and the female superego. Kotschmieren, menses und werbliches uber-ich. *Int. Ztschr. f. Psa.*, 16:43-56. Also in: *Selected Writings of Bertram D. Lewin*, ed. J. Arlow. New York: Psychoanalytic Quarterly Press, 1973, pp 12-25.

This paper presents clinical evidence to support the belief that the female superego is incompletely developed. Lewin speculates that the beginning of menstruation is unconsciously regarded as castration. The castration is denied, and the fantasy appears, "This is not blood; it is feces (urine)." An anal (or urethral) regression takes place. Libido, which at first is genital, becomes anal and is finally displaced to the skin. Lewin reasons, that, since the superego is formed by oral introjection and the oral libidinal cathexis is displaced to the body surface or to anal impulses, there will be less oral libido available for the process of incorporation of objects and therefore less complete introjection and superego formation. This paper is of particular historical interest in demonstrating the era's incomplete analytic knowledge, which was rooted in drive theory.

Horney, Karen (1931). Premenstrual tension. In: *Feminine Psychology*, ed. H. Kelman. New York: Norton, pp. 99-106.

While acknowledging that a rise in libido associated with the premenstruum may share in creating premenstrual tension, Horney attributes premenstrual tension to an unconscious awareness of the physical readiness for pregnancy in women with conflicts about becoming pregnant.

Chadwick, Mary (1932). *The Psychological Effects of Menstruation*. New York: Nervous and Mental Diseases.

Chadwick reviews early superstitions and the writings of ancient medical men about the periodic occurrence of psychological disturbances in women. She also surveys the psychoanalytic literature relating symptoms of menstruating women to the behavior of medieval witches. Developmental factors contributing to menstrual symptoms are discussed. According to Chadwick, women's wishes to be men, together with their "unreliability and dangerous actions" at that time of month, made it necessary for society to develop taboos against menstruating women. Women's wishes evoke fantasies of rage over disappointment at being women rather than men; this rage is discharged through menstrual symptoms. The greater a woman's hostility toward her mother, the more guilt and rage at the self will result, with symptoms derived from fantasies connecting castration to weaning and birth.

Chadwick, Mary (1933). *Women's Periodicity*. London: Noel Douglas.

Chadwick discusses the history of the concept of periodicity from childhood through adult life. She describes the characteristic symptoms of menstrual cycle rhythms, which include 1) physical health symptoms related to the body; 2) output of energy and fatigue; and 3) psychological symptoms and emotional changes. Chadwick assumes that the woman who has no fluctuation of symptoms should be suspected of suffering from penis envy.

Daly, Claude (1935). The menstruation complex in literature. *Psychoanal. Q.*, 4:307-340.

The author discusses literature in which the menstruation complex is a focus. In particular, he reviews René Laforgue's study of the life of the French poet Baudelaire and Edgar Allan Poe's writings. He views the menstruation complex as the nucleus of the Oedipus complex, and he believes it can be seen both in literature and art.

Balint, Michael (1937). A contribution to the psychology of menstruation. *Psychoanal. Q.*, 6:346-352.

The author believes that in certain instances menstruation may be viewed as a conversion symptom. As such, the symptom expresses both a wish and a denial of the woman's sexual excitement, as well as her conflicting wishes to excite and disappoint a man. Clinical vignettes illustrate the author's formulations.

Benedek, Therese and Rubenstein, Boris (1939a). The correlations between ovarian activity and psychodynamic processes I: The ovulative phase. *Psychosom. Med.*, 1:245-270.
Benedek, Therese and Rubenstein, Boris (1939b). The correlations between ovarian activity and psychodynamic processes II: The menstrual phase. *Psychosom. Med.*, 1:461-485.

These important studies on the menstrual cycle experience report data from nine women with 75 menstrual cycles in Part I of the study and 15 women with 125 menstrual cycles in Part II. Part I focuses on the ovulatory phase, and Part II focuses on the menstrual phase. On the basis of daily records of dream content, wishes, fears, and other analytic process notes, Benedek evaluates the dynamic themes and attempts to predict the phase of the menstrual cycle. The psychodynamic material is then compared with physiological data, including daily vaginal smears and basal body temperatures, which are analyzed independently by a gynecologist. The study indicates a correlation of estrogen dominance prior to ovulation with manifest dream content of increasingly active libidinal tendencies; progesterone dominance after ovulation is correlated with passive receptivity and preoccupation with the self. The authors find significant correlations between the physiological and psychological processes. Instinctual drives seem related to specific hormone functions of the ovaries. At the peak of estrogen production, dream content expresses heterosexual object choice, whereas at the peak of progesterone production, dream content expresses infantile or pregenital object choice.

Menninger, Karl (1939). Somatic correlations with the unconscious repudiation of femininity in women. *J. Nerv. Ment. Dis.*, 89: 514-527.

Menninger offers a comprehensive overview of the relationship between a woman's repudiation of her femininity and her somatic symptomatology. He emphasizes that instinctual energies influence the function of the reproductive organs, manifesting themselves in frigidity, and accompanying somatic symptoms such as vaginismus, sterility, hyperemesis gravidarum, amenorrhea, dysmenorrhea, menorrhagia, metrorrhagia, and leucorrhea. He contends that these symptoms simultaneously reflect a rejection of the feminine role, an aggression against the male, and self-punishment. Improvement of symptoms is correlated with a woman's acceptance of femininity.

Menninger, Karl (1941). Psychogenic influences on the appearance of the menstrual period. *Int. J. Psycho-Anal.*, 22:60-64.

Menninger discusses some of the unconscious motivations and wishes that may be gratified by uterine bleeding. Bleeding brought on at times of the month other than the regular menses may serve l) to test whether the man will love the woman in spite of the bleeding; 2) to reject the love object; 3) to avoid coitus; and 4) to symbolize wishes for self-inflicted castration. Clinical examples are included.

Daly, Claude (1943). The role of menstruation in human phylogenesis and ontogenesis. *Int. J. Psycho-Anal.*, 24:151-170.

Daly attempts to show the genetic source of ambivalence, incest dread, sadism, and masochism in the evolution of culture. The biological and physiological evolution of estrus in lower animals is traced through to menstruation in primates. The psychological reactions associated with menstruation are discussed, although no conclusion is drawn. Daly contends that menstruation becomes associated with men's fears of being eaten and castrated. These fears, in turn, affect the repression of incestuous desire.

Gill, Merton (1943). Functional disturbances of menstruation. *Bull. Menn. Clin.*, 7:6-14.

The concept of the menstruating woman as a threat to men's virility is the organizing theme of this article. Women's dangerousness derives from their resentment of monthly menstruation, which is a reminder of their deficient sense of femininity. Gill also describes dysmenorrhea, premenstrual tension, "false pregnancy," menorrhagia, and metrorrhagia in the context of this theme.

Deutsch, Helene (1944). *The Psychology of Women*, Vol 1. New York: Grune and Stratton.

Deutsch's writings reflect early psychoanalytic views similar to those of Freud. Menstruation is viewed as potentially intensifying a woman's preexisting conflicts about pregnancy, parturition, castration, feelings of uncleanliness, lack of control of body functions, aggression, penis envy, and masturbation. This book should be read for its historical interest. [See also Chapter 2.]

Devereux, George (1950). The psychology of feminine genital bleeding. *Int. J. Psycho-Anal.*, 31:237-257.

This article presents an analysis of Mohave Indian puberty and menstrual rites. It is presented in two parts and includes a detailed description of Mohave rites and an analysis of the meaning of female genital bleeding in Mohave Indian society. Menstrual bleeding is seen as ridding the body of its contents, an act that is unconsciously imagined to be the result of aggression. The puberty rituals are a means of binding the anxiety associated with this outward manifestation of an aggressive act.

Silbermann, Isidor (1950). A contribution to the psychology of menstruation. *Int. J. Psycho-Anal.*, 31:258-267.

This theoretical paper proposes that during the menstrual cycle women regress to pregenital levels in response to hormonal changes. Depending on their libidinal development and psychological structure, the same amount of hormone may cause different reactions in different women. He suggests that women with earlier libidinal fixations experience more trauma with more serious symptoms than do women who have attained higher libidinal development. Case illustrations are provided.

Benedek, Therese (1952a). *Studies in Psychosomatic Medicine. Psychosexual Functions in Women.* New York: Ronald Press.

This book presents a detailed account of research done earlier. Fifteen women in analysis are followed for over 100 menstrual cycles, with vaginal smears and basal body temperature readings registering the rise and fall of estrogen and progesterone levels. The aim is 1) to investigate the connection between the physiologic function of ovulation and the emotions and behavior of the women; and 2) to discover the laws governing response to fluctuation in hormone levels. The study finds that increased estrogen levels correlate with increased heterosexual urge, aggressive behavior, anxiety, and highest genital function. The postovulatory, or progesterone, stage is marked by motherliness or dependency, withdrawal, increased narcissistic concerns, and wishes for or defenses against pregnancy. The last four chapters use this psychosomatic model to discuss the mother-infant relationship, menopause, specific sexual disturbances, and the specific problems associated with motherhood.

Rodrigue, Emilio (1955). Notes on menstruation. *Int. J. Psycho-Anal.*, 36:328-334.

This paper describes a portion of the psychoanalysis of a 26-year-old woman that spans three consecutive menstrual cycles. The author traces the patient's initial persecutory anxiety, stirred up by menstruation through its diminution and change into depressive anxiety. Ultimately he describes the appearance of a loving attitude in an object relationship. Rodrigue concludes that the constructive aspects of menstruation need to be more emphasized in clinical work.

Shainess, Natalie (1961). A re-evaluation of some aspects of femininity through a study of menstruation: A preliminary report. *Comp. Psychiat.*, 2:20-26.

The author first reviews the evolution of psychoanalytic thinking about feminine psychology and then reports on a questionnaire she gave to 103 women. The questionnaire elicited brief background data and a detailed menarcheal history. Shainess concludes the following about premenstrual symptoms: 1) they reflect two primary reactions: either helplessness and a need for love, or defensiveness against anticipated attack; 2) they are an expression of the devaluation of the self in relation to femininity; and 3) they relate to unpleasant, humiliating, or unloving experiences with the mother.

Hart, Marion and Sarnoff, Charles (1971). The impact of menarche: A study of two stages of organization. *J. Amer. Acad. Child Psychiat.*, 10:257-271.

The authors describe two stages of organization surrounding menarche:1) a premenarcheal stage, in which there is an upsurge of pregenital bisexual conflicts and fantasies that manifest themselves as confusion and disequilibrium, and 2) a menarcheal stage, in which menstrual bleeding demands a reorganization of the ego around a clearer body image that results in a clarification of sexual role. Menarche acts as an organizer of experience and a nidus for the crystallization of body boundaries. Clinical vignettes illustrate each stage.

Whisnant, Lynn and Zegans, Leonard (1975). A study of attitudes toward menarche in white middle-class American adolescent girls. *Am. J. Psychiat.*, 132:809-814.

Twenty-five premenarcheal and ten postmenarcheal girls are interviewed about their attitudes and feelings concerning menarche. Their responses suggest that the following issues are evoked by menarche: 1) the girl's emerging identity as an adult woman, 2) her newly acquired ability to reproduce, and 3) her changing relationship to her mother. The authors recommend an empirical data base from which to develop clinical guidelines to meet the psychological needs of young adolescent girls. Their attempt to gather such a database is described in the Whisnant, Brett, and Zegans (1979) annotation in this chapter.

Lidz, Ruth and Lidz, Theodore (1977). Male menstruation: A ritual alternative to the oedipal transition. *Int. J. Psycho-Anal.*, 58:17-31.

Based on studies of "male menstruation" rituals in two Papua/New Guinea societies whose way of life differs profoundly from that of Western societies, this article suggests a need for reexamining the functions of the oedipal transition. The initiation rites, which include self-induced bleeding and vomiting, seem to relate to the theme of providing men with powers and attributes that they believe women possess naturally. In the various rites, men are not threatening castration. Rather, the rituals permit physical sexual development and protect the initiate from the malignant emanations of women. From a psychoanalytic viewpoint, male menstruation rites are the means of overcoming boys' symbiotic tie to mother.

Weideger, Paula (1977). *Menstruation and Menopause*. New York: Dell.

This revised and expanded version of an original book (1975), attempts to challenge menstrual taboos. An historical account of menstrual taboos and details of menstrual physiology are provided.

Shuttle, Penelope and Redgrove, Peter (1978). *The Wise Wound: Eve's Curse and Everywomen*. New York: Richard Marek Publishers.

This is one of several popular books published in the 1970s to break the silence surrounding women's menstruation and to challenge prevailing attitudes about menstruation.

Whisnant, Lynn, Brett, Elizabeth, and Zegans, Leonard (1979). Adolescent girls and menstruation. *Adol. Psychiat.*, 7:157-170.

Using empirical data from an interview (70 subjects) and questionnaire survey (171 subjects) of prepubertal, pubertal, and postpubertal adolescent girls, the authors describe how menarche is anticipated, experienced, and perceived afterward. Fantasies about the body, relationships with peers and parents, particularly the mother, and the effect of education about menstruation on the young girl are examined. The significance of the choice and use of napkins or tampons and importance of the circumstances of the first use of tampons are presented. Symbolic meanings of the napkin as connected with excretory soiling and of the tampon as the first object to enter the vagina are elucidated. The discussions connect empirical with psychodynamic developmental theories, including references to Freud, Kestenberg, Lewin, and Deutsch.

Friedman, Richard, Hurt, Stephen, Aronoff, Michael, and Clarkin, John (1980). Behavior and the menstrual cycle. *Signs*, 5: 719-738. Also in: *Women: Sex and Sexuality*, ed. C. Stimpson and E. Person. Chicago, IL: University of Chicago Press, 1980, pp. 192-211.

The authors provide a comprehensive summary of the complex relationships that exist between behavior and the menstrual cycle and suggest relevant issues needing further study. They delineate a model of female functioning in which individual women provide meaning to menstrual cycle physiological changes based on the psychosocial context of the event, their attitudes and expectations about the event, their previous experiences, and their personality structure. The authors caution against generalizing from data on normal women to women with psychopathology.

They recommend further research to replicate earlier studies correlating hormonal events of the menstrual cycle with specific fantasies and to clarify descriptive, etiological, and nosological perspectives on psychopathology in relation to menstrual cycle phenomena.

Notman, Malkah (1982). The psychiatrist's approach. In: *Premenstrual Tension: A Multidisciplinary Approach*, ed. Charles Debrovner. New York: Human Sciences Press, pp. 51-69.

Reporting data from analytic and psychotherapy patients, Notman finds that premenstrual tension may be an expression of an identification with a mother who was also symptomatic. If a woman feels helpless to change her situation or to express aggression directly, premenstrual tension can result, reflecting problems about control, power, and anger that cannot be expressed otherwise.

Nadelson, Carol, Notman, Malkah, and Ellis, Elizabeth (1983). Psychosomatic aspects of obstetrics and gynecology. *Obstet. Gyn.*, 24:871-884.

This article reviews some of the psychosomatic aspects of obstetrics and gynecology in the light of current data about gynecological conditions and in the context of changing views of femininity. Biological factors, psychiatric factors, and reciprocal psychobiologic interactions are described for premenstrual and menstrual behaviors, postpartum reactions, menopause, pelvic pain, and hysterectomy. The authors view variations from normal menstrual cycle phenomena as derived from several possible sources, including 1) identification with a significant woman, 2) somatic expressions of body and self images, and 3) reflections of concepts of femininity. The authors recommend attention to both biological and psychological factors.

Notman, Malkah (1983). Menarche: A psychoanalytic perspective. In: *Menarche*, ed. S. Golub. Lexington, MA: Lexington Books, pp. 271-278.

Notman discusses adolescents' experience of menarche by delineating the developmental tasks of the adolescence. She explains how menarche has a profound effect on the integration of object relations and separation-individuation, self-identity, sexuality, and consolidation of body image. She contends that menarche is one of several psychic organizers of adolescence. Menstruation is important, as it helps consolidate femininity by confirming the existence of the vagina. The developmental tasks of adolescence must be understood in the context of the symbolic meaning of menarche for individual girls.

Manson, William (1984). Desire and danger: A reconsideration of menstrual taboos. *J. Psychoanal. Anthro.*, 7: 241-255.

This article reviews explanations for menstrual taboos and sexual pollution beliefs. It focuses on castration anxiety, ambivalently fearful veneration of female reproductive capacities, and gender polarization.

Renik, Owen (1984). An example of disavowal involving the menstrual cycle. *Psychoanal. Q.*, 53:523-532.

Clinical material illustrates the confusion between reality and fantasy in the tendency of some women in psychoanalysis to disavow menstrual events. Some technical considerations pertaining to the analysis of disavowal as a resistance are described. Renik suggests that women in analysis will tend to disavow mittelschmerz as well as perceptions of other events in the menstrual cycle when such perceptions have consciously gratifying associations.

Delaney, Janice, Lupton, Mary, and Toth, Emily (1988). *The Curse: A Cultural History of Menstruation*. Chicago: University of Illinois Press.

This book covers topics on menstruation, including menstrual taboos in religion, advertising, and literature.

Lander, Louise (1988). *Images of Bleeding: Menstruation as Ideology*. New York: Orlando Press.

The theme of menstruation as a biological, psychological, and social event is developed in an attempt to create a positive "women-centered" way of viewing menstruation.

Meyer, Jon (1988). A case of hysteria, with a note on biology. *J. Amer. Psychoanal. Assn.*, 36:319-346.

The course of psychoanalysis is described for a woman patient who presented with the physical manifestations of hyperprolactinemia, including galactorrhea, amenorrhea, and infertility.
[See Chapter 20 for annotation.]

Severino, Sally (1988) The psychoanalyst in a bio-medical world: New opportunities for understanding women. *Acad. Forum*, 32:10-12.

Severino focuses on the need to modify psychoanalytic metapsychology to include medical advances in neuroendocrinology as a contemporary challenge to psychoanalysts. She also addresses the question of how hormonal changes affect information processing in women. She proposes a cyclic pattern of cognitive functioning that is regulated by menstrual cycle events.

Lupton, Mary (1989). Claude Dagmar Daly: Notes on the menstruation complex. *Amer. Imago*, 46:1-20.

This scholarly paper presents Daly's (1935, 1943) thesis that menstruation is a significant factor in the intrapsychic development of both males and females. Unlike Freud, who emphasized the fear of the castrating father, Daly emphasizes the fear of the menstruating mother as the primary source of castration anxiety.

Severino, Sally, Bucci, Wilma, and Creelman, Monica (1989). Cyclical changes in emotional information processing in sleep and dreams. *J. Amer. Acad. Psychoanal.*, 17:555-577.

This article offers a comprehensive review of the literature on the effects of the menstrual cycle on sleep patterns, dream recall, and dream content. The authors then apply Bucci's dual-code model of the mind to the dreams reported in the Benedek-Rubenstein (1939a,b) and psychoanalytic study of the menstrual cycle that is described in this chapter. Their findings provide preliminary evidence that there are psycholinguistic styles characteristic of different phases of the menstrual cycle and that this variation in verbal expression reflects a correlation between hormone production and the ability to access and communicate nonverbal representations.

Severino, Sally and Moline, Margaret (1989). *Premenstrual Syndrome: A Clinician's Guide*. New York: Guilford Press.

This book is a comprehensive review of the literature on all aspects of premenstrual syndrome (PMS), including etiology, differential diagnosis, treatment, and women's issues. The chapters on the history of PMS and the psychology of the menstrual cycle are of particular interest to psychoanalysts.

# Chapter 11

# Adult Development: Overviews

Sandra Kopit Cohen and Nadine Levinson

This chapter includes overview books and papers on female adult development. Adult development represents a relatively new focus for psychoanalysts. In "Three Essays on the Theory of Sexuality," Freud (1905) proposed a theory of psychosexual development based on libidinal phases that begin in infancy and continue until the attainment of genital sexuality at the end of adolescence. While Freud emphasized the importance of childhood phases in the consolidation of psychic structure, he did not conceptualize developmental events as continuing into adulthood. Erikson (1950) and Mahler (1975) extended Freud's psychosexual model to include additional psychosocial factors and phases of development beyond adolescence into old age.

Contemporary theorists of adult development maintain that psychological development continues throughout the life cycle with new dynamic and phase-specific tasks. The developmental tasks are variable, rather than occurring in biologically predetermined, invariant chronological stages. The theorists argue that structural transformations can and do occur in adulthood. Those changes are influenced by the interaction of biological, psychological, and social events. Conflicts from childhood continue to exert an additional influence on adult life and behavior as well.

Modern theories of adult development have originated from three distinct perspectives: sociological, psychological, and psychoanalytic. Both sociological and psychological models have heuristic value, but they tend to oversimplify by blurring the distinctions between objective life events, such as marriage, childbirth, or parenthood, and the intrapsychic meanings and developmental impetus of those events. The intrapsychic meanings of life events reflect psychological structures derived from early childhood as well as ongoing developmental issues for the adult. Recent psychoanalytic writings on adult development integrate biological, sociological, and psychological viewpoints within a metapsychological framework.

Adulthood is conventionally divided into early adulthood, midlife, and old age. Most models of adult development have been based on observations of the life patterns of men. Yet, women's lives commonly include complexities in the ordering of career, marriage, pregnancy, childbearing, and childrearing. Since male development is not an appropriate prototype for female development, prevailing models have questionable applicability to women.

Several theoretical questions remain unresolved: What relationship exists between social and cultural changes and intrapsychic transformations in the superego and ego ideal? Are certain adult life-challenges or experiences necessary for the completion of adult maturation? Does the achievement of external landmarks necessarily indicate intrapsychic growth? How are self-representations altered by these adult experiences? Whether experiences in adulthood produce developmental, structural transformations or adaptive compromise-formations remains a focus of particular controversy.

This chapter covers theoretical and integrative papers that are relevant to a psychoanalytic inquiry into female adult development. Many articles and books on adult development are not gender specific, but the most important general works are included here, along with those that focus explicitly on female adult development itself. Psychoanalytically oriented readers may criticize the writings in this area as being insufficiently informed by psychoanalytic experience. Indeed, psychoanalytic exploration of female adult developmental issues continues as a prime area for future research.

This chapter primarily contains overviews of female adult development. By contrast, the papers in Chapters 12-15 delineate specific events and developmental challenges in adult life such as falling in love, marriage, pregnancy, motherhood, work, aging, and illness, and explore the relationship of those events to psychological development and vulnerability. (S.K.C., N.L., and E.S.)

### Erikson, Erik (1950). *Childhood and Society*. New York: Norton.

Erikson's epigenetic model proposes that each stage of the life cycle is characterized by certain events or crises that must be resolved in order for development to proceed smoothly. He extends Freud's psychosexual theory of development beyond adolescence by discussing developmental potentials at all stages of life, especially the capacities for intimacy, generativity, and ego integrity.

### Benedek, Therese (1959). Parenthood as a developmental phase. *J. Amer. Psychoanal. Assn.*, 7:389-417.

Adult developmental processes are stimulated by the experience of parenthood. [See Chapter 14 for annotation.]

Bibring, Grete, Dwyer, Thomas, Huntington, Dorothy, and Valenstein, Arthur (1961). A study of the psychological processes in pregnancy and of the earliest mother-child relationships. *The Psychoanalytic Study of the Child*, 16:9-72. New York: International Universities Press.

Life-cycle issues during pregnancy, motherhood, and grandmotherhood are explored. [See Chapter 14 for annotation.]

Miller, Jean Baker (1973). *Psychoanalysis and Women*. New York: Brunner/Mazel.

Miller's collection of 23 psychoanalytic papers explores changing theories of childhood and adult female development. Many papers diverge from the classical Freudian view. In Miller's conclusion, she underscores the divergences between male and female development. The papers by Thompson (1942), M. B. Cohen (1966), and Symonds (1971) address issues specifically related to adult female development, including work inhibitions and sexuality. [See Chapter 12 for annotations.]

Mahler, Margaret, Pine, Fred, and Bergman, Anni (1975). *The Psychological Birth of the Human Infant*. New York: Basic Books,

Mahler proposes a process of separation-individuation and describes the early development of a person's sense of self and of a self in relation to the world around him. She states that the fourth subphase, "Consolidation of Individuality and the Beginnings of Emotional Object Constancy," is an open-ended process that continues over the life cycle. [See also Chapter 6.]

Vaillant, George (1977). *Adaptation to Life*. Boston: Little, Brown.

Using longitudinal data, Vaillant studies the construction of a hierarchy of ego mechanisms as men advance in age. Defenses are organized along a continuum that reflects two aspects of personality development: immaturity-maturity and psychopathology-mental health. Conflict resolution is dependent on the maturation of ego mechanisms of defense throughout the life cycle. Vaillant concludes that adaptive and intrapsychic changes take place throughout life. He also finds that Erikson's model of the life cycle is valid.

Levinson, Daniel, Darrow, Charlotte, Klein, Edward, Levinson, Maria, and McKee, Braxton (1978). *The Seasons of a Man's Life*. New York: Knopf.

Based on a study of personality development of 40 men, Levinson et al. postulate four developmentally discrete, but overlapping eras of development, each lasting 25 years. The evolving sequence of eras and their ages are childhood and adolescence, age 0-22; early adulthood, age 17-25; middle adulthood, age 40-65; and late adulthood, age 60 and up. Four to five year transitional periods alternate with the stable eras.

Notman, Malkah and Nadelson, Carol (ed.)(1978). *The Woman Patient: Sexual and Reproductive Aspects of Women's Health Care*, Vol. 1. New York: Plenum Press.

This collection of 25 chapters concerns women patients and their health care. The chapters related to female adult development are "The Sense of Mastery in the Childbirth Experience," by Seiden; "Adolescent Sexuality and Pregnancy," by Nadelson, Notman, and Gillon; "The Problem of Infertility," by Mazor; "Problems in Sexual Functioning," by Nadelson; "A Psychological Consideration of Mastectomy," by Notman; and "The Woman and Esthetic Surgery," by Goldwyn. Most of the authors have a psychoanalytic or psychodynamic orientation. [See also Chapters 12 and 15.]

Colarusso, Calvin and Nemiroff, Robert (1981). *Adult Development*. New York: Plenum Press.

The authors outline a psychoanalytic framework for adult development that focuses on stages and tasks in the adult life cycle. They emphasize that the development of mental structures continues throughout adulthood in interaction with adult experiences. Part I reviews the history of theories of development; Part II presents the authors' hypotheses; and Part III relates these propositions to clinical work. Colarusso and Nemiroff present seven key ideas: 1) the nature of the developmental process is basically the same in adults as in children; 2) development in adulthood is an ongoing, dynamic process; 3) whereas child development focuses primarily on the formation of psychic structure, adult development is concerned with the continued evolution and use of existing structure; 4) the fundamental developmental issues of childhood continue as central aspects of adult life but in altered form; 5) the developmental processes in adulthood are influenced by the adult past as well as by the childhood past; 6) development in adulthood, as in childhood, is profoundly influenced by the body and physical change; and 7) a central, phase-specific theme of adult development is the normative crisis precipitated by the perception and acceptance of the finiteness of time and the inevitability of personal death. "Female Midlife Issues in Prose and Poetry," by Colarusso, Nemiroff, and Zuckerman, discusses female development. [See Chapter 15 for annotation.]

Gould, Roger (1981). Transformational tasks in adulthood. In: *The Course of Life: Psychoanalytic Contributions Toward Understanding Personality Development, Adulthood and the Aging Process*, Vol. 3, ed. S. Greenspan and G. Pollock. Adelphi, MD: U.S. Department of Health and Human Services, NIMH, pp. 55-90.

Gould asserts that psychological growth occurs when life-cycle stages clash with false childhood assumptions and when a change in the construction of reality results. Men and women have different but overlapping sets of assumptions and myths. Gould contends that women are more likely than men are to believe that life is impossible without a protector. He describes the case of a 36-year-old woman with a work inhibition and a psychosomatic illness.

Greenspan, Stanley and Pollock, George (ed.)(1981). *The Course of Life: Psychoanalytic Contributions Toward Understanding Personality Development, Adulthood and the Aging Process*, Vol. 3, ed. S. Greenspan and G. Pollock. Adelphi, MD: U.S. Department of Health and Human Services, NIMH.

This is the third volume of a set reviewing personality development from infancy through old age. "Transformational Tasks in Adulthood," by Gould, and "Psychoanalysis and Aging: A Developmental View," by Gutman, sketch adult development in women. [See Chapter 15 for annotation.]

Giele, Janet (1982a) Women in adulthood: Unanswered questions. In: *Women in the Middle Years*, ed. J. Giele. New York: Wiley, pp. 1-35.

Giele, reviewing the literature on adult development, notes that male patterns are too often viewed as the norm. She proposes a multidimensional model that embraces aspects of both stage and life-span theory. According to Giele, more distinct stages of adult development are evident in socially complex societies. In contrast, in societies or social classes with greater stability, such stages rarely become discernable. Giele differentiates male and female adult development. She outlines four major areas for future research: 1) the physical domain, 2) psychological issues, 3) social roles, and 4) the institutional and cultural context. The author provides a thorough and intelligent overview of the subject.

Giele, Janet (ed.)(1982b). *Women in the Middle Years*. New York: Wiley.

This book is an outgrowth of the work of a multidisciplinary study group. "Women in Adulthood," by Giele, and "Adult Development and

Women's Development: Arrangements for a Marriage," by Gilligan, are most relevant to the psychoanalytic understanding of female adult development. Other papers focus on various demographic trends and sociocultural changes in women's health, social, and work roles. For the analyst unfamiliar with sociological research, the appendix proves most valuable. In this appendix, by Antonucci, there is a summary of the methods and results of the major longitudinal and cross-sectional data sources on women in the middle years. She provides bibliographic references for most of the published sociological studies. [See this chapter.]

Gilligan, Carol (1982b). Adult development and women's development: Arrangements for a marriage. In: *Women in the Middle Years*, ed. J. Giele. New York: Wiley, pp. 89-114.

Gilligan uses data from the literature and from several small studies to illustrate the divergence of male and female developmental lines in adolescence, young adulthood, and middle age. In contrast to males of the same age, adolescent and young adult females value attachment over autonomy. Gilligan argues that in middle age, men and women can achieve maturity only by balancing autonomy with affiliation. However, men and women experience different psychological and social realities throughout the life cycle.

Nadelson, Carol and Notman, Malkah (ed.)(1982a). *The Woman Patient: Concepts of Femininity and the Life Cycle*, Vol. 2. New York: Plenum Press.

This volume is more psychoanalytically focused than Volume 1. Section I, Theory, contains two chapters presenting critiques of psychoanalytic theories of women: "Feminine Development: Changes in Psychoanalytic Theory," by Notman, and "Changing Views of the Relationship between Femininity and Reproduction," by Notman and Nadelson. Section II, Life Cycle Considerations, comprises four chapters: "To Marry or Not to Marry," by Nadelson and Notman; "Maternal Work and Children," by Notman and Nadelson; "Midlife Concerns of Women," by Notman; and "Separation: A Family Developmental Process of Midlife," by Zilbach. These chapters interrelate psychoanalytic and life-cycle concepts that clarify important developmental issues for women.

Nadelson, Carol, Notman, Malkah, Miller, Jean Baker, and Zilbach, Joan (1982). Aggression in women: Conceptual issues and clinical implications. In: *The Woman Patient: Aggression, Adaptations and Psychotherapy*, Vol. 3, ed. M. Notman and C. Nadelson. New York: Plenum Press, pp. 17-28.

This chapter examines the interrelationship between aggression and self-esteem in women. The authors define aggression as "those actions and impulses toward action and assertion that give expression to the individual's own aims and/or have an effect on others" (p. 19). The authors trace the development of aggressive wishes in girls and the effect of parental and social prohibitions against aggressiveness on girls' ego ideal.

Notman, Malkah (1982a). Feminine development: Changes in psychoanalytic theory. In: *The Woman Patient: Concepts of Femininity and the Life Cycle*, Vol. 2, ed. C. Nadelson and M. Notman. New York: Plenum Press, pp. 3-29.

Notman reviews psychoanalytic theories concerning female development and the essence of normal femininity. By observing that the wish for a baby may represent the expression of a healthy identification with the mother rather than a fantasized reparation for castration, she underscores the importance of recognizing a separate line of development for girls. Drawing on the results of clinical work with adult women, she traces the mutually dependent biological, intrapsychic, and societal influences on the developing girl's sense of gender, femininity, and self-esteem.

Notman, Malkah and Nadelson, Carol (ed.)(1982c). *The Woman Patient: Aggression, Adaptations and Psychotherapy*, Vol. 3. New York: Plenum Press.

The contributors to this volume examine the etiology and adult consequences of women's intrapsychic conflicts concerning their aggressive wishes and behavior. The clinical implications of these observations for the psychotherapy of women patients are explored.

Shainess, Natalie (1982). Antigone: Symbol of autonomy and women's moral dilemmas. *J. Amer Acad. Psychoanal.*, 10:443-455. Also in: *The Psychology of Today's Woman: New Psychoanalytic Visions*, ed. T. Bernay and D. Cantor. Hillsdale, NJ: The Analytic Press, 1986, pp. 105-120.

[See Chapter 12 for annotation.]

Zinberg, Norman (1982). Changing sex stereotypes: Some problems for women and men. In: *The Woman Patient: Concepts of Femininity and the Life Cycle*, Vol. 2, ed. C. Nadelson and M. Notman. New York: Plenum Press, pp. 43-75.

Zinberg explores gender differences in the ways that cultural changes in sex-roles affect intrapsychic functioning. Using historical, social, and clinical data, he concludes that as feminine gender-norms change, women experience more guilt and men experience more anxiety. He explains this gender difference by looking at the relation between passivity and self-esteem. Women experience a moral, superego conflict when activity predominates over passivity. Women also derive ego-syntonic pleasure from activity. In contrast, most men do not derive ego-syntonic pleasure from the gratification of passive wishes. Zinberg makes an important distinction between passivity and activity in overt behavior as contrasted to ego passivity and activity.

Emde, Robert (1985). From adolescence to midlife: Remodeling the structure of adult development. *J. Amer. Psychoanal. Assn.*, 33:59-112.

Emde reviews and discusses five books based on the developmental data collected from four longitudinal studies. Research design and methodology are evaluated. Two of the books, *Lives Through Time*, by Block and Haan and *Present and Past in Midlife*, by Eichorn, Clausen, Haan, Honzik, and Mussen, include women in their samples. Emde selects findings of psycho-analytic importance from these books and concludes that 1) psychological development continues dynamically into midlife with new developmental transformations of self and of defensive patterns; 2) cognitive development continues into midlife; 3) sexuality experiences a resurgence in midlife; and 4) marital satisfaction in midlife is correlated with similar personality characteristics of the spouses.

Nemiroff, Robert and Colarusso, Calvin (1985). *The Race Against Time*. New York: Plenum Press.

The authors present a sequel to their first book, *Adult Development* (1981), and expand on their original psychoanalytic formulations. They illustrate their theories with 10 detailed case histories of adults between the ages of 40 and 89. They include a comprehensive literature review, an analysis of key concepts, and a discussion of critical clinical issues. The last section contains a paper by Notman, "When a Husband Dies," which explicitly concerns issues for women influenced by aging, changes in roles, and the threat of imminent loss and death. [See Chapter 15 for annotation.]

Bernay, Toni (1986). Reconciling nurturance and aggression: A new feminine identity. In: *The Psychology of Today's Woman: New Psychoanalytic Visions*, ed. T. Bernay and D. Cantor. Hillsdale, NJ: The Analytic Press, pp. 51-80.

Bernay examines the conflict between traditional parental expectations that are embedded in the ego ideal of daughters and the changing social expectations of adult women. She asserts that developmental models of feminine identity must include reconciliation of affiliative and aggressive urges. Several examples of conflicts between nurturance and aggression are illustrated clinically.

Bernay, Toni and Cantor, Dorothy (ed.)(1986). *The Psychology of Today's Woman: New Psychoanalytic Visions*. Hillsdale, NJ: The Analytic Press.

Most of the papers in this book are written from an interpersonal psychoanalytic perspective and emphasize the conflict between sociocultural ideals and the development of a mature feminine identity. [Papers by Bernay, Herman and Lewis, Jordan and Surrey, and Shainess are in this chapter; papers by Applegarth, Cantor, Lewis, Person, Semel, Tallmer, Williams, and Ziman-Tobin are annotated in Chapters 12 and 15. See also Chapter 4.]

Herman, Judith and Lewis, Helen (1986). Anger in the mother-daughter relationship. In: *The Psychology of Today's Woman: New Psychoanalytic Visions*, ed. T. Bernay and D. Cantor. Hillsdale, NJ: The Analytic Press, pp. 139-163.

The authors examine the vicissitudes of ambivalence in the mother-daughter relationship in childhood, adolescence, young adulthood, and middle age. They assert that the peak of estrangement occurs during adolescence and young adulthood, when the daughter struggles to differentiate herself from the mother and the mother confronts her own conflicts, which are reawakened by identification with her adolescent child. According to the authors, when the daughter becomes generative, either bearing a child or committing herself to a creative task, a rapprochement between mother and daughter may occur as each negotiates a maturational crisis.

Jordan, Judith and Surrey, Janet (1986). The self-in-relation: Empathy and the mother-daughter relationship. In: *The Psychology of Today's Woman: New Psychoanalytic Visions*, ed. T. Bernay and D. Cantor. Hillsdale, NJ: The Analytic Press, pp. 81-104.

Jordan and Surrey argue that women develop a sense of self in the context of significant relationships rather than in the attainment of autonomy. Concomitant lines of self-development include agency and creativity. The authors define the "self-in-relationship" as demonstrating mutuality rather than a merger of identities. In this model, individual development proceeds by the attainment of more mature relational experiences, rather than by separation. The expectation of mutuality in relationships leads to increased self awareness, purpose, and mutual empowerment. The authors illustrate these concepts with psychotherapy cases.

Settlage, Calvin, Curtis, John, Lozoff, Marjorie, Lozoff, Milton, Silber-schatz, George, and Simburg, Earl (1988). Conceptualizing adult development. *J. Amer. Psychoanal. Assn.*, 36:347-369.

Although this excellent paper does not deal directly with female development, the authors propose basic principles about the developmental process that apply to female adult development. Beginning with the mother-child interaction, the developmental process continues to form structures throughout life. The stimulus for ongoing development is a disturbance in prior self-regulatory and adaptive functions. New disturbances can arise from the vicissitudes of biological maturation, environmental expectations and demands, a loss or other traumatic experience, or a perceived possibility of achieving a better adaptation. Such disturbances can lead to development, to restabilization of the status quo, to regression, or to symptom formation. The authors postulate a sequence of five discrete elements in the developmental process: 1) developmental challenge, 2) developmental tension, 3) internal (intrapsychic) developmental conflict, 4) resolution of developmental conflict, and 5) change in the self-representation. Illustrations of the authors' developmental model are provided from childhood, adolescence, and adulthood.

Chodorow, Nancy (1989a). Psychoanalytic feminism and the psychoanalytic psychology of women. In: *Feminism and Psychoanalytic Theory*. New Haven, CT: Yale University Press, pp. 178-198.

Chodorow addresses two problems that have important implications for theories of adult female development. The first is the epistemological difficulty of combining knowledge from the divergent disciplines of sociology, feminist studies, literature, nonanalytic psychology, and psychoanalysis into a coherent framework. The second is the difficulty of integrating the theoretical developmental and clinical perspectives of interpersonally oriented psychoanalysts, who emphasize cultural pressures and interpersonal relationships, especially the mother-daughter relationship, with those of classical and object-relations analysts, who place greater emphasis on internalizations, unconscious defenses, conflicts, and self- and object representations.

Chodorow, Nancy (1989b). Seventies questions for thirties women: Gender and generation in a study of early women psychoanalysts. In: *Feminism and Psychoanalytic Theory*. New Haven, CT: Yale University Press, pp. 199-218.

Chodorow describes the methodological difficulties that she encountered in questioning early women psychoanalysts about gender issues. She emphasizes that this particular group of 80-year-olds forms a cohort from a specific historical context. She also cautions about the potential difference in meaning of a concept to the researcher and to the population sampled. In studying adults over the course of life, one must consider the cohort effect, which is the effect of societal change during the particular period in which the subject lived.

Mercer, Ramona, Nichols, Elizabeth, and Doyle, Glen (1989). *Transitions in a Woman's Life: Major Life Events in Developmental Context*. New York: Springer Publishing.

The authors report on their retrospective study of the life histories of 80 women over the age of 60. They divide the adult female life cycle into the following chronological and developmental clusters: 1) 16-25, the launch into adulthood; 2) 26-30, leveling; 3) 36-60, liberating; 4) 61-65, regeneration/ redirection; and 5) 80 and over, creativity/destructiveness (in which the subjects experience a surge of creativity as well as loss). Women who were mothers had more variation in sequence and a greater number of transitions than women without children. Motherhood did not significantly alter development over the life span. The relation of the subjects to their own mothers appears to have been more important than the experience of mothering others. Greater differences were seen between married and never-married women. The authors conclude that unexpected, nonnormative transitions have greater mutative power than do expected ones.

Clower, Virginia (1990). The acquisition of mature femininity. In: *Women and Men: New Perspectives on Gender Differences*, ed. M. Notman and C. Nadelson. Washington, DC: American Psychiatric Press, pp. 75-88.

Clower juxtaposes her adult psychoanalytic and psychotherapy cases with published reports of Mahler's observations to illustrate the continuity between childhood and adult feminine development. Primary femininity and the female body as a fundamental aspects of feminine ego development are asserted. Clower also focuses on the crucial experiences of female infants with female primary caretakers. Caretaking experiences are different for male and for female children, as mothers relate to their female children in ways that often foster a mutually adhesive relationship and that make the outcome of the rapprochement crisis problematic. In women, conflicts with autonomy and disturbances with the acquisition of mature femininity reflect incomplete separation from the mother, owing in part to the more complete mutual narcissistic identification between mother and daughter. The depressive affect seen in a little girl may actually indicate mourning the loss of the special closeness to the mother, rather than the acknowledgement of not having a penis. Material from the analyses of two girls illustrates their struggle with separation in the rapprochement phase of development.

Nemiroff, Robert and Colarusso, Calvin (1990). *New Dimensions in Adult Development*. New York: Basic Books.

In their third book on adult development, Nemiroff and Colarusso take a multidisciplinary approach to adult development intended to stimulate growth in the field by entering into a dialogue with creative scholars and clinicians who are working on the cutting edge of theory and research. Each chapter is enhanced by a discussion by the editors. Several chapters, including Bardwick's chapter "Where We Are and What We Want: A Psychological Model," and Nadelson's chapter "Women Leaders: Achievement and Power," deal directly with female development.

# Chapter 12

# Early Adulthood: Identity Consolidation, Autonomy, Attachments, Working, and Parenting

Sandra Kopit Cohen
Additional contributions by Eleanor Schuker

Early adulthood is defined both chronologically and by specific developmental challenges. Major tasks of this period include the formation of affectionate and sexual attachments; the consideration of whether and when to pursue childbearing; the resolution of issues related to choice of career pathway, early experiences of marriage, motherhood, and career; and the resolution of ego-ideal conflicts among all these areas. Many writers assert that female identity-consolidation continues throughout this period as these major tasks are resolved. Researchers continue to debate the relative prominence of social and parental expectations, conscious individual choices, unconscious intrasystemic (ego ideal/ego) conflicts, and intersystemic (id/ego) conflicts in influencing the resolution of the principal life challenges of early adulthood. Theoreticians base their models of female development on observations of both normal development and pathological clinical situations, including work inhibitions, working/parenting conflicts, and autonomy/affiliative conflicts. Some writers emphasize the differential effects of being raised by a parent of the same sex on later conflicts around issues of autonomy, dependency, attachment, competition, and ambition. This chapter includes material on identity consolidation, inhibitions in work and autonomy, and conflicts about childbearing. These isssues usually come into view in early adulthood. Related annotations can be found in Chapters 9, 14, and 20. (S.K.C. and E.S.)

Freud, Sigmund (1916). Some character-types met with in psycho-analytic work. *Standard Edition*, 14:309-333. London: Hogarth Press, 1953.

Drawing on literary works and some of his analytic cases, Freud discusses several women who experienced success neuroses because of id/ego ideal conflicts that interfered with happiness. He describes derivatives of oedipal conflict that produce difficulties with marriage and child rearing. [See also Chapter 1.]

Thompson, Clara (1942). Cultural pressures on the psychology of women. *Psychiat.*, 5:331-339. Also in: *Psychoanalysis and Women*, ed. J. B. Miller. New York: Brunner/Mazel, 1973, pp. 49-64.

Thompson examines the interplay between cultural and unconscious factors that contribute to a masculinity complex in some women. These women compete with men professionally, exhibit hatred of men, and avoid intimate relationships with them. [See also Chapter 4.]

Hayward, Emeline (1943). Types of female castration reaction. *Psychoanal. Q.*, 12:45-66.

[See Chapter 18 for annotation.]

Greenacre, Phyllis 1960. Woman as artist. In: *Emotional Growth*, Vol. 2. New York: International Universities Press, 1971, pp. 575-591.

Greenacre discusses why artistic and scientific creativity historically have appeared less frequently in women. She distinguishes intrinsic creative capacity from creative productivity. Greenacre contends that several factors in female psychosexual development are responsible for the restriction of the capacity for externalization and the expression of creativity. Dynamic forces leading to biological creativity, that is, to the bearing and raising of children, conflict with the development of artistic creative expression. Girls are preoccupied with personal relationships from an early age, and this preoccupation diminishes their capacity for creative expression. By contrast, boys are more physically active and are concerned with external objects. This focused externalization leads to the development of boys' capacity for creative productivity. Gender-related differences in attitudes about their genitals produce different attitudes toward, and contents of, creative fantasies; there is correspondingly less precisely focused externalization in girls. The tendency to identify the vagina with the anus may inhibit creativity. Oedipal castration fears may also interfere with artistic conception. Greenacre reports that owing to early genitalization, gifted girls have heightened sensitivities to stimuli and a strong bisexual empathy, which may lead to later susceptibility to inhibitions or to fears of fraudulence.

Cohen, Mabel Blake (1966). Personal identity and sexual identity. *Psychiat.*, 29:1-14.

Cohen observes that society's traditional definitions of masculine and feminine sex roles exaggerate the degree of dependency and passivity in normal females and the degree of independence and activity in normal males. She illustrates how these cultural stereotypes conflict with optimal personal development for both sexes. She supports her conclusions with data from studies in social and developmental psychology and from her own study of 50 pregnant subjects and their husbands. In examining the maturational challenge posed by pregnancy and childbirth, Cohen notes five predominant patterns of maternal response. These patterns depended on both maternal and paternal personalities. She concludes that the balance of dependence/independence and the distribution of caretaking responsibility between the partners becomes crucial during pregnancy. Those couples who coped least well with the pregnancy demonstrated extreme polarities of activity/passivity and independence/dependence within the marriage.

Symonds, Alexandra (1971). Phobias after marriage—women's declaration of dependence. *Amer. J. Psychoanal.*, 31:144-152.

Symonds describes three women who were active and competent before marriage and who became inhibited and phobic after marriage. [See Chapter 20 for annotation.]

Hoffman, Lois (1972). Early childhood experiences and women's achievement motives. *J. Soc. Iss.*, 28:129-156.

Hoffman reviews and evaluates child development studies and examines the hypothesis that females' affiliative needs interfere with achievement motivation. She observes that female children do not develop confidence in their competence to cope independently with the environment. This lack of confidence results from less parental encouragement for early independent strivings and from delayed or incomplete separation from the mother. Lack of self-confidence leads to fears of abandonment and the need to seek protection from others through affiliation with powerful figures. Hoffman cautions about the limitations of extrapolating from child development data to the behavior of adult women. The article is particularly useful as an introduction to developmental research on sex differences.

Horner, Matina (1972). Toward an understanding of achievement-related conflicts in women. *J. Soc. Iss.*, 28:157-176.

Horner extends her 1968 experimental study of women's motives to avoid success by contrasting the characteristics of women who scored high in avoiding success with those who score low. She emphasizes that women do not avoid success because they seek failure. Women who score high in avoidance of success demonstrated decreased performance in competitive situations, especially when competing with men. This decreased performance correlates with anxiety about the consequences of success and does not correlate with strength of affiliative motives. High-scoring women more often had parents and male peers who considered achievement unfeminine. Low-scoring women had boyfriends who supported their achievement, although both members of these couples believed that men are more intelligent. The high-scoring women showed more frustration, hostility, aggression, bitterness, and confusion in responses to TAT cards than did low-scoring women. Drug use was reported more often in the high-scoring group. Horner concludes that high-scoring women need to inhibit their achievements because of anxiety about anticipated negative consequences of success and that tension and drug use are secondary consequences.

Notman, Malkah (1974). Pregnancy and abortion: Implications for career development of professional women. In: *Women and Success*, ed. R. Kundsin. New York: Morrow, pp. 216-221.

[See Chapter 14 for annotation.]

Applegarth, Adrienne (1976). Some observations on work inhibitions in women. *J. Amer. Psychoanal. Assn.* (Suppl.), 24:251-268.

Vignettes from psychoanalysis and psychoanalytic psychotherapy illustrate the intrapsychic sources of female work inhibitions. Applegarth describes the inhibiting effects of pathological narcissism on learning processes, on the ability to experience gratification from achievement, and on confidence in one's capacities. She reviews Freud's and Horney's conceptions of penis envy in reference to her clinical observation that certain women convey a sense of defectiveness that leads to work inhibition; these women commonly have a fantasy that their grievances will be redressed. Applegarth postulates gender-specific superego contents, rather than structural deficits, to explain women's greater anxiety and conflict over expressing aggression. She asserts that fear of success is unconsciously linked to the preoedipal fears of destruction of rivals or the loss of narcissistic connections.

Galenson, Eleanor (1976b). Reporter, Panel: Report on the psychology of women. (2) Late adolescence and early adulthood. *J. Amer. Psychoanal. Assn..*, 24:631-645.

[See Chapter 9 for annotation.]

Gray, Sheila (1976). The resolution of the Oedipus complex in women. *J. Phila. Assn. Psychoanal.*, 3:103-111.

[See Chapter 7 for annotation.]

Symonds, Alexandra (1976). Neurotic dependency in successful women. *J. Amer. Acad. Psychoanal.*, 4:95-103.

Symonds presents clinical illustrations of two types of women suffering from conflicts about dependency. The first type experiences conflicts between her feminine ego-ideal and the demands of society that she act aggressively in order to achieve career success. The second type of woman has intense, unfulfilled dependency needs and feels inferior as a female. This type may function well professionally but experiences little gratification from professional success, while desperately seeking men whom she fantasizes will fulfill her insatiable dependency wishes. Symonds contrasts differences in prognosis and treatment between the two groups.

Ticho, Gertrude (1976). Female autonomy and young adult women. *J. Amer. Psychoanal. Assn. (Suppl.)*, 24:139-155.

Ticho criticizes Freud and argues instead that women wish to become complete and autonomous as women in their own right. She considers the girl's turning from the mother to the father in the oedipal period as a complex process that is crucial to the integration of genitality and to personality development. She postulates that this partial resolution is repeatedly reworked lifelong as women experience intrapsychic crises triggered by internal or external events. In pathological situations, irreversible regression or overrigidity can lead to neurotic repetition of the initial oedipal situation. Ticho presents a clinical case in which a female patient's sexual and work inhibitions became evident when she left her parental home. Ticho concludes that superego identifications with both parents play a significant role in the formation of a woman's sense of autonomy. This autonomy can be disturbed if there is inordinate pre-oedipal envy and aggression toward the mother. Ticho briefly discusses the effect of the gender of the analyst on female patients' reworking of these identifications. [See also Chapter 9.]

Bernstein, Doris (1979). Female identity synthesis. In: *Career and Motherhood: Struggles For A New Society*, ed. A. Roland and B. Harris. New York: Human Science Press, pp. 103-123.

Bernstein defines "identity synthesis" as an overarching term encompassing gender identity, ego, superego, ideals, and identifications. She postulates that the genital difference makes separation from the mother easier for boys, who are physically different from their mothers and who experience their bodies as having a more focused sexuality. Bernstein emphasizes differences in superego contents between the sexes, rather than differences in structure. She contends that girls must be able to form identifications with aspects of both mother and father. Bernstein notes that not every positive feeling toward a paternal figure should be interpreted as erotic.

Moulton, Ruth (1979). Ambivalence about motherhood in career women. *J. Amer. Acad. Psychoanal.*, 7:241-258.

Using data from psychoanalytic psychotherapy, Moulton discusses career women's ambivalence about motherhood and the psychological factors that influence their decisions about family size. Moulton describes the need to have children, the consequences of having too many children, the external as well as unconscious reasons for wanting children, and the psychological effects of childlessness through default or choice.

Schecter, Doreen (1979). Fear of success in women: A psychodynamic reconstruction. *J. Amer Acad. Psychoanal.*, 7:33-43.

Schecter presents some female patients in analysis to illustrate the preoedipal roots of fear of success in women. She proposes that for many women success unconsciously represents murder of the envied, preoedipal, omnipotent mother. Retaliation is feared as a projection of these murderous urges. Schecter distinguishes two groups of women who present clinically with fear of success. The first group come from families in which the mother was emotionally unavailable and the father was nurturing. The daughter develops a façade of self-sufficiency but in fantasy imagines that her excessive dependency needs will be met by the mother or a mother-substitute when she becomes successful in work or marriage. Analysis reveals rage at and envy of the mother. The second group of women were their mother's special child and were jealously kept from any relationship with the father. The daughters experienced an independent move away from the mother to marriage or a successful career as a hostile attack on the mother. These women developed inhibitions and phobias to avoid breaching their dyadic relationship with their mothers.

Friedman, Gloria (1980). The mother-daughter bond. *Contemp. Psychoanal.*, 16:90-96.

Using an interpersonal psychoanalytic perspective, the author discusses young adult women's difficulties in achieving independence and a sense of adult womanhood. Today's changing roles of women have intensified problems in the continuing of a necessary loving bond between mothers and daughters. Women struggling to become independent and successful often fear some loss in the relationship with their mothers. Cultural differences between the generations may encumber the formation of a loving bond of a common feminine identity during the reworking of separation issues in adolescence and young adulthood. Mothers' ambivalence toward their daughters' separating and becoming women may also interfere with the loving bond. A case highlights clinical issues.

Turkel, Ann (1980). The power dilemma of women. *Amer. J. Psychoanal.*, 40:301-311.

Turkel examines definitions of power, attitudes toward power as related to developmental factors in both sexes, and female difficulties in obtaining power. She emphasizes the inhibiting effects of female social roles in a patriarchy, including female roles of expressing emotions for men, validating their masculinity, decreasing male-male competition by serving as an underclass, and avoiding direct expression of effectiveness.

Colarusso, Calvin and Nemiroff, Robert (1981). Narcissism in the adult development of the self. In: *Adult Development*. New York: Plenum Press, pp. 83-104.

The role of narcissism, the adult developmental process, and further acceptance of sexual differences are discussed. [See Chapter 22 for annotation.]

Nadelson, Carol and Notman, Malkah (1981). To marry or not to marry. *Amer. J. Psychiat.*, 138:352-356. Also in: *The Woman Patient: Concepts of Femininity and the Life Cycle*, Vol. 2, ed. C. Nadelson and M. Notman. New York: Plenum Press, 1982b, pp. 111-120.

[See Chapter 13 for annotation.]

Schecter, Doreen (1981). Masochism in women: A psychodynamic analysis. In: *Changing Concepts in Psychoanalysis*, ed. S. Klebanow. New York: Gardner Press, pp. 169-181.

Schecter suggests that masochistic defenses against women's nuclear preoedipal conflicts may be manifested by fears of success. [See Chapter 21 for annotation.]

Brazelton, T. Berry and Keefer, Constance (1982). The early mother-child relationship: A developmental view of woman as mother. In: *The Woman Patient: Concepts of Femininity and the Life Cycle*, Vol. 2, ed. C. Nadelson and M. Notman. New York: Plenum Press, pp. 95-109.

[See Chapter 14 for annotation.]

Lebe, Doryann (1982). Individuation of women. *Psychoanal. Rev.*, 69:66-71.

Lebe asserts that women do not fully complete their separation-individuation from their mothers until the age of 30 to 40, when life experiences begin to modify self- and object representations from childhood. She describes the analyses of three married women in their 30s who had children and complained of depression. These women were attached to a fantasied, omnipotent, preoedipal mother as demonstrated in the transference to the analyst. Lebe traces the evolution of a shift from idealization of the analyst to idealization of the father and then to more realistic self- and object representations during the course of the analyses.

Menaker, Esther (1982). Female identity in psychosocial perspective. *Psychoanal. Rev.*, 69:75-83.

[See Chapter 20 for annotation.]

Notman, Malkah and Nadelson, Carol (1982a). Changing views of the relationship between femininity and reproduction. In: *The Woman Patient: Concepts of Femininity and the Life Cycle*, Vol. 2, ed. C. Nadelson and M. Notman. New York: Plenum Press, pp. 31-42.

The authors examine feminine development and identity as separate from childbearing. They compare women who choose childlessness with those suffering from involuntary sterility. Noting that few studies of childless couples provide psychological depth, they conclude that voluntarily childless women tend either to devalue or to exaggerate the importance of parenthood. In contrast, sterile women and men have different concerns and, not consciously having realized the importance they placed on having a child, are puzzled by the intensity of their feeling of having been narcissistically injured. Their sense of loss of control over life and mourning for the loss of parenthood eventually leads to a redefinition of their femininity and masculinity. The authors hypothesize that childlessness may constrain mature adult development if the loss is not worked through.

Notman, Malkah and Nadelson, Carol (1982b). Maternal work and children. In: *The Woman Patient: Concepts of Femininity and the Life Cycle*, Vol. 2, ed. C. Nadelson and M. Notman. New York: Plenum Press, pp. 121-133.

[See Chapter 14 for annotation.]

Person, Ethel (1982). Women working: Fears of failure, deviance and success. *J. Amer. Acad. Psychoanal.*, 10:67-84.

Person carefully delineates the major sources of work inhibitions in women 1) role conflicts, 2) ambition without clear-cut goals, 3) fear of failure, 4) fear of deviance, 5) fear of success, and 6) special problems among successful women, including fear of public exposure, the personalization of work, the misunderstanding of power, and the sense of fraudulence. She regards women's fear of the loss of affiliative ties as a significant intrapsychic factor leading to work inhibitions. She emphasizes the importance of analyzing the specific intrapsychic fantasies and conflicts for a given analysand.

Shainess, Natalie (1982). Antigone: Symbol of autonomy and women's moral dilemmas. *J. Amer Acad. Psychoanal.*, 10:443-455. Also in: *The Psychology of Today's Woman: New Psychoanalytic Visions*, ed. T. Bernay and D. Cantor. Hillsdale, NJ: The Analytic Press, 1986, pp. 105-120.

Shainess parallels Freud's use of Oedipus as a model for adolescent maturational conflicts by choosing Antigone as a model for female development. She reflects that Antigone, unlike Electra, embodies the qualities of independent ethics, caretaking, and autonomy. Shainess reasons that Antigone's behavior was not masochistic even though it led to her death, because her motivation was based on an adherence to a higher ideal and not to the pursuit of suffering. A case of a masochistic patient in analysis who suffered from conflicts about autonomy is presented.

Krueger, David (1984). *Success and the Fear of Success in Women*. New York: Free Press.

Emphasizing an intrapsychic perspective, Krueger presents a systematic review of the biological, sociological, psychological, and psychoanalytic writings on fear of success in women. He considers success phobia to be a specific disturbance in the ability to accept achievement, a disturbance that can be exhibited by inhibitions toward marriage, motherhood, or career. His observations are based on ego-psychological principles and provide developmental and clinical data.

Schafer, Roy (1984). The pursuit of failure and the idealization of unhappiness. *Amer. Psychol.*, 39:398-405.

[See Chapter 21 for annotation.]

Bergmann, Maria (1985). The effect of role reversal on delayed marriage and maternity. *The Psychoanalytic Study of the Child*, 40:197-219. New Haven, CT: Yale University Press.

Bergmann discusses six female analytic patients and traces common elements in their development from childhood to midadulthood. All the women were childless and sought analysis toward the end of their childbearing years. Several common clustered psychological features were observed, including intensified separation anxiety, continued symbiosis, inhibited negative oedipal love for the mother, role reversal in relation to the mother, and a seductive relationship with the father that resulted in fantasies of oedipal victory and of having had father's baby. Role reversal with mother in childhood led to rage, loss of differentiation from mother as caregiver, disruption of self-constancy, and impaired self-esteem. Bergmann views the role reversal as a defensive substitute for separation-individuation. In most of her cases, the father remained an idealized object of love and identification and was unconsciously preferred to any male peer. Incestuous guilt based on fantasied oedipal victory was paid for by childlessness. Postadolescent sublimations included 1) asceticism (these women tended to care for the children of other women), and 2) adult love relationships that followed a pattern of idealization, giving way to disappointment. Bergmann integrates concepts of self, object relations, and ego psychology to explain her analysands' shared adult traits of delayed marriage and maternity, self-sacrifice, and professional success.

Kanefield, Linda (1985). Psychoanalytic constructions of female development and women's conflicts about achievement—Parts I and II. *J. Amer. Acad. Psychoanal.*, 13:229-366.

[See Chapter 21 for annotation.]

Moulton, Ruth (1985). The effect of the mother on the success of the daughter. *Contemp. Psychoanal.*, 21:266-283.

Women's reactions to their own professional success are seen as reflecting factors in the mother-daughter relationship. Some women respond to professional success with anxiety; they fear that they have gone "too far" and expect maternal retaliation, envy, and loss of dependency gratification. Discouragement by the mother can produce a tendency to fail, fears of failure, unconscious fears of success, and fantasies of punishment via destruction of childbearing capacity. Preoedipal and oedipal factors in the mother-daughter relationship, as well as the developmental influence of the father are cited in several clinical vignettes.

Schuker, Eleanor (1985). Creative productivity in women analysts. *J. Amer. Acad. Psychoanal.*, 13:51-75.

Schuker's two-year pilot study of articles in *Journal of the American Psychoanalytic Association* and *Journal of the American Academy of Psychoanalysis* demonstrates that female analysts were underrepresented as authors. She explores five possible factors influencing productivity: 1) women analysts may be discouraged from creative productivity during training; 2) gender-related issues may not be represented in the publications; 3) practical cultural aspects, such as family pressures and career opportunities may interfere; 4) personality factors related to feminine role conflicts and fears of deviance may inhibit productivity; and 5) other basic dynamic issues in female psychology, including those related to narcissistic and ego ideal conflicts and to surpassing the oedipal father may cause writing inhibitions. Schuker reviews sociological studies of women in other professions, such as psychology, psychiatry, and law, to provide comparison data and raises provocative questions in need of further study.

Applegarth, Adrienne (1986). Women and work. In: *The Psychology of Today's Woman: New Psychoanalytic Visions*, ed. T. Bernay and D. Cantor. Hillsdale, NJ: The Analytic Press, pp. 211-230.

Applegarth presents a survey of components that may underlie work inhibitions. These factors include narcissistic fantasies of achievement without work or without risking mistakes, penis envy, conflicts over aggression, fears of being alone, and wishes to be dependent. She observes that intense conflicts between work and motherhood may disguise defensive wishes for a child. Applegarth notes that her patients with the most extreme work inhibitions had intense relationships with mothers who discouraged any movement toward independence.

Cantor, Dorothy (1986). Marriage and divorce: The search for adult identity. In: *The Psychology of Today's Woman: New Psychoanalytic Visions*, ed. T. Bernay and D. Cantor. Hillsdale, NJ: The Analytic Press, pp. 195-210.

[See Chapter 13 for annotation.]

Lebe, Doryann (1986). Female ego ideal and conflicts in adulthood. *Amer. J. Psychoanal.*, 46:22-32.

Lebe explores the development of the female ego ideal from childhood through middle age. Using data from psychotherapy, she proposes four common ego-ideal conflicts in adult females. Conflict may arise when the feminine ego ideal 1) requires mothering of others rather than pleasing of oneself, 2) is identified with the required performance of all household chores, 3) forbids the expression of anger, or 4) embraces unrealistically high expectations.

Litwin, Dorothy (1986). Autonomy: A conflict for women. In: *Psychoanalysis and Women: Contemporary Reappraisals*, ed. J. Alpert. Hillsdale, NJ: The Analytic Press, pp. 183-214.

Litwin asserts that autonomy is a universal conflict for women because of women's need for affiliation and attachment. She reviews the evolution of psychoanalytic thinking about preoedipal mother-child relationships, object relations, and ego psychology. Female propensity toward nurturing is seen as conflicting with the social valuation of autonomy, creating an ego-ideal conflict. Litwin seems to confuse intrapsychic differentiation with separation.

Moulton, Ruth (1986). Professional success: A conflict for women. In: *Psychoanalysis and Women: Contemporary Reappraisals*, ed. J. Alpert. Hillsdale, NJ: The Analytic Press, pp. 161-181.

Moulton explores the conflict between autonomy and dependency in women from an interpersonal perspective. Professional success is equated with masculinity by both the culture and the individual's unconscious; this creates conflict. Moulton stresses the greater salience of preoedipal conflicts than of oedipal guilt in work inhibitions. She presents several examples of women who were able to obtain professional success but enacted the fantasy that the mother would retaliate by damaging their sex organs (infertility, cancer) by not marrying or having children. Moulton warns that externalizing blame for lack of professional success to the spouse, society, or children may obscure intrapsychic factors.

Notman, Malkah, Zilbach, Joan, Miller, Jean B., and Nadelson, Carol (1986). Themes in psychoanalytic understanding of women: Some reconsiderations of autonomy and affiliation. *J. Amer. Acad. Psychoanal.,* 14:241-253.

The authors integrate the psychoanalytic literature on female development, autonomy, and affiliation with models from related fields such as cognitive psychology, anthropology, and sociology. They use three clinical vignettes to illustrate the popular confusion between pseudoautonomous manifest behavior and true intrapsychic autonomy. Each patient consciously chose to give low priority to an interpersonal attachment because she thought such a priority was immature. The authors propose that adult maturity rather than regression is signified by the ability to move from childhood maternal attachments to adult mutual interdependence.

Person, Ethel (1986). Working mothers: Impact on the self, the couple and the children. In: *The Psychology of Today's Woman: New Psychoanalytic Visions,* ed. T. Bernay and D. Cantor. Hillsdale, NJ: The Analytic Press, pp. 121-138.

[See Chapter 14 for annotation.]

Williams, Susan (1986). Reproductive motivations and contemporary feminine development. In: *The Psychology of Today's Woman: New Psychoanalytic Visions,* ed. T. Bernay and D. Cantor. Hillsdale, NJ: The Analytic Press, pp. 167-193.

[See Chapter 14 for annotation.]

Ziman-Tobin, Phyllis (1986). Childless women approaching midlife: Issues in psychoanalytic treatment. In: *The Psychology of Today's Woman: New Psychoanalytic Visions,* ed. T. Bernay and D. Cantor. Hillsdale, NJ: The Analytic Press, pp. 305-317.

Ziman-Tobin provocatively suggests that the analyst should pay deliberate attention to a childless analysand's conflicts around pregnancy and motherhood if the patient is between ages 35 and 45, even if the patient treats her own fertility as if it had no time limit. Ziman-Tobin advises the analyst to focus on analyzing conflicts that interfere with the maintenance of heterosexual relationships.

Severino, Sally, McNutt, Edith, and Feder, Samuel (1987). Shame and the development of autonomy. *J. Amer. Acad. Psychoanal.,* 15:93-106.

[See Chapter 20 for annotation.]

Bergmann, Maria (1988). On eating disorders and work inhibition. In: *Bulimia: Psychoanalytic Treatment and Theory*, ed. H. Schwartz. Madison, CT: International Universities Press, pp. 347-371.

[See Chapter 23 for annotation.]

Lachmann, Frank (1988). On ambition and hubris: A case study. In: *Frontiers in Self Psychology: Progress in Self Psychology*, Vol. 3, ed. A. Goldberg. Hillsdale, NJ: The Analytic Press, pp. 195-209.

Two psychoanalyses of a woman by the same analyst are described from the perspective of her dilemma about and conflicts between attachments and ambitious strivings. Lachmann asserts that her incompatible ideals and goals about devoted attachments were in conflict with ruthless ambition and that this is a gender-related conflict shared by many women. He warns against equating female career ambitions with masculine strivings; conflicts about pursuit of realistic ambitions are not necessarily based only on unresolved intrapsychic problems. In the patient's first analysis these conflicts between attachment and ambition reflected preoedipal and oedipally derived conflicts, including oedipal competition, separation fears, defensive needs to be mother's caretaker, and an erotic tie to the father and defensive idealization of him. In the second analysis, 10 years later, the inhibition of ambitions in order to retain the mother as an archaic, mirroring selfobject, or protective presence, was analyzed. Maintenance of an archaic mirroring selfobject transference had necessitated the patient's relinquishing her right to be admired and had restricted her ambitions. With analysis, conflicts between attachment and ambition receded and the discomfort with respect to incompatible ideals and goals was tolerated by an integrated self-organization.

Levenson, Ricki (1988). Boundaries, autonomy and aggression: An exploration of women's difficulty with logical, abstract thinking. *J. Amer. Acad. Psychoanal.*, 16:189-208.

Levenson asserts that constraints on cognitive development in girls are gender linked and are based not only on psychological conflicts in separation-individuation, but also on gender-specific child-rearing practices that prohibit the development of skills necessary for logical, abstract thinking. The author assumes, without substantiation, that different developmental experiences for girls during separation-individuation cause ego constriction.

Reiser, Lynn Whisnant (1988a). Love, work, and bulimia. In: *Bulimia: Psychoanalytic Treatment and Theory*, ed. H. Schwartz. Madison, CT: International Universities Press, pp. 373-398.

[See Chapter 23 for annotation.]

Silverman, Martin (1988). Gender identity, cognitive development, and emotional conflict. In: *Motive and Meaning: Psychoanalytic Perspectives on Learning and Education*, ed. K. Field, B. Cohler, and G. Wool. New York: International Universities Press, pp. 451-478.

Despite improved opportunities available to women for personal expression and achievement in recent years, women and men alike have failed to make use of expanded gender role possibilities because of unconscious factors stemming from the complexities involved in the development of gender identity and gender role identity. These unconscious factors, and the developmental processes underlying them, are examined. Emphasis is placed on the interplay between biological and experiential factors and between cognitive and emotional ones.

Kalinich, Lila (1989). The biological clock. In: *The Middle Years: New Psychoanalytic Perspectives*, ed. J. Oldham and R. Liebert. New Haven, CT: Yale University Press, pp. 123-134.

[See Chapter 15 for annotation.]

Klebanow, Sheila (1989). Power, gender and money. *J. Amer. Acad. Psychoanal.*, 17:321-328.

Klebanow speculates that many women have difficulty understanding that money is equivalent to power. They are less often involved in both the use and the abuse of money as power. Women are frequently inhibited in integrating the power to have money through their own labors rather than through a relationship with a man. They may choose powerlessness over power. Interest in money can be seen as unfeminine, so that a woman may manage a corporation's finances but eschew financial interests of her own. Men and women alike have neurotic problems about equating money with success.

McDougall, Joyce (1989). The dead father: On early psychic trauma and its relation to disturbance in sexual identity and creative activity. *Int. J. Psycho-Anal.*, 70:205-219.

[See Chapters 16 and 19 for annotations.]

Nadelson, Carol (1989). Issues in the analyses of single women in their thirties and forties. In: *The Middle Years: New Psychoanalytic Perspectives*, ed. J. Oldham and R. Liebert. New Haven, CT: Yale University Press, pp. 105-122.

Nadelson reviews the psychoanalytic literature to illustrate the conscious and unconscious determinants of a group of single premenopausal women who enter treatment with the fantasy that the analysis will enable them to find a partner or have a child. Successful analysis requires giving up this specific fantasy of "cure" and replacing it with resolution of intrapsychic conflicts, which can allow generativity with or without child bearing.

Colarusso, Calvin (1990). The third individuation: The effect of biological parenthood on separation-individuation processes in adulthood. *The Psychoanalytic Study of the Child*, 45:179-194. New Haven, CT: Yale University Press.

Colarusso describes parenthood as the third individuation phase and as a time of continuous elaboration of the self and differentiation from objects during early (20-40) and middle (40-60) adulthood. At its core are involvements with the family, especially spouse and children. Parenthood facilitates this third individuation by producing a situation in which infantile themes and relationships can be reworked in relation to adult developmental tasks and conflicts. Conception adds a new dimension to sexual identity, confirms the capability of the sexual apparatus, and leads to a new body image altered to include the newly demonstrated capacity of the genitals. This narcissistic gratification produces a psychological readiness in mothers to engage their babies. After delivery, interactions with infants narcissistically enhance the sense of adult sexual completeness in biological parenthood. The intense fusion of the self with the infant in psychological parenthood completes the mother's experience with symbiosis. The stage is then set for an ongoing process of parental separation from the child, which produces dramatic changes in the self and stimulates the third individuation. Later, continued interest in the next generation is stimulated by the narcissistic injury surrounding an aging body and limited time. Parental individuation continues during the child's oedipal period, latency, and adolescence. The onset of grandparenthood begins the fourth individuation phase.

McDougall, Joyce (1991). Sexual identity, trauma and creativity. *Psych. Inq.*, 11(4).

McDougall uses a three-session vignette from the analysis of a middle-aged female homosexual author to illustrate several theoretical points about trauma, creativity and its inhibition, homosexuality, sexual identity, and somatization. The patient, who lost her father when she was 15 months old, experienced a regressive return of a writing block late in her analysis, following a total hysterectomy for severe endometriosis. McDougall contends that this event proved traumatic in that the patient felt that her body image was damaged and her feminine identity thwarted. McDougall maintains that this trauma gave rise to symptomatic psychic reorganization, because it reactivated early psychic trauma. The patient's internalized mother was experienced as anally intrusive, narcissistically demanding, and attacking of her sexuality and capacity to bear children and create. The patient's unconscious fantasy that her mother was responsible for the surgery, for her earlier damaged feminine body image, and for her father's death overlay another guilty fantasy of her own responsibility for this death and for her mother's psychopathology. McDougall asserts that creative work requires the integration of universal bisexual wishes and an identification with the potential fertility of both parents.

# Chapter 13

# Love, Genital Primacy, and Relations between the Sexes

## Denise Dorsey, with Eleanor Schuker

The psychoanalytic papers reviewed in this chapter cluster around the topics of love, genital primacy, and relations between the sexes. These themes have universal appeal, and the papers encompass ideas beyond a specific psychoanalytic focus and beyond our interest in female psychology. One historical controversy in this area has been whether psychological maturity requires heterosexual gratification. In "Instincts and Their Vicissitudes," Freud (1915b), defined maturity as the attainment of genital primacy. He believed that psychological maturity was evidenced in women by the ability to experience heterosexual coital orgasm, which was based on a shift from clitoral to vaginal cathexis. A more current psychoanalytic view contends that libidinal development and maturation of the personality are independent variables. Both variables are influenced by ego capacities for sublimation and for control of libidinal and aggressive drives. Orgastic gratification itself is not an indication of maturity or of a capacity for mature object relations.

In several recent psychoanalytic papers, the perspectives of object relations, ego psychology, and drive development are combined to evolve new theories of love. Among the ideas offered are the influence of the early mother-child relationship, the necessity of resolving ambivalence about gender differences, and the use of love for creative psychic growth. Other psychoanalytic papers have viewed the subjects of love and relations between the sexes from an interpersonal perspective, exploring cultural attitudes about male supremacy and the effects on love relations of female-dominated child care, and the influence of sociocultural phenomena on the psychology of marriage. It is clear from reviewing these papers that there can be no discussion about mature, loving women without also discussing their relationship to men. (D.D. and E.S.)

Freud, Sigmund (1905b). Three essays on the theory of sexuality. *Standard Edition*, 7:125-243. London: Hogarth Press, 1953.

Freud offers the clinical example of a child sucking at the mother's breast as a prototype of every love relationship. Later in the essay, he elaborates on how the relationships with both parents influence object choice. [See also Chapter 1.]

Freud, Sigmund (1908c). Civilized sexual morality and modern nervousness. *Standard Edition*, 9:179-204. London: Hogarth Press, 1953.

Freud criticizes the societal, cultural, and familial constraints on women's (and men's) sexuality that influence women to escape into marriage. According to Freud, satisfying sexual intercourse during marriage takes place only after several years and only for a few years. The resulting sexual difficulties and a double sexual morality predispose women more than men to neuroses. The neurosis is sought as a refuge from a woman's conflict between her unsatisfied desires and her sense of duty as a faithful wife.

Freud, Sigmund (1912b). On the universal tendency to debasement in the sphere of love. *Standard Edition*, 11:178-190. London: Hogarth Press, 1953.

Freud proposes two currents of love, affectionate and sensual, whose union is necessary for a normal attitude in love, creating normal passion and overvaluation of the love object. The affectionate current is formed on the basis of the interests of the self-preservative instinct and corresponds to the child's primary objects. The sensual current originates at puberty and initially cathects the original infantile objects. The incest barrier results in a new seeking of more suitable objects. In psychical impotence, the sensual current remains fixated to unconscious incestuous fantasies. The main protective measure of this symptom is to maintain a split between two objects, one loved but not desired, and the other desired but not loved. As a result, there is psychical debasement of the sexual object that allows full sensual expression and overvaluation of the incestuous object and its representatives.

Freud, Sigmund (1914). On narcissism: An introduction. *Standard Edition*, 14:69-102. London: Hogarth Press, 1953.

Among other topics discussed in this essay, Freud views secondary narcissism as a normal and necessary stage between autoeroticism and object love. Object choice can be anaclitic or narcissistic. Women tend to the latter if they have a great need to be loved. The concept of the ego ideal, which becomes the container of the self-love enjoyed in childhood, is introduced. Freud notes that the feeling of bliss evoked by loving (projecting one's ego ideal) and being loved in return results in an elimination of tension from a conflict existing between the ego and ego ideal. [See also Chapters 1 and 22.]

Freud, Sigmund (1915b). Instincts and their vicissitudes. *Standard Edition*, 14:111-140. London: Hogarth Press, 1953.

Freud grapples with his previous distinctions between instincts and elaborates on the vicissitudes of the sexual instinct, including its relationship to love. He proposes that love has three paired opposites: loving and hating, loving and being loved, and loving and indifference. Freud recognizes that love cannot simply be a component of the sexual instinct. He suggests that the term love be reserved for the relation of the total ego to its object after there is a synthesis of the component sexual instincts under the primacy of the genitals in the service of reproduction.

Freud, Sigmund (1918b). The taboo of virginity. *Standard Edition*, 11:192-208. London: Hogarth Press, 1953.

[See Chapter 1 for annotation.]

Abraham, Karl (1924). A short study of the development of the libido, viewed in the light of mental disorders. In: *Selected Papers of Karl Abraham, M.D.* New York: Brunner/Mazel, 1979, pp. 418-502.

[See Chapter 2 for annotation.]

Ferenczi, Sandor (1924). Thalassa: A theory of genitality. *Psychoanal. Q.*, 2:361-403, 1933; continued in 3:1-29, 1934.

In this historically interesting article, Ferenczi explains the symbolic meaning of coitus. He focuses especially on the male experience as an attempt to return to the mother's womb through a threefold identification: identification of the whole organism with the genital, identification with the partner, and identification with the sexual secretion. He then extends this explanation to include motives for evolution of the species.

Horney, Karen (1928). The problem of the monogamous ideal. *Int. J. Psycho-Anal.*, 9:318-331.

[See Chapter 2 for annotation.]

Horney, Karen (1932b). Problems of marriage. In: *Feminine Psychology*, ed. H. Kelman. New York: Norton, pp. 119-132, 1967.

Horney explores intrapsychic impediments to the maintenance of a good marriage that are determined by early childhood factors and are independent of the personality of the partner. Most important is the illusion that the spouse will fulfill all of one's desires. Numerous clinical examples are given.

Klein, Melanie (1937). Love, guilt and reparation. In: *Love, Guilt and Reparation*. London: Virago Press, pp. 306-343, 1988.

Klein focuses on the child's early impulses and unconscious feelings and fantasies in relation to later love relations. She argues that the guilt resulting from hate of the frustrating parent can be undone by loving as a spouse and parent. Ideal love relationships in marriage and parenthood are described. The intrapsychic determinants of various pathological relationships between marital partners and within the family are explored.

Zilboorg, Gregory (1944). Masculine and feminine. *Psychiat.*,7:257-296.

Zilboorg explores the role of hostile envy in men's relationships with women and the consequent structuring of male supremacy in society. The author reviews the evolution of changes in the theoretical understanding of female development proposed by various authors. He then draws on cultural observation, literature, and mythology to develop a "gynaecocentric" basis for the "androcentric" bias in psychoanalytic thinking of that time (1944). Paternity is viewed as an attempt to control women, and as a reaction to perceived female superiority because of childbearing. This article remains provocative and of interest. [See also Chapter 4.]

Balint, Michael (1947). On genital love. In: *Primary Love and Psychoanalytic Technique*, ed. E. Jones. New York: Liverright, 1953, pp. 128-140.

Noting the tendency of previous writers to define genital love in terms of what it is not, Balint explores various positive definitions. He contends that genital love is a misnomer for a state of being that does not really exist. The condition referred to as genital love results from a fusion of disagreeing elements: genital satisfaction and pregenital tenderness. The expression of this fusion is "genital identification," and the reward for bearing the strain of this fusion is the joy of full orgasm.

Novey, Samuel (1955). Some philosophical speculations about the concept of the genital character. *Int. J. Psycho-Anal.*, 36:88-94.

The author expands Fenichel's classical definition of the term genital character, which depends on the supremacy of the libidinal drive, as demonstrated by adequate genital functioning to denote maturity. Because this definition does not explain the coincident psychological concomitants of maturity of object relationships and of the aggressive drive, Novey, drawing from Winnicott and Sperling, attempts to supply a theoretical substructure to support his ideas. His thesis is based on a pessimistic attitude that a healthy, mature man assumes the "delusion" that his life is meaningful and that he looks upon himself as purposeful and unitary. Thus, Novey concludes, psychoanalysis does not allow one to deal with "inner reality" but can only alter a malfunctioning personal myth so that it functions better.

Sherfey, Mary Jane (1966). The evolution and nature of female sexuality in relation to psychoanalytic theory. *J. Amer. Psychoanal. Assn.*, 14:28-128.

This article is the first attempt to incorporate Masters and Johnson's (1966) research into psychoanalytic theory. Sherfey disagrees with the concept that the vaginal orgasm is distinct from clitoral orgasm. She contends that the rise of civilization is dependent on the suppression of the cyclic sexual drive of women. Suppression is necessary because women's uncurtailed, continuous hypersexuality drastically interferes with maternal responsibilities, and large families are mandatory for an agricultural economy. Thus, Sherfey adds yet another dimension to the unconscious motive for male supremacy. [See also Chapter 18.]

Berezin, Martin (1969). Reporter, Panel: The theory of genital primacy in the light of ego psychology. *J. Amer. Psychoanal. Assn.*, 17:968-987.

Ross, Myerson, Lichtenstein, Sarlin, and Berezin participate in a panel organized to reexamine one of the oldest, accepted psychoanalytic concepts, genital primacy. The panelists agree that the capacity for orgastic gratification in itself is not an indication that the genital phase has been attained. Sarlin adds that the final stage of psychosexual development refers specifically and exclusively to the development of the ego and to superego control and sublimation of the libidinal and aggressive drives. This panel report proposes a number of theoretical questions to be answered by future research.

Ross, Nathaniel (1970). The primacy of genitality in the light of ego psychology. *J. Amer. Psychoanal. Assn.*, 18:267-284.

Stating that it is no longer possible to maintain that libidinal development and the maturation of the personality are dependent variables, Ross challenges the theory of genital primacy. He cites clinical material that contradicts the theory that firm establishment of genital primacy is dependent on mature object relations. An ego-psychological approach is proposed.

Sarlin, Charles (1970). The current status of the concept of genital primacy. *J. Amer. Psychoanal. Assn.*, 18:285-299.

This theoretical paper defines genital primacy as the end stage of psychosexual development, based on the capacity of the ego for sublimation and control of both libidinal and aggressive instinctual drives. Sarlin cites both cross-cultural customs of maternal infant care and adult symptomatologies to demonstrate that the psychosexual level of development of the mother determines the characterological patterns of both men and women of the next generation. Some of the ideas are useful for teaching, yet also controversial.

Bergmann, Martin (1971). Psychoanalytic observations on the capacity to love. In: *Separation-Individuation. Essays in Honor of Margaret S. Mahler*, ed. J. McDevitt and C. Settlage. New York: International Universities Press, pp. 15-40.

Concepts of love are illustrated by quotations from Greek mythology, the Bible, literature, and numerous psychoanalysts, including Freud, Fromm, Reik, Jacobson, Abraham, and Mahler. Bergmann finds that three perspectives have been present in the theories of love: a genetic perspective, seeing love as a rediscovery of the early love object; an economic perspective, holding that love results from the transformation of narcissistic libido into object libido; and a developmental perspective, in which love is the automatic byproduct of past psychosexual phases in healthy development. According to Bergmann, the work of Mahler provides psychoanalysis with a conceptual framework to clarify the genetic perspective of love. He feels that love revives feelings and archaic ego states that were once active in the symbiotic phase, if not the direct memories themselves. Successful resolution of the separation-individuation phase is necessary for one to be alone with the love object and also separate, thus enabling love. Bergmann contends that only love from one person in early infancy can assure later happiness and that the assumption of maternal functions in early infancy by multiple caretakers, including fathers, later results in people who are incapable of loving. This controversial article demonstrates an impressive breadth of knowledge and can be psychoanalytically useful.

Moulton, Ruth (1972). The fear of female power. *J. Amer. Acad. Psychoanal.*, 5:499-519.

Illustrations of how the new feminism of the last decade has stimulated age-old fears of female power in both men and women are presented. Examples from social anthropology and mythology demonstrate how men learned to use their physical power to combat their fear of magical female power. The clinical material includes treatment of couples and individuals.

Bak, Robert (1973). Being in love and object loss. *Int. J. Psycho-Anal.*, 54:1-8.

Bak views being in love, which he calls the transitory grande passion, as occurring within a triad, midway between mourning and melancholia. All three conditions involve a hypercathexis of and identification with the object and a loss of the object or of symbolic object representations. Bak proposes that being in love is also preceded by separation or loss and aims to undo loss by the restitution of the lost object. When attempts at substitution are unsuccessful, love may turn into acute melancholia and suicide, thus explaining the love and suicide motif in history and literature. Many examples of this motif are offered as Bak integrates the role of aggression with the state of being in love. This article is a major contribution to the psychoanalytic understanding of love.

Kernberg, Otto (1974a). Barriers to falling and remaining in love. *J. Amer. Psychoanal. Assn.*, 22:486-511.

Kernberg proposes that the achievement of two major developmental stages are necessary to the establishment of the normal capacity for falling and remaining in love. The first stage is the integration of early oral and skin erotism with later, more mature object relations. The second stage is the capacity for full genital enjoyment, including complementary sexual identification. Clinical material illustrates barriers particular to different diagnostic categories. Narcissistic personalities must overcome unconscious devaluation of the love object. Borderline patients must work through their reliance on splitting to resolve their pregenital conflicts. Neurotic patients and those with less severe character pathology must resolve unconscious oedipal conflicts to allow the capacity for falling in love to mature into the capacity for a lasting love relation. This is a clearly written article, rich in clinical material and useful for the teaching of psychopathology.

Kernberg, Otto (1974b). Mature love: Prerequisites and characteristics. *J. Amer. Psychoanal. Assn.*, 22:743-767.

Whereas his previous article (Kernberg, 1974a) focused primarily on interferences with the capacity to fall in love, this article illuminates the definition of mature love. Mature love is present when there is confidence that mutual empathy and implicit collusion in full expressions of sexuality, violent anger, attack, and rejection can be contained within an overall loving relation that also has periods of quiet and a sharing of internal life. Kernberg elaborates on the consistencies between his own ideas and those of others. He illustrates the prerequisites for and characteristics of mature love by examples from adolescence and middle age.

Dinnerstein, Dorothy (1976). *The Mermaid and the Minotaur*. New York: Harper and Row.

This book is a thoughtful feminist application of psychoanalytic theory to problems in the organization of the traditional family. It explores the psychological motives for both love and the relationship between the sexes. Dinnerstein traces the intricate network of intrapsychic factors that reinforce such sociocultural standards as female-dominated childcare, male prerogatives for sexual possessiveness, and the long-standing subjugation of women. She offers a detailed explanation of how these arrangements allow both sexes to reexperience the early mother-child relationship. Dinnerstein feels that deep psychological motives maintain these traditional arrangements, which then compromise both sexes, and these motives must be understood in order to fully effect the adaptive changes necessary for survival of our species. She recommends that equal responsibility of the sexes for early infant care could change the common destructive psychological confusion between closeness to women and one's infantile experiences. [See also Chapter 5.]

Woods, Sherwyn (1976). Some dynamics of male chauvinism. *Arch. Gen. Psychiat.*, 33:63-65.

The defensive function of male chauvinism is explored in 11 men. The author illustrates how chauvinistic attitudes defend against anxiety and shame from four prime sources: unresolved infantile strivings and regressive wishes, hostile envy of women, oedipal anxiety, and power and dependency conflicts related to masculine self-esteem. Clinical examples are provided.

Altman, Leon (1977). Some vicissitudes of love. *J. Amer. Psychoanal. Assn.*, 25:35-52.

Altman outlines the vicissitudes of the experience of love that have contributed to the lack of a coherent theory of love. He views fixations at various developmental ages as factors determining future capacity for love. Thus, love for a neonate is objectless and consists of body pleasure. After individuation, a love affair with someone other than oneself becomes possible. This capacity intensifies during latency and adolescence, when love is both instinctualized altruism and self-seeking. These two components are at war until the "flush of love" (p. 40) results, when loved ones are placed above all else. Marriage tests all expectations and overestimations with an inevitable feeling of chagrin. Recompense comes with grandchildren, who restore the wounded narcissism with the illusion of immortality. Altman believes that the transformation of the joys of love into suffering and sorrow occurs through repression and ambivalence. He concludes with an explanation of why women seem to be more faithful to their commitments. He suggests that little girls' renunciation of their mother as love object prepares them for later renunciations. Although the arguments in this article are disjointed, they are thought provoking.

Benedek, Therese (1977). Ambivalence, passion and love. *J. Amer. Psychoanal. Assn.*, 25:53-80.

Benedek offers the concept of primary ambivalence as an alternative theory to the death instinct. The sexual instinct is experienced as a drive. If this drive is intense and frustrated, then the sexual tension dissociates, leading to anxiety and anger, a state of primary ambivalence. Benedek believes that this primary ambivalence was the state that primitive humans needed to repress. Further, it is primary ambivalence of the sexual instinct, along with men's awe of females' procreative ability, that results in men's fear of women. Benedek illustrates these points with examples from primitive cultures epitomized by the Magna Mater. The fear of the other sex, resulting in sexual tension and attraction, is a derivative of the instinctual ambivalence overcome by the ritual of courtship. Benedek contrasts passion, which she equates with sexual love and orgasm, to the love necessary to maintain a lasting marriage. Permanence depends on a stable ego organization that can adapt to the changing aspects of love. Although this article is complicated, it presents a novel perspective on instinct theory and love.

Kernberg, Otto (1977). Boundaries and structure in love relationships. *J. Amer. Psychoanal. Assn.*, 25:81-114.

Kernberg reviews his previous articles on love as well as the work of others, particularly some French authors whose work has not yet been translated. He focuses on the various developmental phases necessary for the attainment of adult genitality in boys and girls. Boys must overcome their primitive envy and fear of women and identify with a generous, non-repressive father. For girls, the mother's conflict over her own femininity brings about inhibited psychosexual development, which is reinforced by penis envy and the repression of sexual competitiveness with the oedipal mother. Holding a secret, unconscious hope that by turning to their father vaginal genitality will be confirmed, girls keep genital issues private. Successful identification with adult genitality enables the experience of sexual passion in orgasm, which is an emotional state that expresses the crossing of boundaries and allows for a transient merger. Orgasm also encompasses the fantasied union of the oedipal parents and a repetition/abandonment of the oedipal relation in a new object relation that reconfirms autonomy and identity. Kernberg stresses that sexual passion is a permanent feature of love relations and provides a consolidation and renovation of love. Clinical examples of mature love and disturbed love relations are offered.

Moulton, Ruth (1977a). Some effects of the new feminism. *Amer. J. Psychiat.*, 134:1-6.

Moulton compares the presenting complaints of female patients in the 1950s with those of female patients in the 1970s. Some of these women were in analysis, but symptoms are described with an emphasis on sociocultural pressures. Women in the earlier period had frequent sexual difficulties, often with total anorgasmia. In the later period, the most common complaints involve conflicts between professional life and family responsibilities resulting in role strain.

Moulton, Ruth (1977b). Women with double lives. *Contemp. Psychoanal.*, 13:64-84.

Twenty-five patients, all professional women who conducted enduring extramarital affairs, are described. They complained that their marriages were failing to provide sufficient intimacy, dependent gratification, or mentorship for professional activity. Analytic findings included negative identifications with mother, fathers who were supportive but then withdrew, and deep dependency conflicts. Some patients had intrasystemic conflicts about autonomy and the feminine ego ideal and sought affairs for reassurance. This article contains clinical examples within an interpersonal approach.

Kaufman, Irving (1978). Marital adaptation in the aging. In: *Normal Psychology of the Aging Process*, ed. N. Zinberg and I. Kaufman. New York: International Universities Press, pp. 187-202.

[See Chapter 15 for annotation.]

Lerner, Harriet (1978). Adaptive and pathogenic aspects of sex-role stereotypes. *Amer. J. Psychiat.*, 135:48-52. Also in: *Women in Therapy*. Northvale, NJ: Aronson, 1988, pp. 79-92.

The author highlights the pitfalls of making generalizations that sex-role stereotypes are either adaptive or pathogenic. Clinical vignettes demonstrate the need to evaluate the defensive or organizing purpose served by the stereotype within the individual. [See also Chapter 5.]

Bergmann, Martin (1980). On the intrapsychic function of falling in love. *Psychoanal. Q.*, 49:56-77.

This article analyzes the metapsychology of loving. A review of the literature includes Freud's thinking about falling in love as well as that of several other psychoanalytic authors. Falling in love is compared to dreaming and is defined as an ego function. The five tasks of the ego for successful loving are: to observe the real qualities of the love object, to integrate the object representations of previous love objects through condensation, to counteract the force of the superego, to counteract the id demand for a replication of symbiosis, and finally, to counteract the pressure of the repetition compulsion in order to find other solutions. Bergmann asserts that a particular person is chosen as a love object when that person fulfills and reinstates the lost ideal ego state of symbiosis. He concludes by discussing the transformation that is required to move from "falling in love" to "enduring love."

Kernberg, Otto (1980). Love, the couple and the group: A psychoanalytic frame. *Psychoanal. Q.*, 49:78-108.

Kernberg asserts that sexual love between a couple always occurs in open or secret opposition to the surrounding social group and that sexual intimacy is by nature rebellious and unconventional. There is an equilibrium between forces for formation and dissolution of couples within the group. Boredom and indifference in marital relationships can be understood as the consequence of both denial of intense ambivalence and lack of contact with intense needs. Sexual experience, object relations, and superego integration all affect the couple's stability within the group. Clinical cases illustrate these ideas and specific psychopathologies.

Person, Ethel (1980). Sexuality as the mainstay of identity: Psychoanalytic perspectives. *Signs*, 5:605-630.

Person notes that women consolidate gender identity by means other than genital (sexual) functioning. The difference in the primacy of sexuality has implications for relations between the sexes, and power and dependency needs. [See also Chapter 18.]

Nadelson, Carol and Notman, Malkah (1981). To marry or not to marry. *Amer. J. Psychiat.*, 138:352-356. Also in: *The Woman Patient: Concepts of Femininity and the Life Cycle*, Vol. 2, ed. C. Nadelson and M. Notman. New York: Plenum Press, 1982b, pp. 111-120.

This article surveys data on marriage with an emphasis on shifts in marriage patterns due to the wider choices available to women and the effect of these shifts on young adult development. The authors note that any decision, whether to marry with or without children or whether to remain single, has unconscious determinants that may be more or less conflictual.

Miller, Jean Baker (1982). Conflict and psychological development: Women in the family. In: *The Women As Patient: Aggression, Adaptations and Psychotherapy*, Vol. 3, ed. M. Notman and C. Nadelson. New York: Plenum Press, pp. 287-299.

Miller uses a case study to illustrate the difficulties which can occur within a marriage when the possibility for continued psychological growth for either partner is curtailed. The couple's collusion to avoid conflict led to the homemaker wife's growing resentment and depression.

Nadelson, Carol, Polonsky, Derek, and Mathews, Mary Alice (1982). Marriage and midlife: The impact of social change. In: *The Woman Patient: Concepts of Femininity and the Life Cycle*, Vol. 2, ed. C. Nadelson and M. Notman, New York: Plenum Press, pp. 145-158.

This chapter focuses on the impact of social change on marital adjustment in midlife. The authors present several case illustrations of middle-aged couples facing various developmental crises.

Cantor, Dorothy (1986). Marriage and divorce: The search for adult identity. In: *The Psychology of Today's Woman: New Psychoanalytic Visions*, ed. T. Bernay and D. Cantor. Hillsdale, NJ: The Analytic Press, pp. 195-210.

Cantor considers marriage as a developmental task requiring the attainment of new object relations and allowing for increased autonomy. She differentiates between marital conflict reflecting unresolved oedipal conflicts and marital conflict related to the separation-individuation of one spouse and the reaction of the other. She applies Mahler's concepts of separation-individuation to her thesis that an adult can experience marriage as a recreation in fantasy of the mother-child dyad. Clinical examples illustrate the theories presented.

Chodorow, Nancy (1986b). Divorce, oedipal asymmetries and the marital age gap. *Psychoanal. Rev.*, 73: 606-610.

This article suggests that prevalent marital patterns, in which men tend to marry younger women or women the same age, enable men to avoid the common male fear of women of equal or superior power. Women, by complement, are likely to find older men somewhat more tolerant of intimacy and dependency needs in themselves and to be more nurturant and capable of intimacy. With the increasing divorce and remarriage rate, with which the marital age gap widens, this solution perpetuates sexual inequality and makes it increasingly hard for heterosexual women to find intimacy as they get older.

Person, Ethel (1986). Working mothers: Impact on the self, the couple and the children. In: *The Psychology of Today's Woman: New Psychoanalytic Visions*, ed. T. Bernay and D. Cantor. Hillsdale, NJ: The Analytic Press, pp. 121-138.

[See Chapter 14 for annotation.]

Bergmann, Martin (1988). Freud's three theories of love in the light of later developments. *J. Amer. Psychoanal. Assn.*, 36:653-672.

Bergmann suggests that Freud formulated three theories of love within the topographic frame of reference. Freud's first theory, appearing in "Three Essays on Sexuality" (1905b), was a genetic theory; the second theory was associated with the discovery of narcissism (1914). The third theory was developed in "Instincts and Their Vicissitudes" (1915b), where Freud shifted from an instinctual to an ego perspective. Bergmann poses and explores the question of why love is so central to human existence.

Goldberger, Marianne (1988). The two-man phenomenon. *Psychoanal. Q.*, 57:229-233.

In this brief article, the not uncommon phenomenon of women who form long-term stable relationships with two men simultaneously is described. Common dynamic features include early marriage, defenses against awareness of unrequited conflicted longings for intimacy with their mothers, reawakening of these longings when their children grow older, and pleasure in the intimacy with lovers that derives from the men's feminine identifications.

Gaylin, Willard and Person, Ethel (ed.)(1988). *Passionate Attachments: Thinking about Love.* New York: Free Press.

Passionate love and other types of attachment are explored in this book which contains a collection of essays by psychoanalysts, philosophers, educators, theologians, and historians. The book evolved out of an interdisciplinary conference about love.

Gilligan, Carol and Stern, Eve (1988). The riddle of femininity and the psychology of love. In: *Passionate Attachments: Thinking about Love*, ed. W. Gaylin and E. Person. New York: Free Press, pp. 101-114.

The authors use the myth of Eros and Psyche to suggest that the issue of objectification is a problem of both Western culture and female adolescent development. Women become aware during adolescence that men's stories about love impose a division between women's roles as mother and as lover and that those stories treat women as the object rather than as the subject of the love experience. In the myth, Psyche struggles against isolation and objectification; she violates the prohibition against seeing her husband Eros, and she gains a sense of her own experience. The authors argue that women must integrate being both mother and lover, so that love becomes a matter of relationship and knowledge rather than of mystery and self-absorption.

Kernberg, Otto (1988). Between conventionality and aggression. In: *Passionate Attachments: Thinking about Love*, ed. W. Gaylin and E. Person. New York: Free Press, pp. 63-83.

This is a complex article in which Kernberg proposes that in healthy sexual passion, polymorphous perverse tendencies are not necessarily subordinate to genital intercourse, but rather are a part of normal love relations. Fantasy heightens sexual passion and allows for the integration of love and aggression within the love relation. Two types of triangulation are described: direct and reverse, which can be either destructive or supportive. Kernberg also elaborates on the role of each partner's superego functioning in the couple's relationship. He concludes with a historical review of the interplay between the dynamics of the couple and those of the social group.

Person, Ethel (1988). *Dreams of Love and Fateful Encounters: The Power of Romantic Passion.* New York: Norton.

This book discusses the phenomenon of falling in love and romantic passionate love from psychoanalytic and philosophical viewpoints. The author contends that romantic love can facilitate change, both through new identifications the lover forms with the love object and by reworking old conflicts. Person discusses differences between the existential, or normal, problems of love (which are intrinsic in the very aims of love) and the neurotic distortions of love. The major distortions of love include surrender, domination, triangulation, and disillusionment. Similarities and differences between falling in love in life and in therapy are explored. Whereas the author posits that the experience of loving is the same for both sexes, she explores the developmental, psychological, and cultural factors that produce somewhat different gender distortions in love. Examples are drawn from life, literature, and film. This book differs from the other major works on love in its emphasis on the transformative nature of love and its creative potential.

Viederman, Milton (1988). The nature of passionate love. *Passionate Attachments: Thinking about Love,* ed. W. Gaylin and E. Person. New York: Free Press, pp. 1-14.

Viederman relates passionate love to mystery and danger, and to the development of new self-representations.

Kirkpatrick, Martha (1989b). Women in love in the 80s. *J. Amer. Acad. Psychoanal.,* 17:535-542.

Kirkpatrick asserts that the basis for the development of the mature capacity to love in women is an early close attachment of daughter to mother, rather than being based on drive development as classical theory had emphasized. Intimacy with other women remains essential support for feminine gender identity and self-worth. The change in sexual object rests on successful internalization of the mother and her approval as well as on father's welcoming and alliance in separating from mother. Girls share the capacity for intimacy with both mother and father, but do not abandon mother. Women suffer more from the isolation of the nuclear family because of its limited intimacy. Lesbian love relations, by contrast, may be troubled by excessive intimacy or by confusion of intimacy with merger. Current marital patterns suggest that mate selection is more practical than romantic, and is related to anticipation of a family. [See also Chapter 18.]

Kernberg, Otto (1991). Perversity and love in the relationship of the couple. In: *The Perversions and Near Perversions in Clinical Practice: New Psychoanalytic Perspectives*, ed. G. Fogel and W. Myers, New Haven, CT: Yale University Press.

Kernberg notes that the recruitment of hatred in the service of love is essential for sexual excitement, romantic love, and commitment. He discusses how the cumulative enactment of dissociated unconscious scenarios between couples may strengthen intimacy or bring about destructive discontinuities.

# Chapter 14

# Pregnancy and Motherhood

Eleanor Schuker and Mary H. Shwetz
Additional contributions by Ingrid Pisetsky

The current psychoanalytic literature on pregnancy and motherhood reflects an expanding and complex field. Pregnancy and motherhood are developmental experiences that may occur as early as adolescence and continue into later adult life. Interest in both childbearing and childrearing has early roots and is affected by many psychodynamic factors during key periods of personality formation as well as by social influences. Freud (1925) viewed the wish for a baby as compensatory, derived from penis envy and then, later, from an identification with maternal activity (Freud, 1933). Deutsch (1945), also writing with an emphasis on instinctual drives, saw maternal functioning as part of the interplay between normal feminine masochism and narcissism. She delineated many aspects of motherliness, including its derivatives in the preoedipal mother-daughter relationship.

By the 1950s and 1960s, analysts were differentiating the motives for childbearing from those for childrearing. Bibring (1959, 1961) and Benedek (1960) undertook systematic studies of the interaction of psychological and physiological factors during pregnancy and the menstrual cycle. These authors conceptualized pregnancy as a developmental crisis entailing a loosening of defenses and an opportunity for reworking unresolved conflicts from all phases of development. This reworking was thought to facilitate the transition to motherhood.

Much of the current literature on the transition to motherhood during pregnancy uses a multidimensional framework involving the drives, object relations, and ego-developmental processes. Many writers contend that the psychobiological vicissitudes of pregnancy and motherhood are not merely adaptations but figure rather as potent psychic reorganizers, adding to the continuum of personality development beyond adolescence. This view remains controversial, however, and some authors (e.g., Lester and Notman, 1988) find evidence that normal regressive processes during pregnancy do not always lead to new psychic reorganization. The qualitative experiences of pregnancy and motherhood may be largely shaped by a woman's preoedipal experience with her own mother. Identifications with the maternal ego ideal, oedipal resolutions, adolescent reworking, cultural influences, and realignments in mental organization during pregnancy may all affect maternal capacities and interests. The experiences of pregnancy and motherhood are now viewed as opportunities rather than requirements for feminine maturity. A woman's sense of her reproductive potential remains an important component of femininity.

This chapter also includes articles on typical developmental problems and challenges related to pregnancy and the mothering experience. It features articles on such subjects as role conflicts, elective abortion, infanticidal conflicts, miscarriage, pseudocyesis, and infertility. These areas are still infrequently explored in the psychoanalytic literature, although some topics have been written about more frequently in sociological, psychological, and general psychiatric journals. The psychoanalytic literature on maternal relinquishment and the experience of adoptive parenthood is surprisingly sparse. Here, hypotheses differentiating pregnancy from motherhood experiences might be well tested. The reader is referred to Chapters 6 and 18 for other annotations studying the interrelation between body-image development and maternal interests and capacities. Chapter 11 includes several articles on motherhood and career issues. (E.S. and M.S.)

**Freud, Sigmund (1917). On transformation of instinct as exemplified in anal eroticism.** *Standard Edition*, 17:126-133. London: Hogarth Press, 1953.

Freud asserts that feces, penis, and baby are interchangeable symbols in the female unconscious. [See Chapter 1 for annotation.]

**Marcinowski, J. (1921). Two confinement dreams of a pregnant woman.** *Int. J. Psycho-Anal.*, 2:432-434.

Material from two brief dreams is presented, as reported by a pregnant woman in analysis four weeks prior to delivery. In both dreams, the dreamer appears to reexperience memories of her own birth.

**Deutsch, Helene (1925a). The psychology of women in relation to the function of reproduction.** *Int. J. Psycho-Anal.*, 6:405-418. Also in: *The Psychoanalytic Reader*, ed. R. Fliess. New York: International Universities Press, 1948, pp. 165-179.

Deutsch regards childbirth and motherhood as a part of normal feminine masochism and a prerequisite for maternal adaptation. Like Freud, she feels that the wish for a baby is secondary to the wish for a penis and that little girls are unaware of the existence of their vagina prior to puberty. Deutsch acknowledges the importance of the pregenital mother-daughter relationship to the sexuality of women. [See also Chapter 2.]

Freud, Sigmund (1925). Some psychical consequences of the anatomical distinction between the sexes. *Standard Edition*, 19:243-258. London: Hogarth Press, 1953.

Freud explicitly states that the wish for a baby is secondary to the wish for a penis. [See Chapter 1 for annotation.]

Horney, Karen (1926). The flight from womanhood. *Int. J. Psycho-Anal.*, 12:360-374. Also in: *Feminine Psychology*, ed. H. Kelman. New York: Norton, 1967, pp. 54-70.

Horney stresses that the wish for motherhood is primary and that motherhood can bring joy and has its own value. [See Chapter 2 for annotation.]

Klein, Melanie (1928). Early stages of the Oedipus conflict. In: *Love, Guilt and Reparation and Other Works: The Writings of Melanie Klein*, Vol. 1. London: Hogarth Press, 1975, pp. 186-198.

According to Klein, girls fear that their mother will destroy their capacity for motherhood and so fear that the contents of their body will be robbed, destroyed, or mutilated. [See Chapter 7 for annotation.]

Freud, Sigmund (1933). Femininity. *Standard Edition*, 22:112-135. London: Hogarth Press, 1953.

Freud views the wish for a baby as derived from penis envy. Girls' wish for a baby is a reparative, secondary, and compensatory wish for the penis their mother failed to give them, in contrast to a primary instinctual wish derived from little girls' feminine identification with their mother. Freud states that early doll play does not express a primary feminine instinctual wish for a baby but, instead, represents a wish to do actively for the doll what was done for the girl by her mother. He asserts that little girls identify with the cared-for baby. [See also Chapter 1.]

Jones, Ernest (1933). The phallic phase. *Int. J. Psycho-Anal.*, 14:1-13.

Jones emphasizes that femininity is primary, as is the wish for a baby. [See Chapter 2 for annotation.]

Payne, Sylvia (1935). A concept of femininity. *Br. J. Med. Psychol.*, 15:18-33.

The need to be pregnant is connected with wishes to control the oral sadistic infant self. [See also Chapter 2.]

Jacobson, Edith (1936). On the development of a girl's wish for a child. *Psychoanal. Q.*, 37:523-538, 1968.

The case illustrates Freud's description of girls' resolution of penis envy by wishing for a child. [See Chapter 2 for annotation.]

Warburg, Bettina (1938). Suicide, pregnancy, and rebirth. *Psychoanal. Q.*, 7:490-506.

The case of a woman with a severe obsessional neurosis and a congenital deformity is presented to demonstrate preoedipal and oedipal factors that underlie her obsession with suicide, pregnancy, and rebirth.

Brunswick, Ruth Mack (1940). The preoedipal phase of the libido development. *Psychoanal. Q.*, 9:293-319. Also in: *The Psychoanalytic Reader*, ed. R. Fliess. New York: International Universities Press, 1948, pp. 261-284.

According to Mack Brunswick, Freud conceded that the wish for a baby preceded the girl's turn to her father. The girl understands that the baby wish, and not the penis wish, is possible and permissible. [See also Chapter 1.]

Kestenberg, Judith (1941). Mother types encountered in child guidance clinics. *Amer. J. Orthopsychiat.*, 11:475-484. Also revised and reprinted in: *Children and Parents*. New York: Aronson, 1975, pp. 63-74.

This is the first of Kestenberg's contributions on the problems of motherhood. She discusses the fantasies of three types of mothers. One type has attempted to solve her infantile problems by means of the fantasy that when she has her own children her difficulties will vanish. A second type, the aggressive mother, manifests the fantasy wish to do to her children what was done to her. The third type, the anxious mother, feels that having children demonstrates genital intactness. Kestenberg notes that many women, not included in these three types, also have the wish to treat their children better than they were treated in childhood.

Moulton, Ruth (1942). Psychosomatic implications of pseudocyesis. *Psychosom. Med.*, 4:376-389.

Symptoms of pseudocyesis are delineated, including amenorrhea (nine months or longer), abdominal enlargement, sensations of fetal movement, breast changes (including secretion), gastrointestinal symptoms, labor pains, and uterine enlargement and cervical softening. Similar symptoms in animal models are reviewed, such as those induced by stimulation of the cervical canal or the anterior pituitary and by use of vitamin E. Several clinical cases with varying aspects of the syndrome are described, including some with persistent corpus luteum. In one adolescent case, hysterical mechanisms, sexual prohibitions with oedipal guilt, and wishes for a baby were prominent. This patient's physical symptoms may have been produced by air swallowing, a lordotic posture, and pituitary suppression of ovarian activity.

Deutsch, Helene (1945). *The Psychology of Women: A Psychoanalytic Interpretation*, Vol. 2. New York: Grune and Stratton.

Deutsch writes comprehensively on the subject of reproductive functioning and mothering in Volume II. Each chapter richly and systematically reviews topics, including the sex act, motherhood, problems with conception, pregnancy, abortion, delivery, lactation, first mother-infant relations, the mother-child relationship, adoption, being a step-mother, and the climacterium. Deutsch differentiates motherhood from motherliness. Motherhood is the psychobiosocial relatedness of the mother to the child, whereas motherliness is the characterological capacity of a woman to relate to a child's helplessness. She observes that mothers want to perpetuate themselves in their relationship with their daughters, and she stresses the importance of the preoedipal mother-daughter relationship in the development of femininity. Deutsch asserts that the qualities that contribute to femininity, including a harmonious interplay between narcissism and masochism, must also be present in motherly women. The chapter on pregnancy describes the natural state of pregnancy, as well as the psychological reasons for sterility and abortion. Many case histories illustrate her salient and timely perspectives. [See also Chapter 22.]

Jacobson, Edith (1946). A case of sterility. *Psychoanal. Q.,* 15:330-350.

The analysis of an anovulatory woman seeking adoption is discussed. [See Chapter 23 for annotation.]

Benedek, Therese (1952b). Infertility as a psychosomatic defense. *Fertility and Sterility*, 3:527-537.

Benedek discusses her psychoanalytic research on the hormonal influences of the different stages of the menstrual cycle. She asserts that both fertility and infertility may be the result of unconscious influences derived from the early mother-daughter interaction. Multiple pregnancies may indicate a fear of sexuality and the wish to avoid it by becoming pregnant. Inability to conceive may represent a somatic defense against conflicts about procreation. Modern society with its emphasis on activity in women may promote conflict with motherhood, a developmental stage that requires a passive-receptive mode.

Bartemeier, Leo (1954). A psychoanalytic study of pregnancy in an 'as if' personality. *Int. J. Psycho-Anal.*, 35:214-219.

Clinical material from the analysis of a woman with an 'as if' personality is presented, including her reactions to pregnancy and delivery and her relationships to her children. The patient was unable to establish true identifications with either parent, so that later parental behavior was narcissistic and ridden with pregenital impulses.

Kestenberg, Judith (1956a). On the development of maternal feelings in early childhood: Observations and reflections. *The Psychoanalytic Study of the Child*, 11:257-291. New York: International Universities Press.

Kestenberg discusses activity and passivity as expressions of vaginal tensions. Passivity enhances the development of affects; activity provides discharge. The biological need to discharge vaginal tensions leads to the development of maternal feeling. Girls' concept of an "anal baby" and an identification with their mother leads them to doll play as a substitute for organ discharge. Vague inner vaginal sensations generate tension and a fertile atmosphere for projection onto body orifices, create an attachment to transitional objects, and lead girls to develop a "fetish" doll baby. Little girls experience the creative illusion of mothering with their doll and its "aliveness." This doll-baby helps them master and discharge inner sensations that cannot otherwise be discharged. With the "death of the doll," girls turn to new phallic-phase interests. Successive and developmentally fixed oral, anal, and phallic representations eventually merge with the final, more realistic image of the vagina and abet the development of motherhood. Each of these representations can contribute to various functions of adult women in their maternal role.

Kestenberg, Judith (1956b). Vicissitudes of female sexuality. *J. Amer. Psychoanal. Assn.*, 4:453-476.

An early preoedipal maternal phase is detailed. [See Chapters 6 and 18 for annotations.]

Fox, Henry (1958). Narcissistic defenses during pregnancy. *Psychoanal. Q.*, 27:340-358.

Clinical material from the analysis of a woman after the birth of her third child and during her fourth pregnancy is presented. While this paper elaborates on dreams and fantasies evoked by pregnancy to illustrate how defenses were used and why pregnancy was so disturbing, the paper fails to provide a cohesive theoretical discussion.

Benedek, Therese (1959). Parenthood as a developmental phase. *J. Amer. Psychoanal. Assn.*, 7:389-417.

This excellent paper proposes that personality development continues beyond adolescence, when psychodynamic processes evoked by reproduction and parenthood act as drive motivations for further psychic development in the mother and father. Reciprocal ego developments take place for both parents and child as an outcome of drive-motivated interpersonal relationships; they are facilitated by the processes of introjection and identification. This article challenges early theories about development, as the author asserts that the Oedipus complex continues to develop with the experience of parenthood, leading to superego modification.

Bibring, Grete (1959). Some considerations of the psychological processes in pregnancy. *The Psychoanalytic Study of the Child*, 14:113-121. New York: International Universities Press.

A significant early contribution to psychoanalytic thinking about pregnancy is presented in this paper. Pregnancy is viewed as a normative crisis and a maturational step that affects all expectant mothers regardless of the state of their psychic health. Women show significant psychological changes during pregnancy, including regression, loosening of defenses agianst early conflicts, and reorganization of defenses. The outcome of pregnancy has profound effects on the subsequent personality development of the mother and the early mother-child relationship.

Benedek, Therese (1960). The organization of the reproductive drive. *Int. J. Psycho-Anal.*, 41:1-15.

Benedek discusses the organization of the reproductive drive and the development of motherliness. The achievement of heterosexual coitus is not the full measure of maturity for female reproductive drive organization. Two additional phases of functioning are necessary, pregnancy and lactation. Benedek reviews her research that uses the psychoanalytic recording of dreams to predict the phases of the menstrual cycle. She finds that sexual inclination is active and object-directed during the estrogen phase of the cycle. Passive and receptive needs occur when progesterone production comes into effect during the luteal phase, and this phase serves as an emotional preparation for motherhood. At the time of ovulation the sexual drive reaches its highest level of integration. Parallel with the low hormonal levels in the premenstrual phase is a regression of psychosexual integration, with a predominance of pregenital manifestations. Benedek concludes that motherliness develops through the cyclic repetition of hormonal stimulation interacting with other aspects of personality development.

Greaves, Donald, Green, Phillip, and West, Louis (1960). Psychodynamic and psychophysiological aspects of pseudocyesis. *Psychosom. Med.,* 22:24-31.

The early psychiatric literature on pseudocyesis is reviewed with a summary of etiology, symptomatology, and treatment. A psychiatric case report illustrates some common psychodynamics, including wishes to secure a husband's unwavering support, fix a failing marriage, bolster femininity, obtain a child as a plaything, and suffer punishment.

Bibring, Grete, Dwyer, Thomas, Huntington, Dorothy, and Valenstein, Arthur (1961). A study of the psychological processes in pregnancy and of the earliest mother-child relationships. *The Psychoanalytic Study of the Child,* 16:9-72. New York: International Universities Press.

The first part of this paper discusses the developmental processes of pregnancy and motherhood and examines the crisis of pregnancy as a normal occurrence and essential part of the growth that precedes and prepares for maturational integration. The second part of this paper is a description and discussion of the methods developed and used for a clinical study of the psychological processes in 15 primigravidae. This paper extends Bibring's (1959) contribution.

Rose, Gilbert (1961). Pregenital aspects of pregnancy fantasies. *Int. J. Psycho-Anal.,* 42:544-549.

Two male cases illustrate how male pregnancy fantasies serve to defend against death wishes, separation anxiety, homosexual anxiety, and omnipotent needs. One female case illuminates how pregenital aspects of pregnancy fantasies contribute to creativity. The author contrasts pre-oedipal hermaphroditic wishes to emulate the active, omnipotent phallic mother who can have babies with later bisexual, oedipal wishes to take mother's place by having babies with father.

Blitzer, John and Murray, John (1964). On the transformation of early narcissism during pregnancy. *Int. J. Psycho-Anal.,* 45:89-97.

The authors review the literature on the meaning of delivery as a narcissistic injury and the role of pregenital fantasies in the genesis of postpartum psychosis and depression. A clinical case illustrates how fantasies of narcissistic entitlement and primitive wish fulfillment may activate postpartum depression. A psychoanalytic understanding of early narcissism can be used in the treatment of pregnant women to prevent postpartum depression. The paper differentiates normal from pathological narcissism in pregnancy.

Moore, Burness (1964). Frigidity: A review of the psychoanalytic literature. *Psychoanal. Q.*, 33:323-349.

Moore views feminine development as predetermined by the biological destiny of motherhood, unless strong disturbances give rise to conflict, which lead to frigidity as a defense. [See Chapter 18 for annotation.]

Gedo, John (1965). Unmarried motherhood: A paradigmatic single case study. *Int. J. Psycho-Anal.*, 46:352-357.

Gedo comments on the paucity of psychoanalytic literature about unmarried motherhood. His patient had given birth to two illegitimate children and placed them for adoption prior to analysis. Genetic and dynamic factors that emerged included the death of her father when she was six-and-a-half years old, identification with an older sister who had an illegitimate pregnancy, and rage and loss connected to a separation from her mother in the second year of life. The conceptions took place on the anniversaries of her father's death, with the pregenital trauma influencing the quality of her oedipal constellation. Revived pregnancy wishes and pseudocyesis emerged during various stages in the transference to relieve empty depression, to reincorporate the father, to regressively deny the need for a man, and to give away a baby to "equalize" the early maternal rejection.

Cohen, Mabel Blake (1966). Personal identity and sexual identity. *Psychiat.*, 29:1-14.

In examining the maturational challenge posed by pregnancy and childbirth, Cohen notes five predominant patterns of maternal response. [See Chapter 12 for annotation.]

Lerner, Burton, Raskin, Raymond, and Davis, Elizabeth (1967). On the need to be pregnant. *Int. J. Psycho-Anal.*, 48:288-297.

The authors review the literature on pregnancy and its motivations and then present the case of a woman with pseudocyesis who had a recurrent wish to live in a pregnant state. Conscious and unconscious motivational factors contributing to the need to be pregnant are discussed in this comprehensive paper. The authors assert that pregnancy in a healthy woman is directed by the desire for motherhood and the capacity for altruistic love. Pregenital needs are viewed as playing a secondary role. As the case illustrates, when pregenital motivations are primary there is a maladaptive effort to resolve conflicts having to do with narcissism, dependency, identity and body image, power, guilt, and pain.

**Schechter, Marshall (1967). Reporter, Panel: Psychoanalytic theory as it relates to adoption. *J. Amer. Psychoanal. Assn.*, 15:695-708.**

Kaplan, Bernard, Lourie, Neubauer and others discuss several issues related to adoptees and adoptive parents, including the typical psychopathologies of adoptees; the timing, nature and mode of "telling" or information transmission; legal issues; and matching of temperaments. Schechter presents a case of a highly disturbed adoptee. Neubauer discusses parental preparation, the family romance, and the incest barrier. Deutsch's comments about adoptive motherhood are quoted extensively by several panelists. Solnit explores narcissistic issues and oedipal conflicts in adoptive mothers and discusses several common fantasies found in analytic material. He expresses optimism for adaptive resolution. Solnit suggests the value of a reciprocating search ("Who am I?" and "Who are you?") over time between adoptive children and parents.

**Calef, Victor (1968). The unconscious fantasy of infanticide manifested in resistance. *J. Amer. Psychoanal. Assn.*, 16:697-710.**

A depressed woman in analysis became pregnant and had an induced abortion. Infanticidal wishes are seen as part of the Oedipus complex, with instinctual and defensive sources. The rational wish to be rid of the pregnancy serves the ego's defensive wish, which arises out of instinctual aggression, but more importantly is determined by the effort to purge oedipal victories and their attendant crimes.

**Abraham, Hilda (1969). New aspects of the psychopathology of patients presenting for termination of pregnancy and abortion on psychoanalytic grounds. *Bull. Menn. Clin.*, 33:265-268.**

Abraham classifies women who sought abortions (and who needed psychiatric permission to do so) according to dynamic factors and unconscious fantasies. The categories of psychopathology ranged from schizoid and psychotic women who used sexual relations as a way of confirming their sense of reality and finding human contact, to more

healthy women who became pregnant during a brief affair. For healthier women, the men were their secret lovers and usually represented the oedipal father.

Calef, Victor (1969). Lady MacBeth and infanticide. *J. Amer. Psychoanal. Assn.*, 17:528-548.

Calef discusses infanticide themes from Shakespeare's "MacBeth." Childlessness is seen as sometimes unconsciously equated with abortion and infanticide. It may represent a defensive wish to deal with oedipal triumphs, which then have to be destroyed. The fantasy of infanticide represents a crime arising from a sense of guilt and an effort to destroy evidence of the more important crime of incest.

Anthony, E. James (1970). The reactions of parents to the oedipal child. In: *Parenthood: Its Psychology and Psychopathology*, ed. E. J. Anthony and T. Benedek. Boston, MA: Little, Brown, pp. 275-288.

Anthony presents clinical vignettes to illustrate the psychodynamic transactions occurring between parents and children of both sexes during the oedipal phase. He asserts that the oedipal phase in children can reactivate the repressed oedipal struggles of their parents, so that the parents transfer onto their children their own sexual and aggressive wishes and feelings from the past.

Anthony, E. James and Benedek, Therese (ed.)(1970). *Parenthood, Its Psychology and Psychopathology*. Boston, MA: Little, Brown.

This richly informative book includes 29 contributions about the psychology and psychopathology of parenthood by many prominent psychoanalytic clinicians as well as by experts from the fields of ethology, anthropology, and sociology. The section on the developmental aspects of parenthood includes clinical papers on pregnancy and on parental reactions to each developmental phase of the child by distinguished experts including Winnicott, Mahler, Anthony, and Kestenberg. The section on clinical attitudes and behavior of parents contains articles about adoption, maternal overprotection, child abuse, and mothers with murderous obsessions. Another section on clinical correlations between parents and children includes studies on the effects of parental pathology on the child. Parenthood is regarded by the editors as a developmental process with psychobiological vicissitudes. [Several contributions are individually annotated in this chapter.]

Anthony, E. James and Kreitman, Norman (1970). Murderous obsessions in mothers toward their children. In: *Parenthood: Its Psychology and Psychopathology*, ed. E. J. Anthony and T. Benedek. Boston, MA: Little, Brown, pp. 479-498.

The authors present their findings on 40 women in therapeutic groups who fell into three diagnostic categories: compulsive-phobic reaction, depressive reaction, and mixed neurotic reaction. The psychodynamics of the murderous relationship between mother and the targeted child in relation to the mother's hostility are presented. Two illustrative clinical cases are discussed.

Benedek, Therese (1970b). Motherhood and nurturing. In: *Parenthood, Its Psychology and Psychopathology*, ed. E. J. Anthony and T. Benedek. Boston, MA: Little, Brown, pp. 153-165.

Benedek proposes that mothering is a drive-motivated function with instinctual origins related not only to pregnancy and the nursing experience but also to the lifelong experience of the sexual response cycle. Primary motherliness is also the result of positive feminine identifications with the preoedipal mother. Motherliness is influenced by ego development, vaginal libido (Kestenberg, 1956a), and maternal identifications involving minute interactions from bodily contact during development. She suggests that there may be subtle restrictions of nursing experiences in our culture that create anxious mothers who lack self-confidence in their intuitive capacities. Maternal separation anxiety may facilitate maternal ambivalence and aggression toward the child. Benedek feels that an active, extraverted "masculine" ego ideal for women in our culture may conflict with the passive and regressive tendencies inherent in propagation, lactation, and bodily care of an infant.

Benedek, Therese (1970c). Parenthood during the life cycle. In: *Parenthood: Its Psychology and Psychopathology*, ed. E. J. Anthony and T. Benedek. Boston, MA: Little, Brown, pp. 185-206.

Benedek regards parenthood as a psychobiologic process that ends only when memory is lost and intrapsychic images fade. Parenthood implies continuous adaptation to physiologic and psychologic changes within the self of a parent, parallel to and in transaction with changes in their children and in their children's expanding world. Benedek organizes parenthood around critical periods divided into early, middle, and late phases. She reviews the manifestations of recurring psychologic conflicts related to parenthood during the life cycle. The early phase of parenthood begins at the conception or birth of the first child and ends when the youngest child

reaches adolescence. The late phase begins with the gradual involution of old age, when grandparenthood is no longer experienced as a new lease on life.

Benedek, Therese (1970d). The psychobiology of pregnancy. In: *Parenthood, Its Psychology and Psychopathology*, ed. E. J. Anthony and T. Benedek. Boston, MA: Little, Brown, pp. 137-151.

Pregnancy is seen as a "critical phase" and a developmental experience that requires physiological and psychological adaptations and leads to a new level of integration. The author reviews her own study of psychological and physiological processes in the menstrual cycle and postulates that pregnancy is an extended luteal (receptive) phase. Psychodynamic processes in normal and pathological pregnancy are discussed in terms of drive organization, regression to the oral (dependent) phase, oedipal derivatives, and infantile fantasies.

Freud, Anna (1970). The concept of the rejecting mother. In: *Parenthood: Its Psychology and Psychopathology*, ed. E. J. Anthony and T. Benedek. Boston, MA: Little, Brown, pp. 376-386.

A. Freud clarifies the concept of the rejecting mother by discussing the various motivations of the mother. She delineates several types of rejection, including rejection resulting from the unwillingness of the mother to take care, abnormality of the mother, separation, inconstancy of feeling, and alternation between rejection and acceptance as well as rejection in spite of devotion. She asserts that only careful evaluation of the reality and fantasy life of the child can help differentiate between willful neglect and fateful situations.

Giovacchini, Peter (1970). Effects of adaptive and disruptive aspects of early object relationships upon later parental functioning. In: *Parenthood: Its Psychology and Psychopathology*, ed. E. J. Anthony and T. Benedek. Boston, MA: Little, Brown, pp. 525-537.

This chapter examines the impact of early object relationships on later parental functioning during children's development. Parents recapitulate with their children the difficulties they had in resolving their own symbiotic phase. Giovacchini, focusing on fixations in the symbiotic phase, found that mothers and fathers who had disturbed early object relations were unable to allow their children to achieve a stage of relative separateness. They required the presence of their children, upon whom they could project unacceptable portions of their destructive self-images, which were largely determined by a nonfunctional, devouring maternal introject.

Jessner, Lucie, Weigert, Edith, and Foy, James (1970). The development of parental attitudes during pregnancy. In: *Parenthood: Its Psychology and Psychopathology*, ed. E. J. Anthony and T. Benedek. Boston, MA: Little, Brown, pp. 209-244.

Using data from a group of culturally similar, contemporary pregnant women who are both married and unmarried, the authors explore aspects of the psychobiology of pregnancy. They discuss the motivations for pregnancy, the development of parental attitudes during pregnancy, and the complexity of problems created by conflicts between the individual's choice and the limitations of his or her personality. They comment briefly on expectant fatherhood.

Kestenberg, Judith (1970). The effect on parents of the child's transition into and out of latency. In: *Parenthood: Its Psychology and Psychopathology*, ed. E. J. Anthony and T. Benedek. Boston, MA: Little, Brown, pp. 289-306.

The author regards parenthood as a developmental phase requiring the flexibility to shift roles and to assign a new identity to children as they mature. In the ego of normal parents, an adaptive regression occurs to the same phase as their children, but this change is limited or isolated from the remainder of parents' ego and superego. Kestenberg includes clinical vignettes and a discussion of her other work on libidinal sensations stemming from the inside of the body during early childhood.

Levy, David (1970). The concept of maternal overprotection. In: *Parenthood: Its Psychology and Psychopathology*, ed. E. Anthony and T. Benedek. Boston, MA: Little, Brown, pp. 387-409.

The chapter reviews earlier theories of maternal overprotection. Levy defines maternal overprotection as excessive maternal care of children characterized by unrestrained contact, infantilization, prevention of independent behavior, and lack or excess of maternal control. The psychopathology of maternal overprotection resembles an obsessional neurosis but may not always be primarily determined by a mother's psychic conflicts, as in the case of a sick child. The relationship between aggressive and maternal behavior is discussed. Levy asserts that a strong maternal drive contributes to the state of being "naturally maternal."

Mahler, Margaret, Pine, Fred, and Bergman, Anni (1970). The mother's reaction to her toddler's drive for individuation. In: *Parenthood: Its Psychology and Psychopathology*, ed. E. J. Anthony and T. Benedek. Boston, MA: Little, Brown, pp. 257-274.

The authors discuss the diverse intrapsychic events in mothers whose toddlers are traversing through the separation-individuation phase. Aspects of object loss and gain in the object relationship to an individuated child are focused on. Data sources include mothers in psychoanalysis, interviews, and an observational study of the mother-child relationship. Clinical vignettes illustrate mothers' reactions to separation-individuation.

Schechter, Marshall (1970). About adoptive parents. In: *Parenthood, Its Psychology and Psychopathology*, ed. E. J. Anthony and T. Benedek. Boston, MA: Little, Brown, pp. 353-371.

Confrontation with infertility is seen as requiring major revision in body image and self-concept. Repeated frustrations in attempts to conceive often contribute to marital tension and sexual constriction. Schechter finds that the wife in an infertile couple often assumes the defect, even if it is not hers, to protect her husband's narcissism. The adoptive parent loses both the opportunity to confirm feminine identification through pregnancy and the support from the community during pregnancy and afterward. Many adoptive families deny differences and feelings of differentness and defect, which are then highlighted by external social attitudes toward adoption. Maladaptive responses of adoptive parents include blaming the child for defect and deprivation; failure to allow separation-individuation in phases from toddlerhood to late adolescence; aggression toward the child for normal omnipotence, aggression, sexuality; and envy of the child's fertility.

Sperling, Melitta (1970). The clinical effects of parental neurosis on the child. In: *Parenthood: Its Psychology and Psychopathology*, ed. E. J. Anthony and T. Benedek. Boston, MA: Little, Brown, pp. 539-569.

Simultaneous and successive analyses of mother and child reveal the subtle verbal and nonverbal communications between mother and child. The significance of the pregenital phase and fixation points in psychosomatic conditions that are consequent to parental neurosis are discussed. The father's role in disturbed mother-child relationships is addressed.

Winnicott, Donald (1970). The mother-infant experience of mutuality. In: *Parenthood: Its Psychology and Psychopathology*, ed. E. J. Anthony and T. Benedek. Boston, MA: Little, Brown, pp. 245-256.

Winnicott asserts that nonverbal experiences between an infant and mother establish a mutuality that unconsciously sets the emotional tone of interpersonal experiences and the emotional coloring throughout life. The meaning of the mutuality of an infant's nonverbal experiences becomes woven into the psychic apparatus and comes into focus in the regression of the psychoanalytic process. A clinical vignette illustrates how primitive mutuality can serve a therapeutic purpose in the psychoanalytic process.

Calef, Victor (1972). The hostility of parents to children: Some notes on infertility, child abuse, and abortion. *Inter. J. Psychoanal. Psychother.*, 1:76-96, 1972.

Using four case histories, two of whom were treated psychoanalytically, Calef discusses the psychological significance of abortion for women. Oedipal dynamics are emphasized; for some women, the pregnancy reflects an oedipal baby that must be destroyed to hide the incestuous wish from early childhood. These women may function well after the abortion. Short-term and long-term effects that follow therapeutic abortion are documented and related to future depressive syndromes. Treatment consists of uncovering the unconscious motivations and linking them to the real loss of the pregnancy. Calef also examines the psychodynamics of infertility, child abuse, and criminal abortion. The paper is clearly written and informative.

Lax, Ruth (1972). Some aspects of the interaction between mother and impaired child: Mother's narcissistic trauma. *Int. J. Psycho-Anal.*, 53:339-344.

A damaged child is experienced by a mother as a narcissistic blow, with ensuing feelings of devaluation of her child and herself and subsequent feelings of depression and worthlessness. The actual magnitude of a child's impairment does not predict the severity of a mother's depression; rather this depends on the extent to which the mother unconsciously perceives her child as an externalization of her defective self and feels symbiotically linked to her child. Lax suggests that similar narcissistic injury and depression can follow the birth of a normal child in attenuated form, to the extent the child does not coincide with the mother's image of the expected and hoped-for baby.

Pines, Dinora (1972). Pregnancy and motherhood: Interaction between fantasy and reality. *Brit. J. Med. Psychol.*, 45:333-343.

Based on her analytic experience with pregnant women, Pines observes that previously repressed fantasies reemerge into preconsciousness and consciousness during pregnancy. The primary task of a pregnant woman and future mother is to integrate reality with her unconscious fantasies, hopes, and daydreams. Pines divides pregnancy into three stages: 1) the time from inception until the baby moves; 2) the time from the recognition of the child as a separate entity; and 3) the final stage, in which a woman prepares for her labor. Pines emphasizes that severe, unresolved conflicts may require psychoanalytic or psychotherapeutic intervention to achieve a successful outcome.

Newton, Niles (1973). Interrelationships between sexual responsiveness, birth and breast feeding. In: *Contemporary Sexual Behavior*, ed. J. Zubin and J. Money, pp. 77-98. Baltimore, MD: Johns Hopkins University Press.

Reproductive behavior of adult females involves coitus, parturition, and lactation. Newton explores the relation of birth behavior and breast feeding to coital orgasm and the relation of coitus, lactation, and birth to environmental disturbances and caretaking behavior. All three aspects of sexual behavior have a common neurohumoral underpinning and tend to be influenced by environmental stimuli. This paper contributes to a fuller understanding of important psychophysiological aspects of reproductive responses in female sexuality.

Fischer, Newell (1974). Multiple induced abortions: A psychoanalytic case study. *J. Amer. Psychoanal. Assn.*, 22:394-407.

The analysis of a married woman who had five induced abortions over a 10-year period is presented. The patient had a history of vaginal discharge at age six; she had multiple examinations and her mother administered suppositories and douches. The multiple pregnancies and abortions were symptomatic dramatizations of unresolved conflicts. Pregnancy represented fulfillment of an incestuous wish for father's penis and for his baby; abortion was the undoing of the wish fulfillment, the expression of rage at father's unfaithfulness, and a repetitive reenactment of the early examinations, fantasied castrations, and homoerotic stimulations. Preoedipal factors influenced the patient's frigidity, including fears of loss of control of all sphincters. In adolescence she had sought to establish a negative identification with her mother to defend against her homosexual attachment and lived out oedipal fantasies through promiscuity.

Notman, Malkah (1974). Pregnancy and abortion: Implications for career development of professional women. In: *Women and Success*, ed. R. Kundsin. New York: Morrow, pp. 216-221.

The author briefly reviews the impact of pregnancy and abortion on the career development of professional women. She asserts that pregnancy for the professionally active woman often provides the first challenge to a previously conflict-free life style. Conscious and unconscious motivations for pregnancy and abortion are considered. Notman emphasizes that past identifications with parents and other important figures may be crucial to the resolution of conflicting ego ideals.

Kohut, Heinz (1975). A note on female sexuality. In: *The Search for the Self*, Vol. 2, ed. P. Ornstein. New York: International Universities Press, 1978, pp. 783-792.

Kohut reviews his own theories and discusses women's wish for a child as a manifestation of their nuclear self, including their central ambitions and ideals, rather than as a wish for a penis. [See Chapter 6 for annotation.]

Blum, Harold (1976). Masochism, the ego ideal, and the psychology of women. *J. Amer. Psychoanal. Assn.* (Suppl.), 24:157-192.

In challenging the coupling of masochism and motherhood, Blum proposes a further examination of the important ingredients for mature mothering. [See Chapters 7 and 21 for annotations.]

Gray, Sheila (1976). The resolution of the Oedipus complex in women. *J. Phila. Assn. Psychoanal.*, 3:103-111.

Freud's ideas about the wish for a baby are reviewed. With the resolution of the Oedipus complex, the vagina can be cathected as an organ of pleasure beyond its function for reproduction. [See Chapter 7 for annotation.]

Kestenberg, Judith (1976). Regression and reintegration in pregnancy. *J. Amer. Psychoanal. Assn.* (Suppl.), 24:213-250.

The author reviews the literature on pregnancy wishes, meanings, and psychological experiences. She then examines her own theory of preparation for parenthood from childhood through adulthood. Kestenberg proposes that pregnancy is perceived as a new edition of the inner-genital phase in early feminine development, and there is a regression during pregnancy to earlier inner-genital phases. Kestenberg describes a study in which she classified material from the analyses of eight expectant mothers treated by colleagues according to her regression typology. During the first trimester, oral incorporative trends were seen. With the establishment of the placenta and a securely attached fetus during the second trimester, anal-retentive trends aided recognition of the fetus as a separate object. During the third trimester, preparation for giving up the fetus was aided by urethral "letting-go" trends.

Parens, Henri, Pollock, Leafy, Stern, Joan, and Kramer, Selma (1976). On the girl's entry into the Oedipus complex. *J. Amer Psychoanal. Assn.* (Suppl.), 24:79-108.

One girl showed the wish for a baby prior to a heterosexual attachment to her father; another showed castration anxiety after demonstating a wish for a baby. [See Chapter 7 for annotation.]

Rossi, Alice (1977). A biosocial perspective on parenting. *Daedelus,* 106:11-31.

This article discusses family tasks and sexual and parental roles as presented in sociological theories. Historical, evolutionary, and current biosocial perspective are examined and compared with past and recent biological views based on endocrinological studies. Rossi emphasizes that current theories in endocrinology stress the interaction between body hormones and social or psychological states. For example, hormonal cycles, pregnancy, and birth all heighten maternal investment in offspring in the first few months of life, an investment that thus exceeds the paternal investment. Therefore, Rossi contends, an egalitarian ideology can interfere with optimal childrearing. The paper raises interesting questions about biological and societal influences on sex roles, parenting, and parent-child relations.

Chodorow, Nancy (1978d). The psychodynamics of the family. In: *The Reproduction of Mothering: Psychoanalysis and the Sociology of Gender.* Berkeley: University of California Press, pp. 191-209.

Chodorow examines the psychodynamic constellations of children raised by female caregivers. She asserts that females raise girl children with, and raise boy children without, the particular psychological capacities and needs to become future primary parents. Chodorow traces the asymmetry of the oedipal situation for boys and girls nurtured by a female primary parent. She concludes that while both sexes seek to return to the gratifications of the early emotional and physical union with mother throughout their lives, only men can find direct gratification of this wish through a heterosexual bond. Women, even when finding erotic gratification with men, often seek important, additional, preoedipally derived emotional gratification in relationships with other women, in relationships with a child, or both.

According to Chodorow, women's heterosexuality is triangular, by which she means that preoedipal and oedipal needs of girls are satisfied in childhood by different objects; thus women require a third person for the structural and emotional completion of their heterosexual relationship. Having a child recreates for a woman the exclusivity of the early mother-child bond, thus satisfying a basic need. However, for the man, a child interrupts his marital edition of this bond, just as his father interfered with his original tie to his mother. Therefore, fathers commonly view children as competitors.

The asymmetry of childhood experiences for girls and for boys also results in girls' developing other characteristics important for their later mothering role. These characteristics include a sense of self that is continuous with others; an increased capacity for primary identification; and a greater ongoing involvement in the preoedipal aspects of relationships. Additionally, a father's role in helping a girl achieve separation and individuation from her mother predisposes her to idealization of him and of men in general, thus contributing to the perpetuation of ideology about male dominance of women. [See also Chapter 4.]

Chodorow, Nancy (1978e). Why women mother. In: *The Reproduction of Mothering: Psychoanalysis and the Sociology of Gender.* Berkeley: University of California Press, pp. 11-39.

Chodorow discusses the psychological nature of mothering activity and the need for mothering capacities to be built into the personality at the deepest level. She asserts that the sexual division of labor, in which almost all significant early child care is done by women, produces gender differences that tend to perpetuate the existing social and economic organization. This phenomenon is known as social reproduction, and women have been key figures in its occurrence. Chodorow delineates and provides critiques for various theories derived from biological, psychological, and sociological perspectives. She concludes that there is no biological reason for women's exclusive care of toddlers and older children. Rather, it is the social and cultural internalization of childbearing and lactation capacities that lead to women's nearly exclusive mothering role. This internalization cannot be explained solely by role training or socialization theories. Instead Chodorow proposes that the explanation for women's mothering behavior is derived from their psychological structure, stemming from their earliest relationship with the mother.

Mazor, Miriam (1978). The problem of infertility. In: *The Woman Patient: Sexual and Reproductive Aspects of Women's Health Care*, Vol. 1, ed. M. Notman and C. Nadelson. New York: Plenum Press, pp. 137-160.

Although the details of the gynecological infertility work-up are dated, the discussion of the psychological aspects of such an evaluation remain timely. In particular, Mazor describes the grief and mourning of couples with confirmed infertility. Whether or not adoption, artificial insemination, or other forms of assisted reproduction are possible, the couple mourns their sense of lost potential. They grieve for their inability to share in what they had expected to be a biological given.

Pines, Dinora, (1978). On becoming a parent. *J. Child Psychother.*, 4:19-30.

An analytic view of the process of becoming a parent is presented with a particular emphasis on the early stages. A distinction is made between the wish to prove one's mature feminine sexual identity and the genuine wish to have a child. The first pregnancy in particular may be seen as a normal developmental crisis for both mother and father. Its impact, together with the reemergence of previously repressed fantasies and conflicts in the mother's inner world, may cause her to act out in her relationship to her child. The relationship between the new parents may be affected by the first pregnancy, as may be a mother's relationship to her own parents. The invaluable role of the family and of the environment in supporting a mother at this time is stressed. Clinical material illustrates these themes.

Moulton, Ruth (1979). Ambivalence about motherhood in career women. *J. Amer. Acad. Psychoanal.*, 7:241-258.

[See Chapter 12 for annotation.]

Feder, Luis (1980). Preconceptive ambivalence and external reality. *Int. J. Psycho-Anal.*, 61:161-178.

Feder describes a preconceptive ambivalent stage reflecting intrapsychic conflict in the biological parents that can cause major or minor difficulties with the child. The ambivalence is manifested by death wishes and fantasied infanticide. Aggressive wishes, abortion, and multiple abortions are discussed.

Kestenberg, Judith (1980a). Maternity and paternity in the developmental context: Contribution to the integration and differentiation as a procreative person. *Psychiatric Clinics of North America: Sexuality*, 3:61-79. Philadelphia, Pennsylvania: W. B. Saunders.

Kestenberg emphasizes that wishes both to procreate and to obtain sexual satisfaction are integrated differently within feminine and masculine drives and ego tendencies. Parental roles are prescribed by culturally established norms and biological sex differences. For a man, coital orgasm and ejaculation of bodily contents into a woman are the same act. A woman can be impregnated without the sexual response of orgasm. Both sexes want to procreate, but the woman is engaged in this process much longer and is primarily responsible for child care. Kestenberg traces the psychological determinants of procreation through the developmental phases.

Kestenberg, Judith (1980b). Pregnancy as a developmental phase. *J. Bio. Exper. Stud.*, 3:58-66.

This paper discusses the results of a movement-analysis study of pregnant women. Pregnancy and delivery trigger a regression that results in a reorganization that assists parenting. This regression is similar to psychoanalytic transference regression and is often seen as a maternal or paternal transference to the obstetrician.

Blum, Harold (1981). The maternal ego ideal and the regulation of maternal qualities. In: *The Course of Life: Psychoanalytic Contributions Toward Understanding Personality Development, Adulthood and the Aging Process*, Vol. 3, ed. S. Greenspan and G. Pollock. Adelphi, MD: U.S. Department of Health and Human Services, NIMH, pp. 91-114.

The first section of this chapter examines the formation and functioning of the maternal ego ideal. Human maternal functioning is highly variable, and maternal attitudes are overdetermined, reflecting unconscious fantasy, cultural custom, and education. The maternal ego ideal develops in response to narcissistic needs and is rooted in early identifications, particularly with the mother, but also with the father. Each developmental phase contributes to the integration of wishful fantasies of being mother or being like her. Conflicts between the maternal ego ideal and rejecting attitudes toward maternity are universal in girls and women. The maternal ego ideal contributes importantly to the female superego, and its content may be significantly different from other areas of the female superego and from the masculine ego ideal.

The second part of the paper describes psychopathology of the maternal ego ideal. The child's demanding and devouring behavior poses a regressive threat to maternal ideals and stimulates infanticidal impulses and the defenses against them. The sources and clinical consequences of the aggressive impulses of parents toward children are reviewed.

Chodorow, Nancy and Contratto, Susan (1981). The fantasy of the perfect mother. In: *Rethinking the Family: Some Feminist Questions*, ed. B. Thorne with M. Yalom. New York: Longman, pp. 54-75. Also in: *Feminism and Psychoanalytic Theory*, New Haven, CT: Yale University Press, 1989, pp. 79-96.

This essay asserts that feminist writings about mothers, like the culture as a whole, accept several problematic assumptions, including a sense that mothers are totally responsible for the outcome of their mothering even if their behavior is in turn shaped by a male-dominant society. Belief in an all-powerful mother includes a tendency to blame the mother, to idealize her, and to assume maternal asexuality or a romanticized libidinal motherhood. Finally, the authors argue, feminist writings invoke an imagery that ties mothers and motherhood to aggression and death; infantile omnipotence is seen as destructive toward mothers, and, reciprocally, mothers can invoke life and death powers over children. These themes reflect a 19th-century cultural ideology and post-Freudian psychology.

Franks, Darrell (1981). Psychiatric evaluation of women in a surrogate mother program. *Am. J. Psychiat.*, 138:1378-1380.

Using MMPI and psychiatric interviews, the author finds no apparent psychopathology in the 10 applicants he studied who wanted to participate in a surrogate mothering program. Their reasons for entering the program seem to have been a mixture of financial and altruistic factors.

Kestenberg, Judith (1981b). Notes on parenthood as a developmental phase. In: *Clinical Psychoanalysis*, Vol. 3, ed. S. Orgel and B. Fine, New York: Aronson, pp. 199-234.

Kestenberg regards parenthood as a developmental phase and an opportunity for the reorganization of psychic structures. She contends that parenthood is anticipated in childhood in each psychosexual stage of development, with the inner-genital phase serving in both sexes as the somatic core for the wish to bear, deliver, and nurture a baby. In the phallic phase, the father and his penis are admired by both sexes as the "generator" of children. In latency, sublimations of the wish for a phallic child are reflected in child care and games of teaching. A renewal of inner-genital tensions in early adolescence intensifies the wish for a child and enhances a reintegration of pregenital and genital drives. In mid- and late adolescence, the baby is linked with incestual oedipal relationships. In adulthood, the wish for a child with a new partner emerges from repression. The previous denial of the importance of inner-genital structures is permanently lifted, and a hypercathexis of the inside of a woman extends to hopes for impregnation, pregnancy, and delivery without injury. There is a renewal of intimacy and a new drive for regenerative reproduction in the phase of grandparenthood.

Brazelton, T. Berry and Keefer, Constance (1982). The early mother-child relationship: A developmental view of woman as mother. In: *The Woman Patient: Concepts of Femininity and the Life Cycle*, Vol. 2, ed. C. Nadelson and M. Notman. New York: Plenum Press, pp. 95-109.

Brazelton and Keefer construct a normal developmental model of becoming a mother that involves a complex sequence of changes. They describe the process of initial attachment and subsequent incremental autonomy that evolves in the mother-infant relationship. They particularly stress the role of individual infants in eliciting reciprocity. In their observational work, they discern predictable patterns of homeostatic attentional cycles between mother and infant where the infant provides important feedback to the mother that increases her self-esteem. Failures of reciprocity can result from problems within either the mother or infant.

Freidman, Rochelle and Cohen, Karen (1982). Emotional reactions to the miscarriage of a consciously desired pregnancy. In: *The Woman Patient: Aggression, Adaptations and Psychotherapy*, Vol. 3, ed. M. Notman and C. Nadelson. New York: Plenum Press, pp. 173-187.

Freidman and Cohen report on their clinical experiences treating women who miscarried in consciously desired pregnancies. A normal mourning process occurs in which the depth of grief is related to the degree of attachment the mother has made to the mental representation of the fetus within her. A sense of narcissistic injury and the loss of fantasies about the self-as-mother also effect the grief process; anger, blame, and guilt emerge along with grief.

Kestenberg, Judith (1982). The inner genital phase: Prephallic and preoedipal. In: *Early Female Development*, ed. D. Mendell. New York: S.P. Medical and Scientific Books, pp. 71-126.

Kestenberg postulates a period between anal and phallic phases called the early maternal or inner genital phase, in which there is a triangular-maternal attitude and projection of inner genital tensions onto representations of the baby. [See Chapter 6 for annotation.]

Notman, Malkah and Nadelson, Carol (1982a). Changing views of the relationship between femininity and reproduction. In: *The Woman Patient: Concepts of Femininity and the Life Cycle*, Vol. 2, ed. C. Nadelson and M. Notman. New York: Plenum Press, pp. 31-42.

[See Chapter 12 for annotation.]

Notman, Malkah and Nadelson, Carol (1982b). Maternal work and children. In: *The Woman Patient: Concepts of Femininity and the Life Cycle*, Vol. 2, ed. C. Nadelson and M. Notman. New York: Plenum Press, pp. 121-133.

Notman and Nadelson emphasize the importance of differentiating between maternal separation and maternal deprivation in evaluating the literature on the effect of mothers' working outside the home on early child development. They review demographic data that show increasing numbers of working women with and without children. Several studies conclude that mothers' outside work has a positive effect on children, particularly daughters. A clinical vignette illustrates the complex interplay of societal, familial, and intrapsychic forces on the working mother.

Pines, Dinora (1982). The relevance of early psychic development to pregnancy and abortion. *Int. J. Psycho-Anal.*, 63:311-319.

A developmental phase of pregnancy and motherhood is described and a little girl's wish to have a child in identification with her mother is discussed. Now, on the basis of a biological foundation, the pregnant woman can identify with the omnipotent, life-giving mother and also with the fetus, as if she were her own child. When her own mother has been "good enough," pregnancy is a pleasurable developmental phase. For other women, the inevitable regression reactivates primitive anxieties and conflicts stemming from their own experience of being mothered. The analysis of a patient who repeatedly allowed herself to become pregnant, but aborted the pregnancy each time, illustrates the intrapsychic experience of abortion and fears of pregnancy.

Rynearson, Edward (1982). Relinquishment and its maternal complications: A preliminary study. *Am. J. Psychiat.*, 139:338-340.

The author used psychiatric interviews to study 20 middle-aged, non-psychotic psychiatric women outpatients, each of whom had relinquished a child for adoption during late adolescence. The women uniformly reported a number of mental and behavioral phenomena that were adaptive adjustments to the relinquishment. They had perceived the relinquishment as an externally enforced decision that overwhelmed their internal wish for continued attachment to the baby. Maternal attachment and identification were intensely sought. In the first two years, there were recurrent dreams concerning loss of the baby, with themes of traumatic separation and joyful reunion, as well as concerns about future infertility. In later marriage and motherhood, attachment to the newborn was particularly strong and protective; fear of adolescent daughters' sexual maturity was high. Symptoms of mourning at the anniversary of relinquishment continued but gradually diminished.

Blum, Harold (1983). Adoptive parents: Generative conflicts and generational continuity. *The Psychoanalytic Study of the Child*, 38:141-163. New Haven, CT: Yale University Press.

The reality of adoption is seen as influencing the activation of, magnitude of, and solution to various psychological conflicts in adoptive parents and grandparents, as well as having an impact on the development of adoptive children. The network of relationships, identifications, shared conflicts and fantasies, and communications among the three generations have complex effects on all. Unconscious fantasies, especially of oedipal constellations in the family romance, the primal scene, and the castration complex (infertility) are linked to issues of generational difference, narcissism, and familial continuity and discontinuity. Using clinical examples, Blum delineates the detrimental effects of unsupportive grandparents who fail to confirm their adult children's parental identity (and reinforce harsh superego conflicts in the parental generation), later contributing to identity confusion and fears of rejection in an adoptive child.

Kestenberg, Judith and Javaid, Ghazala (1983). Entrancement of the mother with her young baby: Implications for the older sibling. *Dynamic Psychotherapy*, 1:63-74.

The authors describe entrancement of the mother with her newborn as like the state of "being in love." This intense feeling of mutual belonging is facilitated by the pleasure of bodily contact and contributes to symbiosis. The duration of entrancement is connected to the reciprocal dependency of mother and baby. In this state, a mother resents any intrusions that may disrupt mutuality between mother and baby. Temporary estrangement can occur between a mother and her older child and the rest of the family.

Parker, Philip (1983). Motivation of surrogate mothers: Initial findings. *Am. J. Psychiat.*, 140:117-118.

Motivational and demographic data derived from a questionnaire and interviews with 125 women who applied to be surrogate mothers are discussed. Complementary motivations included the wish to be pregnant and to "give" a baby, the desire for money, and wishes to resolve internal conflicts such as those related to previous abortion or adoptive relinquishment.

Morris, Muriel (1985). Unconscious motivation in the refusal to have children. In: *Women and Loss: Psychoanalytic Perspectives*, ed. W. Finn, M. Tallmer, I. Seeland, A. Kutscher, and E. Clark. New York: Praeger, pp. 116-123.

Morris describes a continuum of women ranging from those who consciously do not want children to those whose ambivalence about having children suppresses ovulation, causes difficulty with pregnancy and delivery, and produces infertility. She asserts that the psychodynamic conflicts related to psychogenic or hypothalamic infertility, as in all psychosomatic patients, belong to the earliest stages of life. An analytic patient illustrates conscious and unconscious levels of psychogenic infertility. The salient psychodynamic factors include extreme ambivalence about femininity; rage and envy toward men; delusional thinking about the wrongs of society, derived as a projection of a disturbed early relationship with her mother; conflicts about identification with a maternal introject; fears of maternal retaliation for oedipal wishes; and equation of menstruation with oral and anal themes, including excretion, internal damage, and oral birth fantasies. The transference was marked by severe mistrust, magical thinking, and demands for redress of grievances. [See also Chapter 23.]

Hunt, Jennifer and Rudden, Marie (1986). Gender differences in the psychology of parenting: Psychoanalytic and feminist perspectives. *J. Amer. Acad. Psychoanal.*, 14:213-225.

The authors review representative writings on parenthood from the psychoanalytic and feminist literature to explore whether desires to have and nurture children are rooted in universal or specifically feminine developmental and biological experiences. Men and women alike have creative desires that can be expressed in parenting; motherhood allows for expression of a biological potential and a culturally prescribed gender role but can also be a neurotic choice. Exclusively female parenting can reflect, and can lead to, many problems for women and children and can limit men's opportunities to provide active nurturing and to experience the psychological reworking it allows.

Jordan, Judith and Surrey, Janet (1986). The self-in-relation: Empathy and the mother-daughter relationship. In: *The Psychology of Today's Woman: New Psychoanalytic Visions*, ed. T. Bernay and D. Cantor. Hillsdale, NJ: The Analytic Press, pp. 81-104.

[See Chapter 12 for annotation.]

Klyman, Cassandra (1986). Pregnancy as a reaction to early childhood sibling loss. *J. Amer. Acad. Psychoanal.*, 14:323-335.

Women from families with early childhood loss may be left in a state of incomplete mourning, with unconscious wishes to master a trauma by making their passive experience into a life event, pregnancy. These patients present as unconscious searchers for or avoiders of pregnancy. Several clinical cases illuminate other resultant difficulties such as separation anxiety and learning inhibitions in latency, exaggerated pseudo-heterosexuality and other risk-taking behaviors at puberty, problems in self-esteem regulation, and survivor guilt. Reinstating a mourning process for a lost sibling is an essential technical guideline for successful analysis.

Lester, Eva and Notman, Malkah (1986). Pregnancy, developmental crises and object relations. *Int. J. Psycho-Anal.*, 67:357-366.

This article, presenting clinical material from the analyses of three pregnant women, highlights the internal shifts and realignments in their mental organization during their pregnancies. The women consciously wished for a child but were quite anxious about and preoccupied with their pregnancies. One neurotic patient had a positive maternal identification and a deep desire to become a mother. By contrast, the two borderline patients wanted a baby as a narcissistic object and had intense ambivalence toward their maternal object. The authors propose that the course of pregnancy is chiefly determined by a woman's preoedipal experiences with her mother rather than by oedipal conflict. Narcissistic valuation of the body and a poorly integrated body ego may become the sources of serious anxiety which may be somatized during pregnancy.

Person, Ethel (1986). Working mothers: Impact on the self, the couple and the children. In: *The Psychology of Today's Woman: New Psychoanalytic Visions*, ed. T. Bernay and D. Cantor. Hillsdale, NJ: The Analytic Press, pp. 121-138.

Person explores the conscious stresses, conflicts, and guilt that working mothers experience in balancing their dual roles. She also reviews the social, economic, and cultural factors that lead most working mothers to work out of financial necessity rather than for self-fulfillment. She maintains that infant researchers have perpetuated myths that intensify working mothers' guilt. While acknowledging the practical need for competent infant and preschool childcare, Person challenges the myth of "dedicated motherhood," which claims that an infant requires the attention of a single caretaking parent to ensure the child's normal development.

Williams, Susan (1986). Reproductive motivations and contemporary feminine development. In: *The Psychology of Today's Woman: New Psychoanalytic Visions*, ed. T. Bernay and D. Cantor. Hillsdale, NJ: The Analytic Press, pp. 167-193.

This paper looks at the multiple intrapsychic, interpersonal, social, political, and economic motivations for reproduction. Williams notes the influence of sexism and misogyny on women's development and the resultant conflicts about reproduction and caretaking. She argues that the development of effective contraceptives has brought these multiple influences into sharp focus. Clinical material from several female patients in psychotherapy illustrates the conflicts. A new model emphasizing the internalization of sexism as causal in reproductive conflicts is proposed over a biological/instinct model. Although a multidetermined model is proposed, the reality and effect of external factors as etiologic in conflict are stressed over unconscious determinants.

Kestenberg, Judith (1987). Empathy for the fetus: Fetal movements and dreams. In: *Pre- and Perinatal Psychology: An Introduction*, ed. T. Vernay. New York: Human Sciences Press, pp. 138-150.

This paper reports on 13 pregnant women who participated in a study in which they recorded movement changes in their babies, themselves, and their dreams. A correlation was found between fetal movements and movement in dreams. Kestenberg contends that the course of labor and delivery can be predicted from the interrelationships between fetal movements and fantasies evidenced in the dreams.

Appelbaum, Ann (1988). Psychoanalysis during pregnancy: The effect of sibling constellation. *Psychoanal. Inq.*, 8:177-195.

A session-by-session summarized account of 20 sessions of psychoanalytic treatment of a woman in the second trimester of her pregnancy is considered. The author asserts that the patient's identification with the fetus, whose sibling position corresponded to her own, facilitated the recognition of a lost fragment of her identity containing previously unacknowledged strengths. The patient's two older children were girls, and the third child, (who later proved to be a boy), was represented in dreams during treatment as a boy and reactivated images for the patient of herself as a self-sufficient, tomboy child. The case illustrates a pregnant woman's fluidly shifting identifications with both the fetus and her own mother. Also, reworking of the early maternal relationship in the transference led to a noticeable shift in the patient's sense of her maternal capabilities. The author's focus in the discussion is on the identical sibling position of a patient and her unborn child.

Applegarth, Adrienne (1988). Origins of femininity and the wish for a child. *Psychoanal. Inq.*, 8:160-176.

Applegarth disagrees with Freud's view that the wish for a baby is a defensive derivative of penis envy. She argues that the wish for a baby has many intrapsychic determinants, including gratification of genital libidinal drive, identification with the mother, and striving for a feminine ego ideal. She contends that feminine identity is not primarily motivated by penis envy. Applegarth reviews the work of Money and Ehrhardt, Kestenberg, Parens, and others.

Lester, Eva and Notman, Malkah (1988). Pregnancy and object relations: Clinical considerations. *Psychoanal. Inq.*, 8:196-221.

Adding to their 1986 paper, the authors observe psychological aspects of pregnancy and childbirth in three female analysands. One of the three women had two consecutive pregnancies during her analysis. Extensive analytic material from the four pregnancies is provided. The psychological course of pregnancy is determined primarily by factors relating to women's preoedipal experiences with the maternal object, while oedipal conflicts surface but play a less significant role. A woman's healthy identification with her own mother constitutes the basis of motherliness, defined as the desire to care for a child. The woman patient with the second pregnancy repeated conflicts from the first pregnancy rather than achieving a new level of integration, as proposed by Bibring and others. Three separate phases of pregnancy are described, with the quickening representing a demarcation line between the first and second phases.

Meyer, Jon (1988). A case of hysteria, with a note on biology. J. Amer. Psychoanal. Assn., 36:319-346.

The course of psychoanalysis is described for a woman patient who presented with the physical manifestations of hyperprolactinemia, including galactorrhea, amenorrhea, and infertility as well as psychological conflicts about her anatomy and sexual functioning. [See Chapter 20 for annotation.]

Notman, Malkah and Lester, Eva (1988). Pregnancy: Theoretical considerations. Psychoanal. Inq., 8:139-159.

This article is a companion to Lester and Notman (1988). The authors summarize Freud's theories on female sexuality and the wish for a child. The authors review psychoanalytic writings, including the works of Deutsch, Kestenberg, Benedek, Stoller, and Chasseguet-Smirgel on feminine identity, the wish for a child (the procreative urge), pregnancy, and the origins of motherhood. Modern thinking on gender identity, "primary femininity," and the developmental roots of motherhood is synthesized, noting the psychological preparedness for pregnancy and the complex interplay between biological and psychosocial maturational forces. An overview of the phases of pregnancy is provided. The last section describes variations in the experience of pregnancy at specific developmental stages.

Novick, Kerry (1988). Childbearing and childrearing. Psychoanal. Inq., 8:253-259.

Childbearing and childrearing wishes are seen as separate strands in feminine development and as derivatives of phenomena that arise at different developmental stages. Childbearing wishes are first observed in toddlerhood. Toddler girls are particularly vulnerable to narcissistic injury (from the loss of infantile omnipotence and the recognition of anatomical differences); the wish to have a baby is understood as an attempt at narcissistic repair and an identification. In the oedipal period, childbearing fantasies represent rivalry with the mother and the wish for a penis. Childrearing behavior represents an adaptive substitution for the wish to bear a child as well as a defensive identification with the caretaking aspects of the mother. Throughout development there is a tension between childbearing and childrearing wishes, the former representing narcissistic gratification and libidinal wishes, the latter being more closely tied to defensive functions. At the end of adolescence, girls must work through their aggression toward their mother so that their childrearing wishes can be freed of their defensive function. Conflicts of adoptive mothers related to failures in childbearing are discussed briefly.

Pines, Dinora (1988). Adolescent pregnancy and motherhood: A psychoanalytical perspective. *Psychoanal. Inq.*, 8:234-251.

Using analytic material from two adolescent mothers, the author focuses on the unconscious conflicts that prevented these young women from being good-enough mothers. Superficially both women presented with normal adolescent behavior, but both were more deeply disturbed than they at first appeared. The transference and countertransference problems encountered in both analyses confirmed that the patients' pathologies made rejection of their children inevitable. Both patients externalized a harsh, punitive superego figure that was projected onto the analyst and elicited countertransference responses of anger and outrage at the cruelty to their children. Pines feels that her gender was an important factor in working through the material.

Schuker, Eleanor (1988). Psychological effects of the new reproductive technologies. In: *Embryos, Ethics and Women's Rights*, ed. E. Baruch and A. D'Adamo. Haworth Press, New York, pp. 141-147. Also in: *Women and Health* 13, 1/2 (1987).

New reproductive technologies are seen as having the potential to stimulate fantasies and myths in parents and in the children who are products of these technologies, similarly to the way adoption can serve as such a stimulus to both generations. Effective parenting is viewed as being facilitated by early psychologically and legally secure bonds, rather than solely requiring a biological connection. Motivations of surrogate mothers include ideals, altruism, narcissistic needs, and reparative wishes, rather than primarily financial gain.

Silver, Donald and Campbell, Kay (1988). Failure of psychological gestation. *Psychoanal. Inq.*, 8:222-233.

Silver and Campbell coin the term "psychological gestation" and define it as the crucial intrapsychic work that must be done during pregnancy. Failure of psychological gestation is most commonly associated with inadequate social and family support and generally leads to impaired mother-child attachment or infant psychopathology. The authors discuss a variety of conflicts that may be activated during pregnancy. From their clinical experience with patients who failed at psychological gestation, they conclude that women who had unresolved conflicts with abandoning, abusing mothers were driven to neglect themselves during pregnancy and to repeat the cycle of emotional deprivation with their infants.

Stein, Yehoyakim (1988). Some reflections on the inner space and its contents. *The Psychoanalytic Study of the Child*, 43:291-304. New Haven, CT: Yale University Press.

Fantasies about menstruation, pregnancy, and abortion in a young female patient are discussed. [See Chapter 18 for annotation.]

Kalinich, Lila (1989). The biological clock. In: *The Middle Years: New Psychoanalytic Perspectives*, ed. J. Oldham and R. Liebert. New Haven, CT: Yale University Press, pp. 123-134.

[See Chapter 15 for annotation.]

Martinez, Diane (1989). Psychosomatic considerations of infertility. *Medical Psychiatry: Theory and Practice*, Vol. 2, ed. E. Garza-Treviño. Teaneck, NJ: World Scientific Publications, pp. 693-719.

This excellent review article discusses the psychological impact of recent technological innovations in the field of infertility. Providing a brief critique of previous views, Martinez argues that emotional factors are no longer considered the primary etiology of infertility. Infertility challenges a couple's relationship and their self-esteem and involves a multiplicity of losses. Those infertile couples who seek treatment have common personality characteristics, including ambition, perseverance, and the tendency to approach problems cognitively. The specific medical therapies for infertility are reviewed, their particular psychological stresses are delineated, and the indications for psychological intervention are described.

Robinson, Gail and Stewart, Donna (1989). Motivation for motherhood and the experience of pregnancy. *Can. J. Psychiat.*, 34:861-865.

The authors review selected literature on motivation for motherhood and the development of maternal feelings. They argue that sociocultural and psychological motivations for motherhood are crucial, whereas evidence for a biological basis for maternal feelings in human females is less important. Varying psychoanalytic views on whether motherhood is essential to female identity are discussed. The authors stress that a woman does not have to experience motherhood in order to feel feminine, although reproductive capacity and choice are important components of femininity and self-esteem. Psychological changes and adjustments to both normal and complicated pregnancy are also reviewed.

Winestine, Muriel (1989). To know or not to know: Some observations on women's reactions to the availability of prenatal knowledge of their baby's sex. *J. Amer. Psychoanal. Assn.*, 37:1015-1030.

Winestine studied 34 volunteer pregnant women who had amniocentesis; 18 had expressed the wish to know the baby's sex prenatally, and 16 had expressed the wish not to know. Attitudes proved enduring before and after amniocentesis and reflected differing cognitive styles and affective cathexes. Women who wished to know the sex were more invested in their fetus as a real object and favored concrete fantasies; women who wished not to know were more invested in the state of being pregnant for its own sake. The hypothesis that women who had resolved ambivalence about sex preferences would want to know the sex of their fetus was not confirmed. Issues related to mourning both the loss of the fantasy of the sex-preferred child and the loss of the fantasy of the sex opposite to the expected one are discussed.

Brodzinsky, David and Schechter, Marshall (ed.)(1990). *The Psychology of Adoption.* New York: Oxford University Press.

This collection has an excellent bibliography and several noteworthy chapters. Both "A Stress and Coping Model of Adoption Adjustment," by Brodzinsky, and "Adoption from the Inside Out: A Psychoanalytic Perspective," by Brinich, view healthy adjustment to adoption as requiring adaptive mourning by the adoptive parents and the adoptive child. In "The Meaning of the Search," by Schechter and Bertocci, gender differences in adoption and their relation to the search for birthparents is discussed; girls need to develop and resolve their ambivalent feminine identification with a mother who had difficulty bearing babies. In "Surrendering an Infant for Adoption: The Birthmother Experience," Brodzinsky observes that relinquishment may have negative psychological consequences, and she suggests ways of supporting adequate grieving.

Colarusso, Calvin (1990). The third individuation: The effect of biological parenthood on separation-individuation processes in adulthood. *The Psychoanalytic Study of the Child*, 45:179-194. New Haven, CT: Yale University Press.

Parenthood as the third separation-individuation phase is discussed. [See Chapter 12 for annotation.]

Leon, Irving (1990). *When a Baby Dies: Psychotherapy for Pregnancy and Newborn Loss.* New Haven, CT: Yale University Press.

This excellent and analytically informed book contributes to the literature on psychotherapy for perinatal losses. The psychology of pregnancy is discussed, with pregnancy viewed alternately as a developmental stage, an instinctual drive, an object-seeking activity, and an enhancement of the self. Interpersonal and intrapsychic aspects of the psychology of perinatal loss are described. Issues in psychotherapy for the individual woman, couple, and siblings of the lost baby are considered.

Pines, Dinora (1990). Pregnancy, miscarriage and abortion: A psychoanalytic perspective. *Int. J. Psycho-Anal.*, 71:301-307.

Using analytic case material from three female patients, Pines discusses the psychological antecedents that may lead to spontaneous or planned abortion. During pregnancy, the fetus facilitates an experience of primary unity with a woman's own mother and a narcissistic identification with the fetus, as if the fetus were the pregnant woman in her own mother's body. This symbiotic state can activate intense ambivalence and regression. Pines asserts that abortion and miscarriage can represent psychosomatic solutions to the universal dilemma of maternal ambivalence towards the fetus derived from unresolved conflicts. Interpretation of conflict may in some cases lead to a successful pregnancy and birth of a baby.

# Chapter 15

# Adult Development: Midlife Issues, Menopause, and Aging

### Sandra Kopit Cohen

This chapter covers psychoanalytical writings about women during midlife. It addresses such topics as menopause, aging, and the challenges of physical illness. Midlife is often defined as the stage of life beginning in the fifth decade and continuing through the seventh. However, midlife can be better described by phase-specific developmental tasks, rather than any particular chronological age. During this developmental period, the normal adult may experience 1) the physical signs of aging; 2) the movement of children away from home and toward establishing separate families; 3) the eventual death of parents and peers; 4) the failure to fulfill one's ambitions and ideals; and 5) illness and possible death of a spouse and oneself.

The awareness of the finiteness of time and of the inescapability of aging, vulnerability to illness, and eventual mortality ushers in the midlife stage. For women, midlife is marked by a loss of reproductive functioning, as well as changes in bodily appearance, in sexual motivation, and in physical functions that can challenge narcissistic equilibrium. Children grow up, move away, and have their own babies; women are now alone with their mates; they have different learning and work potentials; and they may be required to care for aging parents.

With the exception of papers about the menopause, the psychoanalytic literature about women and midlife is limited. Menopause, which occurs in most women at about age 50, was viewed by early writers (Freud, 1913, Deutsch, 1925) as the salient negative factor in the psychology of women during midlife. Menopausal women were perceived essentially as experiencing diminished reproductive and creative functioning. Deutsch (1945), however, and then Benedek (1950) insightfully observed that women who had established secure identities could experience midlife as a time of freedom, excitement, sublimation, and creative expression.

Contemporary writers have considered midlife issues in a broader context. They explore the predominant conflicts about sexuality and other aspects of the body, intrapsychic changes, and changes in self in relation to family during this period. Colarusso and Nemiroff (1981) argue that middle-age women are more preoccupied with physical signs of aging than are their male counterparts because of prevailing cultural stereotypes that equate femininity and sexual desirability with a youthful body.

A clear definition for senescence (which begins between 65 and 70 years) with a map of its phase-specific developmental tasks, has yet to be satisfactorily delineated in the literature. According to some researchers, senescence is a time for continued adaptive, intrapsychic development despite diminished physical strength. The progressive diminution of physical strength and the inescapability of death call forth either healthy or pathological psychic responses in the elderly. For many women, the final years are a time of emotional growth and reworking of past conflicts. Some psychoanalysts have linked fears of death to castration anxiety, separation fears, or fears of persecutory attack. Curiously, little psychoanalytic literature exists that specifically examines gender differences and aging, with the exception of issues related to menopause. Do women adapt more effectively to old age than do men? Since women live longer than men do, they may experience different adaptive opportunities and different stresses. There is no evidence to support the notion that female and male developmental lines converge with increasing age. The developmental and adaptive vicissitudes for women in this stage of life remain uncharted.

Freud (1933) did not express optimism about the capacity of women over 30 for sublimation, change, or analyzability. He maintained the view (Freud, 1913) that women undergo character change at menopause, with a regression to anal-sadistic traits. Indeed, Freud (1904) believed that few patients over 50 years of age were analyzable. This narrow perspective may have promoted the pejorative attitude among many analysts and impeded the exploration of multiple theoretical and clinical issues related to midlife in general and to aging women specifically. Recent psychoanalytic papers have reexamined the issue of analyzability in the later years. Some papers emphasize the similarities between older and younger analysands, the continuing potential for psychic growth, and the complexity of transferences from past child and adult self-representations that form an integral part of analyses in older patients. It appears that certain character types, as they sense approaching mortality, may actually prove more amenable to analysis at older ages.

This chapter includes annotations for analytic papers focusing on both genders, as well as a sampling of nonanalytic work from sociology, psychology, and physiology that suggests avenues for future analytic research. There has been no attempt to deal in comprehensive fashion with the nonpsychoanalytic literature. Since psychoanalytic investigation proceeds primarily from clinical data, the wider acceptance of the analyzability of older patients may allow for future inquiry and verification of observable behavior documented by other disciplines. Much remains to be learned about women and the feminine experience in relation to adult sexuality, gender identity, narcissism, mind-body linkages, and the intrapsychic meanings of career changes, physical aging, grandmotherhood, menopause, widowhood, and senescence. (S.K.C., N.L., and E.S.)

Freud, Sigmund (1904). On psychotherapy. *Standard Edition*, 7:257-268. London: Hogarth Press, 1953.

Freud asserts that few patients over age 50 are analyzable, because they do not have the necessary elasticity of mental processes. On the basis of his concept of treatment as the removal of repressed mental contents, he contends that the volume of analytic material would prolong the analysis indefinitely.

Freud Sigmund (1913). The disposition to obsessional neurosis: A contribution to the problem of choice of neurosis. *Standard Edition*, 12:317-326. London: Hogarth Press, 1953.

Freud asserts that women undergo a character change at the time of menopause. [See Chapter 20 for annotation.]

Abraham, Karl (1919). The applicability of psycho-analytic treatment to patients at an advanced age. *Selected Papers of Karl Abraham*. New York: Brunner/Mazel, 1979, pp. 312-317.

On the basis of extensive experience with analyses of men and women in their 40s and 50s, Abraham concludes that the prognosis for a successful analysis is favorable when the patient enjoyed several years of normal sexuality and social usefulness after puberty. The age of onset of the neurosis rather than the age at which analysis begins has more significance for analyzability. Abraham found no differences between older and younger analysands' repression of early childhood memories.

Deutsch, Helene (1925b). The menopause. *Int. J. Psycho-Anal.*, 1984, 65:55-62. (Translated from *Psychoanalyse der Weiblichen Sexualfunktionen* [*Psychoanalysis of the Sexual Functions of Women*] by Paul Roazan.)

Deutsch defines the climacterium as beginning with a period of premenopausal psychological changes and extending until the cessation of menses. Using clinical examples to illustrate normal and pathological responses, she defines three climacteric phases: the preclimacteric, the genital, and the postgenital. The particular course of menopause depends on individual dispositional factors. The climacterium constitutes a reversal of the changes of puberty, with a reawakening of oedipal and masculinity conflicts and defensive flight into pubertal fantasies and activities. Depending on previous development, particularly conflict resolution from puberty, the climacterium can be a time of adaptation with creative sublimations. Deutsch recommends beginning analysis before the menopause to facilitate these adaptations.

Freud, Sigmund (1933). Femininity. *Standard Edition*, 22:112-135. London: Hogarth Press, 1953.

[See Chapter 1 for annotation.]

Deutsch, Helene (1945a). Epilogue: The climacterium. *The Psychology of Women*, Vol. 2. New York: Grune and Stratton, pp. 456-487.

Deutsch elaborates on her previous work (Deutsch, 1925), emphasizing that both adaptational and pathological intrapsychic responses to the physiological changes of the climacterium depend on the woman's personality. Menopause is experienced as a narcissistic loss of pubertal gains with the reawakening of early oedipal and bisexual conflicts. These psychological responses reflect not only biological changes but often also concomitant interpersonal and social changes. The adaptive responses serve as a defense against narcissistic loss and as an assertion that the woman has an intelligence and emotional life not only confined to motherhood. Deutsch contends that women's responses to menopause are predictable from their sexual responses to puberty; thus these responses can assist evaluation for psychoanalysis. Sexual excitement outlasts reproductive capacity and may undergo dramatic changes. Depression, which can vary in duration and intensity, is an expectable part of the climacterium. Healthy adaptations to the narcissistic loss of reproductive functioning may include the extension of mothering beyond the family and a shift to masculine, nonsexual sublimations. Adaptive and maladaptive aspects of grandmotherhood are also discussed. Deutsch illustrates the clinical varieties of normal and pathological psychological responses to the physical manifestations of menopause.

Benedek, Therese (1950). Climacterium: A developmental phase. *Psychoanal. Q.*, 19:1-27.

Benedek considers the climacterium as a period of interpersonal reorganization. The responses to menopause arise from the interaction of hormonal changes with the woman's psychosexual past and present psychosexual development. She notes that hormone replacement therapy does not inevitably relieve psychological symptoms. Using anthropological studies, Benedek describes the impact of culture on the individual's experience of menopause. She observes that the climacterium occurs at a time of complex life-cycle tasks; these tasks may activate responses that conflict with the ego ideal. A mature capacity for love is achieved during the reproductive period; this capacity can continue past menopause and be directed inside the family in the role of grandmother or outside the family in other creative roles. Benedict presents two patients suffering from severe climacteric depression. She describes how characterological rigidity and narcissistic vulnerability affected their poor adaptation to menopause. Benedek asserts that shifts in hormonal function and conscious and preconscious manifestations of affects accompanying previous menstrual-cycle experiences prepare women for the final cessation of hormonal production.

Fessler, Laci (1950). The psychopathology of climacteric depression. *Psychoanal. Q.*, 19:28-42.

This survey of 100 psychotherapy patients questions why hormone replacement does not correct psychological responses to menopause. Clinical examples show that climacteric depression is associated with symptoms of conversion and phobia and is similar to hysteria. Fessler proposes that most women experience menopause as an unconscious disappointment that disturbs their defenses against penis envy and reactivates infantile wishes. She asserts that this unconscious disappointment is manifested in her findings that 85% of the menopausal women studied reported prior menstrual and premenstrual difficulties.

Wayne, George (1953). Modified psychoanalytic therapy in senescence. *Psychoanal. Rev.*, 40:99-116.

Psychotherapy with a 66-year-old depressed woman illustrates that the changes of old age can catalyze reversible neurotic reactions to previous unresolved conflicts. Wayne suggests that the depreciated social status of the elderly and their feelings of organic decline rekindle castration fears and feelings of inferiority. This devaluation leads to an unrealistic preoccupation with the body. Technical recommendations for psychoanalytic therapy with the elderly are presented.

Grotjahn, Martin (1955). Analytic psychotherapy with the elderly. *Psychoanal. Rev.*, 42:419-427.

Grotjahn postulates three psychic resolutions to aging: 1) a normal resolution, which allows integration and acceptance of life as lived and an acceptance of one's own death; 2) an increased rigidity of the ego, with attempts to intensify predominant defenses; and 3) a neurotic or psychotic regression. He observes that old age may facilitate therapy by decreasing resistance to unpleasant insights, by softening character defenses through confrontation with reality, and by retrospection that can shift to insight. Grotjahn interprets the fear of death as a form of castration anxiety. He emphasizes the importance of analyzing the reverse Oedipus complex, wherein power shifts from the parent to the child.

Klein, Melanie (1963). On the sense of loneliness. In: *Envy and Gratitude and Other Works, 1946-1963*. New York: Delacorte Press/Seymour Lawrence, 1975, pp. 300-313.

Exploring the internal sense of loneliness, Klein briefly addresses several aspects of normal adaptation to aging. She observes that the capacity for enjoyment throughout the life cycle depends on one's taking pleasure in what is available without excessive greed for inaccessible gratifications or excessive resentment about frustration. The aging person identifies with the satisfactions of youth, just as the child identified with the satisfactions of adulthood. Pathological responses to aging include idealization of the past to avoid acknowledging the frustrations of the present.

Zinberg, Norman and Kaufman, Irving (ed.) (1963). *Normal Psychology of the Aging Process, First Annual Scientific Meeting of the Boston Society for Gerontologic Psychiatry*. New York: International Universities Press. Also revised and expanded as *Normal Psychology of the Aging Process*, ed. N. Zinberg and I. Kaufman, New York: International Universities Press, 1978, pp. 3-156.

This collection of papers examines the effects of aging on the ego. The effects of gender are not examined. Zinberg and Kaufman present a theoretical schema for considering alterations in drive, defense, mental structure, interpersonal relationships, and social, cultural, and physiological manifestations in response to aging. In separate papers, Berezin and Kaufman focus on the timelessness of mental life, and Levin discusses disturbances of libido equilibrium and the limitation of narcissistic gratifications accompanying aging.

Zinberg, Norman (1964). Reporter, Panel: Psychoanalytic consideration of aging. *J. Amer. Psychoanal. Assn.*, 12:151-159.

This panel focuses on the question of analyzability in the elderly. Levin's paper "Distribution of Narcissistic and Object Libido in the Aged" concludes that our culture permits elderly women greater access to bodily contact and libidinal satisfaction with children than is allowed for elderly men.

Berezin, Martin and Cath, Stanley (ed.)(1965). *Geriatric Psychiatry: Grief, Loss, and Emotional Disorders in the Aging Process*. New York: International Universities Press.

This book includes an annotated bibliography of the literature on aging from 1950-1960. Part I contains papers by Zetzel (1965) and Cath (1965) (see this chapter), which provide theoretical models for understanding Busse's data on depression and narcissistic losses in the elderly. Part II focuses on emotional disorders in aging and includes several papers on technical aspects of therapy with the elderly. Gitelson presents a case of erotic transference in an elderly woman to illustrate the timelessness of fantasy and the capacity of aging patients to engage in analytically oriented therapy. Levin views depression in the elderly as resulting from libidinal shifts in response to internal and external cues.

Cath, Stanley (1965). Some dynamics of middle and later years: A study in depletion and restitution. In: *Geriatric Psychiatry: Grief, Loss, and Emotional Disorders in the Aging Process*, ed. M. Berezin and S. Cath. New York: International Universities Press, pp. 21-72.

Cath conceptualizes mental life as a dynamic balance between external and internal depleting and restorative forces. He hypothesizes that the intrapsychic stability derived from several previously held fundamental anchorages about the self and the self in relation to others are threatened with aging. These anchorages include a healthy, intact body and a consolidated body image; acceptable object relations; a secure socioeconomic status; and an integrated identity derived from having a purpose to life. The elderly experience specific anxieties linked to threats of annihilation that can temporarily elicit primitive defenses and regression.

Zetzel, Elizabeth (1965a). Dynamics of the metapsychology of the aging process. In: *Geriatric Psychiatry: Grief, Loss, and Emotional Disorders in the Aging Process*, ed. M. Berezin and S. Cath. New York: International Universities Press, pp. 109-119.

Zetzel contends that adjustment to the inevitable losses that come with senescence demand a mature, passive acceptance that enables the individual to remobilize adaptive capacities in other areas. She proposes that this acceptance depends on satisfactory early object relations and identifications that minimize the intensity of separation anxiety in old age. She notes that early failures of development may not be noticeable until aging exposes the individual's vulnerability. Zetzel asserts that women who have relied heavily on their family for gratification may have more difficulty adjusting to other sublimations.

Bibring, Grete (1966). Old age: Its liabilities and its assets, a psychobiological discourse. In: *Psychoanalysis: A General Psychology, Essays in Honor of Heinz Hartmann*, ed. R. Loewenstein, L. Newman, M. Schur, and A. Solnit. New York: International Universities Press, pp. 253-271.

Bibring views aging as a period of continued development and maturation. For women, these developmental tasks include adapting to menopause, to retirement, and to changes in object relations, including no longer having young children to mother. These changes can lead to a disruption in object ties, isolation, and a loss of significant sublimations. Both men and women face the greater likelihood of physical illness, diminished sensory functioning, the loss of a highly valued physical appearance and peak physical performance, the death of friends and relatives, and the nearing of one's own death. Bibring observes that the specific fantasy behind fears of death varies widely, depending on the predominant unconscious childhood anxiety. Persons who deal best with the developmental tasks of aging are those who have enjoyed previous instinctual gratification, who can tolerate narcissistic injuries without serious regressive reactions, and who have flexible superegos that can modify previous standards. Bibring concludes that mastering the crisis of aging can lead to new freedom from inner and outer pressure and allow greater tolerance for oneself and others.

Neugarten, Bernice (1968). *Middle Age and Aging.* Chicago, IL: University of Chicago Press.

Neugarten reexamines myths about middle age and aging in women and in men from historical, social, and psychological perspectives. She cautions against assuming that biological changes are primary, rather than looking at the importance of psychological responses to biological changes. She provides an overview of biological, psychological, sociological, and ethnological approaches to adult development.

Benedek, Therese (1973). *Psychoanalytic Investigations: Selected Papers.* New York: Quadrangle/New York Times Book Co., pp. 322-323, 343-349.

These papers follow an earlier one (Benedek, 1950) examining the interplay between changes in culture and intrapsychic transformations. She contrasts a "critical period" in men in their 50s with women's experience of menopause. Work is an important psychic organizer for both sexes; it provides narcissistic gratifications that help maintain self-esteem. Women's greater involvement with the family provides a counterbalance to work that men lack. Both sexes become concerned with a decrease in sexual potency with aging, but only women face the cessation of fertility and a period of hormonal imbalance. Benedek contends that as childbearing has become less hazardous, women no longer equate womanliness with fertility, and they are more able to adapt favorably to aging.

Sternschein, Irving (1973). Reporter, Panel: The experience of separation-individuation in infancy and its reverberation through the course of life: Maturity, senescence, and sociological implications. *J. Amer. Psychoanal. Assn.*, 21:633-645.

Papers are presented by I. Sternschein, B. Neugarten, and M. Berezin. Sternschein discusses the similarities in the responses of women and men to narcissistic loss and to the sense of the inevitability of death. He proposes that women mourn the loss of physical attractiveness in contrast to men, who experience more concern over their decreased sexual functioning. Neugarten describes her psychosocial studies of the life cycle. She concludes that the pathogenicity of events depends mostly on the sense of appropriate or unexpected timing of occurrence. She regards midlife as a period when the perception of time sense shifts to thinking about the time remaining until death rather than the time lived since birth. Neugarten provides specific examples to support her conclusion that midlife women experience a new sense of freedom as well as the pain of loss and separation. Berezin emphasizes the timelessness of drives, wishes, and psychic structure in elderly men and women. He presents two cases of women whose previously stable adaptations decompensated with age.

King, Pearl (1974). Notes on the psychoanalysis of older patients. Reappraisal of the potentialities for change during the second half of life. *J. Analyt. Psychol.*, 19:22-37.

Reviewing her work with older analysands, King concludes that middle-age people (40-65) can benefit from analysis and that narcissistic analysands with a false self may respond better than they could at an earlier age. The internal pressure of feeling limited in time and the failure of once-successful defenses under the pressure of aging render the narcissistic analysand more accessible to interpretations about loss and grief. King describes the narcissistic disequilibrium that may occur in this age group from 1) aging, which is perceived as a threat of disintegration; 2) the diminution of sexual potency and the loss of the capacity to have children, causing women to fear losing power over objects they can no longer control; 3) the threat of replacement by younger workers; 4) illness or death of one's own parents, especially for these patients, who never fully completed separation-individuation and treated their parents as an extension of themselves; 5) the inevitability of illness and consequent dependence on others; and 6) awareness of the inevitability of death, which diminishes a sense of omnipotence. King proposes that decreased instinctual impulses with aging means less need for rigid defenses; analysis thus can render archaic parental imagos and object relations less terrifying. At termination, successful analysands are able to assimilate new objects, modify the impossible standards of their ego ideal, incorporate achievable goals and value systems, and establish a new sense of identity with a shift from living through a false self toward a true, creative self.

Barrett, Carol (1977). Women in widowhood. *Signs*, 2:856-868. Also in: *Psychology of Women: Selected Readings*, ed. J. Williams. New York: Norton, 1979, pp. 496-506.

Barrett provides an extensive review of the sociological studies of widowhood. The stresses concomitant with widowhood, as compared with those of married women, include grief, economic burden, loneliness, role dislocation, reluctance to remarry, unavailability of partners for marriage or for sexual gratification, and impairment of physical and mental health. Response to these stressors varies with age, personality, educational level, employment status, children in the home, and social supports. Barrett assesses social policy and the therapeutic implications of these findings. Areas for further research are suggested.

Griffen, Joyce (1977). A cross-cultural investigation of behavioral changes at menopause. *Soc. Sci. J.*, 14:49-55. Also in: *Psychology of Women: Selected Readings*, ed. J. Williams. New York: Norton, 1978, pp. 488-495.

Griffen uses anthropological data on menopause to separate cultural factors from behavioral and physiological factors. She observes the scarcity of anthropologic data on cultural rites that mark women's passage from their reproductive years. In 10 cultures where data exist, ethnographers noted changed behavior for both men and women with increasing age. In eight other cultures, there was no observation of changes in behavior of postmenopausal women. In some cultures, postmenopausal women withdrew from previous activities, while in others women experienced greater freedom and increased power. Griffen proposes that the paucity of data may reflect gender or age bias of the researchers.

Barnett, Rosalind and Baruch, Grace (1978). Women in the middle years: Conceptions and misconceptions. In: *Psychology of Women: Selected Readings*, ed. J. Williams. New York: Norton, pp. 479-487.

Barnett and Baruch provide a methodological critique of theories of adult development that view the developmental process as proceeding in a linear fashion, requiring specific tasks for resolution. According to the authors, this view is based on the male experience of development and does not consider the unique female experience of varying role patterns and changing degrees of commitment and time demands inherent in balancing career, marriage, and children. The effects of cultural and social bias, and false assumptions about biological determinism in women are discussed. Alternative theoretical models and topics for continued research are proposed.

Kaufman, Irving (1978). Marital adaptation in the aging. In: *Normal Psychology of the Aging Process*, ed. N. Zinberg and I. Kaufman. New York: International Universities Press, pp. 187-202.

Kaufman reviews sociological studies of long-term marriages to examine how couples can balance the changing needs of both partners for narcissistic and object supplies in periods of transition. A clinical example describes how the stability of a marriage was interrupted when the wife became depressed after the children left home. The husband reacted to his wife's withdrawal with resentment and withdrawal, increasing her sense of loss. Therapy focused on the underlying personality conflicts in each partner.

Weideger, Paula (1977). *Menstruation and Menopause*. New York: Dell.

[See Chapter 10 for annotation.]

Notman, Malkah (1978). A psychological consideration of mastectomy. In: *The Woman Patient: Sexual and Reproductive Aspects of Women's Health Care*, Vol. 1, ed. M. Notman and C. Nadelson. New York: Plenum Press, pp. 247-255.

Mastectomy is associated with a life-threatening illness, as well as being a loss of an important body part and a threat to the patient's sense of sexuality. Notman stresses the critical importance of the reactions of the family and the medical staff in helping the patient to develop a stable, adaptive resolution to this crisis.

Matthews, Mary (1979). Depression in mid-life: Change or repetition?—Another chance for working through. *J. Ger. Psychiat.*, 12:37-56.

Matthews presents the case of a depressed 58-year-old woman with a primitive hysterical personality. She illustrates how failure to master earlier developmental tasks of autonomy and intimacy can interfere with successful adaptation to aging.

Rubin, Lillian (1979). *Women of a Certain Age: The Midlife Search for Self.* New York: Harper and Row.

Rubin reports on a survey of 160 full-time mothers between the ages of 35 and 54. In a largely anecdotal book, the women's own words about their conscious experiences present rich material about women's reactions to midlife. Rubin defines midlife in women by the functional changes rather than by age. Despite methodological limitations, Rubin provides a large sample of empirical data from nonpatients.

King, Pearl (1980). The life cycle as indicated by the nature of the transference in the psychoanalysis of the middle-aged and elderly. *Int. J. Psycho-Anal.*, 61:153-160.

King presents two detailed analytic reports of middle-age women and one of a middle-age man to illustrate the common reality pressures and intrapsychic conflicts associated with aging. She emphasizes the centrality of working through developmental issues of adolescence as they reemerge in the transference. King contends that changes in the life situation of middle-age patients that disturb previously stable adaptations also introduce a sense of urgency and immediacy about actual loss. This loss facilitates the analysand's acknowledgment of paranoid and depressive anxieties and the initiation of mourning.

Moulton, Ruth (1980). Divorce in the middle years: The lonely woman and the reluctant man. *J. Amer. Acad. Psychoanal.*, 8:235-250.

Moulton focuses on social and interpersonal aspects of the causes and results of divorce in midlife. Five pseudoindependent professional women experienced reemergence of dependency feelings, loneliness, and needs for reassurance about their femininity in the postdivorce period. Their male counterparts feared renewed dependence on women and remained ambivalent and unattainable.

Colarusso, Calvin, Nemiroff, Robert, and Zuckerman, Susan (1981). Female midlife issues in prose and poetry. In: *Adult Development*, ed. C. Colarusso and R. Nemiroff. New York: Plenum Press, pp. 141-165.

This paper surveys the literature on female adult development in midlife. The authors compare and contrast male and female development by describing midlife themes of the body, object relations, work, time, and death. Prose and poetry vividly illustrate the developmental hurdles, intrapsychic conflicts, and possible resolutions that women face in midlife. Women experience more pain and are more preoccupied with physical signs of aging than are their male counterparts. The authors suggest that prevailing cultural stereotypes that equate femininity and sexual desirability with a youthful body may predispose middle-age women to these reactions.

Gutmann, David (1981). Psychoanalysis and aging: A developmental view. In: *The Course of Life: Psychoanalytic Contributions Toward Understanding Personality Development, Adulthood and the Aging Process*, Vol. 3, ed. S. Greenspan and G. Pollock. Adelphi, MD: U.S. Department of Health and Human Services, NIMH, pp. 489-518.

Gutmann views old age as a time for continued growth and evolution, rather than as a time only for losses and diminished capabilities. He stresses the phase of parenthood for women as an important developmental milestone. With motherhood, women have an opportunity for decisive separation from their own mothers and acceptance of their own mortality. He proposes that depression in women may be a consequence of developmental failure in this phase. Using cross-cultural data, Gutmann maintains that strictly delineated sex roles are essential during early parenthood. With time, men become more open to feminine roles and women take active leadership positions in the community. Although the cross-cultural perspective provides interesting data, Gutmann does not convincingly prove his allegation that these are optimal normative patterns.

Alonso, Anne (1982). Leftover life to live: Issues of entitlement, power, and generativity. *J. Ger. Psychiat.*, 15:155-164.

Alonso's contribution to a symposium on "The Displaced Homemaker: A Crisis of Later Life" focuses on those women who are not able to adapt after losing their role as caretaker to husband, children, or parents. She proposes that these women suffer from serious deficits in their sense of entitlement, power, and generativity that derive from conflicts over aggression and autonomy.

Blau, David (1982). Discussion. Leftover life to live: Issues of entitlement, power and generativity. *J. Ger. Psychiat.*, 15:165-172.

Blau's discussion of Alonso (1982) focuses on delineating the differences in defensive structures and conflicts between those women who experience difficulties after a change in marital status and those who do not. He cautions that women who have recently suffered a loss may be experiencing a temporary loss of self-esteem rather than a characterological depression or narcissistic disorder.

Cath, Stanley (1982). Discussion. Development and adaptation in aging. *J. Ger. Psychiat.*, 15:33-42.

Cath's discussion of A.M. Sandler's (1982) paper focuses on 1) the central theme of neurosis throughout the life cycle and 2) the accessibility to analysis for older patients. He cautions against compressing midlife and old age into one stage. Cath views the 40s and 50s as a period of physical and functional depletion with fear of loss of sexual attractiveness and potency. By contrast, in the 60s and 70s the primary fears are of organic deterioration, disease, and loss of significant others. He emphasizes a cycle of depletion of the selfobject world, to which individuals respond with some despair followed by creative attempts at restitution. Cath postulates that resolution can proceed by 1) constructive resolution, reconciliation with fate, and more creative use of self and selfobjects, 2) a rigid holding action, or 3) a regression to a primitive level of adaptation. Cath presents a speculative reconstruction of Sandler's patient from a self-psychological perspective. The case emphasizes the depletion inherent in the challenge of concomitant physical and emotional aspects of aging, rather than a breakdown of adaptive defenses.

Genevay, B. (1982). In praise of older women. In: *Women's Sexual Experience: Explorations of the Dark Continent*, ed. M. Kirkpatrick. New York: Plenum Press, pp. 87-101.

Genevay criticizes cultural attitudes and social realities that militate against older women's comfortably expressing their sexuality. She illustrates a continuum of modes of sexual fulfillment available to older women, including denial of desire, remembrances, fantasy and dreams, self-touching, affectional exchanges, unsanctioned partners (younger men or other women), partial relationships, and full relationships.

Giele, Janet (ed.)(1982b). *Women in the Middle Years.* New York: Wiley.

[See Chapter 11 for annotation.]

Kirkpatrick, Martha (ed.)(1982). *Women's Sexual Experience: Explorations of the Dark Continent*. New York: Plenum Press.

Kirkpatrick presents a diverse collection of essays on women's sexuality. Papers by Rubin (1982), and Genevay (1982) address sexual issues of middle age and later. [See also Chapter 18.]

Lax, Ruth (1982). The expectable depressive climacteric reaction. *Bull. Menn. Cl.*, 46:151-167.

Lax provides a comprehensive review of the literature on the climacterium. She considers a depressive reaction to the climacteric as a normal response to the physical, psychical, and interpersonal changes occurring at menopause that interfere with women's achievement of their wishful self-image. Lax observes that this depressive reaction does not necessarily lead to regression of the ego or to overt clinical depression. In healthy women, this reaction can resolve by working through the narcissistic injury, with a resulting increase in creative and libidinal fulfillment.

McCrady, Barbara (1982). Women and alcohol abuse. In: *The Woman Patient: Aggression, Adaptations and Psychotherapy*, Vol. 3, ed. M. Notman and C. Nadelson. New York: Plenum Press, pp. 217-243.

McCrady traces the changing patterns and consequences of women's alcoholism during each stage of the life cycle. She emphasizes the paucity of information on the psychological and demographic aspects of alcoholism in women.

Nadelson, Carol, Polonsky, Derek, and Mathews, Mary Alice (1982). Marriage and midlife: The impact of social change. In: *The Woman Patient: Concepts of Femininity and the Life Cycle*, Vol. 2, ed. C. Nadelson and M. Notman, New York: Plenum Press, pp. 145-158.

[See Chapter 13 for annotation.]

Notman, Malkah (1982b). Midlife concerns of women: Implications of the menopause. In: *The Woman Patient: Concepts of Femininity and the Life Cycle*, Vol. 2, ed. C. Nadelson and M. Notman. New York: Plenum Press, pp. 135-144.

Notman conceptualizes the middle years as a time of change and development, rather than predominantly as a time of loss. With middle age comes a sense of the finiteness of time, which for women is linked to their reproductive potential. She challenges the assertion that childless women are more distressed by menopause than are women who have borne children. Instead, Notman observes that women whose identities have been closely tied to motherhood may experience greater distress at menopause. Childless women may become aware of the finiteness of time at a younger age.

Notman, Malkah (1982c). The midlife years and after: Opportunities and limitations—clinical issues. *J. Ger. Psychiat.*, 15:173-191.

Notman's contribution to a panel on "The Displaced Homemaker: A Crisis of Later Life" consists of a series of clinical anecdotes illustrating the complex interweaving of intrapsychic and environmental factors in the responses of women to losing their role as homemaker.

Rubin, Lillian (1982). Sex and sexuality: Women at mid-life. In: *Women's Sexual Experience: Explorations of the Dark Continent*, ed. M. Kirkpatrick. New York: Plenum Press, pp. 61-82.

Rubin presents data on sexuality from her 1979 study of middle-age women. She finds that middle-age married women experience increased sexual satisfaction as they become older. She questions the cohort effect on these women, who reached adulthood in the 1940s and 1950s and who now are responding to societal changes as well as to increasing age. Cohort effect refers to the sociocultural influence of the time in which the group of women lived.

Sandler, Anne-Marie (1982). A developmental crisis in an aging patient: Comments on development and adaptation. *J. Ger. Psychiat.*, 15:11-32.

Sandler reports the analysis of a depressed 69-year-old woman. She demonstrates how characteristic defenses and modes of self-esteem regulation are interfered with by the internal and external changes of aging. Sandler suggests that the goal in analysis with aging patients, as in child analysis, is to facilitate progressive development. She reports that the analysand was better able to tolerate genuine feelings of affectionate attachment at termination, without accompanying fears of being abandoned or shame about her emotions.

Corby, Nan and Zarit, Judy (1983). Old and alone: The unmarried in later life. In: *Sexuality in the Later Years, Roles and Behavior*, ed. R. Weg. New York: Academic Press, pp. 131-145.

Corby and Zarit present a sociologic and demographic description of widows, divorced women, and women who have never married. They contrast the differences in terms of satisfaction, adaptations to loneliness, and strategies for obtaining sensual and sexual gratification. Women who have never married report satisfaction equal to that of married women and greater than that of divorced women or widows. Widows are less likely to remarry than are divorced women.

Livson, Florence (1983). Gender identity: A life-span view of sex-role development. In: *Sexuality in the Later Years, Roles and Behavior*, ed. R. Weg. New York: Academic Press, pp. 105-127.

On the basis of her studies of the evolution of gender identity over the life cycle in both men and women, Livson concludes that women form a separate sense of identity later than men. Most women experience an increase in satisfaction in the middle years. One subgroup of women, the feminine submissives, report satisfaction in their marriages but have great difficulty adjusting to widowhood and divorce as compared with more independent women.

Weg, Ruth (ed.)(1983). *Sexuality in the Later Years, Roles and Behavior*. New York: Academic Press.

Weg's anthology of psychological, sociological, and physiological essays confronts the stereotype of the elderly as asexual. Although both genders are considered, the psychological, cultural, and demographic difficulties faced by older women seeking to fulfill their sexuality and sensuality are reviewed. The papers by Corby and Zarit (1983), and Livson (1983) [see this chapter] discuss women in midlife and senescence.

Barnett, Rosalind (1984). The anxiety of the unknown—Choice, risk, responsibility: Therapeutic issues for today's adult women. In: *Women in Midlife*, ed. G. Baruch and J. Brooks-Gunn. New York: Plenum Press, pp. 341-357.

Barnett contends that women have difficulty integrating newly available social roles with their conscious sense of what constitutes femininity and that this difficulty leads to diminished self-esteem, anxiety, and depression. Using case material from psychotherapy, she argues that mother-daughter controversies over the daughter's life choices exacerbate the daughter's conflicts.

Baruch, Grace (1984). The psychological well-being of women in the middle years. In: *Women in Midlife*, ed. G. Baruch and J. Brooks-Gunn. New York: Plenum Press, pp. 161-180.

Baruch presents her own study and delineates the difficulties in defining and measuring the psychological well-being of women during midlife. She studies the relation between role and an individual sense of mastery and pleasure in women. Six groups of women are studied: never married and working; divorced and working; married without children and working; married without children and not working; married with children and working; and married with children and not working. All four groups of employed women scored high in mastery. Those women having a single role scored lower for pleasure. Motherhood did not enhance feelings of well-being. The highest scores in well-being were those for women combining career, marriage, and children. These findings challenge the view that multiple roles produce greater stress and conflict.

Baruch, Grace and Brooks-Gunn, Jeanne (ed.)(1984). *Women in Midlife.* New York: Plenum Press.

This collection of essays examines the impact of social change on women. The first section contains papers discussing the conceptual and methodological difficulties of studying midlife development in women. The second section considers the issues of social role and psychological health. The final section evaluates the impact of social change on women's well-being.

Luria, Zella and Meade, Robert (1984). Sexuality and the middle aged woman. In: *Women in Midlife*, ed. G. Baruch and J. Brooks-Gunn. New York: Plenum Press, pp. 371-397.

Luria and Meade review several general studies on female sexuality and conclude that women's enjoyment of sex remains the same or increases after menopause. They compare the age-related sexual behaviors of homosexual and heterosexual couples, widows, and unmarried and divorced women.

Myers, Wayne (1984). *Dynamic Therapy of the Older Patient.* New York: Aronson.

Using his analytic experience with patients over age 50, Myers elucidates the psychodynamic aspects and technical issues of working with aging patients. He presents four analyses and two psychotherapies of men and women from 54 to 71 years of age. Specific issues in analyzability, the impact of loss on the sense of self, the "empty nest" syndrome, retirement, changes in object relationships, and self-esteem regulation are discussed. Myers describes how external dislocations can lead to disconcerting upsurges in instinctual drive derivatives. He agrees with King (1974, 1980) that closeness to death gives impetus to the desire to change, rendering narcissistic defenses more accessible to analysis. He concludes that older patients are as analyzable as younger patients. To the usual criteria for analyzability Myers adds the capacity to come to terms with individual limitations. Intense envy is a poor prognostic sign for analysis.

Notman, Malkah (1984). Reflections and perspectives on therapeutic issues for today's adult woman. In: *Women in Midlife*, ed. G. Baruch and J. Brooks-Gunn. New York: Plenum Press, pp. 359-369.

Notman reviews the intrapsychic determinants of role conflicts that women project onto their mothers or externalize onto society. She defines midlife by the individual's recognition of the finiteness of life. Notman presents several clinical examples in which women consciously experience conflict over success but unconsciously experience aggressive and sexual conflicts. Disappointment in fulfillment of unconscious wishes often initiate inhibitions in pursuing personal or professional ambitions.

Stueve, Ann and O'Donnell, Lydia (1984). The daughter of aging parents. In: *Women in Midlife*, ed. G. Baruch and J. Brooks-Gunn. New York: Plenum Press, pp. 203-225.

Stueve and O'Donnell survey 81 Caucasian women from age 30 to 60 who have a living mother older than 70 years of age. They conclude that the current mother-daughter relationship depends on the daughter's psychic and emotional separation from her parents, the intensity of the parents' needs, and the ages of the daughter's own children. Social class appears to be the most salient variable, with working class daughters more involved in their parents' lives.

Bergmann, Maria (1985). The effect of role reversal on delayed marriage and maternity. *The Psychoanalytic Study of the Child*, 40:197-219. New Haven, CT: Yale University Press.

[See Chapter 12 for annotation.]

Notman, Malkah (1985). When a husband dies. In: *The Race Against Time*, ed. R. Nemiroff and C. Colarusso. New York: Plenum Press, pp. 229-240.

Notman provides a case report of a psychoanalytic psychotherapy with a 65-year-old. The therapy began when the patient's husband was diagnosed as having a terminal illness and continued for one and one-half years, until his death. During the treatment, the patient developed greater autonomy, after having perceived herself for years as in the shadow of her successful husband. Although focused initially on the patient's impending loss, the therapy extended over time to include her wider psychic functioning and interpersonal relationships.

Erikson, Joan, Erikson, Erik, and Kivnick, Helen (1986). *Vital Involvement in Old Age*. New York: Norton.

The authors analyze data from interviews with 29 octogenarians who had been followed for most of their adult lives as parents in the Berkeley Guidance Study. Data from the recent study was compared with data from the Guidance Study; retrospective distortions were observed. The authors consider the critical task of adulthood as the ability to care for the next generation. The achievement of wisdom, which they define as the detached concern with life itself in the face of death, is the central developmental task of old age. Material from the interviews and from literature shows the continued salience of earlier developmental stages to adaptations to old age. Despite the small sample, the authors differentiate gender specific responses to aging.

Formanek, Ruth (1986). Learning the lines: Women's aging and self esteem. In: *Psychoanalysis and Women: Contemporary Reappraisals*, ed. J. Alpert. Hillsdale, NJ: The Analytic Press, pp. 139-157.

Formanek surveys the negative social and cultural pressures on women's self-esteem in relation to physical signs of aging. Stage and life-span theories are evaluated from the perspective of female development. The intrapsychic correlates of self-esteem for women in middle and old age are examined from classical psychoanalytic, Kleinian, and self-psychological perspectives. Formanek notes the decreased effectiveness of narcissistic defenses for older women. Healthy adaptation for women, as for men, requires increasing self-esteem by turning to reminiscences, depersonified abstract ideals and interests, and intimate relationships with family and friends.

Kivnick, Helen (1986). Grandparenthood and a life cycle. *J. Ger. Psychiat.*, 19:39-56.

Kivnick explores the psychological meanings of grandparenthood throughout the life cycle by focusing on five dimensions: 1) the centrality of grandparenthood to a sense of identity; 2) the sense of being a valued elder who can experience oneself as a source of wisdom; 3) a sense of immortality through the clan, or the experiencing of grandchildren as a continuation of the family line; 4) reinvolvement with one's personal past through identification with one's own grandparents; and 5) pleasure in being able to indulge grandchildren. Gender-specific issues are not mentioned.

Kornhaber, Arthur (1986). Grandparenting: Normal and pathological—a preliminary communication from the Grandparent Study. *J. Ger. Psychiat.*, 19:19-38.

Kornhaber reports on his large-scale study of grandparents and grandchildren. He finds that grandparents and grandchildren play a significant role for each other in the mutually supportive family. He contrasts this mutually supportive position to several pathological situations, which reflected the grandparent's psychopathology. Intrapsychic representations and fantasies of grandparents and grandchildren are not discussed.

Miller, Nancy (1986). Reporter, Panel: The psychoanalysis of the older patient. *J. Amer. Psychoanal. Assn.*, 34:163-177.

The panelists, E. Simburg, P. King, A.M. Sandler, and N. Miller, provide theoretical and clinical evidence that psychoanalysis can facilitate developmental and structural change in the middle and later years of life. They provide theoretical and clinical evidence that human object-needs and transference potentials occur throughout the life cycle. Preoedipal and oedipal material is readily available from early childhood. Sexual and work inhibitions can be shifted, and modification of self-representations and the ego ideal can take place. The analyses of several women over 60 with depressive and masochistic symptoms are discussed.

Semel, Vicki (1986). The aging woman: Confrontations with hopelessness. In: *The Psychology of Today's Woman: New Psychoanalytic Perspectives*, ed. T. Bernay and D. Cantor. Hillsdale, NJ: The Analytic Press, pp. 253-269.

Semel uses a review of the psychoanalytic literature to illustrate how symptoms such as loss of memory or rigidity of character, which appear to be a consequence of organic deficits, may actually result from intrapsychic conflict that can be treated. She asserts that responses to aging are complex and variable and are dependent on level of health, social situation, and character structure. She demonstrates this diversity with three case histories of women with severe preoedipal pathology, but with distinct patterns of predominant defenses.

Severino, Sally, Teusink, J. Paul, Pender, Vivian, and Bernstein, Anne (1986). Overview: The psychology of grandparenthood. *J. Ger. Psychiat.*, 19:3-17.

The literature on grandparenthood is reviewed with an emphasis on the intrapsychic changes involved in adapting to the developmental tasks of this phase. The authors discuss a 40-year-old woman who became depressed when her children left home. The patient identified with the hated aspects of her maternal grandmother, whom she had represented intrapsychically as a "bad" mother, and directed her hostility against herself as she approached grandmotherhood. The authors delineate the ways in which grandparenthood can serve to successfully rework old conflicts or can precipitate new maladaptations.

Tallmer, Margot (1986). Empty-nest syndrome: Possibility or despair. In: *The Psychology of Today's Woman: New Psychoanalytic Perspectives*, ed. T. Bernay and D. Cantor. Hillsdale, NJ: The Analytic Press, pp. 231-252.

Tallmer challenges the view that mothers predominantly experience both menopause and their children's leaving home as losses. She cites several studies indicating that the departure of the last child does not correlate with emotional distress. Tallmer suggests that women at midlife can be stimulated by changes and may return to unresolved issues of identity and autonomy. Emotional distress may result from the return of adult children or the presence of ill parents in the home just as the mother is eager to relinquish the caretaking role. Tallmer provides a critical review of theories of adult development.

Ziman-Tobin, Phyllis (1986). Childless women approaching midlife: Issues in psychoanalytic treatment. In: *The Psychology of Today's Woman: New Psychoanalytic Visions*, ed. T. Bernay and D. Cantor. Hillsdale, NJ: The Analytic Press, pp. 305-317.

[See Chapter 12 for annotation.]

Meyer, Jon (1988). A case of hysteria, with a note on biology. *J. Amer. Psychoanal. Assn.*, 36:319-346.

The analysis of an hysterical neurosis with somatic illness is discussed. [See Chapter 20 for annotation.]

Weller, Malcolm (1988). Hysterical behavior in patriarchal communities. *Brit. J. Psychiat.*, 152:687-695.

[See Chapter 20 for annotation.]

Auchincloss, Elizabeth and Michels, Robert (1989). The impact of middle age on ambitions and ideals. In: *The Middle Years: New Psychoanalytic Perspectives*, ed. J. Oldham and R. Liebert. New Haven, CT: Yale University Press, pp. 40-57.

The evolution of ambitions and ideals in midlife is examined by integrating three models of adult midlife development. The first model focuses on midlife events that are reworked in the light of childhood fantasies. In the second model, midlife challenges elicit new defensive styles and adaptations. The third model proposes continual changes in the self-representation. Analytic case material, Freud's life, and examples from literature illustrate the authors' contention that middle age brings an awareness of the inevitability of death and a potential shift toward creativity and generativity.

Hiller, Janet (1989). Breast cancer: A psychogenic disease? *Women and Health*, 15:5-18.

Hiller critically assesses early historical and current psychiatric, psychosomatic medicine, and psychoanalytic literature for their psychological theories about 1) the etiology of breast cancer and accompanying depression, 2) the link between conflicts about masculine activities and the development of various female reproductive illnesses, 3) psychoanalytic formulations of disease etiologies based on conflict over femininity and sexual repression, and 4) current ideas that disease in general results from repressed anger. She concludes that these theories all reflect social views of women rather than medical realities. Her observations of flawed research designs and confusion of cause and effect, even in recent explorations of the relationship between breast cancer and character, provide a framework for initiating new research on this topic.

Kalinich, Lila (1989). The biological clock. In: *The Middle Years: New Psychoanalytic Perspectives*, ed. J. Oldham and R. Liebert. New Haven, CT: Yale University Press, pp. 123-134.

Kalinich presents several vignettes about resistance, transference, and countertransference issues in analyzing perimenopausal women who are attempting to conceive.

Kernberg, Otto (1989). The interaction of middle age and character pathology: Treatment implications. In: *The Middle Years: New Psychoanalytic Perspectives*, ed. J. Oldham and R. Liebert. New Haven, CT: Yale University Press, pp. 209-223.

Kernberg provides a conceptual framework for the developmental tasks of midlife (ages 40-60). Using clinical examples, he suggests that most patients with a neurotic personality organization can benefit from treatment at this age; certain patients with narcissistic personality disorder may actually be better able to benefit from treatment at midlife than at an earlier age. Kernberg feels that the prognosis for treatment at midlife for most borderline character disorders is generally poor.

Kirkpatrick, Martha (1989a). Lesbians: A different middle age? In: *The Middle Years: New Psychoanalytic Perspectives*, ed. J. Oldham and R. Liebert. New Haven, CT: Yale University Press, pp. 135-148.

Lesbians are a diverse group for whom aging may be less stressful than for heterosexual women. For the 25-35% of homosexuals who are parents, the phases of their adult life have been organized around children. A study of divorced homosexual mothers showed them to be less bitter than divorced heterosexual mothers are; the homosexual women ascribed their marital failure to lack of intimacy. They did worry about being devalued by adolescent children because of societal prejudices. Another subgroup of long-married women who changed sexual orientation to homosexual in midlife were seeking intimacy and relief of loneliness rather than sexual gratification. These women feel new self-esteem and pride in the discovery of the capacity for intimate feelings toward women. Lesbian women are less likely to lose their partner in middle age than are heterosexual women; they hold higher-paying jobs; and they are used to managing their own financial affairs. The search for intimacy has a special imperative in the lives of lesbians.

According to Kirkpatrick, lesbians' sexual relations are likely to be better than heterosexual women's in midlife, resting on the valuation of mutual nurturing and similar levels of sexual interest. The heterosexual women more often experience incompatibilities with their partners in midlife. Lesbian couples suffer instead from excessive intimacy or merger, including an inability to tolerate separate feelings and differences, and excessive demands to supply their partner's narcissistic needs. This can lead to symptoms of partner dissatisfaction, depression, loss of libido, and phobic states.

Martinez, Diane (1989). Psychosomatic considerations of infertility. *Medical Psychiatry: Theory and Practice*, Vol. 2, ed. E. Garza-Treviño. Teaneck, NJ: World Scientific Publications, pp. 693-719.

[See Chapter 14 for annotation.]

Meyers, Helen (1989). The impact of teenaged children on parents. In: *The Middle Years: New Psychoanalytic Perspectives*, ed. J. Oldham and R. Liebert. New Haven, CT: Yale University Press, pp. 75-88.

Meyers describes a regression undergone by middle-age parents of adolescents, which can reawaken their own adolescent conflicts. This regression can lead to impairment of previously functional compromises or to the formation of more adaptive solutions. Intimacy with one's adolescent child offers the opportunity to rework infantile conflicts and facilitate mature adaptation. Positive opportunities for the midlife parent include guiding the adolescent, sharing the adolescent's experience, and experiencing his growth. Parental conflicts about loss, sexuality, disappointment, and competition can lead to difficulty in the parent. Both positive and negative outcomes are illustrated.

Nadelson, Carol (1989). Issues in the analyses of single women in their thirties and forties. In: *The Middle Years: New Psychoanalytic Perspectives*, ed. J. Oldham and R. Liebert. New Haven, CT: Yale University Press, pp. 105-122.

[See Chapter 12 for annotation.]

Oldham, John (1989). The third individuation: Middle-aged children and their parents. In: *The Middle Years: New Psychoanalytic Perspectives*, ed. J. Oldham and R. Liebert. New Haven, CT: Yale University Press, pp. 89-104.

Oldham draws parallels between individuation in adolescence and in midlife. In adolescence, individuation involves emotional turbulence, disengagement from parents, and modification of parental object representations. By contrast, midlife individuation involves relinquishing the illusion of the immortality of one's parents and oneself. If an elderly parent requires prolonged caretaking, dies prematurely, or does not die at the expected time, resolution of this phase becomes more complicated.

Pathological resolutions may lead to dysfunctional attachments or to avoidance of the elderly parent.

**Oldham, John and Liebert, Robert (ed.)(1989). *The Middle Years: New Psychoanalytic Perspectives*. New Haven, CT: Yale University Press.**

The middle years are conceptualized from the perspectives of ego psychology, self psychology, object relations theory, and family therapy. Most papers consider the experiences of both men and women at midlife (ages 30-60). Auchincloss and Michels (1989) review theoretical questions about changes versus fixity in intrapsychic life. Fantasies, self-representations, and ego-ideals of midlife are explored in relation to their constancy in childhood. Three chapters specifically deal with midlife development in women: "Issues in the Analyses of Single Women in their Thirties and Forties" by Nadelson [reviewed in Chapter 12], "The Biological Clock" by Kalinich, and "Lesbians: A Different Middle Age?" by Kirkpatrick.

**Viederman, Milton (1989). Middle life as a period of mutative change. In: *The Middle Years: New Psychoanalytic Perspectives*, ed. J. Oldham and R. Liebert. New Haven, CT: Yale University Press, pp. 224-239.**

Viederman addresses the intrapsychic effect of sudden and severe physical illness before old age. Although he focuses on middle age, his observations apply throughout the life cycle. He describes a married, 40-year-old mother who was able to mourn after her own mastectomy and the simultaneous loss of a close friend who died of breast cancer and thus successfully developed a more mature self-representation.

**Bell, Susan (1990). The medicalization of menopause. In: *The Meanings of Menopause: Historical, Medical and Clinical Perspectives*, ed. R. Formanek. Hillsdale, NJ: The Analytic Press, pp. 43-63.**

Bell traces the sociological impact of the designation of menopause as a deficiency disease in the 1930s and 1940s. In the 19th century, menopause was viewed as a normal physiological crisis. Bell proposes that employing the disease model for a normal process has had adverse implications for menopausal women's self-image.

**Bowles, Cheryl (1990). The menopausal experience: Sociocultural influences and theoretical Models. In: *The Meanings of Menopause: Historical, Medical and Clinical Perspectives*, ed. R. Formanek. Hillsdale, NJ: The Analytic Press, pp. 157-176.**

Bowles explores the interplay of biological, psychological, and sociocultural factors in women's experiences of menopause. She concludes that women's reporting of symptoms varies across cultures and across subgroups within a culture. She reviews several theoretical models.

Datan, Nancy (1990). Aging into transitions: Cross-cultural perspectives on women at midlife. In: *The Meanings of Menopause: Historical, Medical and Clinical Perspectives*, ed. R. Formanek. Hillsdale, NJ: The Analytic Press, pp. 117-132.

Datan reports the results of a large-scale study of five subpopulations of menopausal Israeli women to assess the relationship between the modernity of culture and the responses to menopause. The findings of the demographic study indicated that 1) women in all groups unanimously welcomed menopause even if they previously had wanted more children, 2) menopausal symptoms varied between groups, 2) the group experiencing the greatest cultural transition reported the highest levels of stress. The author concludes that ease of adaptation to developmental tasks is facilitated by the stability of cultural context, rather than by the specific contents of cultural beliefs. Menopause was demonstrated to be primarily experienced as a time of transition and change rather than of loss.

Formanek, Ruth (1990a). Continuity and change and "the change of life": Premodern views of the menopause. In: *The Meanings of Menopause: Historical, Medical and Clinical Perspectives*, ed. R. Formanek. Hillsdale, NJ: The Analytic Press, pp. 3-41.

Formanek provides an extensive review of historical attitudes toward menopause from Galen through the discovery of sexual hormones in the 1920s. She notes the paucity of data in the gynecological and psychoanalytic literature about women's experience of menopause.

Formanek, Ruth (ed.)(1990b). *The Meanings of Menopause: Historical, Medical, and Clinical Perspectives*. Hillsdale, NJ: The Analytic Press.

This book is a collection of essays that comprehensively survey the historical, cultural, sociological, medical, psychological, and psychoanalytical aspects of menopause. The book is divided into three sections: 1) History and Theory; 2) Psychosocial, Cross-Cultural, and Research Perspectives; and 3) Endocrinology, Clinical and Experiential Studies, and Literary Aspects. The papers demonstrate that almost every aspect of menopause continues to be the subject of controversy. Most of the papers are annotated separately in this chapter.

Goodman, Madeleine (1990). The biomedical study of menopause. In: *The Meanings of Menopause: Historical, Medical and Clinical Perspectives*, ed. R. Formanek. Hillsdale, NJ: The Analytic Press, pp. 133-156.

Goodman reviews the current biomedical understanding of menopause and uses cross-cultural data to demonstrate that the biology of menopause cannot be studied in isolation from the life circumstances and health status of the target population.

Greene, John (1990). Psychosocial influences and life events at the time of the menopause. In: *The Meanings of Menopause: Historical, Medical and Clinical Perspectives*, ed. R. Formanek. Hillsdale, NJ: The Analytic Press, pp. 79-115.

Greene reviews empirically based studies of women during menopause. He reports that climacteric women have a greater vulnerability to stressful life events as compared with premenopausal women. He contends that their greater vulnerability could exacerbate preexisting psychopathology, marital discord, or social isolation. Greene concludes that in the absence of contributing factors, menopause need not be associated with physical or psychological illness.

Harris, Helena (1990). A critical view of three psychoanalytical positions on menopause. In: *The Meanings of Menopause: Historical, Medical and Clinical Perspectives*, ed. R. Formanek. Hillsdale, NJ: The Analytic Press, pp. 65-77.

Harris contrasts the early Freudian model espoused by Deutsch (1925, 1945), Benedek's (1973) ego psychological model, and Lax's (1982) object relational model. She proposes a self-psychological model, stressing the importance of women's selfobject functioning in maintaining equilibrium and self-esteem during menopause.

Kaplan, Helen (1990). Sex, intimacy, and the aging process. *J. Amer. Acad. Psychoanal.*, 18:185-205.

Kaplan summarizes the age-related changes in sexual functioning of both sexes. Reviewing work with 400 patients between 50 and 92 years of age, she focuses on the interplay of cultural, intrapsychic, and relationship factors within the couple that may temper or exacerbate these sexual changes. Kaplan describes a psychodynamically based treatment program for psychosexual rehabilitation of the older couple that enables continuing pleasurable sexual activity. Women who can accept a more active sexual role with increasing age have more healthy sexual adaptations.

Maxwell, Marilyn (1990). Portraits of menopausal women in selected works of English and American literature. In: *The Meanings of Menopause: Historical, Medical and Clinical Perspectives*, ed. R. Formanek. Hillsdale, NJ: The Analytic Press, pp. 255-279.

Maxwell presents examples of literary images of middle-age women from 1621 to the 1950s to illustrate her observation that until publication of recent feminist literature, middle-age women were depicted stereotypically as diseased, as unnaturallly sexual, and as behaving irrationally.

Notman, Malkah (1990). Varieties of menopausal experience. In: *The Meanings of Menopause: Historical, Medical and Clinical Perspectives*, ed. R. Formanek. Hillsdale, NJ: The Analytic Press, pp. 239-254.

Notman discusses several menopausal patients whose physical symptoms could be linked to a variety of individual symbolic meanings. Menopause is viewed as just one of many life transitions, this one occurring at midlife, although a woman may experience the change as a central physical and psychological marker in her life. Notman contends that the individual woman's sense of femininity, identity, and self-esteem depends on complex intrapsychic dynamics that may be influenced by the cessation of reproduction but does not necessarily depend on it.

Phillips, Suzanne (1990). Reflections of self and other: Men's views of menopausal women. In: *The Meanings of Menopause: Historical, Medical and Clinical Perspectives*, ed. R. Formanek. Hillsdale, NJ: The Analytic Press, pp. 281-295.

Phillips investigates men's views of menopausal women and the reciprocal effect of these views on women's redefinitions of themselves. She uses both clinical observations and a questionnaire examining male and female attitudes in midlife. Phillips concludes that men experience confusion, crisis, and collusion along with concern and empathy in facing their partner's menopause.

Vinokur, Amiram, Threatt, Barbara, Vinokur-Kaplan, Diane, and Satariano, William (1990). The process of recovery from breast cancer for younger and older patients: Changes during the first year. *Cancer*, 65:1242-54.

This article reports data from a large-scale, collaborative study of the mental health of postmastectomy female patients, controlling for age and severity of disease. Assessment was based on psychological tests, self-reports, and reports by significant others. Contrary to their initial hypothesis, the authors found that the perception of threat from breast cancer was not correlated with the actual stage of the disease (true risk of recurrence). The threat was experienced as greater by younger patients than older patients. Predictors of poor mental health at follow-up were strongly correlated to increased appraisal of threat in younger women and to greater physical impairment in older women.

# Chapter 16

# Fathers and Daughters

Nadine Levinson

Even in Freud's earliest writings (1895), fathers were considered to be of primary importance in the development of their daughters. He insisted that the deepest affection of girls was for their fathers, who played a central role in the etiology of their neurosis. Later, Freud modified this conviction as he developed his theory of female development (1925, 1931a) to reflect his discovery that the most intense attachment of girls was actually for their mothers, with fathers subsequently assuming major significance in the acquisition of femininity during oedipal-phase development and adolescence. Fathers were now seen as objects of love, admiration, protection, and authority. Freud also believed, however, that turning to the father represented a secondary formation after an early phase of competitive rivalry with the father for the mother. He offered no further discussion from his own clinical work with women about how these negative oedipal wishes originated, became transformed into positive oedipal strivings, or finally attained resolution.

From Freud's death until the 1970s, a gap developed in the literature. The 1970s ushered in a burgeoning of interest in fathers in many allied disciplines, including developmental psychology, psychiatry, cognitive psychology, and ethology. Father-infant studies focused on the differences and similarities between mothers and fathers and the differential emotional and behavioral responses of their infants. Investigators recognized that mothers were not reliable informants about fathers' parenting behaviors. Scientists began observing fathers in the laboratory and in natural settings. These studies pointed to an earlier, unrecognized appreciation of the father's significance to the infant as more than a protector, but also as an attachment object and an important facilitator of ego development.

Recent psychoanalytic literature has reflected these provocative findings by shifting focus from the oedipal father or "forgotten father" to an assessment of the vicissitudes of the preoedipal father-daughter relationship. Areas of interest include stranger anxiety, attachment behavior, cognitive, psychosexual, and gender development, affect control, normal narcissism, gender identity, and self- and object representations. These developmental challenges and the internalizations that result from them are parallel to, yet separate from, the preoedipal relationship of girls with their mothers, although these early experiences do later influence the oedipal constellation. [Other annotations on the relationship of fathers to their daughters may be found in Chapters 21 and 24.]

Freud, Sigmund (1919). A child is being beaten. *Standard Edition*, 17:177-204. London: Hogarth Press, 1953.

Masochistic fantasies as a compromise solution for girls' oedipal yearnings for father are detailed. [See Chapters 1 and 21 for annotations.]

Freud, Sigmund (1925). Some psychical consequences of the anatomical distinction between the sexes. *Standard Edition*, 19:243-258. London: Hogarth Press, 1953.

Freud asserts that the libidinal attachment to the father is a consequence of penis envy. [See Chapter 1 for annotation.]

Lampl-de Groot, Jeanne (1927). The evolution of the Oedipus complex in women. *Int. J. Psycho-Anal.*, 9:332-345. Also in: *The Psychoanalytic Reader*, ed. R. Fliess. New York: International Universities Press, 1948, pp. 180-194.

Lampl-de Groot describes how the girl's first oedipal attachment to mother precedes her erotic oedipal attachment to father. The girl's competitive, oedipal relationship with her father is detailed. [See Chapter 2 for annotation.]

Freud, Sigmund (1931a). Female sexuality. *Standard Edition*, 21:223-243. London: Hogarth Press, 1953.

Freud notes that an intense father attachment only reflects an earlier exclusive attachment to the mother. [See Chapter 1 for annotation.]

Klein, Melanie (1932b). The effects of early anxiety-situations on the sexual development of the girl. In: *The Psychoanalysis of Children*, London: Delacorte Press, 1975, pp. 194-239.

Klein elaborates an early oedipal fantasy of an oral incorporative wish for the paternal penis, which girls see as belonging to mother, who keeps it in her body. Klein, however, emphasizes libidinal motivation for girls' wish for father's penis (as a substitute for the frustrating breast), rather than narcissistic reasons to introject it as a masculine attribute of their own. [See also Chapter 6.]

Eisendorfer, Arnold (1943). Clinical significance of single parent relationship in women. *Psychoanal. Q.*, 12:233-239.

Two cases demonstrate the impact of a single mother's libido on her daughter, who lost her father before six months of age. Oral fixation and an intense homosexual relationship between mother and daughter were found to exist. The author suggests that a severe superego develops as a defense against unassimilated id forces.

Lacan, Jacques (1958). *Ecrits: A Selection*, London: Tavistock, 1977.

Lacan views the unconscious as structured like a language, a specific language that reflects the values of a patriarchal society. Lacan writes not about the oedipal father, but about a symbolic primal father, with absolute phallic power, who intervenes into the "imaginary" mother-child dyad. Sexuality for both sexes is rooted in the unconscious and hinges on resolution of the castration complex.

Weissman, Philip (1964). Psychosexual development in a case of neurotic virginity and old maidenhood. *Int. J. Psycho-Anal.*, 45:110-120.

Frigidity is linked to a nonoedipal father fixation, which overlays a preoedipal fixation to the mother. [See Chapter 18 for annotation.]

Forrest, Tess (1966). Paternal roots of female character development. *Contemp. Psychoanal.*, 3:21-38.

The unique paternal contributions to female psychological development and character formation are described. Fathers from early infancy help children individuate by breaking into the biopsychic symbiotic bond (primary dependency) with the mother. They preserve the mother's feminine identity and help her from being totally absorbed in motherhood. Paternal trust is derived from fathers' affirmation of their daughters' femininity and is necessary for their future relationships with men. The character formations of the daughter resulting from three types of marital constellations are conjectured: 1) a hysterical character, when a father is rejecting and the daughter is abandoned to the dyadic mother-daughter unity, 2) an impulsive character disorder, when the daughter is preferred to the mother by the father and incestuous impulses are overstimulated, and 3) an obsessional character, when both mother and father are rejecting. A case history of a young woman who suffered paternal deprivation is presented.

Leonard, Marjorie (1966). Fathers and daughters: The significance of fathering in the psychosexual development of the girl. *Int. J. Psycho-Anal.*, 47:325-334.

Using material from the therapies of six adolescent girls, Leonard discusses aspects of the father-daughter relationship that contribute to psychopathology. Leonard contends that the father has a central influence on the libidinal development of his daughter. The quality of the father's participation and his availability to give protection, support, and approval is significant. The father must be optimally available to love and be loved at the time the girl changes from the preoedipal to the oedipal relationship, and then during preadolescence to affirm her budding sexuality. A lack of attention is experienced by the girl as rejection, interferes with her sense of self and self-esteem, and increases difficulties in relinquishing the preoedipal attachment to mother. Pathologic fathering attitudes are illustrated, including nonparticipating, possessive, clingy, identifying, and seductive fathers. Leonard concludes that the father must have resolved his own oedipal conflict to be able to offer his daughter affection at crucial stages of her development.

Spiegel, Rose (1966). The role of father-daughter relationships in depressive women. In: *Science and Psychoanalysis*, ed. J. Masserman. New York: Grune and Stratton, pp. 105-120.

Although discussing the multiple theories and etiologies of depression in women, Spiegel emphasizes the traumatizing role of the unavailable father at preadolescence and adolescence. The daughter reacts with anticipatory depression and a self-effacing self-image, which negatively affects subsequent relationships with men. The clinical material from three analyses is diffuse.

Prosen, Harry (1967). Sexuality in females with "hysteria." *Amer. J. Psychiat.*, 124:141-146.

Prosen asserts that an intense preoedipal attachment to the father led to the development of hysteria. [See Chapter 20 for annotation.]

Benedek, Therese (1970a). Fatherhood and providing. In: *Parenthood: Its Psychology and Psychopathology*, ed. E. J. Anthony and T. Benedek. Boston, MA: Little, Brown, pp. 167-183.

Benedek asserts that fatherhood (the male's role in procreation) has instinctual roots beyond the drive organization of procreation and includes a reciprocal developmental experience for the father as he forms relationships with his children. Two sources of motivation are asserted in the relationship of the father with his child: the identification with his child and the identification with his father. There is no discussion of the relationship of the father to female development.

Chasseguet-Smirgel, Janine (1970). Feminine guilt and the Oedipus complex. In: *Female Sexuality: New Psychoanalytic Views*, ed. J. Chasseguet-Smirgel. Ann Arbor: University of Michigan Press, pp. 94-134.

The author reaffirms that fathers are crucial for their daughters' psychosexual development and influence such traits of female sexuality as penis envy, masochism, and superego formation. [See also Chapters 7 and 21.]

Abelin, Ernest (1971). The role of the father in the separation-individuation process. In: *Separation-Individuation*, ed. J. McDevitt and C. Settlage. New York: International Universities Press, pp. 229-252.

Using observational research on 14 mother-infant pairs throughout the separation-individuation process, Abelin studies the role of the father in early development and asserts that fathers play a special role in the growth and autonomy of ego functions. Specific importance is attributed to fathers during the "practicing subphase" when they encourage exploration and identification. The social smile in response to fathers is the key behavioral milestone Abelin focuses on as an indicator of specific attachment. He finds that girls attach to their fathers as early as seven months, earlier and with more intensity than do boys. Abelin proposes triangulation (the process of the father's being a specific and important identificatory object for the infant) as the mechanism causing the transformation from sensorimotor thought to symbolic formation, resulting in the formation of a first self-image. [See also Chapter 6.]

Burlingham, Dorothy (1973). The preoedipal infant-father relationship. *The Psychoanalytic Study of the Child*, 28:23-47. New Haven, CT: Yale University Press.

Burlingham describes the reciprocal effects of interactions between infants and fathers by reviewing data from parent and child observation, fathers in analyses, and fathers in literature. The multiple roles of fathers in Freud's writings are reviewed, as are the relationship of fathers to infants. Burlingham finds that fathers' fantasies about their infant daughters concern how their daughters will respond to their own loving feelings and, later, whether they will have many suitors. Burlingham reviews the effect of and response to fathers through various developmen-

tudes, including gaze, smiling response, stimulation, and preference for fathers over mothers. Fathers, more than mothers, stimulate and excite both their boys and their girls. Fathers, however, treat their sons as like objects, whereas they relate to their daughters according to their attitudes toward femininity and the feminine part of themselves. The importance of girls' innate femininity is left as an open question. Burlingham concludes that the preoedipal interactions and resulting identifications with fathers are different from those with mothers, but that those differences are based on fathers' personality and specific patterns of handling.

Maccoby, Eleanor and Jacklin, Carol (1974). *The Psychology of Sex Differences.* Stanford, CA: Stanford University Press.

Social-psychological research on fathers and young daughters supports the idea that fathers are a potent force in defining and expecting feminine behavior from their daughters. [See also Chapter 5.]

Biller, Henry (1976). The father and personality development: Paternal deprivation and sex-role development. In: *The Role of the Father in Child Development,* ed. M. Lamb. New York: Wiley, pp. 89-156.

This comprehensive chapter assesses important empirical developmental research about fathers. One section reviews the research on the effect of fathers on girls' emotional and interpersonal functioning. Problems with sex-role and personality development are linked to paternal deprivation. Numerous studies showed that women with inadequate or disturbed paternal relationships are more likely to become homosexual. There are few references to psychoanalytic studies, but the paper amasses a large bibliography from other disciplines that examines father absence and inadequate fathering and psychopathology.

Lamb, Michael (1976). The role of the father: An overview. In: *The Role of the Father in Child Development,* ed. M. Lamb. New York: Wiley, pp. 1-63.

This chapter reviews the psychologic and psychoanalytic developmental literature about the role of the father up to 1976. A critical appraisal of theoretical and empirical developmental studies is undertaken, with a synthesis of the diverse analytic and nonanalytic viewpoints. The data show that infants reveal precursors of specific and differential attachment to the father. In order for an attachment to take place, fathers must have both a quantitative and a qualitative interaction in the first few months. References to fathers and sex-role adaptation are numerous.

Chodorow, Nancy (1978). *The Reproduction of Mothering.* Berkeley: University of California Press.

Chodorow notes that in the preoedipal period fathers are less important than mothers for the determination of a sense of self, for they are not as internalized and thus much less of an object subject to ambivalence, repression, and splitting of good and bad aspects. She details a developmental explanation for the change of objects from mother to father as the girl enters the oedipal phase. Chodorow argues that girls may want a penis libidinally, but that does not mean they want it narcissistically, or as a part of their own body. She observes that the father must encourage his daughter's feminine/heterosexual attachment to him, yet the quality of his relationship with her, based on his own personality or socialization as a father, will not have the same impact on her as that of her mother (her primary caretaker). Chodorow emphasizes that although the daughter takes father as an erotic object and has a heterosexual orientation, her relationship of love, dependence, attachment, and symbiosis still continues with her mother.

Abelin, Ernest (1980). Triangulation, the role of the father, and the origins of core gender identity during the rapprochement subphase. In: *Rapprochement,* ed. R. Lax, S. Bach, and J. Burland. New York: Aronson, pp. 151-179.

A more fully developed "tripartite model" of early triangulation and the role of the father in core gender identity is proposed to account for gender differences in the evolution of symbol formation and self- and object representation. The data are derived from an observational comparison longitudinal study of a brother and sister and other observations gathered over years in Mahler's research nursery. Abelin proposes that gender identity emerges earlier and more readily in boys, and generational identity emerges earlier in girls. He contends that symbol formation and the symbolic mental image of self originate in male infants' full-blown identification with their father at 18 months. Girls' sexual-core-self classification is acquired later, at three years of age. He assumes that girls' core self-image constellation is, "I (a child) want mommy (big); or I (a child) want baby (small)" and that girls cannot establish gender identity because they have not yet formed an attachment to a different kind of object, the male father. The core self-image is thought to be feminine, like the mirrored mother, but not in reference to the unlike self, the father, who is still peripheral. By contrast, for boys, "the father becomes the primary attachment object" in a triadic relationship that does not exist for girls. Other data from academic psychology, French psychoanalysts, ethology, and biology are employed to buttress Abelin's paradigmatic model. The paper is valuable in its effort to explain the role of fathers in the transformation of sensorimotor schemata to symbolic thought and core gender identity.

Ekstein, Rudolph (1980). Daughters and lovers. In: *Women's Sexual Development: Explorations of Inner Space*, ed. M. Kirkpatrick. New York: Plenum Press, pp. 207-237.

A blueprint of the life cycle of the father-daughter relationship and the reciprocal developmental tasks is proposed by Ekstein, using examples from literature and child observation.

Cath, Stanley, Gurwitt, Alan and Ross, John (ed.)(1982). *Father and Child: Developmental and Clinical Perspectives*. Boston, MA: Little, Brown.

The role of the father throughout the life cycle is elucidated in this scholarly and comprehensive psychoanalytically oriented volume. It provides solid evidence for the different, but equally important, parental roles that fathers and mothers play in relationship to their children. The book is divided into five sections. The History and Review section contains several chapters critically reviewing the existing literature on fathering. The next two sections focus on developmental perspectives in the early and later phases of the life cycle, including topics on gender identity, aggression, and the preoedipal father, mother, and daughter. Sociocultural and historical views are presented in the fourth section. Finally, the fifth section concentrates on clinical problems and applications and examines such issues as incest, divorce, and the father's impact on psychopathology. [Several chapters are annotated in this chapter.]

Galenson, Eleanor and Roiphe, Herman (1982). The preoedipal relationship of a father, mother, and daughter. In: *Father and Child: Developmental and Clinical Perspectives*, ed. S. Cath, A. Gurwitt, and J. Ross. Boston, MA: Little, Brown, pp. 151-162.

From infant observation, the authors trace the preoedipal interactions between a little girl, Mary, and her mother and father. The report emphasizes the developmental vicissitudes of the growing identification with both parents. The mother's conscious and unconscious wish to undo her painful experiences with her own father, coupled with Mary's father's willingness, led Mary to a similar, early erotic attachment to her father and an early flirtatiousness with other men. The authors describe the child's responses to the discovery of the anatomical differences, which revived for both mother and daughter earlier fears of anal and object loss. Whereas the mother idealizes the penis to make up for previous losses, Mary shows heightened genital curiosity, denial of genital difference, and increased capacity for symbol formation. Clearly, the mother's unconscious conflicts and fantasies about her father from childhood colored her daughter's perceptions and actions with her father.

Gunsberg, Linda (1982). Selected critical review of psychological investigations of early father-infant relationship. In: *Father and Child: Developmental and Clinical Perspectives*, ed. S. Cath, A. Gurwitt, and J. Ross, pp. 65-82. Boston, MA: Little, Brown.

Pitfalls in methodology are stressed in this critical review of the literature on fathers. The topics covered include father-infant interaction studies, direct and indirect influence of the father in the father-mother-infant triad, the father's influence on cognitive development and gender identity, and suggestions for future research. Gunsberg asserts that less is known about father's role in girls' preoedipal development than in boys'.

Herzog, James (1982). On father hunger: The father's role in the modulation of aggressive drive and fantasy. In: *Father and Child: Developmental and Clinical Perspectives*, ed. S. Cath, A. Gurwitt, and J. Ross. Boston, MA: Little, Brown, pp. 163-174.

Through examination of fantasy, play, and dreams collected from the psychoanalytically oriented psychotherapy of 70 children with absent fathers, Herzog postulates a specific role of the father as modulator of affect-drive fantasy. The children were grouped by age from 18 to 28 months, 36 to 60 months, and 60 to 84 months. The two youngest groups consisted mainly of boys who had significant difficulty with their aggression and who developed nightmares and phobic defenses to deal with the loss of their father. The father's return was restitutive. The older group consisted of half each of boys and girls whose main defense was aggression turned toward the self. On the basis of the data, Herzog asserts that fathers serve a critical function for children as the modulator of aggression for preoedipal boys and oedipal boys and girls. The paper raises questions about why the father's absence does not occasion the same dyscontrol of aggressive affect in preoedipal girls.

Lachmann, Frank (1982b). Narcissistic Development. In: *Early Female Development*, ed. D. Mendell. New York: S.P. Medical and Scientific Books, pp. 227-248.

Lachmann discusses "penis envy" and the role of the father as an "ideal." [See Chapters 21 and 22 for annotations.]

Stolorow, Robert and Lachmann, Frank (1982). Early loss of the father: A clinical case. In: *Father and Child: Developmental and Clinical Perspectives*, ed. S. Cath, A. Gurwitt, and J. Ross. Boston, MA: Little, Brown, pp. 535-542.

The case of a psychoanalytically treated woman who lost her father when she was four years old illustrates the crucial developmental importance of the father as an idealized selfobject and illuminates the consequences of his loss. The loss took place just prior to the girl's oedipal phase, causing disturbances in her self-image, sexual identity, self-esteem, and subsequent interactions with men in her life. The patient, however, had stable self- and object differentiation, reflecting consolidation of earlier structural achievements. The authors show how the fantasies she developed to explain her father's absence underwent psychosexual transformations that were woven into a complex denial system, constituting the core of her neurotic personality organization.

Tessman, Lora (1982). A note on the father's contribution to the daughter's way of loving and working. In: *Father and Child*: Developmental and Clinical Perspectives, ed. S. Cath, A. Gurwitt, and J. Ross. Boston, MA: Little, Brown, pp. 219-238.

Tessman claims that the preoedipal, oedipal, and adult father contributes to his daughters' capacity for pleasure in loving and working. This capacity for pleasure in loving and working occurs through emotional attachment and engagement with the father by way of her response to and internalization of his attitudes and feelings about his daughter and her strivings. Tessman proposes that fathers have a different role than mothers in the acceptance and transformation of erotic (loving) excitement and endeavor (work) excitement. Endeavor excitement occurs in the second year of life and is defined as girls' interest in autonomy and work (play) projects. Erotic excitement begins in the third and fourth year and is tied to oedipal feelings for the father. These libidinal connections with him help form and become assimilated into girls' ego ideal. Mastery of excitement with the father may contribute to affect tolerance and ego strength. Clinical examples illustrate the relationship of the mother-daughter dyad to the father-daughter relationship. A theoretical hypothesis for female structuralization and the role of the father is cogently discussed.

Ornstein, Anna (1983). Fantasy or reality? The unsettled question in pathogenesis and reconstruction in psychoanalysis. In: *The Future of Psychoanalysis*, ed. A. Goldberg. New York: International Universities Press, pp. 281-296.

The case of a little girl whose primary caretaker was her father is reconsidered. [See Chapter 22 for annotation.]

Pruett, Kyle (1983). Infants of primary nurturing fathers. *The Psychoanalytic Study of the Child*, 38:257-277. New Haven, CT: Yale University Press.

This is a prospective clinical inquiry into the development of nine infants from two-parent families where the father was the primary caretaker. A second control group, where the mother was the primary caretaker was also investigated. By the use of analytically oriented interviewing techniques, home visits, naturalistic observations, and developmental testing, data were collected on infants from two months to 24 months. The infants for whom the father was the primary dyadic object developed exceptionally well in terms of ego function and object relationships. Pruett suggests that the superior development of the infants might be due to having two nurturing caretakers, that is, a mother and a father. A methodological problem in this research may be that it actually studied conjoint nurturing parents rather than the father as primary caretaker. Complementary questions are raised about why father selected the nurturing role and why mother relinquished it. Questions concerning the effect on gender identity of having a father as the primary identificatory object are raised. Pruett claims that no deviant gender identity was observed.

Herzog, James (1984). Fathers and young children: Fathering daughters and fathering sons. In: *Frontiers of Infant Psychiatry*, Vol. 2, ed. J. Call, E. Galenson, and R. Tyson. New York: Basic Books, pp. 335-342.

This paper reports findings from a home-based, naturalistic study of four boys and four girls from eight families. Herzog discusses the various paternal functions and patterns in two of the families, and explores the complex effects on the personality of the child. Data pertinent to female psychology can be summarized as follows: 1) The father tends to disrupt calm and peaceful states the child shares with the mother; he seems to be the organizer and modulator of intense affect paradigms. 2) Symbiosis with the mother is disrupted through gross motor activity, which the father demonstrates less with his daughter than with his son. 3) Interactions with daughters seem more "protoerotic" or "protoheterosexual" despite the fathers' stating that they want free choices for their daughters in their future careers or life styles. Herzog suggests that the sex of the first child influences the interaction of the father with the second child. Observational material supports and documents analytic theories about the father and psychosexual development, cognitive aspects of parenting, and separation-individuation.

Eisnitz, Alan (1984-1985) Father-daughter incest. *Int. J. Psychoanal. Psychother.*, 10:495-503.

Eisnitz proposes that father-daughter incest is not as deleterious as mother-son incest. [See Chapter 24 for annotation.]

Soll, Maxwell (1984-1985) The transferable penis and the self-representation. *Int. J. Psychoanal. Psychother.*, 10:473-493.

Soll suggests that an incestuous father-daughter postoedipal relationship results in serious bisexual conflicts, consisting of fantasies of being a male and possessing a penis. [See Chapter 24 for annotation.]

Spieler, Susan (1984). Preoedipal girls need fathers. *Psychoanal. Rev.*, 71:63-68

Spieler contends that the father's optimal and available role in the preoedipal phase of development is necessary for successful entry into the oedipal phase and the subsequent resolution of oedipal conflict. Classical psychoanalytic views in the literature about fathers are critically reviewed, along with nonanalytic and psychoanalytic developmental research. Spieler asserts that little girls also form an important relationship with their father before the oedipal phase, that he is not a stranger at eight months, and that attachment to the father may be even more intense than it is to the mother. Spieler concludes that preoedipal fathers foster ego development and autonomy, promote healthy narcissism and positive self-esteem, and that their absence results in distorted fantasies and developmental deficits that can be missed clinically if analysts do not observe their importance and instead misinterpret the material as representing mother-daughter relationships or oedipal father-daughter relationships.

Burgner, Marion (1985). The oedipal experience: Effects on development of an absent father. *Int. J. Psycho-Anal.*, 66:311-320.

Thirteen children in analysis whose fathers left through parental divorce or separation in the first five years are studied to determine the effects on children's oedipal development. In addition to difficulties with ego development and harsh superego formation, girls showed problems with establishing a feminine identity. Bisexual conflicts were enhanced by the perception of mothers as conflictual identificatory models to whom girls are tied. Many girls viewed their father's leaving as a confirmation of their own inadequate bodies, with resulting low self-esteem, dissatisfaction, and depression. Complete family and complete body became psychic equivalents. Continuation of these problems is illustrated by the analysis of an adult female patient.

Pruett, Kyle (1985). Oedipal configurations in young father-raised children. *The Psychoanalytic Study of the Child*, 40:435-455. New Haven, CT: Yale University Press.

Pruett's (1983) longitudinal study is continued by his examination of the oedipal configuration of the same children four years later. Using the play material of two children, Pruett describes their oedipal development. Pruett does not find any overt psychopathology in children raised primarily by fathers. The children have rich and flexible maternal and paternal identifications. The only unique organizing fantasy may center on the father as a nurturing force, but at a pregender level. How this affects gender development is not addressed. A six-year-old girl is described as bright, articulate, feminine, and engaging in play that has "an unconflicted phallic tinge." The boys with primary-care fathers, like girls raised by mothers, had more difficulty at age three to four years in relinquishing their fathers to the mother/rival.

Benjamin, Jessica (1986a). The alienation of desire: Women's masochism and ideal love. In: *Psychoanalysis and Women: Contemporary Reappraisals*, ed. J. Alpert, Hillsdale, NJ: The Analytic Press, pp. 113-138.

Fathers who do not help their daughter with separation from the mother during rapprochement may contribute to their daughter's masochism. [See Chapter 21 for annotation.]

Chused, Judith (1986). Consequences of paternal nurturing. *The Psychoanalytic Study of the Child*, 41:419-438. New Haven, CT: Yale University Press.

The intrapsychic effects and characterologic complexities of a young woman whose father was the primary nurturing object throughout her life and sole caretaker when she was two-and-one- half to four years are explored. Her individual responses to a primary paternal object include idealization of the penis to symbolize powerful, preambivalent, protecting, and nurturing qualities, and an extreme conflictual oedipal situation. The penis was magically endowed with protective and nurturing qualities, not unlike idealization of the penis encountered in women who have a poor mother-daughter relationship. Although the father was able to provide the continuity and nurturance to complete separation-individuation, the patient defended against the awareness of the important preoedipal relationship with her father because of the enormity of her oedipal guilt connected with her mother's illness. The repression seemed to lead to an unusually intense vulnerability to sexual rejection and a masochistic perception of every relationship. The paper does not clarify or separate out the difficulties that may have stemmed from the early loss of the maternal object and that would significantly effect the patient's self-esteem and masochistic character. The psychological consequences of the father as nurturer and his effect on female gender and personality development are documented.

Galenson, Eleanor (1986b). Early pathways to female sexuality in advantaged and disadvantaged girls. In: *The Psychology of Today's Woman: New Psychoanalytic Visions*, ed. T. Bernay and D. Cantor. Hillsdale, NJ: The Analytic Press, pp. 37-48.

Galenson links the role of the absent father and the ambivalent mother to the daughter's sadomasochistic sexuality. [See Chapter 21 for annotation.]

Pruett, Kyle (1987). *The Nurturing Father*. New York: Warner Books.

This book reviews the research studies published in Pruett's 1983 and 1985 papers.

Rees, Katherine (1987). "I want to be a daddy!": Meaning of masculine identifications in girls. *Psychoanal. Q., 56*:497-522.

Feminine and masculine identifications are formulated as being neither primary nor secondary, but rather as the outcome of complex developmental processes that influence conflict resolution and defensive transformation. Three analytic cases show the origins of, and intrapsychic processes connected with, masculine identifications for girls at each developmental stage. Rees views the negative oedipal phase or girls' wish "to be a daddy" as having multiple meanings and functions and being in the service of healthy feminine gender identification. The role of the father as an object for identification can be either useful or potentially deleterious, depending on the total family constellation and the psychic structuring of the daughter. A complex interaction exists between the real relationship with the parents, the father's personality, and the pregenital fantasies of daughters. This article takes issue with a unicausal meaning of the negative oedipal phase, "castration shock," primary femininity, and masculine identification and proposes a more complex approach.

Balsam, Rosemary (1989). The paternal possibility: The father's contribution to the adolescent daughter when the mother is disturbed and a denigrated figure. In: *Fathers and Their Families*, ed. S. Cath, A. Gurwitt, and L. Gunsburg. Hillsdale, NJ: The Analytic Press, pp. 245-263.

Balsam presents illustrative vignettes from the analyses of five young women who had disturbed or denigrated mothers but active and involved fathers during adolescence. Sexual development and transference manifestations are highlighted. The author contends that in spite of the child's apparently diminished contact with an early nurturing mother, vigorous and energetic character traits come from identification with a father who is involved during adolescence. The female analyst is readily taken in as a feminine ego ideal, which suggests the importance of analysts' gender for young adult women. Androgyny is proposed as a gender defense against the feminine self.

Cath, Stanley, Gurwitt, Alan, and Gunsberg, Linda (ed.)(1989). *Fathers and Their Families*. Hillsdale, NJ: The Analytic Press.

This sequel to *Father and Child* (1982) explores the changing role of fathers and interacting intrapsychic, developmental, familial, and social dimensions. A section on father-daughter relationships highlights the importance of the father's role in girls' sense of self and feminine identification. Several of the chapters are individually annotated.

Galenson, Eleanor (1989). Factors affecting the pre-oedipal and oedipal paternal relationship in girls: The collusion to exclude father. In: *Fathers and Their Families*, ed. S. Cath, A. Gurwitt, and L. Gunsburg. Hillsdale, NJ: The Analytic Press, pp. 491-505.

Paternal emotional availability during the infant's second year of life is a critical factor in enabling an adaptive handling of normally developing aggression of that period. The father's presence modifies the intensity of girls' normal aggression toward mother and provides an alternative object for both libidinal and aggressive impulses. In the absence of the father's influence, girls remain regressively fixed in an overrigid identification with their mother, whereas boys in similar circumstances have difficulty in self-object differentiation and in the establishment of a stable sense of male identity. A clinical case illustrates the principles discussed.

Lamb, Michael and Oppenheim, David (1989). Fatherhood and father-child relationships: Five years of research. In: *Fathers and Their Families*, ed. S. Cath, A. Gurwitt, and L. Gunsburg. Hillsdale, NJ: The Analytic Press, pp. 11-26.

Although not specifically focusing on the father-daughter relationship, this paper reviews the developmental, psychiatric, and sociobiological research of the previous five years that examines the extent, determinants, and consequences of paternal involvement in child care, and summarizes the salient trends.

McDougall, Joyce (1989). The dead father: On early psychic trauma and its relation to disturbance in sexual identity and creative activity. *Int. J. Psycho-Anal.*, 70:205-219.

Using process notes from the psychoanalysis of a woman whose father had died when she was 15 months old, leaving her with a disturbance in sexual identity and creative activity, McDougall poignantly illustrates the important contributions of identifications with both parents to the formation of subjective and sexual identity. Clinical and theoretical issues concerning the nature of psychic trauma, the father's role in the origins of sexual identity and creativity, and the resolution of bisexual (homosexual) wishes are explored. [See also Chapter 19.]

Pacella, Bernard (1989). Paternal influence in early child development. In: *Fathers and Their Families*, ed. S. Cath, A. Gurwitt and L. Gunsburg. Hillsdale, NJ: The Analytic Press, pp. 225-244.

Pacella presents a summary of the basic psychoanalytic assumptions regarding the role, function, and influence of preoedipal fathers. Brief sketches of the analyses of two girls with paternal preoedipal deprivation illustrate the concepts reviewed. Pacella contends that for girls, the father is the preoedipal hero who provides them with incentives for relinquishing their attachment to their mother, facilitates their secondary narcissistic interests as feminine women, and helps shift their libidinal interests to men.

Richards, Arnold (1989). Self-mutilation and father-daughter incest: A psychoanalytic case report. In: *Fantasy, Myth, and Reality: Essays in Honor of Jacob A. Arlow*, ed. H. Blum, Y. Kramer, A. Richards, and A. Richards. Madison, CT: International Universities Press, pp. 465-478.

[See Chapter 24 for annotation.]

Tessman, Lora (1989). Fathers and daughters: Early tones, later echoes. In: *Fathers and Their Families*, ed. S. Cath, A. Gurwitt, and L. Gunsburg. Hillsdale, NJ: The Analytic Press, pp. 197-223.

Tessman elaborates material from her 1982 paper, which postulates the father's preoedipal and oedipal role in endeavor and erotic excitement as two aspects of women's ego ideal and gender identity. Drawing on empirical material from interviews with adult women, she further explores these intrapsychic concepts, developmental transformations, and the interrelationships among them.

Ross, John (1990). The eye of the beholder: On the developmental dialogue of fathers and daughters. In: *New Dimensions in Adult Development*, ed. R. Nemiroff and C. Colarusso. New York: Basic Books, pp. 47-72.

Ross discusses the importance of fathers to daughters during the pre-oedipal phase of development. He explores Freud's preoedipal-father countertransference block with Dora, and provides a refreshing reinterpretation of something else that went awry in Dora's treatment. He asserts that fathers help their daughters disengage from the mother during separation-individuation by their admiration and gaze, which reciprocates girls' feminine (not masculine) exhibitionistic wishes. Penis envy alone is not responsible for the intense exhibitionistic wishes present in many women. The wish to attract father is one of the developmental mechanisms necessary to break the "erotic attachment" to mothers and to further continued psychic structuralization, which includes sexual and self-identity, self-love, and daughters' relationship to others. Psychoanalytic case material and child observation illustrate the thesis. This paper is important in refocusing the function of the father from incestuous object to differentiating object.

Bernstein, Doris (1991a). The female Oedipal complex. In: *The Personal Myth and Psychoanalytic Theory*, ed. I. Graham and P. Hartocollis. Madison, CT: International Universities Press.

Bernstein pays special attention to the father and issues in female development. [See Chapter 7 for annotation.]

# Chapter 17

# *Siblings*

Barbara Rosenfeld

Beginning with Freud's writings, the psychoanalytic literature has included references to the developmental importance and influence of siblings on ego formation, drive regulation, sense of self, narcissistic progression, character formation, the Oedipus complex, object relations, and object choice. The birth of a sibling may heighten issues related to anatomical differences and maternal identifications and may influence a girl's feelings about childbearing and childrearing. Parental responses and family dynamics may also be shaped by the parents' own past sibling experiences. Some authors propose a separate developmental line for sibling experiences. Very few references in the literature focus on the effects of siblings on feminine development, even though sibling relationships may have a profound impact on that development. [B.R. and E.S.]

Freud, Sigmund (1900). Interpretation of dreams. *Standard Edition*, 4:250-255. London: Hogarth Press, 1953.

Freud uses dream material to emphasize the intensity of early rivalrous and jealous feelings in children towards their brothers and sisters. A much older female sibling will feel "maternal instincts" toward a newcomer.

Freud, Sigmund (1916-1917). Introductory lectures. *Standard Edition*, 16:333-334. London: Hogarth Press, 1953.

Freud discusses the displacement of oedipal feelings from the primary object toward siblings. He notes that when siblings are born the Oedipus complex transforms into a family complex. An older male sibling may be taken as an oedipal object if a girl experiences a loss of interest from her father. She may also view a younger sister as the baby from her oedipal father.

Freud, Sigmund (1919). A child is being beaten. *Standard Edition*, 17:177-204. London: Hogarth Press, 1953.

In analyzing manifest beating fantasies, Freud notes that siblings are most often included in the beating fantasy. The male sibling is usually substituted for the girl, who abandons her feminine role to avoid oedipal disappointment by the father. Girls are represented in the sadomasochistic fantasies as whipping-boys. [See also Chapters 1 and 21.]

Freud, Sigmund (1920). The psychogenesis of a case of homosexuality in a woman. *Standard Edition*, 18:146-172. London: Hogarth Press, 1953.

In the analysis of a young homosexual woman, Freud discusses the role of both the younger and the older brother in influencing a girl's choice of object. The older brother was perceived as a heterosexual object and a competitor, contributing to her penis envy. The younger brother, born during the revival of the girl's infantile Oedipus complex in puberty, intensified her oedipal disappointment with her father. [See also Chapters 1 and 19.]

Freud, Sigmund (1931a). Female sexuality. *Standard Edition*, 21:223-243. London: Hogarth Press, 1953.

Freud notes that the birth of a sibling during a girl's phallic phase frustrates her desire to give her mother a baby. This frustration hastens the turning away from her mother, and the move towards her father. [See also Chapter 1.]

Greenacre, Phyllis (1950a). Special problems of early female sexual development. *The Psychoanalytic Study of the Child*, 5:132-134. New York: International Universities Press. Also in: *Trauma, Growth and Personality*. New York: Norton, 1952, pp. 237-258.

Greenacre observes that the birth of a younger sibling when the older female sibling is still preverbal contributes to the development of intense oral and visual envy. If the baby is a boy or if a boy is born within the next two to three years, the oral and visual envy is converted into a severe castration complex and penis envy. Guilt may develop over strong oral aggressive components directed toward the father. The negative effect on girls of multiple sibling births during early childhood is also discussed. [See also Chapter 6.]

Bonaparte, Marie (1953). *Female Sexuality*. New York: International Universities Press.

Bonaparte describes how a girl who is too disappointed in her father may transfer her oedipal longings to a brother, thus remaining heterosexual. Incestuous activity with a brother close in age or younger sometimes may be beneficial, but sexual activity with an older brother may be harmful.

Balint, Michael (1963). The younger sister and Prince Charming. *Int. J. Psycho-Anal.*, 44:226-227.

Using clinical material, Balint discusses typical characterologic features that occur when two sisters are close in age. The older sister is usually openly feminine, often somewhat narcissistic, while the younger one, prevented by the older from more feminine development, develops bisexuality with greater penis envy.

Mahler, Margaret (1966). Notes on the development of basic moods: The depressive affect. In: *Psychoanalysis—A General Psychology: Essays in Honor of Heinz Hartmann*, ed. R. Loewenstein, L. Newman, M. Schur, and A. Solnit. New York: International Universities Press, pp. 152-168.

In the course of describing the separation-individuation process, Mahler gives a case history of a girl whose younger sister was born during her rapprochement phase. Shortly after the birth, pregnancy and birth fantasies were expressed by pernicious withholding of feces, and penis envy directed toward her older brother increased.

Bank, Stephen and Kahn, Michael (1982). *The Sibling Bond*. New York: Basic Books.

Utilizing clinical material and reviewing research on siblings from the psychological, psychoanalytic, and social science literature, the authors detail the pervasive importance of siblings throughout the life cycle. Vignettes illustrate a variety of psychological issues for both same- and opposite-sex sibling combinations. The authors' literature review and their own clinical interview study of childhood sibling incest leads them to conclude that the long-term effects of incest are more pernicious for women than for men.

Abarbanel, Janice (1983). The revival of the sibling experience during the mother's second pregnancy. *The Psychoanalytic Study of the Child*, 38:353-379. New Haven, CT: Yale University Press.

Abarbanel focuses on the experience of a second pregnancy as it affects the relationship between pregnant mothers and their female toddlers. The author postulates that the quality of the experience depends on the childhood relationship of a mother with her own mother and siblings. One mother who had been cut off from her mother as an unwanted second child, duplicated this experience with her own second child. Rivalry with her older sister interfered with her ability to prepare her daughter for the new baby's arrival. By contrast, another pregnant woman, not preoccupied with rivalries and jealousies, could identify with her mother, empathize with her older sister, and thus prepare her daughter for the new birth.

Colonna, Alice and Newman, Lottie (1983). The psychoanalytic literature on siblings. *The Psychoanalytic Study of the Child*, 38:285-309. New Haven, CT: Yale University Press.

The authors selectively review early psychoanalytic writings on siblings, emphasizing the importance Freud placed on the role of siblings. The literature that stresses sibling rivalry and sibling love and negative reactions to sibling births is examined. The authors present the existing conflicting views on the possibly traumatic, beneficial, or harmless effects of sibling seductions. An overall paucity in the literature on siblings is noted.

Kestenberg, Judith and Javaid, Ghazala (1983). Entrancement of the mother with her young baby: Implications for the older sibling. *Dynamic Psychotherapy*, 1:63-74.

[See Chapter 14 for annotation.]

Kris, Marianne and Ritvo, Samuel (1983). Parents and siblings: Their mutual influences. *The Psychoanalytic Study of the Child*, 38:311-324. New Haven, CT: Yale University Press.

This chapter emphasizes both how parental attitudes modulate sibling relationships and how sibling relationships have profound effects on instinctual development, ego development, the Oedipus complex, and adult object relations. An example is given of a father who transferred his affection from a first-born daughter to the second at the time of her birth, identifying the now older sister with his own hated older sister.

Neubauer, Peter (1983). The importance of the sibling experience. *The Psychoanalytic Study of the Child*, 38:325-336. New Haven, CT: Yale University Press.

The important vicissitudes in the sibling situation and the distinctions between rivalry, envy, and jealousy are explored. Because the observation of anatomical differences occurs before the phallic phase, early sibling reactions reflecting envy, as differentiated from jealousy, influence the role and intensity of penis envy and castration fears and color the outcome of the castration complex in girls.

Abend, Sander (1984). Sibling love and object choice. *Psychoanal. Q.,* 53:425.

This is a brief case description of a younger sister who was attracted to her older brother. He had been at the height of his oedipal stage when she was born. He was seductive and unusually interested in her, while the father was difficult to love and admire because he had a serious illness. Later, she chose a man who resembled her brother in personality and body type, indicating her brother's role as an object choice that substituted for the unavailable father.

Herzog, James (1984). Fathers and young children: Fathering daughters and fathering sons. In: *Frontiers of Infant Psychiatry,* Volume 2, ed. J. Call, E. Galenson, and R. Tyson. New York: Basic Books, pp. 335-342.

Herzog suggests that the sex of the first child influences the interaction of the father with the second child. [See Chapter 16 for annotation.]

Klyman, Cassandra (1986). Pregnancy as a reaction to early childhood sibling loss. *J. Amer. Acad. Psychoanal.,* 14:323-335.

This article explores the psychological effects of an early loss of a sibling. [See Chapter 14 for annotation.]

Agger, Eloise (1988). Psychoanalytic perspectives on sibling relationships. *Psychoanal. Inq.,* 8:3-30.

Agger maintains that character and object relations are determined by early sibling relationships. The intrapsychic meanings of sibling rivalry, new births, sibling losses, and sibling identifications, the quality of both sibling love (aim inhibited, erotic, or incestuous) and attachments (predominantly anaclitic or narcissistic), all influence both ego development and identity formation. Case examples describe the place of siblings in maintaining a fragmented female role; a sense of inadequacy as a female; a position as victim of sexual exploitation; and a life excluding sexual intimacy, marriage, and childbearing. Agger contends that when an object choice is based on an unconscious primary investment in a sibling during a critical developmental phase, the incest barrier set up against the sibling love causes conflict in a later marital relationship.

Appelbaum, Ann (1988). Psychoanalysis during pregnancy: The effect of sibling constellation. *Psychoanal. Inq.*, 8:177-195.

This patient's identification with the fetus, whose sibling position corresponded to her own, facilitated the recognition of a lost fragment of her identity containing previously unacknowledged strengths. [See Chapter 14 for annotation.]

Parens, Henri (1988). Siblings in early childhood: Some direct observational findings. *Psychoanal. Inq.*, 8:31-50.

Parens proposes that 1) from the middle of the first year siblings are experienced as specific objects, significantly invested with libido and aggression; 2) they occupy a unique experiential position, especially the older, but also the younger, one, and can be used jointly and alternately as parent substitute, peer, other family member, and member of the extrafamilial environment; and 3) in both hypotheses, the sibling is used in a number of experiential spheres and in ways that serve adaptation and development. Examples of siblings as erotic objects include a woman whose masochism derived from incestuous play with her brother during adolescence. Parens suggests that sometimes sibling incest fantasies and actual enactments may be adaptive; the turn to the sibling relieves the pressure from threat of parental incestuous fantasies and paves the way for normal attachment to peers, especially in adolescence. Young oedipal girls, pressured by their wishes for a baby from their father, experience pain and hostility toward younger siblings. They commonly cope with their frustration through a fantasy that the sibling is their own baby. Under the heading of sibling as hostile/hated object, Parens traces back to age six to nine months the wish to have what the other has. He contends that these earlier experiences may play a significant part in intensifying girls' wishes for a penis.

Graham, Ian (1988). The sibling object and its transferences: Alternate organizer of the middle field. *Psychoanal. Inq.*, 8:88-107.

Graham notes that an exclusive emphasis on the primary relationship with parents has relegated sibling relationships to a "real object" model while ignoring siblings' effects on developmental and structural characteristics. A dyad with a sibling holds a lesser cathexis than that with parents, but is also a triadic relationship vis-à-vis the mother. This first experience of rivalry, where the sibling is a competitive intruder into the symbiotic dyad, has a different character from that of the oedipal phase, when the child is a competitor in the phallic triad. Material is presented from the transference/countertransference perspective, revealing a sibling profile in both patient and analyst, to underline the structural and phenomenological significance of siblings. Examples of the powerful influence of siblings on each developmental phase are included. Sibling rivalry in adolescence can paralyze or inhibit peer relations, attachments, and achievements. The consolidation of sexual identity, body image, and the development of initiative can also be negatively affected. The separation-individuation process with siblings has a separate line of development distinct from that with the mother. Graham presents a number of case examples, including one of a woman who used a relationship with her brother to avoid grieving for her deceased father. Another woman patient tried to model herself after her fantasy of a dead brother to please her mother and achieve positive status in the family.

Lazes, Pedro (1990). Fact and fantasy in brother-sister incest. *Int. Rev. Psycho-Anal.*, 17:97-113.

Using descriptions of incestuous fantasies concerning siblings found in literature and mythology, Lazes proposes that these fantasies are pre-oedipal, not oedipal in nature.

Lax, Ruth (1991). An imaginary brother. His role in the formation of a girl's self-image and ego ideal. *The Psychoanalytic Study of the Child*, 46. New Haven, CT: Yale University Press.

The analysis of a masochistic 40-year-old woman who had conflicting identification systems is presented. Her wished-for autonomous self-image was based on the fantasy of an imaginary older brother with whom she identified. Her submissive self-image was determined by an unconscious ideal modeled on her mother, and this had determined her masochistic object choices. The persistent older-brother fantasy served narcissistic needs and defended against her succumbing to the unconscious pathological feminine ideal.

# Section III

# Female Sexuality, Character, Psychopathology

# Chapter 18

# Sexuality

Eleanor Schuker
Additional contributions by Nadine Levinson,
Mary Ann Delaney, Lesley Braasch,
Edith McNutt, William Sommer

Freud's conceptualization of "female sexuality" encompassed all aspects of female psychosexual development, psychopathology, body image, identity, character, and relationships—indeed material covered in the entire contents of this book! An understanding of female sexuality has changed in parallel with changes in psychoanalytic theory. Research on female sexuality focuses more narrowly today than formerly on sexual functioning, theories of sexuality, the relation between sexuality and feminine identity, and sexual pathology. These components of female sexuality are viewed from multiple frames of reference, which encompass not only the vicissitudes of the sexual drive, but also aspects of ego psychology and the study of object relations. Female sexuality thus is seen as influencing and being influenced by multiple variables. Consequently, many articles found elsewhere in the bibliography have relevance to this topic; the most highly pertinent are cross-indexed. [The reader is also referred to Chapters 5, 6, 7, 8, 9, 10, 13, 14, 19, 20, and 21.]

This chapter delineates five specific areas of female sexuality.

1)  Historically important papers on femininity, sexual identity, and sexual drive development. These include classical papers on bisexuality, penis envy, castration anxiety, and the role of the vagina. Some papers on these topics, included in Chapter 6, are also cross-indexed here. Several papers that focus on wishes for a baby and motherhood are annotated in Chapter 14.

2)  The female sexual response cycle, including material on masturbation, arousal patterns, and orgasm. Although the biological dimensions of female sexuality have always interested theoreticians, Masters and Johnson's work spurred intense debate and a notable reassessment of psychoanalytic thinking in the 1960s. More recent sex research has not yet been fully integrated with psychoanalytic thinking, but some papers relevant to such an integration are also included here. Love and

relations between the sexes are discussed in Chapter 13.

3)  Psychological aspects of sexual functioning, erotic excitement, and sexual inhibitions in women (including "frigidity," clinical symptoms, and related character problems). Gender pathology and the ego-dystonic homosexualities are annotated in Chapter 19. Hysterical character is annotated in Chapter 20.

4)  Writings on feminine body image and psychic representations of the female genitals, feminine body anxieties, and related conflicts. Provocative, controversial, and contradictory ideas may be found in these papers. Modern studies add new dimensions and revise classical ideas about female genital anxieties and feminine body image.

5)  Global theories of sexuality and theories of female sexuality. Papers on the development of gender identity and femininity and on sexuality and its relation to identity are included. (E.S.)

Freud, Sigmund (1905b). Three essays on the theory of sexuality. *Standard Edition*, 7:125-243. London: Hogarth Press, 1953.

Among the most influential of Freud's contributions, this paper serves as a theoretical and clinical basis for his later theories of female sexuality and character development. Infantile sexuality is postulated as the central factor in both normal and neurotic development. Libidinal phases are delineated. Many of Freud's early ideas about female development are also found here. [See Chapter 1 for annotation.]

Freud, Sigmund (1912a). Contributions to a discussion of masturbation. *Standard Edition*, 12:239-254. London: Hogarth Press, 1953.

Freud reviews contemporary knowledge about masturbation. He emphasizes the developmental stages of masturbation, the return of masturbation during therapy, and the role of fantasy and unconscious guilt. [See Chapter 1 for annotation.]

Tausk, Victor (1912). On masturbation. *The Psychoanalytic Study of the Child*, 6:61-79. New York: International Universities Press, 1951.

Tausk outlines the essential elements of masturbation, including the origins, aims, and pathogenic effects. Female sexuality is not described separately, and illustrative material is about males. Tausk defines masturbation as involving solitary manipulation of the genitals, with the aim of direct discharge of sexual tension. The contents of masturbatory fantasies are traced through all stages of development. Sadomasochistic components of the sexual instinct are of particular significance as a precipitating factor in childhood masturbation. Conflicts with masturbation occur primarily during the transition to the latency stage and in adolescence. Consequences of masturbation may reflect the struggle to abstain, somatic effects, and psychological influences, including anxiety, guilt, and damage to object choice if sexuality is kept at an infantile (incestuous) level. Tausk disagrees with Freud that the "actual neurosis" is caused by the toxic products of masturbation. Masturbation can be either normal or destructive, depending on developmental, sociocultural, or constitutional factors.

Freud, Sigmund (1918b). The taboo of virginity. *Standard Edition*, 11:192-208. London: Hogarth Press, 1953.

This article includes a discussion of the clinical problem of frigidity in women. [See Chapter 1 for annotation.]

Abraham, Karl (1924). A short study of the development of the libido, viewed in the light of mental disorders. In: *Selected Papers of Karl Abraham, M.D.* New York: Brunner/Mazel, 1979, pp. 418-502.

Abraham discusses the vicissitudes of object love in relation to sexual aims and provides a table with six developmental stages. [See Chapter 2 for annotation.]

Freud, Sigmund (1924b). The dissolution of the Oedipus complex. *Standard Edition*, 19:172-179. London: Hogarth Press, 1953.

Freud first notes that the course of delopment of sexuality is different for girls and boys. [See Chapter 1 for annotation.]

Horney, Karen (1924). On the genesis of the castration complex in women. *Int. J. Psycho-Anal.*, 5:50-65. Also in: *Feminine Psychology*, ed. H. Kelman. New York: Norton, 1967, pp. 37-53.

Horney describes primary and secondary penis envy and the secondary nature of the neurotic castration complex. [See Chapter 2 for annotation.]

Deutsch, Helene (1925a). The psychology of women in relation to the function of reproduction. *Int. J. Psycho-Anal.*, 6:405-418. Also in: *The Psychoanalytic Reader*, ed. R. Fliess. New York: International Universities Press, 1948, pp. 165-179.

Deutsch outlines normal female libidinal development throughout the life cycle. [See Chapter 2 for annotation.]

Deutsch, Helene (1925b). The menopause: Psychoanalysis of the sexual functions of women. *Int. J. Psycho-Anal.*, 65:55-62, 1984.

Deutsch asserts that women's loss of reproductive capacity is accompanied by a decathexis of the vagina as somatic changes necessitate regressive libidinal shifts. [See Chapter 2 for annotation.]

Freud, Sigmund (1925). Some psychical consequences of the anatomical distinction between the sexes. *Standard Edition*, 19:243-258. London: Hogarth Press, 1953.

This paper includes a clear description of Freud's theory of the development of femininity. Freud discusses the dissimilarity in sexual development between boys and girls, focusing on the castration complex and penis envy as pivotal responses to the discovery of the anatomical differences. [See Chapter 1 for annotation.]

Horney, Karen (1926). The flight from womanhood. *Int. J. Psycho-Anal.*, 12:360-374. Also in: *Feminine Psychology*, ed. H. Kelman. New York: Norton, 1967, pp. 54-70.

This paper was one of the first to consider the motives for female frigidity and masturbatory inhibition. Female genital anxiety as differentiated from castration anxiety is observed and discussed. Horney proposes a primary and an innate femininity. [See also Chapter 2.]

Stekel, Wilhelm (1926). *Frigidity in Woman in Relation to Her Love Life*, Vol. 1 and 2. New York: Boni and Liveright.

The origins of frigidity in women are comprehensively discussed and illustrated with many analytic case examples. Nine chapters in Volume I cover such topics as falling in love, sexual trauma, infantile fixations, menstruation, and the psychology of frigid women. In Volume II, disorders of the instincts and the emotions are considered in discussions about homosexuality, dyspareunia, transvestism, and other issues. The topics are richly illustrated by analytic cases.

Jones, Ernest (1927). The early development of female sexuality. *Int. J. Psycho-Anal.*, 8:459-472.

Jones postulates the fear of "aphanisis" (the complete extinction of the capacity for sexual enjoyment) as central in both sexes. An innate femininity is implied. [See Chapter 2 for annotation.]

Horney, Karen (1928). The problem of the monogamous ideal. *Int. J. Psycho-Anal.*, 9:318-331.

Frigidity and impotence in relation to marital conflicts are traced to underlying hostility and guilt. [See Chapter 2 for annotation.]

Deutsch, Helene (1930). The significance of masochism in the mental life of women. *Int. J. Psycho-Anal.*, 11:48-60. Also in: *The Psychoanalytic Reader*, ed. R. Fliess. New York: International Universities Press, 1948, pp. 195-207.

Deutsch discusses the origin of femininity, the central importance of masochism to feminine psychology, and the nature of frigidity. [See Chapters 2 and 21 for annotations.]

Yates, Sybille (1930). An investigation of the psychological factors in virginity and ritual defloration. *Int. J. Psycho-Anal.*, 11:167-184.

Motives underlying attitudes toward virginity in both men and women are examined through psychoanalytic and cultural analyses. Women's valuation of virginity may be motivated both by the wish to preserve it for the ideal man and by the fear of losing something precious. Menstruation and defloration are associated with fantasies of genital damage. Yates describes how these fears are reflected in primitive customs and rituals surrounding virginity and first intercourse.

Freud, Sigmund (1931a). Female sexuality. *Standard Edition*, 21:223-243. London: Hogarth Press, 1953.

Freud delineates two additional developmental tasks for girls: the change in libidinal object from mother to father and the change in girls' sexual zone and aim. The little girl's sexual life begins with a normal masculine phase, and then after the recognition of the anatomical differences, changes to a feminine one. Other possible outcomes include a neurotic masculinity complex or an inhibition. The influences of the preoedipal relation with mother are also discussed. [See Chapter 1 for annotation.]

Brierley, Marjorie (1932). Some problems of integration in women. *Int. J. Psycho-Anal.*, 13:433-448.

Brierley correlates drive integration along feminine lines with physiological factors determining the development of the female body. Women must retain some oral cathexis (in a mouth-anus-vagina displacement series) for normal genital functioning, whereas males can better

sublimate their oral interests. Several women patients who are sexually inhibited and fixated halfway between homo- and heterosexuality are described. A primary preoedipal difficulty with oral sadism underlies their oedipal conflicts. Their equating the vagina with a biting mouth leads to inhibitions in vaginal erotism, since the vagina is experienced as orally aggressive, or as endangered by projected aggression.
[See also Chapter 2.]

Klein, Melanie (1932). *The Psychoanalysis of Children*. New York: Norton.

Klein argues that girls have a dominant feminine instinctual disposition and that penis envy originates secondarily from oral envy of the maternal breast and the mother's body and contents. [See Chapters 2, 8, 16, and 22 for annotations.]

Freud, Sigmund (1933). Femininity. *Standard Edition*, 22:112-135. London: Hogarth Press, 1953.

Freud reiterates his views on the vicissitudes of normal female sexuality, discussing normal bisexuality and feminine character traits. [See Chapter 1 for annotation.]

Horney, Karen (1933a). The denial of the vagina. *Int. J. Psycho-Anal.*, 14:57-70. Also in: *Feminine Psychology*, ed. H. Kelman. New York: Norton, 1967, pp. 147-161.

This paper includes observations and discussions of spontaneous vaginal sensations in children and conflicts about vaginal experiences. [See Chapter 2 for complete annotation.]

Horney, Karen (1933b). Psychogenic factors in functional disorders. *Amer. J. Ob. Gyn.*, 25:694-704. Also in: *Feminine Psychology*, ed. H. Kelman. New York: Norton, 1967, pp. 162-174.

In a chapter that is relevant to the current debate about the roles of psychological and physiological factors in sexual dysfunction, Horney asserts that intrapsychic conflict is the major factor in the etiology of functional sexual disorders in women. She feels that functional disorders include not only pseudocyesis, vaginismus, frigidity, menstrual disorders, and hyperemesis, but also some forms of premature delivery, sterility, leucorrhea, and pruritus. Using material from her psychoanalytic cases, Horney illustrates psychodynamic and developmental determinants. Symptoms of frigidity are derived from early developmental experiences and often are connected with ambivalence toward men or toward a female role associated with fears and fantasies about menstruation, pregnancy, and masturbation. Horney concludes that her findings would be validated by using analytic methodology to study female psychosexual experiences. She feels that employing analytic treatment would also result in resolution of conflicts and amelioration of symptoms.

**Jones, Ernest (1933). The phallic phase.** *Int. J. Psycho-Anal.*, 14:1-13.

Jones elaborates on the phallic phase, proposing an innate primary femininity. [See Chapter 2 for annotation.]

**Lampl-de Groot, Jeanne (1933). Problems of femininity.** *Psychoanal. Q.*, 2:489-518. Also in: *Man and Mind: Collected Papers of Jeanne Lampl-de Groot.* New York: International Universities Press, 1965, pp. 12-31.

Lampl-de Groot stresses the passivity and masochism in normal development that derives from the narcissistic injury of penislessness. [See Chapter 2 for annotation.]

**Rado, Sandor (1933). Fear of castration in women.** *Psychoanal. Q.*, 2:425-475.

Rado asserts that the narcissistic injury of castration may cause women to give up masturbation and turn to masochistic fantasy gratification. Frigidity is a defense against masochistic dangers. [See also Chapter 2.]

**Fenichel, Otto (1934). Further light upon the preoedipal phase in girls.** In: *The Collected Papers of Otto Fenichel.* New York: Norton, 1953, pp. 241-288. First published in *Int. Zeitschr. Psa.*, 20:151-190, 1934.

Fenichel stresses the importance of preoedipal antecedents in female sexuality. [See Chapter 2 for annotation.]

**Payne, Sylvia (1935). A concept of femininity.** *British J. Med. Psychol.*, 15:18-33.

Payne views the feminine body and reproductive functions as central to femininity and explores the psychological characteristics of genitally mature women. [See Chapter 2 for annotation.]

**Brierley, Marjorie (1936). Specific determinants in feminine development.** *Int. J. Psychoanal.*, 17:163-180.

In an attempt to understand specific factors affecting adult female heterosexuality, Brierley targets the earliest phases of ego integration and connects oral pathology with sexual symptoms and development. [See Chapter 2 for annotation.]

Hitschmann, Eduard and Bergler, Edmund (1936). *Frigidity in Women: Its Characteristics and Treatment. Nervous and Mental Disease Monograph Series No. 60.* Washington, DC: Nervous and Mental Disease.

Using Freud's views of female development as the basis for understanding female sexual life and frigidity, the authors propose multiple causations for frigidity such as changes in libido, penis envy, changes in erogenous zones in female development, inversion and perversion, affects, and incompetence of the male partner. Chapter 2 provides a concise review of female sexuality and libidinal development along the lines that Freud proposed. In Chapter 3, descriptions of symptomatology, nosology, and degrees of frigidity are detailed, with frigidity defined as the inability to have a vaginal orgasm (despite possible excitement and lubrication). Clitoral orgasm is viewed as masculine. Eighteen clinical categories of frigidity are outlined from different developmental stages, with illustrations of defenses and symptomatology by clinical vignettes. The last chapter presents two psychoanalytically cured cases.

Jacobson, Edith (1937). Ways of superego formation and the female castration complex. *Psychoanal. Q.*, 45:525-538, 1976.

This article contains important ideas on feminine castration conflicts and genital self-image. Fantasies of an inner organ or an invisible penis can be an early reaction to the castration complex and can be a preparation for later normal genitality. Whereas in the developmental history of the "traditional" feminine woman the narcissistic genital cathexis is transferred onto the father, an alternative female "vaginal" character takes a different normal developmental path. Rapid discovery of the female genital allows resolution of the castration complex, and the child's female self-esteem is restored with the belief that she possesses an equally valuable genital. This valued genital self-image sets female development along the path toward active-genital love relations, and an anaclitic choice of love object, including independence in relation to the love object and successful development of an independent superego. Castration fear has a female counterpart in fear of injury to the female genital. [See also Chapters 2 and 7.]

Barrett, William (1939). Penis envy, urinary control, pregnancy fantasies, constipation. *Psychoanal. Q.*, 8:211-218.

[See Chapter 6 for annotation.]

Eissler, Kurt (1939). On certain problems of female sexual development. *Psychoanal. Q.*, 8:191-210.

Eissler presents cases from the nonanalytic literature that report about vaginal sensations in young girls to shed light on the controversy about early feminine sexual experience. He also discusses Freud's theory of girls' developmental shift in sexual object, change from activity to passivity, and change in erotogenic zone. [See Chapter 2 for annotation.]

Lorand, Sandor (1939). Contribution to the problem of vaginal orgasm. *Int. J. Psycho-Anal.*, 20:432-438.

Lorand discusses the analyses of women who complain of sexual anesthesia or inability to reach vaginal orgasm during intercourse. He finds that these women have preoedipal-phase conflicts with their mothers. Their flight from femininity is related to resentment toward their mother, their own aggression toward and consequent fear of their mother, wishes to deny their mother's pleasure in intercourse, resulting in inhibitions in identifying with their sexual mother, and feelings of inferiority that express not only penis envy but a deeper comparison of mother and child. Analysis of emerging vaginal sensations reveals strong oral and oral-aggressive themes, with the vagina=mouth equation. Lorand affirms concepts of early femininity; early vaginal awareness with infantile masturbation involving the clitoris, labia, and vagina; and the importance of early preoedipal attachments and their relation to disturbances of female sexuality.

Hayward, Emeline (1943). Types of female castration reaction. *Psychoanal. Q.*, 12:45-66.

Hayward discusses two types of adult women who orient their lives around penis envy, Abraham's (1927) "wish-fulfillment" and "revengeful" types. Hayward sees these types as evolved from an emotionally meaningful discovery of the penis in different developmental stages. Penis envy from the (preoedipal) anal-sadistic stage leads to the revengeful type of woman. Preoedipal penis envy often occurs when girls repeatedly confront anatomical differences from brothers who are near their own age. An accusation of castration/deprivation is directed against the mother, and future relationships are corrupted by this ambivalence and hostile identification. The wish-fulfillment type of woman becomes preoccupied with penis envy after reaching a phallic level, where the penis is seen as having pleasure-giving attributes and bringing admiration. She wants a penis and feels deprived because of what a penis can do; but she does not feel that this lack deters her from success and she may develop a penis-equivalent such as using her intellectual potentialities. Anxieties focus around the fear that she will be exposed as being "only a woman" despite apparent success in masculine endeavors. Interesting clinical material is included.

Deutsch, Helene (1944e). The 'active' woman: The masculinity complex. In: *The Psychology of Women*, Vol. 1. New York: Grune and Stratton, pp. 279-324.

Deutsch uses an extensive bibliographical study of Georges Sand to discuss the masculinity complex and to differentiate it from a description of the active-feminine woman. The masculinity complex is characterized by active and aggressive tendencies that conflict with the environment and the feminine inner world. Fears of femininity mobilize masculine tendencies, with the masculinity complex concealing fears of feminine functions and role. Intellectual women show thwarted femininity, conflicted elimination of the mother-identification, and identification with the father. The "feminine core" is a product of external and internal inhibitions of aggression but is still accompanied by a number of uninhibited active and aggressive tendencies in equilibrium. The normal early identification with an active mother is intensified in puberty. An erotic active feminine type, similar to matriarchs and to that found in the Demeter myth, develops greater activity, both outward and inward, than does the erotic-feminine (passive) woman; this activity serves nonerotic aims, including actual or sublimated motherhood. If motherly activity is inhibited by conflict or by the environment of this active-motherly woman, then reactions reflecting direct or concealed aggression appear, including the masculinity complex. Thus, if women's activity oversteps definite limits, feminine-erotic experiences are restricted. Active, provocative coquetry is seen as reflecting aggression, as a mask of femininity that is a flight from repressed feminine desires. Carmen's coquetry in Bizet's opera constitutes archfeminine masochism covered by aggression; some women use activity as a defense against fears of passivity.

Deutsch, Helene (1944a). Eroticism: The feminine woman. In: *The Psychology of Women*, Vol. 1. New York: Grune and Stratton, pp. 185-218.

Sublimated eroticism or inner erotic fantasies and longings are inherent in the adolescent feminine psyche. The ability to gradually shape these erotic longings so they do not negate the direct experience of sexuality is a goal of female adulthood and sexual maturity. [See Chapter 20 for annotation.]

Deutsch, Helene (1944c). Feminine passivity. In: *The Psychology of Women*, Vol. 1. New York: Grune and Stratton, pp. 219-238.

Passivity becomes a central aspect of femininity as a consequence of vaginal unresponsiveness and genital trauma in the phallic phase. [See Chapter 20 for annotation.]

Agoston, Tibor (1945). Some psychological aspects of prostitution: The pseudo-personality. *Int. J. Psycho-Anal.*, 26:62-67. Addendum in: *Int. J. Psycho-Anal.*, 27:59, 1946.

The essential psychological factor in prostitution is the development of a pseudo-personality, which is manifested by the prostitute's psychological incognito or mask, her false tales about herself, and her false toughness. Agoston argues that prostitutes are shy people with pregenital symptoms, who suffer from existential global castration fears and unresolved oedipal anxieties. Using the mask of not being affectively present, through their sexual behavior and false money-madness they conceal infantile perversions and regressive trends. Etiology includes actual emotional rejection by both parents as well as childhood threats of total devastation such as being "in the gutter."

Deutsch, Helene (1945b). The psychology of the sex act. In: *The Psychology of Women*, Vol. 2. New York: Grune and Stratton, pp. 183-112.

Deutsch contends that intercourse serves both individual sexual satisfaction and reproduction; the two components are not quantitatively the same for both sexes. Women psychologically perceive coitus as the beginning of a process that culminates in delivery, as evidenced by women's fantasies. Coitus heals women's genital trauma by enabling them both to receive the penis and discover the vagina. Narcissistic self-love and masochistic pleasure without damaging the ego are both satisfied. Direct coital experience leads to vaginal erotization, and the clitoris is replaced as the central organ of spontaneous sexual excitation. The association of pleasure and pain in defloration creates constitutional readiness for the masochistic character of female sexuality. Orgasm is a biologically determined function that becomes possible by overcoming constitutional inhibitions to vaginal eroticism and by managing feminine masochism. A "malicious" orgasm found in masculine-aggressive women involves rhythmic contractions that disregard men's rhythm. Women's orgasm, often later than men's, is a relaxing gratification in the slow course of an excitation curve and subsides later and gradually. [See also Chapter 22.]

Greenacre, Phyllis (1945). Urination and weeping. *Amer. J. Orthopsychiat.*, 15:81-88. Also in *Trauma, Growth and Personality*, New York: Norton, 1952, pp. 106-119.

Neurotic feminine weeping of two types, shower weeping (flooding) and stream weeping (crocodile tears), are both derived from conflicts about urination in the infantile period. In both there is strong penis envy or fascination with urinary function. The first involves continuing to weep excessively about the absence of the penis. The second type substitutes weeping for the male urination that was observed in childhood, with periodic aggressive demands for the male organ and illusional ideas of its possession. Greenacre describes two patients who also wept about their sensations of vaginal dryness in intercourse. One patient had a bland lack of emotion, urinary frequency, and vaginal dryness, as well as a strong body-phallus identification. She had extraordinary stream weeping, often only from the eye closest to the analyst, in relation to penis envy themes. The relations between weeping, visual focusing, and urination are traced from infancy, with sex differences noted in urination from about seven months. Girls at age 10-12 months laugh during urination, whereas urination becomes a serious business for boys and an outlet for aggressive discharge. In girls, urination usually remains a simpler tension reliever. Girls are susceptible to visual erotization of male urination, which can then take over the castration problem.

Keiser, Sylvan (1947). On the psychopathology of orgasm. *Psychoanal. Q.*, 16:378-390.

Investigating male and female patients who can enjoy intercourse but cannot achieve orgasm because of neurotic disturbances, Keiser studies fantasies and feelings in the period prior to orgasm. Analysis reveals that both sexes fear the hostility that is activated by their oral conflicts. Women may equate a fantasied penis with the maternal nipple and may fear loss of control, addiction, passive yielding, and the vagina's becoming too full and exploding. The author describes a female patient whose fantasies include masochistic themes and phallic wishes.

Spitz, Rene and Wolf, Katherine (1949). Autoerotism. *The Psychoanalytic Study of the Child*, 3/4: 85-120. New York: International Universities Press.

This classic paper describes observations on three autoerotic activities—genital play, rocking, and fecal play—in a group of 170 children in the first year of life. The authors find that autoerotic activities are a function of object relations; thus, when object relations are normal, genital play results. When object relations are contradictory, making object formation impossible, rocking results; when object relations change in an intermittent manner, fecal play results. There are no autoerotic activities if object relations are absent. Gender differences are not noted.

Greenacre, Phyllis (1950a). Special problems of early female sexual development. *The Psychoanalytic Study of the Child*, 5:122-138. New York: International Universities Press. Also in: *Trauma, Growth and Personality*. New York: Norton, 1952, pp. 237-258.

This paper clarifies the relationship between the two main zones of erotogenic pleasure in women, the clitoris and the vagina. Greenacre argues that there are varying configurations of this relationship in the preoedipal phase, as well as in the phallic and oedipal phases. She takes issue with Freud's assumption that the vagina is without sensation until puberty. Greenacre speculates that vaginal sensations may develop in the preoedipal period in infants subject to intense overstimulation, which causes diffuse and disorganized discharge through many channels, including the genitals. She also suggests that vaginal sensations may be derived from early anal stimulation. In addition, oral stimulation and frustration may influence vaginal awareness and reactivity. Early vaginal awareness is more apt to be present than is early clitoral awareness, which more typically develops in the phallic phase. Greenacre describes ways in which experiences of vaginal sensitivity and experiences of clitoral sensitivity may develop and interact with each other and with various phases of psychosexual development, and how these may have a role in the production of psychopathology. A particular female character, "the Medea complex," develops in girls to whom one sibling is born before they are 16 months old and another sibling arrives when the girl is about three years old. In these girls, oral envy of the mother's breast is admixed with penis envy and a particular fixation on the testicles. Such women are narcissistically vulnerable to loss or to rejection by their partners and they lack maternal tenderness.

Lampl-De Groot, Jeanne (1950). On masturbation and its influence on general development. *The Psychoanalytic Study of the Child*, 5:153-174. New York: International Universities Press.

The author describes the uses of masturbation during various phases of libidinal development in boys and in girls. She discusses the significance of renouncing or continuing masturbation during the latency period and adult life. The author recognizes that little girls have knowledge of their vagina and engage in vaginal masturbatory activity. She attempts to explain why girls continue to masturbate after having become aware of the "defectiveness" of their genital.

Nydes, Jule (1950). The magical experience of the masturbation fantasy. *Amer. J. Psychother.*, 4:303-310.

This paper explores the popular fallacy that "masturbation drives one crazy" or is harmful. Nydes focuses on the sense of power from the physical sensations of arousal and orgasm that become connected to the masturbation fantasy and that impart a sense of reality. The masturbatory activity creates an illusion of reality because the orgasm is actually happening, thus fortifying the hallucinatory quality of the experience and the sense of magical omnipotence. The sense of hallucinatory power in the fantasy-making process, rather than a "loss of self-control," lends credence to the idea that masturbation causes insanity. A contrast between the grandiose power of the masturbation fantasy and the consciousness of reality limitations contributes to feelings of depression in the aftermath.

Thompson, Clara (1950). Some effects of the derogatory attitudes toward female sexuality. *Psychiat.*, 13:349-354. Also in: *Psychoanalysis and Women*, ed. J. B. Miller. New York: Brunner/Mazel, 1973, pp. 65-74.

Cultural and socioeconomic factors are delineated that produce effects on women's attitudes toward their own sexuality. The major sexual problem for women in this culture is to acknowledge their own sexuality. Penis envy is seen as a symptom of failure to achieve this acknowledgment. Conventional ideas interfere with women's natural self-expression and spontaneity and can result in resentment and envy. Women's devaluation of their own sexual organs in this culture is seen as more basically problematic than is penis envy. Cultural attitudes that derogate female sexuality are described. Thompson does not explore psychoanalytically the intrapsychic sources of the fixity of culturally widespread distortions. [See also Chapter 13.]

Bergler, Edmund (1951). Neurotic counterfeit sex. In: *Impotence, Frigidity, "Mechanical" and Pseudosexuality, Homosexuality*. New York: Grune and Stratton. Also in: *Counterfeit-Sex, Homosexuality, Impotence, Frigidity*, (2nd, enlarged edition of *Neurotic Counterfeit-Sex*, 1951). New York: Grune and Stratton, 1958.

Discussing the superiority of vaginal orgasm over other female sexual pleasures, Bergler suggests that orgasm produced by other routes implies frigidity and necessitates psychoanalytic treatment. "Counterfeit sex" is the term he uses for women's faking of orgasm. Involuntary contraction of the pelvic and perineal muscles at the end of intercourse signifies that the woman is not faking orgasm. For women, masochism and passivity in relation to their mother is common, yet is the source of sexual pathology. [See also Chapter 19.]

Kris, Ernst (1951). Some comments and observations on early autoerotic activities. *The Psychoanalytic Study of the Child*, 6:95-116. New York: International Universities Press.

Early autoerotic activities may promote or impede ego development. A disturbed 8-year-old female masturbator is described.

Levine, Milton (1951). Pediatric observations on masturbation in children. *The Psychoanalytic Study of the Child*, 6:117-124. New York: International Universities Press.

Masturbation is viewed as a normal activity of childhood. This pediatrician's observations include those of female children from 16 months through eight years. Vaginal insertion is noted in some children from age three on.

Reich, Annie (1951). The discussion of 1912 on masturbation and our present day views. *The Psychoanalytic Study of the Child*, 6:80-94. New York: International Universities Press. Also in: *Psychoanalytic Contributions*. New York: International Universities Press, 1973, pp. 155-178.

Reich summarizes the rich discussions on masturbation that took place during the Vienna Psychoanalytic Society's 1912 meeting and contrasts those views with the ideas prevailing in 1950. She reviews Freud's emphasis on the harmfulness of masturbation, which could be grouped in three ways: organic damage, psychic patterns, and fixation of infantile sexual aims. Masturbation accompanied by an incomplete sexual discharge could cause an "actual neurosis." The work of the other participants, Tausk, Stekel, Ferenczi, Federn, Nunberg, Rank, and Hitschmann, is examined. Tausk emphasized the importance of guilt feelings stemming from oedipal fantasies; the harmfulness of masturbation depended on the psychosexual stage of development. Stekel, taking an extreme view, proposed that masturbation was a necessary and universal form of sexual gratification. Whereas many participants were interested only in the physical effects of masturbation, Ferenczi and Federn introduced the concept of disturbed sexual rhythm and disturbed sexual excitement. Nunberg emphasized that lack of gratification from masturbation resulted from the failure to cathect real objects. Rank and Hitschmann discussed character formation. Female masturbation per se is not addressed.

De Monchy, Rene (1952). Oral components of the castration complex. *Int. J. Psycho-Anal.*, 33:450-453.

The author argues that oral experiences do not merely color the castration complex, but rather have a primary influence. The child's observation of anatomical differences is compared to the "congenital reaction schemes," or potential for imprinting, that was described by animal behaviorist Lorenz. The infant immediately perceives the nipple and then the penis as designated for the mouth. De Monchy describes a woman patient whose ambivalent longings for the mother's breast are intermixed with penis envy. Working through her oral frustration was essential to working through her castration complex.

Greenacre, Phyllis (1952a). Pregenital patterning. *Int. J. Psycho-Anal.*, 33: 410-415.

Greenacre discusses pregenital stimulation and its influences on the libidinal phases of development. [See Chapter 6 for annotation.]

Bonaparte, Marie (1953). *Female Sexuality*. New York: International Universities Press.

Bonaparte describes four types of orgastic experiences: an (infantile) clitoral orgasm; clitoral orgasm with some vaginal sensations; vaginal orgasm requiring clitoral participation; and (seldom) complete vaginal orgasm for which clitoral participation is unnecessary. Complete vaginal orgasm is felt to be the peak of mature femininity. [See also Chapter 2.]

Spitz, Rene (1952). Authority and masturbation: Some remarks on a bibliographical investigation. *Psychoanal. Q.*, 1:490-527.

Spitz traces the historical literature on repression of masturbation from the Bible to past and current medical writings. Campaigns against masturbation in children seemed to increase with an awareness of infantile sexuality and female masturbation at about 1700. Pediatric textbooks through the 1930s prescribed sadistic "treatments" for female masturbation, including corporal punishment, clitoridectomy, and cauterization of the genitals and thighs. Spitz illustrates that the radical change in attitudes in the medical community by the 1940s, was directly attributable to psychoanalytic education.

Bornstein, Berta (1953). Masturbation in the latency period. *The Psychoan-alytic Study of the Child*, 8:65-78. New York: International Universities Press.

Bornstein observes that there is a strong repression of sexuality and an intense masturbatory struggle at the end of the oedipal phase, a struggle that leads to latency and to strictness of the superego. [See Chapter 8 for annotation.]

Kinsey, Alfred, Pomeroy, Wardell, Martin, Clyde, and Gebhard, Paul (1953). *Sexual Behavior in the Human Female*. Philadelphia: London: Saunders.

Kinsey et al. present data about sexual behavior and responses from a nonclinical population of 16,000 women, including a sample of 5,940 American white women who were personally interviewed. The sample represents a broad although incomplete spectrum. The authors find that human sexual response comprises a whole system of responses involving the entire body, not merely the genitals. There is great individual sexual variation among women as well as in any single woman over time and circumstances. Anatomical and physiological similarities between men and women are striking, differences partly reflecting culturally disparate psychologies. The authors delineate "slower responses" in women, more erogenous zones, earlier sexual development, physiologically unique female orgasms, and greater emotional content in sexual responsivity. The authors contend that a vaginal orgasm achieved by sexual intercourse is not necessarily superior to an orgasm achieved by other means, nor is it a sign of sexual maturity. This book had significant historical impact.

Rangell, Leo (1953). The interchangeability of phallus and female genital. *J. Amer. Psychoanal. Assn.*, 1:504-509.

This article explores unconscious fantasies of the interchangeability of male and female sexual organs as a common expression of bisexual impulses. The genital of either sex can be used, in fantasy or act, to represent the genitality of the opposite sex. A woman patient with prominent masculine drives had a dream and an associated fantasy of blowing a condom outward from her vagina, the balloonlike projection being a penis-equivalent if sticking out, a receptive vagina if pushed in. Another woman had unconscious ideas of the vagina being an inverted penis and vice-versa, as an attempt to deny anatomical facts. Male cases are also discussed.

Kramer, Paul (1954). Early capacity for orgastic discharge and character formation. *The Psychoanalytic Study of the Child*, 9:128-141. New York: International Universities Press.

The effects on character formation of traumatic sexual overstimulation in childhood without physiological opportunity for discharge are discussed, and the beneficial effects of the physiological capacity for orgasm in female children are described. Sexually overstimulated boys who did not have the capacity for orgastic discharge later developed shame, awe of women, masochism, and a quest for excitement. Two overstimulated girls who masturbated to orgasm at ages three and four by contrast developed adaptive defenses to express their genital excitement and aggression. A third female patient with serious ego deficits gave a history of masturbation with orgasmlike experiences in childhood, but these had been stimulated by traumatic seduction by an adult.

Marmor, Judd (1954). Some considerations concerning orgasm in the female. *Psychosom. Med.*, 16:240-245.

Marmor challenges Freud's assertion that normal psychosexual development in women requires a progression from clitoral orgasm to vaginal orgasm. He reviews anatomical, histological, sociological, and physiological evidence to support his thesis that orgasm in normal women results from clitoral stimulation before and during intercourse. The author describes normal psychosexual response patterns and suggests that understanding the mechanism of orgasm can be of great clinical value in treating "frigidity" or anorgasmia.

Abraham, Hilda (1956). A contribution to the problem of female sexuality. *Int. J. Psycho-Anal.*, 37:351-353.

The author discusses the treatment of several women referred for vaginismus and other forms of frigidity. She describes two types of fixations in these women, a more common father fixation and a less common mother fixation. In the father-fixation type, the father is usually less available and the daughter clings to her masculine identification and wants to be mother's protector. These women are usually sadistic to their husbands. In the second type, the girl clings to a strong passive wish in relation to the phallic mother.

Fleiss, Robert (1956). *Erogeneity and Libido*. New York: International Universities Press.

Fleiss examines three hypotheses that he feels are presented in Freud's works: the dual instinct theory, the assumption of phylogenetic inheritance, and the hypothesis of libido. He supports the second hypothesis through a discussion of Little Hans and other works, and through a discussion of Freud's three concepts of repression. He describes three different definitions of libido in Freud's work and distinguishes between erogeneity, which is the functioning of an erogenic zone, and libido, which is the energy of the sexual instincts. Fleiss presents a detailed exposition of the libidinal phases of development, including many rich clinical descriptions. The first and second oral phase, the anal-sadistic phases, the phallic phase, and the genital phase are described. In discussing the genital phase, he includes clinical examples of female genital representation, oral and anal-sadistic themes, and typical dreams during the menstrual cycle. He closes with a chapter on erogenic (regressively partial-erotic) uses of language.

Kestenberg, Judith (1956a). On the development of maternal feelings in early childhood: Observations and reflections. *The Psychoanalytic Study of the Child*, 11:257-291. New York: International Universities Press.

The biological need to discharge vaginal tensions leads to the development of maternal feeling. [See Chapter 14 for annotation.]

Kestenberg, Judith (1956b). Vicissitudes of female sexuality. *J. Amer. Psychoanal. Assn.*, 4:453-476.

Kestenberg discusses the role of the vagina in development. There is evidence of vaginal sensations early in the preoedipal period. This inner activity creates a need for discharge, which leads to the development of maternal feelings in a preoedipal maternal phase by way of the projection of inner vaginal tensions onto the doll/baby. This phase ends with the "death of the baby," or the realization that the doll is inanimate. The girl then shifts into the phallic phase. Active experiences, rather than passivity, are required for the development of organ images and boundaries. The experiences of intercourse and delivery are required for full mastery of the vagina. "True feminine passivity can only be achieved with the repeated experience of vaginal gratification." [See also Chapter 6.]

Benedek, Therese (1960). The organization of the reproductive drive. *Int. J. Psycho-Anal.*, 41:1-15.

Benedek discusses female reproductive drive as requiring two steps beyond heterosexual coitus for maturity, achievement of pregnancy and of lactation. She also disagrees with the clitoral-vaginal transfer theory. [See also Chapter 14.]

Deutsch, Helene (1960). Frigidity in women. In: *Neuroses and Character Types.* New York: International Universities Press, 1965, pp. 358-362.

Deutsch asserts that the clitoris is the female sexual organ and the vagina is primarily an organ of reproduction. She notes that most women reach orgasm via the clitoris. Although some women experience vaginal orgasms, for most women vaginal contractions offer a passive receptive gratification. The clitoris, as the sexual organ, is the focus of castration fears. The vagina, as the organ of reproduction, is the focus of anxieties about death. Deutsch feels there is a misperception that frigidity is increasing and a preoccupation with experiencing vaginal orgasms, based on the misconception that the vaginal orgasm is the norm.

Greenacre, Phyllis (1960). Woman as artist. In: *Emotional Growth*, Vol. 2. New York: International Universities Press, 1971, pp. 575-591.

According to Greenacre, dynamic forces leading to biological or reproductive creativity conflict with the development of artistic creative expression. [See Chapter 12 for annotation.]

Hammerman, Steven (1961). Masturbation and character. *J. Amer. Psychoanal. Assn.*, 9:287-311.

The significance of masturbation and of masturbation fantasy in psychic development is discussed. The author suggests that analysis of the precursors of genital masturbation fantasies can shed light on early self- and object representations. These precursors are reflected in the adult's genital masturbation activities and fantasies and in behavioral patterns. As a patient in analysis can tolerate more adequate object relationships in the external world, the need to maintain archaic object relations in fantasy lessens, as does overt or covert masturbatory activity. This article contains four case studies of male patients, all of whom had significant preoedipal conflicts that interfered with adult sexual functioning. Whether similar ideas about masturbation would be supported by clinical material from women is not discussed, although it is noted that preoedipal interferences had previously been ascribed only to women.

Harley, Marjorie (1961). Masturbation conflicts. In: *Adolescents: Psychoanalytic Approach to Problems in Therapy*, ed. S. Lorand and H. Schneer. New York: Hoeber, pp. 51-77.

[See Chapter 9 for annotation.]

Hollender, Marc (1961). Prostitution, the body, and human relatedness. *Int. J. Psycho-Anal.*, 42:404-413.

Two analytic cases are presented in this study of why women become prostitutes (call girls). The women turned to prostitution as a way of finding an impersonal type of relatedness, wherein the interpersonal relationship provides tension relief using another's body and one's own body, rather than a relation to a specific person. Object relations were on an oral or predifferentiation level. They sought escape from an enmeshed disturbing mother-daughter relationship that was eroticized. Both women identified with the mother's promiscuity, and with the mother's word and example that sexuality was acceptable only as a relationship of bodies and not of persons. Masturbatory fantasies were of women, and included direct eroticized longings for the mother's love. Neither patient had a sustained father-figure, both feared or hated men, and one had a history of sexual abuse and accidental vulval injury. The behavior provided the veneer of adult femininity. Partial self-destruction, the reaction to a difficult mother-daughter entanglement, is also a social consequence of prostitution.

Lichtenstein, Heinz (1961). Identity and sexuality: A study of their interrelationship in man. *J. Amer. Psychoanal. Assn.*, 9:179-260.

This important and influential paper is a theoretical study of the function of human sexuality, emphasizing its relation to identity. The article does not address aspects of sexuality that are gender specific. Lichtenstein asserts that the maintenance of identity supersedes both the reality and the pleasure principles. The main function of nonprocreative sexuality is to maintain identity, which was originally and unconsciously imprinted on the infant by the sensual ministrations of the mother during the early symbiotic relationship. The case of a woman is presented to illustrate this hypothesis. Another section discusses Freud's theoretical shift toward a dual instinct theory to account for the repetition compulsion. Lichtenstein postulates that the repetition compulsion can be better explained as the consequence of a person's primary need to maintain his "identity theme."

Moore, Burness (1961). Reporter, Panel: Frigidity in women. *J. Amer. Psychoanal. Assn.*, 9:571-584.

Helene Deutsch chaired this historically interesting panel. She notes that frigidity, as defined as failure to experience vaginal orgasm, has a high incidence in women, has disappointing results from psychoanalytic treatment despite other gains, and often shows no correlation with psychopathology. Deutsch argues that the clitoris is the sexual organ and the vagina is primarily the organ of reproduction. She raises the questions of why and how are some women endowed with vaginal orgasm and asserts that most women experience vaginal lubrication and mild slow vaginal relaxation. This passive-receptive gratification should be considered normative for women. Lack of vaginal orgasm may be psychogenic, constitutional, or anatomical.

Moore asserts that most psychoanalysts have accepted the idea that frigidity implies the incapacity to have vaginal orgasm. He outlines theories about etiology, including frigidity as a defensive compromise resulting from excessive activity, bisexuality, masochism, maternal fixation, and frustrated orality. He argues that erotic needs can be gratified in motherhood rather than in orgastic discharge. Heiman reports on Masters' new revolutionary physiological investigations of normal sexual response, including the discovery of vaginal lubrication and muscular contractions, resulting in a physiological climax. Heiman believes that this hormonally mediated sensory experience provides the basis for the emotional experience of orgasm. He argues that the dual functions of the vagina in sexual pleasure and reproduction cannot be separated and proposes that frigidity is a defense against devouring oral tendencies.

Benedek's paper emphasizes that pregnancy and lactation complete female psychosexual and reproductive maturity. The full transference of sensation from the clitoris to the vagina is inconsistent with physiology. Pleasurable sensations begin in the clitoris and spread to the vaginal walls and the whole body in orgasm; this spread and the way it may be psychologically experienced are affected by emotional and personality factors. Frigidity is a complex defense mechanism against those anxieties--including fears of transient ego regression, of helplessness, or of being at the mercy of one's impulses--that would be mobilized by complete (including vaginally perceived) orgasm. Bychowski's paper focuses on preoedipal and oedipal pathologies that lead to clitoral hypercathexis and vaginal anesthesias.

Heiman, Marcel (1963). Sexual response in women: A correlation of physiological findings with psychoanalytic concepts. *J. Amer. Psychoanal. Assn.*, 11:360-387.

Heiman views physiological studies such as Masters' preliminary findings as useful for understanding psychoanalytic and physiological correlations with respect to the functions of the vagina, the nature of female orgasm, and the relationship between female orgasm and reproduction. Coitus is one phase in a total female reproductive process, and the vagina has the functions of reproduction and sexual pleasure, with vaginal orgasm considered here as the norm. The two manifestations of sexual response are vaginal lubrication and muscular contractions. The vagina is self-lubricating, and severe frigidity (vaginismus or lubrication difficulties) may impair reproduction. Intercourse is always psychologically connected to reproduction. The muscular contractions in the vagina and the uterus that occur during orgasm are related psychologically to infantile oral sucking. Uterine and vaginal contractions of orgasm are also essential to sperm transport; the penis-vagina-uterus form a single functioning unit for pleasure and reproduction. Heiman argues that the female is "active" in her sexuality and has active biological functioning toward propagation. Female coital pleasure and orgasm have physiological and psychological (sensual-emotional) components. There are neurohormonal connections between coitus, sexual pleasure with contractions and sperm transport, birth, and nursing, all of which are oxytocin mediated. During coitus a woman projects herself "progressively" into the place of her future baby; identification with the baby satisfies her own passive-dependent suckling needs; and the identifications unite three generations. Brain research supports the central role of oral factors.

Sarlin, Charles (1963). Feminine identity. *J. Amer. Psychoanal. Assn.*, 11:790-816.

Sarlin defines feminine identity in relation to ego structure, which is in turn rooted in biology and thus is influenced by capacities for lactation and gestation. He proposes that to establish feminine identity, two tasks proposed by Freud must be resolved: renouncing clitoridal sexuality and relinquishing maternal attachment. The normal outcome is progression to oedipal conflict and heterosexual object relations. Since Sarlin assumes that genital primacy cannot be established in the phallic phase, the development of nipple erotism with pubertal enlargement of the breasts and other associated physical changes is seen as the decisive physiological step for the development of femininity. This allows a shift from the erectile clitoris with its phallic significance to the nipples with their erectile capacity but feminine connotation. Frigidity, or vaginal unresponsiveness, is connected with the inability to establish genital primacy because of regressive pregenital oral and sadistic trends and bisexual conflicts. A clinical case is detailed.

**Segal, Morey (1963). Impulsive sexuality: Some clinical and theoretical observations. _Int. J. Psycho-Anal._, 44:417-425.**

Patients with intermittent episodes of sexually impulsive behavior are described. In men, this sexual behavior consists of promiscuous and perverse relationships, often with prostitutes. In women, the behavior consists of promiscuity with many partners and involves caressing, kissing, and bodily contact, but seldom coitus, which evokes disgust. The genital form of sexual expression is absent, and pregenitality predominates for both sexes. Impulsive sexuality is understood as a screen for desire for symbiotic fusion with the mother and as an attempt to repair primitive depressive affect. The depression is precipitated by imagined or real object loss; the behavior is an attempt at restitution with an object who responds to the intense pregenital needs. Female patients may experience a temporary decrease in sexual impulsivity during pregnancy and the postpartum period, when their infants are anaclitically dependent.

**Moore, Burness (1964). Frigidity: A review of the psychoanalytic literature. _Psychoanal. Q._, 33:323-349.**

This is a scholarly review of psychoanalytic thought on female frigidity beginning with Freud and other early contributors. While noting that the psychoanalytic literature on frigidity has too often focused on problems in the transfer of erotogenic zones, Moore maintains that vaginal orgasm is a valid subjective phenomenon. He states that biological factors may contribute to a lack of sexual responsivity in some women. Those factors include weakening of libido by change in object and erotogenic zone; bisexuality, which interferes with full erotic pleasure; and possible neuroanatomical differences, including lessened cortical influence in women. Emphasizing the classical Freudian schema, he focuses on the vicissitudes of female psychosexual development and the unconscious processes that may impair female erotic life. The essential change from activity to passivity may be interfered with by penis envy, identification with an active phallic mother, and failure to identify with a feminine mother. Moore also elaborates classical ideas of the masculinity complex, hostile wishes for revenge, and difficulty accepting masochistic wishes as contributors to frigidity. He sees feminine development as predetermined by the biological destiny of motherhood, unless strong disturbances give rise to conflict, which lead to frigidity as a defense. Moore concludes that neither the compromise nature of frigidity as a symptom nor the metapsychology of orgasm and frigidity have been adequately understood. The relationship between erotic needs and the functions of motherhood also is not yet clarified. There is a comprehensive bibliography.

Weissman, Philip (1964). Psychosexual development in a case of neurotic virginity and old maidenhood. *Int. J. Psycho-Anal.*, 45:110-120.

A case of neurotic virginity and old maidenhood with an unconscious fear of sexual intercourse is presented. In her relationships, the patient avoided intercourse but permitted clitoral masturbation. An intense nonoedipal defensive fixation on the father was found to represent an extension of a strong preoedipal fixation on the mother, including wishes for a penis from mother and regressive oral and sadistic longings and fears. The fear of intercourse was related to uneven maternal nurturing. A defensive attachment to the heterosexual object was accompanied by deeply repressed phallic aims toward the phallic mother. The interrelation between instinctual pathology and the development of object relations is discussed, especially with regard to the incompleteness of the oedipal attachment to the father.

Barnett, Marjorie (1966). Vaginal awareness in the infancy and childhood of girls. *J. Amer. Psychoanal. Assn.*, 14:129-140.

Vaginal awareness and stimulation occur in the infant and neonate but are later repressed. Barnett explores possible factors in the repression of vaginal awareness: 1) the lack of voluntary muscular control over the vagina is a threat to body integrity (anxiety about penetration or loss of body contents); 2) characteristics of the vagina as a cavity, and the consequent difficulty in visualizing it, make it difficult for girls to incorporate the vagina into their body image; and 3) the inability to maintain awareness of the vagina without anxiety leads to decathexis of this organ and clitoral hypercathexis, which emerges to assist in vaginal repression. Barnett states that the complete sequence of normal female development may be based on orifice and cavity cathexis. Clinical material from two girls is included.

Masters, William and Johnson, Virginia (1966). *Human Sexual Response.* London: J. and A. Churchill.

This landmark book summarizes extensive research on the physiological responses to sexual stimulation of male and female volunteers. A basic response pattern of excitement, plateau, orgasm, and resolution is delineated in both men and women, with differences found between the sexes and within each sex. Orgasm in women is produced by clitoral stimulation, which can occur either directly or indirectly by the traction caused by penile thrusting. This finding necessitated a critical reexamination of Freud's hypothesis that women must evolve from clitoral to vaginal orgasm as development proceeds and highlighted the role of inadequate clitoral stimulation in anorgasmia.

Moulton, Ruth (1966). Multiple factors in frigidity. In: *Science and Psychoanalysis: Sexuality of Women*, ed. J. Masserman. New York: Grune and Stratton, pp. 75-93. Also in: *Women, Body and Culture*, ed. S. Hammer. New York: Harper and Row, 1975, pp. 156-171.

Moulton describes several determinants of frigidity and divides them into specific sexual fears and nonsexual characterological distortions. Classical ideas about penis envy, the role of the vagina, the equation of passivity with femininity, and the nature of female orgasm are all seen as based on misconceptions about female sexuality. Moulton summarizes her clinical experience with patients with sexual dysfunctions and describes their difficulties with oedipal and preoedipal relationships. Two-thirds of her female cases had some degree of frigidity. Two analytic cases, one with vaginismus, illustrate the various therapeutic considerations.

Sherfey, Mary Jane (1966). The evolution and nature of female sexuality in relation to psychoanalytic theory. *J. Amer. Psychoanal. Assn.*, 14:28-128.

This article is of historical significance as a controversial first attempt to reevaluate psychoanalytic theory in the light of Masters and Johnson's research and major advances in embryology. It merits study in conjunction with Heiman et al. (1968) and Barker's (1968) panel report. Sherfey reviews female genital anatomy, the phases of sexual arousal for men and women, and female functioning during sexual activity. She discusses physical etiologies for female sexual dysfunction. Sherfey's ideas include 1) There is no biological basis for the psychoanalytic theory of bisexuality; the embryological anlage develops in a female direction unless androgens induce male development. 2) Clitoral erotism is the only erotism, as shown by Masters and Johnson; it is a physical impossibility to separate the clitoral from the vaginal orgasm. Intravaginal coition produces orgasm by the preputial-glandar mechanism of stimulating the clitoris. 3) Female orgastic response, especially in multiparas, is insatiable. 4) Female sexuality has necessarily been suppressed for the evolution of civilized society. Sherfey does not integrate her work with other psychoanalytic contributions. [See also Chapter 13.]

Prosen, Harry (1967). Sexuality in females with "hysteria." *Amer. J. Psychiat.*, 124:141-146.

[See Chapter 20 for annotation.]

Shopper, Moisy (1967). Three as a symbol of the female genital and the role of differentiation. *Psychoanal. Q.*, 36:410-417.

Clinical material from the analysis of an adult woman and her dream shows the feminine significance of the number three as a symbol. The symbol three may symbolize the differentiated feminine genital apparatus, rather than necessarily relating to penis envy or male genitals. The patient began analysis with a cloacal concept of her female genitals, connected to self-devaluation. She denied masturbation, avoided vaginal exploration, and had problems with constipation and delayed urination. While becoming aware of and sorting out genital sensations and working through her cloacal fantasies, the patient had a dream with the image of a building with three tiers and a swimming pool. The author suggests that dream symbolization can serve as an index of the degree of differentiation of the genital apparatus. Enclosed cavity symbols (box, room) may refer to the female genitalia as a whole or to the more specifically differentiated vagina. Female genital symbolization may develop from a unitary beginning (cloaca) and return again to a unitary symbol at maturation (vagina), with an intermediary tripartite phase of increasing differentiation in which the woman acknowledges the distinctness of bladder, vagina, and rectum, each with contents, sensations, and sphincteric functions. The role of differentiation in the attainment of vaginal dominance is discussed.

Barker, Warren (1968). Reporter, Panel: Female sexuality. *J. Amer. Psychoanal. Assn.*, 16:123-145.

This is an excellent report of a panel that integrated anatomic and physiological research with psychoanalytic theory and observations. The panel was a response to Masters and Johnson's research and Sherfey's 1966 paper. The four panel presentations are interspersed with discussions illustrating the vigorous struggle to understand, rework, and integrate the new information with psychoanalytic theory. In the first paper, "On the Nature of Female Sexuality," Benedek presents a consolidated view of female sexual development using the recent findings of embryological and physiological research. Orr, in his paper, "The Female Sexual Role: Historical Notes," responds to Sherfey's work and questions some of her findings; he disagrees with her views about the role of sexuality in the evolution of civilized society. Moore's paper, "Psychoanalytic Reflections on the Implications of Recent Physiological Studies on Female Orgasm," looks at the psychic representations of sexuality and sexual gratification in conjunction with physical changes and development. Finally, Barnett, in "Psychoanalytic Implications of a Sexual Training Program," considers the transferential elements in Masters and Johnson's sex training. Together the four papers and discussions are a thorough review of psychoanalytic thought on female sexuality and female sexual responses at that time. Several of the papers were also published separately.

Barnett, Marjorie (1968). I can't versus he won't. *J. Amer. Psychoanal. Assn.*, 16:588-600.

This article reconsiders positive oedipal development in the light of new anatomic and physiological information regarding differences between the sexes. Biological differences are reflected in gender-specific object relationships, in successful resolution of the Oedipus complex, and as organizers for adult sexual object choice. Barnett's title refers to a simplification of the childhood positive oedipal position. The girl has conflicts around the father's unwillingness to penetrate her (he won't), and the boy has conflicts around his inability to penetrate the mother (I can't). Barnett hypothesizes that Masters and Johnson's sex training is effective with patients having unresolved oedipal conflicts because the therapists temporarily provide less harsh maternal and paternal superego models. They override the patients' own internalized prohibitions and parental introjects.

Francis, John (1968). Reporter, Panel: Masturbation. *J. Amer. Psychoanal. Assn.*, 16:95-112.

Francis notes that normal genital play in the first two years serves the development of body image and establishment of object relatedness. Masturbation, with associated fantasy, is established in the phallic-oedipal period. Among several papers on masturbation, Geleerd presents "Guilt and Masturbation in an Adolescent Girl," describing the analysis of a 16-year-old who was depressed and had masochistic beating fantasies. Buxbaum presents a paper, "Anal Masturbation, Breathing Difficulties and Mourning in a Four-and-a-half-year old Girl," in which symptoms reflected mourning for a dead brother.

Glenn, Jules and Kaplan, Eugene (1968). Types of orgasm in women: A critical review and redefinition. *J. Amer. Psychoanal. Assn.*, 16:549-564.

The terms vaginal orgasm and clitoral orgasm, which Freud did not employ, are widely used but ill-defined. The authors suggest that one should refer instead to the area stimulated and the location of the orgastic experience. More than one area may be stimulated, and the area or areas in which the orgasm is felt need not be the same. The anatomic and physiologic changes during orgasm are essentially the same and always include vaginal contractions regardless of the area of stimulation or the experience of orgasm. The type and location of the experience depends largely on the mental representations of specific areas and the nature of the person's fantasies. Both drive satisfaction and defenses influence the quality and location of the orgastic experience.

Heiman, Marcel (1968). Female sexuality: Introduction. *J. Amer. Psychoanal. Assn.*, 16:565-568.

This short paper comprises the introductory comments for a 1967 panel on Female Sexuality (summarized by Barker, 1968) which were then also published separately. Heiman reviews criticisms of Masters and Johnson's work, including the absence of psychological data, the emphasis on physiological reactions, and the methodology. He expresses the hope that Masters and Johnson's and Sherfey's work will cause a reexamination of the role of sexuality and orgasm in the psychology of women.

Heiman, Marcel, Kestenberg, Judith, Benedek, Therese, and Keiser, Sylvan (1968). Discussions of Mary Jane Sherfey: The evolution and nature of female sexuality in relation to psychoanalytic theory. *J. Amer. Psychoanal. Assn.*, 16:406-456.

This article and Barker's (1968) panel on Female Sexuality are necessary companions to Sherfey's (1966) paper. Because of the intense interest generated by Sherfey's paper, editors of the *Journal* invited these written discussions of the controversial points. All four discussants present well-developed critiques, which include the noting of Sherfey's biases, inaccuracies, tone, and lack of psychoanalytic validation. 1) Heiman disputes Sherfey's interpretation of embryological data and her dismissal of a biological basis for bisexuality; he states that embryological data do not contribute to understanding the psychopathology of clitoral erotism; 2) Kestenberg focuses on Sherfey's misinterpretation of biological data, including her overlooking the role of the proximal portion of the vagina, her disregard for the role of the male in organizing woman's full genital capacity, and her disregard for the unconscious; Kestenberg's (1968) position is elaborated elsewhere; 3) Benedek emphasizes bisexuality as a psychological concept; she sees sexual response as integrated into reproductive function and its psychic representations and notes that the functions of the sexual organs are organized via psychic representations within the personality; 4) Keiser critiques Sherfey's sarcasm, lack of psychoanalytic correlations and invalid generalizations; he fails to find clinical validation for her concepts of female sexual insatiability, the immediacy of male erections, and the lack of existence of psychopathological clitoral fixations.

Kestenberg, Judith (1968). Outside and inside, male and female. *J. Amer. Psychoanal. Assn.*, 16:457-510.

Kestenberg reviews the psychoanalytic literature and the research of Masters and Johnson as background for presenting her view of female and male sexual development and their interrelatedness. Her emphasis is on "inner" and "outer" genitality and how developmental phases vary in significance for males and females. Through developmental schemas and clinical material, she demonstrates the relevance and importance of these differences. On the basis of this "inner" and "outer" orientation, she hypothesizes that women need men to "complete [their] sexual development" and that psychoanalysis can "make woman teachable but cannot teach her." Kestenberg's position predates recent research on gender identity and infant development.

Laufer, Moses (1968). The body image, the function of masturbation, and adolescence. *The Psychoanalytic Study of the Child*, 23:114-137. New York: International Universities Press.

Laufer examines the role of adolescent masturbation and masturbation fantasies in establishing genital primacy and an integrated body image that includes mature genitals. [See Chapter 9 for annotation.]

Moore, Burness (1968). Psychoanalytic reflections on the implications of recent physiological studies on female orgasm. *J. Amer. Psychoanal. Assn.*, 16:569-587.

Moore's discussion extends his presentation in the Barker (1968) panel. Moore raises important and still controversial issues concerning female orgasm and genital psychic representation. He disagrees with Sherfey (1966), who stated "that there is no such thing as psychopathological clitoral fixation." Moore asserts that Sherfey overemphasized anatomical and physical facts rather than their psychic representation. Tracing the development of the psychic representation of female sexual organs, Moore reviews the literature, delineating women's difficulties in developing a psychic representation of the vagina, an invisible organ having vague and diffuse sensations and lacking sphincter control. Persistent clitoral orgasm may or may not hinder a satisfying sexual relationship, because the clitoris is also necessary for vaginal arousal. Moore uses coital orgasm as the sine qua non for female orgasm. Anorgasmia can sometimes be nonpathological, as when an active-erotic woman is with a male partner who is threatened by her orgastic response and has his own sexual dysfunction. Moore concludes that the significant therapeutic factors are the intrapsychic representation of the genitals, especially of the vagina, the cathexis of coitus, and improvement of object relations.

Shainess, Natalie (1968). The problem of sex today. *Amer. J. Psychiat.*, 124:1076-1085.

This article criticizes the research of Masters and Johnson as reinforcing social attitudes that dehumanize sex and separate it from human relationships. Shainess feels that the research laboratory situation focuses artificially on sexual physiology. On the basis of her analytic experience, Shainess questions Masters and Johnson's findings that there is only one type of female orgasm and related physiological pattern of sexual arousal. Also in this article, Lief rebuts Shainess's arguments and defends Masters and Johnson's methodology. He contends that responsivity of the vagina is added to that of the clitoris. These articles reflect the controversy stimulated by Masters and Johnson's research.

Sperling, Melitta (1968). Trichotillomania, trichophagy, and cyclic vomiting: A contribution to the psychopathology of female sexuality. *Int. J. Psycho-Anal.*, 49:682-690.

[See Chapter 23 for annotation.]

Stoller, Robert (1968b). The sense of femaleness. *Psychoanal. Q.*, 37:42-55. Also in: *Psychoanalysis and Women*, ed. J. B. Miller. New York: Brunner/Mazel, 1973, 231-244.

The earliest phase of femininity, core gender identity, is seen as the acceptance of the body ego, "I am female." Core gender identity forms unequivocally when the parents have no doubt that their infant is female. This sense of femaleness develops regardless of defects in anatomy, genetics, or physiology. Several types of patients are described to explore this thesis: 1) females who are without vaginas but otherwise biologically normal, 2) females who are biologically neuter but whose external genitalia at birth looked normal so there was no doubt about the infant's sex in the parents' minds, 3) females whose external genitalia were masculinized, but who were reared unequivocally as girls, and 4) females who are biologically normal (with vaginas) except for masculinization of their external genitalia, but who were reared unequivocally as boys. The first three types develop female core gender identity, which is maintained even after discovery of their anatomical defects; the fourth type regard themselves as boys. Stoller speculates about females born without the clitoris as well. He asserts that definitive signs of primary femininity are present before the phallic phase, from at least the first year of life.

Yazmajian, Richard (1968). Dreams completely in color. *J. Amer. Psychoanal. Assn.*, 16:32-47.

This article on technicolor dreams includes clinical material on the psychic representation of the vagina. Yazmajian discusses a woman patient with frigidity and multiple phobias. She had been unable to integrate her vagina into her body image because of the narcissistic wound of penislessness and an inability to conceptualize and organize into a Gestalt her internal vaginal sensory perceptions. She had repressed vaginal sensations and developed an illusory penis fantasy. In the course of working through conflicts about her vagina, she had a technicolor dream. Associations indicated that the technicolor image represented an illumination of the interior of the vagina. The invisible body part was represented as hypervisible by use of reversal and projection during dreaming.

Gillespie, William (1969). Concepts of vaginal orgasm. *Int. J. Psycho-Anal.*, 50:495-497.

The author suggests that revisions in Freud's theories of the psychology of women are necessitated by the findings of Masters and Johnson on the physiology of orgasm. In particular, two significant hypotheses suggested by Freud are in need of revision: 1) that to achieve psychosexual maturity a woman must substitute vaginal orgasm for clitoral orgasm, and 2) that a woman must substitute a passive aim for an active one. Masters and Johnson's findings make it clear that vaginal orgasm does not exist independent of clitoral orgasm. Therefore, it becomes physiologically impossible for a woman to achieve what Freud viewed as psychosexual maturity. The author also suggests that women may actively desire the penis as the source of the stimulation necessary for orgasm given their physiological needs.

Clower, Virginia (1970). Reporter, Panel: The development of the child's sense of his sexual identity. *J. Amer. Psychoanal. Assn.*, 18:165-176.

This panel report reviews current concepts of gender identity in 1970 as presented by Settlage, Stoller, Bell, and Kleeman. [See Chapter 6 for annotation.]

Fink, Paul (1970). Correlations between 'actual' neurosis and the work of the Masters and Johnson. *Psychoanal. Q.*, 39:38-52.

This article discusses the clinical phenomena noted by Masters and Johnson in their research with prostitutes who repeatedly experienced sexual excitation without experiencing orgasm. These women developed pelvic vasocongestion characterized by multiple somatic and psychological symptoms, including irritability, difficulty sleeping, and other signs of emotional distress. The symptoms were relieved by achieving orgasm through masturbation. The author compares these symptoms with those described by Freud in his work on the "actual neurosis," and notes that both conditions are similar. Fink presents clinical material from female patients illustrating the effect of unsatisfactory sexual experiences. He cautions against assuming that symptoms occurring after sexual contact arise predominately from intrapsychic conflict. They may be due to insufficient sexual stimulation to achieve orgasm.

Grunberger, Belá (1970.) Outline for a study of narcissism in female sexuality. In: *Female Sexuality: New Psychoanalytic Views*, ed. J. Chasse-guet-Smirgel. Ann Arbor: University of Michigan Press, pp. 68-83.

[See Chapter 22 for annotation.]

Kaplan, Eugene (1970). Congenital absence of the vagina. *Psychoanal. Q.*, 39:52-70.

Eleven cases of congenital absence of the vagina are studied, the literature is reviewed, and implications for hypotheses about the role of the premenarchal vagina in psychosexual development are discussed. This anomaly constitutes a severe narcissistic disturbance compromising sexual identity, body image, and self-esteem, with denial of defect, feelings of being the exception, and exacerbation of bisexual and exhibitionistic conflicts. Orgasms after surgical reconstruction are described as being of a different quality and with more vaginal location. Surgery can offer concrete resolution of bisexual conflicts, with the vagina being equated with femininity. Kestenberg's concepts of diffuse vaginal tensions needing discharge, Greenacre's contrasting idea of early vaginal sensations within the body image, and the hypothesis that the discovery of the introitus in the phallic phase is anxiety provoking in female development are discussed in the light of the clinical data on this anomaly.

Lichtenstein, Heinz (1970). Changing implications of the concept of psychosexual development. *J. Amer. Psychoanal. Assn.*, 18:300-318.

Lichtenstein proposes that sexuality is the most archaic mode capable of conveying the conviction of one's existence or identity. Freud's concept of the central importance of sexuality in human development has been challenged by 1) a lack of clear correlation between emotional maturity and "genital primacy" and 2) sexuality's being seen by ego psychologists as only one among several independent variables affecting personality development. According to Lichtenstein, sexuality must be accorded some central "exemplary function" (Freud) if we are to understand the unique driving power over the human personality of longings for sexual ecstasy. This exemplary function is the ability of sexuality to provide emotional affirmation of the reality or truth of personal existence. Aggression is seen not as an independent variable on a par with sexuality as a drive, but as a secondary means of obtaining personal affirmation by coercion of others. This article does not address aspects of sexuality that are gender specific.

Moulton, Ruth (1970a). A survey and reevaluation of penis envy. *Contemporary Psychoanalysis*, 7:84-104. Also in: *Psychoanalysis and Women*, ed. J. B. Miller. New York: Brunner/Mazel, pp. 207-230, 1973.

Moulton asserts that penis envy occurs frequently but is neither primary nor universal in female development. [See Chapter 6 for annotation.]

Moulton, Ruth (1970b). Sexual conflicts of contemporary women. *Interpersonal Explorations in Psychoanalysis*, ed. E. Witenberg. New York: Basic Books, pp. 196-217.

Writing about the sexual revolution from an interpersonal viewpoint, Moulton stresses that intrapsychic changes lag behind external cultural changes, sometimes by many generations. While overt restrictions on women have lessened, internal inhibitions and concepts of sexual role do not fade quickly. Contemporary educated women who struggle to combine professional and domestic roles illustrate role conflicts, the search for identificatory models, fear of other women's envy, sexual and marital difficulties, and work and sexual inhibitions. Inhibitions of orgasm may be related to early preoedipal dependency needs, unresolved oedipal conflicts, fears of submission to male dominance, performance pressure, or wishes to withhold a demanded response. Female orgasm is different from male orgasm. The amount of cooperation required for satisfying and meaningful sex is probably greater than that required in most other human relationships and reflects the ability of a couple to cooperate in other aspects of living.

Torok, Maria (1970). The significance of penis envy in women. In: *Female Sexuality*, ed. J. Chasseguet-Smirgel, Ann Arbor: University of Michigan Press, pp. 135-170.

[See Chapter 6 for annotation.]

Glenn, Jules (1971). Regression and displacement in the development of the body-phallus equation. In: *The Unconscious Today*, ed. M. Kanzer. New York: International Universities Press, pp. 274-289.

This paper examines the fantasy of certain male and female patients that their body equals a phallus. Two of Glenn's patients, one a woman, experienced the Isakower phenomenon, a regressive experience in which one attains preoedipal oral satisfaction. This ego state in which the body feels as if it were swollen was complemented by displacement of feelings of swelling from the genitals, including the phallus, to the rest of the body in the formation of the body-phallus equation. In the female patient, the Isakower phenomenon appeared when she was pregnant, because of her guilt over oedipal wishes and conception. The patient did not perceive her clitoris' swelling as her body seemed to swell. Her body-phallus equation and the experience of the swollen body acted as a compensation for her absent penis. Her identification with her baby, her wish to keep her baby inside her and not give birth, the latter in part a derivative of early toilet training experiences, and her desire to retain contact with her mother all expressed themselves through the Isakower phenomenon.

Kleeman, James (1971a,b). The establishment of core gender identity in normal girls: Part I. Introduction: The development of the ego capacity to differentiate; Part II. How meanings are conveyed between parents and child in the first three years. *Arch. Sex. Behav.*, 1:103-116, 117-129.

Kleeman reviews the research showing differences in gender behaviors during the preoedipal period. Girls establish a sense of their femaleness long before the phallic phase or the discovery of anatomical differences, and feminine gender identity is well established by about the third year. Reviewing the multiple mechanisms for the creation of gender identity,

Kleeman specifically highlights the central role of the process of cognition and the ego's capacity to differentiate. This article contains an excellent and extensive review of the literature from many disciplines. In part II, Kleeman describes in rich detail the evolution of a girl's sense of feminine gender identity, including (by age three) her awareness of pregnancy and birth processes, her recognition of genital differences, and her preliminary genital schematization. Conflictual and nonconflictual elements are described. [See also Chapter 6.]

Fraiberg, Selma (1972). Some characteristics of genital arousal and discharge in latency girls. *The Psychoanalytic Study of the Child*, 27:439-475. New York: Quadrangle.

Three cases are discussed, including the psychoanalysis of an adult woman and the psychotherapy of two latency-age children who suffered from an early loss of genital sensation following overwhelming excitement. Fraiberg reviews the psychoanalytic and physiologic literature to confirm the early occurrence of vaginal awareness, excitation, and orgasm in females. Her cases suggest a link between frigidity in the adult female and childhood erotic experiences that are tied to dread of penetration or fears of overwhelming excitement or orgastic discharge.

Green, Andre (1972). Aggression, femininity, paranoia and reality. *Int. J. Psycho-Anal.*, 53:205-211.

The integration of aggressive drives in femininity is discussed from a Kleinian viewpoint. Aggressive cathexes are directed toward internal retention in girls. This internal orientation and inhibitory retention have many consequences, including 1) a reinforcement of some narcissistic defenses, 2) endangering of object cathexes, and 3) impeding of development of erotic cathexes. Too free an outward expression of aggressive drives may cause excessive masculine identification. Mother-daughter relations are always an inextricable mixture of love and hate, parallel to the paranoid relation. Female sexual difficulties with incorporating the penis involve fears of hurting or of being hurt by the penis; fantasies of incorporating and destroying the penis resonate with earlier oral fantasies. Women compromise between fears of object loss and dangerous incorporation. An intermediate position between an object too exclusively internal (fused, devoured) or too overtly external (disavowed, rejected, subject to loss) is the required compromise. A protecting virile man may be sought and used as if he were a mother, a common transference to a male analyst. This article is densely written, with several unproven hypotheses.

Sherfey, Mary Jane (1972). On the nature and evolution of female sexuality. In: *Psychoanalysis and Women*, ed. J. B. Miller. New York: Brunner/Mazel, 1973, pp. 115-129.

The author hypothesizes that women possess a "biologically determined" heightened sexual drive that has been culturally suppressed in order to insure stable child-rearing practices. [See Chapter 5 for annotation.]

Stoller, Robert (1972). The "bedrock" of masculinity and femininity: Bisexuality. In: *Psychoanalysis and Women*, ed. J. B. Miller. New York: Penguin, 1973.

Stoller revises Freud's belief in a "bedrock" of constitutional bisexuality. He argues that the female's wish for a penis and the male's repudiation of femininity, rather than reflecting fundamental biological qualities, are defensive maneuvers that follow upon little girls' initial primary femininity and little boys' earlier primary identification with the mother. He asserts that although recent findings support the idea that biological mechanisms can influence the balance of masculine and feminine behaviors in one individual, fundamental masculinity and femininity can be permanently established in earliest life under the influence of psychological forces in opposition to the biologic state of the individual.

Blum, Harold (1973). The concept of erotized transference. *J. Amer. Psychoanal. Assn.*, 21:61-76.

The erotized transference is viewed as a distorted form of the erotic transference. Erotization can be a defensive attempt to master trauma by repetition, or can defend against hostility, homosexuality, loss, or unconscious conflicts. [See Chapter 25 for annotation.]

Fisher, Seymour (1973). *The Female Orgasm*. New York: Basic Books.

Results from a questionnaire study of 300 middle-class wives on feelings and fantasies aroused during sexual intercourse and other sexual states are reported in this book. The author delineates psychological factors facilitating or inhibiting women's capacity for excitement and satisfaction. Anxiety about loss of love objects and difficulties with the father are associated with problems in obtaining orgasm. The author also addresses the personal correlates of how orgasm is experienced, clitoral-vaginal preferences, intercourse frequency, narcissism, and various attitudes toward masturbation. Although not analytic, this book contains many provocative ideas.

Halpert, Eugene (1973). On a particular form of masturbation in women: Masturbation with water. *J. Amer. Psychoanal. Assn.*, 21:526-542.

Halpert studies masturbation with water to elucidate the relationship between the physical form of masturbation and the contents of the unconscious fantasy expressed. He describes three women patients who use masturbation with water as an exclusive or preferred technique. The unconscious associated fantasy is of having the paternal phallus, which then can be controlled to masturbate and urinate. Halpert also proposes that masturbation with water represents a cleansing or undoing, revenge against the father's penis with castration by means of a destructive urinary stream, pleasure in control of the masturbatory tool, and other oedipal and oral conflicts. These patients appeared to have experienced intense early passive stimulation and narcissistic traumata in connection with water and urination and the simultaneous demand for control of discharge.

Kestenberg, Judith (1973). Nagging, spreading excitement, arguing. *Int. J. Psychoanal. Psychother.*, 2/3:265-297. Also in: *Children and Parents*. New York: Aronson, 1975, pp. 75-100.

In this controversial article, the "typically feminine" moods of nagging, passing excitement on to others, and argumentatively trying to fix the blame on men are correlated with female genital tensions, and their origin is traced back to early phases of development. Nagging originates in a specific inner genital phase in response to nagging feelings from within the vagina. The passing on of excitement is derived from the end stages of this phase and is associated with feelings of swelling and intolerable spreading of waves of excitement. Argumentativeness begins at that time also but becomes dominant in the late phallic-oedipal stage, when the need to project forbidden wishes and guilt onto men arises from inner-genital tensions. In adolescence, with increasing inner-genital sensations, the revival of old wishes and earlier modes of defense intensifies nagging, passing on of excitement, and argumentativeness. Adult women can still be subjected to these typically feminine types of moods, which can be correlated with cyclic changes and other factors producing inner-genital tensions.

Newton, Niles (1973). Interrelationships between sexual responsiveness, birth and breast feeding. In: *Contemporary Sexual Behavior*, ed. J. Zubin and J. Money, pp. 77-98. Baltimore, MD: Johns Hopkins University Press.

[See Chapter 14 for annotation.]

Stoller, Robert (1973a). The impact of new advances in sex research on psychoanalytic theory. *Amer. J. Psychiat.*, 130:241-251.

Drawing on recent advances in sex research, Stoller reevaluates five concepts of sexuality in Freud's writings: bisexuality, infantile sexuality and the Oedipus complex, libido theory, the primacy of the penis, and conflict. Data from such allied fields as genetics, neurophysiology, behavioral research, and anthropology, are reviewed. Freud's concepts of libidinal zonal phases, conflict, and the influence of parental relationships early on and in the oedipal configuration remain valuable. New research shows evidence of biological bisexual potentialities, but the human capacity to symbolize and fantasize remains unique. Early parental attitudes and handling create conflict-free femininity by age one. Despite attacks on conflict theory, other fields have not yet clarified the mechanisms of human sexual behavior.

Abrams, Samuel and Shengold, Leonard (1974). The meaning of "nothing." *Psychoanal. Q.*, 43:115-119.

"Nothing" in a woman patient's associations, and in King Lear, may refer to the female genital from the vantage point of the centrality of the penis in the phallic phase. Other meanings from different developmental phases may include flatus, the helplessness of separation, and the all-or-nothing values of the early narcissistic period, wherein the "nothing" response to the female genitals involves fear, denigration, and feelings of being presented with a castrated genital instead of with the omnipotent fulfillment of oral, anal, and sexual desires.

Irigaray, Luce (1974). This sex which is not one (translation). In: *New French Feminisms*, ed. E. Marks and I. de Courtivron. Amherst: University of Massachusetts Press, 1980, pp. 99-106.

This paper offers a poetic challenge to traditional Freudian concepts and typifies French feminist writings. Irigaray feels that female sexuality has been incorrectly "theorized within masculine parameters." She metaphorically contrasts men's autoerotism, which requires an instrument and activity, with women's "touching herself constantly . . . for her sex is composed of two lips which embrace continually." Phallic intrusion interrupts this pleasure experience. Women do not distinguish between activity and passivity. Our phallocentric culture and linguistic patterns misleadingly enumerate everything, whereas women are "neither one nor two" and have multiple sexual organs. Feminine language, imagination, and thought are different.

Joseph, Edward (1974). An aspect of female frigidity. *J. Amer. Psychoanal. Assn.*, 22:116-122.

Joseph reports the analysis of a woman who seldom achieved orgasm and saw sex as a duty. As various masochistic and revenge fantasies about men were analyzed, the patient developed warm sensual responses spreading from her vaginal area, which Joseph describes as a vaginal type of orgasm. However, a scotoma with regard to the clitoris became evident with the analysis of certain oedipal themes. The patient had avoided clitoral stimulation in masturbation and in the marital relationship in order to maintain an oedipal fantasy of a special relationship with her father and with the analyst in the paternal transference. Joseph contends that the patient's frigidity was a form of libidinal gratification of an infantile (feminine) oedipal fantasy, rather than serving expression of aggressive or envious impulses. Clitoral sensations and their psychic representation are seen as a normal component of adult female sexuality.

Kubie, Lawrence (1974). The drive to become both sexes. *Psychoanal. Q.*, 43:349-426.

This last contribution from Kubie asserts that Freud underestimated the role of the preconscious wish to achieve mutually irreconcilable, dual sexual identities. He believes that these confused gender identities contribute to the genesis of the neurotic process and psychotic disorganization. Kubie differentiates the conscious, preconscious, and unconscious sources of the wish to become both sexes and finds that art and literature are the most obvious vehicles for the expression of this preconscious wish. Clinical manifestations of the drive to become both sexes include 1) an angry and perpetual search for the ideal mother-father parental figure, 2) insatiability or the demand to remain a bisexual child who is suckled, comforted, and made love to by the parent with whom there is also competition, 3) the wish to become and thus displace both the mother and father, and 4) the need to replace a younger sibling of opposite sex while remaining the same sex oneself. A variety of clinical phenomena and life situations in relation to the drive to become both sexes are traced in neuroses and psychoses. Kubie presages the work of Fast and others.

Schafer, Roy (1974). Problems in Freud's psychology of women. *J. Amer. Psychoanal. Assn.*, 22:459-485. Also in: *J. Amer. Psychoanal. Assn.* (Suppl.), 24:331-360.

Schafer discusses problems in Freud's psychology of women under three headings—1) the problem of women's morality and objectivity, 2) the problem of neglected prephallic development, and 3) the problem of naming. [See Chapter 7 for annotation.]

Stoller, Robert (1974). Facts and fancies: An examination of Freud's concept of bisexuality (1973). In: *Women and Analysis*, ed. J. Strouse. New York: Grossman, pp. 343-364.

Challenging Freud's theory of the biological basis of homosexuality, the author proposes that the fear of homosexuality, so prevalent in males, results from fantasied loss of gender identity as a result of merger with the overpowering preoedipal mother. Using clinical examples of intersex patients who were sexually misassigned at birth, Stoller demonstrates that belief in one's gender is the crucial determinant of core gender identity. At the opposite extreme is the psychological homosexuality of the male transsexual, whose primary feminine identification with the too gratifying mother is so intense that he experiences himself as a psychological female, though a biologically intact male. Despite their heterosexual object choice, boys have a shakier start in psychological heterosexuality than girls do because they must disidentify from mother. In girls, the pull toward merger strengthens core gender identity. The article contains an extensive bibliography. [See also Chapter 19.]

Waltzer, Herbert (1974). The umbilicus as vagina substitute. *Psychoanal. Q.*, 43:493-496.

A case is described in which a borderline psychotic woman treats her invaginated umbilicus as though unconsciously it were the vagina, with rituals related to menstrual hygiene and sexuality.

Clower, Virginia (1975). Significance of masturbation in female sexual development and function. In: *Masturbation: From Infancy to Senescence*, ed. I. Marcus and J. Francis, New York: International Universities Press, pp. 107-144.

Clower carefully delineates the meanings, forms, and functions of masturbation for women throughout the life cycle. She reviews the psychoanalytic and physiologic literature, including Freud, Spitz, Kleeman, Kinsey, and Masters and Johnson. She includes many detailed examples of normal and conflicted masturbatory activities and fantasies for each age group. Girls masturbate differently than boys do, and latency girls may use indirect means. The extension of clitoral to vaginal responsiveness may be gradual and dependent on experience. Clinical illustrations also include two adult women who had inhibitions in integrating a functioning internal genital (vagina) because of sadomasochistic conflicts.

Francis, John and Marcus, Irwin (1975). Masturbation: A developmental view. In: *Masturbation: From Infancy to Senescence*, ed. I. Marcus and J. Francis. New York: International Universities Press, pp. 9-43.

The authors describe the developmental phases of masturbation and review the psychoanalytic literature in each phase, including: autoerotism in the first year, the specific genital self-stimulation of the second year, the phallic-oedipal stage, the latency period, and masturbation in puberty. Masturbation in preadolescent and adolescent girls and the psychopathology of sexual trauma are also discussed.

Hollender, Marc (1975). Women's use of fantasy during sexual intercourse. In: *Masturbation: From Infancy to Senescence*, ed. I. Marcus and J. Francis. New York: International Universities Press, pp. 315-328.

Fantasy during coitus is used to derive gratification that otherwise could not be attained. It may be either a transitory or a fixed phenomenon. Women may use fantasies to shorten the time for arousal and orgasm, substitute an attractive partner for an unattractive one, convert the sexual act into one consonant with what is found sexually exciting, relieve anxiety, be in control, combat guilt feelings, or dampen sexual gratification. Fantasies may involve changes in the act, partner, oneself, or setting. These fantasies are usually identical with those used effectively with masturbation.

Kleeman, James (1975). Genital self-stimulation in infant and toddler girls. In: *Masturbation: From Infancy to Senescence*, ed. I. Marcus and J. Francis. New York: International Universities Press, pp. 77-106.

[See Chapter 6 for annotation.]

Kohut, Heinz (1975). A note on female sexuality. In: *The Search of the Self*, Vol. 2, ed. P. Ornstein. New York: International Universities Press, 1978, pp. 783-792.

Kohut agrees with Freud that girls inevitably suffer a narcissistic injury when they recognize the anatomical differences, but he strongly disagrees that this recognition is the significant genetic factor either in the wish to have a child or in narcissistic personality disorders in women. [See Chapters 6 and 22 for annotations.]

Marcus, Irwin and Francis, John (ed.)(1975). *Masturbation: From Infancy to Senescence*. New York: International Universities Press.

This comprehensive work emphasizes a developmental point of view. Several pertinent chapters from this book are reviewed individually in this section. These include "Masturbation, A Developmental View," by Francis and Marcus, "Masturbation in Female Sexuality," by Clower, "Women's Fantasies During Sexual Intercourse," by Hollender, and "Genital Self-Stimulation in Infant and Toddler Girls," by Kleeman. Clinical material on female patients can also be found in other chapters.

Bettleheim, Bruno (1976). The animal groom cycle of fairy tales. In: *The Uses of Enchantment: The Meaning and Importance of Fairy Tales*. New York: Knopf, pp. 277-310.

Bettleheim contends that fairy tales provide children with a means to work at mastering developmental conflicts by conveying developmental concerns and their solutions in symbolic form. They provide intuitive understanding of the psychological accomplishments that are necessary to achieve maturity and fulfillment. Bettleheim's chapter on the animal groom cycle is relevant to female sexual development. The animal groom cycle includes fairy tales in which an ugly, frightening animal is transformed into an acceptable mate through the love of a young woman. These stories deal with the girl's need to master fears and repulsions connected with childhood images of sexual relations with a male partner. Some fairy tales in this group emphasize the role of a loving father in enabling the girl to transfer her love and sexual interest to a new object.

Chasseguet-Smirgel, Janine (1976). Freud and female sexuality: Some consideration of the blind spots in the exploration of the "dark continent." *Int. J. Psycho-Anal.*, 57:275-286.

Chasseguet-Smirgel challenges Freud's concepts of sexual phallic monism (the idea of a single genital) and the child's supposed ignorance of the vagina. Rather, these are understood as defensive constructs held by children that function on two levels. On the oedipal level, such phallocentric concepts allow for the denial of the narcissistic wound and the feelings of helplessness that are created by recognition of the difference between generations, since if the vagina did not exist male children would not need to feel inadequate in either the negative or the positive oedipal position. On a more archaic level, children of both sexes deny their sense of inadequacy in comparison with the primal maternal image and break away from the omnipotent mother by denying the vagina and projecting her power onto the father and his penis. Thus, both phallic monism and penis envy are defensive denials of the primal maternal image.

Clower, Virginia (1976). Theoretical implications in current views of masturbation in latency girls. *J. Amer. Psychoanal. Assn.* (Suppl.), 24:109-125.

Clower discusses masturbation in latency-age girls and in women throughout the life cycle. She challenges several classical psychoanalytic assumptions about female sexuality by proposing that 1) latency-age girls do not turn away from clitoral masturbation and develop persistent penis envy as a necessary step in development; 2) in latency there is a better balance between drive and ego, and therefore a relative decrease in drive intensity; and 3) latency-age girls do masturbate, but the activity takes a variety of specifically feminine forms and is different from that of boys. Masturbation in latency girls typically involves indirect clitoral stimulation by rhythmic activities and pressure, sometimes to climax. The clitoris functions by initiating and elevating levels of tension, a biological capacity it retains throughout the female life cycle. Phase-specific defenses and transference resistances play a role in limiting the analyst's exposure to latency sexual activities and fantasies.

Strong superego prohibitions and oedipal guilt may interfere with focused genital stimulation. Complete repression of masturbation can be pathological and produces regressive symptoms, whereas genital anesthesias may be based on anxieties about overwhelming excitement rather than on feelings of inferiority. The transient loss of ego boundaries during orgasm threatens some girls and provokes repression.

Clower asserts that a girl who has abandoned genital self-arousal entirely is suffering from an interference in normal development. Clower goes on to describe the normal masturbatory developmental sequence of fantasy and behavior from latency to adulthood. She criticizes several points in Freud's theories, including his downplaying both feminine reproductive capacities and the impact of parental attitudes toward gender. Clower views both sexes as struggling to individuate from symbiotic ties with the mother and to recognize their sex and affirm and integrate their gender. The girls' anxieties about being female and becoming feminine are well matched by similar anxieties in boys. Persistent penis envy is defensive and pathological, indicating incomplete resolution of separation conflicts and boding ill for future feminine development.

Feigelson, Charles (1976). Reconstruction of adolescence (and early latency) in analysis of an adult woman. *The Psychoanalytic Study of the Child*, 31:225-236. New Haven, CT: Yale University Press.

[See Chapter 9 for annotation.]

Galenson, Eleanor (1976b). Reporter, Panel: Psychology of women. II. Late adolescence and early adulthood. *J. Amer. Psychoanal. Assn.*, 24:631-645.

[See Chapter 9 for annotation.]

Galenson, Eleanor and Roiphe, Herman (1976). Some suggested revisions concerning early female development. *J. Amer. Psychoanal. Assn.* (Suppl.), 24:29-57.

Using child observation, the authors confirm and modify several aspects of Freud's theory of female sexuality. An "early genital phase" emerging between 16 to 19 months was observed in 70 children in a research nursery. The impact of the discovery of the anatomical difference, occurring within the context of heightened genital awareness and curiosity characteristic of this phase and resonating with earlier drive organization, object relations, and issues of object and anal loss, elicits differing responses in girls and boys. All the girls showed mild to profound degrees of castration reaction, whereas few boys showed overt disturbance. From this point on, marked differences appear in the psychological development of boys and girls in the areas of sexual identity, object relations, basic mood, and many aspects of ego functioning. The authors contend that their research validates Freud's original position that sexual drive organization, including female castration complex and penis envy, exerts a special and exemplary role during the various psychosexual stages. Modifications include the early timing of the castration reaction, the influence of object relations, and a prior "vague sense of sexual identity" contributed to by early genital-zone experiences.

Grossman, William and Stewart, Walter (1976). Penis envy: From childhood wish to developmental metaphor. *J. Amer. Psychoanal. Assn.* (Suppl.), 24:193-213.

Three cases illustrate the effect of inexact and explanatory use of the concept of penis envy, and the necessity to analyze penis envy rather than consider it "bedrock." [See Chapter 6 for annotation.]

Grossman, William (1976). Discussion of "Freud and Female Sexuality." *Int. J. Psycho-Anal.*, 57:301-305.

[See Chapter 3 for annotation.]

Heiman, Marcel (1976). Sleep orgasm in women. *J. Amer. Psychoanal. Assn.* (Suppl.), 24:285-304.

The analysis of two women with sleep (dream) orgasm provides support for the hypothesis that the nursing female infant experiences vaginal sensations that are stimulated from within. One patient's sleep orgasm was associated with oral needs and the nursing situation. In another case, the orgasm was associated with a dream of intense, flooding, anally derived anger, which Heiman speculates might have stemmed from earlier frustrations in the nursing situation. Heiman believes that sleep orgasm represents gratification of unacceptable disguised pregenital wishes, or aggressive wishes, or both; it thus can occur unrelated to orgasms experienced while awake.

Kleeman, James (1976). Freud's views on early female sexuality in the light of direct child observation. *J. Amer. Psychoanal. Assn.* (Suppl.), 24:3-27.

Kleeman examines Freud's assumptions about early female sexuality in the light of findings from direct child observation. He suggests that modifications are indicated in the following areas: onset, nature of, and reasons for alterations in genital self-stimulation; the presence of femininity in the first year of life and its relation to the emergence of early gender identity; the importance of the father in girls' early development; and the relative importance of learning, cognitive functions, and language, compared with penis envy, in the emergence of femininity. Kleeman traces the development of gender identity as established before the phallic phase and as influenced by learning experiences, the maturation of cognitive functioning, and especially language or capacity for labeling, which serves as a basic organizer. Girls turn to their fathers very early, with object relations rather than instinct appearing to be primary in early gender identity, so that penis envy and feelings of inferiority are relegated to a less universal and less necessary place. The observable manifestations of early genital self-stimulation have a feminine character and variable patterning. Genital self-stimulation and sensations are felt to contribute to feminine identity but are not a major organizer of behavior. This article has observations and conclusions that contrast yet overlap with those of Galenson and Roiphe (1976).

Klein, George (1976). Freud's two theories of sexuality. *Psychological Issues*, Monogr. 36. New York: International Universities Press.

This influential paper is relevant for the development of a theory of sexuality. Klein discusses two models of sexuality that he finds implicit in Freud's work: a drive/discharge theory and a clinically based meaning/motivation theory. He elaborates the advantages he perceives in the latter model, particularly for explaining clinical phenomena. He proposes that the consequence of the unchallenged preeminence of the drive model has been a lack of investigation of the intrapsychic meanings and sources of drive and the relative neglect of testing the clinical theories of sexuality through systematic clinical observation. He briefly notes that the symbolic elaboration of sexual experience will be different in men and women.

Lerner, Harriet (1976). Parental mislabeling of female genitals as a determinant of penis envy and learning inhibitions in women. *J. Amer Psychoanal. Assn.* (Suppl.), 24:269-283. Also in: *Women in Therapy.* Northvale, NJ: Aronson, 1988, pp. 25-41

Using case material, Lerner suggests that the failure of parents to properly label the genitals is a factor in penis envy and the castration complex. [See Chapter 6 for annotation.]

Moore, Burness (1976). Freud and female sexuality: A current view. *Int. J. Psycho-Anal.*, 57:287-300.

Freud's concepts of bisexuality, the prolonged preoedipal period, the role of penis envy, the transfer of erotogenic zones, the nature of superego formation, and the traits of passivity, narcissism, and masochism are reviewed. Moore distinguishes between biological and psychological bisexuality (identifications), but describes psychoanalytic findings that both sexes unconsciously regard the clitoris as an inferior penis. Moore delineates recent emphases on the pregenital period in girls and the psychic differentiation of gender identity. He revises Freud's statement that the sexuality of girls is wholly masculine. He agrees with Kleeman (1976) that the psychic differentiation of gender identity requires that the ego has developed the capacity to differentiate (symbolization) and the capacity for reality testing (cognitive organization). However, Moore agrees with Galenson and Roiphe (1976) when he concludes that genital sensation and masturbation, or the development of the libidinal drive, is the major organizer of gender differentiation in the second year of life, in the context of separation-individuation. He concurs with Freud that girls have a longer preoedipal period, and he emphasizes that the inadequate genital schematization of girls leads to the desire that any object replacing the mother "serve the same passive needs for pregenital gratification." He feels that an inadequately narcissistically cathected genital and its close relationship with object loss may account for an apparently greater object relatedness and dependency in women. Moore retains the concept of a universal negative oedipal phase.

Turning to a discussion of transitional objects and the use of dolls, Moore sees dolls as aiding girls in changing to an active identification with their mother, in mastering vaginal tensions, and in assuaging anxiety aroused by the instability of body image connected with the lack of an external, easily controlled genital. Passivity, narcissism, and masochism, which Freud associated with females, are likely to be produced by disturbances in separation-individuation and early genital schematization. Thus, they may be observed in women with severe penis envy or in men with passive feminine tendencies.

With respect to superego differences between the sexes, Moore asserts that Freud erroneously made value judgments about differing potentialities. Moore's article provides an excellent summary of conservative analytic revisions of Freud's concepts, while continuing to emphasize the centrality of the castration complex, penis envy, and an inadequately narcissistically cathected female genital in feminine development and in the progression to the positive Oedipus complex.

Stoller, Robert (1976a). Primary femininity. *J. Amer Psychoanal. Assn.* (Suppl.), 24:59-78.

[See Chapter 6 for annotation.]

Stoller, Robert (1976b). Sexual excitement. *Arch. Gen. Psychiat.*, 33:899-909.

Noting the dearth of writings about the dynamics of sexual excitement, Stoller offers a tentative hypothesis: the crucial thematic element in conscious erotic scripts or daydreams is the desire to harm someone, or hostility. The unconscious fantasy converts frustration and trauma to triumph, and revenges and reverses childhood victimization. Erotic fantasy converts painful experiences to pleasurable triumph. Factors that produce sexual excitement include a balance of traumatic or fear-producing and safety elements, such as dehumanization, hostility, control over mystery and risk, and reversal of painful childhood experiences. There is a continuum in the degree of hostility manifested, from the bizarre psychotic to the rare contented, affectionate person. Stoller argues that hostility always remains an element in sexual excitement. He uses studies of gender development, perversion, fantasy, and pornography to support his thesis.

Eissler, Kurt (1977). Comments on penis envy and orgasm in women. *The Psychoanalytic Study of the Child*, 32:29-84. New Haven, CT: Yale University Press.

This lengthy and controversial article covers psychoanalytic, biological, historical, sociological, and cultural aspects of differences between the sexes, focusing on the concepts of penis envy and vaginal orgasm. Eissler regards penis envy as universal, noting that "the little girl perceives an organ at a place where she has none"(sic) and stating that adult women are seldom free of it. He agrees with Freud's (1925) findings on activity/passivity and superego differences in men and women and he adds differences in wishes to penetrate/be penetrated. Discussing vaginal orgasm, Eissler argues that all orgasms are not psychologically the same, despite Masters and Johnson's data on a single physiological pattern of orgasm. He presents a clinical case to illustrate the perception of a different sexual sensation in vaginal orgasm, with different defenses and inhibitions. He sees vaginal orgasm as a goal of female psychosexual development, proposes that the erogenous genital zones in women are divided, and notes that psychic fusion in intercourse is enhanced when simultaneous orgasm is achieved. Women whose sexual life is centered on healthy, noncastrative vaginal orgasm and who have outgrown clitoral primacy are seen as less ambivalent in their object relations. Eissler notes clinical exceptions wherein vaginal orgasm may reflect a castrative triumph over the penis, or other aggressive or narcissistic object relations. He speculates that vaginal orgasm evolved biologically in relation to fertilization and species propagation; thus Freud's female developmental path was an evolutionary schema. He comments further on obstacles to creativity in women and ends with a vehement critique of the feminist movement.

Fast, Irene (1979). Developments in gender identity: Gender differentiation in girls. *Int. J. Psycho-Anal.*, 60:443-453.

[See Chapter 6 for annotation.]

Galenson, Eleanor and Roiphe, Herman (1979). The development of sexual identity: Discoveries and implications. In: *On Sexuality, Psychoanalytic Observations*, ed. T. Karasu and C. Socarides. New York: International Universities Press, pp. 1-18.

[See Chapter 6 for annotation.]

Stoller, Robert (1979). *Sexual Excitement: Dynamics of Erotic Life*. New York: Pantheon.

Stoller draws on previous writings (1976a, 1976b) that describe primary femininity and sexual excitement, and then explores the dynamics of erotic behavior and erotic daydreams or fantasies through the detailed presentation of a female analytic case. He proposes that hostility enhances sexual excitement and fantasy and is an attempt to triumph over childhood traumas. Childhood frustrations are transformed into sexual arousal patterns in adulthood; the erotic scripts repair these traumas and contain the history of a person's psychic life. The extensive detailing of the case of Belle depicts a prolonged erotized sadomasochistic transference, early abandonment traumata, and exhibitionistic sexualized defenses.

Chiland, Colette (1980). Clinical practice, theory and their relationship in regard to female sexuality. *Int. J. Psycho-Anal.*, 61:359-365.

Chiland uses Freud's statements about female sexuality to demonstrate the role that theory may play in obscuring rather than clarifying clinical data. Freud's statements contain three main assumptions: 1) the equations between activity and masculinity and passivity and femininity; 2) the primacy of the phallus (the opposite of phallic is castrated); and 3) the perception of the clitoris as a little penis. Chiland disputes these assumptions and indicates how Freud was hindered by them, as well as by his own psychology, in his efforts to develop a theory of female sexuality. She speculates that Freud was inhibited in identifying with a woman, which for him meant identifying with a castrated being and perhaps also regressing to a primary identification with his mother.

Jayne, Cynthia (1980). The dark continent revisited: An examination of the Freudian view of the female orgasm. *Psychoanal. Contemp. Thought*, 3:545-568.

The author argues that Freud's "pine-shavings" theory of the clitoris' role and its relationship to the vagina may find confirmation in the work of Masters and Johnson. Tracing Freud's views of female sexuality and orgasm, she argues that he sees the adult vagina as the site of end-pleasure (orgasmic response) but that transfer from clitoris to vagina does not necessarily imply total renunciation of the clitoris. Freud viewed clitoral masturbation as masculine but varied in his view of whether the clitoral zone is given up or continues to function as "pine shavings" (tinder) as part of adult female sexual response. The transfer of erotogenic zones could be understood as part of a gradual reintegration of earlier libidinal phases, with earlier (clitoral) zones playing a role in adult sexual gratification as part of forepleasure and increasing sexual tension. Thus, the clitoral versus vaginal orgasm controversy is seen as misrepresenting Freud.

The author notes that Masters and Johnson, Kinsey, and several other researchers have found that orgasms induced by coitus are more psychologically satisfying than are the more physiologically intense orgasms of clitoral masturbation. Orgasm itself in women is not equated with satisfaction or relief of sexual desire, while orgasm consistency (correlated with early experience) is a variable distinct from sexual satisfaction (correlated with current psychological factors). Masters and Johnson find that the clitoris is the focus of sensual response and must be retained in the adult female but that vestibule sensitivity (rather than vaginal) also occurs. The author argues that the idea of clitoral sensitivity must be retained but that Freud's "pine shavings" theory is substantially correct in that the indirect clitoral stimulation provided in coitus gradually replaces direct clitoral stimulation. This "tinder" role for the clitoris is not transitory but is an integral and enduring part of the physiological response. Freud's view of the clitoris as the homologue of the masculine penis is wrong; the clitoris has its own essential functions. The psychological importance of the vagina as the sine qua non of heterosexual relations overrides its physiological role in orgasm.

Kestenberg, Judith (1980c). The three faces of femininity. *Psychoanal. Rev.*, 67:313-335.

Three typical feminine conflicts are described: motherhood and eroticism; motherhood and competitive work outside the home; and feminine eroticism and intellectual or career achievement. Within this larger frame, Kestenberg outlines three subphases of femininity: 1) the inner-genital preoedipal-maternal subphase, 2) the phallic-negative oedipal-rivalrous subphase, and 3) the phallic-positive oedipal-heterosexual subphase. Adult and child case material and Kestenberg's research project on movement patterns of communication and expression provide data bases for her concepts.

Kirkpatrick, Martha (1980). *Women's Sexual Development; Explorations of Inner Space*. New York: Plenum Press.

[See Chapter 4 for annotation.]

Person, Ethel (1980). Sexuality as the mainstay of identity: Psychoanalytic perspectives. *Signs*, 5:605-630. Also in: *Women: Sex and Sexuality*, ed. C. Stimpson and E. Person. Chicago, IL: University of Chicago Press, 1980, pp. 31-61.

This paper breaks new ground while reevaluating psychoanalytic paradigms and their implications for a theory of sexuality. Person challenges psychoanalytic and popular assumptions that sexuality is an innate force achieving ideal expression free of cultural inhibitions and that female sexuality is inhibited while male sexuality is the norm. She views sexuality as a motivational system derived from the psychological record of sensual experiences and integrated through a series of object relations. Sexuality maintains a unique position in psychic development through its crucial role in identity formation via the mediating structures of gender and the "sex print" (the individual's irreversible erotic script). Implications for differences in male and female sexuality are evaluated. Freud's libido (drive) theory is reviewed and contrasted with an appetitional (cultural conditioning) theory of sexual motivation.

Person then develops a third paradigm, an amalgam of Freud's clinical-psychological theory of sexuality and of object relations theory (i.e., a new theory of internalizations). Early object relations can shape the experience of desire, and sensuality then becomes a vehicle of object relations and can express a variety of motivations. Gender development orders sexuality. Female sexual inhibition, as understood within this paradigm, may reflect inhibitions of assertiveness and of sexual desire, relatively low sexual drive, and the muting effects of internalized object relations (such as the homosexual nature of the first erotic object, or oedipal girls' dependency on the rival maternal figure). Female sexuality is less compulsive or driven than is male because it is not used as extensively to confirm and consolidate gender. Nonsexual meanings of sexuality in power and dependency conflicts are traced to the history of object relations and the female monopoly of child care.

Roiphe, Herman and Galenson, Eleanor (1981). *Infantile Origins of Sexual Identity*. New York: International Universities Press.

In the 14 chapters of this book, most of which are revisions of previously published journal articles, the authors rework and further explicate their findings and conclusions about the development of sexual identity during the latter half of the first year and the second year of life, as based on observations made of children and their mothers in a research nursery setting. They describe a previously unidentified phase of instinctual development, which they term the "early genital phase," and delineate its differing evolution in boys and girls in interaction with concomitant object relations, self-object differentiation, oral and anal phase development, and aspects of ego development. Chapters are devoted to discussions of how such factors as object loss, congenital defect, and narcissistic or depressed mothering affect can distort the typical unfolding of the development of sexual identity during the first two years of life. These factors can lead to such phenomena as heightening of early castration reactions, more than usually profound effects on mood and ego organization, and disturbed sexual identity formation. The research methodology is described in detail. The concept of the "infantile fetish" is discussed. Extensive observations of children illustrate typical and atypical paths of sexual identity formation. [See also Chapter 6.]

Silverman, Martin (1981). Cognitive development and female psychology. *J. Amer. Psychoanal. Assn.*, 29:581-605.

Silverman proposes that core feminine gender identity, which may be irreversible by the middle of the second year, is mediated more by cognitive development and learning than by the observation of genital differences. Discovery of the differences between the sexes takes place at a time when cognitive immaturity makes it impossible for girls to appreciate their largely internal, nonvisualizable, nonpalpable, female sexual organs. Penis envy and narcissistic vulnerability are unavoidable though temporary. In optimal circumstances, they will be eliminated in the course of further development. A healthy self-image and self-esteem will take their place. Persistence of penis envy into adulthood is not a normal phenomenon. Data from child observation and clinical experience are included.

Bassin, Donna (1982). Woman's images of inner space: Data for expanded interpretative categories. *Int. Rev. Psycho-Anal.*, 9:191-204.

Bassin argues that positive categories for women's psychic experiences have not been sufficiently developed and elaborated within traditional psychoanalysis, nor within language and culture. Women's art, especially poetry, contains pervasive inner-space and central core imagery and metaphors. Bassin feels that these images illuminate the existence of a bodily schema for productive inner space that goes beyond maternal/reproductive functions. These symbolic images are hypothesized as connected with biological origins and early bodily experiences that serve as a base for construction of a category of experience or a mode of cognition, similar to phallic activity and its representations.

Formanek, Ruth (1982). On the origins of gender identity. In: *Early Female Development*, ed. D. Mendell. New York: S.P. Medical and Scientific Books, pp. 1-24.

Sex, gender, and core gender identity are defined, and the physical contributions to gender identity are reviewed. Formanek provides a critical review of studies of hormones and behavior and of psychoanalytic infant research. [See Chapter 6 for annotation.]

Glover, Laurice and Mendell, Dale (1982). A suggested developmental sequence for a preoedipal genital phase. In: *Early Female Development*, ed. D. Mendell. New York: S.P. Medical and Scientific Books, pp. 127-174.

On the basis of the analysis of dreams of six adult females, the authors propose a preoedipal developmental phase occurring between the anal and the oedipal periods in which the dominant zone is genital and the dominant task is the defining of self as female. [See Chapter 6 for annotation.]

Kestenberg, Judith (1982). The inner genital phase: Prephallic and preoedipal. In: *Early Female Development*, ed. D. Mendell. New York: S.P. Medical and Scientific Books, pp. 71-126.

Kestenberg postulates a period between anal and phallic phases called the early maternal or inner genital phase, in which there is a triangular-maternal attitude and projection of inner genital tensions onto representations of the baby. [See Chapter 6 for annotation.]

Kirkpatrick, Martha (ed.)(1982). *Women's Sexual Experience: Explorations of the Dark Continent*. New York and London: Plenum Press.

Contributors to this volume address diverse issues pertaining to female sexuality from a general psychological viewpoint. Topics include sexuality and ethnicity, sexuality and aging, incest, teenage pregnancy, pregnancy, childlessness, sterilization, extramarital sex, sexually transmitted diseases, sexuality at midlife, and the sexuality of Black and American Indian women. Each paper is followed by a brief discussion by another author. [See also Chapter 15.]

Laufer, M. Egle (1982). Female masturbation in adolescence and the development of the relationship to the body. *Int. J. Psycho-Anal.*, 63:295-302.

Laufer proposes that for both sexes the hand is unconsciously identified with the mother's active handling of the child's body. The child needs to masturbate to internalize a positive narcissistic cathexis of the body and to separate from the mother's body. When the girl recognizes that she cannot fulfill the wish to identify her body with her mother's by being able to produce a baby, the activity of her hand becomes the source of anxiety and is given up during latency. The girl finds masturbation an even greater threat at puberty, since it represents passivity and a homosexual object choice. This threat may explain intense struggles against masturbation in some adolescent girls, and the compelling need of other adolescents to attack the body actively with the hand. The choice of wrist or arm as an area for attack can be understood as part of the effort to control the hand by symbolically removing it from the body. The variety of other methods used by females in masturbation, such as "indirect" masturbation, and their meanings, are not discussed. Laufer and Laufer (1984) expand these ideas.

Menaker, Esther (1982). Female identity in psychosocial perspective. *Psychoanal. Rev.*, 69:75-83.

[See Chapter 20 for annotation.]

Meyer, Jon (1982). The theory of gender identity disorders. *J. Amer. Psychoanal. Assn.*, 30:381-413.

[See Chapter 19 for annotation.]

Oliner, Marion (1982). The anal phase. In: *Early Female Development: Current Psychoanalytic Views*, ed. D. Mendell. New York: S.P. Medical and Scientific Books, pp. 25-60.

[See Chapter 6 for annotation.]

Tyson, Phyllis (1982). A developmental line of gender identity, gender role, and choice of love object. *J. Amer. Psychoanal. Assn.*, 30:61-86.

Tyson views gender identity in a broad sense as composed of three interacting aspects: core gender identity, gender role identity, and sexual partner orientation. [See Chapter 6 for annotation.]

Dahl, Kirsten (1983). First class or nothing at all? Aspects of early feminine development. *The Psychoanalytic Study of the Child*, 38:405-428. New Haven, CT: Yale University Press.

[See Chapter 6 for annotation.]

De Cereijido, Fanny Blanck (1983). A study on feminine sexuality. *Int. J. Psycho-Anal.*, 64:93-104.

Material from the Kleinian analysis of a 40-year-old married professional woman is discussed to evaluate theoretical positions on feminine development with respect to two questions: when do girls consider themselves feminine, and if difficulties in sexual identification (homosexual trends) arise, do these reflect developmental arrests or a regression from the triadic situation? The author's clinical material supports the idea of early femininity and the pattern of regression from oedipal material in the presence of deficiencies in the primary (maternal) object relation as the basis for homosexual trends. Positive elements in the tie to fathers support feminine development. Clinical material from the analysis of a woman with somatic symptoms, frigidity, unconscious homosexuality, and narcissistic and melancholic trends illustrates these concepts.

Montgrain, Noel (1983). On the vicissitudes of female sexuality: The difficult path from "anatomical destiny" to psychic representation. *Int. J. Psycho-Anal.*, 64:169-186.

Montgrain considers the nature of female sexual experience and posits that female orgasmic pleasure is experienced as diffuse waves of pleasurable sensation spreading within the body and lacking precise limits. Similarly, females often perceive their genitals as lacking definition, causing women difficulty in creating a mental representation of their sexual pleasure and anatomy. These factors contribute to a view of sexual impulses as fearful and uncontrollable. The wish to have a penis can be understood as a wish for a discrete organ of pleasure that can be easily represented mentally, and whose threatened removal can help to limit the drives. Persistence of young girls' sexualized, fusional attachment to the preoedipal mother is seen as another factor interfering with the achievement of adult sexuality in women. The girl's relation to her mother, particularly the bodily contact with her, is perceived as the essential site of pleasure. Femininity is experienced in bodily events that stimulate archaic feelings and fears and inescapably underscore the identification with woman-as-mother. Clinical material is presented.

Person, Ethel and Ovesey, Lionel (1983). Psychoanalytic theories of gender identity. *J. Amer. Acad. Psychoanal.*, 11:203-226.

[See Chapter 6 for annotation.]

De Goldstein, Raquel Zak (1984). The dark continent and its enigmas. *Int. J. Psycho-Anal.*, 65:179-189.

The author attempts to revise Freud's (1933) views on female sexuality by means of a Lacanian approach. She asserts that both sexes suffer a "cut" from fusion with the mother, so that the first notion of identity in infants is that of the mirror image and the gaze from an "alien" mother. These experiences differ by sex, but each searches for something uncanny that has been lost from their earliest experiences. Boys separate very early from closeness with mother's body, whereas girls are held in that closeness. The experience of maternity may involve a belated realization that one is separate from mother. Masculinity and femininity develop differently on the basis of reactions to the discovery of the otherness of the primal love object. Girls remain within an affectionate attachment to their mother, which causes some primitivity and shapes the Oedipus complex and the acquisition of autonomy. Girls are absorbed by ambivalence conflicts and are preoccupied with their mother's body, integrity, and possessions. The author proposes a normal hypochondriacal phase based on the anticipation of the experiences of menarche, defloration, and maternity. Remnants of the early fusional state with the primal mother become normal fetishes in both sexes. In women, remnants of this state are transformed into exhibiting of femininity or becoming "the lure."

Fast, Irene (1984). *Gender Identity: A Differentiation Model.* Hillsdale, NJ: The Analytic Press.

Expanding on her previous work (1978, 1979), Fast proposes that the child's earliest gender experience is undifferentiated rather than male or female. [See Chapter 6 for annotation.]

Laufer, Moses and Laufer, M. Egle (1984). The female adolescent, the relationship to the body, and masturbation. In: *Adolescence and Developmental Breakdown*, ed. M. Laufer and M.E. Laufer, New Haven: Yale University Press, pp. 49-63.

[See Chapter 9 for annotation.]

Ritvo, Samuel (1984). The image and uses of the body in psychic conflict: With special reference to eating disorders in adolescence. *The Psychoanalytic Study of the Child*, 39:499-469. New Haven, CT: Yale University Press.

[See Chapters 9 and 23 for annotations.]

Gray, Sheila (1985). "China" as a symbol for vagina. *Psychoanal. Q.*, 54:620-623

In this brief article, a patient uses the highly condensed dream symbol of wedding china to represent her vagina. Her belief that she had a damaged genital was associated with marital sexual inhibition and a core neurotic conflict about the dangers of feminine creative and independent functioning.

Mayer, Elizabeth (1985). Everybody must be just like me: Observations on female castration anxiety. *Int. J. Psycho-Anal.*, 66:331-348.

Mayer presents toddler observations and clinical data from adult analyses to demonstrate a specific form of female castration anxiety that involves fantasies of loss of the female genitals or of the capacity to be genitally open. [See Chapter 6 for annotation.]

Person, Ethel (1985). Female sexual identity: The impact of the adolescent experience. In: *Sexuality: New Perspectives*, ed. Z. DeFries, R. Friedman, and R. Corn. Westport, CT: Greenwood Press, pp. 71-88.

[See Chapter 9 for annotation.]

Benjamin, Jessica (1986). A desire of one's own: Psychoanalytic feminism and intersubjective space. In: *Feminist Studies/ Critical Studies*, ed. T. De Lauretis. Bloomington: Indiana University Press, pp. 78-101.

This paper presents a thesis similar to that of "The Alienation of Desire," by Benjamin, 1986; [see chapter 21 for annotation], but formulated in the context of current feminist theory. After briefly discussing female masochism, Benjamin focuses on the problem of how women can become "subjects of desire" if they identify with a mother who only has object status in the gender system and if the phallus is privileged to represent all desire. Benjamin argues that women's experience of sexuality and of the relationship between self and other leads to a different representation of desire from that of men. This representation, which is oriented to the inter-subjective components of self and sexuality, is spatial rather than symbolic and thus is not related to a single anatomical organ.

Chehrazi, Shalah (1986). Female psychology: A review. *J. Amer. Psychoanal. Assn.*, 34:141-162.

Summarizing and integrating the contributions from preoedipal infant observation, Chehrazi details how current theories and their clinical applications differ from the early psychoanalytic views. [See Chapter 6 for annotation.]

Gillespie, William (1986). Woman and her discontents: A reassessment of Freud's views on female sexuality. In: *The British School of Psychoanalysis: The Independent Tradition*, ed. G. Kohon. New Haven, CT: Yale University Press, pp. 344-361.

[See Chapter 4 for annotation.]

McDougall, Joyce (1986). Eve's reflection: On the homosexual components of female sexuality. In: *Between Analyst and Patient: New Dimensions in Countertransference and Transference*, ed. H. Meyers. Hillsdale, NJ: The Analytic Press, pp. 213-228.

McDougall elaborates Freud's concept of the two tasks encountered by girls in the development of their femininity: coming to terms with their anatomy, including the changing from clitoral to vaginal cathexis, and changing their object from mother to father. Unconscious remnants of psychological bisexuality have an impact on adult love relationships. Infantile homosexual desires always have the double aim of possessing the same-sex parent and identifying with the opposite sex. These wishes are frequently associated with strong aggressive feelings. McDougall enumerates five areas in which feminine homosexual libido is invested and expressed in normal (heterosexual) adult life. In an interesting case vignette the author describes how her own countertransference blind spot, with respect to her homosexual desires for her mother, interfered with her ability to help her analysand deal with unacknowledged homosexual wishes for her mother. She does not differentiate homosexual libido from other aspects of the preoedipal attachment to mother. This readable paper contributes to the understanding of the homosexual aspect of female sexuality. [See also Chapter 25.]

Tyson, Phyllis (1986). Female psychological development. *The Annual of Psychoanalysis*, 14:357-373. New York: International Universities Press.

Tyson describes the establishment of primary femininity and female gender role, wishes to create and nurture babies, early steps in superego formation, and anal/rapprochement conflicts between wishes to be "at one with" an ideally viewed mother and, at the same time, be autonomous from her. [See Chapter 6 for annotation.]

Bernstein, Isidor (1988). A woman's fantasy of being unfinished: Its relation to Pygmalion, Pandora, and other myths. *Fantasy, Myth, and Reality: Essays in Honor of Jacob A. Arlow, M.D.*, ed. H. Blum, Y. Kramer, A. Richards, and A. Richards. Madison, CT: International Universities Press, pp. 217-232.

Analytic material illustrates how a woman patient developed a fantasy of herself as incomplete or unfinished. This fantasy was the outcome both of traumatic experiences and attempts to resolve intrapsychic conflicts. [See Chapter 22 for annotation.]

Chasseguet-Smirgel, Janine (1988). A woman's attempt at a perverse solution and its failure. *Int. J. Psycho-Anal.*, 69:149-161.

This article describes a woman patient who defensively sexualizes relationships. [See Chapter 19 for annotation.]

Dahl, Kirsten (1988). Fantasies of gender. *The Psychoanalytic Study of the Child*, 43:351-365. New Haven, CT: Yale University Press.

Gender is a complex psychological construction of the mind, drawing together during development some aspects of ego functioning, infantile sexual drives in the context of object relations, narcissism, and aggression. It centers on the body, interactions with the bodies of others, and the drives. The appearance of fixity obscures the fact that gender organization is not a dichotomous variable. Gender constancy develops over time, is potentially transmutable, and involves various subjective states, especially as revealed in fantasy configurations. It includes the possibility of retroactive transformations of previous meanings. Three clinical vignettes, including one about a female adolescent, illustrate the complexity of gender identity and of fantasies about gender. The author disagrees with Stoller's formulation that pathologies of gender result from failure to differentiate from a primary feminine matrix. Children construct their own gender choices from multiple paths of conflict resolution.

Pines, Dinora (1988a). A woman's unconscious use of her body: A psychoanalytic discussion. (Wozu Frauen ihren Korper unbewusst benutzen: Eine psychoanalytische Betrachtung.) *Zeitschr. f. psychoanal. Theorie und Praxis*, 3:94-112.

[See Chapter 6 for annotation.]

Stein, Yehoyakim (1988). Some reflections on the inner space and its contents. *The Psychoanalytic Study of the Child*, 43:291-304. New Haven, CT: Yale University Press.

Using data from the analysis of a young woman, Stein describes themes concerning the "dangerous" contents of her patient's body and the symbolism of a menstruation-pregnancy-abortion cycle that were central in her neurosis. As sadomasochistic fantasies were analyzed, the patient felt more comfortable with her femininity and had better relationships with men. Fantasies about her perception of her inner body were analyzed by using her body language and symbolism. Her skin represented the border between inside and outside; it protected against the outside world and contained and bound the inside. Males often repress their anxieties about the body interior, while females, through the events of menstruation, pregnancy, and parturition, are more likely to be conscious of inner body fantasies and anxieties.

Kirkpatrick, Martha (1989b). Women in love in the 80s. *J. Amer. Acad. Psychoanal.*, 17:535-542.

This essay asserts that attachment and bonding are seen as better models for the development of the capacity to love in women, than is the classical theory that love originates from sexual drive. Kirkpatrick argues that feminine gender identity arises from the special bonding with the mother, including social and sensual exchanges, rather than from innate vaginal sensations, discovery of inner generativity, or penis envy. Intimacy with other women remains essential support for and characteristic of femininity. Both core feminine identity and the capacity for love derive from the early intimacy with mother. Intimacy, rather than orgasm, restores feminine self-worth and validates individuality for women; sexual freedom has not provided as much gain as anticipated. Processes of erotization are not well understood. [See also Chapter 13.]

Mayson, Sterrett (1989). Reporter, Panel: Personal reflections on the role of sexuality in the etiology and treatment of the neuroses. *J. Amer. Psychoanal. Assn.*, 37:803-812.

Changes over the years in approaches to understanding the relation between sexuality and the neuroses are discussed, with personal anecdotes, by Sachs, Spruiell, Gardner, Rocah, and Boesky. Several panelists have become more aware of preoedipal issues over the years. Rocah discusses a female patient who turned from her mother because of disillusionment with the mother's actual limitations rather than because of maternal castration. Rocah feels that her patient's oedipal conflicts could not be resolved solely through interpretation, a view which Boesky criticizes.

**Person, Ethel, Terestman, Nettie, Myers, Wayne, and Goldberg, Eugene (1989). Gender differences in sexual behaviors and fantasies in a college population. *J. Sex and Marital Ther.*, 15:187-198.**

Responses to a written questionnaire by 193 university students allow comparison of sexual experiences and fantasies of males and females. The only behavioral difference was that females masturbated less and used less pornography. Females also fantasized about sex less frequently and had less interest in partner variation and dominance or submission. The majority of men and women did not report fantasies or behaviors supporting the stereotypes of male sexuality as aggressive or sadistic and female sexuality as passive or masochistic. One third of the males had the fantasy of "forcing sexual partner to submit" but this was not matched by any equivalent fantasy need for submission and masochism on the part of the women. Both sexes reported about the same level of masochistic fantasies. These findings challenge classical psychoanalytic theories.

**Tyson, Phyllis (1989). Infantile sexuality, gender identity, and obstacles to oedipal progression. *J. Amer. Psychoanal. Assn.*, 37:1051-1069.**

Infantile sexuality is considered as one of several variables in the broader perspective of gender identity. Rapprochement conflict and hostility toward mother interfere with oedipal progression. [See Chapter 6 for annotation.]

**Vogel, Sara (1989). Reporter, Panel: Current concepts of the development of sexuality. *J. Amer. Psychoanal. Assn.*, 37:787-802.**

This 1987 panel discusses the vicissitudes of sexuality in relation to developmental processes of early childhood, emphasizing normal development as well as deviations. Scharfman notes the contributions of Freud (1905) and of Mahler. Friedman stresses the importance of biological factors in male homosexuality and boyhood effeminacy as well as the role of boys' moving away from females and toward other males. Galenson discusses her studies of sexual and erotic development in the second year of life. She emphasizes the dynamic relationship between sexual development and the ambivalent object relations of this period. She notes girls' apparently greater vulnerability to the realization of anatomical differences and the vicissitudes of their increased anger toward and disappointment with the mother. The task of girls is to relinquish the libidinal tie to the mother without losing their sense of femininity.

Stoller emphasizes the atraumatic formation of some aspects of gender identity in all individuals, and the role of defenses against conflict in other aspects of gender identity formation. He views a disruption in mother-infant symbiosis as leading to risks of masculine development in girls, risks that are increased if fathers are intrusively present and encouraging their daughter to be like them.

Tyson discusses ways in which all evolving developmental currents converge around the oedipal conflict. Prolonged symbiosis may interfere with separation and oedipal progression but also fosters feminine core gender identity formation, which is facilitated by identification with the primary object. Excessive hostility toward mother may block oedipal progression and feminine identifications. Since girls' genitals are internal and give rise to internally experienced sensations, anxieties about genital damage are not as frequent in girls as in boys.

Ritvo, in his discussion, comments that girls do not relinquish the tie to mother but, rather, learn to deal with their aggression against the mother while retaining the tie. He notes the importance of the body ego. He agrees with Tyson's description of girls' narcissistic vulnerability to having their sense of femininity disrupted; aggression toward mother may compromise that object relation and imbue girls' sexuality with sadomasochistic features.

**Bernstein, Doris (1990). Female genital anxieties, conflicts, and typical mastery modes. *Int. J. Psycho-Anal.*, 71:151-165.**

How females experience their own bodies developmentally is seen as having a unique influence on psychic structure. Three anxieties—access, penetration, and diffusivity—represent dangers to body integrity comparable to but different from male castration anxiety. Different modes of mastery (and defense) arise from the feminine genital experience and shape character. Incomplete visual and tactile access to their own genitals can lead girls to rely on proprioception, symbolization, and utilization of other people to aid in defining genital experience. The object embeddedness seen in the feminine character may be a consequence. The spreading of genital sensations rather than the heightened focus that results from stimulation can lead to diffusion, including defensively diffuse thinking styles. Penetration anxiety may involve lack of control over access to the genital, fears of damage, struggles with boundaries and self-definition, and, in adolescence, further anxieties related to "wetness" and menstruation.

These issues of access, definition, and control are all central to achieving female individuation. The genital experience may be mastered effectively by defenses, including regression, identification, externalization, and penis envy. Turning to mother and to increased identification with her in order to master female genital anxieties may produce new conflicts. Recent developmental research is reevaluated using the framework of mastery of female genital anxieties rather than "castration" reactions. These issues are also illustrated with extensive material from the analyses of adult women.

Schmukler, Anita and Garcia, Emanuel (1990). Special symbols in early female oedipal development: Fantasies of folds and spaces, protuberances and cavities. *Int. J. Psycho-Anal.*, 71:297-307.

[See Chapter 6 for annotation.]

Tyson, Phyllis and Tyson, Robert (1990). Gender development: Girls. *Psychoanalytic Theories of Development: An Integration.* New Haven, CT: Yale University Press, pp. 258-276.

[See Chapter 6 for annotation.]

Kulish, Nancy (1991). The mental representation of the clitoris. *Psycho-anal. Inq.*

This paper explores the many possible mental representations of the clitoris. Kulish notes that although the clitoris has been a pivotal focus in early psychoanalytic theories of female sexuality, the specific nature of that clitoral sexuality has been unexplored. She explores the following questions: 1) What is the nature of clitoral sexuality? 2) What is the role of penis envy in terms of clitoral sensations and fantasies? 3) Is clitoral sexuality masculine? 4) Are there distinct types of orgastic experiences associated with clitoral and vaginal areas? Kulish argues that clitoral sensations can be associated with phallic or masculine fantasies, but also with distinctly female sensations and fantasies; the clitoris is an intrinsic part of normal feminine sexual functioning and development. In addition to developmental issues—the clitoris' lack of visibility and localization, there are also powerful psychological motivations to suppress and repress mental imagery of the clitoris. These motivations have more to do with guilt and fear of the nature of female sexuality (characterized by overwhelming genital excitement with the clitoris as a trigger), rather than with penis envy. Kulish explores the avoidance of discussion of the clitoris in scientific writings, myths, fairy tales, dreams, and neurotic symptoms related to clitoral sexuality and presents anthropological data about female circumcision and clitoridectomy. She argues that the experience of sexual excitement for females has a distinct character of spinning and is more circular than linear. Material from the analysis of a young woman revealed obsessions and compulsions that contained a representation of the clitoris as a switch to forbidden sexual impulses. Her clitoris was represented as a cut off penis, but also as a specifically feminine image of a button or secret key that could unlock female sexual knowledge, feelings, and excitement. A distinctively female sexual developmental line for female sexuality and orgastic response is depicted.

McDougall, Joyce (1991). Sexual identity, trauma and creativity. *Psych. Inq.*

[See Chapter 12 for annotation.]

Person, Ethel (1991). The "construction" of femininity: Its influence throughout the life cycle. In: *The Course of Life: Adolescence*, Vol. 4, ed. S. Greenspan and G. Pollock. Madison, CT: International Universities Press.

Person discusses the evolution of femininity throughout the life cycle by summarizing the development of gender identity and reviewing modern theories of sexual functioning and the role of clitoral eroticism. She proposes that gender is a central organizing schema in personality development, which in turn shapes sexual development. She asserts that a coherent theory of gender integrates object relations, the symbolic investment of the genitals, sexual differences, and input from cultural prescriptions. Gender becomes a scaffolding for self-identity that predisposes one to specific adaptive strategies. Differences and similarities between men and women with respect to sexual behavior, eroticism, and the primacy of sexuality (centrality to the personality) are examined. Gender identity (rather than biological sex) launches the individual into a particular pathway that is decisive for the shape of object relations, for the configuration and contents of fantasy life and eroticism, and for specific fears and longings. Questions about the rigidity of gender divisions are raised.

Renik, Owen (1991). A case of premenstrual distress: Bisexual determinants of woman's fantasy of damage to her genital. *J. Amer. Psychoanal. Assn.*

Case material is used to illustrate specific clinical applications of the concept of primary femininity. Some contemporary contributions to the psychoanalytic theory of female psychosexual development are presented as complementary with, rather than contradictory to, more familiar, long-standing formulations that emphasize phallic strivings in women. In the clinical example reported, a fantasy of genital damage underlay a female patient's premenstrual distress. Aspirations and concerns related to both aspects of her fundamental bisexuality participated in symptom formation and had to be investigated in order to achieve symptom relief. As the analytic work unfolded, the patient's awareness of her feminine aims served defensively to keep her masculine aims out of awareness, and vice versa.

# Chapter 19

# Gender Identity Disorders, Paraphilias, and the Ego-Dystonic Homosexualities in Women

Brenda Solomon, Eleanor Schuker,
Mary Ann Levy, and Diane Martinez
Additional contributions by Nadine Levinson

This chapter traces the evolution of psychoanalytic concepts regarding disorders of gender and sexual identity in women. It covers gender-identity disorders, paraphiliac disorders (perversions), and ego-dystonic homosexualities. Regrettably, knowledge about these disorders remains incomplete. Theoretical explanatory emphases have shifted from an early historical focus on oedipal dynamics and pathologies to the more recent interest in preoedipal, object-relational, and self-psychological issues. These theoretical shifts also reflect the modern conception of gender identity as separate and distinct from sexual identity and behavior.

Gender-identity disorders and paraphilias (the term paraphilia is now thought to be less pejorative than perversion) are usually described as occurring less frequently in women than in men because of differing vicissitudes in separation-individuation. Certain recent theorists argue that some of these disorders can be hidden behind a mask of conventional femininity. Recent hypotheses about etiologies for both gender-identity disorders and paraphilias in women stem from analysis of specific female developmental vicissitudes. Gender disorders may be related to difficulties in separation-individuation combined with familial confusion and distortion about gender issues. A poor early preoedipal maternal relationship, often with a depressed, absent, or intrusive mother, seems to be a significant etiological factor. Paraphilias have classically been viewed as related to oedipal castration anxiety, but recent writers have emphasized distortions of both gender and sexuality. Modern theorists have identified such etiological factors as distortions in ego development and the defenses, vicissitudes of aggression, separation-individuation difficulties, body-image instability, needs to maintain self-esteem and self-cohesion, and genital anxieties and gender-identity anxieties (for both sexes). How erotic feelings and the sense of one's femininity (or masculinity) come to serve defensive purposes remains an area of continued interest. Further study of this subject may shed new light on female gender disorders, paraphilias, and normal femininity.

Some writers have included the homosexualities among paraphilias, while others maintain that the homosexualities should be discussed separately because of multiple and differing etiologies for homosexual behavior. These multidetermined etiologies encompass not only preoedipal gender disorders and disorders involving defenses against oedipal conflict, but likely biological influences as well. In discussing the homosexualities here with other gender disorders, we are not implying that all cases of homosexuality necessarily indicate psychopathology. Indeed, prevailing psychiatric thinking, as exemplified in the current DSM-III, no longer regards homosexuality as a gender disorder or other pathological entity unless it becomes ego dystonic. The term ego dystonic, does not help discriminate issues such as repression or denial of unconscious feelings. Rather than categorize a group of individuals by a specific shared behavior or common fantasy, one must understand the evolution of each individual's sex print.

The literature on female homosexualities encompasses many etiological explanations, among them oedipal issues; castration anxiety; excessive aggression; triumph over traumatic experiences or gender prejudices; disturbances in gender identity, feminine identification, or separate identity; ego adaptations to disturbed preoedipal maternal object relations; an adaptive search for greater intimacy; and normal biological variance. The female homosexualities might be studied with more clarity if sexual orientation were defined precisely and broken down into its several components, including erotic fantasy, interpersonal experience, and sense of identity and social role. New ideas in the psychoanalytic literature about male homosexualities may also stimulate reexamination of theories about female homosexualities. In this chapter, articles that discuss gender disorders, paraphilias, and homosexualities in both men and women are included where relevant to understanding female pathologies. Psychoanalytic awareness of the salience of gender and sex in development and identity formation generally will facilitate and enhance research on the subjects discussed below. (E.S.)

Freud, Sigmund (1905a). Fragment of an analysis of a case of hysteria. *Standard Edition*, 7:3-122. London: Hogarth Press, 1953.

Freud discusses unconscious homosexual tendencies in this well-known case (Dora). [See Chapter 1 for annotation.]

Freud, Sigmund (1905b). Three essays on the theory of sexuality. *Standard Edition*, 7:125-243. London: Hogarth Press, 1953.

In Section I, The Sexual Aberrations, Freud discusses homosexuality as a reflection of bisexuality, and of constitutional and accidental factors. For both male and female homosexuals, sexual aim and sexual object have changed. The female homosexual usually exhibits masculine characteristics and makes a narcissistic object choice, reflected by her preference for femininity in the sexual object. The sexual aims in female homosexuals are diverse, with special predilection for the mucous membranes of the mouth. [See Chapter 1 for annotation.]

Freud, Sigmund (1915a). A case of paranoia running counter to the psychoanalytic theory of the disease. *Standard Edition*, 14:262-272. London: Hogarth Press, 1953.

Freud links a woman's paranoid delusions to an unconscious homosexual attachment. [See Chapter 1 for annotation.]

Freud, Sigmund (1920). The psychogenesis of a case of homosexuality in a woman. *Standard Edition*, 18:146-172. London: Hogarth Press, 1955.

Freud's major paper about female homosexuality describes an 18-year-old girl who falls in love with an older woman in order to defy her father, as well as to secure love from a mother substitute. The patient had a strong masculinity complex, as noted in her activity, competitiveness, penis envy, and rebellion against being a woman. She also had a strong infantile attachment to her mother and had been traumatized by the birth of another brother when she reached puberty. This revived oedipal trauma of not being able to have father's male child led to bitter rejection of her father and all men and an identification with them that was manifested in the development of a masculine attitude toward female objects. Her homosexual object choice was also an attempt to substitute a more tender, loving, female object for the disappointing mother. Thus, she avoided competition with her mother, while expressing open antagonism for her father for not giving her a baby. Freud formulates the patient's suicide attempt as a compromise formation that unconsciously symbolizes a phallic union with her father (by falling from the embankment), and a punishment for the wish. In his discussion of homosexuality, Freud differentiates between object choice, mental masculinity or femininity, and physical sexual characteristics. Although Freud states that the homosexuality was nonconflictual and the patient was not neurotic, this paper, predating his discovery (1931) of girls' intense preoedipal attachment to their mother, highlights the centrality of oedipal and preoedipal conflicts.

Abraham, Karl (1922). Manifestations of the female castration complex. *Int. J. Psycho-Anal.*, 3:1-29. Also in: *Selected Papers*. London: Hogarth Press, 1927, pp. 338-369.

In Part III, Abraham describes perverse resolutions, such as homosexuality, the fantasy of having a penis, and the conscious wish to castrate the man. [See Chapter 2 for annotation.]

Horney, Karen (1924). On the genesis of the castration complex in women. *Int. J. Psycho-Anal.*, 5:50-65. Also in: *Feminine Psychology*, ed. H. Kelman. New York: Norton, 1967, pp. 37-53.

"Secondary penis envy" is discussed as a symptomatic aspect on a continuum from normal development through the "castration complex" to homosexuality. [See Chapter 2 for annotation.]

Jones, Ernest (1927). The early development of female sexuality. *Int. J. Psycho-Anal.*, 8:459-472.

Analyses of five overtly homosexual women show that homosexuality is a defensive oedipal phenomenon secondary to an unusually strong infantile fixation to the mother from the oral (sadistic) phase. Aphanisis, the fear of total extinction of sexual capacity and enjoyment, is more threatening than castration for both sexes. In resolving oedipal conflict, both sexes are threatened with aphanisis and must renounce "either their sex or their incest." The homosexual solution occurs when union between penis and vagina is bound up with the dread of aphanisis and genital integrity is identified with possession of the organ of the opposite sex. Homosexual girls become pathologically dependent either on possession of the penis or on having unobstructed access to the man with whom they have identified themselves. Jones distinguishes two broad groups of female homosexuals. If oral eroticism is prominent, the inversion takes the form of dependence on another woman and a lack of interest in men; the subject is masculine but enjoys femininity through identification with a feminine woman whom she gratifies by a penis substitute, typically the tongue. If oral sadism is prominent, there are wishes to obtain from men the recognition of one's masculine attributes, resentment against men, and castrating (biting) fantasies. Homosexual women alternate between inverted gratification and aphanisis based on dread of the father. [See also Chapters 2 and 7.]

Riviere, Joan (1929). Womanliness as a masquerade. *Int. J. Psycho-Anal.*, 10:303-313. Also in: *Psychoanalysis and Female Sexuality*, ed. H. Ruitenbeek. New Haven, CT: College and University Press, 1966, pp. 209-220.

Oscillations between a masculine identification and a pseudo-feminine identification to protect against the emergence of a genuine feminine identity are stressed. [See Chapter 2 for annotation.]

Deutsch, Helene (1932). On female homosexuality. *Psychoanal. Q.*, 1:484-510.

This is an historic report of the analyses of 11 cases of female homosexuality. Each case had strikingly strong aggressive feelings toward the preoedipal mother, as well as intense reactions to the castration complex and the Oedipus complex. Sadistic impulses toward the mother in the phallic phase facilitated passive masochistic attitudes toward the father and a "thrust into passivity." Deutsch posits that female homosexuality involves more than reaction formations and a fixation on the mother with an unsuccessful change of object. Rather, in the phallic-oedipal phase there is a return to mother because of dangers in the new passive attitude toward father and guilt feelings toward mother. Concepts of penis envy, the wish for a baby, revenge directed toward the mother, bisexual oscillations in object choice, moral masochism, and regression are described. The phallic-masculine forms of homosexuality are seen as most common, although pregenital levels occasionally dominate. Girls' special difficulties in overcoming the Oedipus complex at puberty are illustrated. This paper is still relevant and clearly expresses Deutsch's pioneering work.

Klein, Melanie (1932a). An obsessional neurosis in a six-year-old girl. In: *The Psychoanalysis of Children*. New York: Norton, 1975, 35-57.

Klein presents the analysis of Erna, a precocious girl suffering from sleeplessness, depression, inability to learn, obsessional behavior, and open excessive masturbation. Dominated by vivid, anal-sadistic fantasies in which she was being cruelly persecuted by her mother, Erna defended against intense feelings of hatred for her mother. Her homosexual tendencies came to light after a period of obstinate and lengthy resistance. Persecution fantasies and homosexuality emerged, alternating with love for the mother, in a process understood as similar to projection. Klein believes that beneath the homosexuality was an intense hatred of mother derived from the child's early oedipal situation and her oral sadism. The analysis highlights some of Klein's theories that were viewed as controversial, including the preoedipal origin of sexual identity, early identification of both sexes with the mother, unconscious awareness of the vagina and vaginal sensations, and the preoedipal roots of the superego. Many of these observations have been confirmed by recent psychoanalytic research and are now accepted as accurate.

Freud, Sigmund (1940b). Splitting of the ego in the process of defense. *Standard Edition*, 23:273-278. London: Hogarth Press, 1953.

This classic paper describes splitting of the ego, or defensive disavowal of reality, as the central mechanism in formation of a fetish. A three-year-old boy, caught masturbating by his father and threatened with castration, developed a fetish. He was previously seduced into sexual activity by an older girl and observed that she had no penis. The castration threat revived the memory of the genital perception, which now is understood as a dreaded confirmation of castration. The boy created a fetish, which was a substitute for the penis he saw as missing in females, transferred the importance of the penis to the fetish, and continued to masturbate. The defensive disavowal of reality was demonstrated by his apparent indifference to the castration threat and by the emergence of new symptoms of fears of being eaten by his father and of having his little toes touched.

Reich, Annie (1940). A contribution to the psychoanalysis of extreme submissiveness in women. *Psychoanal. Q.*, 9:470-480. Also in: *Psychoanalytic Contributions*. New York: International Universities Press, 1973, pp. 85-120.

Primarily on the basis of psychoanalyses of two women, the author discusses the dynamics and etiology of extreme submissiveness in women, which she considers to be a perversion. [See Chapter 21 for annotation.]

Deutsch, Helene (1944d). Homosexuality. *The Psychology of Women*, Vol. 1. New York: Grune and Stratton, pp. 325-353.

Using some data from her previous papers on this topic, Deutsch delineates two types of homosexual women: those who have a feminine body constitution and those who have physical masculine traits. Usually, female homosexuality is psychologically determined, but in some cases activity and aggression may have subtle physiological components. Patterns of relationships, including triangles and the influence of sisters, universal bisexuality, events of puberty, transformations of hate for the mother, and sibling rivalry are discussed. In most cases, the urge for union with the mother is predominant, with infantile regressive elements or defenses against hate leading to the homosexual outcome. This tendency is strengthened by disappointment with the father during puberty.

Bergler, Edmund (1951). Neurotic counterfeit sex. In: *Impotence, Frigidity, "Mechanical" and Pseudosexuality, Homosexuality.* New York: Grune and Stratton. Also in: *Counterfeit-Sex, Homosexuality, Impotence, Frigidity,* (2nd, enlarged edition of *Neurotic Counterfeit-Sex*, 1951). New York: Grune and Stratton, 1958.

[See Chapter 18 for annotation.]

Blos, Peter (1957). Preoedipal factors in the etiology of female delinquency. *The Psychoanalytic Study of the Child,* 12:229-249. New York: International Universities Press.

Delinquency in girls is related to the perversions in that it is a form of sexual acting out and defends against the regressive pull to the preoedipal mother. [See Chapter 9 for annotation.]

Socarides, Charles (1962). Reporter, Panel: Theoretical and clinical aspects of overt female homosexuality. *J. Amer. Psychoanal. Assn.,* 10:579-592.

This rich extensive panel on overt female homosexuality includes Serota, Socarides, Weiss, Clyne, Davis, Kestenberg, Rogers, and Rappaport as participants. Serota reviews the issues to be discussed, which include object loss and dread of aphanisis (Jones, 1927), the frequent suicide attempts provoked by threat of female object loss, the mechanism of turning aggression against the self, the strong proclivity for regression towards the early maternal relationship, the relationship of bisexuality to female homosexuality, oedipal difficulties, the homosexual's "living by identification" (Serota), and finally, the dynamics of the gradual shift during therapy from the pregenital homosexual aim of binding aggression and libidinal drives to that of actual heterosexual object relations. Serota notes that the therapist should be a man, since the father is the person from whom the homosexual woman has regressed.

Socarides' paper discusses constitutional versus acquired factors, the concept of bisexuality, Freud's contributions, developmental factors, contributions from ego psychology, nosology and the relationship to other perversions and psychosis, and therapy. He correlates therapeutic success with bisexual organization. The low incidence of fetishism in women is ascribed to the female's ability to disguise a lack of orgastic response and thus escape narcissistic mortification.

Weiss's paper reiterates a strong belief in biological bisexuality. The more the ego fails to express the tendencies of the opposite sex, the more it feels anatomically mutilated. In normal development, females give up a masculine identification and are satisfied vicariously in relations with a man. Female homosexuals need to establish greater stability in the balance between masculine and feminine longings. Some feminine women whose vaginal erotism is blocked may need to counteract this obstruction by identifying themselves with a vaginally aroused woman; this is a type of female homosexuality that can occur around puberty and may be followed by the unblocking of feminine eroticism and of wishes for a relationship with a man. Homosexual women have either suffered a severe disturbance in their relationship to the father or have repressed frightening incestuous wishes.

Seeing female homosexuality as a result of failure to sexualize the vagina, Kestenberg characterizes homosexual women as "eternally virginal." Externalization operates in conjunction with the glorification of virginity and renunciation of motherhood. Case presentations include Rogers's case of homosexuality acted out behind a veneer of an apparently heterosexual life.

Socarides, Charles (1963). The historical development of theoretical and clinical concepts of overt female homosexuality. *J. Amer. Psychoanal. Assn.*, 11:386-414.

Socarides summarizes the existent significant work on homosexuality under several headings, including constitutional versus acquired factors, the concept of bisexuality, Freud's view of developmental factors, contributions from ego psychology, the relationship of female homosexuality to other perversions and psychoses, nosological considerations, and therapy. The work of Freud, Deutsch, Fenichel, Glover, Greenacre, Horney, Jones, Klein, and several others is considered.

Wilbur, Cornelia (1965). Clinical aspects of female homosexuality. In: *Sexual Inversion: The Multiple Roots of Homosexuality*, ed. J. Marmor. New York: Basic Books, pp. 268-301.

This chapter is primarily of historical interest. It reviews possible etiologies, family constellations, role behavior, relationships to peers, patterns of sexual object-choice, sexual behavior, and treatment. The controversial conclusions assert that treatment orientation should be toward heterosexuality.

Spiegel, Nancy (1967). An infantile fetish and its persistence into young womanhood: Maturational stages of a fetish. *The Psychoanalytic Study of the Child*, 22:402-425. New York: International Universities Press.

A shoestring was used as part of a masturbatory ritual by a 19-year-old woman analysand who presented with symptoms of excessive masturbation and feelings of emptiness. Although Spiegel refers to the object as a fetish, the shoestring was not always used to achieve orgasm and seemed to be used for defensive undoing of loss. The patient had manipulated this string since losses associated with a brother's birth when she was two-and-one-half years old. Various defensive uses of the string play throughout her development are traced. The patient had been subjected to early traumata, including repeated enemas from nine months to eight years, maternal deficits, and early exposure to an overstimulating grandfather.

Bak, Robert (1968). The phallic woman: The ubiquitous fantasy in perversions. *The Psychoanalytic Study of the Child*, 23:15-36. New York: International Universities Press.

Bak summarizes his earlier thoughts about the integration of castration anxiety, aggressive conflicts, and early identifications in the dynamics of perversions. He theorizes that in all perversions denial of castration is acted out through the regressive revival of the fantasy of the maternal or female phallus; fetishism is the basic perversion. This primal fantasy constitutes the psychological core of bisexual identification. Six case vignettes contain fetishism, self-flagellation, masochism, homosexuality, voyeurism, exhibitionism, transvestism, sadism, and transsexualism. One of the cases describes an obsessional, neurotic female who is preoccupied with transsexual wishes. Her progression from beating fantasies and homosexuality to this "near-delusional" idea of transsexualism is briefly described.

Greenacre, Phyllis (1968). Perversions: General considerations regarding their genetic and dynamic background. *The Psychoanalytic Study of the Child*, 23:47-62. New York: International Universities Press. Also in: *Emotional Growth*, Vol. 1. New York: International Universities Press, 1971, pp. 300-314.

Greenacre does not discuss female perversion per se, but her formulations about preoedipal factors in the perversions (including homosexuality), which focus on early disturbances of ego development, are of interest. She notes that a disturbed mother-infant relationship can lead to instability of genital body outline, prolongation of the introjective-projective stage in which there is incomplete separation of self and other, and persistence of primary identification. Penis envy and castration fears occurring well before the phallic phase may reflect problems of body narcissism, anal and aggressive conflicts, and disturbances in pregenital object relationships. Any obligatory need to believe in the phallic mother must be preceded by disturbances in separation-individuation. Actual traumas at ages two and four, such as witnessing or experiencing bleeding or injury, may play an important role in some cases of perversion. All perversions show an increase in sadomasochistic behavior and aggression. Weakness in body image, self-image, and especially genital self-image because of pregenital disturbances, become significant during the phallic and oedipal periods. Aggression is aroused by castration fears. Maturing sexual drives are then distorted in the interest of narcissistic needs to bolster the body image and to discharge aggression.

Sperling, Melitta (1968). Trichotillomania, trichophagy, and cyclic vomiting: A contribution to the psychopathology of female sexuality. *Int. J. Psycho-Anal.*, 49:682-690.

Sperling discusses hair-pulling and hair-swallowing as fetishistic acts. [See Chapter 23 for annotation.]

Morgenthaler, Fritz (1969). Introduction to panel on disturbances of male and female identity as met with in psychoanalytic practice. *Int. J. Psycho-Anal.*, 50:109-112.

Morgenthaler asserts that in homosexuals an unevenness of developmental progression between the developmental lines of ego and drive brings about disturbances of narcissism and of sexual identity. This unevenness occurs in the late preoedipal phase at the time of recognition of the anatomical differences. Sexual identity, self-representation, and gender role representations are distorted. In treatment, a narcissistic disturbance of sexual identity becomes apparent with transference regression. Common transference manifestations include attempts to compel the analyst to become intolerant of homosexual tendencies, the perception of the analyst as sexually undifferentiated, and the need to make the analyst into an idealized object in order to ward off castration anxiety and maintain a narcissistic equilibrium. Guidelines for clinical interventions are proposed. While focusing on male homosexuals, some treatment principles are applicable to females.

Bychowski, Gustav (1970). Reporter, Panel: On disturbances of male and female identity as met in psychoanalytic practice. *Int. J. Psycho-Anal.*, 51:251-254.

Panel presentations by Kestenberg, Moore, Barande, Herman, and Langer respond to a paper by Morgenthaler. [See annotation for Morgenthaler (1969) in this chapter.] Kestenberg discusses the development of early sexual identity. In order to establish an independent, sex-specific identity, the three-year-old must integrate pregenital and inner-genital drive components and isolated nuclei of identity into an organized unit. This integration forms the basis for the phallic body ego of the four to five year old. Clinical examples suggest that the arrested child who does not become heterosexual uses abnormal sexual practices to avoid disintegrative anxiety. Moore describes a pathological symbiosis between mother and child that interferes with the formation of a differentiated identity and sexual identity. Barande describes a woman with a sexual-identity disturbance and the clinical resolution of her archaic masculine identifications.

McDougall, Joyce (1970). Homosexuality in women. In: *Female Sexuality: New Psychoanalytic Views*, ed. J. Chasseguet-Smirgel. Ann Arbor: University of Michigan Press, pp. 171-212.

McDougall views female homosexuality as a compromise that maintains a precarious sense of identity in patients with preoedipal and gender identity disturbances and a specific oedipal constellation. The homosexual woman achieves detachment from an idealized, yet dangerous, all-forbidding, controlling maternal image by unconsciously identifying with the paternal object, who is decathected libidinally but possessed symbolically via regression to an anal-sadistic identification. This identification with a fecal phallus is a bulwark against psychotic dissolution. Idealized aspects of the mother are sought in the female partner, who is also seen as providing freedom from the real mother and triumph over her. The regression from oedipal triangulation to dyadic relationships is accompanied by the incorporation of the symbolic anal-phallus. Patients have a disturbed body image, confused sexual identity, splitting of parental imagos, and part-object relationships.

McDougall discusses the analytic treatment of four homosexual women and highlights developmental and clinical issues. The homosexual solution contains new dangers since the new partner becomes reduced to a part-object, as the homosexual woman was in her infantile relation to her mother. McDougall believes the homosexual's character structure is not neurotic or psychotic, but rather "perverse," in the sense of the homosexual's continual acting out of an internal drama in an attempt to maintain ego identity. Severe depressive or paranoid psychotic episodes are likely when defenses fail.

Zavitzianos, George (1971). Fetishism and exhibitionism in the female and their relationship to psychopathy and kleptomania. *Int. J. Psycho-Anal.*, 52:297-305.

This article reviews the literature on perversion, fetishism, and exhibitionism and discusses the analytic treatment of a 20-year-old psychopathic female fetishist. The symptom of kleptomania emerged as the fetish became detached from its sexual function. Zavitzianos concludes that exhibitionism, kleptomania, and psychopathy can derive from fetishism. In addition to contributing to the scant literature on female fetishism, the article explores the relevance of disturbances in the early mother-child relationship, in contrast to the classical view of fetishism as a defense against castration anxiety.

Stoller, Robert (1973b). *Splitting*. New York: Dell/Quadrangle Books.

This book contains detailed transcripts of the treatment process, the history, and a discussion of a disturbed masculine woman who had a fantasy of a penis inside her pelvis. Multiple personalities, homosexual and masochistic behavior, violations of the law including murder and armed robbery, suicide attempts, and a severely deprived childhood are part of the clinical picture. [The case was summarized by Stoller, 1975a, in this chapter.]

Green, Richard (1974). *Sexual Identity Conflict in Children and Adults*. New York: Basic Books.

Green provides a cross-cultural, historical, nonpsychoanalytic psychological view of deviations from masculinity and femininity. Scientific work on sex and gender and theories about the origin of sexual deviations are reviewed. Green's data bases for the study of the forces shaping sexual identity and gender role include interviews and psychological testing of individuals and their families whose development has been atypical and a longitudinal study of children who showed early deviations. Adult female transsexuals are found to demonstrate pervasive childhood gender-role disturbances, including fantasies of wanting to be a boy, tomboy behaviors, dislike for girls' toys, preference for boys' clothes, wishes for boy playmates, feelings of being male, and wishes to love another female as a male. The following histories are common: a masculine name for the female child; a stable, warm father; an unpleasant relationship with the mother; and repetitive rough and tumble play. Female transsexuals have a masculine gender-role identity, do not consider themselves homosexual, and seek surgery as a solution to their conflicts. Girlfriends and wives of adult female-to-male transsexuals are described as heterosexuals who have become orgasmic for the first time with the transsexual woman partner and are not "homosexual" but desire a relationship with a "man" who lacks a penis. Postsurgical adjustment is good. Green's work is descriptively useful.

Ostow, Mortimer (1974). *Sexual Deviation: Psychoanalytic Insights.* New York: Quadrangle/New York Times Book Co.

This book summarizes the clinical efforts of a collaborative research group. None of the most detailed case studies are of women, and no women analysts collaborated. Women are viewed as less in need of the compromise formation represented by a perversion because our culture conspires to permit greater erotization and pregenital gratification with their bodies and the physical requirements of intercourse do not cause "failure" if there is not a threshold level of excitement. Pregenital needs may also be gratified in play with children. The suggestion is made that sociocultural changes may ultimately produce an increase in the incidence of overt sexual perversion in women when behavioral expectations change.

Stoller, Robert (1974). Facts and fancies: An examination of Freud's concept of bisexuality. In: *Women and Analysis*, ed. J. Strouse. New York: Viking Press, pp. 343-364.

Stoller feels that Freud's concept of "bisexuality" was overinclusive and was used inaccurately to explain homosexuality and other distortions of gender development. Stoller conceptually differentiates biological from psychological etiologies. The homosexuality or bisexuality that Freud claimed was biological is more precisely a nonbiological threat to core gender identity, to which males are more vulnerable. Men's fear of homosexuality is actually a fear of the loss of gender identity. Psychological forces are seen as crucial in forming human gender behavior, regardless of whether or not biological bisexuality (intersexuality) exists. For example, transsexuals have normal biology but a primary feminine-core gender identity, which Stoller ascribes to a prolongation of a blissful symbiotic merger with the mother. Freud's Schreber case is discussed. Femininity is seen as having a more stable base than masculinity in primary identification with the mother, so that fears of homosexual accusations are less frequent in psychotic and nonpsychotic women than in men. Homosexual experimentation is less guilt inducing and impeding of emotional growth in women than in men, and for the girl merging with mother is seen as strengthening her sense of femaleness. Stoller does not discuss the dynamics of female gender disorders directly.

Stoller, Robert (1975a). *Perversion: The Erotic Form of Hatred.* New York: Pantheon Books.

Perversion consists of a fantasy that is usually acted out and becomes habitual and obligatory for sexual satisfaction. The perversion is motivated by hostility and is used to preserve gender identity in the face of a threat to gender. The fantasy takes the form of revenge hidden in the actions that make up the perversion and serves to convert childhood trauma to adult triumph. Stoller postulates an etiological childhood trauma that was severe and threatening to the child's sexuality or to parts of the body capable of erotic and sexual pleasure. Perversion is seen more frequently in men than in women because it may serve as a defense against early primary identification with the mother (merger threat). In women, the tendency to merge is less threatening to gender identity and may sustain femininity. However, failure to separate predisposes the person to a perversion later in life.

In Chapter 9, "A Crime As A Sexual Act," Stoller describes the therapy of a disturbed woman who commits a crime as part of a complicated sexual ritual. Her criminal act is perverse; the behavior is repetitive, gratifying, and based on hostility. The patient uses the defense of transforming passive to active by being the victor rather than the victim. The perverted act is primarily hostile rather than erotic. This woman searches for her identity and is convinced that she possesses a penis inside her pelvis. Having felt unwanted and "frozen out" by her mother, she became "male" by age four to prevent feelings of abandonment and humiliation. Compulsive stealing was a revenge against an ungiving mother but required punishment, and the woman arranged to be raped. Treatment enabled her to give up her wish to have or be a penis and to relinquish the craving to steal.

Stoller, Robert (1975b). *Sex and Gender: The Transsexual Experiment,* Vol. 2. London: Hogarth Press, 1976, and New York: Aronson.

Stoller presents clinical data on the syndrome of transsexualism. He asserts that male transsexualism is created by an excessively prolonged blissful symbiosis with the mother, wherein the son serves as the mother's feminized phallus. The mother's history includes dissatisfaction with femininity and longings for a penis, and the father fails to serve as a strong masculine model or to interrupt the mother-son symbiosis. One chapter devoted to female transsexualism describes this syndrome as different clinically and dynamically from that of the male. Histories are of a noncuddly infant; a removed, depressed mother; and a daughter who is influenced by both parents to be the mother's caretaker or a substitute husband to assuage the mother's depression. The daughter develops a masculine identity by both encouragement and identification with the father. Several cases are described to differentiate between masculine female transsexuals and female homosexuals. Stoller also reports on two female identical twins, one of whom became feminine and the other transsexual. Stoller states that normal mother-infant symbiosis creates and augments femininity and that femininity has a more solid base in primary identification than does masculinity. He concludes, therefore, that homosexuality is less threatening for women.

Zavitzianos, George (1977). The object in fetishism, homeovestism and transvestism. *Int. J. Psycho-Anal.*, 58:487-496.

Homeovestism is a perverse behavior that involves erotic wearing or masquerading in the clothes of the parent of the same sex with whom the patient wishes to identify; it is regarded as closer to transvestism than to fetishism. The case of a 20-year-old woman who felt like an imposter is described. At age three she closely identified with the body image of her pregnant mother. With the birth of a brother, she developed castration anxiety at the sight of his penis, at noticing her mother's "distressing change" in body shape, and at observing her mother's menstruation. The patient's dreams, fantasies, and acting out via compulsive erotic dressing in her mother's clothes and stealing female clothes are attempts to feel phallic and pregnant and to reestablish the mother-child unity and a maternal identification. The homeovestite, dressing up as mother, stabilized a precarious body image and relieved castration anxiety, separation anxiety, and disintegration anxiety. In women, homeovestism can also be a form of imposture that creates the illusion of possessing a maternal phallus and avoids masturbation.

DeFries, Zira (1978). Political lesbianism and sexual politics. *J. Amer. Acad. Psychoanal.*, 6:71-78.

Nine college students in a cultural atmosphere in which feminist ideology was often used for consolidation of sexual identity and preference are studied. The students sought therapy because of confusion and anxiety occasioned by alternating homo- and heterosexual acting out. Of the nine students, two retained a lesbian identity; one, a bisexual identity; and six, a heterosexual identity after one to five years of psychotherapy. An evolution from political lesbian feminist to nonlesbian feminist or to lesbian with secondary feminist politics followed a sequence in which sexual roles, power, competition, and dependency issues became comprehended as more complex and integral to hetero- or homosexual relationships.

### Socarides, Charles (1978). *Homosexuality*. New York: Aronson.

This comprehensive book discussing intrapsychic determinants of homosexuality in men and women uses data from psychoanalysis and psychoanalytic psychotherapy with over 100 homosexual patients. Socarides asserts that the widespread incidence of homosexuality results from unsuccessful resolution of the separation-individuation phase of early childhood. This phase is decisive for gender identification. Although most of his patients are men, Socarides proposes many interesting concepts pertaining to homosexual women. In Chapter 7, "Basic Concepts: Female Homosexuality," he discusses his ideas about the development of female homosexuality. He views homosexual women as having preoedipal distortions, which lead to regression from oedipal conflict. Rejection by a woman partner may impel the patient into treatment, although there may be little conscious guilt and no wish to change her homosexuality. Homosexual women are in flight from men because of childhood feelings of rage, hate, and guilt toward mother. Preoedipal fears of being poisoned and devoured by the mother have made them unable to handle any real or imagined positive oedipal disappointments or rejections from the father. A state of constant, impending narcissistic injury and mortification results in a turning back to the mother (the new homosexual partner) while also remaining fearful of merger, in an attempt to gain love and alleviate murderous aggression. Socarides' female homosexual analysands have frequent masochistic fantasies that heterosexual intercourse would repeat an injury already experienced from the mother or that disembowelment or impotence could result from homosexual intercourse. Homosexual women, renouncing their femininity, usually identify with the father. Finally, Socarides proposes nine homosexual subgroups that are based on different ego structures, libidinal development, and object relations.

### DeFries, Zira (1979). A comparison of political and apolitical lesbians. *J. Amer. Acad. Psychoanal.*, 7:57-66.

The author compares apolitical lesbian college students with lesbians whose sexual preference was entwined with feminist politics and social activism in the early 1970s. Political lesbians had more conflict about lesbian activities, were preoccupied with the problem of sexual identity, were initially ambivalent about therapy, were more often virulently hostile to men, and were psychologically introspective. Nonpolitical lesbians were not concerned either with sexual preference or with sex role stereotyping and feminist issues, were more inhibited in discussing sexual matters, appeared more fragile, and reported more social isolation and distance from their family. Tomboy behavior and early crushes were not differentiating factors. The author asserts that nonpolitical lesbians may have shortcircuited curiosity about sexual identity by early acceptance of lesbianism, whereas political lesbians use ideology and group experience as part of a process of identity consolidation in late adolescence, which enlarges affective and cognitive horizons and affords additional behavioral options.

Khan, Masud (1979). *Alienation in Perversions*. London: Hogarth Press.

In the chapter "The Role of Infantile Sexuality and Early Object," Masud offers clinical material from the analysis of a young female patient who had an intense and overt homosexual attachment during her analysis. Khan sees homosexuality as an attempt to repeat and elaborate conflicts from an archaic and collusive relation to the mother, which had been required because of the mother's depressive pathology. The patient's infantile sexuality and transference repetition of a disturbed symbiotic mother-child relationship are described. Castration anxiety, penis-awe, body-ego distortions, and modifications of the Oedipus complex contribute to the dynamics. There is a distortion of superego (ego-ideal) development through a regressive idealization of early body-care experiences with the mother. The role of acting out in the treatment of homosexuality and problems in the transference are discussed. Pregenital fantasizing and pseudo-hostility are used to defend against passivity, surrender, and dependency in the early phases of transference repetition. This is a rich, dense chapter with interesting clinical material.

Kirkpatrick, Martha and Morgan, Carole (1980). Psychodynamic psychotherapy of female homosexuality. In: *Homosexual Behavior*, ed. J. Marmor. New York: Basic Books, pp. 357-375.

After reviewing the psychoanalytic literature on etiology and treatment of homosexual women, the authors conclude that very little has been reported about the actual treatment of lesbian women, despite the relatively high frequency of homosexual behavior. They feel that homosexual behavior may have many different meanings, including a developmental phase related to the consolidation of feminine identity, a reactive means of restoring self-esteem in response to a disappointment, a regression from oedipal competitive anxieties, and a preoedipal gender disorder with a specific narcissistic defect. The authors assert that women with little psychopathology may experience homosexual relationships. Those patients who have a preoedipal gender disorder experience longings for intimate physical contact with a female. These longings produce sexual arousal accompanied by 1) underlying confusion about gender identity, 2) a limitation in the ability to value and enjoy feminine proclivities, and 3) an inhibition in experiencing sexual intimacy (rather than inhibited sexual arousal) with a man. The authors highlight the homosexual transference as it appears with therapists of either gender and emphasize that it must be identified correctly as an aspect of the sexualization or sexual experiencing of maternal interactions rather than as oedipally based.

McDougall, Joyce (1980). *Plea for A Measure of Abnormality*. New York: International Universities Press.

This book continues McDougall's (1970) work and is a valuable contribution to the understanding of perversions and homosexuality. Perversion is seen as a product of the child's infantile fantasies, but based on a core infantile trauma in relation to the mother. Sexual overstimulation and parental pathology create an illusion in the child that the child's pregenital sexuality is adequate to satisfy the mother. The child replaces the father's phallic function (primal scene fantasy), thus bolstering the denial of sexual realities. Individuation is impaired, and the child uses action tendencies to resolve conflicts that cannot be resolved in fantasy. A phallic object or "barrier" is required to differentiate mother from self and to prevent psychotic decompensation.

In the chapter "The Homosexual Dilemma: A Study of Female Homosexuality," female homosexuality is viewed as an attempt to resolve conflict between the two poles of psychic identity, an identity as a separate individual and a sexual identity. Homosexual women's profound castration anxiety is not limited to phallic anxiety about sexual differences but serves to defend against overwhelming anxiety concerning separateness and fear of disintegration, as the mother was experienced as rejecting of the daughter's body, sexuality, and separate existence. Female homosexuals' identification with their father prevents further ego disintegration, although it also has crippling consequences for the ego. The mother image is idealized in order to repress hostile, destructive primal scene fantasies. Analytic cases illustrate homosexual women's oedipal structure, the erotization of defenses against anxiety, and ego defenses, especially splitting mechanisms and the pathological introjection of the father figure. If depressive anxiety predominates, the homosexual aim of repairing the partnership is uppermost. Those patients in whom persecutory anxiety predominates have an overwhelming need to dominate the object erotically.

McDougall discusses penis envy and wishes for the phallus in homosexual women that keep feminine sexual desires dormant, as well as accomplish other defensive purposes. The chapter also discusses contributions of others and reflects on limitations in the treatment of homosexual women.

Ponse, Barbara (1980a). Finding self in the lesbian community. In: *Women's Sexual Development: Explorations of Inner Space*, ed. M. Kirkpatrick. New York, Plenum Press, pp.181-200.

Distinguishing between homosexual activity and sexual identity, Ponse uses the term "women-related women" to encompass those who have had or anticipate sexual and emotional relationships with women, so as to include a multiplicity of identifications including lesbian, bisexual, heterosexual, and celibate. Contact with the lesbian community may occur prior to a lesbian resolution of identity. Couple relationships in a variety of contexts are described. Biographies of primary lesbians are distinguished from those of "elective" lesbians, who usually come to identify themselves as lesbian later in life.

Ponse, Barbara (1980b). Lesbians and their worlds. In: *Homosexual Behavior*, ed. J. Marmor. New York: Basic Books, pp. 157-175.

Ponse describes her analysis based on interviews with 75 "women-related" women, of the secretive and activist lesbian worlds. She depicts aspects of the lesbian world, including "gay referencing" (labeling of places and persons as gay), rules of access into this world, strategies of passing, counterfeit secrecy (mutual pretense with one's family not to acknowledge the gay self), restriction, and the "aristocratization" of lesbianism. In discussing the activist lesbian world, she describes political challenges to the existing heterosexual order and how lesbian life styles and culture are supported and maintained. During a "coming out" process, the lesbian begins to disclose the gay self before an expanding series of audiences, beginning with the personal or true self. Ponse concludes that the lesbian world provides both support and pressures for conformity.

Stolorow, Robert and Frank Lachmann (1980). *Psychoanalysis of Development Arrests: Theory and Treatment.* New York: International Universities Press.

In the chapter "Sexual Fantasy and Perverse Activity," the authors review the literature and assert that normal psychosexual experiences, fantasies, and acts serve as psychic organizers and as indications of consolidation of self- and object representations. [See Chapter 22 for annotation.]

Roiphe, Herman and Galenson, Eleanor (1981). *Infantile Origins of Sexual Identity*. New York: International Universities Press.

Disturbances in sexual identity and the infantile fetish are discussed. [See Chapter 18 for annotation.]

Eisenbud, Ruth-Jean (1982). Early and later determinants of lesbian choice. *Psychoanal. Rev.*, 69:85-109.

The author postulates that primary lesbian erotic love originates in a precocious initiation of erotic desire mandated by an ego that is responding to a lack of 'good enough' or 'long enough' primary bliss and seeks closeness and inclusion by a sexual bond, sexual wooing, and arousal. The girl is excluded from identification with the mother, who demands that the child serve her in a masculine fashion as a boy, further contributing to confusion about gender. Thus, erotism is the child's defense against merging and engulfment. Eisenbud describes technical problems wherein the patient denies infantile sexuality and defends against using Freudian theory on political grounds. She also describes the analyst's countertransference feelings, which may be useful in highlighting the patient's attempts to form a primary sexual bond. Eisenbud suggests that therapists must recognize that the patient's erotic struggle is for the primary purpose of avoiding a new exclusion or narcissistic insult within the treatment.

Meyer, Jon (1982). The theory of gender identity disorders. *J. Amer. Psychoanal. Assn.*, 30:381-418.

This article is an outgrowth of ten years of clinical experience with male and female patients with severe gender disturbances. Reviewing several hypotheses, Meyer explains transsexualism and other gender disorders on the basis of preoedipal conflict. The quest for sex reassignment is a defensive symptom. It expresses a compromise, reflecting developmental trauma caused by peculiar symbiotic and separation-individuation-phase relationships. The child is used in fantasy by the mother to deny sexual differences and to repair her body image. Perverse patients express similar fantasies on a symbolic or ritual level rather than concretely. Gender identity is a tertiary phenomenon of the developing personality; it begins with the archaic body ego, continues with early structuring of the body image and primitive selfness, and then extends and integrates these into the sexual and reproductive spheres. In pathological gender development, the integration of bodily attributes into the ego is affected, body image is disturbed, the distinction between self and others is blurred, reproductive potential is denied, and there is overall severe ego impairment.

Waites, Elizabeth (1982). Fixing women: Devaluation, idealization, and the female fetish. *J. Amer. Psychoanal. Assn.*, 30:435-439.

This article explores a prevalent ideal of femininity—that of the aesthetically flawless but behaviorally nonaggressive woman—and the perverse defensive structure with which this ideal can be associated. The author presents male and female cases to demonstrate how narcissistic people with repressed conflicts involving perceptions of the female can use the ideal feminine representation defensively. The possible relationship of this structure to a transitional object and to a fetish is discussed.

The female case was a young homosexual model who sought treatment to separate from her parents. She eventually stabilized her intermittent psychosis through the elaboration of defensive patterns with fetishistic features and later through exhibitionism. While outwardly feminine by virtue of meticulous dressing and body adornment, she viewed her outward presentation as false and felt enraged toward men who were attracted to her. Her fetishistic self-representation of femininity, accomplished by dressing and adornment, defended against a self-representation of being damaged. Her fantasy life, masturbatory practices, and homosexual relations involved attempts to gain contact with her own femaleness and to obtain the narcissistic supplies she needed because of a severe disturbance in her maternal relationship. A frightening, controlling father also made heterosexuality dangerous. The childhood masturbatory fetish—her mother's menstrual pad—reminded her of the pleasurable body fusion she still sought with female lovers. An image of a passively seductive female was an outgrowth of a series of psychological developments, reflecting early idealization and devaluation of the mother as a mirror of the child's narcissism and later issues in differentiation of gender, self, and (devalued) nonself. This image enabled an illusion of separation while maintaining compulsive control over the needed object.

Zavitzianos, George (1982). The perversion of fetishism in women. *Psychoanal. Q.*, 51:405-425.

The question of whether fetishism as defined by Freud in males can exist in females is discussed. Clinical material supports the author's assertion that female fetishism does exist and serves as a defense against castration anxiety arising from the perception of the female genital. He suggests that in females the fetish represents the penis of the father, rather than that of the mother. The discussion includes thoughts on the relationship between female fetishism, kleptomania, and sexual promiscuity in women.

Lothstein, Leslie (1983). *Female-to-Male Transsexualism: Historical, Clinical, and Theoretical Issues.* Boston: Routledge and Kegan Paul.

This is the first book to examine the phenomenon of female-to-male transsexualism as a distinct clinical entity. In Chapter 6, "Psychological Issues and Theories," Lothstein states that the major organizing principle of female transsexualism is the girl's preoedipal relationship with her mother, as well as the effect of joint parental and familial borderline dynamics influencing the structuring of the self. The parents communicate and transmit distorted gender meanings to their daughters. Consequently, by the second half of the second year of life, these girls are unable to establish a core female gender identity and a nuclear self system. Self psychology is used to offer new constructs for understanding transsexuals' self-deficiencies. These girls have defective ego mechanisms regulating their gender-self constancy. They manifest a borderline personality organization, employing rigid and pathological defenses. They constantly experience a sense of dread that they will go "crazy," and they resort to cross-gender behavior and unconscious fantasies. The transsexual woman's wish for gender reassignment is viewed as a reparative attempt to restore cohesion. The girl's overidealization of her father distorts the daughter's sense of reality because the father reinforces his daughter's hatred of her female body. Primary gender pathology is differentiated from pathology related to diagnoses of psychosis or schizophrenia. Lothstein concludes that long-term psychotherapy, not sexual reassignment surgery, is the treatment of choice.

Person, Ethel and Ovesey, Lionel (1983). Psychoanalytic theories of gender identity. *J. Amer. Acad. Psychoanal.*, 11:203-226.

Femininity and masculinity are viewed as parallel constructs in development. Attempts to master separation anxiety by use of merger fantasies are seen as having differing consequences for gender identity development in boys and in girls. In both sexes, perpetuation of merger fantasies disrupts the sense of self, object relations, and certain ego functions. In boys, merger fantasies may also be accompanied by gender pathology. Where the merger fantasy persists or is reinvoked after imitative motor behavior and cognitive awareness have emerged, ambiguous core gender and cross-gender behavior and cross-gender identification may appear in males with resultant cross-gender disorders and increased castration anxiety. Merger fantasies in females do not carry gender connotations. Female gender disorders are not specifically discussed, though the preponderance of gender disorders in males is explained by the gender marker that accompanies some merger fantasies. [See also Chapter 6.]

Hopkins, Juliet (1984). The probable role of trauma in a case of foot and shoe fetishism: Aspects of the psychotherapy of a 6-year-old girl. *Int. Rev. Psycho-Anal.*, 11:79-91.

A six-year-old psychotic girl who believed she was a boy showed erotic excitement about feet and shoes as well as fetishistic masturbation. Treatment uncovered traumatic, life-threatening assaults, primal scene exposure, and probable incestuous seduction and sexual assaults by the father. Interest in feet and shoes began at seven months while the child was playing with her father. The mother, who as a child had been abused by a stepfather with a shoe fetish, was also physically abusive and unprotective. Hopkins suggests that the psychotic illness and masculine identity in this girl served defensive purposes, including identification with the aggressor. This symbolic recreation of traumatic sexual acts in the foot fetishism and masturbatory fetishism was accompanied by disavowal of sexual differences and a fantasy of possessing a penis in order to protect herself from violation. When the patient relinquished the fetish, aggression in her object relationships escalated. The illusory phallus and castration anxiety in female fetishism may be secondary to the terror of violation.

Coen, Stanley (1985). Perversion as a solution to intrapsychic conflict. *J. Amer. Psychoanal. Assn.* (Suppl.), 33:17-57.

This comprehensive article reviews and critiques the central ideas of four books on the perversions: Joyce McDougall's *Plea for a Measure of Abnormality*, Mortimer Ostow's *Sexual Deviation: Psychoanalytic Insights*, and Robert Stoller's *Perversion: The Erotic Form of Hatred* and *Sexual Excitement: Dynamics of Erotic Life*. Each of these books emphasizes that perversions can be understood and treated psychoanalytically. Coen reviews historical hypotheses about the perversions, including infantile trauma versus defensive functions, defenses against oedipal castration anxiety, defenses against hostile aggression, and superego functioning and weakness in the perversions. The newer contributions include McDougall's ideas of a core infantile preoedipal seduction, requiring development of a phallic barrier to validate the distinction between mother and oneself, injured narcissism in the primal scene, and higher level conflicts screened under seemingly more primitive fixations. Stoller emphasizes hostile aggression or mastery of an actual infantile trauma directed to one's gender identity, and sexual excitement as a defense against anxiety. Coen also reviews and summarizes many other earlier contributions. He highlights Khan's work (1979), which describes organized defenses against maternal depression via libidinizing of the body and genitals and maintenance of a separate secret self, the latter validated in masturbatory ritual. The Ostow book discusses behavioral enactment of masturbatory fantasies, use of erotization as a defense because of seduction experiences and as a form of identification with the aggressor, and the role of magical events as repair in action.

Coen proposes three factors in the development of perversions: 1) intense early sensual feelings, contributed to by the mother's seductive over-stimulation of the child, 2) the promotion of sexualized defense in the mother-child relationship, and 3) the usefulness of sexualized defense for mastering large quantities of hostile aggression. To compensate for maternal emotional unavailability and relative neglect of the child's emotional needs, the child turns to sexual stimulation as a mode of relating to the mother. When the mother's own predominant mode of defense has been sexual, identification with the mother combines with the child's need for defense. Efforts to master sexual overstimulation by active repetition recreate a mode in which other multiple defensive functions can be simultaneously served. Coen describes the role of masturbation and masturbation fantasy in the future pervert's childhood in providing the child with the sense of magical control and omnipotence over the genitals and the world. Later, omnipotence and control are demonstrated in perverse behavior in relation to a partner or substitutive object.

Coen highlights the pervert's urgent transference demands for gratification, love, and affirmation from the analyst. He feels that, for the analytic process to develop, the analyst must interest the pervert in understanding this urgent demand and the defensive purposes it serves. Coen views sex and gender, as well as disturbances in masculinity and femininity, as first developing in relation to separation-individuation conflicts. He argues that feminine wishes and wishes for merger with a maternal introject are not the same in either males or females. Identification with mother in both feminine and nonfeminine ways can occur. Coen agrees that premature interruption of maternal symbiosis interferes with femininity in girls; but he asserts that for women to become fully heterosexual, psychic independence and selective partial identification with the mother's role as a heterosexual woman are required. He disagrees with Stoller and argues that the female homosexual is not simply feminine, nor do wishes for merger with a maternal introject make her more feminine.

Stoller, Robert (1985). *Observing the Erotic Imagination*. New Haven, CT: Yale University Press, pp. 184-200.

In the chapter "One Homosexual Woman," Stoller illustrates his thesis that all erotic choice has a central mental mechanism, undoing, which effects a change from trauma to triumph. In this book he adds that much of erotism is energized by variations on themes of hostility. In the case he presents, Lisa's homosexuality is seen as an erotic neurosis, not an aberrant one. Stoller argues against a single etiologic constellation to account for all homosexual behavior. This case includes central separation-individuation issues, the repetition compulsion, and a negative therapeutic reaction when relinquishing of symptoms seemed like a loss (of passion). During the treatment, in relationship to parents, lovers, and analyst, there is a progression of Lisa's themes from "I am crazy" to "who is crazy?" to "they are crazy."

Eisenbud, Ruth-Jean (1986). Lesbian choice: Transferences to theory. In: *Psychoanalysis and Women: Contemporary Reappraisals*, ed. J. Alpert, Hillsdale, NJ: The Analytic Press, pp. 215-233.

Eisenbud candidly describes her changing theoretical loyalties and improved clinical work with lesbian patients between 1969 and 1986. Her psychoanalytic work is based on the idea that lesbian choice is not generated simply by biology, neurosis, or social learning. She suggests that the preoedipal ego can use sexual feelings in its struggle for relatedness and autonomy in three ways: 1) crying for mother's care can turn passivity into precocious sexual yearning. Active courtship may develop in the interest of controlling individuation and avoiding merger with mother by seizing the initiative; 2) when exclusion from mother is a determinant, a struggle for a "way in" may take the form of "turning-on"; or 3) when mother gives a double bind message of "be a little girl, but be my support," there is a push to identification with father's role. In any of these three situations, the father may or may not be available for nurturance, identification, or rescue. If he is absent, abusive, pitiful, or compromised, the father may become negatively internalized, and masochism and dependence on the primary love of the mother is reinforced.

McDougall, Joyce (1986). Eve's reflection: On the homosexual components of female sexuality. In: *Between Analyst and Patient*, ed. H. Meyers. Hillsdale, NJ: The Analytic Press, pp. 213-228.

This readable paper contributes to the understanding of the homosexual aspect of female sexuality. [See Chapters 18 and 25 for annotations.]

Schwartz, Adria (1986). Some notes on the development of female gender role identity. In: *Psychoanalysis and Women: Contemporary Reappraisals*, ed. J. Alpert. Hillsdale, NJ: The Analytic Press, pp. 57-79.

The developmental sequence leading to female gender role identity includes rapprochement, triangulation, adolescence, work, and mother-hood. Schwartz feels that triangulation can lead to lesbian rather than heterosexual object choice; lesbianism occurs if the daughter feels excluded from identification or competition with the mother but is designated to replace father as mother's confidante or to serve as mother's male self. Escaping "inclusion," the girl may seek erotic domination of mother in lieu of identification with her. Where maternal failure as a role model is due to mother's passivity or inadequacy that reinforces gender role stereotypes, deidentification with the mother as female results. The daughter gives up the dangerous, elusive father as her love object, identifies with him, and seeks an idealized mother in a homosexual relationship. Schwartz asserts that lesbian choice may also be an active resistance to perceived male privilege when this privilege is reflected in the nuclear family constellation and the culture. Transient lesbian choice may appear during adolescence when menstruation is not celebrated as a rite of passage, but, rather, met with cultural fear and defensive devaluation. The father's role is to consolidate the daughter's gendered self as subject and object of desire and give his daughter knowledge of gender privilege.

Gardiner, Judith (1987). Self psychology as feminist theory. *Signs*, 12:761-780.

Gardiner proposes that self psychology provides gender-neutral constructs for the study of gender development and separates the development of self-esteem from that of sexual desire; thus lesbian development can be conceptualized as including a clear feminine gender identity and a strong self-image. [See Chapter 23 for annotation.]

Wolfson, Abby (1987). Reporter, Panel: Toward the further understanding of homosexual women. *J. Amer. Psychoanal. Assn.*, 35:165-173.

This report summarizes contributions by Applegarth, Kirkpatrick, McDougall, Stoller, Nadelson, and Wolfson. Applegarth reviews classical and revised explanations for gender identity, object choice, and interest in motherhood. She suggests that homosexual outcome may reflect complicated structures of gratification and defense. Stoller presents a clinical paper, "One Homosexual Woman" (See Stoller, 1985), in which he notes that there are "female homosexualities" reflecting multiple etiologies. Kirkpatrick, reporting her study of 20 divorced lesbian mothers, highlights findings that the children of lesbians show no evidence of disturbed gender development, at least by ages five to twelve. Lesbian women's marriages fail because of lack of intimacy, not because of a lack of sexual gratification. Kirkpatrick feels that homosexual orientation does not have a disruptive effect on character development or on the capacity to function as an analyst. The psychoanalytic (male) model that identifies genital release as the major organizing and motivating factor in psychological development is described as inadequate for female development, where object relations are more central. For some women, lesbianism is a means of finding intimacy and pursuing personal development. Maternal desire and competence has its own developmental line separate from object choice.

McDougall presents analytic material from women who were almost exclusively homosexual. This group of patients presented with professional inhibitions, deep depression, phobic body anxieties, and intense dependency on lovers. Analytic work revealed a split-off narcissistic maternal image who demanded total power over her child's body. The lesbianism of these patients may be understood as a quest not only for love and erotic sharing, but also for psychic survival of individual and sexual identity.

Nadelson discusses the concept of plural homosexualities and suggests that developmental dynamics do not necessarily determine ultimate sexual object choice. She questions whether homosexuality should be viewed as an illness. Wolfson highlights the panel's contributions to a revision of theories of normative development, including challenges to ideas of penis envy, penis-baby equation, castration anxiety versus the female castration complex, and superego weakness in females. She concludes that these papers provide evidence that penis envy is not the bedrock of female psychological structure but rather may serve defensive functions. The papers demonstrate that the drive to have a baby follows a separate developmental line not dependent on object choice or wishes for a penis, and finally, that girls fear for the integrity of their female genitals.

## Chasseguet-Smirgel, Janine (1988). A woman's attempt at a perverse solution and its failure. *Int. J. Psycho-Anal.*, 69:149-161.

A psychoanalytic case in progress is presented in which a young woman defensively sexualizes all relationships to avoid narcissistic pain reflective of an inadequate mother-child relationship. Her sexuality is viewed as a failing, a perverse solution that expresses hostility and revenge against the primary object. Chasseguet-Smirgel proposes that the perversion, involving idealization of pregenitality and anality and manifested by primal scene fantasy, does not provide an organizing function for the female as it does for the male pervert. She hypothesizes that the mother projects less of her narcissism onto her daughter and thus makes the idealization of pregenitality less enticing than for the male. The male pervert is seduced by the mother into believing that the male genital ego ideal is valueless, whereas his pregenitality is idealizable.

Siegel, Elaine (1988). *Female Homosexuality: Choice Without Volition.* Hillsdale, NJ: The Analytic Press.

This book discusses the etiology, theory, and clinical issues pertaining to homosexuality in women. Siegel describes the analyses of eight female homosexuals with the common symptoms of incomplete body image, lack of stable object relations leading to narcissistic injuries and cognitive arrests, and unconscious denial of differences between the sexes. She outlines recurring treatment phases that typified these analyses and offers formulations based on ego-developmental, object-relational, and self-psychological perspectives. Siegel contrasts early psychoanalytic views with current thinking about female psychological development, describes a distinctive pathogenesis, and proposes guidelines for treatment of lesbian patients. These women struggle with developmental deficits and primitive conflicts that prevent the emergence of a gender identity. Specifically, their incomplete body image lacks schematization of the vagina, leading to a self-representation that searches to complete itself in the actual and metaphorical mirror of the same-sex partner.

Siegel differs from other self theorists in that she claims that internal structure is built upon experiential interchange with the surround. Other specific findings in her patients were a childhood preferred mode of playing consisting of motoric tension discharge without fantasy content and an absence of doll play. The chapter on "Countertransference Regression and Empathy," includes a review of the literature and the author's valuable, candid countertransference insights, including ideas about societal assumptions about sexuality and their impact on the analyst. The analyst must often use her own body sensations to decode verbally what has been transmitted nonverbally. Siegel explores her responses of feeling sleepy when patients were negating her gender. Because analysands project the kind of object they need, Siegel maintains that analysts of either gender can analyze female homosexuals. This book also contains two clinical chapters and a short chapter on parental profiles as they emerged in the daughters' analyses.

Blum, Harold (1989). Shared fantasy and reciprocal identification, and their role in gender disorders. In: *Fantasy, Myth, and Reality: Essays in Honor of Jacob Arlow,* ed. H. Blum, Y. Kramer, A. Richards, and A. Richards. Madison, CT: International Universities Press, pp. 323-338.

Blum suggests that shared unconscious fantasies between parent and child may have a developmental influence on the evolution of perversion. Features of shared fantasies are delineated. Stoller's transsexual case is reevaluated as an example of three generations of shared unconscious fantasy of the phallic woman and denial of gender, compatible with preoedipal distortions of the Oedipus complex in the transsexual child rather than as an example of symbiosis.

Kirkpatrick, Martha (1989a). Lesbians: A different middle age? In: *The Middle Years: New Psychoanalytic Perspectives*, ed. J. Oldham and R. Liebert. New Haven, CT: Yale University Press, pp. 135-148.

[See Chapter 15 for annotation.]

McDougall, Joyce (1989). The dead father: On early psychic trauma and its relation to disturbance in sexual identity and in creative activity. *Int. J. Psycho-Anal.*, 70:205-219.

McDougall argues that sexual deviancy (homosexuality) and creativity may be traced back to early psychic trauma; both phenomena are seen as "solutions" to overcoming the trauma. McDougall's patients often seek help because of professional inhibitions. The analysis of a homosexual writer who presented with the symptoms of a writing block and tension in her homosexual love-relations is described. Her narcissistic pathology is traced to the death of her father at age 15 months and the mother's disturbed way of handling the death by hiding it from the child. The mother was seen as obliterating and controlling, regarding the patient as a narcissistic extension, attempting to deny the child's paternal relationship, and thus forcing her child into a magical identification with the dead father. McDougall feels that the parental couple may hinder or help the young child to come to terms with the sexual difference and give up universal wishes to be bisexual and incestuous, favoring or not favoring a deviant sense of core gender and sexual identity (gender role). Different identifications with both parents structure the sense of sexual identity for all children. [See also Chapter 16.]

Quinodoz, Jean-Michel, (1989). Female homosexual patients in psychoanalysis. *Int. J. Psycho-Anal.*, 70:55-63.

The author reviews and summarizes the early literature on female homosexuality including the work of Freud, Abraham, Jones, and Klein. Female homosexuality is linked to oedipal pathology, and identification with the penis is a predominant dynamic. Quinodoz proposes an alternative model in which identification with the baby is the primary characteristic. In that group of patients, fixation is at an earlier developmental level and differentiation is less well established. Quinodoz discusses homosexuality as a dual defense, blocking regression toward psychosis and against progression toward the oedipal situation. He also comments on the differing transference relationship in manifest and latent female homosexuality. Like Klein, he views homosexuality as a defense against paranoid and depressive anxieties and advises working through the defenses against these anxieties to allow for the integration of the early internal object relations contained in the homosexual fixation.

Raphling, David (1989). Fetishism in a woman. *J. Amer. Psychoanal. Assn.*, 37:465-491.

A clinical illustration of fetishism in an adult woman confirms the existence of this perversion in females. Raphling reviews the literature on fetishism and compares and contrasts female and male fetishism. He suggests that fetishism, involving id derivatives as well as ego defenses against castration, is more complex in women than in men. The author contends that female fetishism, existing in a well-disguised form, may be more prevalent than previously realized.

Richards, Arlene (1989). A romance with pain: A telephone perversion in a woman? *Int. J. Psycho-Anal.*, 70:153-164.

Richards notes that female perversions are seldom discussed in the literature because the perverse sexuality is hidden, just as female sexual anatomy is hidden. She conceptualizes perversion as a symptom or compromise formation. An analytic patient's clinging and persistent calls are seen as reflecting a sadomasochistic perversion based on the central fantasy of phallic intrusion on the mother. Richards asserts that the perverse female, like the male, has pregenital conflicts about identification with her mother, in addition to later conflicts with identifications with her father.

Vogel, Sara (1989). Reporter, Panel: Current concepts of the development of sexuality. *J. Amer. Psychoanal. Assn.*, 37:787-802.

This 1987 panel discusses the vicissitudes of sexuality in relation to developmental processes of early childhood, emphasizing normal development as well as deviations. [See Chapter 18 for annotation.]

Kaplan, Louise (1990). *Female Perversions: The Temptations of Emma Bovary*. New York: Doubleday.

Exploring male and female perversion, Kaplan redefines traditional views of perversion based on castration anxiety to include also female anxiety about destruction of the female genitals. Male perversion involves the expression of shameful feminine strivings and hostile aggression toward the female body hidden by infantile male gender stereotypes of virility. Female perversions are disguised in social gender stereotypes of femininity. They include extreme submissiveness, transvestism, homeovestism, other masquerades and impersonations of femininity, kleptomania, delicate self-cutting, trichotillomania, cosmetic surgery as a polysurgical addiction, and anorexia. Social roles assigned to women and gender stereotypes of femininity collaborate in the structure of the perverse symptom. Kleptomania is seen as related to consumerism, where material goods are substituted for emotional needs, rather than as related to penis envy. Child abuse is discussed as a perversion.

Lawrence, Lauren (1990). The psychodynamics of the compulsive female shopper. *Amer. J. Psychoanal.*, 50:67-70.

Lawrence proposes that castration anxiety is the primary motive responsible for compulsive shopping in females. The female child unconsciously harbors unrelenting sorrow for the missing penis and seeks to replace it in adulthood. The greater the feeling of early loss of the mother, the greater a need to find an object replacement by identification with the father and by compulsive purchasing of symbolically phallic objects.

Richards, Arlene (1990). Female fetishes and female perversions: Hermine Hug-Hellmuth's "A Case of Female Foot or More Properly Boot Fetishism" reconsidered. *Psychoanal. Rev.*, 77:11-23.

Richards translates Hug-Hellmuth's (1915) German-language paper, which describes a 30-year-old woman from a military family who had a fetish for men's shiny riding boots and the men who wore them. She claimed, "The man is his foot." Her marriage and sexual life were unhappy for she was aroused by the boots but disgusted by naked feet and by intercourse. Hug-Hellmuth describes derivations of the fetish from identification with the father, wishes to be a boy, idealization of the father, masochistic elements, and displacement of shock and attraction onto the substitute penis, defended in the service of idealization of the object. Hug-Hellmuth rejects narcissism as an etiological factor, though it is an outcome. Richards defines the fetish as a perversion either when it replaces the object or when it is an adjunct to intercourse to cover sexual dysfunction. She reviews the literature on female perversion and on perversion in general. A view of perversion as a form of self-esteem regulation involving special sensitivities is contrasted with that postulating castration anxiety and substitution for the female phallus as a central dynamic. Clinically, this patient showed lack of shame, rather than the more common secrecy. Richards emphasizes that perverse symptoms in women may be often missed.

Fogel, Gerald and Myers, Wayne (ed.)(1991). *The Perversions and Near Perversions in Clinical Practice: New Psychoanalytic Perspectives.* New Haven, CT: Yale University Press.

This book includes new and revised views of perversion presented at a Columbia Psychoanalytic Center symposium that discussed perverse phenomena, including both fixed obligatory perversions and transient or facultative perverse phenomena of everyday clinical practice. Contributors include Cooper, Stade, Stoller, Bach, Arlow, H. Meyers, L. Kaplan, O. Kernberg, and McDougall. Several writers refer to gender differences, and Kaplan's article, "Women Masquerading as Women," specifically discusses perverse pathology in women. Cooper suggests that perversions may be less apparent in women because the conflict over separation from the mother is not compounded by the task of gender differentiation. Kernberg's chapter, "Perversity and Love in the Relationship of the Couple," discusses aggression, excitement, and romantic love.

Kaplan, Louise (1991). Women masquerading as women. In: *The Perversions and Near Perversions in Clinical Practice: New Psychoanalytic Perspectives,* ed. G. Fogel and W. Myers, New Haven, CT: Yale University Press, pp. 127-152.

Kaplan asserts that stereotypic femininity in women often has the same underlying structure and analogous purposes as classic perversions in males. Biological differences are exploited to accomplish conscious and unconscious purposes. Perversions are viewed as pathologies of gender identification, rather than as pathologies of sexuality, as they derive much of their emotional force from social gender stereotypes. Kaplan discusses individual and societal psychopathology and the interplay between them. Perverse strategies are regressive compromise solutions to oedipal crises that use preoedipal and presexual gender identifications and become caricatures of mature sexuality. Personal conflicts, familial necessity, and societal reenforcement draw women into perverse solutions. Society's own distorted purposes are met by defining these complex characterological personal pathologies as normal. Homeovestism, female impersonations by females (*Playboy* centerfolds, fashion models), and masquerades of womanliness (character perversions) demonstrate the use of a stereotyped femininity to mask forbidden (masculine or preoedipal) strivings.

McDougall, Joyce (1991). Sexual identity, trauma and creativity. *Psych. Inq.*

McDougall uses a three-session vignette from the analysis of a middle-aged female homosexual author to illustrate several theoretical points about trauma, creativity and its inhibition, homosexuality, sexual identity, and somatization. [See Chapter 12 for annotation.]

# Chapter 20

# Aspects of Female Character

Eleanor Schuker and Ingrid Pisetsky
Additional contributions by Nadine Levinson

This chapter comprises a broad group of writings about the character styles and character traits that have commonly been associated with femininity. A full discussion of the concept of character, its evolution, and its role in psychoanalytic theory lies beyond the scope of this chapter. Baudry (1983) delineates the evolution of the psychoanalytic concept of character in Freud's writings, including its relation to theories of neurotic-symptom formation. Stein (1969) and Baudry (1984) review some dilemmas in character theory. Character derives from ego development, traumata, conflict resolution, and endogenous constitutional factors. It results from a complex interaction of drive derivatives, defenses, superego constituents, and identifications, shaped by multiple developmental factors and integrated into an enduring personality organization. Discussions of gender proclivities for particular character styles and traits reflect conceptual and definitional changes in the psychoanalytic understanding of character over the years.

Historically, writers beginning with Freud asserted that various character types were predominant among women—the hysterical, oral, depressive, narcissistic, and masochistic characters. Character traits associated with femininity, such as narcissism, masochism, passivity, lessened aggressiveness, dependency, inhibited autonomy, susceptibility to shame, jealousy, and, more recently, relatedness and concern for others have been designated as attributes of women. These are viewed as derived from constitutional predisposition, developmental processes, or cultural prescription.

Current psychoanalytic thinkers, however, have noted that the character typology attributed by Freud to femininity (passivity, masochism, narcissism) was based on conventional stereotypes, rather than on psychoanalytic data about the range of possible developmental paths (Grossman and Kaplan, 1989). Feminine traits and character types that were assumed to be linked ineluctably to femininity thus may have reflected, at least in part, social gender stereotypes and developmental vicissitudes in a given culture rather than biological predispositions or inevitable developmental paths. While Freud described a unilinear normal feminine developmental path, analysts now believe that many developmental narratives are possible. Hence each person's dynamic life story must be understood as conveying its own individual complexity as well as common gender-role pressures and other inescapable factors (Tyson, 1991). Which, if any, factors related to gender are immutable still form the subject of debate; arguments have been advanced for constitution, temperament, body-image development, and other specific developmental vicissitudes. Moreover, the psychoanalytic classification of character types has been further confused by the mixing of terms from different levels of abstraction, for example, according by libidinal phase (such as oral character), by defenses, or by manifest behaviors. This difficulty is reflected in the variety of approaches taken by papers annotated in this chapter.

Character formation may be understood as beginning with prenatal and postnatal temperamental differences, which, together with body image development, preoedipal object relations, and other dynamic elements can influence the shape of separation-individuation and early defensive patterns. Character is shaped further by oedipal resolution, superego formation, preoedipal, oedipal, and postoedipal identifications, and the development of a gendered self. Culture and gender role conventions interact with inevitable and variant developmental processes in the evolution of the character structure of the individual. The issues covered in this chapter are thus have broad ramifications.

Primarily, this chapter includes articles that posit the presence of common elements in feminine character and discuss the etiologies of presumed feminine character traits. Considerable attention has been devoted in the literature to the topic of the hysterical character. In addition, selected general articles relevant to a psychoanalytic understanding of character have been incorporated into this chapter. Since the topics of narcissism and masochism have been written about so extensively in relation to female character, and since they are subject to their own specific controversies, they are relegated to separate chapters (see chapters 21 and 22) that can be read as companions to this one. The reader is also referred to Section II: Developmental Perspective and chapters 18 and 19. (E.S.)

Freud, Sigmund (1893-1895). Studies on hysteria II. Case Histories. *Standard Edition*, 2:19-181. London: Hogarth Press, 1953.

Freud proposes that hysteria results from the repression of traumatic sexual memories and their conversion into physical symptoms. [See also Chapters 1 and 24.]

Freud, Sigmund (1894). The neuro-psychoses of defense. *Standard Edition*, 3:43-61. London: Hogarth Press, 1953.

Freud discusses three forms of hysteria—hypnoid, defense, and retention hysteria.

Freud, Sigmund (1896a). Further remarks on the neuro-psychoses of defense. *Standard Edition*, 3:159-185. London: Hogarth Press, 1953.

Freud distinguishes hysteria from obsessional symptoms. In hysteria, a passive sexual experience takes place, while in obsessional neurosis an active one occurs. [See also Chapter 24.]

Freud, Sigmund (1896b). The aetiology of hysteria. *Standard Edition*, 3:189-221. London: Hogarth Press, 1953.

In this early attempt to understand the etiology of neurotic symptoms and traits, Freud states that certain traumatic childhood sexual experiences, which have been initiated by adults, are later reproduced in the psychical life of hysterics by mechanisms of defense in the form of symptoms that have symbolic meaning. Hysterical reactions may not begin until puberty, when childhood experiences are reawakened.

Freud, Sigmund (1905a). Fragment of an analysis of a case of hysteria. *Standard Edition*, 7:3-122. London: Hogarth Press, 1953.

[See Chapter 1 for annotation.]

Freud, Sigmund (1905b). Three essays on the theory of sexuality. *Standard Edition*, 7:125-243. London: Hogarth Press, 1953.

Several comments throughout the *Three Essays* specifically refer to aspects of character. In Part I, Freud notes that "character-inversion" is regularly seen in homosexual women, but not as regularly in homosexual men. Women with inversion of sexual object choice also have other masculine mental qualities, instincts, and character traits. In Freud's discussion of sadism and masochism, he apposes the groupings of active/sadistic/masculine with passive/masochistic/feminine. In Part II, active and passive forms of masturbation are used as prototypes of active and passive character traits. Part III directly discusses character. Masculine and feminine character traits become distinguished at puberty, when a fresh wave of repression affects clitoral sexuality. The girl's masculine sexuality is repressed, and she transfers her excitement to the vagina. This change is the chief determinant of women's greater proneness to neurosis, especially hysteria. In the summary, Freud notes that instincts, transformed by the processes of sublimation and reaction formation, lead to the building up of character.

[See also Chapter 1.]

Freud, Sigmund (1908a). Hysterical fantasies and their relation to bisexuality. *Standard Edition*, 9:157-166. London: Hogarth Press, 1953.

Describing the nature of hysterical symptoms from different points of view, Freud presents a theory of symptom formation. Hysterical symptoms 1) are mnemic symbols; 2) are substitutes via "conversion" for traumatic experiences; 3) express wish fulfillment; 4) are the realization of an unconscious fantasy which serves wish fulfillment; 5) serve sexual satisfaction; 6) correspond to a return to an infantile repressed mode of sexual satisfaction; 7) arise as a compromise between two opposite affective and instinctual impulses; and 8) take over the representation of unconscious impulses that are not sexual but have sexual significance. Freud added the new idea that hysteria is the expression of bisexual (both masculine and feminine) unconscious sexual fantasy. [See also Chapter 1.]

Freud, Sigmund (1908b). Character and anal erotism. *Standard Edition*, 9:169-175. London: Hogarth Press, 1953.

Freud describes three character traits—orderliness, parsimony, and obstinancy—that are regularly combined. These traits are seen as the consequence of sublimation of and reaction formations against anal erotism. In this paper, Freud integrates the effect of masturbation and the struggle against sexual urges into an early character theory.

Freud, Sigmund (1908c). Civilized sexual morality and modern nervousness. *Standard Edition*, 9:179-204. London: Hogarth Press, 1953.

Discussing the role of sexual instincts in determining many aspects of behavior, Freud notes (pp. 197-199) the harmful effects that the demand for abstinence before marriage produces in the nature of women. These effects include frigidity and inhibitions in intellectual matters. [See also Chapter 13.]

Freud, Sigmund (1913). The disposition to obsessional neurosis: A contribution to the problem of choice of neurosis. *Standard Edition*, 12:313-326. London: Hogarth Press, 1953.

Freud discusses the disposition to obsessional neurosis and to anal character traits and contrasts the processes of symptom formation and character development. He contends that with the loss of their "genital function," women undergo a character change at menopause and regress to what has been sometimes satirized as the "old dragon." They become "quarrelsome, vexatious and overbearing, petty and stingy; that is they exhibit typically sadistic and anal-erotic traits which they did not possess earlier, during their period of womanliness" (pp. 323-324). Another woman, who develops obsessional symptoms with the onset of her husband's impotence, is also described.

Freud, Sigmund (1916). Some character-types met with in psychoanalytic work. *Standard Edition*, 14:310-333. London: Hogarth Press, 1953.

This paper is an early reference to a woman's need to be special or an exception because narcissistic injury has led to resentment toward the mother for having damaged her by not giving her a penis. [See Chapters 1 and 12 for annotations.]

Freud, Sigmund (1919). A child is being beaten. *Standard Edition*, 17:177-204. London: Hogarth Press, 1953.

Freud briefly notes the effects of unconscious fantasies on character. [See Chapters 1 and 21 for annotations.]

Sachs, Hanns (1920). The wish to be a man. *Int. J. Psycho-Anal.*, 6:262-267.

[See Chapter 2 for annotation.]

Freud, Sigmund (1923a). The ego and the id. *Standard Edition*, 19:3-66. London: Hogarth Press, 1953.

Identifications, which substitute for the lost object, contribute significantly to the structure of the ego and its character. [See also Chapter 1.]

Freud, Sigmund (1925). Some psychical consequences of the anatomical distinction between the sexes. *Standard Edition*, 19:243-258. London: Hogarth Press, 1953.

Freud states that women have less sense of justice and more emotionality than do men as a result of their castration complex and their weaker superego. [See Chapter 1.]

Freud, Sigmund (1926). Inhibitions, symptoms and anxiety. *Standard Edition*, 20:77-174. London: Hogarth Press, 1953.

In the Addenda, Freud contrasts the results of reaction formations in hysteria and in obsessional neuroses (pp. 157-158). Reaction formations in hysteria may be confined to particular relationships, so that an hysterical woman may be especially affectionate with her own children, whom she hates, but will not be loving in general. He describes scomatization, or the hysterical anticathexis that is directed outward against dangerous perceptions. [See also Chapter 1.]

Riviere, Joan (1929). Womanliness as a masquerade. *Int. J. Psycho-Anal.*, 10:303-313. Also in *Psychoanalysis and Female Sexuality*, ed. H. Ruitenbeek. New Haven, CT: College and University Press, 1966, pp. 209-220.

[See Chapter 2 for annotation.]

Freud, Sigmund (1931b). Libidinal types. *Standard Edition*, 21:216-220. London: Hogarth Press, 1961.

Freud describes three types of libidinal characters: the erotic, the narcissistic, and the obsessional type. Erotic characters share a primary interest in being loved; they are dominated by fear of loss of love and are especially dependent. Obsessional types are dominated by the superego and fear of conscience; they are self-reliant but have an internal dependence. Narcissistic types have no tension between their ego and superego and no preponderance of erotic needs. Their interest is directed to self-preservation; their ego has a large amount of aggressiveness, and loving is preferred to being loved. Narcissistic types are independent and not open to intimidation. Many persons are mixed rather than pure types. Freud notes that with the onset of illness, there is no evidence to infer that erotic types develop hysteria, obsessional types develop an obsessional neurosis, or narcissistic types develop psychosis. Since neuroses arise from internal conflicts between psychic agencies and drives, it is the task of psychoanalysis to discover the individual pathogenic processes. This paper uses concepts from both structural and libido theory.

Brierley, Marjorie (1932). Some problems of integration in women. *Int. J. Psycho-Anal.*, 13:433-448.

Brierley discusses oral aggression in relation to identity and sexuality. [See Chapters 2 and 18 for annotations.]

Freud, Sigmund (1933). Femininity. *Standard Edition*, 22:112-135. London: Hogarth Press, 1953.

Freud considers different psychical peculiarities (character traits) of mature femininity, including narcissism, jealousy, shame, vanity, and masochism. Penis envy, an intense early attachment to the mother, hostility toward the mother, suppression of aggression, and cultural factors are considered as sources of feminine character traits. Shame is viewed as a feminine characteristic "which has as its purpose . . . concealment of genital deficiency (p. 132)." [See also Chapter 1.]

Horney, Karen (1935a). Personality changes in female adolescents. *Amer. J. Orthopsychiat.*, 5:19-26. Also in: *Feminine Psychology*, ed. H. Kelman. New York: Norton, 1967, pp. 234-244.

[See Chapter 9 for annotation.]

Payne, Sylvia (1935). A concept of femininity. *Br. J. Med. Psychol.*, 15:18-33.

Payne views the feminine body and reproductive functions as central to femininity and explores the psychological characteristics of genitally mature women. [See Chapter 2 for annotation.]

Freud, Sigmund (1937). Analysis terminable and interminable. *Standard Edition*, 23:211-253. London: Hogarth Press, 1953.

Freud feels that unalterable ego states serve as character resistances. Penis envy is not capable of further analysis. [See also Chapter 1.]

Jacobson, Edith (1937). Ways of superego formation and the female castration complex. *Psychoanal. Q.*, 45:525-538, 1976.

Jacobson suggests that the superego in women has its origin in preoedipal castration conflicts. In a 1976 note, she suggests that an ever-increasing group of women, whom she labels "the female 'vaginal' character" rather than the "masculine woman," have a self-image that includes a valued female genital, an independent superego, a strong effective ego, and a healthy, expansive sexuality. [See also Chapters 2, 7, and 18.]

Hayward, Emeline (1943). Types of female castration reaction. *Psychonal. Q.*, 12:45-66.

[See Chapter 18 for annotation.]

Jacobson, Edith (1943). Depression: The Oedipus conflict in the development of depressive mechanisms. *Psychoanal. Q.*, 12:541-560.

Jacobson contends that the preoedipal and oedipal stages of development are crucial in the subsequent formation of a depressive condition. Following a brief overview of the development of depressive mechanisms, Jacobson presents the case of a severely depressed 24-year-old woman. This patient demonstrated an earlier failure to establish normal object relationships with her parents and had experienced previous depressive periods at age three-and-a-half and at puberty. There was also a family history of depression. A series of traumatic events triggered regression to her previous primal depression at three-and-a-half, which served as the nucleus of her pathogenic conflict.

Deutsch, Helene (1944a). Eroticism: The feminine woman. In: *The Psychology of Women*, Vol. 1. New York: Grune and Stratton, pp. 185-218.

Deutsch discusses several feminine traits, including eroticism, a tendency to (narcissistic) identification, passive-receptiveness (activity turned inward), masochism, and intuition. Sublimated eroticism or inner erotic fantasies and longings are inherent in the adolescent feminine psyche. The ability gradually to shape these erotic longings so that they do not negate the direct experience of sexuality is one of the goals of female adulthood and sexual maturity. Deutsch derives healthy erotic feminine types of character from an interplay between narcissism and masochism. Narcissism has positive value, contributing to strength of character, self-confidence, self-respect, and feminine charm. She asserts that women's sexual goals are dangerous for their ego, as they are masochistic, and narcissistic protective reactions become the "guardian" of a passive-masochistic position. On the basis of different functions of the guardian in the psychological structure, three feminine erotic types are differentiated. Object choices and the quality of the relationship with the love object for these three groups are also influenced by previous emotional ties to the mother and father. All these feminine erotic women have had good relationships with their mothers and have complete sexual readiness toward partners, provided their passivity is overcome by arousal by the partner. Women have some degree of constitutional sexual inhibition. Further sources of frigidity lie in excessive narcissism, masochism, ties to former objects, and motherliness.

Deutsch, Helene (1944c). Feminine passivity. In: *The Psychology of Women*, Vol. 1. New York: Grune and Stratton, pp. 219-238.

Passivity as a central attribute of femininity is discussed using Deutsch's clinical work and phylogenetic animal data. Two factors cause girls' primary genital trauma: the inadequacy of the clitoris for gratification of active and aggressive instinctual impulses during the phallic phase; and the lack of responsiveness of the vagina to which the girl turns when active expression is inhibited. Genital trauma (organlessness) is the basis for women's essential conflicts rather than penis envy, which Deutsch contends can become a secondary consequence. She asserts that the later awakening of the vagina is dependent on the man's capacity for arousing the woman.

Deutsch, Helene (1944e). The "active" woman: The masculinity complex. In: *The Psychology of Women*, Vol. 1. New York: Grune and Stratton, pp. 279-324.

The active-feminine woman is differentiated from the masculine woman. [See Chapter 18 for annotation.]

Greenacre, Phyllis (1948). Anatomical structure and superego development. *Amer. J. Orthopsychiat.*, 18:636-648. Also in: *Trauma, Growth, and Personality*, New York: Norton, pp. 149-164.

Greenacre proposes that children's character and superego may be influenced by their reactions to their physical bodies. [See Chapter 7 for annotation.]

Fessler, Laci (1950). The psychopathology of climacteric depression. *Psychoanal. Q.*, 19:28-42.

[See Chapter 15 for annotation.]

Greenacre, Phyllis (1950a). Special problems of early female sexual development. *The Psychoanalytic Study of the Child*, 5:122-138. New York: International Universities Press. Also in: *Trauma, Growth and Personality*. New York: Norton, 1952, pp. 237-258.

A particular female character, "the Medea complex," develops in girls who experience two sibling arrivals, the first coming before age 16 months and the second before age three. [See Chapter 18 for annotation.]

Greenacre, Phyllis (1950b). The prepuberty trauma in girls. *Psychoanal. Q.,* 19:298-317. Also in: Trauma, Growth and Personality. New York: Norton, 1952, pp. 204-223

[See Chapter 9 for annotation.]

Goldman, F. (1950/51). Breastfeeding and character formation: The etiology of the oral character in psychoanalytic theory. *J. Pers.*, 19:189-196, Durham, NC: Duke University Press. Also in: *Scientific Evaluation of Freud's Theories and Therapies*, ed. S. Fisher and R. Greenberg. New York: Basic Books, 1978, pp. 80-87.

Goldman studied 100 adult male and female subjects for the personality trait of "oral pessimism/optimism" on the basis of verbal rating scales. These scores were correlated with the age of the subjects at the time of weaning from breastfeeding as reported by the subjects' mothers. The authors found a significant correlation between early weaning (less than four months) and "oral pessimism." Prolonged breastfeeding beyond nine months resulted in scores that were significantly "optimistic" as compared with the early weaning group.

Leuba, John (1950). Women who fall. *Int. J. Psycho-Anal.*, 31:6-7

This brief paper describes the syndrome of women who stumble or trip frequently. The roots are found in ego weakness and unconscious aggressive and erotic impulses.

Marmor, Judd (1953). Orality in the hysterical personality. *J. Amer. Psychoanal. Assn.*, 1:656-671.

In reevaluating the psychodynamics of the hysterical character, Marmor hypothesizes the following: 1) Oral fixations give the Oedipus complex of hysterics a strong pregenital cast, resulting in clinical resistance to change, immaturity, and instability of ego structure; there is also increased frequency of addictions, depressions, and schizophrenia. 2) The greater incidence of hysteria in women as compared with men may be a cultural phenomenon; hysterical traits such as oral receptivity, dependency, and passivity are considered by our society as feminine and more acceptable in women. 3) Oral fixations can be neurotic or psychotic, depending on the balance between ego strength and ego stress. A case study illustrates an hysteric character with an oral libidinal fixation.

Kramer, Paul (1954). Early capacity for orgastic discharge and character formation. *The Psychoanalytic Study of the Child*, 9:128-141. New York: International Universities Press.

The effects of traumatic sexual overstimulation in childhood on character formation are discussed. [See Chapter 18 for annotation.]

Ovesey, Lionel (1956). Masculine aspirations in women. *Psychiat.*, 19:341-351.

Masculine aspirations expressed by women are seen as adaptations to a male-oriented society in which the position of women is devalued. Even if women consciously reject this devalued view of themselves, unconsciously they must struggle against the inevitable injury to self-esteem. For neurotic women, the penis can become a symbol of masculine superiority. Unconscious fantasies of having, acquiring, or incorporating a penis represent wishes for magical repair by the acquisition of masculine traits and the positive social attributes that accompany them. Conversely, unconscious fantasies of castration become the symbol of feminine inferiority. Ovesey presents clinical material from the analysis of a woman who wished to be a man.

Chodoff, Paul and Lyons, Henry (1958). The hysterical personality and "hysterical" conversion. *Amer. J. Psychiat.*, 114:734-740.

This article clarifies various uses of the term hysteria. Hysterical personality disorder is defined using distinctive behavioral characteristics. Conversion reaction disorders are classified as symptoms of the voluntary nervous system that represent symbolic resolution of emotional conflicts. The authors examine historical and cultural factors in the relatively higher frequency of hysteria in women. The female predisposition to hysteria was explained by Freud (1905b) as caused by repression and by oedipal-phase fixations from castration reactions. Chodoff and Lyons note that some hysterical personality traits are socially sanctioned, since they are regarded by society as more feminine. This disorder has usually been described in female patients by their male psychiatrists and is seen as a "caricature of femininity."

Brenner, Charles (1959). The masochistic character: Genesis and treatment. *J. Amer. Psychoanal. Assn.*, 7:197-226.

[See Chapter 21 for annotation.]

Greenacre, Phyllis (1960). Woman as artist. In: *Emotional Growth*, Vol. 2. New York: International Universities Press, 1971, pp. 575-591.

Greenacre discusses why artistic and scientific creativity is seen less often in women than in men. [See Chapter 12 for annotation.]

Hammerman, Steven (1961). Masturbation and character. *J. Amer. Psychoanal. Assn.*, 9:287-311.

The author suggests that analysis of the precursors of genital masturbation fantasies can shed light on early self- and object representations. [See Chapter 18 for annotation.]

Lichtenstein, Heinz (1961). Identity and sexuality: A study of their interrelationship in man. *J. Amer. Psychoanal. Assn.*, 9:179-260.

[See Chapter 18 for annotation.]

Lustman, Seymour (1962). Defense, symptom, and character. *The Psychoanalytic Study of the Child*, 17:216-244. New York: International Universities Press.

The analysis of a four-and-a-half year old girl is used to illustrate the sources of character traits (bravery) and symptom formation (obsessive cleansing). These sources include constitutional factors, identifications, reactions to trauma, and development of defenses. Themes of masculine strivings, sexual confusion, penis envy, sibling rivalry, and seduction experiences are discussed. Defense, symptomatic act, and character are intimately interrelated, with the difference between character and symptom being a quantitative one related to the degree of internalization of the superego.

Witkin, Herman, Dyk, Ruth, Paterson, Hanna, Goodenough, Donald, and Karp, Stephen (1962). *Psychological Differentiation: Studies of Development*. New York: Wiley.

The authors observe that "the way in which each person orients himself in space is an expression of a more general preferred mode of perceiving, which, in turn, is linked to a broad and varied array of personal characteristics involving a great many areas of psychological functioning" (p. 1). The ability to separate body from field, or field independence, is correlated with a relatively well-developed body image or body concept. Field dependence is associated with a less well-developed body concept. Women are found to be more field dependent, at least after age eight. They tend toward a global field approach in perceptual and intellectual functioning rather than an analytical approach.

Balint, Michael (1963). The younger sister and Prince Charming. *Int. J. Psycho-Anal.*, 44:226-227.

Using clinical material, Balint discusses typical characterologic features that occur when two sisters are close in age. [See Chapter 17 for annotation.]

Sarlin, Charles (1963). Feminine identity. *J. Amer. Psychoanal. Assn.*, 11:790-816.

[See Chapter 18 for annotation.]

Winter, Harold. (1964). Pre-oedipal factors in the genesis of hysterical character neurosis. *Int. J. Psycho-Anal.*, 45:338-343.

Winter emphasizes preoedipal factors in the analyses of several young men whom he diagnoses as having hysterical character neuroses. Their symptoms include inhibited assertiveness, sexual difficulties, primitive "fused" object relationships, fears of dependence, and needs to please and be loved. The patients tended to regress to a fused identification with the mother.

Easser, Barbara and Lesser, Stanley (1965). Hysterical personality: A re-evaluation. *Psychoanal. Q.*, 34:390-405.

This article reviews analytic case material from six female patients who were diagnosed as hysterical personalities. Hysterical personalities are vividly differentiated from a more disturbed group of patients who use hysterical mechanisms but who are diagnosed as "hysteroid." The following traits are seen in the hysterical personality 1) labile emotionality; 2) direct engagement with the human world, related to the need to love and be loved; 3) poor responses to frustration and to excitement, even though the hysteric may instigate excitement; 4) the existence of a close relationship between excitability and its accompanying romantic fantasy; 5) defenses against suggestibility; 6) a dislike of the exact, rote, and mundane; and 7) a seemingly irresponsible, flighty quality and a self-presentation as a child/woman. Hysterical defense mechanisms involve the substitution of emotions, one for the other, or a shift in the quality of emotional responses. Emotionality conceals core conflicts. Patients with a "hysteroid" diagnosis range from immature and dependent to borderline or even psychotic. They act as caricatures of the hysterics, with erratic adaptive functioning, difficulty in maintaining object relations, core problems with the maternal object, and tendencies toward emotional and impulse dyscontrol. Clinical examples and dreams are presented to demonstrate these diagnostic differences.

Shapiro, David (1965). *Neurotic Styles*. New York and London: Basic Books.

This classic book describes four neurotic forms or styles of functioning, thinking, and perceiving, which are factors in determining defense mechanisms, traits, and symptoms. Shapiro discusses obsessive-compulsive, paranoid, hysterical, and impulsive styles, based on his psychoanalytically oriented clinical work and knowledge of projective tests. Hysterical personality traits are mediated by particular cognitive styles, including impressionistic distortions of experience, short-circuited appraisal of meanings, and limited categories and availability of memory. Hysterical emotionality is illustrated by a clinical vignette of a woman.

Zetzel, Elizabeth (1965b). The incapacity to bear depression. In: *Drives, Affects, Behavior*, Vol. 2., ed. M. Schur. New York: International Universities Press, pp. 243-274. Also in: *The Capacity for Emotional Growth*. New York: International Universities Press, 1970, pp. 85-114.

In this developmental study of depression and depressive affect, Zetzel comments on differences between males and females in the ability to experience and tolerate depression. Components of the ability to tolerate and master depressive affect include good object relations, the ability to accept the limitations of reality, and the capacity to renounce an omnipotent self-image. More women than men, in Zetzel's clinical experience, complain of depression as a presenting symptom, but more women can better tolerate this affect. Men who complain of depression tend to be more disturbed and have passive-dependent characters and problems in masculine identification. Zetzel postulates two phases in the development of the capacity to tolerate and master depressive affect, which differ in emphasis for each sex. The first phase involves tolerance of the passivity inherent in the inability to modify painful realities. The second phase involves an adaptation to reality by mobilization of available areas of gratification and achievement. Men tend to overemphasize the second phase because of the importance of activity in association with their masculine ego ideal and thus may have difficulty in tolerating passivity. In women, a good adaptation to passivity may be followed by excessive passivity and helplessness reinforced by the oedipal period. This leads to problems in active mastery (or phase-two adaptations) and vulnerability to or narcissistic injury. Good pregenital identifications with mother can stimulate independence and autonomy, but excessive emphasis on active achievement as a mode of gaining approval can also lead to difficulties, such as disavowal of passive goals, overcompensatory activity, and defensive reinforcement of penis envy.

Cohen, Mabel Blake (1966). Personal identity and sexual identity. *Psychiat.*, 29:1-14.

Cohen observes that society's traditional definitions of masculine and feminine sex roles exaggerate the degree of dependency and passivity in normal females and the degree of independence and activity in normal males. [See Chapter 12 for annotation.]

Forrest, Tess (1966). Paternal roots of female character development. *Contemp. Psychoanal.*, 3:21-38.

Paternal contributions to female character formation are described. [See Chapter 16 for annotation.]

Lazare, Aaron, Klerman, Gerald, and Armor, David (1966). Oral, obsessive, and hysterical personality patterns. *Arch. Gen. Psychiat.*, 14:624-630.

Clusters of traits found on a 200-item self-rating scale administered to 90 recently discharged psychiatric patients were compared using historical data and clinical descriptions of hysterical, oral, and obsessive personality types. The self-rating scale was designed to measure 20 personality traits. The responses to the rating scale formed three clusters or factors. Factor I consisted of traits related most closely to clinical descriptions of hysterical personality. Aggression and "oral" aggression were highly predicted traits in the factor analysis of the self-rating scale but were not included in historical and clinical descriptions of the hysterical personality type. Conversely, suggestibility and fear of sexuality, both considered hallmarks of the hysterical personality in past clinical descriptions, clustered in factor II rather than factor I. Factor II corresponded to the historical descriptions of the oral personality, although the fit between this cluster and the clinical description was the poorest of the three. There was a close relationship between factor III and the clinical descriptions of the obsessive personality, including traits of orderliness, severe superego, perseverance, obstinancy, rigidity, rejection of others, parsimony, and emotional constriction. This research attempts to integrate psychological and statistical methods to validate and extend psychoanalytic observations.

Prosen, Harry (1967). Sexuality in females with "hysteria." *Amer. J. Psychiat.*, 124:141-146.

Prosen presents two cases to challenge the idea that frigidity is an invariable part of the hysterical personality. Both his patients had intense attachments to their fathers, who had functioned as mother substitutes. Both women developed heterosexual relationships characterized by hypersexuality. One patient described her sexual pleasure as an euphoric sense of union or oneness. The other patient used sexual activity as a defense against feelings of disappointment and anger connected to her father. Both patients experienced decreased sexuality after treatment. Prosen suggests that pregenital contributions are important in the hysterical personality.

Zetzel, Elizabeth (1967). The so-called good hysteric. *Bul. Phila. Assn. Psychoanal.*, 17:177-188. Also in: *Int. J. Psycho-Anal.*, 49:256-260, 1968.

On the basis of a review of several hundred psychoanalytical diagnostic evaluations of nonpsychotic women, four subgroups of female patients with hysterical symptoms are described and classified according to analyzability. The four subgroups include: 1) the true good hysteric with oedipal (triangular) conflicts, who is ready for analysis; 2) the potential good hysteric who is less intrapsychically ready for analysis; 3) the patient with underlying depressive character structure disguised by hysterical symptoms; 4) the florid hysteric who lacks the ability to tolerate triangular relationships and to distinguish internal and external relationships; and who is frequently unanalyzable. The author gives a useful description of the specific developmental hazards faced by each of these groups.

Kestenberg, Judith (1968). Outside and inside, male and female. *J. Amer. Psychoanal. Assn.*, 16:457-510.

(See Chapter 18 for annotation.]

Cleghorn, R. (1969a). Hysteria: Multiple manifestations of semantic confusion. *Canad. Psychiatr. Assn. J.*, 14:539-551.

Cleghorn addresses the confusion that has surrounded the use of the term "hysteria." An historical perspective on the etiology, diagnosis, and treatment of hysterical women and men is presented. Dysmnesic (dissociative) disorders, conversion reactions, and the hysterical or histrionic personality are differentiated and delineated.

Cleghorn, R. (1969b). Hysterical personality and conversion: Theoretical aspects. *Canad. Psychiat. Assn. J.*, 14:553-565.

Cleghorn reviews the historical development of the concept of conversion. Conversion reactions are defenses linked to somatization that are used by many different personality types. Voluntary or autonomic innervation can occur in both somatization and conversion disorders. Studies supporting the contribution of oral traits to the hysterical or histrionic personality and challenging the invariability of frigidity are reviewed.

Stein, Martin (1969). The problem of character theory. *J. Amer. Psychoanal. Assn.*, 17:675-701.

Stein questions why a comprehensive theory of character has not evolved with the elegance of the theory of symptom formation. Obstacles include denial of sex differences, prejudicial value judgments associated with delineation of character traits, the lack of an agreed upon theory of aggression and action, and technical difficulties involving analytic limitations in the observation of behavior. In addition to sociocultural forces, he argues that anatomical differences play a decisive role in establishing differences in character through influences from body perceptions and body image and developmental processes. These gender-related character differences are often denied by analysts. He reviews Witkin's (1962) work on increased field dependence in women as compared to men.

Broverman, Inge, Broverman, Donald, Clarkson, Frank, Rosenkrantz, Paul, and Vogel, Susan (1970). Sex-role stereotypes and clinical judgements of mental health. *J. Consult. Clin. Psychol.*, 32:1-7.

This classic article demonstrates that sex-role stereotypic beliefs among clinicians about differing character traits in men and women lead to clinicians' holding a double standard of mental health. [See Chapter 5 for annotation.]

Cloninger, Robert and Guze, Samuel (1970). Female criminals; their personal, familial, and social backgrounds; the relation of these to the diagnoses of sociopathy and hysteria. *Arch. Gen. Psychiat.*, 23:554-558.

Cloninger and Guze examine the relationship between hysteria and sociopathy by describing the social and personal background of 66 female felons. The authors support the theory that certain personality disorders, such as borderline, narcissistic, histrionic, and antisocial personalities, cluster in the same group. Psychodynamics are not discussed.

Sandler, Joseph and Dare, Christopher (1970). The psychoanalytic concept of orality. *J. Psychosom. Res.*, 14:211-222. Also in: *From Safety to Superego*, ed. J. Sandler. New York: Guilford Press, 1987, pp. 301-314.

Early life experiences and modes of functioning are explored in relation to their influences on adult character formation. The relationship between orality and the oral character is emphasized. Oral character traits such as the need to be fed are viewed from an object relations perspective. The authors assert that although psychobiological life experiences in the first year can affect character formation, adult behavior with an oral cast or oral fantasies in the adult do not necessarily have their origin in the oral phase of development. Dependent, oral longings for an object as a provider are at their greatest intensity in the second year of life, during separation-individuation and the anal phase.

Jaffe, Daniel (1971a). The role of ego modification and the task of structural change in the analysis of a case of hysteria. *Int. J. Psycho-Anal.*, 52:375-393.

The author illustrates modifications of ego structure in the extensive description of an analysis of a female hysteric with sexual inhibitions, anxiety, and self-destructive thoughts. Clinical issues such as infantile sexuality and its derivatives, bisexual conflicts, pregenital influences on the oedipal struggle, penis envy, the castration complex, and primal scene reconstruction are illustrated through all phases of the analysis.

Jaffe, Daniel (1971b). Postscript to the analysis of a case of hysteria. *Int. J. Psycho-Anal.*, 52:395-399.

Following the termination of a three-year analysis (Jaffe, 1971a), the patient again sought help. In the ensuing sessions, the patient's magical expectations about her termination, her ego structure, and the further tasks remaining for resolution of the transference neurosis were discussed. Clinical material centers on problems the patient encountered following the birth of her baby nine months after the termination of her analysis. The analysis helped the patient to minimize her losses and maximize opportunities for satisfaction.

Kernberg, Paulina (1971). The course of analysis of a narcissistic personality disorder with hysterical, compulsive features. *J. Amer. Psychoanal. Assn.*, 19:451-471.

Primitive superego introjects, infiltrated by the patient's oral aggression and her projected oedipal rivalry, were seen as protecting the patient from further narcissistic wounds. [See Chapter 22 for annotation.]

Levin, Sidney (1971). The psychoanalysis of shame. *Int. J. Psycho-Anal.*, 52:355-362.

Levin discusses shame as an affect that limits self-exposure, compromises libidinal investment, and discourages aggression by projection onto others. He considers defenses against shame and elaborates on how shame is incorporated into the ego ideal. Clinical examples illustrate such issues as secondary shame about blocking thoughts in a psychoanalysis; shame-induction by the analyst; "shame anxiety," or fear of experiencing shame; "countershame"; shame as a painful symptom to be eradicated; and shame at being teased.

Symonds, Alexandra (1971). Phobias after marriage—women's declaration of dependence. *Am. J. Psychoanal.*, 31:144-152.

Symonds describes a group of previously capable and self-reliant women who married and subsequently developed depression with increased dependency needs, phobias, and constriction of self. These patients equated self-assertion with hostility. Their suppressed hostility led to depression and phobic symptoms. These women had common childhood experiences in which self-reliance and control of feelings were rewarded or were necessary for survival. Dependency feelings were repressed until marriage and then resurfaced as wishes to be totally dependent and cared for.

Green, Andre (1972). Aggression, femininity, paranoia and reality. *Int. J. Psycho-Anal.*, 53:205-211.

Green proposes that freedom in aggressive-drive expression may cause excessive masculine identification. [See Chapter 18 for annotation.]

Wolowitz, Howard (1972). Hysterical character and feminine identity. In: *Readings of the Psychology of Women*, ed. J. Bardwick. New York: Harper and Row, pp. 307-314.

Wolowitz reviews common antecedents and dynamic functions of both feminine identity and hysterical character. He asserts that hysterical character and cognitive-perceptual style have maladaptive and adaptive features. He notes that a nonneurotic form of hysterical character is developmentally appropriate in women. Hysterical characteristics fall along a continuum from normal feminine identity to hysterical pathology. Female development emphasizes emotional responsivity to and from others, so that one's sense of identity and worth as a female may be based on the ability to elicit strong primitive emotional responses from others. Emphasis on emotional responsivity may be normative or pathological, depending on how much the focus on evoking positive reactions diminishes the self-experience. The hysteric's use of sexuality, the substitution of feelings and its relation to a diminished sense of self, and the role of a sense of personal injustice in the development of hysterical character are discussed.

Sperling, Melitta (1973). Conversion hysteria, conversion symptoms: Revision of concepts. *J. Amer. Psychoanal. Assn.*, 21:745-771.

Sperling summarizes the diagnosis, psychodynamics, and treatment of conversion hysteria and conversion symptoms. Material from two analyses is presented. The first case, Mrs. A, is compared to Freud's Dora. Early trauma influenced her fantasy life and choice of a symptom, food allergies. The second case was a 16-year-old with pernicious vomiting that started when she began menstruating. Both patients were able to control their seemingly involuntary somatic symptoms in the first few months of treatment, before the underlying dynamics were analyzed. Sperling proposes that the initiation of the conversion process is related to a mother who encourages a psychosomatic type of object relationship by intolerance of overt expressions of aggression, sexuality, and anxiety in her child. The analyst substitutes for the parental ego and superego and assists the patient in tolerating uncomfortable affects without regressing.

Laplanche, John (1974). Reporter, Panel: On hysteria today. *Int. J. Psycho-Anal.*, 55:459-469.

Beres, Brenman, Green, and Namnum discuss hysteria in terms of 1) definitions that differentiate between symptoms and a personality disorder, 2) classic psychodynamics versus ego-psychological formulations, and 3) oedipal level versus preoedipal level of psychopathology. Gender issues and biases are not addressed. Beres emphasizes the aggressive components of libidinal oedipal conflict. Namnum notes that current formulations about hysterical personalities overemphasize the expression and exhibition of instinctual impulses, a "perverse counterpart" of obsessional characters, rather than the classical concept of defenses against instinctual expression. Brenman describes a case with preoedipal dynamics. The patient's hysterogenic mother was overwhelmed by anxiety, maintained a model of perfection, encouraged negation of psychic truth, and indulged in excessive physical stimulation that promoted greedy dependency and hypersexuality. Green describes hysterical symptoms as a fantasy creation, as a container for primitive defenses against narcissistic injury from rejection, and as a nuclear issue of loss and the threat of depression. Laplanche discusses preoedipal overstimulation from pathological maternal care that induces passivity.

Lerner, Harriet (1974a). Early origins of envy and devaluation of women: Implications for sex-role stereotypes. *Bull. Menn. Cl.*, 38:538-553. Also in: *Women in Therapy*, Northvale, NJ: Aronson, 1988, pp. 3-24.

Lerner proposes that devaluation of women by both sexes defends against intense feelings stemming from children's original dependency on the all-powerful mother and her breast. For men, there is a "defensive reversal" of the early mother-child relationship in which the adult male can feel dominant and controlling over the devalued female. Women collude in this reversal as a way of assuaging their own envy and fear of their mothers. Additionally, women are encouraged to be infantile, dependent, weak, and passive in this culture. Lerner suggests that shared parenting would defuse the original envy and fear of the all-powerful maternal image.

Lerner, Harriet (1974b). The hysterical personality: A woman's disease. *Comp. Psychia.*, 15:157-164. Also in: *Women in Therapy*. Northvale, NJ: Aronson, 1988, pp. 103-118.

Lerner discusses the reasons for the frequent diagnosis of hysteria in women and its infrequent appearance in men. She proposes that preoedipal and oedipal factors are secondary to cultural and social factors. Social and cultural pressures tend to favor the development of cognitive styles and personality traits in women that lend themselves to a diagnosis of hysterical personality on psychological tests and in diagnostic interviews. Diagnostic criteria for and behavioral characteristics of hysterical personality are proposed. Behavioral characteristics include defensive use of repression, imprecise intellectual styles, sociability, the seeking of approval, and emotional lability. Lerner notes that there is great overlap between the hysterical character and the stereotype of the feminine character. She concludes that role pressures can lead to the formation of an hysterical style, whereas women who have repressive styles of defense may not be diagnosed as hysterical. Suppression of intellectual skills and an emphasis on social success can lead women to develop hysterical characteristics. Recent trends in diagnosis of hysterical personality stress psychodynamic factors rather than descriptive symptoms.

Schafer, Roy (1974). Problems in Freud's psychology of women. *J. Amer. Psychoanal. Assn.*, 22:459-485. Also in: *J. Amer. Psychoanal. Assn.* (Suppl.), 24:331-360.

Schafer comments on obsessive versus hysterical morality and on value judgments about traits linked to femininity in Freud's writings. He notes that Freud did injustice to his own psychoanalytic method in discussing feminine traits. [See Chapter 7 for annotation.]

Mahler, Margaret, Pine, Fred, and Bergman, Anni (1975). *The Psychological Birth of the Human Infant.* New York: Basic Books.

The authors describe a greater tendency for depressive moods in women, related to conflicts in the rapprochement phase and the discovery of anatomical differences. [See Chapter 6 for annotation.]

Blum, Harold (1976). Masochism, the ego ideal and the psychology of women. *J. Amer. Psychoanal. Assn.*, (Suppl.), 24:157-192.

Blum asserts that the occurrence of more accessible and ego-syntonic masochistic fantasies in women than in men is not evidence of greater innate masochism, nor is masochism an essential organizing attribute of mature femininity. [See Chapters 7 and 21 for annotations.]

Lewis, Helen Block (1976). *Psychic War in Men and Women.* New York: New York University Press. Also published as: *Sex and the Superego: Psychic War in Men and Women.* Hillsdale, NJ: Lawrence Erlbaum Associates, 1987.

Sources of shame, guilt, and aggression in women are discussed. Women are seen as more vulnerable to shame than guilt. [See Chapter 4 for annotation.]

Moore, Burness (1976). Freud and female sexuality: A current view. *Int. J. Psycho-Anal.*, 57:287-300.

Moore suggests that an inadequately narcissistically cathected genital and its close relationship with object loss may account for an apparently greater object relatedness and dependency in women as compared to men.

Symonds, Alexandra (1976). Neurotic dependency in successful women. *J. Amer. Acad. Psychoanal.*, 4:95-103.

Symonds discusses two types of women suffering from conflicts about dependency. [See Chapter 12 for annotation.]

Ticho, Gertrude (1976). Female autonomy and young adult women. *J. Amer. Psychoanal. Assn.* (Suppl.), 24:139-155.

Ticho asserts that superego identifications with both parents play a significant role in the formation of a woman's sense of autonomy. [See Chapters 9 and 12 for annotations.]

Weissman, Myrna (1976). Depressed women: Traditional and nontraditional therapies. In: *Successful Psychotherapy*, ed. J. Claghorn. New York: Brunner/Mazel, pp. 170-188.

Weissman reviews the data on sex differences in rates of depressive disorders and examines the evidence from controlled studies on the efficacy of psychotherapy in depression. She finds a predominance of depression in women. Nontraditional psychotherapies for depression are described.

Wells, Charles (1976). The hysterical personality and the feminine character: A study of Scarlett O'Hara. *Compr. Psychia.*, 17:353-359.

The author examines the concept of the hysterical personality in relation to feminine character styles that result from social forces. Using descriptive-behavioral characteristics consistent with DSM-II, he briefly reviews the definition of hysterical personality and then adds a psychoanalytic perspective and a theory of cognitive style. The character Scarlett O'Hara is viewed as the prototypical Southern Belle, raised in an ideal climate for the production of an hysterical personality. She fulfills the criteria for diagnosis of hysterical personality from a descriptive standpoint (DSM-II) but cannot be considered hysterical using psychoanalytic criteria or a cognitive style assessment.

Horowitz, Mardi (1977). Hysterical personality: Cognitive structure. *Int. Rev. Psycho-Anal.*, 4:23-50.

Horowitz complements psychoanalytic theories and the psychoanalytic process by adding cognitive formulations and interventions. Cognitive process includes habitual styles of ideation, emotion, and defense, that is, ego functions. The psychoanalysis of a young woman is discussed from the developmental/adaptational, structural/topographic, and dynamic/economic points of view. Repression and denial were the predominant initial defenses. Horowitz conceptualizes hysterical personality primarily as an oedipal configuration. Techniques for the modification of self- and object representations and hysterical cognitive processes are provided. The learning of new, undistorted ways of processing information is a component of working through.

Thomas, Alexander and Chess, Stella (1977). *Temperament and Development.* New York: Brunner/Mazel.

The following categories of temperament are identifiable in early childhood and influence personality development: 1) activity level, or the proportions of active and inactive periods during the day; 2) rhythmicity, or the predictability of such functions as hunger, feeding pattern, elimination, and the sleep-wake cycle; 3) approach or withdrawal speed and ease with which behavior is modified in response to altered environment; 4) intensity of reaction, or energy level; 5) threshold of responsiveness to sensory stimuli, the environment, and human relationships; 6) quality of mood (pleasant and social versus unpleasant and unsocial); 7) distractibility; and 8) attention span and persistence.

Weissman, Myrna, and Klerman, Gerald (1977). Sex differences and the epidemiology of depression. *Arch. Gen. Psychiat.*, 34:98-111.

The authors critically review the evidence that there is a preponderance of women among depressives. After analyzing the various explanations for this phenomenon, they suggest that there may be multiple etiological factors requiring future research. Possible alternative explanations include differences in help-seeking patterns and affective experiencing of stress; biological susceptibility (including genetic and endocrine); psychosocial factors such as discrimination; an association between depression, marriage, and poverty; and female learned-helplessness and dependency.

Chodorow, Nancy (1978). *The Reproduction of Mothering: Psychoanalysis and the Sociology of Gender.* Berkeley, CA: University of California Press.

Asymmetries in family experiences, growing out of women's mothering, affect differential gender identity development in both females and males. [See Chapters 4, 5, 6, 7, 14, and 18 for annotations.]

Krohn, Alan (1978). Hysteria: The elusive neurosis. *Psychological Issues*, Monogr., 45:1-345.

This monograph is divided into five chapters. The first chapter traces the history of Freud's theories about hysteria from the "Studies on Hysteria" (1893) with Breuer, through the abandonment of the seduction theory, the case of Dora (1905a), the "Introductory Lectures" (1916-1917), and finally, the structural theory (1923a). Krohn notes that Freud focused on hysterical symptoms and not on hysterical character. Krohn speculates that this approach reflected Freud's assumption that the hysterical character of his female patients represented an exaggeration of the cultural norm for

Victorian women. Chapter 2 is a broad historical survey of hysteria, including descriptions, definitions, psychological testing and research findings, and theories of etiology, spanning a period from the early Egyptians and Greeks to contemporary psychoanalytic writers. Chapter 3 reviews the multiple etiologies of hysteria. Family dynamics, the effect of loss, and constitutional influences on ego-organizing modes are considered. Gender issues related to development and to the incidence of hysteria are explored. Chapter 4 discusses cross-cultural perspectives on hysteria; it posits that hysterics in all cultures adopt a caricature of an accepted societal role in an unconscious attempt to promote a "myth of passivity." A contemporary form of hysteria uses externalization to locate the source of all personal problems in political and social oppression. Krohn proposes that hysterics contribute to social stability by remaining within the limits of convention. Chapter 5 presents clinical material to illustrate the development of a comprehensive model of hysteria and the hysterical personality. Krohn concludes that in female hysterics the sources of depression are predominantly phallic conflicts rather than oral ones.

Lerner, Harriet (1978). Adaptive and pathogenic aspects of sex-role stereotypes. *Am. J. Psychiat.*, 135:48-52. Also in: *Women in Therapy.* Northvale, NJ: Aronson, 1988, pp. 81-92.

Sex-role stereotypes are seen as having both positive and negative effects. The degree to which sex-role stereotypes are adaptive is inversely related to the degree to which a person has consolidated a stable gender identity. Dichotomous notions of gender are of greater psychological value to male children because of castration anxiety and the need to differentiate from the primary caretaker. Defensive conformity to sex-role stereotypes may shore up a fragile identity. For a healthy patient, the restrictive, inhibiting consequences of sex-role stereotypes need to be analyzed. [See also Chapter 5.]

Lewis, Helen Block (1978). Sex differences in superego mode as related to sex differences in psychiatric illness. *Social Science and Medicine,* 12B:199-205.

Lewis reviews the literature on sex differences in superego modes of functioning and proneness to psychiatric illnesses. Women's superego functioning is characterized by a greater tendency to shame, whereas men are more "guilt prone." Lewis claims that there is empirical evidence for connections between field dependence and perceptual style, gender, depression, and shame. She argues that women are vulnerable to depression because of their shame-prone superego mode. Lewis reviews similar data on the hysterias, obsessions and compulsions, and schizophrenia. She suggests that better attention to sex differences in superego mode can enhance clinical management of the transference and help prevent the negative impact of unanalyzed shame.

Warner, Richard (1978). The diagnosis of antisocial and hysterical personality disorders. An example of sex bias. *J. Nerv. Ment. Dis.*, 166:839-845.

The author discusses similarities in hysterics and sociopaths from behavioral, epidemiological, psychophysiological, and psychometric testing perspectives. He proposes that these character disorders are actually a single condition that has been shaped by cultural forces and stereotypes into different presentations. Hysteria predominates in women, sociopathy in men. This categorization is further reinforced by the sex bias of therapists employing these diagnoses. Implications for clarification of the core problems, treatment options, and research are discussed. Warner confines his focus to descriptive behaviors and speculation about cultural forces.

Bernstein, Doris (1979). Female identity synthesis. In: *Career and Motherhood: Struggles For A New Society*, ed. A. Roland and B. Harris. New York: Human Science Press, pp. 103-123.

Bernstein defines "identity synthesis" as an overarching term encompassing gender identity, ego, superego, ideals, and identifications. [See Chapter 12 for annotation.]

Brenner, Charles (1979). Depressive affect, anxiety, and psychic conflict in the phallic-oedipal phase. *Psychoanal. Q.*, 48:177-197.

Brenner focuses on the relative roles of anxiety and depression in boys and in girls during the phallic-oedipal phase. Depressive symptoms in adulthood emerge as a result of inadequate defenses and may originate in unresolved phallic-oedipal conflicts, as well as in preoedipal factors. Narcissism is discussed in relation to fluctuations of self-esteem through the inevitable narcissistic injuries in the phallic-oedipal phase that result from perceived physical inadequacies of the body. Brenner asserts that narcissistic issues in this developmental stage are crucial for superego formation. [See also Chapter 7.]

Lewis, Helen Block (1979). Gender identity: Primary narcissism or primary process? *Bull. Menn. Cl.*, 43:145-160.

Lewis, exploring the development of gender identity, cites studies from embryology, genetics, anthropology, primatology, the social sciences, and epidemiology to support her conclusions. She views gender-identity development as a process that is influenced by children's relationships with their mothers and fathers, by their social environment and the social inferiority of females, and by biological factors. She contrasts her views with those of Freud, who emphasized parallel but individualistic and narcissistic aspects of gender-identity formation in males and females. Lewis argues that women have an easier task in gender-identity formation, as they only have to recognize they are like their mother, to whom they are attached. Males have more difficulty with gender identity as they must first differentiate themselves from their mother. Lewis cites the greater incidence of gender-identity symptoms in men as clinical justification for her position. She further asserts that men must deny their affectionate nature in order to assume a competitive, masculine role in a patriarchal society. Societal and later intrapsychic devaluation of women's affectionate and nurturing identity predisposes women to problems with shame and depression.

Meissner, William (1979a). A study on hysteria: Anna O. *The Annual of Psychoanalysis*, 7:17-52. New York: International Universities Press.

Meissner reviews data on the Anna O. case (Breuer and Freud, 1893) and the biography of Bertha Pappenheim to argue that a diagnosis of borderline psychopathology with hysterical features was most likely. [See Chapter 3 for annotation.]

Meissner, William (1979b). Studies on hysteria—Katarina. *Psychoanal. Q.*, 48:587-618.

[See Chapter 3 for annotation.]

Sugarman, Alan (1979). The infantile personality: Orality in the hysteric revisited. *Int. J. Psycho-Anal.*, 60:501-513.

Sugarman differentiates hysterical character structure from the infantile personality. He prefers the term infantile personality to that of hysteroid because of the intense oral characteristics and childlike behavior. Sugarman, describing the differences in representational world, ego strength, and cognitive and affective organization, demonstrates that the infantile personality may be differentiated from the hysterical personality along structural as well as phenomenological lines of development. The borderline features of the infantile personality are illustrated with several clinical vignettes of women.

Lerner, Harriet (1980b). Internal prohibitions against female anger. *Am. J. Psychoanal.*, 40:137-148. Also in: *Women in Therapy.* Northvale, NJ: Aronson, 1988, pp. 57-75.

Lerner argues that women tend to be more inhibited than men in directly expressing realistic anger and protest because of both intrapsychic and cultural factors. Anger is considered unfeminine, and socialization pressures combine with neurotic inhibitions against its legitimate expression. Girls' freedom to express anger and aggression, or competitive and self-assertive behavior, is culturally restricted. Two intrapsychic determinants are central in women's fear of their own anger: 1) Women fear their own omnipotent destructiveness. Primitive projections in childhood give rise to an early maternal imago as vengeful, angry, possessive, and restrictive. Identification with the mother may involve this omnipotent destructive image, so the girl defensively shifts to a self-experience of being castrated and helpless, with a related idealization of men. Devaluation of female genitals may also defend against the image of a dangerously incorporative vagina. 2) Separation-individuation difficulties in the mother-daughter relationship may leave women unable to tolerate the sense of separateness and differentness and the loss of connection inherent in the experiences of anger and autonomy. A feeling of separateness promoted by angry feelings evokes separation anxiety and unconscious fears of object loss, so that masochistic solutions such as crying, apologizing, self-criticism, and expressions of hurt and depression may be used in attempts to repair the relationship. Since differentiation involves assimilation of sameness and identification with mother, the girl is likely to feel unfeminine when she is more autonomous. Women have been taught that their value and their identity rest largely on their loving and being loved.

Person, Ethel (1980). Sexuality as the mainstay of identity, psychoanalytic perspectives. *Signs*, 5:605-630.

Person argues that female sexuality is less driven because it is less central to the maintenance of gender identity and may be muted by female internalized object relations. [See Chapter 18 for annotation.]

Stone, Michael (1980). Traditional psychoanalytic characterology reexamined in the light of constitutional and cognitive differences between the sexes. *J. Amer. Acad. Psychoanal.*, 8:381-401.

Biological antecedents of the sex differences in certain cognitive capacities, behavioral tendencies, and personality types are examined. Stone notes the uneven distribution between the sexes of diagnoses of hysterical and obsessional personalities. A more complete model of character development and pathology takes into account biological differences that reflect sexual dimorphism in certain neurophysiological mechanisms, leading to divergent developmental paths. Data is presented from animal studies, studies of abnormal human sexual development, studies on sexual differences in the development of and functional balance between the cerebral hemispheres, and developmental and clinical studies. [See also Chapter 5.]

Thomas, Alexander and Chess, Stella (1980). *Dynamics of Psychological Development.* New York: Brunner/Mazel.

Thomas and Chess's experimental research using longitudinal studies of normal and handicapped children clearly indicates that development plays a central role in influencing individual differences and temperamental qualities and that there is a high level of plasticity in the developmental process. Temperament, like other psychological characteristics, does not show linear continuity over time. The categorization of temperament is derived from a group of behaviors exhibited at any one age. These behaviors result from the interaction of past and present influences in a constantly evolving interactional process. Thomas and Chess assert that their interactional approach to development is more correct than an early psychoanalytic drive/conflict model of character formation, which they find reductionistic.

Anthony, E. James (1981). Shame, guilt, and the feminine self in psychoanalysis. In: *Object and Self: A Developmental Approach*, ed. S. Tuttman, C. Kaye, and M. Zimmerman. New York: International Universities Press, pp. 191-234.

This comprehensive chapter addresses the history of the concept of shame in psychoanalysis, with special emphasis on women. Anthony reviews theoretical questions and offers analytic treatment strategies for shame reactions in women. He agrees with Freud's view of primary shame in women as a reaction to the absence of a penis. Cultural, physiologic, physical, and developmental factors are considered and account for the greater shame-proneness in women. Anthony finds that childrearing techniques of shaming versus those of inducing guilt are etiologic. Reviewing Jacobson's clinical differentiation between guilt and shame, he links both guilt and shame to depression and paranoia. In each of the vignettes of female patients, shame phenomena are linked to the transference feeling of threat of abandonment by the analyst. Tact, flexibility, and sensitivity are required when working with shame issues.

Lewis, Helen Block (1981). Shame and guilt in human nature. In: *Object and Self: A Developmental Approach,* ed. S. Tuttman, C. Kaye, and M. Zimmerman. New York: International Universities Press, pp. 235-265.

Lewis proposes that shame and guilt are derived from social interactions and that men and women differ in their prevailing superego mode. Using object relations theory, she asserts that women, on the basis of same-sex anaclitic identifications, are more prone to shame. She asserts that shame and guilt arise from an interpersonal attachment matrix, and she disagrees with the analytic hypothesis of a superego ruled by guilt rather than by shame. Experimental findings are reviewed with respect to male-female differences in field dependent versus field-independent personality types. Women as a group are more field dependent. Lewis connects this data with more shame proneness, depression, and hysteria in women. By contrast, men tend to be more field-independent, guilt prone, and obsessive-compulsive. Lewis contends that shame and guilt phenomena are aimed at restoring lost or threatened attachments. Shameful states also help to maintain a sense of separate identity. Because women differentiate from a same-sex primary attachment figure (the mother), they are more vulnerable to shame reactions; men have more sexual identity problems. Clinical vignettes illustrate shame reactions and their complicated defenses. In one case, a paranoid projection of rage was used as a defense against feelings of shame; this defense elicited guilt over the shame.

Mahler, Margaret (1981). Aggression in the service of separation-individuation: Case study of a mother-daughter relationship. *Psychoanal. Q.,* 50:625-638.

Mahler describes how girls use aggression in pathologic and normal situations to defend against wishes to merge and to help extricate themselves from the symbiotic bond with the mother in order eventually to attain self- and gender identity. At the same time, aggressive distancing maneuvers are undone or negated by defensive clinging. [See Chapter 6 for annotation.]

Roiphe, Herman and Galenson, Eleanor (1981). *Infantile Origins of Sexual Identity*, New York: International Universities Press.

The authors discuss infant observational research and its relationship to sexual identity. They illustrate how such factors as object loss, congenital defect, and narcissistic or depressed mothering can shape and distort the development of sexual identity during the first two years of life. [See Chapter 18 for annotation.]

Bassin, Donna (1982). Woman's images of inner space: Data for expanded interpretative categories. *Int. Rev. Psycho-Anal.*, 9:191-204.

[See Chapter 18 for annotation.]

Chodoff, Paul (1982). Hysteria and women. *Am. J. Psychiat.*, 139:545-551.

The author explores the relationship between hysteria and women by reviewing biological, ethological, psychological, and sociocultural data. The hysterical (histrionic) personality includes traits of emotional reactivity, superficial seductiveness, interpersonal dependency needs, and a diffuse and global cognitive style. Chodoff contends that hysterical behavior represents an exaggeration of normal behavior influenced by patriarchal cultural pressures. He also concludes that femininity itself is a product of inborn personality differences between the sexes. He notes that the hysterical personality caricatures femininity, in parallel to the sex-role distortion of "machoism," which caricatures masculinity.

Gilligan, Carol (1982a). *In A Different Voice: Psychological Theory and Women's Development*. Cambridge, MA: Harvard University Press.

Women's moral development differs from men's. Feminine attributes include emphasis on caring and concern. [See Chapters 4 and 7 for annotations.]

Lax, Ruth (1982). The expectable depressive climacteric reaction. *Bull. Menn. Cl.*, 46:151-167.

Lax considers a depressive reaction to the climacteric as a normal response to the physical, psychical, and interpersonal changes occurring at menopause that interfere with women's achievement of their wishful self-image. [See Chapter 15 for annotation.]

Lebe, Doryann (1982). Individuation of women. *Psychoanal. Rev.*, 69:66-71.

[See Chapter 12 for annotation.]

Menaker, Esther (1982). Female identity in psychosocial perspective. *Psychoanal. Rev.*, 69:75-83.

Menaker writes that female sexual identity develops in a familial, social, cultural, and historical framework. There are inherent gratifications in femaleness that precede motherhood, but pleasure in femininity may be conflictual. Envy and feelings of inferiority from internalization of maternal and paternal attitudes toward a girl's body, as well as later social influences play a role. Observation of anatomical differences need not produce envy and feelings of inferiority; the sight of a penis might function as a release for receptive sexual desire. Social changes, including career and sexual opportunities, have altered women's self-image and identity. The wish to avoid repeating one's mother's life is not due solely to oedipal rivalry, but also to mothers' disparagement of their own female identity and communication of chronic dissatisfaction. Fear of being merged with the maternal introject leads many women to disavow almost totally their identification with their mothers and to thus undermine integration of their female identity. This disavowal can lead to feelings of emptiness and depression. A loving early bond, corrective experiences, and social support can help resolve feminine identity conflicts.

Nadelson, Carol, Notman, Malkah, Miller, Jean Baker, and Zilbach, Joan (1982). Aggression in women: Conceptual issues and clinical implications. In: *The Woman Patient: Aggression, Adaptations and Psychotherapy*, Vol. 3, ed. M. Notman and C. Nadelson. New York: Plenum Press, pp. 17-28.

This chapter examines the interrelationship between aggression and self-esteem in women. [See Chapter 11 for annotation.]

Notman, Malkah (1982a). Feminine development: Changes in psychoanalytic theory. In: *The Woman Patient: Concepts of Femininity and the Life Cycle*, Vol. 2, ed. C. Nadelson and M. Notman. New York: Plenum Press, pp. 3-29.

[See Chapter 11 for annotation.]

Oliner, Marion (1982). The anal phase. In: *Early Female Development: Current Psychoanalytic Views*, ed. D. Mendell. New York: S.P. Medical and Scientific Books, pp. 25-60.

Anal-phase developmental conflicts in girls are highlighted. [See Chapter 6 for annotation.]

ShaLness, Natalie (1982). Antigone: Symbol of autonomy and women's moral dilemmas. *J. Amer Acad. Psychoanal.*, 10:443-455. Also in: *The Psychology of Today's Woman: New Psychoanalytic Visions*, ed. T. Bernay and D. Cantor. Hillsdale, NJ: The Analytic Press, 1986, pp. 105-120.

[See Chapter 12 for annotation.]

Zinberg, Norman (1982). Changing sex stereotypes: Some problems for women and men. In: *The Woman Patient: Concepts of Femininity and the Life Cycle*, Vol. 2, ed. C. Nadelson and M. Notman. New York: Plenum Press, pp. 43-75.

Zinberg explores gender differences in the ways that cultural changes in sex-roles affect intrapsychic functioning. [See Chapter 11 for annotation.]

Baudry, Francis (1983). The evolution of the concept of character in Freud's writings. *J. Amer. Psychoanal. Assn.*, 31:3-32.

Baudry traces the development of the psychoanalytic concept of character in Freud's writings and relates changes in this concept to Freud's changing theories of neurosis. Major determinants of character include 1) libidinal drives; 2) unconscious fantasies, often masturbatory; 3) identifications; 4) individual solutions to critical (castration and oedipus) complexes; 5) constitutional influences; 6) defense mechanisms, including denial, projection, reaction formation, introjection, and displacement; 7) reaction to trauma; 8) superego; and (9) the attempt to deal with a neurosis or ego distortion. Baudry notes that factors proposed by Freud as constitutional bedrock, such as the resistance of penis envy, have subsequently been shown to be accessible to further analysis. Baudry applies Freud's (1908) ideas about symptom formation and bisexuality to character formation.

Herman, Martha (1983). Depression and women: Theories and research. *J. Amer. Acad. Psychoanal.*, 11:493-512.

Herman delineates five common features used to describe both women and depressed patients in the psychoanalytic literature: low self-esteem; dependency; passivity; aggression turned inward, guilt, or masochism; and heightened emotionality or tolerance of affect. She reviews the psychoanalytic and traditional psychological literature on sex differences and depression and thus provides a useful bibliography. Herman contrasts studies emphasizing biological differences with those emphasizing psychological and cultural differences, including socialization of women to powerlessness as an exaggeration of feminine role. She argues that research on less traditional subgroups may differentiate the effects of sexual stereotypes. College students showed no significant sex predominance in depression in her survey, but women were more likely to be precipitated into depression by interpersonal events and to seek out others rather than withdraw. Herman asserts that depression is not fundamental to feminine psychology, from either biological predispositions or early psychological experiences, as demonstrated by this survey. The five traditional features should be redefined to clarify negative and positive qualities, such as whether dependency is equated with helplessness or with empathic connectedness.

Lerner, Harriet (1983). Female dependency in context: Some theoretical considerations. *Amer. J. Ortho.*, 53:697-705. Also in: *Women in Therapy.* Northvale, NJ: Aronson, 1988, pp. 178-194.

Lerner asserts that male therapists tend to overlook the adaptive function of dependent behavior in their female patients and to underestimate the degree of penalty some women face for independence, such as loss of love and rejection by family members. This view is based on her experience supervising male therapists and in applying a family-systems point of view to psychoanalysis. Manifest dependent behavior in women is distinguished from degree of psychic differentiation. Male therapists who authoritatively press their own point of view by expecting compliance to an ideal of being more independent actually may cause an enactment. Only by understanding the protective aspect of female dependency as a way to safeguard vital emotional ties can more adaptive change be achieved.

Baudry, Francis (1984). Character: A concept in search of an identity. *J. Amer. Psychoanalytic Assn.*, 32:455-478.

Baudry clarifies clinical usages of the concept of character. Character formation and neurotic symptoms are both possible paths for conflict resolution. Character establishes a relation between a superficial attribute and deep structures and represents the core of the individual in relation to the outside world. Baudry examines and provides definitions for the terms character trait, character, and character disorder.

Bernstein, Anne and Warner, Gloria (1984). *Women Treating Women.* New York: International Universities Press.

[See Chapter 4 for annotation.]

De Folch, T. Eskelinen, Adroer, S., Oliva, M, and Tous, J. (1984). Hysteric's use and misuse of observation. *Int. J. Psycho-Anal.*, 65:399-410.

The authors discuss the ability of hysterical patients to observe their own and others' behavior and their tendency to distort and blur their observations in order to avoid change. These patients verbalize fantasies and adapt to the analyst's interpretations in a manner easily mistaken for a good analytic alliance. Instead, their behavior is geared toward establishing an intense, exciting relationship with the analyst. Two female cases are presented to illustrate the authors' formulations.

Kohon, Gerald (1984). Reflections on Dora: The case of hysteria. *Int. J. Psycho-Anal.*, 65:73-84.

Kohon uses a critique of Freud's case of Dora to posit a correlation between femininity and hysteria. He suggests that a hysterical stage characterized by "divalence" occurs in the development of all women. Divalence describes the moment when the subject is confronted within the context of the oedipal drama with the difficult task of change of object. Fixation at this stage produces the hysteric, who is a caricature of the normal feminine woman. Kohon asserts that hysterics are unable to choose between mother and father and are incapable of defining themselves as women or men.

Morrison, Andrew (1984). Working with shame in psychoanalytic treatment. *J. Amer. Psychoanal. Assn.*, 32:479-507.

Shame, reflecting feelings of defect, inferiority, and failure of the self, is seen as the central affect in narcissistic pathology, with internal shaming permeating the treatment. In neurotic patients, shame reflects partial failures of the self, and is reactive to internal conflict, castration fears, and intermixed oedipal issues. Clinical vignettes from the treatments of a female and a male patient illustrate Morrison's approach. In the clinical sequence, shame must be first recognized, accepted, and empathically investigated before exploring conflictual and genetic derivatives.

Person, Ethel (1985). Female sexual identity: The impact of the adolescent experience. In: *Sexuality: New Perspectives*, ed. Z. DeFries, R. Friedman, and R. Corn. Westport, CT: Greenwood Press, pp. 71-88.

[See Chapter 9 for annotation.]

Benjamin, Jessica (1986). A desire of one's own: Psychoanalytic feminism and intersubjective space. In: *Feminist Studies/ Critical Studies*, ed. T. De Lauretis. Bloomington: Indiana University Press, pp. 78-101.

Benjamin explores women's difficulty experiencing their own sexual arousal and agency. [See Chapter 18 for annotation.]

Bernay, Toni (1986). Reconciling nurturance and aggression: A new feminine identity. In: *The Psychology of Today's Woman: New Psychoanalytic Visions*, ed. T. Bernay and D. Cantor. Hillsdale, NJ: The Analytic Press, pp. 51-80.

Bernay asserts that developmental models of feminine identity must include reconciliation of affiliative and aggressive urges. [See Chapter 11 for annotation.]

Jordan, Judith and Surrey, Janet (1986). The self-in-relation: Empathy and the mother-daughter relationship. In: *The Psychology of Today's Woman: New Psychoanalytic Visions*, ed. T. Bernay and D. Cantor. Hillsdale, NJ: The Analytic Press, pp. 81-104.

The concept of the self-in-relation is distinguished from merger. [See Chapter 11 for annotation.]

Litwin, Dorothy (1986). Autonomy: A conflict for women. In: *Psychoanalysis and Women: Contemporary Reappraisals*, ed. J. Alpert. Hillsdale, NJ: The Analytic Press, pp. 183-214.

The conflict between autonomy and women's needs for affiliation and attachment is explored. [See Chapter 12 for annotation.]

Bergman, Anni (1987). On the development of female identity: Issues of mother-daughter interaction during the separation-individuation process. *Psychoanal. Inq.*, 7:381-396.

[See Chapter 6 for annotation.]

Severino, Sally, McNutt, Edith, and Feder, Samuel (1987). Shame and the development of autonomy. *J. Amer. Acad. Psychoanal.*, 15:93-106.

The development of the ability to experience the affect of shame is seen as crucial for growth toward autonomy. Men and women differ in the ways they experience, elaborate, and manage shame because they have had different developmental tasks. The capacity to tolerate shame, like the capacity to tolerate anxiety and depression, is an element of ego strength and is required for further growth. Women tend to experience shame more than men do because of developmental factors, including the narcissistic injury incurred with the discovery of genital differences, the different prevailing superego modes based on same-sex identifications, and the tendency towards better passive tolerance of affects, but with an associated helplessness and use of avoidance as a defense. The management of shame is connected with self-esteem regulation and is necessary for identity formation. Tolerance of shame without regression stimulates adaptation, whereas the inability to experience shame or any deficiency in oneself requires continual defensive efforts. Excessive traumatic experiences of shame, however, can lead to regression and can interfere with the development of autonomy when shame is associated with a sense of destruction of the self, inhibitions, or defensive denial. The need to keep hidden a defective sense of self prevents self-assertion, sexual and aggressive drive expression, and learning from failures. Clinical examples include a woman with feelings of shame about "childlike" aspects of herself that disrupted her sense of self, and an analytic patient who uncovered her shame-laden, repressed belief in a defective body image, which was vertically split off from other aspects of ego development at each stage. The authors agree with Freud that shame conceals an internalized defective body image but disagree that shame is a feminine characteristic.

Silverman, Doris (1987b). What are little girls made of? *Psychoanal. Psychol.*, 4:315-334.

Silverman stresses the early powerful bonding proclivities of females and relates this ability to women's vulnerability to depression and to conflicts about autonomy. [See Chapter 6 for annotation.]

Benjamin, Jessica (1988). *The Bonds of Love: Psychoanalysis, Feminism, and the Problem of Domination*. New York: Pantheon.

The dynamics of dominance and submission in women in relation to masochism and the death instinct are reassessed. [See Chapter 4 for annotation.]

Kestenberg, Judith (1988). Der komplexe charakter weiblicher identitat. Betrachtungen zum entwicklungsverlauf. [The complex character of feminine identity: Observations on the developmental process.] *Psyche*, 42:349-364.

[See Chapter 6 for annotation.]

Lerner, Harriet (1988). *Women in Therapy*. Northvale, NJ: Aronson.

[See Chapter 4 for annotation.]

Levenson, Ricki (1988). Boundaries, autonomy and aggression: An exploration of women's difficulty with logical, abstract thinking. *J. Amer. Acad. Psychoanal.*, 16:189-208.

Levenson proposes that deficiencies in cognitive development are gender-linked to differences in caretaking that block the necessary skills for future abstract thinking in girls. [See Chapter 12 for annotation.]

Meyer, Jon (1988). A case of hysteria, with a note on biology. *J. Amer. Psychoanal. Assn.*, 36:319-346.

The course of psychoanalysis is described for a woman patient who presented with the physical manifestations of hyperprolactinemia, including galactorrhea, amenorrhea, and infertility, as well as psychological conflicts about her anatomy and sexual functioning. She suffered from an hysterical neurosis, with conflicts at all levels of development. The author proposes that unconscious fantasies and conflicts influenced or partially regulated the physical symptoms. As the unconscious meanings of the conflicts were analyzed, symptom remission occurred. This article attempts to integrate psychoanalytic and neurobiologic data and discusses inferences, research difficulties, and future research possibilities.

Silverman, Martin (1988). Gender identity, cognitive development, and emotional conflict. In: *Motive and Meaning: Psychoanalytic Perspectives on Learning and Education*, ed. K. Field, B. Cohler, and G. Wool. New York: International Universities Press, pp. 451-478.

[See Chapter 12 for annotation.]

Weller, Malcolm (1988). Hysterical behavior in patriarchal communities. *Brit. J. Psychiat.*, 152:687-695.

Weller describes four case vignettes of young adult Cypriot women who presented with hysterical episodes. These women came from traditional, repressively domineering, patriarchal families. The high educational aspirations of the families brought the women into close contact with English peers and values, which amplified the tension between the ethos of the immigrant and host cultures. In all the cases, the hysterical behavior provided a secondary gain in allowing the patients to challenge overwhelming parental authority with the impunity of "illness." These cases illustrate the idea that culture contributes to patterns of psychological defense and entry into the sick role. The author discusses the differential diagnosis of hysteria. Weller points to the striking parallels between these cases and Freud's patients Anna O., Emmy von N., and Rosalia H.

Auchincloss, Elizabeth and Michels, Robert (1989). The impact of middle age on ambitions and ideals. In: *The Middle Years: New Psychoanalytic Perspectives*, ed. J. Oldham and R. Liebert. New Haven, CT: Yale University Press, pp. 40-57.

[See Chapter 15 for annotation.]

Fuerstein, Laura (1989). Some hypotheses about gender differences in coping with oral dependency conflicts. *Psychoanal. Rev.*, 76:163-184.

[See Chapter 23 for annotation.]

Grossman, William and Kaplan, Donald (1989). Three commentaries on gender in Freud's thought: A prologue on the psychoanalytic theory of sexuality. In: *Fantasy, Myth, and Reality: Essays in Honor of Jacob A. Arlow*, ed. H. Blum, Y. Kramer, A. K. Richards, and A. D. Richards. Madison, CT: International Universities Press, pp. 339-370.

Freud's view of allegedly feminine traits (e.g., passivity, masochism, narcissism) in relation to female sexuality, gender differences, and social conformity are examined. [See Chapter 3 for annotation.]

Lax, Ruth (1989). The narcissistic investment in pathological character traits and the narcissistic depression: Some implications for treatment. *Int. J. Psycho-Anal.*, 70:81-90.

This article examines the developmental history of pathological character traits, their role in adult psychic equilibrium and maladaptive functioning, and the implications for treatment. Because character traits by definition are ego syntonic, it is difficult to make them a focus of analytic investigation. Lax discusses from a developmental standpoint the reasons why patients seem invested narcissistically in such traits. The initial treatment task is to interpret contradictions in the patient's behavior and attitudes so as to make the traits ego dystonic. The patient reacts with anger related to a new psychic disequilibrium and to a perceived repetition of the analyst/parent forcing the patient/child to give up a valued part of himself. Later a period of depression leads to the patient's mourning the loss of the fantasized grandiose self. Eventually, the patient develops an empathy for himself and a more realistic wishful self-image. Two case vignettes, one male and one female, are used to illustrate Lax's points. Particular character traits were unconsciously selected by the child as a way to maintain loving ties with parents and as an identification with the aggressor.

Bernstein, Doris (1990). Female genital anxieties, conflicts, and typical mastery modes. *Int. J. Psycho-Anal.*, 71:151-165.

Bernstein discusses how feminine genital experiences shape character. [See Chapter 18 for annotation.]

Clower, Virginia (1990). The acquisition of mature femininity. In: *Women and Men: New Perspectives on Gender Differences*, ed. M. Notman and C. Nadelson. Washington, DC: American Psychiatric Press, pp. 75-88.

[See Chapter 11 for annotation.]

Gillman, Robert (1990). The oedipal organization of shame: The analysis of a phobia. *The Psychoanalytic Study of the Child*, 45:357-376. New Haven, CT: Yale University Press.

Gillman discusses details from the analysis of a phobic woman whose shame and fear of exposure were linked to bodily and sexual concerns and reflected complex compromises of impulse, fantasies, and defense. The patient had been sexually overstimulated and exploited as a child. Her preoedipal experiences of shame, associated with loss of control, became incorporated into new meanings derived from oedipal conflicts. The affects of shame and guilt played an important role in the oedipal period as a source of unpleasure and as a signal affect. Signal shame anxiety warded off guilty sexual and aggressive fantasies and motivated character traits, including the renunciation of ordinary caring. Gillman provides a thoughtful review of the literature on shame.

Tyson, Phyllis and Tyson, Robert (1990). Gender development: Girls. In: *Psychoanalytic Theories of Development: An Integration.* New Haven, CT: Yale University Press, pp. 258-276.

A developmental line of gender identity in relation to the contributions from ego, superego, and object relations is traced from infancy through adolescence. [See Chapter 8 for annotation.]

Kaplan, Louise (1991). Women masquerading as women. In: *The Perversions and Near Perversions in Clinical Practice: New Psychoanalytic Perspectives*, ed. G. Fogel and W. Myers. New Haven, CT: Yale University Press, pp. 127-152.

Kaplan asserts that stereotypic femininity in women often has the same underlying structure and analogous purposes as classic perversions in males. [See Chapter 19 for annotation.]

Person, Ethel (1991). The "construction" of femininity: Its influence throughout the life cycle. In: *The Course of Life*, Volume 4, ed. S. Greenspan and G. Pollock. Madison, CT: International Universities Press.

[See Chapter 18 for annotation.]

Tyson, Phyllis (1991). Some nuclear conflicts of the infantile neurosis in female development. *Psychoanal. Inq.*

Tyson describes many possible developmental narratives in female development. She emphasizes a narcissistically valued sense of femininity, resolution of rapprochement conflict, and the wish to retain the love of the idealized mother as central to superego development. [See Chapter 6 for annotation.]

# Chapter 21

# Masochism

Nadine Levinson

Psychoanalytic interest in masochism dates back to an 1870 publication by Lepold von Sacher-Masoch, *Venus in Furs*. Freud, in his "Three Essays on Sexuality" (1905), began discussing masochism and sadism as paired, opposite-component drives, where sexual excitement figures as a derivative of pain. Later, in 1919, Freud emphasized the centrality of unconscious guilt as stemming from oedipal wishes in the dynamics of masochism. He viewed beating fantasies as a regressive substitute for girls' sexual relationship with their father. Although at the time Freud postulated identical lines of development for both boys and girls, this paper suggests different developmental paths at least in relation to masochism. In 1924, Freud addressed the clinical aspects of masochism and described three types: feminine masochism, erotogenic masochism, and moral masochism. Freud viewed masochism in males as a passive feminine wish and as a defense against castration. He contended that girls, upon recognizing anatomical differences, internalize their aggression, change from active to passive, and submit to father to obtain the penis-baby. In 1933, he suggested further that social proscriptions for suppression of aggression in women merely augmented a strong biological tendency toward masochistic impulses.

The culture-bound assumption that women are naturally (i.e., biologically) submissive, passive, and masochistic was elaborated by Helene Deutsch. She contended that masochism was rooted in the psychobiological experiences of menses, defloration, childbirth, and child care. Later psychoanalytic papers do not view women as having an intrinsic propensity toward masochism. Instead, they consider masochism to be the result of a complex relationship between perversion, character pathology, and gender, along with contributions of such salient developmental factors as preoedipal influences, object relationships, feminine superego formation, aggression, and defensive, adaptive, and narcissistic needs. This chapter also includes some general articles on masochism that do not focus exclusively on women but nevertheless prove useful for an understanding of masochism in women and the broader issues of feminine personality structure.

Freud, Sigmund (1905b). Three essays on the theory of sexuality. *Standard Edition*, 7:135-243. London: Hogarth Press, 1953.

Freud discusses masochism and sadism as paired instincts. [See Chapter 1 for annotation.]

Freud, Sigmund (1919). A child is being beaten. *Standard Edition*, 27:179-204. London: Hogarth Press, 1955.

This paper summarizes an exhaustive analytic study of four women and two men and the vicissitudes of their conscious and unconscious masochistic fantasies. Freud sees the beating fantasy as originating in the incestuous attachment to the father. The subject's masochistic fantasy has three phases: 1) father is beating the child (whom I hate); 2) I am being beaten by father (this is the central unconscious masochistic phase); and 3) a number of children (usually male) are being beaten by a father figure. The choice of boys in the final version expresses the girl's rejection of her femininity. The second phase expresses a reaction to the Oedipus complex. Male patients defend against passive homosexual wishes for the father, and female patients expiate themselves for oedipal guilt by repression, regression, and transformation of sadism to masochism. Remnants of the unconscious wish are noted in the associated sexual excitation, which finds its outlet in masturbation. Freud found no exact parallel between male and female cases. This paper is historically valuable as one of Freud's earliest views on masochism as being derived from attempted resolution of the Oedipus complex. Later, in his 1924 paper, he equates masochism with femininity.

Freud, Sigmund (1924a). The economic problem of masochism. *Standard Edition*, 19:159-172. London: Hogarth Press, 1961.

A revision of the metapsychology of masochism is formulated by Freud to better approximate his clinical findings and account for the concept of primary masochism. Three types of masochism are proposed: primary, or erotogenic masochism (sexual pleasure with pain), feminine masochism, and moral masochism. Masochistic perversions and fantasies are linked to oedipal guilt, erotogenic masochism, and feminine masochism. The victim is characterized as taking a passive, feminine position by being castrated, copulated with, or injured by childbirth. Freud claims that feminine masochism is based on the normal expression of the feminine nature. Interestingly, the cases illustrating feminine masochism are about males with neurotic conflicts.

Muller-Braunschweig, Carl (1926). Genesis of the feminine superego. *Int. J. Psycho-Anal.*, 8:359-362.

Penis envy is seen as a defensive reaction formation against the masochistic wish to be violated by the father. [See Chapter 7 for annotation.]

Deutsch, Helene (1930). The significance of masochism in the mental life of women. *Int. J. Psycho-Anal.*, 11:48-60. Also in: *The Psychoanalytic Reader*, ed. R. Fleiss, 1948, New York: International Universities Press, pp. 195-207.

Deutsch questions the origin of the feminine passive-masochistic disposition in women. Deutsch speculates that girls give up active phallic wishes and the clitoris as a phallic organ because of guilt about active sadistic impulses toward the mother and because of their perception of the anatomical differences. The active-sadistic libido that is denied little girls when they must give up the clitoris for the passive vagina is deflected in a regressive direction towards masochism, with the wish, "I want to be castrated by my father." Other masochistic wishes are 1) sublimated into maternity or caring for others, 2) expressed in perversion, or 3) repressed (leading to symptoms of penis envy, narcissism, and particular object choices). Masochism is thus seen as biological destiny. The manifest content of a dream is offered to support Deutsch's hypotheses, yet it only raises a question with regard to her methodology. This paper is historically valuable for Deutsch elucidates and elaborates Freud's early theories of female psychology. Her ideas now may be viewed as based on several false assumptions and misinterpretations of biological and psychological events.

Klein, Melanie (1932b). The effects of early anxiety-situations in the sexual development of the girl. In: *The Psychoanalysis of Children*, London: Delacorte Press, 1975, pp. 194-239.

Klein proposes that the deepest root of feminine masochism relates to fears of internalized dangerous objects. Hence, masochism only reflects the woman's own projected sadism. [See also Chapters 2 and 6.]

Bonaparte, Marie (1935). Passivity, masochism and femininity. *Int. J. Psycho-Anal.*, 16:325-333.

Bonaparte asserts that women must give up their masculinity complex to attain a passive masochistic position. [See Chapter 2 for annotation.]

Horney, Karen (1935b). The problem of feminine masochism. *Psychoanal. Rev.*, 22:241-257. Also in: *Feminine Psychology*, ed. H. Kelman. New York: Norton, 1967, pp. 214-233.

The meaning of a sociocultural perspective and its connection to psychoanalytic theory current in the 1930s is investigated in this classic paper. Biological and genetic factors in female development are emphasized. Horney asserts that specifically feminine forms of masochism may not be pathologic, but simply represent a "normal" female attitude. This paper implies that there are normal and pathologic forms of masochism and questions the origin of masochistic behavior.

Jacobson, Edith (1936). On the development of a girl's wish for a child. *Psychoanal. Q.*, 37:523-538, 1968.

An early female masochistic stage characterized by pregenital and phallic-sadistic strivings and originally directed against the mother and turned back on the self is clinically illustrated in the analysis of a little girl from age three to five years old. Later, in the oedipal phase, masochistic fantasies with the father become prominent. With the girl's renunciation of the wish for a penis, the masochistic and oral sadistic fantasies are lessened. [See also Chapter 2.]

Lampl-de Groot, Jeanne (1937). Masochism and narcissism. In: *The Development of the Mind*. New York: International Universities Press, 1965, pp. 82-92.

Lampl-de Groot discusses factors that make a person seek unpleasure or suffering and how these unpleasant experiences eventually become pleasurable. She proposes that the typical beating fantasy, "I was deprived of my penis as a punishment for masturbation," which is often observed in little girls who have begun to notice anatomical differences, is more tolerable than is acceptance of her physical defect of penislessness. The pleasure in being beaten serves to deny the narcissistic injury of not having a penis. This early fantasy does not originate from oedipal incestuous guilt, but rather from preoedipal phase hostility towards the mother for taking away her penis. Rage towards mother is turned inward as masochism and undoes the powerlessness resulting from narcissistic injury. Moral masochism, or the need to seek punishment and suffering, is the outcome of conflict between a sadistic superego and a masochistic ego.

Reich, Annie (1940). A contribution to the psychoanalysis of extreme submissiveness in women. *Psychoanal. Q.*, 9:470-480. Also in: *Psychoanalytic Contributions*. New York: International Universities Press, 1973, pp. 85-120.

Primarily on the basis of psychoanalyses of two women, the author discusses the dynamics and etiology of extreme submissiveness in women, which she considers to be a perversion. She defines extreme submissiveness as a special dependency of one adult on another, the impossibility of living without the partner, and the sacrificing of all self-interests, including independence and self-reliance, to comply with the wishes of the object. In these women, sexual intercourse is overvalued—yet through coitus, the woman regains, through identification, her renounced narcissism. Anxiety, despair, and feelings of helplessness are experienced in the absence of the object. These women tend to fall in love with men who abuse and humiliate them. Reich hypothesizes that this pathology has its roots in unresolved hostility to the mother and intense penis envy. The hostility is transformed into masochism, is repressed, but then is explosively discharged upon the self during intercourse through identification with a brutal, sadistic man who has the penis. The masochism is also reflected in the woman's self image—"I have no penis; I cannot do anything alone" (p. 91). This is a clearly written, clinically rich article that elucidates some of the dynamic factors contributing to the tendency of some women to be extremely submissive to sadistic, narcissistic men. It deserves consideration in the light of more recent attempts to understand the psychology of abused women.

Thompson, Clara (1942). Cultural pressures on the psychology of women. *Psychiat.*, 5:331-339. Also in: *Psychoanalysis and Women*, ed. J. B. Miller. Brunner/Mazel, 1973, pp. 49-64.

Thompson contends that Freud's concept of masochism is erroneous as it ignores cultural factors. [See Chapter 4 for annotation.]

Deutsch, Helene (1944b). Feminine masochism. In: *The Psychology of Women: A Psychoanalytic Interpretation*, Vol. 1. New York: Grune and Stratton, pp. 239-278.

Deutsch outlines her views of female masochism. She agrees with Freud, who viewed masochism as destructive tendencies turned inward; but Deutsch also tentatively speculates that the origin of feminine masochism is related to an interplay between narcissism and masochism. Narcissistic self-love protects the ego from destructive impulses yet also predisposes women to masochism. The process of self-love protects normal women from inflicting moral or physical pain upon themselves in order to derive pleasure. Only later, in relation to reproductive functioning, are both pain and pleasure experienced. Deutsch defines feminine masochism as erotic pleasure in pain and moral masochism as a consequence of the need to suffer.

The development of masochism and passivity in female personality formation is reviewed. Girls use hostility to help them turn from the mother to the father. An additional source of anger for girls is their reaction to the genital trauma of lacking an active organ, the penis. Mothers and fathers both have inhibiting influences on their daughters' activity. Active games that become erotic influence girls to give up their aggressivity and turn their aggression inward. In order to be loved by father, they renounces their active aims and aggressive drive and take on a passive-masochistic attitude in relation to him. The developmental significance of masochistic fantasies in puberty and adulthood of different masochistic psychopathologic characters and the contribution of masochistic aims to the reproductive function are elaborated. Feminine sexuality acquires a masochistic coloring because of the effects of coitus, defloration, and parturition. Deutsch asserts that masochism helps adjustment of the ego to reality. [See also Chapter 22.]

**Berliner, Bernhard (1947). On some psychodynamics of masochism. Psychoanal. Q., 16:459-471.**

Moral and sexual masochism are viewed as disturbances in object relations where the introjected sadism of the love object is turned upon the self. According to this concept, masochism is viewed neither as an inevitable consequence of the death instinct nor as a component of the sexual drive in a desexualized form (moral masochism.) The disturbances in interpersonal relations are maintained by the masochistic character formation, a defensive formation of the ego against an instinctual conflict between the need for love and the hostility that such love is not provided. Berliner feels that the provocations of masochistic patients express a masochistic wish either to be loved by the feared, frustrating transference object or to punish the love object, thus becoming the active adult victimizer, rather than being the passive child victim. Helpful analytic clinical illustrations, with technical recommendations for treatment, are provided. This remarkable paper adumbrates many later contributions to the idea that masochistic phenomena are rooted in preoedipal pathology.

Brenman, Margaret (1952). On teasing and being teased: And the problem
of "moral masochism." *The Psychoanalytic Study of the Child*, 7:264-285.
New York: International Universities Press.

Moral masochism is discussed in the context of the treatment of a 15-
year-old-adolescent girl inpatient, a "comic teasee" who evokes mistreat-
ment. Brenman elucidates the components of the complex psychological
functions played by the masochistic character, expressing drives, defenses,
and adaptational purposes. The masochistic pattern not only expresses a
need for punishment, but also maintains a balance between primitive
aggressive and libidinal drives. Specific ego defenses, including introjection,
denial, reaction formation, and projection, as well as certain ego-adaptive
functions, are described. These vary with the level of ego functioning. This
is one of the first papers to clarify the confusion about masochism that has
resulted from the blurring of different levels of abstraction in psychoanalytic theorizing.

Menaker, Esther (1953). Masochism: A defense reaction of the ego.
*Psychoanal. Q.*, 22:205-220.

Masochism viewed from the perspective of the ego explains how the
masochistic attitude serves a self-protective function. A vitally needed love
relationship with a cruel object is preserved and defends against feelings of
abandonment and loss, resulting in self-depreciation. Menaker discusses the
case of a female analysand who had early psychic trauma from insufficient
love from her mother and resultant malformation of the ego. The
masochistic reaction is a way to maintain the illusion of ideal mother love
in order to cope with the trauma. The patient blamed herself in order to
protect the image of an all-powerful and loving mother. This paper marks
a shift of emphasis from drive theory to an appreciation of object relations,
patterns of internalizations, and self-preservative functions of the ego as
motives for moral masochism.

Gardiner, Muriel (1955). Feminine masochism and passivity. *Bull. Phila.
Assn. Psychoanal.*, 5:74-79.

This article considers several questions about masochism including: 1)
Is masochism truly feminine? 2) Is it a necessary corollary of passivity? 3)
Should masochism be considered normal for women? Like her predeces-
sors, Gardiner attempts to answer these questions by way of an instinctual
explanatory model. She agrees with Freud that passivity, a biological and
evolutionary factor, is an expression of feminine nature but also disagrees
by stating that masochism is not a normal female characteristic. For both
men and women, she sees masochism as a regression from the genital

libidinal attachment to the father. Therefore, she argues, it is not an essential ingredient of feminine sexual fulfillment. In this article she takes issue with Deutsch's 1925 and 1930 papers that assert that the functions of pregnancy, parturition, and coitus are masochistic and a necessary basis for femininity. Gardiner also disputes Bonaparte's (1935) contention that female maturity is dependent on women's ridding themselves of the infantile fear that has its origin in the sadistic conception of coitus. Gardiner contends that feminine masochism does not exist without passivity, but that passivity can and does exist without being a masochistic gratification. Gardiner's contribution is to separate passivity from masochism and to place the essential functions of women as pleasurable components of the reality and pleasure principles. This article is a departure from the earlier views of feminine masochism, but it antedates the psychoanalytic understanding of the importance of preoedipal developmental issues.

Lester, Milton (1957). The analysis of an unconscious beating fantasy in a woman. *Int. J. Psycho-Anal.*, 38:22-31.

A clinically informative analytic case history shows the vicissitudes of a beating fantasy in the masochistic character formation of a young woman. The case illuminates Freud's formulation in his 1919 paper, "A Child is Being Beaten," that an infantile masochistic perversion can continue throughout adult life, not as a perversion, but as a character disorder. Lester postulates that the patient's lifelong need to be beaten repetitively is a way of disavowing her oedipal competition with her mother and an expression of her attachment to her father. To quote the patient, "It's better to be beaten than to be ignored." The paper is valuable in showing the clinical working through of a masochistic personality disorder. Its theoretical discussion emphasizes oedipal relationships rather than preoedipal formulations.

Brenner, Charles (1959). The masochistic character: Genesis and treatment. *J. Amer. Psychoanal. Assn.*, 7:197-226

Masochism is considered as a paradox that challenges Freud's view that human beings seek pleasure rather than pain. A succinct summary of Freud's papers and later authors is offered. Next, Brenner suggests some formulations concerning the genesis of the masochistic character. Masochism is the legacy of infantile (principally oedipal) conflict and should not be identified as specifically feminine. Finally, a discussion of treatment and specific technical problems is presented. The clinical material is especially useful for understanding Brenner's point that masochistic fantasies and behaviors can serve many developmental functions.

Kestenberg, Judith (1961). Menarche. In: *Adolescents: Psychoanalytic Approach to Problems and Therapy*, ed. S. Loran and H. Schneer. New York: Hoeber Press, pp. 19-50.

Kestenberg asserts that feminine masochism becomes more developed after menarche. [See Chapter 9 for annotation.]

Chasseguet-Smirgel, Janine (1970). Feminine guilt and the Oedipus complex. In: *Female Sexuality: New Psychoanalytic Views*, ed. J. Chasseguet-Smirgel. Ann Arbor: University of Michigan Press, pp. 94-134.

Chasseguet-Smirgel offers another perspective on masochism that incorporates both the Kleinian preoedipal experience and oedipal wishes. Masochism is linked to the guilt that results from wanting to be freed of the omnipotent mother and from repressed aggressive wishes toward an idealized father. [See also Chapter 7.]

Luquet-Parat, Catherine (1970). The change of object. In: *Female Sexuality: New Psychoanalytic Views*, ed. J. Chasseguet-Smirgel. Ann Arbor: University of Michigan Press, pp. 84-93.

This paper traces a Kleinian developmental view of femininity and proposes that the shift from the maternal to the paternal object is primarily accounted for by the onset and progression of a normal feminine masochistic phase during the pregenital stage. Femininity is achieved when girls actively adopt the passive or receptive aim, thus diverting an earlier sadistic drive directed toward their father's penis. If these masochistic fantasies and the strong affects connected to them are not tolerated and accommodated to, girls will suffer insuperable anxiety and ego and drive regression. An alternative meaning of the wish for the penis may be the wish to have it for themselves so they will not be hurt by it. The assumption seems to be made that the wish for penetration is a masochistic wish. [See also Chapter 7.]

Novick, Jack and Novick, Kerry (1972). Beating fantasies in children. *Int. J. Psycho-Anal.*, 53:237-242.

The authors review, concur with, and elaborate on, Freud's (1919) work on beating fantasies in children. They narrowly define the beating fantasy as a fulfillment in conscious or unconscious thought of the sexualized wish to be beaten, usually observed in the form of daydreams (and different from beating games or beating wishes). Two types of beating fantasies are found, a normal transitory one and a fixed fantasy. The transitory fantasies are more often found in girls, arise postoedipally, and give way to interpretation of oedipal strivings. Fixed fantasies occur more in boys, take years of interpretive work to abate, and reflect preoedipal pathology from the first few months of life. In girls, there is first an aggressive beating wish at the anal phase, followed by a sexualized phallic beating game, leading in some latency-aged girls to a wish-fulfilling beating fantasy. Beating wishes and fantasies are viewed by the authors as reflecting positive oedipal strivings as well as punishment for incestuous wishes. These wishes and fantasies help girls move into a passive feminine position with age-appropriate derivative wishes. The authors conclude that for girls, the beating fantasy is a normal transitional component of intense oedipal wishes for the father, whereas for boys, it is rooted in an early sadomasochistic relationship to the mother. The importance of preoedipal determinants and the relationship to the mother in the formation of the fantasy is emphasized.

Person, Ethel (1974). Some new observations on the origins of femininity. In: *Women and Psychoanalysis*, ed. J. Strouse, New York: Grossman/ Viking Press, pp. 250-261.

Person reviews and revises in the light of contemporary research, the formulations put forth by Bonaparte (1935) in her article "Passivity, Masochism and Femininity." Person focuses on Bonaparte's discussion of the origin of female character traits, particularly feminine masochism. In reviewing Bonaparte's views, Person shows that Bonaparte agreed with Freud as to the importance of the discovery of the anatomical difference in the phallic oedipal phase for the development of femininity. However, Person points out that it is not the anatomic difference per se which ushers in the divergence in female personality development, but instead, it is the girl's symbolic meaning and elaboration of the perception. While Person agrees with Bonaparte that feminine masochism is the outcome of developmental issues derived from many sources and serving different adaptive needs, she disagrees with Bonaparte's emphasis on the role of instinct and the importance of the discovery of anatomical differences. Person views specific attributes of femininity, such as masochism, as adaptive neurotic solutions derived from early developmental struggles around dependency, from child-rearing practices, and from sociocultural roles. This paper is valuable as a reevaluation and revision of early formulations on femininity and female masochism. [See also Chapter 3.]

Schafer, Roy (1974). Problems in Freud's psychology of women. *J. Amer. Psychoanal. Assn.*, 22:459-486. Also in: *J. Amer. Psychoanal. Assn.* (Suppl.), 24:331-360.

Schafer asserts that Freud made erroneous generalizations by linking together the terms female, feminine, passive, masochistic, and submissive. [See Chapter 7 for annotation.]

Bernstein, Isidor (1976). Masochistic reactions in a latency-age girl. *J. Amer. Psychoanal. Assn.*, 24:589-607.

This article reports the analysis of an eight-year-old girl with masochistic patterns of behavior and adds to recent psychoanalytic revisions about psychosexual development of women by providing child observation. The analysis of this girl revealed a number of factors that combined to interrupt her progress into and through normal latency. They include repeated early primal scene exposure, represented by arguments between the parents; an inhibition of outward expression of aggression and its direction against her own body; a masochistic oedipal fantasy of penetration and impregnation by the male, which she viewed as potentially destructive to her body; a prolonged, traumatizing illness (ear infection) necessitating a series of painful injections; identification with a suffering mother; and seductive stimulation and teasing by members of her family and her peers. These are factors that can promote masochism in both men and women. Bernstein does not equate masochism with femininity, but rather, sees it as a distorted view of women's role based on unconscious fantasy and reinforced by cultural proscriptions against the expression of aggression in women.

Blum, Harold (1976). Masochism, the ego ideal, and the psychology of women. *J. Amer. Psychoanal. Assn.* (Suppl.), 24:157-192.

Blum reformulates the origins of masochism from a developmental, biopsychological, and sociocultural viewpoint. He provides a critique of earlier works by Freud as well as by other analytic writers, with a reminder of the speculative nature of Freud's propositions. Freud based his model for feminine masochism on observations of men and also by proposing a biological basis for the tendency toward internalization of aggression. Feminine development consisted of a series of disappointments, including penis envy, the castration complex, and oedipal defeat, with unconscious irrational fantasies of defect, renunciation, and envy. Masochism was a consequence of drive endowment, anatomical differences, developmental vicissitudes, and oedipal fantasies. Blum reproaches Deutsch for failing to distinguish between masochistic goals and the enduring of suffering in the service of an ego interest or ego ideal. Sexual receptivity or nurturing are not equivalent to masochistic submission.

Blum asserts that a modern view of feminine personality development now includes preoedipal development of cohesive self- and object representations, identity and gender identity, and the postoedipal evolution of a feminine and maternal ego ideal. The occurrence of more accessible and ego-syntonic masochistic fantasies in women is not evidence of greater innate masochism, nor is it an essential organizing attribute of mature femininity. Men may be more heavily defended against masochistic fantasies and thus more likely to manifest masochistic perversion. Blum views masochism as a residue of unresolved infantile conflict that is neither essentially feminine nor a valuable component of mature female functioning and character. The roots of sadomasochism in girls are traced to pregenital libidinal conflicts, the intensification of aggression from unresolved separation-individuation conflicts and pathological object relations, differences in socialization and its effect on identification, and ego ideal conflicts. [See also Chapter 7.]

Moore, Burness (1976). Freud and female sexuality: A current view. *Int. J. Psycho-Anal.*, 57:287-300.

Masochism in women is ascribed to difficulties in separation-individuation rather than reflecting an aspect of normal development. [See Chapter 3 for annotation.]

Lax, Ruth (1977). The role of internalization in the development of certain aspects of female masochism: Ego psychological considerations. *Int. J. Psycho-Anal.*, 58:289-300.

Using case material from the analysis of three masochistic women who were professionally assertive and achieving but self-defeating in their personal lives, Lax describes the deviant ego structure that results from pathological early object relations and internalizations. Maternal failure to "refuel" led to the women's failure to master the rapprochement subphase, resulting in an unconscious, devalued maternal representation (related to the mother's narcissistic devaluation of her daughter) and an overidealized paternal representation; the patient consciously identified with both of these. The pathologically devalued and aggressive representations were elaborated in sadomasochistic masturbatory fantasies that were multiply determined. These fantasies served as an atonement for oedipal incestuous wishes, expressed identification with the sadistic male, and attained unconscious gratification of positive and negative oedipal wishes through "total enactment of the perceived parental interaction." This article is a valuable contribution to the understanding of female masochism and its relationship to internalization, ego, and superego development.

Benjamin, Jessica (1980). The bonds of love: Rational violence and erotic domination. *Feminist Studies*, 6:144-175. Also in: *The Future of Difference*, ed. H. Eisenstein and A. Jardine. Boston, MA: G. K. Hall, 1980, pp. 41-70.

This paper presents a theory of domination that joins Hegel's analysis of the master-slave relationship to the psychoanalytic theory of self-other differentiation. It argues that erotic domination represents a failure of self-other differentiation. Benjamin explains how the common gender positions of male domination and female submission derive from the opposite positions adopted by each sex toward the mother in the early differentiation process.

Galenson, Eleanor (1980). Preoedipal determinants of a beating fantasy. *Int. J. Psychoanal. Psychother.*, 8:649-652.

Galenson discusses Myers' (1980) paper by elaborating on pregenital factors contributing to the female beating fantasy. She concurs that the fantasy of being beaten by the father is determined by earlier fantasies of being beaten by the mother. She asserts that the wish to be beaten by the mother is common and perhaps universal in girls during the anal stage of psychosexual development.

Lerner, Harriet (1980b). Internal prohibitions against female anger. *Amer. J. Psychoanal.*, 40:137-148. Also in: *Women in Therapy*. Northvale, NJ: Aronson, 1988, pp. 57-75.

This article discusses two intrapsychic determinants for women's anger: 1) irrational fear of their omnipotent destructiveness and 2) difficulties with separation-individuation. Women's self-experience of being weak or castrated is a defensive stance against the fear of being destructive and castrating to both the preoedipal mother and the idealized male. Lerner proposes separation anxiety as the second source of fear of anger. If the girl has not completed separation and individuation, she will not be able to tolerate her own anger since it means separateness. An attempt is made to look at the differences between men and women based on these dynamics. This article does not make explicit an equation between being weak or castrated and being masochistic.

Myers, Wayne (1980). The psychodynamics of a beating fantasy. *Int. J. Psychoanal. Psychother.*, 8:623-638.

The case of a woman with a beating fantasy who was treated in psychoanalytic psychotherapy is discussed. The fantasy of being beaten by the father was found to defensively screen even more ego-dystonic wishes to be beaten by the mother.

Schecter, Doreen (1981). Masochism in women: A psychodynamic analysis. In: *Changing Concepts in Psychoanalysis*, ed. S. Klebanow. New York: Gardner Press, pp. 169-181.

Masochism is viewed as an unconscious or conscious self-destructive behavior that is a pathologic self-protective defense of the ego, aimed at warding off a dangerous conflictual situation. Masochistic defenses are seen to originate more from preoedipal rather than oedipal guilt. Schecter feels that the key to the nuclear conflict is fear of success, which is unconsciously perceived as a threat to the primary dyadic bond with the mother, with accompanying fears of retaliation by her in the form of abandonment. Masochistic defenses undo the fear of object loss, ensure survival, and are reparations to the mother by token submission. Analytic case examples of two types of family constellations seen in the fear-of-success syndrome illustrate the developmental dynamics underlying masochistic behavior. Schecter thinks that girls may be more prone to preoedipal guilt and masochistic defenses than boys, as mother is both the girl's protector and the oedipal rival. This is a valuable paper linking success phobia, unconscious guilt, and masochistic behavior in women.

Lachmann, Frank (1982b). Narcissistic development. In: *Early Female Development*, ed. D. Mendell. New York: S.P. Medical and Scientific Books, pp. 227-248.

Although Lachmann discusses other aspects of feminine development and narcissism, the particular interplay of masochism and narcissism is detailed. Deutsch's theory of female psychosexual development is reviewed, and Lachmann comments that the psychologically healthy woman described by Deutsch would be diagnosed today as having a masochistic character disorder. He reinterprets a dream presented in Deutsch's (1930) paper on masochism, and emphasizes the narcissistic importance of the preoedipal mother and how phallic strivings must be reconciled with preoedipal longings. The masochistic fantasy is viewed as a defensive and compensatory reflection of the preoedipal and unresolved conflict of separation and individuation to avert further regression or self-devaluation. [See also Chapter 22.]

Bernstein, Isidor (1983). Masochistic pathology and feminine development. *J. Amer. Psychoanal. Assn.*, 31:467-486.

This article looks critically at the genetic and developmental factors contributing to masochistic trends and character formation in women. Four analytic cases representing moral and erotogenic masochism are discussed in the context of more recent advances in female psychology. Bernstein uses the case material to illustrate several well-known positions about feminine etiologic developmental factors that increase masochistic tendencies. These include 1) early identification with a mother who negatively regards her femininity, 2) narcissistic injury from anatomical observation, 3) anatomical closeness of vagina and anus, 4) frustration of aggression by society and parents, and 5) inner-directedness. Applying newer formulations about female psychology, this article emphasizes the importance of stable and valued self-representations from the preoedipal phase and from positive maternal and paternal ego ideals. The development of pathological masochistic patterns and character is contrasted with the development of positive, less conflictual aspects of femininity, which progress toward the goal of becoming mature women, capable of sexual, maternal, and creative fulfillment.

Caplan, Paula (1984). The myth of women's masochism. *Amer. Psychol.*, 39:130-139.

Caplan provides a feminist criticism of the psychoanalytic theory of masochism based on apparent misunderstandings about nosology, descriptive versus explanatory theorizing, and a lack of appreciation for the multidetermination of symptom formation. In stating that "women are innately masochistic," she falsely assumes that this viewpoint is a "widely accepted formulation by psychoanalysts," while also ignoring both older and more recent psychoanalytic articles that clarify the complementary role of biological, psychological, and sociocultural dimensions. She makes a useful point that seeking pain to expiate guilt is not genuine masochism, or the enjoyment of pain, but the wish to end the unpleasure. Caplan mistakenly, however, generalizes this dynamic to all female masochistic behavior or fantasies. This article is valuable for some of its well-reasoned counterpoints to early psychoanalytic theories, although it sets psychoanalysis up as a straw man for feminist, socially based theories.

Schafer, Roy (1984). The pursuit of failure and the idealization of unhappiness. *Amer. Psychol.*, 39:398-405.

Contradictory infantile meanings of success, unhappiness, and failure are explored for patients with intense masochistic psychical suffering.

Schafer finds that although there is disturbance in ideal-self development for both men and women, masochism is manifested in men by the unconscious pursuit of failure and in women by the unconscious idealization of unhappiness. He attributes these differences to dissimilarities in early development, to sexist influences, and to reactions to the analyst's interpretative activity. Useful clinical examples with practical technical guidelines are suggested.

Friedman, Lester (1985). Beating fantasies in a latency girl: Their role in female sexual development. *Psychoanal. Q.*, 54:569-596.

The vicissitudes of beating fantasies in a latency-age girl are explored using analytic case material. Friedman's data affirms Freud's (1925) formulation that the perception of anatomical differences initiates the female Oedipus complex. The data from the analysis of a latency-age child support the conclusion that beating fantasies evolve at age five as a defense against oedipal wishes and fears of vaginal penetration and as a substitute for genital sensations. Other issues discussed are onset and effects of vaginal sensations, penis envy, and castration anxiety. This article emphasizes psychosexuality and says little about internalization and the preoedipal mother-father-infant relationship. It is valuable for its rich analytic clinical material.

Kanefield, Linda (1985). Psychoanalytic constructions of female development and women's conflicts about achievement—Parts I and II. *J. Amer. Acad. Psychoanal.*, 13:229-366.

This two-part article discusses the psychodynamics of women's conflicts with achievement and emphasizes the interactive role of intrapsychic, preoedipal, and oedipal development and sociocultural ideals. Kanefield contends that penis envy and masochism are crucial dynamics underlying women's conflicts about their own autonomous achievements. In part I she reviews the early literature and contrasts it with the changing concepts of femininity.

In part II, Kanefield proposes that masochism and penis envy serve defensive functions in female separation-individuation. Like Schecter (1981), she sees masochism as a way of sacrificing the self in order to maintain symbiotic closeness to the mother and to preserve the maternal ego ideal. Success is seen as a breach of the dyadic unity. A review of penis envy and its developmental and metaphorical significance in separation-individuation is presented. Girls may wish for a penis to mask their autonomous strivings and may feel guilty for abandoning their mother and their feminine identification. This article is a salient summary of the concepts of masochism and penis envy and their role in female psychological development and achievement.

Maleson, Franklin (1985). The multiple meanings of masochism in psychoanalytic discourse. *J. Amer. Psychoanal. Assn.*, 32:325-326.

This article describes the growing complexity of the term masochism, which includes an ongoing tension between a wide range of nonsexual and sexual clinical phenomena, dynamic factors, and theoretical considerations. The dynamic factors emphasize the following diverse aspects: harsh superego; conflicts over aggression; anal-sadistic regressions or fixations; disturbances in object relations derived from early deprivation, feminine traits, or unconscious or conscious beating fantasies. The theoretical issues can refer to the death instinct, sadistic and masochistic component sexual drives, and innate feminine proclivities toward pain. Maleson systematically reviews and clarifies the psychoanalytic literature with regard to the origin, scope, and clinical implications of the complex terminology. The tension between metapsychological and clinical perspectives for all forms of masochism is considered. There is a critical exposition of the emergence of the confusing and ambiguous concepts of feminine masochism that were rooted in instinctual theory. For example, masochism was seen either as a component, transformed sexual drive resulting from guilt, as a regression to the sadistic-anal phase, or as a sadistic or masochistic drive reflecting different developmental roots of masculinity or femininity. A comprehensive review is undertaken of the newer formulations that emphasize preoedipal attachments, identifications, and other developmental forces and transformations. Feminine masochism and paired sadomasochistic drive are not congruent with a clinical model of multiple functions that determine human behavior.

Mayer, Elizabeth (1985). Everybody must be just like me: Observations on female castration anxiety. *Int. J. Psycho-Anal.*, 66:331-348.

Mayer illustrates the uniquely feminine fears of genital damage and a masochistic oedipal fantasy of genital loss. [See Chapter 6 for annotation.]

Benjamin, Jessica (1986a). The alienation of desire: Women's masochism and ideal love. In: *Psychoanalysis and Women: Contemporary Reappraisals*, ed. J. Alpert, Hillsdale, NJ: The Analytic Press, pp. 113-138.

In this comprehensive paper, early and later psychoanalytic concepts of feminine masochism are reviewed. Several salient points are raised: 1) the reality of pain is different from the symbolic meaning of pain; 2) masochism is seen as a compromise formation; 3) submission (and its erotization), not pain, is the crucial concept in feminine masochism; and 4) female masochism is a variant of a type of object relationship called ideal love. Ideal love and masochism result from difficulties in girls' early efforts to identify with father to help themselves separate from mother during rapprochement.

Benjamin views masochism and ideal love as alienated attempts to resolve active female desire stemming from difficulty arising from the tension between identifying with and separating from a desexualized mother and between wishing for and being unable to identify with a father who stands for an erotic object of desire. Whereas in normal male development, the paternal identification constitutes an erotic bond that confirms boys' sense of themselves as subject and not object of desire; instead, in female development, girls see themselves as the object in an idealized love relation with their father. The case of an adult woman illustrates the dynamics of ideal love and masochistic surrender to a father figure with whom she wants to identify in order to overcome rapprochement conflicts and separation anxiety stemming from her preoedipal relationship with her mother. Pathological idealization and masochism are thus the products of incomplete separation-individuation and the need to supply self-structure.

Benjamin, Jessica (1986b). A desire of one's own: Psychoanalytic feminism and intersubjective space. In: *Feminist Studies/ Critical Studies*, ed. T. De Lauretis. Bloomington: Indiana University Press, pp. 78-101.

[See Chapter 18 for annotation.]

Galenson, Eleanor (1986b). Early pathways to female sexuality in advantaged and disadvantaged girls. In: *The Psychology of Today's Woman: New Psychoanalytic Visions*, ed. T. Bernay and D. Cantor. Hillsdale, NJ: The Analytic Press, pp. 37-48.

Galenson discusses the different patterns of gender-identity formation in the second year of life in advantaged girls and contrasts these to the distortions in development in disadvantaged girls. Data are derived from a longitudinal study of 70 normal families and 8 disadvantaged ones. An early genital phase, occurring at 16-24 months, was observed. Infants who suffered insult or bodily damage or an impaired maternal relationship developed more severe reactions to the awareness of anatomical differences. In the disadvantaged girls, aggression and a sadomasochistic tie to mother were intensified rather than attenuated because the father figure was distant or absent. Galenson suggests that the erotic turn to father helps girls disengage from a disturbed, ambivalent maternal attachment. This paper is valuable in reviewing and contrasting gender-identity development in infancy and linking the role of the absent father and the ambivalently viewed mother to sadomasochistic sexuality.

Grossman, William (1986). Notes on masochism: A discussion of the history and development of a psychoanalytic concept. *Psychoanal. Q.*, 55:379-413.

Masochism is reviewed and reconsidered in relation to the evolution of psychoanalytic theory and technique. It is suggested that masochism should no longer be used as a superordinant explanatory concept, because other psychoanalytic issues, such as the development of the regulation of aggression, internalization of authority, and restoration of narcissistic equilibrium, may be more salient. This article is essential reading for the understanding, usage, definitions, and nosology of masochism. From that understanding, a critical study of masochism and women can be undertaken.

Novick, Kerry and Novick, Jack (1987). The essence of masochism. *The Psychoanalytic Study of the Child*, 42:353-384. New Haven, CT: Yale University Press.

From their study (Novick and Novick, 1972) of beating fantasies in children, the authors found two types of beating fantasies; a normal transitory fantasy and a fixed fantasy. On the basis of Freud's (1919) idea that the beating fantasy is the essence of masochism, and using the model of the fixed beating fantasy, the authors trace the developmental line of masochism. Child observation and case material from 11 children with beating fantasies and child and adult analyses serve as the data base that elucidates the dynamic, adaptive, and genetic points of view.

The Novicks suggest that masochistic pathology grows out of a myriad of painful externalizations of blame, failure, and devalued aspects of the parent onto the child that are elaborated at each developmental stage. Autonomy is compromised as the mother needs to see the child as helpless. Children struggle to maintain the image of an idealized, loving mother and deal with their aggression by denying any signs of hostility. Fathers of girls with fixed beating fantasies usually encourage denigration of the mothers and are involved in overstimulating relationships from the oedipal phase on; the result is an intense, bisexual conflict and penis envy as a component of the masochistic pathology. The pathology of delusions of omnipotence and the libidinization of painful experiences persists in adult patients. The Novicks did not find a necessary relationship between masochism and feminine functions. Technical implications and guidelines for interpretation are given. They conclude by viewing masochism as an adaptation to an early disturbance in the relationship with the mother, a defense against destructive wishes toward the object, and a gratification in the participation in a sadomasochistic relationship.

Simons, Richard (1987). Psychoanalytic contributions to nosology: Forms of masochistic behavior. *J. Amer. Psychoanal. Assn.*, 35:583-608.

This article summarizes current psychiatric nosology and uses masochistic behavior as a clinical example of how psychoanalytic understanding can enrich the evolution of psychiatric nosology. Simons reviews the various forms of masochistic behavior. He suggests that without needing to adhere to Freud's metapsychological speculations or theories, masochistic behavior can be thought of as separated into behavior in which there is a conscious link of pain with pleasure, and behavior where that link is predominantly unconscious. Both unconscious and conscious categories of masochistic behavior exist in normal and pathologic forms. Normal masochistic behavior is evident at all developmental stages where pain and loss accompany individuation. Simons regards feminine masochism as normal, but only in those normal female psychosexual experiences where pain and pleasure may be consciously linked, such as during menses, first intercourse, and childbirth. Useful clinical vignettes assist differential diagnosis of masochistic personality disorders and moral masochism.

Benjamin, Jessica (1988). *The Bonds of Love: Psychoanalysis, Feminism, and the Problem of Domination.* New York: Pantheon.

[See Chapter 4 for annotation.]

Cooper, Arnold (1988). The narcissistic-masochistic character. In: *Masochism: Current Psychoanalytic Perspectives*, ed. R. Glick and D. Meyers. Hillsdale, NJ: The Analytic Press, pp. 117-138.

This article proposes that narcissism and masochism are intimately intertwined in both normal and pathological development and in clinical presentation. Cooper further emphasizes the centrality of preoedipal narcissistic development with ubiquitous masochistic defenses as a key to the understanding of this clinical finding. A brief review of the literature on definitions and theories of masochism as proposed by Freud, Rado, Brenner, and Bergler is saliently summarized. Cooper links narcissism and masochism by looking at the pleasure and narcissistic benefits of experiencing pain. He concludes: 1) pain is a necessary concomitant of separation and individuation and fosters self-definition; 2) the inevitable disappointments of separation-individuation that threaten omnipotent control as the child feels passive and helpless are seen as narcissistic injuries; and 3) the child responds by defensively restoring self-esteem by disavowing passivity and helplessness and reasserts control by making the suffering ego syntonic: "I am frustrated because I want to be." Alternatively, narcissistic equanimity is maintained by the child's equating the familiar with the pleasurable to deal with more than ordinary pain or displeasure. It is postulated that masochistic-narcissistic defenses are not used to achieve fantasied reunion with the gratifying and loving preoedipal mother, but rather for control over the cruel or damaging mother. The pleasure is not oedipal, genital-sexual, but preoedipal. A clinical vignette from the psychoanalysis of a masochistic young woman illuminates the relationship of the narcissistic importance of her self-representation as an abandoned martyr. Her own provocative behavior produced a repetition of the preoedipal painful relationship with her mother but with the hidden gratification of autonomy, narcissistic control, and masochistic satisfaction.

Galenson, Eleanor (1988). Masochism, protomasochism: Early roots of masochism. In: *Masochism: Current Psychoanalytic and Psychotherapeutic Contributions*, ed. R. Glick and D. Meyers. Hillsdale, NJ: The Analytic Press, pp. 189-204. Also in a shortened version as: The precursors of masochism. In: *Fantasy, Myth, and Reality: Essays in Honor of Jacob A. Arlow*, ed. H. Blum, Y. Kramer, A. K. Richards, and A. D. Richards. Madison, CT: International Universities Press, 1989, pp. 371-380.

Galenson postulates that masochism, or the capacity for experiencing pleasure in pain, is preceded by a protomasochistic phase that takes place in the latter part of the first year and the second year of life. This article emphasizes the multiple sources of aggression from developmental conflicts, environmental stress, and aggressive conflicts of the parents, which interfere with the capacity for internalization of positive parental attributes. Galenson states that these early aggressive experiences are transformed into a protomasochistic precursor of masochism as they give rise to an unduly harsh maternal response, which is then identified with or defended against by the infant. The resulting distortion in the development of aggression leads to a variety of clinical syndromes: 1) psychosis in physically abused children, 2) psychosis in young infants, 3) deviant patterns of sexual development in females, 4) failure to thrive, and 5) infantile autism. These clinical syndromes are characterized by a predominantly sadomasochistic object relationship, with a basic instability in the sense of masculinity in boys and excessive passivity with regressive clinging to the mother in girls. In proposing that girls are more masochistic than boys, Galenson elevates description of clinical phenomena to explanatory levels.

Glick, Robert and Meyers, Donald (ed.) (1988). *Masochism: Current Analytic Perspectives*. Hillsdale, NJ: The Analytic Press.

This book contributes to the psychoanalytic understanding and clinical treatment of masochism and its many levels and functions. Glick and Meyers provide a clear and comprehensive review of the early theories of masochism from Sacher-Masoch to Freud through post-Freudian contributions. It is from this historical framework that the current perspectives on masochism are considered by the different authors. Separation-individuation, preoedipal and oedipal conflict resolution, developmental factors, narcissism and self-psychological experiences, ego-psychological, and object relational perspectives are all represented.

Meyers, Helen (1988). A consideration of treatment techniques in relation to the functions of masochism. In: *Masochism: Current Analytic Perspectives*, ed. R. Glick and D. Meyers, Hillsdale, NJ: The Analytic Press, pp. 175-188.

Masochism is considered as multiply determined and grounded in different developmental levels with different functions and meanings that vary from patient to patient and within the same patient from time to time. Meyers outlines the various functions of masochism and makes recommendations for clinical technique with such patients. These separate functions include masochism and guilt, maintenance of object relations, masochism and self-esteem, and masochism and self-definition. Feminine masochism is separately discussed with a concise critique of Freud and Deutsch, who narrowly saw masochism in relation to false assumptions about female biology and women's far greater intrinsic need to suffer than exists in men. Meyers states that there is no more masochism among women than men, but "perhaps it surfaces in different areas" because of differences in the contents of ego ideals and superego. She distinguishes between faithful support of a loved one and masochistic renunciation. Meyers raises questions about the effects of the analyst's gender on the availability of preoedipal masochistic transferences.

Montgomery, Jill and Greif, Ann (1989). *Masochism: The Treatment of Self-Inflicted Suffering*. Madison, CT: International Universities Press.

Based on a five-year analytic study of masochism, the authors focus on their clinical experiences. Three premises about masochism are proposed: 1) masochism is viewed as having real precipitants, with real effects on interpersonal relationships and self representations, 2) an inadequate sense of self is always coupled with a sense of pain and oppression, and 3) dysfunctions in living result from failure in symbolic activity and the inability to transform events into personal experiences. Traditional psychoanalytic formulations and interpretations stressing aggression, instinctual gratification, and superego retaliation are demonstrated to be inadequate in light of interpretations that conceptualize masochism as a necessary part of an object relationship. The patients continue to suffer in order to stay alive and attached, staving off identity diffusion and psychotic regression. Masochism is seen as derived from early maternal identifications, where the mother's own life experiences of shame, regret, and depression foster the same character traits in her daughter. These character tendencies are not rooted in penis envy, but rather in the wish to be loved by the preoedipal mother. Most of the chapters present case material of women with masochistic disorders.

Person, Ethel, Terestman, Nettie, Myers, Wayne, and Goldberg, Eugene (1989). Gender differences in sexual behaviors and fantasies in a college population. *J. Sex and Marital Ther.*, 15:187-198.

Most female students did not report patterns of masochistic or passive behavior or fantasies. [See Chapter 18 for annotation.]

Lax, Ruth (1992). A variation of Freud's theme in "A Child is Being Beaten": Mother's role—Some implications for superego development. *J. Amer. Psychoanal. Assn.*

Lax discusses the masturbatory beating fantasies of several female patients treated by psychoanalysis. The fantasies followed slightly different patterns with contents different from those found by Freud (1919). Lax finds that the beating fantasy is multidetermined. She proposes three important dynamics: 1) the girl is punished but also gratified by the beating; 2) the father, by way of the beating, commits the incestuous act; and 3) the mother, not the father, figures as the punisher. Lax asserts that the unconscious perception of mother as punisher has profound developmental effects on superego structuralization and contents. The superegos of her female patients reflected extreme harshness stemming from reintrojection of the patients' rage toward their mothers and identification with their violating fathers. Girls' superegos are formed by identification with the aggressor-mother and manifested by "thou shall and shall not," and also by identification with the feminine mother, who desires and wins the father. Thus, the fantasy of the punishing mother forms the moral nucleus of the superego.

# Chapter 22

# *Narcissism*

Brenda Clorfene Solomon and Diane Martinez,
with Nadine Levinson and Eleanor Schuker

This chapter includes articles about women and narcissism as seen from various psychoanalytic perspectives. The term narcissism has been used differently by diverse psychoanalytic writers over the years, resulting in a lack of conceptual clarity. Freud (1914) discussed the concept of narcissism by considering its primary and secondary states and by defining narcissism as the libidinal investment of the ego with its specific attributes of self-regard and the ego ideal. He proposed a developmental schema for narcissism that involved an antithesis between libido directed toward the self (ego) or toward objects, with symptoms related to excessive investment in either direction. Freud used both developmental and energic concepts of narcissism in delineating its participation in normal sexual development, perversions, schizophrenia, and hypochondriasis. He also explicated the connections between narcissism, penis envy, and the development of femininity. Freud (1914, 1925, 1933) felt that narcissism was a universal feminine character trait and that women were more narcissistic than men because they inevitably felt castrated.

Hartmann's redefinition of narcissism as the libidinal investment of the self (1950) shifted the focus on the concept of narcissism to an ego psychological perspective. Object relations theorists shifted psychoanalytic interest toward object representations, the ego, and the self. Jacobson (1964) espoused that clear differentiation from others reflected the achievement of drive regulation and neutralization. She followed Hartmann's position that the self emerges vis-à-vis objects, and her work serves as a basis for many theorists who envision self and objects in terms of multiple developing relationships.

In the 1960s, many psychoanalysts noted that narcissistic character defenses occur in patients of both sexes and often originate with developmental vicissitudes of separation-individuation. Galenson and Roiphe (1976) observed that discovery of anatomical differences occurs before a stable sense of self and object have been consolidated. They suggest that genital anxieties may be indissolubly linked with anxieties about object loss and the intactness of the self. Thus, feelings about genital anatomy may resonate with narcissistic issues.

More recently, psychoanalytic theories on narcissism have been substantially enriched by the contrasting contributions of Kohut and Kernberg. There is vigorous debate about the relative merits of self-psychological or standard psychoanalytic approaches to the analysis of narcissistic phenomena at each developmental level. (See P. Kernberg, 1971 or Freyberg, 1984.) Kohut's contribution, like Deutsch's (1944, 1945) stresses the developmental and adaptive aspects of narcissism. This contribution provides a corrective balance to Freud's emphasis on narcissistic injury derived from recognition of anatomical differences as the central issue in female development. Self psychologists emphasize that a positive narcissistic investment in being female contributes to self-esteem and is derived from adequate selfobject experiences in early relationships. Specific narcissistic issues for women at each developmental phase are only now beginning to be elaborated. Recent psychoanalytic literature focusing on distinctive narcissistic factors in the development of female children explicates the relevant features of the preoedipal mother-daughter relationship, narcissistic vulnerabilities at each level of psychosexual development, the components of superego formation in girls, the multiple meanings of penis envy, and the mother's and father's roles both as idealizable and emotionally responsive objects. Because narcissistic issues are present in each developmental phase, articles in other chapters may prove relevant to narcissistic issues in female psychology. [See especially Chapters 6, 7, 9, 13, 14, 18, and 26.]

**Freud, Sigmund (1914). On narcissism: An introduction. *Standard Edition*, 14:69-102. London: Hogarth Press, 1959.**

Proposing both developmental and energic concepts for narcissism, Freud struggles with the definitions of primary and secondary narcissism. He recognizes not only narcissism's regular occurrence in human sexual development and erotic life, but also its presence in the perversions, schizophrenia, and hypochondriasis. Narcissism is viewed both as a developmental stage midway between autoeroticism and object love and as a drive that oscillates between ego libido and object libido. Thus, object love (the state of being in love) is depleted in direct proportion to an increase in ego libido and vice-versa. A dual instinct theory, comprising ego instincts (nonsexual, self-preservative) and sexual instincts is proposed.

In part II, Freud elaborates on the narcissistic importance of children's earliest sexual objects. Freud outlines two types of object choice, an anaclitic (attachment) and a narcissistic type. Men characteristically choose the anaclitic type, attaching to a woman who feeds or protects. Women usually chose the narcissistic type of object love, based on what they themselves are, what they were, or what they would like to be. Women tend toward narcissistic object choice as a perpetuation of their childhood narcissism. At puberty, girls experience an intensification of primary narcissism and have a need to be loved. Freud asserts that women can experience complete object love after bearing a child, as a part of their own body, which they can then give their complete love. Another road to object love for women is by masculine identification. In part III, Freud briefly mentions the developmental experience of penis envy and its narcissistic impact on femininity. [See also Chapters 1 and 13.]

Freud, Sigmund (1916). Some character types. *Standard Edition*, 14:310-333. London: Hogarth Press, 1955.

This early paper makes reference to a woman's need to be special. [See Chapter 1 for annotation.]

Andreas-Salomé, Lou (1921). The dual orientation of narcissism. *Psychoanal. Q.*, 1962, 31:1-30. (Translated from *Narzissmus als Doppelrichtung* by Stanley Leavy. *Imago*, 7:361-386.)

Andreas-Salomé emphasizes that the concept of primary narcissism includes not only self-love, but also the persistent feeling of identification with the totality. [See Chapter 2 for annotation.]

Harnik, Jeno (1924). The various changes undergone by narcissism in men and women. *Int. J. Psycho-Anal.*, 5:66-83.

Harnik proposes that girls substitute whole body narcissism for the "loss" of the penis at puberty. [See Chapter 2 for annotation.]

Freud, Sigmund (1925). Some psychical consequences of the anatomical distinction between the sexes. *Standard Edition*, 19:243-258. London: Hogarth Press, 1953.

Freud asserts that one of the consequences of girls' reaction to the anatomic differences is penis envy and a conviction that they are castrated. The resulting narcissistic vulnerability and sense of inadequacy is a crucial factor in girls' development of femininity. [See also Chapter 1.]

Freud, Sigmund (1933). Femininity. *Standard Edition*, 22:112-135. London: Hogarth Press, 1953.

Narcissistic aspects of female character are briefly discussed. [See Chapter 1 for annotation.]

Lampl-de Groot, Jeanne (1937). Masochism and narcissism. In: *The Development of the Mind*. New York: International Universities Press, 1965, pp. 82-92.

The girl's masochistic wish to be punished for having masturbated avoids or denies the narcissistic injury of not having a penis. [See Chapter 21 for annotation.]

Deutsch, Helene (1944, 1945). *The Psychology of Women: A Psychoanalytic Interpretation*, Vol. 1 and 2. New York: Grune and Stratton.

Deutsch, like Freud and Hartmann, defines narcissism as self-love. However, her exploration of the "feminine core" and feminine development goes beyond this restricted definition and presages a self-psychological perspective. Deutsch views narcissism as having both healthy and pathological aspects. Narcissism is the basis for self-confidence in women and protects the personality against masochistic tendencies that derive from early development and the "genital trauma" in the phallic phase. In Volume I, Deutsch discusses feminine development and personality. The first four chapters organize feminine development through the beginning of menstruation. In "Puberty and Adolescence," Deutsch discusses the importance of narcissism for maturation during this developmental phase. Her definition of "narcissistic" reflects the ego's drawing advantages for itself. She sees this dynamic as playing a particular role in adolescence by "extending the limits" of adolescent girls' weak egos and increasing their self-confidence. Relationships with girlfriends also enhance adolescent narcissism. The negative aspects of a heightened narcissistic focus in adolescence account for difficulties in interpersonal relations, owing to the associated disappointments and frustrations. Interestingly, Deutsch cautions against viewing adolescent girls' wishes to be loved by many men as narcissistic, in that their goal may be to win the respect of their parents as adult females. Deutsch also describes mother-daughter relationships in which the daughter is unable to resolve her dependency conflicts. The girl puts every gesture and experience before the mother or her substitute, and her happiness is absolutely dependent upon this evaluation. (Deutsch views these actions as a consequence of adolescent narcissism and anticipates a self-psychological view.)

In "Menstruation," Deutsch discusses narcissistic reactions to the bodily changes of adolescence that may lead a girl to enhance or to neglect her physical attractiveness or to have anxieties about her genitals that may expand into a generalized hypochondriasis. Deutsch devotes individual chapters to feminine eroticism, passivity, and masochism. In "Eroticism: The Feminine Woman," Deutsch offers a nonpejorative context to narcissism in women. The appeal of "erotic feminine types" is derived from an interplay between healthy narcissism and masochism. Deutsch asserts that the heightened self-confidence that is characteristic of these women defends against the narcissistic mortification of penis envy. Yet, opposing other psychoanalytic theorists, Deutsch does not see penis envy as the main source of feminine narcissism. In "Feminine Masochism," she further elaborates her thesis that narcissism balances feminine masochism and extends this view into a discussion of the role each plays in relation to reproductive functions. In "The Active Woman," she reiterates her position that the narcissistic mortification of seeing the penis in the phallic phase, while producing injured self-esteem and masochistic tendencies, is not the only factor contributing to feminine development. In particular, she stresses the shaping of feminine development by biology.

In Volume II, Deutsch explores the psychological impact of the multiple roles women play as "servant of the species." Narcissism is referred to in most of the chapters. In "Motherhood, Motherliness and Sexuality," she notes how the narcissistic wish to be loved is transferred from the ego of the woman to her children. Depending on the woman's personality, she may experience her ego as having been expanded, or she may feel restricted and impoverished. In the "Psychology of the Sexual Act," Deutsch proposes that men have an impervious physiological urge, accompanied by psychical elements, to complete the sexual act. In contrast, for women, the process is primarily psychological and supported by biological factors. Deutsch describes sexual wishes in women as consisting of yearnings for erotic pleasure, narcissistic needs to be loved, and a masochistic striving to give to others. Feminine women, who are character-ized by a struggle for balance between the narcissistic forces of self-love and the masochistic forces of giving, find fulfillment in the sexual act in relation to their partners and potential children.

In "Pregnancy," Deutsch discusses the role of the "narcissism of pregnancy" in erasing the boundaries between "the I" and "the you." This narcissism persists after the birth of a child to the extent that the child is loved as part of the mother's self. In "Confinement and Lactation," Deutsch notes that for some time after delivery, the mother's world is perceived as identical with her ego. Narcissistic self-love can be strengthened later on during motherhood as a defense against excessive masochism, particularly in schizoid women, who are disappointed in their expectation that their children will release them from their inner rigidity and coldness. In "The Mother-Child Relation," maternal love is depicted as a peculiar mixture of narcissism and object love or as the most selfless self-love. In "Stepmothers," Deutsch proposes that it is the nature and degree of a woman's narcissism which determines her fate as a stepmother. In "The Climacterium," menopause is seen as a narcissistic mortification to women, that sets up a struggle for the preservation of femininity in which the forces of the ego are mobilized to achieve a better adjustment to reality. Deutsch discusses how different types of women handle these developmental conflicts. A certain form of feminine narcissism seems to constitute a psychical cosmetic, which allows some women to remain young and beautiful into old age. [See also Chapters 2, 9, 14, 15, and 18.]

Hartmann, Heinz (1950). Comment on the psychoanalytic theory of the ego. In: *Essays on Ego Psychology*. New York: International Universities Press, 1964, pp. 113-141.

Hartmann makes a significant early attempt to clarify the psychoanalytic definition of the self by equating the self with one's own person. He differentiates the self from objects, just as the ego, as a psychic system was differentiated from other substructures of the personality. Hartmann's use of the term "objects" refers to cathexes of representations and not to cathexes of real people, just as Freud himself originally differentiated between mental representations of objects and the objects themselves.

Hartmann, Heinz (1953). Contributions to the metapsychology of schizophrenia. In: *Essays on Ego Psychology*. New York: International Universities Press, 1964, pp. 182-206.

Hartmann notes that object relations must proceed from an initial ability to distinguish between objects and activities to a later differentiation between the activity and the object to which the activity is directed. Ultimately, self becomes differentiated from objects.

Reich, Annie (1953). Narcissistic object choice in women. *J. Amer. Psychoanal. Assn.*, 1:22-44. Also in: *Annie Reich: Psychoanalytic Contributions*. New York: International Universities Press, 1973, pp. 179-208.

Reich's paper applies Freud's ideas on narcissistic object choice to women. Two categories of object choice are clinically detailed, women who manifest extreme submissiveness and women who experience multiple transitory infatuations. Reich hypothesizes that narcissistic object choices for women are based on regression in response to the discovery of the lack of a penis; the motive for the choice of object is the restoration of self-esteem with the aggrandized phallus. Reich sees these attachments as based predominantly on homosexual fixations stemming from the preoedipal mother-daughter relationship. [See also Chapter 7.]

Blitzer, John and Murray, John (1964). On the transformation of early narcissism during pregnancy. *Int. J. Psycho-Anal.*, 45:89-97.

The authors review the literature on the meaning of delivery as a narcissistic injury and the role of pregenital fantasies in the genesis of postpartum psychosis and depression. [See Chapter 14 for annotation.]

Jacobson, Edith (1964). *The Self and the Object World.* New York: International Universities Press.

Jacobson employs the economic definition of narcissism as the libidinal cathexis of the self and does not devote her specific focus to female development. Nevertheless, many of her comments are relevant to understanding female development and reflect a broader perspective of narcissism and the development of a cohesive self. In Chapter 5, Jacobson discusses the impact of girls' perception of their genitals as damaged. This perception leads to an increased narcissistic involvement with their face and figure. She speculates that the revival of infantile castration conflicts by menstruation and the resultant withdrawal of narcissistic involvement from the genitals may fortify girls' defenses against sexual involvement. In Chapter 6, Jacobson refers to the narcissistic injury of the discovery of the genital differences and how this effects the development of female object relations; she suggests that women may have more complex narcissistic conflicts and more disturbed object relations than men.

In Chapter 7, Jacobson discusses whether the superego of males is superior to that of females due to the lack of castration fears. She argues that girls find the idea of castration unacceptable, suffer transient castration fears, and eventually acknowledge their castration. The consequent devaluation of self and mother facilitates a shift to father as the sexual love object and the establishment of the feminine narcissistic goal of physical attractiveness. During the oedipal phase, the loss of the father's love also represents a narcissistic injury, that is, the loss of their father's penis. In Chapter 10, Jacobson briefly discusses the mingled feelings of shame and pride that girls experience around their pubertal physical development. Emotional and physical relations between adolescents serve primarily narcissistic aims of self-assertion, rather than attainment of genital level of object relations. [See also Chapter 7.]

Grunberger, Belá (1970.) Outline for a study of narcissism in female sexuality. In: *Female Sexuality: New Psychoanalytic Views*, ed. J. Chasseguet-Smirgel. Ann Arbor: University of Michigan Press, pp. 68-83.

This essay attempts to integrate the theory of narcissism with instinct theory and female sexuality. Grunberger observes that women seek narcissistic gratification (the need to be loved) at the expense of their own sexual needs. He proposes that difficulties in girls' narcissism are rooted in their early, deficient, and ambivalent relationship with their mothers. Because the mother is the same sex, she can not be a satisfactory sexual object for her daughter, as she is for her son, thus causing frustration and narcissistic vulnerability in the pregenital stages. Girls must turn to themselves for narcissistic confirmation to make up for this inherent maternal deficiency. These efforts fail, so girls are more dependent on their love objects; they despise and feel guilty about their pregenital sexuality, and then turn to their fathers with blame and anger for not making their pregenital experiences better. An equivalence exists between possession of the paternal penis and narcissistic adequacy. Women sometimes become the phallus themselves (becoming beautiful and charming) and thus achieve a state of narcissistic autonomy, often to the detriment of object relations. Grunberger disagrees with Freud about the deficient nature of the female genital apparatus. The mysterious guilt accompanying narcissism is viewed as the outcome of having a clitoris, an organ whose only function is to provide great pleasure. Women's difficulties in the sexual act are related to women's dependence on the cluster of pregenital components incompletely gratified by the mother.

Kernberg, Paulina (1971). The course of analysis of a narcissistic personality with hysterical and compulsive features. *J. Amer. Psychoanal. Assn.*, 19:451-471.

This case illustrates the complex diagnostic and transference difficulties encountered in the evaluation and treatment of narcissistic personalities. Intense negative transferences between the female analyst and female patient were attributed to the female analyst's being experienced as reflecting the patient's own negative self-representations about the defective and devalued aspects of her body and also her penis envy. Primitive superego introjects, infiltrated by the patient's oral aggression and her projected oedipal rivalry were seen as protecting the patient from further narcissistic wounds.

**Lax, Ruth (1972). Some aspects of the interaction between mother and impaired child: Mother's narcissistic trauma. *Int. J. Psycho-Anal.*, 53:339-344.**

Lax asserts that the actual magnitude of a child's impairment does not predict the severity of a mother's depression; rather this depends on the extent to which the mother unconsciously perceives her child as an externalization of her defective self and feels symbiotically linked to her child. [See Chapter 14 for annotation.]

**Sternschein, Irving (1973). Reporter: Panel: The experience of separation-individuation in infancy and its reverberation through the course of life: Maturity, senescence, and sociological implications. *J. Amer. Psychoanal. Assn.*, 21:633-645.**

Narcissistic issues in aging women are discussed. [See Chapter 15 for annotation.]

**Kohut, Heinz (1975). A note on female sexuality. In: *The Search for the Self*, ed. P. Ornstein. New York: International Universities Press, 1978, pp. 783-792.**

This valuable paper is the only one that Kohut devoted entirely to female sexuality. It summarizes his major contributions. Kohut agrees with Freud that girls inevitably suffer a narcissistic injury when they recognize the anatomical differences, but he strongly disagrees that this recognition is the significant genetic factor either in the wish to have a child or in narcissistic personality disorders in women. Instead, Kohut postulates that developing girls, if their nuclear self is appropriately mirrored by their selfobjects, will eventually grow to be women who seek self-expression in a variety of ways, often including the wish to have a child. In the obverse, girls who are unempathically responded to will hypercathect the experience of isolated drives and isolated body parts in order to stimulate themselves. The addictionlike intensity of perverse activities or the hunger for enhancement of self-esteem in the (nonperverse) narcissistically disturbed is not due to a cravings activated by the drives, but rather to the intense need to fill a structural defect. [See also Chapter 6.]

Sarnoff, Charles (1975). Narcissism, adolescent masturbation fantasies, and a search for reality. In: *Masturbation: From Infancy to Senescence*, ed. I. Marcus and J. Francis. New York: International Universities Press, 11:277-304.

This chapter contains literature review on the relation between masturbation and narcissistic fantasy.

Grossman, William and Stewart, Walter (1976). Penis envy: From childhood wish to developmental metaphor. *J. Amer. Psychoanal. Assn.* (Suppl.), 24:193-213.

Two patients with narcissistic character disturbances had a sense of inferiority at not having a penis. This reflected other, more global aspects of envy, identity conflicts, narcissistic sensitivity, and conflicts about aggression. [See Chapter 6 for annotation.]

Lerner, Harriet (1976). Parental mislabeling of female genitals as a determinant of penis envy and learning inhibitions in women. *J. Amer Psychoanal. Assn.* (Suppl.), 24:269-283. Also in: *Women in Therapy*. Northvale, NJ: Aronson, 1988, pp. 25-41.

Lerner discusses how girls are inhibited in taking pride in their femininity because of parental failures and how penis envy may serve defensive narcissistic functions. [See Chapter 6 for annotation.]

Moore, Burness (1976). Freud and female sexuality: A current view. *Int. J. Psycho-Anal.*, 57:287-300.

Narcissistic traits in women are reviewed. [See Chapter 18 for annotation.]

Goldberg, Arnold (1978)(ed.) *The Psychology of the Self: A Case Book*. New York: International Universities Press.

This book is a compilation of analytic case reports written in collaboration with Heinz Kohut. Two of the case presentations are of female patients. Both cases demonstrate how problems around feminine identity and sexuality are better understood from a self-psychological perspective, rather than from the viewpoint of oedipal conflict.

Rothstein, Arnold (1980). *The Narcissistic Pursuit of Perfection*. New York: International Universities Press, pp. 195-209

Rothstein uses the character of Anna Karenina, in Tolstoy's novel, as a basis for his chapter, "Anna: A Stereotypical Female Narcissistic Personality Disorder." Anna invests in her physical beauty to capture a sense of narcissistic perfection; this quest for a perfect existence tragically destroys her real life. She is unable to relinquish the wish to be the central, admired, overvalued object. Thus, she cannot invest in objects such as her children or in functions related to her identity as a mother and wife. Anna experiences being ignored by her husband as a humiliating mortification and responds with narcissistic rage. Her search for admiration and adulation is reflected in her affairs, attempts at seduction, and in homosexual trends. Suicide offers the illusion of turning passive humiliation into active mastery.

Stolorow, Robert and Frank Lachmann (1980). *Psychoanalysis of Development Arrests: Theory and Treatment*. New York: International Universities Press.

The authors explore the concept of the developmental arrest as the basis of psychopathology and, focusing on treatment of the narcissistic personality disorder, investigate its clinical and theoretical implications. Narcissistic pathology that serves as a defense against intrapsychic conflict (Kernberg) is distinguished from pathology that results from developmental arrests (Kohut). The clinical cases include several women. The authors present the case of a woman whose rape fantasies during intercourse served the narcissistic function of restoring a positive self-representation. The "rapist" was a derivative of the phallic mother. Dreams of possessing a penis appeared as the patient worked through these fantasies, which the authors understood as reflecting the attainment of a new developmental step in the realm of self- and object separation. Intense penis envy was interpreted as marking the new acceptance of genital differences and the integration of gender-specific limitations into her self-representation, thus serving as a developmental indicator of the consolidation of her representational world. In the chapter "Sexual Fantasy and Perverse Activity," the authors review the literature and assert that normal psychosexual experiences, fantasies, and acts serve as psychic organizers and as indications of consolidation of self- and object representations. Perverse sexual fantasies and acts are viewed as ways of maintaining self-cohesion, particularly in developmentally arrested or sexually traumatized persons. Masochism can serve narcissistic functions.

Blum, Harold (1981). The maternal ego ideal and the regulation of maternal qualities. In: *The Course of Life: Psychoanalytic Contributions Toward Understanding Personality Development, Adulthood and the Aging Process*, Vol. 3, ed. S. Greenspan and G. Pollock. Adelphi, MD: U.S. Department of Health and Human Services, NIMH, pp. 91-114.

Blum asserts that the maternal ego ideal develops in response to narcissistic needs and is rooted in early identifications, particularly with the mother, but also with the father. [See Chapter 14 for annotation.]

Colarusso, Calvin and Nemiroff, Robert (1981). Narcissism in the adult development of the self. In: *Adult Development*, ed. C. Colarusso and R. Nemiroff. New York: Plenum Press, pp. 83-104.

Colarusso and Nemiroff focus on the role of narcissism in the developmental process and especially in the development of the self. They propose that one of many sexual themes, the acceptance of sexual differences, is further elaborated in adulthood. Women must accept their female sexuality as different, not defective. Repeated experiences with intimacy and sexuality lead to a more thorough understanding of the complementary differences between male and female genitalia. The experience of pregnancy validates the necessity of both male and female genitals. Sexual identity is sharpened by the experience of parenthood with a positive narcissistic investment in the child. Infantile sexuality is reworked with parenting of the child, but from the vantage of adult experience.

Colarusso, Calvin, Nemiroff, Robert, and Zuckerman, Susan (1981). Female midlife issues in prose and poetry. In: *Adult Development*, C. Colarusso and R. Nemiroff. New York: Plenum Press, pp. 141-165.

This article discusses middle-aged women's more narcissistic preoccupation with the physical signs of aging. [See Chapter 15 for annotation.]

Lachmann, Frank (1982a). Narcissism and female gender identity: A reformulation. *Psychoanal. Rev.*, 69:43-62, 1982.
Lachmann, Frank (1982b). Narcissistic Development. In: *Early Female Development*, ed. D. Mendell. New York: S.P. Medical and Scientific Books, pp. 227-248.

In these two very similar papers, Lachmann presents an historical review of female narcissistic development, including writings by Freud, Deutsch, Kohut, and Stolorow. He proposes that sex differences do not influence structure formation (of the self) per se but are important in the contents of the self-representation and in the defenses and compensations for structural vulnerabilities. Lachmann elaborates on three issues in the consolidation of female narcissistic development: the role of the preoedipal mother-daughter relationship, the role of the psychosexual phases and "penis envy," and the role of the father as an "ideal." Masochistic tendencies can serve the narcissistic need of consolidating a self-representation different and separate from the preoedipal mother. Oral and anal phase derivatives can support a vulnerable self-representation. Castration fears and penis envy are not viewed as "bedrock" for girls, but rather they are better understood as developmental stepping stones toward mature self-representations. Clinical examples of the various meanings of women's penis envy are provided. Diminution of themes of pathological awe and idealization of a father can be associated with the emergence of penis-envy imagery, suggesting a new parity between father and daughter, and an increase in paternal identifications and sharing of father's idealized qualities. This decreased idealization of the father is associated with a reduced need to maintain the mother as a selfobject in order to retain a sense of self-cohesion and self-esteem. Lachmann's papers are valuable for their innovative conceptualizations, clinical examples, and self-psychological critique of classical theory. [See also Chapter 21.]

Lebe, Doryann (1982). Individuation of women. *Psychoanal. Rev.*, 69:66-71.

Lebe traces the evolution of a shift from idealization of the analyst to idealization of the father and then to more realistic self- and object representations during the course of analysis. [See Chapter 12 for annotation.]

Glenn, Jules (1983). Forms of narcissism in literary characters. *Hillside J. Clin. Psychiat.*, 5:239-258.

Glenn describes a sequence in the development of narcissism, which he defines as libidinal cathexis of the self or self-representation. He gives examples of narcissistic configurations from literary characters, including some women.

Ornstein, Anna (1983). Fantasy or reality? The unsettled question in pathogenesis and reconstruction in psychoanalysis. In: *The Future of Psychoanalysis*, ed. A. Goldberg. New York: International Universities Press, pp. 281-296.

The case of Dorothy (Kris, 1956) is reconsidered to demonstrate the effect of the gender of the caretaker who served as primary selfobject on the child's oedipal experience. Dorothy's father was her primary caretaker in her early years. Ornstein explores whether the early identification with the father was a primary or compensatory (defensive) psychological structure. Reconstruction of pathogenic aspects of the parents' personalities and parent-blaming are considered. Ornstein argues that unconscious oedipal (sexual and aggressive) fantasies are not pathogenic in themselves, but rather that the failure of empathic or partially empathic parental responses to the child's legitimate selfobject (mirroring and idealizing) needs produced Dorothy's pathology.

Freyberg, Joan (1984). The psychoanalytic treatment of narcissism. *Psychoanal. Psychol.*, 1:99-112.

Narcissism is viewed as a dimension of psychopathology found at all levels of psychic functioning, at the core of which are characteristic ego and superego deficits around self-cohesion, self-continuity, and self-esteem regulation. Freyberg argues that traditional Freudian or ego-psychological techniques are applicable and that the treatment of narcissism does not require a new theory separate from that of object relations. Detailed clinical material from a female patient illustrates how psychological phenomena are overdetermined and may contain aspects of unresolved preoedipal and oedipal conflicts. At each stage of development, critical issues in self-cohesion, continuity, and esteem must be understood and interpreted, in addition to structural conflicts. The author illustrates the interpretive skills that are required to discern narcissistic and object-relations aspects of the clinical material. Although empathy aids self-cohesiveness, the interpretation of rage is also decisive. Countertransferences related to the analyst's own narcissism are also emphasized. This rich article is a persuasive attempt at integrating concepts of narcissism with object relations and structural theory.

Lang, Joan (1984). Notes toward a psychology of the feminine self. In: *Kohut's Legacy*, ed. P. Stepansky and A. Goldberg. Hillsdale, NJ: The Analytic Press, pp. 51-70.

Using concepts from self psychology, Lang explores the process of consolidation of the feminine self. She questions whether it is possible for girls to experience a freely responsive, mirroring milieu because fixed cultural ideas of gender stereotypes have an impact on the developing female self. The attributes that are presented to children as attainable and worthy of admiration are also gender specific. Lang demonstrates that the development of both poles of the feminine self, nuclear ambitions and guiding ideals, are highly influenced by gender-determined selfobject experiences, including patterns of parenting. She hypothesizes that cultural influences promote depression, low self-esteem, and lack of self-cohesion in women. Although children's archaic idealizations of the mother are disrupted, she is still usable as a mirroring selfobject by both sexes. Because of the mother's culturally influenced low self-esteem, she can not be a valid, idealized selfobject for girls. Girls may retain a secure sense of having a feminine self, but the development of a girl's nuclear self, which is organized around ideals and values, may be derailed, arrested, or disavowed. This delayed development of the nuclear self accounts for the longstanding psychoanalytic conceptualization of the feminine superego as being "weaker." Arrested development in girls may impair separation and individuation, so that they retain their mother as an archaic selfobject.

Dalsimer, Katherine (1986b). *Female Adolescence: Psychoanalytic Reflections on Literature*, New Haven, CT: Yale University Press.

In the introductory chapter and in literary illustrations, Dalsimer discusses narcissistic issues in relation to the adolescent girl's needs for new relationships, for developing pride and pleasure in her own genitals, and for the delimitation of life goals. [See Chapter 9 for annotation.]

Fenster, Sheri, Phillips, Suzanne, and Rapoport, Estelle (1986). *The Therapist's Pregnancy: Intrusion in the Analytic Space*. Hillsdale, NJ: The Analytic Press.

Narcissistic issues in the pregnant analyst are discussed. [See Chapter 26 for annotation.]

Lester, Eva and Notman, Malkah (1986). Pregnancy, developmental crises and object relations. *Int. J. Psycho-Anal.*, 67:357-366.

A female patient is described who used her unborn baby to rescue her sense of self. [See Chapter 14 for annotation.]

Benjamin, Jessica (1987). The decline of the Oedipus complex. In: *Critical Theories of Psychological Development*, ed. J. Broughton. New York: Plenum, pp. 211-244.

Benjamin challenges the contention that narcissism reflects a failure of oedipal internalization of paternal or parental authority. She notes that current theories of narcissism imply that early failures in resolving issues of separation and dependency transpire within the preoedipal mother-child dyad. She contests the psychoanalytic theory that gives fathers a preeminent role in fostering separation. Benjamin argues that the theory of oedipal repudiation of femininity and identification with paternal autonomy distracts from emphasis on an earlier process, in which mother and child must recognize each other as simultaneously separate and connected.

Gardiner, Judith (1987). Self psychology as feminist theory. *Signs*, 12:761-780.

Self psychology as a theoretical system is viewed as being useful for feminist theory, since it provides gender-neutral constructs for the study of gender development, character, superego, and the development of values. Self psychology separates the development of self-esteem from that of sexual desire; thus lesbian development can be conceptualized as including a clear feminine gender identity and a strong self-image. By stressing the formation of goals, values, and self-esteem, self psychologists show how the larger culture and the early caretaking environment influence children's development. A mother who prefers her son to her daughter or who has negative feelings about the female body will produce a self-devaluing daughter. The author feels that girls have a wider range of empathic capacities because of selfobject ties to mothers. The article reflects feminist criticisms, as well as correcting misconceptions about psychoanalysis.

Bernstein, Isidor (1988). A woman's fantasy of being unfinished: Its relation to Pygmalion, Pandora, and other myths. *Fantasy, Myth, and Reality: Essays in Honor of Jacob A. Arlow, M.D.*, ed. H. Blum, Y. Kramer, A. Richards, and A. Richards. Madison, CT: International Universities Press, pp. 217-232.

An analytic case illustrates how a woman patient developed a fantasy of herself as incomplete or unfinished. Factors that led to her creation of this personal myth include 1) deficits in early maternal care or interest, 2) identification with a mother who had narcissistic problems regarding her femininity, 3) prolonged and repeated anal stimulation and erotization, 4) traumatic experiences, including surgery that resulted in fantasies of having been damaged, 5) a family constellation that depreciated the importance of women, and 6) a need to defend against oedipal wishes. Bernstein discusses the Pandora and Pygmalion myths as societal elaborations of similar ideas that a woman is unfinished.

Lachmann, Frank (1988). On ambition and hubris: A case study. In: *Frontiers in Self Psychology: Progress in Self Psychology*, Vol. 3, ed. A. Goldberg. Hillsdale, NJ: The Analytic Press, pp. 195-209.

[See Chapter 12 for annotation.]

Novick, Kerry (1988). Childbearing and childrearing. *Psychoanal. Inq.*, 8:253-259.

Novick asserts that throughout development there is tension between wishes for childbearing and childrearing. The former wish represents narcissistic and libidinal gratification, whereas the latter wish is more closely tied to defensive functions and identifications. [See Chapter 14 for annotation.]

Siegel, Elaine (1988). *Female Homosexuality: Choice Without Volition.* Hillsdale, NJ: The Analytic Press.

Siegel discusses early phases of female narcissism and its relationship to homosexuality. A narcissistic defect, with incomplete schematization of the body image, leads to a search for mirroring in the same-sex partner. [See also Chapter 19.]

Lax, Ruth (1989). The narcissistic investment in pathological character traits and the narcissistic depression: Some implications for treatment. *Int. J. Psycho-Anal.*, 70:81-90.

Lax discusses from a developmental standpoint, the reasons why patients seem invested narcissistically in pathological character traits. [See Chapter 20 for annotation.]

Ornstein, Anna (1989). "Klinische darstellung" [Clinical examples of a female patient's transference to her female analyst]. In: *Selbst Psychology, Verlang Internationale Psychoanalyse.* Munchen: Wien.

This paper, published in German, examines the development of gender esteem and emphasizes the process of transmuting internalization. Two developmentally crucial selfobject functions are related to gender-linked psychological characteristics: 1) the same-sex parent is idealizable as a male or female according to the "standard" of what constitutes "feminine" or "masculine" in the particular culture, and 2) the idealized parent delights in, and responds enthusiastically to, the gender-linked attributes of the same-sex child. The analysis of a female patient who had a sense of defectiveness about her femininity demonstrates these developmental needs and how they emerged in the transference and countertransference. The erotization of the longing to be looked at and found irresistible is explained as an intense need for mirroring by the idealizable same-sex parent. Ornstein maintains that traditional psychoanalysis has failed to integrate social and political realities into a depth-psychological understanding of patients. The concept of the superego has not been useful in this respect because the superego, like the concept of identification, calls for a conceptualization of the psyche as a closed system after the resolution of the Oedipus complex. The concept of the selfobject bridges the intrapsychic and interpersonal.

Eber, Milton (1990). Erotized transference reconsidered: Expanding the countertransference dimension. *Psychoanal. Rev.*, 77:25-40.

[See Chapter 25 for annotation.]

Horner, Althea (1990). From idealization to ideal—from attachment to identification: The female analyst and the female patient. *J. Amer. Acad. Psychoanal.*, 18:223-232.

This paper discusses the female therapist's role in facilitating positive feminine identifications in nonborderline patients with oedipal and postoedipal identificatory conflicts with a devalued mother. Identification is a process central to the resolution of separation-individuation and oedipal conflicts, as well as to the resolution of these conflicts when they recur during adolescence. Many women make a primary identification with their preoedipal mother but later, defensively refuse to identify with her and take her as an ego ideal. Determinants of this disparagement of mother as a model worthy of identification include inevitable preoedipal maternal failures, difficulties with differentiation, and oedipal rivalry. Deidentification with the mother protects the developing ego ideal but interferes with achievement of assimilations and identifications necessary for object constancy and emotional autonomy and thus leads to emotional dependency and proneness to depression. With a male analyst, these oedipally fixated women may fail to analyze the hidden transference resistance of devaluing women and overvaluing men. With a female analyst, the wish for lost maternal nurturance may be heightened. Some of these patients may have experienced good-enough early mothering (and consequently there was a cohesive feminine self) but had parents who projected hated aspects of themselves onto their oedipal children and were unacceptable models for later ego and superego identifications. The therapeutic limitations of the analyst's gender are discussed.

Imber, Ruth (1990). The avoidance of countertransference awareness in a pregnant analyst. *Contemp. Psychoanal.*, 26:223-236.

Narcissistic fulfillment in the pregnant analyst is discussed. [See Chapter 26 for annotation.]

Lang, Joan (1990). Self psychology and the understanding and treatment of women. *Rev. Psychiat.*, 9:384-402.

Lang asserts that self psychology offers a basis within psychoanalysis to meet critical challenges from feminist scholars without abandoning depth psychology. Such controversial formulations about women, including femininity as a compensatory formation, the inferior feminine superego, morality, and penis envy are contrasted from classical and self-psychological perspectives. The concept of the selfobject is important because it is gender neutral and offers a mediator between psyche and culture. This is a valuable review of self psychology and its potential for understanding and treating women.

Tyson, Phyllis and Tyson, Robert (1990). Gender development: Girls. In: *Psychoanalytic Theories of Development: An Integration*. New Haven, CT: Yale University Press, pp. 258-276.

The Tysons explore the relationship between narcissism and gender identity in girls. A girl's narcissistic pride in her feminine body has its beginnings in the vicissitudes of separation-individuation and her struggle for autonomy in relation to her mother. Early superego formation, penis envy, the mother's sense of her own femininity, and the father's role in affirming his daughter's femininity all have an impact on narcissistic development. [See also Chapter 6.]

Tyson, Phyllis (1991). Some nuclear conflicts of the infantile neurosis in female development. *Psychoanal. Inq.*, 11(4).

Tyson proposes the central rapprochement fear of loss of love and the wish to retain the love of the idealized same-sex object, rather than castration anxiety, as an influential motivator for feminine development, narcissism, and self-esteem. [See Chapter 4 for complete annotation.]

# Chapter 23

# *Eating Disorders*

Nadine Levinson, Thomas Hessling, Muriel Morris

This chapter includes psychoanalytic papers on the eating disorders that are strongly preponderant in women: anorexia nervosa and bulimia. These disorders occur in women approximately ten times as often as they do in men. The chapter does not systematically cover the general psychiatric literature, nor does it address the literature pertaining to other eating disorders, such as obesity, pica, rumination, and neonatal feeding disturbances. The term anorexia is a misnomer, since the severe weight loss characteristic of this illness is not due to loss of appetite, but instead represents a refusal to eat, a fear of gaining weight, and a significant disturbance of body image. The term bulimia describes a disorder characterized by relatively normal weight, with episodic binge eating followed soon after by purging. Often the two conditions coexist and are referred to as bulimarexia.

Anorexic and bulimic symptoms were described as far back as the third century. Sours (1980) provides a review of the early literature. Anorexia was identified as a discrete syndrome in the 17th century, but the syndrome of bulimia did not achieve clinical recognition until the 1940s. Historically, most of the medical literature contained graphic descriptions of clinical phenomena, but little awareness of the psychological origin of these conditions. The etiology of anorexia was thought to stem from an organic dysfunction of the pituitary gland or the hypothalamus, and minimal attention was paid to intrapsychic factors. Gradually, in the 20th century, analysts and psychiatrists have brought to light the psychological components of both disorders, including severe distortions in body image, need for control, oral fixations, oedipal conflicts, conflicts in expressing aggression, and accompanying personality disorders.

Analysts initially linked anorexia and bulimia to such other diagnostic entities as hysteria, obsessional neurosis, depression, and schizophrenia. The psychoanalytic literature, beginning with Freud's early writings, focused on psychological factors and the symbolic meanings of the symptoms. In a letter to Fliess, Freud (1899) noted pregnancy wishes underlying hysterical vomiting in a female patient. While reporting on the case of Dora, Freud (1905a) expressed the view that anorexia was related to melancholy and occurred in sexually underdeveloped girls. He observed (1905b) the frequent universal childhood fantasy that a baby can be conceived by kissing or by eating, a fantasy which merges oral-incorporative and oedipal-genital wishes. Later, in "An Infantile Neurosis," Freud (1918) remarked that anorexia figured as a means for prepubertal girls to express aversion to sexuality at puberty.

In the 1940s, interest in psychosomatic disorders led to a deeper understanding of eating disorders that emphasized oral-sadistic wishes as well as reaction formations against incorporative wishes and longings for oral mothering. Anorexia, with its accompanying symptoms of starvation and amenorrhea, was viewed as a defense against or rejection of the forbidden wish to be pregnant. Sperling (1949), in a pathbreaking study, called attention to the "psychosomatic dyad" and stressed the role of the pathogenic mother who predisposed her child to an eating disorder because of her own unconscious libidinal, aggressive, and narcissistic conflicts. The mother of the psychosomatically symptomatic child perceives the child as a literal extension of her own ego. Thus anorexia was explained by early psychoanalysts as stemming from a fixation at the oral phase with the gratifying or frustrating maternal object or as reflecting oedipal conflicts around incestuous desires and wishes for pregnancy with a defensive regression from genital expression. Psychodynamic formulations reflecting these differences in emphasis continue to exist today.

In the last 40 years psychoanalytic interest and research in the area of eating disorders have increased. Formulations centering on fixation and regression of the psychosexual drives have become less fashionable. Current psychoanalytic literature, while still acknowledging the contributions of drive manifestations, focuses on disturbances in early object relations and separation-individuation, within the comprehensive framework of a structural perspective. This perspective stresses the multidetermined and individual nature of the symptomatology, with its complex layering of childhood developmental levels expressing infantile wishes, defenses, and needs for punishment.

Patients suffering from anorexia and bulimia exhibit a broad spectrum of characterologic disorders and possess body-image disturbances and conflicts from every developmental stage. Often the two syndromes are arbitrarily lumped together, causing conceptual confusion and contradictory clinical findings. The puzzling 10:1 prevalence of anorexia and bulimia in females as compared with males remains to be explained. This variance may reflect a substantial dissimilarity in the quality of the early mother-child relationship between males and females. Body isomorphism between females leads to stronger mutually narcissistic identifications between mother and daughter and lends a different quality to the separation-individuation phase. Ritvo (1989) suggests that the strong bodily tie to the mother and unresolved ambivalence predisposes the daughter to oral symptoms, which are especially adaptable to the representation of incorporative, sadomasochistic, and bisexual conflicts. An ideal research model would consider such multiple factors as character style, personality malformation, body-image problems, ego and superego defects, developmental variables, object relations, and organic predispositions.

While papers in the psychiatric literature stress medical, interpersonal, familial, and social factors in these disorders, psychoanalysis provides parallel data focusing on the unconscious pregenital and oedipal conflicts that play central role in the etiology and eventual symptom resolution. The nature of the early mother-daughter relationship, the family pathology, organic predisposition, and ego and superego development in relation to choice of symptom or predominance of eating disorders in women constitute fruitful areas for further research. (N.L.)

Freud, Sigmund (1899). Extracts from the Fliess papers, Letter 105. *Standard Edition*, 1:278. London: Hogarth Press, 1953.

Freud reports on pregnancy wishes underlying hysterical vomiting in a female patient.

Freud, Sigmund (1905a). Fragment of an analysis of a case of hysteria. *Standard Edition*, 7:3-122. London: Hogarth Press, 1953.

Freud expresses his view that anorexia is related to melancholia. [See also Chapters 1 and 20.]

Freud, Sigmund (1905b). Three essays on the theory of sexuality. *Standard Edition*, 7:125-243. London: Hogarth Press, 1953.

In discussing universal childhood fantasies, Freud observes the fantasy that "a baby can be gotten by a kiss" or by eating, which merges oral incorporative and oedipal-genital wishes. [See Chapter 1 for annotation.]

Abraham, Karl (1916). The first pregenital stage of the libido. In: *Selected Papers*. London: Hogarth Press, 1948, pp. 248-279.

Abraham, describing several female patients who suffer from ravenous hunger and compulsive eating, connects the symptoms to repressed orality.

Freud, Sigmund (1918). An infantile neurosis. *Standard Edition*, 17:106. London: Hogarth Press, 1953.

Freud discusses the dynamics of the Wolf Man's fear of being eaten by the wolf. Freud links this fear to the oral phase and a disturbance of the nutritional instinct. He relates this impairment to a neurosis that occurs in girls during puberty and that expresses itself as an aversion to sexuality by means of anorexia.

Abraham, Karl (1924). A short study of the development of the libido viewed in the light of mental disorders. In: *Selected Papers*. London: Hogarth Press, 1954, pp. 418-501.

Abraham describes a female patient with psychogenic vomiting and a body-phallus fantasy. The fantasy originates as an intrapsychic compromise for narcissistic mortification, schizophrenia awe, and oral-incorporative wishes directed at the paternal phallus. [See also Chapter 2.]

Waller, John, Kaufmann, Ralph, and Deutsch, Felix (1940). Anorexia nervosa: A psychosomatic entity. *Psychosom. Med.*, 2:3-16.

This article reviews the phenomenology and psychodynamics of anorexia nervosa. The cases of two female patients illustrate the relationship between gastrointestinal symptoms and infantile fantasies of oral impregnation. The authors show how the disgust for food experienced by one patient derived from a symbolic equivalence in which eating represented forbidden sexuality. Constipation represented the pregnant abdomen, and increased fluid intake expressed a cleansing and purification ritual. Reaction formations used the body to defend against incestuous wishes. A psychological transfer of transgenerational traits and behaviors from parent to child are demonstrated.

Masserman, Jules (1941). Psychodynamisms in anorexia nervosa and neurotic vomiting. *Psychoanal. Q.*, 10:211-242.

This analytic report of an anorexic woman emphasizes psychodynamics, including oedipal and preoedipal conflicts, fantasy life, and early experiences and their relationship to functional and organic symptomatology. The patient was rejected for being a girl, was admired for her boyish appearance, and was indulged for passive-dependent and incestuous behavior. Cannibalistic and oral incorporative tendencies, riddance phenomena, sexual inhibitions, rejection of femininity, and marital and pregnancy conflicts were observed. Masserman describes the wish to possess the father's penis in order to satisfy her mother and replace her father. There is an extensive bibliography of early contributions.

**Sterba, Edith (1941). An important factor in eating disturbances of childhood. *Psychoanal. Q.*, 10:365-372.**

Sterba observes that eating conflicts are important and frequent manifestations in young neurotic children. Using classical libido theory, she describes two preoedipal children in the anal stage of development who regressed to the oral stage while being toilet trained. They developed an eating disorder that symbolized in oral terms their resistance to giving up their feces. Sterba emphasizes the symbolic elements of the eating disorder, sees it as a compromise solution to conflict, and stresses the role of genitalization of the mouth.

**Moulton, Ruth (1942). A psychosomatic study of anorexia nervosa including the use of vaginal smears. *Psychosom. Med.*, 4:65-74.**

Moulton views the act of manually stimulating the throat in purging as a masturbatory act representing a fellatio and impregnation wish.

**Eissler, Kurt (1943). Some psychiatric aspects of anorexia nervosa. *Psychoanal. Rev.*, 30:121-145.**

This extensive case history of a severely disturbed anorexic patient was written at a time when anorexia was viewed as an endocrine disorder and psychological mechanisms were poorly understood. In an attempt to control overwhelming greed and desire for the maternal object, the patient denied her instinctual yearnings and lived a passionless existence. She became preoccupied with food and eating rather than with relationships and other developmental tasks such as vocational pursuits. The mother's failure to provide physical affection influenced the patient's ability to experience internal emotional responses to inner sensations, to feel alive, and mentally to represent her body and its feelings. The patient felt enslaved to the maternal object. Development was arrested, and the patient was unable to handle conflict during puberty and adult life. Eissler distinguishes between anorexia as a symptom and as a disease entity or illness.

**Lorand, Sandor (1943). Anorexia nervosa: A report of a case. *Psychosom. Med.*, 5:282-292.**

Lorand summarizes typical features in the analysis of a female with anorexia nervosa. He notes that the analysis had to be modified because of difficulties in establishing the transference. Depression, with self-destructive and suicidal desires, was prevalent owing to an excessively punitive superego and unconscious guilt related to impregnation fantasies. Food symbolically represented the vehicle of love (impregnation) and punishment related to those wishes. Food is unconsciously equated with the paternal phallus, and ingestion undoes castration and conceives the oedipal baby. The author emphasizes the reality of the patient's feelings of not belonging and being unwanted in her hostile family.

Rose, John (1943). Eating inhibitions in children in relation to anorexia nervosa. *Psychosom. Med.*, 5:117-124.

Rose asserts that understanding and interpreting the psychodynamics of eating disorders are crucial for the treatment of anorexic patients. He briefly reviews 10 child therapy cases where resistance to eating was a prominent symptom. He finds that anorexia or the suppression of eating is used as a defense against fears of change from growth at all developmental stages. The taking of food symbolically represents giving up the old for the new. Typical conflicts, family constellations, life crises, and cultural demands are discussed. Rose recommends simultaneous treatment of parents.

Sylvester, Emmy (1945). Analysis of psychogenic anorexia and vomiting in a four-year-old child. *The Psychoanalytic Study of the Child*, 1:167-187. New York: International Universities Press.

This paper presents the analysis of a four-year-old anorexic girl with severe pregenital conflicts. Sylvester observes that the intrapsychic factors contributing to the somatic manifestations in this child closely correspond to the psychodynamic of threatened object loss related to melancholic depression in adults. The patient was traumatized and had her anaclitic needs frustrated by sudden weaning precipitated by the mother's pregnancy and then again, at 13 months, in relation to another pregnancy. The little girl presented with the following conflicts: oral pregnancy wishes and fantasies, sibling rivalry toward both her brothers and sisters, aggression and hostile dependency toward a mother who was insufficiently available, and oedipal jealousy of the father. The vomiting was a defense against her destructive, incorporative tendencies and a means to restore regressively her dependent relationship with her mother. During treatment, autoplastic manifestations of her organ neurosis were converted to alloplastic behavior demonstrated in the transference neurosis.

Jacobson, Edith (1946). A case of sterility. *Psychoanal. Q.*, 15:330-350.

Jacobson reports the analysis of an amenorrheic, anovulatory woman who had extreme ambivalence about adopting a baby. The patient evidenced clinical signs, history, and psychodynamics of a patient with anorexia nervosa. Medical approaches were ineffectual in treating her glandular disturbance. Analysis of the patient's traumatic family history and personal conflicts around the issues of pregnancy and birth facilitated a subsequent birth of her own child.

Lehman, Edward (1949). Feeding problems of psychogenic origin. *The Psychoanalytic Study of the Child*, 3/4:461-488. New York: International Universities Press.

Lehman surveys the psychiatric and psychoanalytic literature on the significance of eating. Developmental factors, including the psychic importance of eating, breastfeeding, nursing, and weaning; effects of emotions on appetite; and effects of parental attitudes are discussed. In his review of pathological factors, the topics of zone displacements, phobic anxiety, sadism, masochism, food idiosyncracies, and food displacement are explored. Lehman proposes that psychogenic disorders of feeding can occur almost immediately after birth. Unconscious attitudes, often expressing opposite poles of the same psychic complex, may be expressed symbolically by food aversion or craving.

Sperling, Melitta (1949). The role of the mother in psychosomatic disorders in children. *Psychosom. Med.*, 11:377-385.

Using the simultaneous analyses of both mother and child, Sperling explores the nature of the unconscious and pathologic bond that exists between the child with a psychosomatic disorder and the mother. The mother and child represent a psychosomatic dyadic entity, wherein the child acts out the mother's unconscious needs. Sperling finds that the child often represents a hated sibling or parent or is a narcissistic projection of a part of the mother's own body, the wished-for penis. As the child gets better, the mother often develops depression and sometimes even an eating disorder.

Jessner, Lucie and Abse, Wilfred (1960). Regressive forces in anorexia nervosa. *Brit. J. Mod. Psychol.*, 33:301-312.

This article summarizes psychoanalytic thinking about anorexia at a time that drive theory was emphasized. The authors' observations and inferences from two cases support a psychodynamic etiology, in contrast to existing theories of organic etiology stemming from pituitary and hypothalamic dysfunction. The authors view anorexia as a psychological restitutive mechanism that includes the following dynamic elements: 1) early oral deprivation is followed by a period of closeness and gratification. The frustration during the sucking period enforces biting tendencies, resulting in severe ambivalence toward a feeding or starving mother; 2) anal defiance is displaced to the father, and oedipal aims are renounced in order to maintain closeness with the mother; and 3) traumatically induced preverbal oral fixations lay the groundwork for a sequence in which frustration leads to immediate action-patterns without the normal endopsychic displacements required for thought and use of language.

Sperling, Melitta (1968). Trichotillomania, trichophagy, and cyclic vomiting: A contribution to the psychopathology of female sexuality. *Int. J. Psycho-Anal.*, 49:682-690.

The successful analytic treatment of a teenage girl suffering from hair-pulling, hair-eating, and vomiting is presented. Sperling shows how the patient's physical symptoms are related to her distortions of body image and to an ambivalent and disturbed mother-child relationship, usually stemming from the mother's own unresolved pregenital conflicts. The patient's original relationship with her mother was of the psychosomatic type in which her dependent needs were rewarded by special attention when she was sick, but rejection followed when she was healthy and independent. After the birth of a male sibling, the relationship with her mother turned to a more overt acting-out type, with fetishistic attempts to separate from the mother. The cyclic vomiting at adolescence, which reestablished the psychosomatic relationship between mother and daughter, was a way for the patient actively to master unconscious conflicts in relation to her mother. Issues of control, dependency, separation and aggression, and dread of adult female sexuality are discussed in relation to the eating disorder.

Sandler, Joseph and Dare, Christopher (1970). The psychoanalytic concept of orality. *J. Psychosom. Res.*, 14:211-222. Also in: *From Safety to Superego*, New York: Guilford Press, 1987, pp. 301-314.

Oral character and its relationship to psychosomatic problems is discussed. An oral symptom, fantasy, or behavior may actually be expressing an oral mode, not an oral drive derivative. [See Chapter 20 for annotation.]

Friedman, Stanley (1972). On the presence of a variant form of instinctual regression: Oral drive cycles in obesity-bulemia. *Psychoanal. Q.*, 41:242-364.

Friedman's research considers the relationship between psychopathology and its correlate in the central nervous system. Oral activity cycles, an equivalent in waking life to REM cycles during sleep, are used as a biological marker to infer that increased instinctual drive activity is present. The author hypothesizes that states of tension are related to short oral activity cycles; these activity cycles resemble those of young children, rather than those of adults. The test subjects were obese persons whose oral activities, such as eating and smoking, were studied, quantified, and compared with those of nonobese controls. The findings indicate instinctual regression and failure of sublimation in the obese subjects as compared with the controls. Friedman speculates that psychosomatic illnesses, including eating disorders, may be related to chronic states of shortened activity cycles or to a continuous state of regression. These activity states may be the biological underpinning for psychoanalytic drive theory about the onset and progression of psychosomatic illness.

Bruch, Hilde (1973). *Eating Disorders*. New York: Basic Books.

This comprehensive book explores the medical, biochemical, and physiologic literature; research; treatment methods and goals; and the various family constellations and social backgrounds associated with obesity and anorexia in females and males. The historical and political background of the eating function throughout history and in many cultures is reviewed. Bruch notes that in American culture anorexia is linked to chronic depression. She provides vivid descriptions of eating disorder phenomenology and psychiatric and medical treatment modalities. Many of the patients who have a poor prognosis have suffered from severe early pathology. She believes that classical psychoanalytic theory and treatment, focusing on drives, oral dependency, and pregnancy conflicts, are not useful for understanding and treating eating-disorder patients. She proposes that the failure to achieve an integrated self-concept and self-esteem regulation must take precedence over conflict resolution; apparently she assumes that a psychoanalytic approach does not take these elements into consideration.

Sperling, Melitta (1973). Conversion hysteria, conversion symptoms: Revision of concepts. *J. Amer. Psychoanal. Assn.*, 21:745-771.

[See Chapter 20 for annotation.]

Selvini-Palazzoli, Mara (1974). *Self-Starvation: From the Intrapsychic to the Transpersonal Approach in Anorexia Nervosa.* London: Human Context Books. Retitled: *Self-Starvation: from Individual to Family Therapy in the Treatment of Anorexia Nervosa,* 1978, New York: Aronson.

This monograph summarizes the author's clinical experiences and reflections. Part I reviews the historical and clinical aspects of anorexia nervosa, including descriptions and differential diagnosis. Part II reports on the social and family background of anorexic patients and provides a psychodynamic formulation of anorexia that is rooted in early object relations theory. The author's developmental model contains a description of an overprotective mother who sees her daughter as a narcissistic extension of herself. Compliance with the mother takes priority and results in a child who lacks effectiveness in thought and action and who experiences depression related to oral helplessness. The anorexic views her body as an incorporated object that she sees as bad. The bad object is repressed and causes a splitting of the ego. Body image disturbances occur because the body is equated with the bad object and there is an inability to recognize body needs and signals. Part III discusses treatment. In her later editions of her book, retitled *Self-Starvation: from Individual to Family Therapy in the Treatment of Anorexia Nervosa,* (1978), Selvini-Palazzoli stresses the importance of family intervention and discusses family therapy.

Sours, John (1974). The anorexia nervosa syndrome. *Int. J. Psycho-Anal.,* 55:567-576.

Sours contends that anorexia nervosa is not a single nosological entity with predictable findings and a predictable grave outcome. He believes that there are two groups of female anorexic patients. In the first, more seriously disturbed group, the syndrome reflects an ineffective ego structure. Functional ego regression is more prominent than drive regression because of instinctual fixation, unresolved infantile object dependency, and failure in achieving autonomy. With the increase in instinctual drives at puberty, these girls regress to primary object relations and pregenital drive discharge. They are unable to enter the second separation-individuation phase of adolescence unless they can relinquish their infantile inner objects and move toward external and extrafamilial ambivalent objects. Fears of merger mobilize magical devices to save the self from merging with a primitive identification with the omnipotent mother. In the second group, there are no striking deviations in the mother-child dyad during the first separation-individuation phase, and autonomy is achieved. The resurgence of oedipal feminine wishes during adolescence leads to regressive solutions. These adolescent girls pull away from sexual fantasies and wishes, regressing to an oral-aggressive position. Incorporative fantasies give rise to the fear of destruction of the maternal object. Sours emphasizes that the second group of patients with anorexia nervosa can be treated with traditional psychoanalysis and will respond to the resolution of the transference neurosis.

Chediak, Charles (1977). The so-called anorexia nervosa: Diagnostic and treatment implications. *Bull. Menn. Clin.*, 41:453-474.

Chediak summarizes the physical and psychological symptoms of anorexia nervosa and relates these symptoms to a developmental sequence. He postulates that vicissitudes in the rapprochement crisis bring about an unsatisfactory resolution of the separation-individuation phase and lead to a narcissistic overvaluation of the body and its functions. A regressive reenactment of the rapprochement crisis in early adolescence occurs as a desperate attempt to turn away from sexual, vocational, and other identity choices. This sequence is viewed as responsible for the emergence of anorexia in the adolescent who otherwise has been thought of as developing favorably. A psychoanalytic case illustrates these ideas.

Bruch, Hilde (1978). *The Golden Cage: The Enigma of Anorexia Nervosa.* Cambridge, MA: Harvard University Press.

This clear and comprehensive introduction to the anorexia syndrome provides clinical information for both the educated lay person and the mental health professional. Drawing on her extensive clinical experience, Bruch describes the psychodynamic issues, including feelings of powerlessness, a need to comply, and a desperate need to gain control. The nature of the family dysfunction and how intrafamilial pressures maintain the illness are detailed. Difficulties in openly expressing aggression are cited as a central etiologic factor. Numerous informal case descriptions shed light on the experience of medical and psychiatric interventions with these patients and their enmeshed families. Bruch does not emphasize a psychoanalytic treatment approach.

Blinder, Barton (1980). Developmental antecedents of the eating disorders: A reconsideration. In: *Psychiatric Clinics of North America*, 3: 579-592. Philadelphia: W. B. Saunders.

Blinder focuses on the importance of developmental antecedents for anorexia nervosa and bulimia. He proposes that careful conceptual distinctions for eating disorders should be made in three areas: 1) early feeding experiences, including a pathological mother-child relationship, which may be related to anxiety, overindulgence, or deprivation; 2) oral factors and their influence on personality development as differentiated from later specific eating disorders; and 3) specific eating disorders that represent significant psychobiologic regression, distorted body image awareness, or possible neurophysiologic dysfunction such as impairment in appetite regulatory centers. Blinder finds that specific developmental factors are less consistently correlated with pathology. He discusses the efficacy of different treatment modalities, including operant techniques for weight gain, education, and behavioral integration.

Mogul, Louis (1980). Ascetism in adolescence and anorexia nervosa. *The Psychoanalytic Study of the Child*, 35:155-175. New Haven, CT: Yale University Press.

Asceticism and anorexia in adolescence is considered as a defense against drives, as a defense against the sense of powerlessness, and as the expression of a wish for aesthetic and moral transcendence. The onset of anorexia nervosa usually follows a disengagement from the mother. This disengagement is viewed by the teenager as a threat to longings for closeness, often causing a regressive retreat. Mogul contends that stubborn negativism, expressed by a refusal to eat, is a way to exert control over self and objects.

Sours, John (1980). *Starving to Death in a Sea of Objects: The Anorexia Nervosa Syndrome*. New York: Aronson.

This book provides a scholarly description of theoretical and clinical aspects of anorexia nervosa. Sours asserts that the eating disorder is related to a desperate search for perfection and autonomy, important ideals in our society. The second section of the book consists of a short novel depicting the disease progression of a prototypic patient, a teenage girl, and her family, who are involved in a hostile and enmeshed relationship. The remainder of the book focuses on various family patterns involved in the etiology and maintenance of the disease, developmental issues, and treatment guidelines.

Sugarman, Alan, Quinlan, Donald, and DeVenis, Luanna (1981). Anorexia nervosa as a defense against anaclitic depression. *Int. J. Eat. Dis.*, 1:44-61.

This article offers a developmental understanding of the type of anaclitic depression that frequently underlies the form of anorexia nervosa that consists of gorging and purging. Familial lapses in transactional boundaries are viewed as leading to a maternal overinvolvement or unavailability during the practicing subphases of the separation-individuation process. Consequently, the future anorectic becomes arrested at a sensorimotor level of self- and object representations with no ability to evoke a representation of the object in its absence. Vulnerability to separation experiences results in depression, loss, and helplessness. The authors assert that many anorectic symptoms can be regarded as a defense against separation and the accompanying loss of self-other boundaries. This paper bridges familial and intrapsychic contexts and conceptually explains the accompanying depression.

Risen, Stephen (1982). The psychoanalytic treatment of an adolescent with anorexia nervosa. *The Psychoanalytic Study of the Child*, 37:433-459. New Haven, CT: Yale University Press.

Although anorexia nervosa is a syndrome embedded in various psychiatric diagnoses, Risen stresses that the indications for analysis of an anorexic are not different from those for other cases. He asserts that other treatment approaches, such as behavioral and family therapies, differ from psychoanalysis as they do not change the underlying intrapsychic conflicts. With many anorectics, oedipal conflicts have to be considered along with preoedipal conflicts of autonomy, control, and dependency. Successful treatment can occur with analysis and resolution of the transference neurosis. Risen discusses the five-year analysis of a 14-year-old girl with anorexia nervosa.

Mushatt, Cecil (1982). Anorexia nervosa: A psychoanalytic commentary. *Int. J. Psychoanal. Psychother.*, 9:257-265.

Mushatt asserts that separation-individuation conflicts are central to the development of anorexia nervosa. He observes that the greater the impairment of separation of self from object, the more severe the symptoms. The desire for thinness seems related to fears of voraciousness and insatiability and associated narcissistic vulnerability. Several brief analytic case vignettes illustrate intense primitive guilt, fear of destruction of the object, lack of clear sexual identity, and sexualization of all relationships. Even those patients with more mature egos have significant developmental failures from early development.

Sugarman, Alan and Kurash, Cheryl (1982). The body as a transitional object in bulimia. *Int. J. Eat. Dis.*, 1:57-67.

This article explores the body's unique meaning for the bulimic patient. In contrast to Selvini-Palazzoli's (1974) view of the body as a persecutory object, the authors suggest that a more primitive meaning or function underlies the role of the body in bulimia. Specifically, the body becomes a transitional object or a vehicle for both representing the maternal object and repudiating her. The bulimic symptom reflects a developmental arrest at the practicing subphase of separation-individuation. A synthesis of the cognitive and object relations lines of development to clarify the meaning of the body for the bulimic is outlined.

**Wilson, C. Philip (1982). The fear of being fat and anorexia nervosa. *Int. J. Psychoanal. Psychother.*, 9:233-255.**

The markedly greater incidence of restrictor and bulimic anorexia nervosa (fat phobia) in women is caused primarily by the female's unique superego structure. Important determinants of the fear of being fat include 1) the fear of loss of impulse control; 2) the fear of regression; and 3) the fear of undoing the ego's defenses of denial, repression, and displacement, with the danger of the emergence of oral, anal, and oedipal conflicts. Dysfunctional parent-child relationships and parents who have intense fears of being fat are predisposing factors in the development of anorexia. Other secondary reinforcing factors include medical, societal, and cultural influences.

**Goodsitt, Alan (1983). Self-regulatory disturbances in eating disorders. *Inter. J. Eat. Dis.*, 2:51-60.**

Goodsitt examines Sugarman and Kurash's (1982) hypothesis that bulimic patients use their bodies as transitional objects. He feels that evidence does not support this proposition. He proposes, instead, that much of the behavior of anorexics and bulimics is better understood as autoerotic-like phenomena and that these patients actually reveal defects in transitional object relatedness. He argues that these patients have severe defects in self-organization and self-regulation. Much of the symptomatology, including starvation, bingeing, vomiting, and hyperactivity, is better understood as a desperate attempt to drown out states of overstimulation and fragmentation.

**Boris, Harold (1984a). The problem of anorexia nervosa. *Int. J. Psycho-Anal.*, 65:315-322.**

Using object relations theory, Boris discusses the role of unconscious fantasy, including overwhelming feelings of envy and greed for the desired maternal object, needs to devalue all important objects, and displacement of conflicts with these objects into the eating domain. The author describes how anorexic patients suffer from developmental arrests, poor ego boundaries, and brutal superegos. He notes the intransigence of these cases and their risk of fatality, and proposes expanding treatment approaches to include family therapy in some cases.

Boris, Harold (1984b). The treatment of anorexia nervosa. *Int. J. Psycho-Anal.*, 65:435-442.

Boris describes the severe transference-countertransference reactions that arise in analysis with anorexic patients. Feeling that her eating-disorder condition is not a problem but the solution, the patient usually tries to manipulate the analyst to want something from her in order to deny her own neediness and to maintain the illusion that she wants nothing from anyone. Using projection and externalization, she contrives to see her therapist as greedy, intemperate, enslaving, and thus devalued. Clinical vignettes illustrate the primitive object relations, defenses, and analytic interventions.

Ritvo, Samuel (1984). The image and uses of the body in psychic conflict: With special reference to eating disorders in adolescence. *The Psychoanalytic Study of the Child*, 39:499-469. New Haven, CT: Yale University Press.

Ritvo reviews the psychoanalytic literature on body image, which he relates to eating disorders. He supports A. Freud's contention that the ego begins first as a body ego. He cites Lewin's writings about children's use of the image and perception of the body to externalize instinctual wishes in an effort to achieve mastery over their drives. Ritvo asserts that the image of the body as sexually mature is most vulnerable to psychic conflict. Because the mouth and eating serve for both incorporation and expulsion, oral activity is especially suitable for representation of ambivalence by externalization onto the body, when oral sadism is a major source of conflict. Eating can be used to express conflicts over loving and being loved, loving and hating, attacking and being attacked, and punishing and being punished. Analyses of several young women with eating disorders illustrate the multiple functions of using the body for externalization of psychic conflict. [See also Chapter 9.]

Morris, Muriel (1985). Unconscious motivation in the refusal to have children. In: *Women and Loss: Psychoanalytic Perspectives*, ed. W. Finn, M. Tallmer, I. Seeland, A. Kutscher, and E. Clark. New York: Praeger, pp. 116-123.

The analysis of an amenorrheic woman with eating disorder dynamics (obsession with control, fear of being fat, and preoccupation with body image) as well as fears of pregnancy is discussed. [See Chapter 14 for annotation.]

Wilson, C. Philip, Hogan, Charles, and Mintz, Ira (1985). *The Fear of Being Fat: The Treatment of Anorexia Nervosa and Bulimia*. Northvale, NJ: Aronson.

This collection of 17 papers takes a psychoanalytic perspective on anorexia nervosa and bulimia. Based on data from 44 analyzed cases, the psychodynamics, etiology, and psychoanalytic techniques for treatment of restrictor and bulimic anorexics are provided. M. Sperling's (1949) work about the importance of mother-infant relationships in predisposing to psychosomatic disorders is acknowledged. The authors explore the structure of the ego and superego and the nature of object relations. One chapter addresses the important dynamic differences in the personality characteristics of male and female anorexics. The high incidence of eating disorders in females is attributed to the different nature of the early mother-infant relationship in males and in females. Special difficulties in treatment are discussed, including an exploration of pregenital conflicts and past object relations, management guidelines for acting out, and conjoint therapy of the parents in adolescent cases. The risks and complications of the concomitant use of medication and analysis are also explored.

Schwartz, Harvey (1986). Bulimia: Psychoanalytic perspectives. *J. Amer. Psychoan. Assn.*, 34:439-462.

Schwartz provides an encyclopedic, theoretical view of the psychoanalytic literature on bulimia. Bulimia, or the syndrome of bingeing and purging, derives from pathological early object relations and later intrapsychic conflicts over incestuous impregnation wishes. Schwartz observes that the early psychoanalytic literature focuses on the pathogenic role of the mother's unconscious psychic life, which leads to the child's eating disorder. He discusses the common body-phallus fantasy (Abraham, 1924) found in bulimics. This fantasy originates as a compromise for narcissistic mortification, scoptophilic wishes, and oral-incorporative wishes for the paternal penis. Often the child experiences herself as the penis of the mother. The mother views herself as castrated and uses the child as a compensatory extension of herself to repair her own self-esteem. The child becomes dependent on the mother; there is a hypercathexis of exhibitionistic aspects of the body, lack of differentiation, and the intergenerational transmission of a defective feminine ego-ideal.

Schwartz suggests a structural perspective to view symptom formation. He stresses the symptom's symbolic and conflictual configuration. Symptoms are viewed as compromise formations derived from different developmental levels and expressing childhood wishes, defenses, and punishment. He disagrees with those analysts who view bulimic disturbances as a fixation at the presymbolic oral-separation levels, rather than as a regression and displacement from genital wishes. He asserts that an exclusive focus on dependency issues with the mother often obfuscates the defensive elements of the negative oedipal constellation.

Bergmann, Maria (1988). On eating disorders and work inhibition. In: *Bulimia: Psychoanalytic Treatment and Theory*, ed. H. Schwartz. Madison, CT: International Universities Press, pp. 347-371.

In her work with eating disordered patients, Bergmann has noted a correlation between bulimia and work inhibition. She postulates that overindulgence on the part of the mother results in an excessive symbiotic bond and the failure of the child to transcend the use of the body to express frustration and aggression, resulting in marked deficiencies in learning and productivity. Thus, the joy of mastery is not experienced, except in the service of the mother's narcissistic needs. In psychoanalytic treatment, the bulimic-anorectic's difficulty with taking in food can often be equated with her difficulty with "taking in" interpretations. The analytic setting may then serve as a model for "an intake process," in which the patient identifies with the analyst who takes in what the patient presents. Along with the analysis of the psychic conflict regarding intake and output, the patient learns to hold in and retain what was assimilated without feeling forced and to use it autonomously. Four analytic case examples illustrate the major theoretical and clinical points.

Boris, Harold (1988). Torment of the object: A contribution to the study of bulimia. In: *Bulimia: Psychoanalytic Treatment and Theory*, ed., H. Schwartz. Madison, CT: International Universities Press, pp. 89-110.

Boris discusses his analytic work with a bulimic patient who was initially seen for several sessions with her family and then psychoanalyzed. Focusing on both the material from the family work and the analysis, Boris demonstrates the therapist's availability as both an observer of the patient's intrapsychic fantasies and as an object of the fantasies themselves. Because the patient's internal images are psychically unavailable, the patient tends to fill in with outside objects; there is a lack of differentiation between self and others. In the treatment setting, the patient uses others (the therapist) as containers for her projections and introjections through the processes of projective identification and introjective identification. The initial therapeutic task is to increase the patient's own self-awareness.

Krueger, David (1988). Body self, psychological self, and bulimia: Development and clinical considerations. In: *Bulimia: Psychoanalytic Treatment and Theory*, ed., H. Schwartz. Madison, CT: International Universities Press, pp. 55-72.

Krueger reviews the histories of over 300 patients with eating disorders who were treated either in an inpatient setting or in outpatient therapy with either psychotherapy or psychoanalysis. He finds that the bulimic's failure to develop a distinct and separate body self, boundaries, and an accurate body image occurs as the result of a preverbal developmental arrest. Lack of integration of mind and body (rather than defensive splitting) is directly related to deficiencies in self-regulation, pathological narcissism, and separation-individuation difficulties. The resulting maladaptive behaviors represent deficits rather than conflicts. Since disturbances in differentiating self and other affect the ability to create symbols of the body self and affective self, distinctions between the symbol and the object symbolized are incomplete. Thus, thinking is concrete and lacks the capacity for abstraction or representation of the body and its contents, including feelings. The patient, rather than denying painful affects, may not have developed the capacity to recognize or distinguish different affects and bodily sensations. The symptomatic act of the bulimic is an attempt at restitution of the defective or incomplete body self.

Mintz, Ira (1988). Self-destructive behavior in anorexia and bulimia. In: *Bulimia: Psychoanalytic Treatment and Theory*, ed. H. Schwartz. Madison, CT: International Universities Press, pp. 127-171.

Three case examples treated with psychoanalysis and psychoanalytic psychotherapy focus on the self-destructive aspects of both anorexia and bulimia. Differences in ego structure between the two syndromes result in variations in the manifestations of self-destructive behavior and the meaning of this behavior. The starving anorexic displaces onto food her conflicts related to feeling out of control with people. With the intact part of her ego structure and primitive superego she controls her food and weight and inhibits her impulse to eat, as a way of repressing her destructive impulses toward people. She directs her aggression against herself to satisfy the needs of a primitive, punitive superego and avoids interpersonal relations. The bulimic-anorexic feels out of control in her relationships and displaces this feeling to her control conflicts involving food. Unable to contain her impulses, she attacks the food the way she would like to attack people. Without an intact ego structure, she is unable to contain impulses. Attacking food symbolically gratifies aggressive, sexual, and dependency needs.

Oliner, Marion (1988). Anal components in overeating. In: *Bulimia: Psychoanalytic Treatment and Theory*, ed. H. Schwartz Madison, CT: International Universities Press, pp. 227-254.

Oliner cautions against viewing overeating merely as a manifestation of oral conflicts related to dependency and stresses that overeating can be a derivative of anal drive conflicts. An analytic case illustrates a female overeater who had fantasies of her body as a container of bad substances, such as garbage, fecal material, and waste, which she could control and manipulate by vomiting or overeating. Overeating enabled the patient to reverse the flow of anal sadism from the object to herself, which then allowed her to be free of the object, discharge the impulse, and punish herself. In the process, she saw herself as separate, but possessing a bad or undesirable body.

Reiser, Lynn Whisnant (1988a). Love, work, and bulimia. In: *Bulimia: Psychoanalytic Treatment and Theory*, ed. H. Schwartz. Madison, CT: International Universities Press, pp. 373-398.

Reiser presents analytic case material of a 25-year-old female patient who developed bulimia after a career promotion. She demonstrates how a single case complements and supplements survey studies of risk factors in larger populations. The patient's psychodynamics are presented to clarify some of the reasons for onset of bulimic symptoms. This paper highlights the overdetermination of the bulimic syndrome.

Reiser, Lynn Whisnant (1988b). Reporter, Panel: Obesity and related phenomena. *J. Amer. Psychoanal. Assn.*, 36:163-171.

Reviewing the early psychoanalytic contributions about obesity, Castelnuovo-Tedesco emphasizes oral drive manifestations, incapacity of ego functions, and pathology in self-representation. Personality characteristics of the obese, including the use of food for self-soothing and as a replacement for disappointing objects (to achieve pseudoindependence), are derived from anal and phallic-oedipal levels. Other presentations focus on recent biological contributions; psychodynamics, including defenses against pathological orality, diffuse rage, introjective responses to loss, pregnancy wishes, affects, and distortions in self-representation; and treatment perspectives. Several female cases are discussed, but without special emphasis on the role of gender or of female sexuality.

Risen, Stephen (1988). Reporter, Panel: Anorexia nervosa: Theory and therapy—a new look at an old problem. *J. Amer. Psychoanal. Assn.*, 36:153-161.

Castelnuovo-Tedesco traces how psychobiological and psychoanalytic perspectives on eating disorders over the years have emphasized the role of unconscious pregnancy fantasies regressively experienced in oral terms, reaction-formations against anal-sadistic impulses, failure to neutralize drive regression, defects in ego functioning, preoedipal issues, separation-individuation factors, and the influence of self psychology. Wilson's paper, "The Psychoanalytic Treatment of Anorexia Nervosa and Bulimia," classifies eating disorders as psychosomatic conditions with predominant preoedipal conflicts. Eating disorders are rooted in oral sadomasochistic conflicts with overcontrolling parents, who overemphasized food and eating as symbols of love, and thus caused inhibitions of normal development in their anorexia-prone children. Anorexia is a neurotic symptom-complex that is accompanied by a character disorder and a split in the ego, but with areas of ego functioning that remain relatively intact so that the patient is capable of a transference relationship. The term "fat phobia" (fear of being fat) should replace the term anorexia. Wilson details a parental psychological profile that appears etiologic for later manifestations of anorexia. Guidelines for treatment include 1) early interpretation of masochism, harsh superego trends and guilt, and the need for instant gratification; 2) interpretation of defenses against acknowledging masochistic behavior; 3) interpretation of defenses against aggressive and libidinal impulses, with a relatively healthy ego; and 4) after a shift from part-object relations to whole-object relations, interpretation of triadic oedipal material. Anorexics seem to have better ego structure than do bulimics.

Ceaser presents the paper "Anorexia Nervosa and Bulimia," emphasizing oral incorporation fantasies as the single unifying concept in all eating disorders. The anorexic wants to deny oral incorporative fantasies, while the bulimic surrenders to them. He recommends antidepressant treatment for those selected patients with accompanying mood disorders and discusses indications for analysis. Gehrie's presentation, "Comment on Eating Disorders: Dynamics of Treatment," describes three female bulimic patients who could not tolerate a classical analysis and who suffered from intense anxiety, fragmentation, and overwhelming needs to control the analyst to validate their own self-experience. For these patients with narcissistic vulnerability, eating served to maintain narcissistic connections and to defend against the pain of loss; eating was an important path to connectedness to an idealized parent.

Blinder's presentation elaborates on several neurobiological systems that are involved in eating disorders. He suggests that eating disorders may be conceptualized as intermediate phenomena, reflecting both brain function and behavior. He classifies the broad category of eating disorders into three separate areas: early feeding disturbances, oral personality traits, and eating disorders proper. Hitchcock discusses the conceptual differences between preoedipal, presymbolic, and preconflictual phenomena and notes the importance of healthy expression of aggression for children.

Fuerstein, Laura (1989). Some hypotheses about gender differences in coping with oral dependency conflicts. *Psychoanal. Rev., 76*:163-184.

The author focuses on the defensive use of overeating, restrictive eating, and vomiting, and the reasons for gender differences. Women act out oral dependency conflicts particularly with food, whereas men use alcohol and sexualization. Female patients may use food in the service of defense, such as for repression, denial, or displacement of primitive anxieties around dependency. Culturally approved defensive expressions of dependency may result in a negatively altered body, which then becomes a target of superego and external censure. Weight change is also part of women's normal psychophysiological experiences of puberty, pregnancy, and the menstrual cycle and is associated with issues in various stages of separation-individuation. Fuerstein delineates some aspects of female development, including the "same-gender identity" with mother, that make women more likely to use food and eating defensively with less anxiety. Female patients employ food as a symbolic means of inviting or avoiding merger with the maternal object in the transference. These hypotheses were tested during the analyst's two pregnancies. The defensive choices for her female patients included overeating and an alternating of open expressions of anger at abandonment and at the fetus with wishes to be the analyst's oral infant. Male patients employed the defenses of denial, reaction formations, and acting out with sex and alcohol. For both men and women, when the body is used defensively to express psychic conflict, there is resistance to the development of transference as conflicts are introjected.

Ritvo, Samuel (1989). Mothers, daughters, and eating disorders. In: *Fantasy, Myth, and Reality: Essays in Honor of Jacob A. Arlow*, ed. H. Blum, Y. Kramer, A. K. Richards, and A. D. Richards. Madison, CT: International Universities Press, pp. 371-380.

Ritvo reviews the role of aggression in the early mother-daughter relationship and the contribution of unresolved ambivalence to the subsequent development of eating disorders. He observes that there is a strong bodily tie with the mother that is relinquished with difficulty, predisposing girls to conflict and symptoms. Oral themes in fantasy and behavior are especially adaptable to the representation of incorporative, introjective, sadomasochistic strivings and the expression of bisexual conflicts. The girl, by adopting a masculine shape, can fantasize herself as her mother's sexual partner and thus defend against merger fantasies, the greatest wish/fear derived from the preoedipal mother-daughter attachment. The role of the father as a major determinant in eating disorders is also discussed. Four analytic cases illustrate the treatment of eating disorders.

Kaplan, Louise (1990). *Female Perversions: The Temptations of Emma Bovary*. New York: Doubleday.

Female perversions are disguised in social gender stereotypes of femininity, often manifested as an eating disorder. [See Chapter 19 for annotation.]

Reiser, Lynn Whisnant (1990). The oral triad and bulimic quintet: Understanding the bulimic episode. *Int. Rev. Psycho-Anal.*, 17:239-248.

Reiser describes phenomena characterizing bulimic episodes and links bulimic phenomena to infantile eating behaviors and the oral triad. The oral triad consists of wishes to eat, to sleep, and to reach a state of relaxation, which normally occurs in conjunction with nursing. The triad resembles five manifest clinical behaviors of bulimics: 1) restlessness and craving, 2) eating and feeling full, 3) nausea and vomiting, 4) purging, and 5) an altered state of consciousness. Three clinical vignettes of female patients illustrate the continuum of eating behaviors that can exist from patient to patient and in the same patient at different times.

# Chapter 24

# Sexual Abuse

## Alice Brand Bartlett and Eleanor Schuker

This chapter annotates writings on the psychological consequences of sexual assault experiences, including both incest and rape. Freud (1893-1895) brought the reality of the crippling effects of childhood seduction and sexual abuse to the attention of the world, although he has been also criticized (Masson, 1985) for avoiding the truth about the widespread nature of abuse and for deemphasizing the role of trauma. This censure reflects a misunderstanding of the nature of Freud's work, including his discovery of and interest in psychic unconscious factors in the etiology of neurosis. Psychoanalysts since Freud have tried to explicate the complex interplay between traumatic external events and the development of psychical reality and psychic structure. Both Ferenczi (1949) and Greenacre (1949, 1950b, 1952a) wrote about the dramatic effects of sexual abuse on the development of children.

The effects of both incestuous and rape experiences on children and adults, and their widespread occurrence, became a major focus for psychoanalytic writers only in the 1970s. During that decade, psychoanalysts built upon a dynamic understanding developed out of studies of traumatic and war neuroses, acute grief reactions, and crisis theory. Since 1970, over 3000 books and papers have been written on sexual abuse, including incest and sexual assault.

This chapter selects from the many publications about the consequences of sexual assault—those that have been written by psychoanalysts, are considered classical works, or contribute principally to a psychoanalytic understanding. Several salient points are emphasized 1) Incest and rape experiences can profoundly influence ego and symbolic mental functioning. Many factors, including age, relationship to the assailant, and the nature of the attack, influence the trauma. Because of the traumatic effects, repair may take precedence or may limit psychoanalytic exploration. 2) The relationship between external reality and patients' preexisting psychological conflicts, especially for children in incestuous families and for recidivist rape victims, can be complex. 3) Early trauma can interfere with the achievement of a cohesive identity and sense of self and can operate as a potential pathway for the development of a borderline personality structure. 4) Intense transferences and countertransferences occur in the treatment of patients who are incest victims. 5) Analytic treatment of adults who were victims of incest and of those who survived sexual assaults can be successful.

The psychology of recidivist victims of rape, a quarter of whom have a history of incest, is poorly understood and rarely discussed; research would be useful in this area. The compulsion to repeat traumata, the need to disavow danger and avoid self-protection, and the use of sexualized modes of defense, all must be differentiated from the inappropriate blaming of victims or denial of assailants' pathologies. The assailants of female victims of rape and incest are usually male, and papers focusing on the psychology of male assailants are not included here. However, the psychology of female incest perpetrators and female rapists is still largely unexplored. Although the psychiatric literature on battered and physically abused women is extensive, this topic rarely has been studied by psychoanalysts. A few useful general articles and the relevant psychoanalytic papers have been included.

**Freud, Sigmund (1893-1895). Studies on Hysteria II. Case Histories.** *Standard Edition*, **2:19-181. London: Hogarth Press, 1953.**

Freud briefly touches on the role of childhood sexual experiences in the etiology of hysteria. He presents two case histories of young women (Rosalia and Katharina), detailing early sexual abuse by their uncles. Later, Freud admitted that the real abusers were the fathers of the girls. [See also Chapter 1.]

**Freud, Sigmund (1896a). Further remarks on the neuro-psychoses of defense.** *Standard Edition*, **3:159-185. London: Hogarth Press, 1953.**

Freud reports that in 13 female cases of hysteria that he analyzed, there was a passive sexual experience before puberty. He emphasizes that it is not the sexual experience itself that is traumatic, but rather the revival of the experience as a memory after the patient enters sexual maturity. Sexual experiences in early childhood are also etiologic in the development of obsessional neuroses; mastery of the passive sexual experience is attempted through aggressive sexual activity. Freud originally attributed the sexual seductions to nursemaids and governesses. Later, in a private communication to Fleiss, he acknowledged that a significant number of female patients had been seduced by their fathers. [See also Chapter 20.]

Freud, Sigmund (1896b). The aetiology of hysteria. *Standard Edition*, 3:189-221. London: Hogarth Press, 1953.

Freud observes that certain traumatic sexual experiences initiated by adults are later reproduced in the psychical life of hysterics by mechanisms of defense in the form of symptoms that have symbolic meaning. [See Chapter 20 for annotation.]

Freud, Sigmund (1905b). Three essays on the theory of sexuality. *Standard Edition*, 7:125-243. London: Hogarth Press, 1953.

Freud revises his seduction theory to include the role of internal psychic factors in the etiology of neurosis. Although he does not discount the effects of true seduction, he emphasizes that seduction is neither universal nor sufficient to cause neurosis. [See also Chapter 1.]

Reich, Annie (1940). A contribution to the psychoanalysis of extreme submissiveness in women. *Psychoanal. Q.*, 9:470-480. Also in: *Psychoanalytic Contributions*. New York: International Universities Press, 1973, pp. 85-120.

Dynamic factors applicable to the understanding of the psychology of abused women are discussed. [See Chapter 21 for annotation.]

Bornstein, Berta (1946). Hysterical twilight states in an eight-year-old child. *The Psychoanalytic Study of the Child*, 2:229-240. New York: International Universities Press.

Bornstein provides rich clinical material to show how infantile sexual trauma and preoedipal and oedipal factors formed the core of a neurosis in an eight-year-old latency girl who suffered from severe fugue and twilight states. The girl had been seduced by an uncle at the time of the birth of a younger sister. She developed gonorrhea, necessitating vaginal douches by both parents, who had to hold her down. The cessation of the gratifying vaginal douches triggered the fugue symptom. Aggression and jealousy occurred during the twilight states, which were linked to oedipal incestuous wishes toward the father; angry, competitive feelings for the mother; and a defense against and simultaneous discharge of these conflicting wishes, which merged with the feelings from the original seduction by the uncle. The analysis was interrupted before primal-scene material could be recovered. Bornstein observes that ego and superego development were only minimally weakened with regard to management of the girl's oedipal strivings but did not affect her control over pregenital impulses, cognitive development, or capacity for sublimation.

Ferenczi, Sandor (1949). Confusion of tongues between the adult and the child; (the language of tenderness and of passion). *Int. J. Psycho-Anal.*, 30:225-230.

Ferenczi's paper describes the transference manifestations of adults who have experienced childhood sexual assault and their identification with the aggressor.

Greenacre, Phyllis (1949). A contribution to the study of screen memories. *The Psychoanalytic Study of the Child*, 3-4:73-84. New York: International Universities Press. Also in: *Trauma, Growth and Personality*. New York: Norton, 1952, pp. 188-203.

The analysis of an adult woman with a latency screen memory of having witnessed the primal scene led to the uncovering of a repressed traumatic rape at age five or six.

Greenacre, Phyllis (1950b). The prepuberty trauma in girls. *Psychoanal. Q.*, 19:298-317. Also in: *Trauma, Growth and Personality*. New York: Norton, 1952, pp. 204-223.

Greenacre examines trauma occurring in the prepuberty period that appears as undistorted memories of the events that contributed to neuroses in four adult women. [See Chapter 9 for annotation.]

Greenacre, Phyllis (1952a). Pregenital patterning. *Int. J. Psycho-Anal.*, 33: 410-415.

Premature and overstimulating genital arousal is discussed. [See Chapter 6 for annotation.]

Bonaparte, Marie (1953). *Female Sexuality*. New York: International Universities Press.

Bonaparte describes the consequences of incestuous activity between a brother and sister. [See Chapter 17 for annotation.]

Factor, Morris (1954). A woman's psychological reaction to attempted rape. *Psychoanal. Q.*, 23:243-244.

Factor briefly describes a segment of an analysis of a young woman who was raped. He explores the hostile and erotic components of the transference prior to the rape and reports a dream following the rape, which he believes clearly expresses feelings of guilt due to the woman's unconscious complicity.

**Gordon, Lillian (1955). Incest as revenge against the preoedipal mother. *Psychoanal. Rev.*, 42:284-292.**

Gordon presents a clinical example of a woman who had acted out incestuous behavior as a child, primarily as revenge against her rejecting mother and as a defense against masochistic dependence on her. Although on the surface the patient appeared too attached to her father, she did not view men as objects in themselves but rather as weapons to be used in a preoedipal struggle with her mother.

**Devereux, George (1957). The awarding of a penis as a compensation for rape. *Int. J. Psycho-Anal.*, 38:398-401.**

Using an infantile-mythological theory of the female penis fantasy, Devereux proposes that myths frequently represent the projection of ego-dystonic insights that are too powerful to be repressed. In the Greek myth, Kainis was raped by Poseidon, who then offered to grant her any request. She chose to be changed into a man, Kaineus, and to be made invulnerable so that no one could rape her again. In her male form, Kaineus worshiped only his spear, an identification with the aggressor. Devereux adds that some women with "penis awe" experience the phallus narcissistically as a split-off part of their own body image, incorporated through identification with the sexual partner via the vagina.

**Shengold, Leonard (1963). The parent as sphinx. *J. Amer. Psychoanal. Assn.*, 11:725-751.**

Shengold describes seductions in early childhood by psychotic parents as revealed in adult analyses. Traumatic overstimulation was perceived as cannibalistic aggression, and these patients became fixated at this level as adults, with a compulsion to repeat aggressive, perverse acts. They identified with the parent/aggressor and with the parent's denial, while taking over the guilt and the need for punishment that the parent should have had.

**Sachs, Lisbeth (1966). Disdain as defense against paternal seduction. *J. Amer. Acad. Child Psychiat.*, 5:211-225.**

Four girls demonstrated a disdainful attitude toward their fathers as an attempt to defend against their own sexual impulses in the presence of their seductive, emotionally dangerous fathers. The disdain was a reaction formation, rather than an identification with their mothers, even though the mothers reinforced the disdainful attitude. As repression lifted in treatment, the girls' positive libidinal attachment to their fathers and their oedipal anger toward their mothers became manifest.

Blum, Harold (1973). The concept of erotized transference. *J. Amer. Psychoanal. Assn.*, 21:61-76.

Blum reports that in analyses of relatively healthy patients without pregenital fixations, the emergence of an erotized transference may reflect a repetition as a distorted attempt to master a parental sexual seduction in childhood. [See also Chapter 25.]

Katan, Annie (1973). Children who were raped. *The Psychoanalytic Study of the Child*, 28:208-224. New Haven, CT: Yale University Press.

Katan presents two detailed reports representative of a group of six patients who had early sexual assaults. All the patients showed marked tendencies to repeat the traumatic incidents. All were preoccupied with the fantasied acquisition of a penis and an aggressive identification with men and felt that they were neither men nor women. They continued to perceive sex as primarily aggressive. Katan attributes their severe pathology to a disturbance in the fusion of the drives and to a lack of integrative capacity of the ego.

Burgess, Ann and Holmstrom, Lynda (1974). Rape trauma syndrome. *Amer. J. Psychiat.*, 131:981-986. Also in: *Rape: Victims of Crisis*. Bowie, MD: Robert J. Brady, 1974, pp. 37-50.

This article and the more comprehensive book are among the earliest descriptions of rape trauma syndrome. The authors describe two phases of the acute reaction, an "expressed style" and a more frequent "controlled style," reflecting shock and denial. Crisis treatment is described.

Brownmiller, Susan (1975). *Against Our Will: Men, Women and Rape*. New York: Simon and Schuster.

Brownmiller's forceful book is a landmark in the study of sexual assault. She documents that sexual assault has been a frequent phenomenon over generations and across cultures. Aspects of male psychology and cultural factors are implicated in its etiology. She criticizes the use of Freud's (1924a) and Deutsch's (1930) conceptualizations of female masochism as a justification for blaming the victim or for seeing rape as an archetypal female experience.

Francis, John and Marcus, Irwin (1975). Masturbation: A developmental view. In: *Masturbation: From Infancy to Senescence*, ed. I. Marcus and J. Francis. New York: International Universities Press, pp. 9-43.

The relationship of masturbation to sexual trauma is discussed. [See Chapter 18 for annotation.]

Hilberman, Elaine (1976). *The Rape Victim*. New York: Basic Books.

This comprehensive volume reviews the literature, phenomenology, social factors, and acute treatment of rape victims from a general psychiatric point of view.

Notman, Malkah and Nadelson, Carol (1976). The rape victim: Psychodynamic considerations. *Amer. J. Psychiat.*, 133:408-413.

The authors discuss the sequelae to rape and their view of rape as a trauma that challenges the ability of women to maintain their defenses, thus arousing feelings of irrational guilt, anxiety, and inadequacy. In assessing the rape victim, a therapist must take into account the life stage of the victim, her defensive structures, her previous adjustment, and her current life circumstances.

Margolis, Marvin (1977). A preliminary report of a case of consummated mother-son incest. *Ann. Psychoanal.*, 5:267-293.

This preliminary report is annotated as a follow-up case report in Margolis (1984) in this chapter.

Meissner, William (1979b). Studies on hysteria—Katharina. *Psychoanal. Q.*, 48:587-600.

Meissner discusses the consequences of an incestuous father-daughter relationship and the dynamics of hysteria. [See Chapter 3 for annotation.]

Nadelson, Carol and Notman, Malkah (1979). Psychoanalytic considerations of the response to rape. *Int. Rev. Psycho-Anal.*, 6:97-103.

The authors consider rape to be the ultimate violation of the self. Rape evokes previous sexual and aggressive conflicts, fantasies, and experiences. The actual helplessness of the woman who is raped reinforces feelings of powerlessness and vulnerability derived from early life. Restitution is often interfered with by lack of support and by condemnation, which reinforce guilt feelings and lower self-esteem. Since women are expected to exert impulse control in sexual encounters, rape victims' sense of failure in setting limits, impossible though this may have been, contributes to their sense of guilt. Since revealing the rape is often experienced as humiliating, victims may perceive medical or psychiatric intervention as equivalent to another rape. Interventions should be aimed at facilitating victims' reestablishment of a sense of control and mastery.

Rosenfeld, Alvin, Nadelson, Carol and Krieger, Marilyn (1979). Fantasy and reality in patients' reports of incest. *J. Clin. Psychiat.*, 40:159-164.

The majority of the literature emphasizes the overwhelming reality of childhood sexual assault. However, the interplay of fantasy and reality is still an important consideration, especially for forensic work. The authors provide questions for clinicians to review before making judgments about the reality of a report of incest, especially when legal procedures are involved.

Schuker, Eleanor (1979). Psychodynamics and treatment of sexual assault victims. *J. Amer. Acad. Psychoanal.*, 7:553-573.

Schuker addresses the narcissistic injury caused by sexual assault. She describes a hospital-based program of crisis intervention, short-term individual and group therapies, and long-term therapy with victims of childhood assault. In the acute aftermath of sexual assault, victims' normal grandiose fantasies of invulnerability to attack are shattered, leaving the ego helpless and overwhelmed. Victims sustain a loss of normal fantasies of being in a safe environment and protected from injury by idealized parental figures. Therapists may serve the temporary role of narcissistic object while helping victims to resume functioning. Long-term therapy with victims of assault focuses on working through impounded rage and recovery of repressed memories.

Shengold, Leonard (1979). Child abuse and deprivation: Soul murder. *J. Amer. Psychoanal. Assn.*, 27:533-559.

The author asserts that actual abusive experiences during childhood have a different and more profound destructive and pathogenic effect than do children's sexual fantasies. Experiences of repetitive and chronic over-stimulation alternating with emotional deprivation, deliberately brought about by another individual, result in "soul murder." These traumas mobilize splitting and idealizing defenses, which have structural implications and interfere with emotional and intellectual development.

Silber, Austin (1979). Childhood seduction, parental pathology and hysterical symptomatology: The genesis of an altered state of consciousness. *Int. J. Psycho-Anal.*, 60:109-116.

Silber describes the analysis of a man who was repeatedly sexually assaulted by his mother between the ages of three and four. He experienced these as physical assaults; however, he was also overwhelmingly sexually excited. He dealt with the trauma by evoking dreamlike images in an hypnotic state that frequently reappeared in the course of the analysis. Silber considers this hypnoid fantasy formation to be the patient's attempt to master what was in reality a lack of control over the functioning of his mind and body during the seduction/assault. The use of the hypnoid state was overdetermined. Through the fantasy, the patient used the hypnoid state as both a denial of reality and as a means of maintaining an emotional tie to his mother. By becoming limp and hypnotic, he actively thwarted his mother's pleasure and in the transference, his analyst's pleasure. Interpretive efforts failed when he was in this state, because the fantasies acted as a barrier to ward off his experiencing the destruction of his sense of himself as an integrated person.

Hilberman, Elaine (1980). Overview: The "wife-beater's wife" reconsidered. *Amer. J. Psychiat.*, 137:1336-1347.

Hilberman argues that masochism is not an adequate theoretical construct to explain why women stay in violent marital relationships. She identifies a specific stress response syndrome caused by violent abuse that includes a state of overwhelming passive terror and denial of rage, similar to the pathological transferences of hostages, in which external choice is restricted. Intrapsychic limitations to change, such as depression, passivity, and self-blame, are often accompanied by external limitations, including economic dependence, physical disability, and homicidal threats from the husband. Societal attitudes that normalize family violence and sex roles that leave women vulnerable to assault are also discussed.

Shengold, Leonard (1980). Some reflections on a case of mother/adolescent son incest. *Int. J. Psycho-Anal.*, 61:461-476.

Shengold discusses the possible reasons for the paucity of case reports of mother-son incest and presents a lengthy vignette describing the psychoanalysis of a 30-year-old man who recovered memories of intercourse with his mother during the analysis. The incest at puberty seemed to have helped reverse the patient's psychic position of subjection to the preoedipal mother, modified his rage, and reinforced his masculinity. Arrogance also resulted, with an accompanying need for failure and punishment.

Stolorow, Robert and Lachmann, Frank (1980). *Psychoanalysis of Developmental Arrests: Theory and Treatment.* New York: International Universities Press.

Included in the book is a chapter about a woman with a rape fantasy and a discussion of its multiple defensive functions. [See Chapter 22 for annotation.]

Cohen, Jonathan (1981). Theories of narcissism and trauma. *Amer. J. Psychother.*, 35:93-100.

Cohen asserts that psychic trauma, such as father-daughter incest during childhood, interferes with normal development. Memory, affects, the sense of time, reality testing, and other ego functions are disturbed, resulting in a deficiency in the cohesion of self- and object representations. These traumatically induced microstructural deficits respond to analytic technique, provided attention is paid to the level of ego functioning and object relatedness and the organization of unconscious content. When memories emerge from repression, they will be in a primitive or proto-symbolic form, which needs to be structured.

Freud, Anna (1981). A psychoanalyst's view of sexual abuse by parents. In: *Sexually Abused Children and Their Families,* ed. P. B. Mrazek and C. Kempe. New York: Pergamon Press, pp. 33-34.

Anna Freud presents a brief overview of the effects of child sexual abuse. She explains that children do not hate or shun abusing or sadistic parents because fear and love of the parent, coupled with natural dependency, give rise to a passive-submissive attitude that makes suffering exciting and ties the victim to the aggressor. In the incestuous relationship, children's anal-sadistic wishes and impulses are gratified, forcing the children into premature phallic or genital development while legitimate needs are ignored. The gratification of oedipal fantasies binds the children more tightly to the aggressors and interferes with age-appropriate separation from the family. Aftereffects may be that 1) the adult longs for repetition in the role of seducer or seduced or 2) there is massive denial, repression, and inhibition of sexuality, leading to frigidity or impotence.

Goodstein, Richard and Page, Ann (1981). Battered wife syndrome: Overview of dynamics and treatment. *Amer. J. Psychiat.*, 138:1036-1044.

The authors review the clinical and therapeutic issues related to the battered wife. They classify family backgrounds and individual dynamics.

Both partners in the family system must be understood, since the woman may be an unwitting collaborator.

Herman, Judith (1981). *Father-Daughter Incest*. Cambridge, MA: Harvard University Press.

This landmark study of 40 incest victims and their families describes the prevalence and adverse effects of incest and summarizes Herman's clinical and feminist analyses of the etiology and impact of incest. She argues that incest is the result of the patriarchal power structure that makes fathers all-powerful and female children defenseless. Mothers in the study were either dysfunctional or overwhelmed with illness and childrearing responsibilities. The daughters felt responsible for nurturing both parents and for keeping father happy. Adult women described feelings of isolation and self-hatred, yet, as a defense against childhood helplessness, also felt that they had unique and special powers over others. Sixty percent had major depressive symptoms; twenty percent abused alcohol or drugs. Relationships were usually unstable and often abusive, with periods of compulsive sexual activity or sexual abstinence.

Bank, Stephen and Kahn, Michael (1982). *The Sibling Bond*. New York: Basic Books.

The authors' literature review and their own clinical interview study of childhood sibling incest lead them to conclude that the long-term effects of incest are more pernicious for women than for men. [See Chapter 17 for annotation.]

Blum, Harold (1982). Psychoanalytic reflections on the "beaten wife syndrome." In: *Women's Sexual Experience: Explorations of the Dark Continent*, ed. M. Kirkpatrick. New York: Plenum Press, pp. 263-267.

Blum considers "wife-beating syndrome" as a complex issue with socio-cultural, sexual, and psychological dimensions. A woman may remain in a situation where she is mistreated because of many factors, including crippling dependence that is psychological, social, and physical; the result of regressive personality disorganization derived from traumatic abuse; safety concerns; isolation; cultural sanction; and the effects of drugs. Blum notes that masochism may play some part; women may seek their own form of misery in a sadomasochistic relationship that is provoked by both partners. Guilt-ridden women and masochistic characters may seek pain, humiliation, punishment, an identification with their sadistic partners, and an acting out of beating fantasies. Assault can activate sadomasochistic tendencies and fantasies of punishment. Masochism does not account for all cases and causes of battering and in no way provides an excuse for the physical or psychological abuse.

Aggressive proclivities are universally found, and victimized women are at risk as perpetrators of child abuse. Issues of internal controls, self-regulation, and failure to sublimate aggressive and sadomasochistic tendencies are also important.

Kaufman, Irving (1982). Father-daughter incest. In: *Father and Child: Developmental and Clinical Perspectives*, ed. S. Cath, A. Gurwitt, and J. Ross. Boston, MA: Little, Brown, pp. 491-507.

Kaufman reviews current perspectives on incest, including the family dynamics and psychodynamics. Father-daughter incest is frequently a search for nurturing for both parties and a shared expression of anger at mothers for desertion. The intense affective interaction binds the family members together. Most father and daughter participants are depressed; a smaller group are schizophrenic. This sexual union is a manifestation of the symbiotic process. A third group of fathers are sadomasochistic, and the sexual act is a manifestation of their perversion. Most of the mothers were rejected daughters and use their own daughters as substitute mothers because they are often threatened by their husband's sexual wishes. The daughters frequently function well until the incest is disclosed. Legal intervention can cause more severe iatrogenic trauma than the sexual encounter. The severity of the consequences of incest depends on the personality matrix of both the family and the girl. Character disorders with accompanying acting out are the most frequent outcome for these daughters. Primary goals of therapy are to further separation-individuation and autonomy for daughters and to treat unresolved parental pathology.

Lister, Eric (1982). Forced silence: A neglected dimension of trauma. *Amer. J. Psychiat.*, 139:872-876.

Lister discusses the value of communicating the fact of incest to the therapist for patients for whom such communication had implicitly or explicitly been prohibited. Recounting the trauma breaks a promise, retaliation by the perpetrator then becomes possible, and a secret relationship with the internalized image of the perpetrator is disrupted. Disclosure requires the victim to undergo a separation that may feel like the loss of a primary object tie. The explicit rendering of details in treatment is likely to be preceded by subtle and perhaps unconscious clues, with the therapist cast into the role of the caring parent who notices these clues or the abandoning parent who fails to notice them. Direct disclosure is defended against because of shame, guilt, and fear of rejection. Magical thinking to avoid disclosure of memories is a common defense mechanism. Disclosure may be accompanied by genuine terror, as though the patient and therapist were in the presence of the perpetrator.

Gelinas, Denise (1983). The persisting negative effects of incest. *Psychiat.*, 46:312-332.

This comprehensive article discusses the presentation of disguised but persisting effects of incest in the adult patient. A chronic traumatic neurosis, problems in interpersonal relationships, and increased intergenerational risks of incest are common findings. Most adults seek treatment for elaboration of the symptoms of traumatic neuroses: chronic depression, poor self-esteem, suicidal ideation, chronic anxiety, irritability, and impulsive behavior. Gelinas argues against the diagnosis of borderline personality disorder for most victims. She differentiates between a chronic state of trauma and ego weaknesses. Although she appreciates the need for long-term, expressive treatment for these patients, she underestimates the transference/countertransference difficulties.

Kramer, Selma (1983). Object-coercive doubting: A pathological defensive response to maternal incest. *J. Amer. Psychoanal. Assn.* (Suppl.), 31:325-351.

Kramer describes the pathological consequences of a mother's extended and repeated play with her child's genitals and contrasts this with previous reports of mother-son sexual intercourse. The mother's forced denial of the genital arousal, coupled with masturbatory prohibitions, rendered the child unable to separate, unable to believe his own perceptions, and needing to coerce repeated external confirmation.

Eisnitz, Alan (1984-1985). Father-daughter incest. *Int. J. Psychoanal. Psychother.*, 10:495-503.

This paper is a clinical and theoretical discussion of Soll's (1984-1985) paper, "The Transferable Penis and the Self-Representation," which emphasizes the role of father-daughter incest in female psychic development. Although a range of psychopathology results from incest, the most serious problems are in the area of self-representation, with the need to seek a narcissistic object choice to shore up a faulty self-representation. Eisnitz finds that father-daughter incest is not as deleterious as mother-son incest, because the relationship with the father defends against an early maternal merger. He disagrees with Soll that the father's penis is transferred to the daughter (in fantasy); it is instead actually shared, reflecting a defect in the self-object boundary.

Hopkins, Juliet (1984). The probable role of trauma in a case of foot and shoe fetishism: Aspects of the psychotherapy of a 6-year-old girl. *Int. Rev. Psycho-Anal.*, 11:79-91.

[See Chapter 19 for annotation.]

Margolis, Marvin (1984). A case of mother-adolescent son incest: A follow-up study. *Psychoanal. Q.*, 53:355-385.

Both this article and Margolis (1977) discuss the case of a young man who sought psychotherapy because he had sexually assaulted his mother and threatened to kill her and her boyfriend. Margolis discards the hypothesis that this behavior was a direct behavioral expression of oedipal fantasies. Instead, he postulates, the repression of major aspects of a positive oedipal drive was necessary for the incest to occur. Castration anxiety, guilt, and repression were present. Margolis considers the incest behavior to be a complex compromise formation that allowed limited and defensively altered expression of oedipal and sadomasochistic preoedipal urges. The patient's superego was pathologically malformed as a result of a traumatic childhood and adolescence.

Masson, Jeffrey (1984). *The Assault on Truth: Freud's Suppression of the Seduction Theory.* New York: Farrar, Straus and Giroux.

Masson criticizes Freud's abandonment of the seduction theory. His controversial and provocative book also contains a valuable review of some French publications on childhood sexual abuse. These serve as evidence that Freud learned about sexual abuse while studying under Charcot. Masson argues that Freud abandoned his seduction theory because he was professionally isolated and therefore was looking for a less controversial theory and because of his guilt over the incident with Emma Eckstein. Fleiss had operated on Eckstein's nose, causing her to experience severe pain and bleeding. Initially, Freud dismissed her symptoms as hysterical until it was determined that Fleiss had left surgical gauze in her nose. Masson asserts that Freud was forced to abandon his emphasis on the role of real trauma in the etiology of neurosis in order to maintain his idealized relationship with Fleiss.

Smith, Sydney (1984). The sexually abused patient and the abusing therapist: A study in sadomasochistic relationships. *Psychoanal. Psychol.*, 1:89-98.

Smith explores the dynamics of therapist-patient sexual relationships. The abusing therapist maintains the unrealistic expectation that the patient should be a primary source of comfort. This narcissistic sense of entitlement interferes with reality testing. The therapist's goal is sadistic seduction, despite any conscious profession of love. Often the patient was a past victim of childhood incest, and the treatment evokes a childhood wish to be special, leading to a repetition of masochistic submission to the abuser in order to maintain the relationship.

Soll, Maxwell (1984-1985). The transferable penis and the self-representation. *Int. J. Psychoanal. Psychother.*, 10:473-493.

Soll presents analyses of several nonborderline women who experienced incestuous postoedipal relationships with their fathers. He proposes that a bisexual self-representation is maintained by these women who have serious conflictual feelings about their functional sexual identity. The bisexual fantasy consists of being male and possessing a penis. However, this forbidden male aspect of the self-representation is intensely defended against, resulting in ego distortion, limited drive gratification, and disturbances in object relationships. In all the cases, maternal loss, deprivation, or pathology was apparent and complicated the attribution of pathological findings solely to the father-daughter object relationship.

Juda, Daniel (1985). Psychoanalytically oriented crisis intervention and treatment of rape co-victims. *Dynamic Psychother.*, 3:41-58.

Juda describes the impact of rape on the co-victim (the person closest to the victim at the time of the offense). The co-victim empathically and vicariously recapitulates the victimization psychologically and passes through the normal crisis response in tandem with the victim. Juda provides a model of the co-victim's response based on his or her fantasy of the crime, own personality and characteristic defensive style, and relationship with the victim. Juda recommends immediate crisis intervention for the co-victim as well as for the rape victim. Further psychotherapy may be indicated when the rape coincides with repressed, forbidden fantasies.

Winestine, Muriel (1985b). Compulsive shopping as a derivative of a childhood seduction. *Psychoanal. Q.*, 54:70-72.

A brief clinical vignette describes a woman with uncontrollable, compulsive shopping sprees. Through analytic work she recalled a memory of early abuse, which she had not fully repressed. During her sprees she had the fantasy of being the wife of a famous multimillionaire who had the power and funds to give her whatever she wished. Thus, she reversed her actual feelings of helplessness in yielding to her impulses and staved off feelings of humiliation and worthlessness for being out of control. The sprees were reenactments of her early abuse, elaborated through fantasy and symptom formation.

Adams-Silvan, Abby (1986). The active and passive fantasy of rape as a specific determinant in a case of acrophobia. *Int. J. Psycho-Anal.*, 67:467-473.

Associations, memories, and the analysis of a reenactment in the treatment of a young woman demonstrated that the wish to rape and be raped were specific determinants of her severe acrophobia. Preoedipal fears of abandonment and anal-sadistic impulses were predisposing factors coloring her oedipal struggles.

Hodges, Jill (1986). Provisional diagnostic profile on a sexually abused girl. *Bull. Anna Freud Cent.*, 9:235-267.

This diagnostic report of a 16-year-old female who presented with atypical pain and swelling in her legs is a detailed case example of the lingering effects of childhood sexual abuse.

Rose, Deborah (1986). "Worse than death": Psychodynamics of rape victims and the need for psychotherapy. *Amer. J. Psychiat.*, 143:817-824.

Rose proposes a treatment model for rape victims based on the psychodynamics of psychic trauma and of loss. A transference/counter-transference paradigm, "therapist as rapist," contributes to a misalliance when both patient and therapist use denial and avoidance.

Russell, Diana (1986). *The Secret Trauma; Incest in the Lives of Girls and Women*. New York: Basic Books.

Russell provides a comprehensive epidemiologic study of female sexual assault. Sixteen percent (or approximately one of every six) of the women in a random sample had experienced incest; only two percent of these experiences were reported to authorities. The trauma was greater when positive feelings or ambivalence about the incest were present than when the experience was felt to be unwanted. Stepfather-daughter incest occurred seven times more frequently than biological father-daughter incest. Female perpetrators were rare and tended to be less abusive.

Solin, Cynthia (1986). Displacement of affect in families following incest disclosure. *Amer. J. Orthopsychiat.*, 56:570-576.

Solin applies her understanding of psychological defenses to the family system. Just after disclosure, incestuous family members typically displace their feelings of rage and betrayal onto therapists and agencies, in an attempt to maintain the family system. If not dynamically understood, such displacement can impede treatment.

Cohler, Jonas (1987). Sex, love and incest. *Contemp. Psychoanal.*, 23:604-621.

Cohler reviews the literature on the centrality of incest in the evolution of neuroses and developmental fixations. Three clinical cases illustrate the linkage between the trauma of incest, developmental disturbances, and intrapsychic elaboration in fantasy. For each woman, the incest trauma confirmed a deep distrust in men and engendered pervasive rage and chronic feelings of victimization. They compulsively sought new male objects as substitutes for their fathers, to master and control the trauma-related anxiety, to find the powerful, strengthening phallus acquired in fantasy during father-daughter incest and to seek punishment for the incest crime. The incestuous relationship destroyed the primary bond with mother, with the girl turning to father as the object of identification, creating an internal distortion of the self-representation. Screen memories served as partitions for earlier repressed memories and affects. Since oedipal fantasies had become real, a defective sense of reality developed. Confronting and mourning the loss of omnipotence and magical thinking were necessary parts of treatment. Therapeutic change was attributed to repetition and working through in the transference, rather than merely to genetic reconstruction, recall of memories, and integration of the patient's personal history.

Ehrenberg, Darlene (1987). Abuse and desire: A case of father-daughter incest. *Contemp. Psychoanal.*, 24:593-604.

Dissociation or denial of her own responsive participation in an incestuous relationship became the basis for a woman patient's alienation from and repudiation of all her desires in any future relationships.

Gluckman, Caroline (1987). Incest in psychic reality. *J. Child Psychother.*, 13:109-123.

This article discusses how incest impedes the capacity for symbol formation. When father-child incest occurs, generational differences are blurred and the child becomes a container for the father's projections. Omnipotent thinking develops defensively in abused children, including a triumphant attitude over the mother as a defense against feelings of guilt and depression. In fantasy, the father's penis is incorporated at the expense of the mother, who is seen as robbed, attacked, and damaged. For the father, the child is a narcissistic object, representing an adored and possessed child-part of himself. Children must cope with unmetabolized stimulation by ridding themselves of persecutory and painful feelings through identification with the corrupting parental figures, projective identification, denial, or psychosis. Early incest may lead to massive body/mind confusion and the inability to differentiate self and objects. Psychoanalysis can modify the psychic impact of incest.

Herman, Judith and Schatzow, Emily (1987). Recovery and verification of memories of childhood sexual trauma. *Psychoanal. Psychol.*, 4:1-14.

This article discusses trauma and defense in 53 women outpatients who participated in short-term psychotherapy groups for incest survivors. Massive repression was the main defense available to patients who were abused early in childhood or who suffered violent abuse. These patients most closely resembled Freud's classic hysterics, both in their symptomatology and in their cathartic responses to the breakthrough of previously repressed memories. Women whose predominant experience of abuse was in latency and whose abuse was not particularly violent or sadistic seemed to employ a combination of defenses, including partial repression, dissociation, and intellectualization. Those women whose predominant experiences of abuse had occurred in adolescence generally preserved conscious memory and presented a constellation of defenses different from that of women who had been abused in early childhood. Preservation of memories did not prevent the formation of classic hysterical symptoms. The authors assert that psychotherapy, including the temporarily disorganizing or painful experience of recovery of repressed memories, promotes integration and recovery.

Matas, M. and Marriott, A. (1987). The girl who cried wolf: Pseudologia phantastica and sexual abuse. *Can. J. Psychiat.*, 32:305-309.

The authors review the literature on pseudologia phantastica, which is characterized by gross falsifications that begin as conscious deceptions but become extensive and complex fantasies that take on a life of their own. They present one example of an incest and rape accusation/fantasy. The authors describe their countertransference reactions as they realized that the patient had not told them the truth. They propose that the fantasy or lies represented a wish fulfillment and were an example of the patient's psychic functioning.

Nachmani, Gilead (1987). Fathers who mistake their daughters for their mothers. *Contemp. Psychoanal.*, 23:621-630.

Nachmani analyzed four women who had incestuous relationships with their fathers during adolescence. He applies psychoanalytic methods to the family systems to present a theoretical description of the incestuous family and its members. The incestuous fathers grew up with cold mothers and distant, idealized fathers and longed to achieve heroic roles in adolescence to repair a sense of inadequacy and lack of intimacy. As adults, they were self-absorbed and preoccupied with fantasies of achievement, and they sought self-definition. They chose wives who regarded marriage as a rescue from a dreadful world rather than as a relationship, a hoped-for maternal symbiosis in which to contain projective identifications. The husband was attracted to the wife's grandiose attributions and expectations. Relatedness thus was based on magical hopes, delusion, and then despair, rage, and emptiness. The mother gave "as if" narcissistic child care, resented the daughter's dependency needs, and failed to treat her as a person in her own right. The child's self-experiences were at variance from parent to parent. The daughter was caught between the parental needs and propelled by her maternal deprivation toward the father. Father found in his daughter the idealization he needed to affirm omnipotent fantasies of perfection. Both father and daughter were seeking a maternal experience.

O'Brien, John (1987). The effects of incest on female adolescent development. *J. Amer. Acad. Psychoanal.*, 15:83-92.

On the basis of work with 60 adolescent female victims of incest and their families, the author asserts that the adolescent developmental tasks of separation from the family and establishment of a positive sense of self, development of reality testing, establishment of heterosexual relationships, consolidation of body image, attainment of a sense of mastery over the environment, and reaffirmation of basic trust are all seriously compromised by the incest experience.

Schimek, Jean (1987). Fact and fantasy in the seduction theory: A historical review. *J. Amer. Psychoanal. Assn.*, 35:937-965.

Schimek reviews Freud's changing versions of the seduction theory from 1896-1933. She argues that Freud based his theory on the reconstruction of childhood sexual seductions of his adult patients rather than on evidence of actual seductions. Further, his theory of external trauma was not meant to account by itself for the appearance of later neurotic symptoms. The relevance of the evolution of Freud's theories for understanding current issues about the roles of external trauma, fantasy, and reconstruction are discussed.

Skues, Richard (1987). Jeffrey Masson and the assault on Freud. *Brit. J. Psychother.*, 3:305-314.

Skues argues that previous papers have dismissed Masson without seriously answering his challenge. He states that Masson's historical reconstruction is unsound on its own internal evidence and that the theoretical conclusions he draws are based on a gross misunderstanding not only of psychoanalysis and the role of fantasy, but also of the seduction theory itself.

Fehrenbach, Peter and Monastersky, Caren (1988). Characteristics of female adolescent sexual offenders. *Amer. J. Orthopsychiat.*, 58:148-151.

Previously published research on female sexual offenders emphasized that these females are usually accompanied or coerced by a male offender. The authors interviewed 28 female adolescent offenders who had been convicted of either rape or indecent liberties. With one exception, the victims were all children 12 years or younger. All offenders knew their victims. Half of the offenders had been sexually abused as children. None had been coerced or accompanied by a male. There was no indication of the repetitive patterns of sexual offense often found with male offenders. On the basis of this sample, prior sexual abuse alone does not explain becoming an offender.

Ganzarain, Ramon and Buchele, Bonnie (1988). *Fugitives of Incest: A Perspective from Psychoanalysis and Groups*. New York: International Universities Press.

Drawing from their clinical work with over 90 adult patients seen in individual psychotherapy, group psychotherapy, and consultations, the authors provide an excellent description of the development of the self of the incest victim, the psychopathology induced by the defenses used by victims following their incest experiences, and the intense trans-ference/countertransference dynamics in their treatment. This approach to working with problematic, acting-out behavior demonstrates the need for a psychodynamic understanding of the interaction of trauma and conflict. The authors recommend long-term psychoanalytically oriented group psychotherapy led by male and female cotherapists to temper countertransference emotions, offer a surrogate "parental couple," and, through the group-as-a-whole, provide the members a good-enough mothering atmosphere in which it is safe to be oneself.

MacCarthy, Brendan (1988). Are incest victims hated? *Psychoanal. Psychother.*, 3:113-120.

The prevalence of self-hatred in incest victims is examined. Because new objects are experienced by incest victims as disappointing and hate is unconscious, negative therapeutic reactions are frequent. MacCarthy views the incestuous father's motive as a wish to achieve symbiotic contact not available with the mother. The child attempts to repair the weak and helpless father and also searches for sexual excitement and relief. The paper explores the intense transferences, the victim's difficulty acknowledging having experienced gratification, and the countertransferences, including hate and distancing.

Parens, Henri (1988). Siblings in early childhood: Some direct observational findings. *Psychoanal. Inq.*, 8:31-50.

Parens suggests that sometimes sibling incest fantasies and actual enactments may be adaptive; the turn to the sibling relieves the pressure from threatening parental incestuous fantasies and paves the way for normal attachment to peers, especially in adolescence. [See Chapter 17 for annotation.]

Sinason, Valerie (1988). Smiling, swallowing, sickening and stupefying: The effect of sexual abuse on the child. *Psychoanal. Psychother.*, 3:97-111.

Using child observation data, Sinason asserts that even in a loving home, unattuned parents can respond inappropriately to their children. She proposes a continuum in which children must struggle at times to keep an image of a good parent by smiling, becoming sick, or becoming stupid or blinded to what is happening to them. These infantile defensive processes are described using clinical examples from the psychoanalytic psychotherapy of two sexually abused patients. A five-year-old girl utilized layers of stupidity and numbing to accommodate abuse. A boy struggled with his identification with the aggressor.

Ulman, Richard and Brothers, Doris (1988). *The Shattered Self: A Psychoanalytic Study of Trauma*. Hillsdale, NJ: The Analytic Press.

Using the theories of self psychology, the authors discuss rape and incest victims and Vietnam combat veterans. They argue that trauma results from real occurrences whose unconscious meaning is the shattering of central organizing fantasies of self in relation to selfobject. The shattering and faulty restoration of such archaic narcissistic fantasies are expressed in the symptoms of posttraumatic stress disorder (PTSD). Instead of viewing PTSD as an anxiety disorder (as in DSM-III), the authors consider the critical clinical feature to be the dissociations. The authors include an excellent review of the trauma literature and many case vignettes.

Van Leeuwen, Kato (1988). Resistances in the treatment of a sexually molested 6-year-old girl. *Int. Rev. Psycho-Anal.*, 15:149-156.

Van Leeuwen presents a case illustrating the profound effect of sexual abuse on the development and character structure of a six-year-old girl who had functioned relatively well before the traumatic events. The question of whether a seduction had taken place was affirmed only after considerable therapy, with great hesitation, unexpectedly and suddenly; the confession then was quickly retracted and denied. The resistance to revelation was difficult to overcome. The author emphasizes that the symptoms of sexual abuse are detectable and require quiet, unexcited, reassuring resolution.

Bernstein, Anne (1989). Analysis of two adult female patients who had been victims of incest in childhood. *J. Amer. Acad. Psychoanal.*, 17:207-221.

The history of the seduction theory in psychoanalysis is reviewed. Symptoms in adult analysands who had been sexually molested as children include depression, defective sense of ownership of self, disturbed object representations and ego functioning, somatization, doubting of reality with cognitive confusion, sleep disorder, and identification with the aggressor. Transference manifestations include difficulty establishing basic trust, the need for a real relationship with the analyst, and transference wishes to be seduced. The analyst may be seen as the perpetrator, as the seductive parent, or as the wished-for good parent. Two analytic cases illustrate de-repression of the trauma and recovery of memories, with panic and depersonalization. Countertransference reactions to the projective identification and to the patient's panic and wishes for protection are discussed. These intense panic states and transferences threaten the integrity of an analysis in ways that fantasies of seduction do not.

Bigras, Julien (1989). Father-daughter incest: 25 years of experience of psychoanalytic psychotherapy with victims. *Can. J. Psychiat.*, 34:804-806.

Theoretical and clinical issues are discussed using data from psychoanalytic psychotherapy with 12 adolescent girls during violent crises and 12 former adult victims with no apparent crisis. Classical psychoanalytic psychotherapeutic treatment was found ineffective; more supportive, yet firm, therapy was found helpful.

Bollas, Christopher (1989). The trauma of incest. In: *Forces of Destiny: Psychoanalysis and Human Idiom.* London: Free Association Press, pp. 171-180.

According to Bollas, when a father commits incest he represents the body of the mother and annihilates the phallus as an intrapsychic object that can facilitate the evolution to independence. The child's sexual desire then becomes misdirected in a regressive fashion. Mental representations of self and other blur selectively, and dreams may be filled with electrifying anxiety. The child has difficulty distinguishing dream from reality. This blurring of reality results in an impairment in reverie, and one's internal space no longer serves as a good container that can transform life experiences into nurturing psychic material. In analysis, incest victims may resist experiencing sexual feelings and needs in the paternal transference and may show defensive contempt for the analyst. Countertransferences include the feeling that the analyst has lost the right to analyze, just as the patient has lost her right to dream, fantasy, play, desire, and form new relationships.

Dewald, Paul (1989). Effects on an adult of incest in childhood: A case report. *J. Amer. Psychoanal. Assn.*, 37:997-1014.

Dewald presents clinical material on a middle-aged woman with symptoms of anxiety, depression, low self-esteem, and unfulfillment. She had been flooded with images of ego-alien sexual fantasies and desires, including sex with strangers or with children, and homosexual and exhibitionistic fantasies and impulses. During analysis, images and memories of sexual interactions with her father emerged. Dewald states that none of the patient's multiple characterological and symptomatic disturbances were specific for incest. He proposes that in cases of overt incest, alloplastic modes of expression of oedipal conflict are observable in physical activity, acting out, and other manifest behaviors. This behavioral repetition derives from the experiencing of the original oedipal conflict in previously condoned overt behaviors, so that the overstimulation limited successful discharge by autoplastic (fantasy) means. By contrast, when parent-child interaction is at the level of fantasy and verbalization, autoplastic intrapsychic symptom formation and character disturbances result. Patients with a history of incest test the analyst and the analytic situation repeatedly and expect themselves to be responsible for behavioral control of the relationship boundaries. Even minor transference gratifications may intensify conflict and increase resistance to a full exploration of the trauma.

Diamond, Diana (1989). Father-daughter incest: Unconscious fantasy and social fact. *Psychoanal. Psychol.*, 6:421-437.

Two cases illustrate the ways in which the external reality of incest combines with pervasive fantasies at particular developmental stages to determine the nature and extent of the pathology of incest victims. An analysis of the mental representation of the incest experience in fantasy is crucial to the success of treatment.

Marcus, Barbara (1989). Incest and the borderline syndrome: The mediating role of identity. *Psychoanal. Psychol.*, 6:199-215.

Marcus reviews empirical studies that suggest a relationship between borderline psychopathology and a history of incest. She suggests that incest is one of a class of events that potentially disrupt the establishment of boundaries crucial to identity formation. Through a review of child development research and psychoanalytic object relations theory, she uses incest as a prototypical model to illustrate how borderline psychopathology emerges in response to persistent and traumatic actual breaches of the boundary between children's wishes and the wishes of caretakers, also considering genetic endowments.

Richards, Arnold (1989). Self-mutilation and father-daughter incest: A psychoanalytic case report. In: *Fantasy, Myth, and Reality: Essays in Honor of Jacob A. Arlow, M.D.*, ed. H. Blum, Y. Kramer, A. Richards, and A. Richards. Madison, CT: International Universities Press, pp. 465-478.

Richards presents the case of a young woman who repeatedly and severely burned herself and engaged in such other self-destructive acts as promiscuity, drug abuse, and suicidal gestures. The self-mutilation, including cutting her breasts and genitals, burning her skin, and aggravating existing sores, was shown in the analytic material through transference manifestations to be a symbolic representation of early traumatic and sadomasochistic experiences with her father, mother, and sisters. Analysis of the transference was central to an understanding of her self-mutilative behavior and to her eventual recovery.

Shengold, Leonard (1989). *Soul Murder: The Effects of Childhood Abuse and Deprivation.* New Haven, CT: Yale University Press.

This volume, a compilation of Shengold's previously published papers, draws on clinical material as well as literary analysis to highlight the crippling effects of abuse and deprivation on the psychic development of the child. [See annotations for Shengold, (1979, 1980) in this chapter.]

Bernstein, Anne (1990). The impact of incest trauma on ego development. In: *Adult Analysis and Childhood Sexual Abuse*, ed. H. Levine. Hillsdale, NJ: The Analytic Press, pp. 65-91.

Clinical material about two patients who remembered incest trauma in the course of long analyses is similar to that described by Bernstein (1989). Emergence of memories was associated with panic and depersonalization. Ego damage in these patients included a defective sense of ownership or control of the self, cognitive deficits with doubt of reality, defensive somatization, identification with the aggressor, internally disturbed object representations, impaired capacity to trust, need for a real relationship with the analyst, vertical splitting, compartmentalization of the incest trauma, depressive affect, and impaired self-esteem. Bernstein asserts the need to find a balance in the countertransference between providing a reparative, caretaking relationship and taking an analytic stance.

Bigras, Julien (1990). Psychoanalysis as incestuous repetition: Some technical considerations. In: *Adult Analysis and Childhood Sexual Abuse*, ed. H. Levine. Hillsdale, NJ: The Analytic Press, pp. 173-196.

Female incest victims who seek treatment with a male analyst after either a seduction or a disappointment with a prior male therapist may sometimes be enacting a sadomasochistic repetition. Male therapists encounter difficulty with the seductive behavior of incest victims and with their underlying profound oral deprivation. The task is to be kind without being overprotective, present without being intrusive, available without being aloof. Female analysts encountering massive sadomasochistic maternal transferences may experience overcompassion, overidentification with needs for revenge, or excessive defensive remoteness. The incestuous negative maternal transference is difficult for analysts of both genders. Termination for incest victims may involve the need to continue the caring relationship with the real person of the analyst, in the form of extra sessions.

Burland, J. Alexis and Raskin, Raymond (1990). The psychoanalysis of adults who were sexually abused in childhood: A preliminary report from the discussion group of the American Psychoanalytic Association. In: *Adult Analysis and Childhood Sexual Abuse*, ed. H. Levine. Hillsdale, NJ: The Analytic Press, pp. 35-41.

In this discussion group's experience, resultant trauma is related to the developmental timing of sexual abuse. Difficulty with self-other boundaries often results from abuse in the first three years, whereas vulnerability to experiencing guilt and responsibility results from abuse in the oedipal period. Certain clinical features should alert therapists to possible sexual abuse: unusually intense castration fears; repetitive traumatic dreams; the need to distance oneself from others; basic depressive affect; periods of cognitive confusion and dissociative states, particularly when repressed memories of abuse are being recovered; doubting of associations; inability to differentiate between fantasies and memories of abuse; and a need to disbelieve one's thoughts. During the analyses of abused patients, periods occurred where grasp on reality collapsed and self-doubting and confusion intensified, despite these patients' prior high functioning. The patients reverted to previously adequate functioning as memories were recovered and acknowledged. Other clinical issues include splitting of self-image and parental images when the abuser was a parent, difficulty developing trust, negative transferences, erotized masochistic transferences as resistance, actualization of memories as resistance, and countertransference reactions of guilt, anxiety, overinvolvement, and resistance to hearing memories. The previous maternal deprivation and inadequate protection of abused patients, as reflected in negative dyadic transferences, need to be analyzed before memories of abuse surface.

Huizenga, Judith (1990). Incest as trauma: A psychoanalytic case. In: *Adult Analysis and Childhood Sexual Abuse*, ed. H. Levine. Hillsdale, NJ: The Analytic Press, pp. 117-135.

Material from the analysis of a woman who had intercourse with her father at age nine illustrates the traumatic impact of incest. Dream material is presented and technical difficulties in analyzing posttraumatic dream material are discussed. The patient had an unconscious fantasy that her father had damaged her genitals and uterus.

Kramer, Selma (1990). Residues of incest. In: *Adult Analysis and Childhood Sexual Abuse*, ed. H. Levine. Hillsdale, NJ: The Analytic Press, pp. 149-170.

Kramer explores the long-term consequences of incest by examining two phenomena that she believes are residues of parental sexual abuse: 1) somatic memories, comprising physical sensations and disturbances in sexual functioning, and 2) general and specific learning problems. Somatic memories of incest include great displeasure, aversion, or pain during foreplay or coitus, anorgasmia, and occasional, inexplicable furious rage during sexual activity. In analytic sessions, these patients complained of hyperacusis, hyperosmia, and excessive sensitivity to touch. Traumatic incidents and affects that are otherwise repressed or denied persist in these somatic forms and result in learning difficulties and muting of affects. These learning problems are partly a function of powerful resistances to remembering events and feelings connected with the incest. Other factors in learning problems include identification with the abusing parent's distortion of reality, obeying parental admonitions to not know, and shame and guilt in the older child. These patients are unable to trust themselves or others, including the analyst. Three female cases and one male case are discussed in this excellent chapter. The effects of abuse by mother or by father are differentiated.

Lazes, Pedro (1990). Fact and fantasy in brother-sister incest. *Int. Rev. Psycho-Anal.*, 17:97-113.

[See Chapter 17 for annotation.]

Levine, Howard (ed.)(1990a). *Adult Analysis and Childhood Sexual Abuse.* Hillsdale, NJ: The Analytic Press.

Organized around clinical issues in the psychoanalytic process, this book presents case material from the analyses of adults who were sexually abused or involved in incest in childhood. The topics discussed include modes of presentation for treatment, diagnostic issues, problems in particular phases of analysis, difficulties in transference and countertransference, and long-term consequences of abuse for ego development, including sexual dysfunctions, somatization, learning disabilities, and difficulties with symbolization. These patients often experience the transference as a threatened traumatic repetition, while they simultaneously act out aspects of their identification with the abuser. Doubting or distortions in the sense of reality, especially in regard to the specifics of the sexual trauma, are common. Implications for technique are addressed and analyses of adults and children who were sexually abused are compared. Contributors to this volume include Steele, Burland and Raskin, Raphling, Bernstein, Sherkow, Huizenga, Lisman-Pieczanski, Kramer, Bigras, and Levine. In the introduction, Levine includes extensive case material documenting the profound impact of a single sexual trauma on a two-and-a-half-year-old girl.

Levine, Howard (1990b). Clinical issues in the analysis of adults who were sexually abused as children. In: *Adult Analysis and Childhood Sexual Abuse*, ed. H. Levine. Hillsdale, NJ: The Analytic Press, pp. 197-218.

For many incest victims, the actual childhood trauma tends to organize and unconsciously inform their experience of an analysis and may dominate the transference. The childhood trauma is associated with a loss of parental protection, resulting in feelings of abandonment and problems with trust. Transference pressures to reexperience and relive the sexual abuse can be enormous, beyond the usual intensity of a transference neurosis. The "as if," illusory quality of the transference may disappear, so that the analytic situation can become a traumatic seduction or a failure to protect. Technical issues, including the development of the therapeutic alliance and countertransferences, are discussed. Levine highlights clinical phenomena including the victim role, difficulties with assertiveness, desire, and the sense of owning one's body; doubting; transference demands for help to know what happened; and countertransference pressures to enact the seductive or the wished-for protective parent.

Lisman-Pieczanski, Nydia (1990). Countertransference in the analysis of an adult who was sexually abused as a child. In: *Adult Analysis and Childhood Sexual Abuse*, ed. H. Levine. Hillsdale, NJ: The Analytic Press, pp. 137-141.

Strong countertransference feelings of deadness, disillusionment, helplessness, irritation, outrage, and disbelief emerge in this incomplete Kleinian analysis of a woman who was sexually abused in childhood by her godfather. The patient was severely disturbed, with primitive object relationships. She had had an affair with a previous therapist and came for "supervision" in her first visit with Lisman-Pieczanski. Dream material is included.

Raphling, David (1990). Technical issues of the opening phase. In: *Adult Analysis and Childhood Sexual Abuse*, ed. H. Levine. Hillsdale, NJ: The Analytic Press, pp. 45-64.

Several clinical vignettes of opening-phase material illustrate modifications in technique that may be required to establish an analytic process with some abused patients. Raphling suggests that these modifications may not preclude successful analysis, as they may be subsequently explored and interpreted. These patients often have strong feelings of vulnerability, expectations of empathic failure, susceptibility to re-creation of past trauma, fears of betrayal, and impaired ego capacities such as difficulty with reality testing and boundary formation. These traumatized patients also demonstrate an inability to distinguish past from present and fantasy from reality. Raphling discusses erotic transferences, erotization as a defense against aggression, and the gender of the analyst in relation to the gender of the abusing parent.

Sherkow, Susan (1990a). Consequences of childhood sexual abuse on the development of ego structure: A comparison of child and adult cases. In: *Adult Analysis and Childhood Sexual Abuse*, ed. H. Levine. Hillsdale, NJ: The Analytic Press, pp. 93-115.

Extensive clinical material from two female child patients and a male adult patient who had been abused in childhood illustrates that ego disturbances seen in abused children also are seen in the adult. These ego disturbances include an intensification of early castration anxiety, body-boundary difficulties, fears of object loss, interference with rapprochement, interference in consolidation of self-esteem, blurring of the ability to discriminate self and object, and interference with consolidation of gender identity. Certain features of play behavior in the children were exaggerated in the adult patients, such as stereotyping of symbolic functioning and use of primitive defenses in the context of relatively intact ego functioning. All patients were preoccupied with the question of fantasy versus reality.

Sherkow, Susan (1990b). Evaluation and diagnosis of sexual abuse of little girls. *J. Amer. Psychoanal. Assn.*, 38:347-369.

The ability to diagnose sexual abuse early in treatment is important since the analyst treats an abused child differently from one who wishes or fears sexual contact with an adult. Sherkow presents clinical material and outlines the following diagnostic criteria suggesting early sexual abuse 1) intense, sexualized play appearing very early in the consultation or treatment; 2) distinctive, driven intensity and a compulsive quality to the play; 3) preoccupation with a single, idiosyncratic kind of play; 4) extremely hostile aggressiveness; 5) stereotyping of symbolic play; 6) exaggeration of normal curiosity about sexual issues and genital differences; and 7) persistent retractions or preoccupation with reality versus fantasy.

Steele, Brandt (1990). Some sequelae of the sexual maltreatment of children. In: *Adult Analysis and Childhood Sexual Abuse*, ed. H. Levine. Hillsdale, NJ: The Analytic Press, pp. 21-34.

Abusive sexual activities are defined as those instigated by a person older than the child and extending beyond the child's ability to understand or manage the affects and conflicts that are generated. Lifelong sequelae include 1) difficulty in seeking and enjoying pleasure, 2) forming attachments to abusive love objects, 3) experiencing pervasive depressive feelings about never being able to have a rewarding intimate relationship as an adult, and 4) failing to form a coherent sense of self. The quality of relationships existing between the child, its caregivers, and with the molester are as important as the sexual act itself in the development of residual problems. Thus, abuse perpetrated by family members or friends tends to be more damaging. In parent-child incest, the child inevitably feels uncared for and the search for pleasure and need satisfaction becomes linked with feeling exploited and disregarded. A case example illustrates transgenerational transmission of maladaptive patterns.

Terr, Lenore (1990). Who's afraid in Virginia Woolf? Clues to early sexual abuse in literature. *The Psychoanalytic Study of the Child*, 45:533-546. New Haven, CT: Yale University Press.

The fictional characters in Virginia Woolf's novels manifest signs and symptoms common to victims of childhood traumas, such as fears, perceptual repetitions, and repetitive behaviors. In cases of long-standing sexual psychic trauma, sexual anesthesias, emotional distancing or numbing, self-hypnosis, splitting, and dissociation are observed. Virginia Woolf admitted long-standing and repetitive sexual abuse in her own childhood. Terr uses Woolf's fiction and autobiographical writings to discuss these symptoms and the possible defensive reaction of adults and readers to these abuses, including boredom, disbelief, and failure to respond.

# Section IV

# Clinical Concepts

# Chapter 25

# Gender Issues in Transference and Countertransference

Judith Chertoff and Nancy Kulish,
with Nadine Levinson and Eleanor Schuker

The papers in this chapter explore the ways in which gender influences the transference and countertransference. Most of the papers focus on the effects of gender on psychoanalytic treatment; a few examine such effects on psychotherapy and on the process of training and supervising therapists. Landmark papers on the erotized transference, as it emerges in both female and male patients, are also included.

The influence of the analyst's gender has been debated since Freud (1931a) first suggested that female analysts might have access to transferences not readily observable by male analysts. Several authors have asserted that the gender of the analyst directly influences the nature of the transference. Others believe that the analyst's gender not only affects the timing and intensity of classical analyses, but may become more influential in psychotherapies and incomplete analyses. The controversy about these issues may be followed here. Some authors discuss the ways in which gender affects the specific unfolding of transference in the four patient-analyst gender combinations: female patient/female analyst, female patient/ male analyst, male patient/female analyst, and male patient/male analyst. Countertransference issues in these dyads are also considered, with attention to potential transferences that may be missed because of gender factors. Several papers in this chapter discuss other clinical topics where gender is pertinent. These include the patient's choice of an analyst by gender, the dynamic implications of such a choice, and the way in which gender may influence transference and countertransference in supervision and training. The study of gender differences in transference/countertransference interactions may shed light on aspects of female and male psychology. [See Chapter 26 for transference/countertransference issues of the analyst's pregnancy.]

Freud, Sigmund (1915c). Observations on transference-love. *Standard Edition*, 12:158-171. London: Hogarth Press, 1953.

Freud describes the common situation where a female patient falls in love with her (male) doctor. He understands this erotic transference as a repetition of childhood experiences and reactions, rather than as arising from the reality situation. Freud points out that it is equally disastrous for the analysis if the patient's craving for love is gratified or if the yearning is suppressed. Transference love feels like genuine love, as it is provoked by the analysis, intensified by resistance, reproduces states of early infantile love, and lacks a degree of reality and regard for consequences. One group of women who cannot be analyzed are those "children of nature" and of elemental passion who insist on gratification. Freud conceptualizes transference love as a resistance or a defensive response that needs to be understood in the analytic situation and not acted on.

Freud, Sigmund (1920). The psychogenesis of a case of homosexuality in a woman. *Standard Edition*, 18:146-172. London: Hogarth Press, 1953.

Freud suggests that a female therapist would have been preferable for his female homosexual patient. [See also Chapters 1 and 19.]

Freud, Sigmund (1931a). Female sexuality. *Standard Edition*, 21:223-243. London: Hogarth Press, 1961.

Freud explicitly comments that female analysts are more likely than himself to elicit preoedipal maternal transferences. [See also Chapter 1.]

Bibring-Lehner, Grete (1936). A contribution to the subject of transference-resistance. *Int. J. Psycho-Anal.*, 17:181-189.

Bibring observes that a seemingly intractable transference-resistance can become accessible to analysis after a change to an analyst of the opposite sex. She describes two cases in which a change of analyst had beneficial effects. In these cases, the gender of the first analysts in conjunction with certain real features of their personalities matched those of the parent who had a strong influence on the patient. The effects of this similarity were 1) the illusory quality of the transference broke, 2) the patient's conflicts could not emerge gradually, 3) a fixation emerged to a certain rigid conflicted transference picture, and 4) the positive transference necessary for analytic work could not form. This article is one of the earliest to suggest a possible effect of the reality of the analyst's gender on the transference. Also of value is the clear and convincing clinical material.

**Thompson, Clara (1938). Notes on the psychoanalytic significance of the choice of analyst. *Psychiat.*, 1:205-216.**

Thompson describes and illustrates with clinical material, the neurotic and realistic reasons for the choice of an analyst of one gender or the other. She emphasizes that the defensive character of the choice can still be honored and worked through unless the analyst, in reality, fits or reinforces the patient's fantasies or needs for defense. She concludes that the analyst's personality is more important than gender in therapeutic outcome. Inasmuch as the patient's choice of an analyst of a given gender contributes to the transference, this article is helpful in understanding the unconscious meanings of this choice.

**Gitelson, Maxwell (1952). The emotional position of the analyst in the psycho-analytic situation. *Int. J. Psycho-Anal.*, 33:1-10.**

This article on countertransference includes a case in which a first dream of the patient's being in bed with the undisguised analyst indicates an unmanageable transference and countertransference.

**Rappaport, Ernest (1956). The management of an erotized transference. *Psychoanal. Q.*, 25:515-529.**

Erotization is understood as an especially strong resistance, usually in patients with defects in reality testing and critical judgment, so that the patient demands that the analyst be the parent, rather than seeing him "as if" he were the parent. These patients are angry, demanding, and cannot tolerate lack of gratification. Same-sex and opposite-sex dyads are described. Rappaport suggests technical application of the concept of "corrective emotional experience," which he defines as the analyst's being his (analytic) self, alert to blind spots wherein the patient may try to transform and control him.

**Tower, Lucia (1956). Countertransference. *J. Amer. Psychoanal. Assn.*, 4:224-255.**

Tower describes her countertransference reactions to four patients and deals extensively with the theoretical implications of these reactions. Three of her patients were male, and their analyses required the working through of paternal and homosexual material. The article adds clinical material to the literature on the male patient/female analyst dyad. It is of interest that one of these three cases was very successful, one was terminated prematurely, and one was unsuccessful. Tower describes the transference and countertransference interactions in one successful and one unsuccessful case. She believes the failed case had a narcissistic personality disorder. She postulates that he was unanalyzable by a woman because the defect in his masculine ego was reparable only by identification with, and actual incorporation of, a masculine ego in a treatment situation with a man.

Greenacre, Phyllis (1959). Certain technical problems in the transference relationship. *J. Amer. Psychoanal. Assn.*, 7:487-502. Also in: *Emotional Growth*, Vol. 2, 1971, pp. 651-669, and in: *Psychoanalytic Explorations of Technique*, ed. H. Blum. New York: International Universities Press, 1980, pp. 419-440.

Greenacre addresses the transference and reality aspects of the sex of the analyst. A patient's questions about choice of an analyst according to sex of analyst may actually reflect anxieties about beginning an analysis. Greenacre warns analysts against being overly active, establishing a real relationship that would overpower the transference, or joining in a reenactment of a past relationship. She discusses the "reality contact" between analyst and analysand in terms of the influence of the gender of the analyst.

Greenacre suggests that the analyst's gender may have an apparent effect if the analyst is pulled into reenacting within the analytic relationship the role of a parent of the same sex. In such cases, it is not the gender of the analyst that is the crucial variable but the reenactment. The sex of the analyst may be the vehicle to convey other, less apparent partial realities, such as particular transferences or homosexual fears. Some stalemated analyses receiving the recommendation for a new analyst of the opposite sex may be reflecting the analyst's resistance to examine other reasons for the stalemate. This article is important for its historical influence and has a helpful discussion of clinical issues.

Saul, Leon (1962). The erotic transference. *Psychoanal. Q.*, 31:54-61.

Saul emphasizes why the analyst must analyze emotional blocks based on childhood patterns rather than provide gratification of love needs for the patient with an erotic transference. Basic principles include: the analyst needs to help the patient find satisfactions in real life; transference longings are in essence infantile and incestuous; the analysis of the transference is the basis of analytic treatment and must be kept as uncomplicated as possible; and hostility and guilt are associated with frustrated love needs, which otherwise would have found prior satisfaction. Brief vignettes are about female patients.

Lax, Ruth (1969). Some considerations about transference and counter-transference manifestations evoked by the analyst's pregnancy. *Int. J. Psycho-Anal.*, 50:363-371.

[See Chapter 26 for annotation.]

Swartz, Jacob (1969). The erotized transference and other transference problems. *Psychoanal. For.*, 3:307-333, ed. J. Lindon.

Swartz describes four cases of erotized transference, including three of the female patient/male analyst dyad. In each of these three cases, the erotized transference indicated a failure of the therapeutic alliance or of the development of an analyzable transference neurosis. Patients' excessive, inappropriate, and unrealistic demands were related to earlier experiences, often derived from preoedipal factors. In the discussion of Swartz's paper, four analysts present their ideas. Solomon emphasizes weak ego structures, negative and hostile transference components, and the use of an erotized transference as a defense against a true object relationship. MacLeod stresses the patients' preoedipal pathology and oral deprivation. Rappaport relates the failure to disguise the analyst in the first dream to ego weakness. Knapp feels these cases exhibit "erotized anti-transference," resembling a "transference perversion" because of the tenacious acting out and difficulty appreciating the analyst's neutrality.

Broverman, Inge, Broverman, Donald, Clarkson, Frank, Rosenkrantz, Paul, and Vogel, Susan. (1970). Sex-role stereotypes and clinical judgments of mental health. *J. Consult. Clin. Psychol.*, 32:1-7.

This article suggests that sex-role biases affect clinical work and research about gender characteristics. [See Chapter 5 for annotation.]

Kernberg, Paulina (1971). The course of analysis of a narcissistic personality with hysterical and compulsive features. *J. Amer. Psychoanal. Assn.*, 19:451-471.

Intense negative transferences between the female analyst and female patient are attributed to the female analyst's being experienced as reflecting the patient's own negative self-representations about the defective and devalued aspects of her body and also her penis envy. [See Chapter 22 for annotation.]

Balint, Enid (1973). Technical problems in the analysis of women by a woman analyst: A contribution to the question "What does a woman want?" *Int. J. Psycho-Anal.*, 54:195-201.

Balint clarifies some technical problems in the analyses of women whose attachment to their mothers persists into adult life. She describes two patients, both of whom entered analysis because of marital difficulties. These cooperative patients were skilled at pleasing the female analyst, and it was initially difficult to detect the transference meaning of their behavior. In both cases, fantasies of exciting the analyst sexually derived from unresolved conflicts in the patients' relationships with their emotionally unavailable mothers. Neither patient repressed heterosexual drives, but nevertheless, both centered their lives around their mothers. By choosing husbands who seemed never able to satisfy them, these women repeated, but defensively reversed, childhood interactions in which they had been unable to satisfy their mothers. Balint discusses the theoretical aspects of these cases and suggests that despite the homosexual wishes of these patients, heterosexual strivings seemed primary. The wish to care for mother (and analyst) arose partly in response to the hostility of the oedipal phase, but also as an attempt to master the feelings associated with the mother's early depression and withdrawal. This is a useful article that helps to elucidate some aspects of the theory of female development and adds to our understanding of certain female patients.

Blum, Harold (1973). The concept of erotized transference. *J. Amer. Psychoanal. Assn.*, 21:61-76.

This excellent article reviews the concept of erotized transference and explores its pathogenesis, dynamics, and related clinical issues. Blum views the erotized transference as a particular distorted form of the expectable erotic transference, in which an intensely vivid, irrational preoccupation with the analyst is characterized by overt, seemingly ego-syntonic demands for love and sexual fulfillment. Erotization is often a distorted attempt to master trauma by active repetition. The erotization serves resistance and defends against hostility, homosexuality, loss, and other unconscious conflicts. Freud's (1915c) observations of the analyzable erotic transference are contrasted with several clinical descriptions of erotization in which a tenacious resistance and strong pregenital factors replace a workable transference neurosis in patients with deficient reality testing. Many of these patients resemble love addicts in their early ego impairment and use of projection and denial. Blum emphasizes, however, that some patients with erotized transference are not psychotic and do not have marked preoedipal fixations but, rather, are experiencing a revival of incestuous oedipal love and disappointment. Erotization masks a trauma of repeated oedipal seduction, overstimulation, and lack of parental, phase-appropriate protection, with resultant distrust and sadomasochistic masturbatory fantasies. Primal scene exposure, parental exhibitionism, and intrusion into the child's privacy are common genetic factors, and oedipal fantasies have some validation in reality. This sexual overstimulation contributes to a sense of omnipotence, confusion of fantasy and reality, and the development of a seductive style of defense.

Blum notes that florid erotic transferences can occur when analyst and patient are of the same sex. Analyzability of the erotic transference depends on intact ego functions. The analyst's resemblance to a childhood object in appearance or attributes is not significant per se, but only because the patient invests this resemblance with transference fantasy. The analytic task remains to differentiate past from present and fantasy from reality. Countertransference can be intense and play a role in erotized transference, but, Blum reminds his readers, the source of transference is the endogenous fantasies and unconscious past conflicts of the patient. His case examples are of the male analyst/female patient dyad.

Aaron, Ruth (1974). The analyst's emotional life during work. *J. Amer. Psychoanal. Assn.*, 22:160-169.

This report summarizes the proceedings of a panel about analysts' useful and problematic countertransference reactions. The panelists include Tolpin, Van Leeuwen, Baum, and Greenson. Tolpin describes a paternal transference of her male patient to herself as an admired and wise father, and her response of surprise. Van Leeuwen describes the transference and countertransference reactions to her pregnancy.

Viederman, Milton (1976). The influence of the person of the analyst. *Psychoanal. Q.*, 45:231-249.

Viederman describes a patient whose defective feminine self-representation was modified through transference fantasies about the analyst's wife, and through perceptions developing over the years of analysis about the analyst's attitude toward femininity. The case is discussed in the context of a review of the literature on the influence of the real person of the analyst. Viederman discusses changes in the patient's self-representation through the mechanism of identification as well as through transference interpretation. He contributes to our theoretical understanding of the analytic process in this attempt to document and explain what he believes was a structural change in his patient. He also illustrates how change in the self-representation can take place in a female patient treated by a male analyst.

Goldberg, Jane (1979). Aggression and the female therapist. *Mod. Psychoanal.*, 4:209-222.

Goldberg discusses culturally linked differences in the ways aggression is expressed by and toward male and female therapists. Her data are largely nonanalytic, drawing from sociological theory and from research on group and individual therapy. She concludes that when women behave contrary to cultural expectations, as in the analyst's impersonal, nonreciprocal role, they provoke frustration and aggression. In contrast, men who deviate from the usual authoritative role by being nurturing provoke less aggression. In the sections devoted to transference and countertransference, Goldberg further elaborates these conclusions. She suggests that the female therapist is more often the target of negative transferences than is the male therapist and may have a need to be more supportive than males. This article is interesting as background to the questions of gender, transference, and countertransference, but its conclusions are derived from sociological concepts and data from research on psychotherapy, so are not necessarily applicable to the psychoanalytic situation.

Kaplan, Alexandra (1979). Toward an analysis of sex-role related issues in the therapeutic relationship. *Psychiat.*, 42:112-120.

This paper is not analytic but may be a useful starting point for discussion by analysts who supervise and teach psychotherapy. It deals primarily with countertransference difficulties theorized to be characteristic of the male or female beginning therapist because of differences in the socialization and development of boys and girls. Kaplan provides evidence to support her supposition that men have difficulty with empathy but not with authority and that the opposite is true of women. She advocates that training programs openly address these differences in order to help beginning therapists overcome the countertransference difficulties that typify their gender.

Karme, Laila (1979). The analysis of a male patient by a female analyst: The problem of the negative oedipal transference. *Int. J. Psycho-Anal.*, 60:253-262.

This article describes the negative oedipal phase in the analysis of a male patient by a female analyst. Karme asserts that although paternal transference feelings were present, there was no sustained paternal transference neurosis. Karme believes that analysts have been reluctant to look at the differences in the analytic process that result from the gender of the analyst, and she attempts to clarify these differences on the basis of evidence from her case report. She concludes that preoedipal transferences are not influenced by the gender of the analyst, but that oedipal transferences develop according to the gender of the analyst. Oedipal transferences based on the parent of the opposite sex from the analyst are displaced onto someone outside the analysis. Karme adds interesting clinical material to the literature on this subject, although her theoretical conclusions have been questioned.

**Ottenheimer, Lilly (1979). Some psychodynamics in the choice of an analyst. *J. Amer. Acad. of Psychoanal.*, 7:339-344.**

Ottenheimer describes a female patient who was transferred to her after a male analyst's termination due to illness. The patient had initially insisted on a male analyst. Ottenheimer believes that the work with the male analyst had provided a corrective emotional experience for this patient, whose father had been passive and unavailable, and had thus played a necessary part in her recovery. The analyst's actual personality characteristics were also considered significant. The patient was later able to work with Ottenheimer. Ottenheimer includes a brief clinical vignette and occasional theoretical references but does not discuss the many conflicting points of view on this topic. The article was originally presented as a tribute to the male analyst involved in the case.

**Kirkpatrick, Martha and Morgan, Carole (1980). Psychodynamic psychotherapy of female homosexuality. In: *Homosexual Behavior*, ed. J. Marmor. New York: Basic Books, pp. 357-375.**

The authors discuss the homosexual transference to male and female therapists alike and view it as a sexualization of the maternal transference rather than as oedipally based. [See Chapter 19 for annotation.]

**Myers, Wayne (1980). A transference dream with superego implications. *Psychoanal. Q.*, 69:284-307.**

A particular type of transference dream is described in which a male analyst is initially represented as his usual male self but as the dream proceeds is transformed into a woman. For female patients with this type of dream, the transformation serves as a wishful undoing of transference revivals of the narcissistic mortifications inflicted by the father in his rejection of his daughter's emerging femininity and sexuality during the oedipal phase and later. These traumata appear to have had an important organizing effect on patients' negative view of femininity and feminine sexuality. The patients' mothers were also perceived as having been rejected by the fathers, and the bond formed between the mothers and daughters neutralized preoedipal aggressive investment in the maternal imago.

Superego formation for these patients followed sex-linked developmental lines, with protective, comforting currents from the mother and hostile elements from the father. Particularly at points of separation from the analyst, the narcissistic mortifications at the hands of the traumatizing father were revived in the transference and led to prolonged acting out and to the dream-transformations.

Tyson, Phyllis (1980). The gender of the analyst in relation to transference and countertransference manifestations in prelatency children. *The Psychoanalytic Study of the Child*, 35:321-338. New Haven, CT: Yale University Press.

Tyson explores the impact of the analyst's gender on the analysis of the prelatency child. She reviews the literature on the variety of transferences involved in the analysis of children and the literature on the influence of gender on the analytic process. Several cases illustrate the ways in which the gender of the analyst can be used by a child for defensive purposes, to complete a developmental step, and for working through specific conflicts. Although the unfolding of conflicts will sometimes be influenced by gender (and Tyson also presents cases where gender is not influential), she emphasizes that the "primary motivating manifestations stem from the pressure of the child's intrapsychic world." She describes one situation, the analysis of a girl fixated at the level of a preoedipal ambivalent relationship with her mother, where the female analyst may be at a disadvantage. Such a child, when seen by a man, may be able to use the real male analyst to move forward developmentally so that the preoedipal struggle becomes attenuated and more easily worked through. With the female analyst, resistance is greater and such movement more difficult. Tyson also describes cases in which paternal and negative oedipal transferences were clearly worked through in a male child treated by a female analyst. She adds considerably to our clinical and theoretical understanding of the impact of the gender of the analyst on the unfolding transference manifestations and resistances in analysis of prelatency children.

Beiser, Helen (1982). Styles of supervision related to child-analysis training and the gender of the supervisor. *The Annual of Psychoanalysis*, 10:57-76. New York: International Universities Press.

This study investigates child-analysis training and gender as factors influencing the characteristics of adult psychoanalytic case supervisors, as perceived by students at the Chicago Institute. The analytic students Q-sorted statements "most characteristic" to "least characteristic" of their supervisors. Gender differences were found to be greater than those related to child-analysis training. Women supervisors were perceived as a more uniform group, described as more open about themselves, more supportive and helpful, more flexible, and more aware of outside forces both in the patient's life and in the life of the student within the Institute. Men supervisors were seen as more task oriented, more intellectual, more oriented to resistances, more likely to have personal biases interfering with the acceptance of students' ideas, and having more individual variation. Supervisors were also asked to rate themselves. They predicted the perceived differences poorly. They did predict that women supervisors would be more aware of the meaning of external relationships; women supervisors, but not men supervisors, predicted that the men would have personal biases. The study's meaning and validity is discussed and related to questions of supervisory assignment.

Mogul, Kathleen (1982). Overview: The sex of the therapist. *Amer. J. Psychiat.*, 139:1-11.

This useful and inclusive review article by a psychodynamically oriented author covers the literature pertaining to the impact of the gender of the therapist in both psychoanalysis and psychotherapy. Mogul critically reviews the pertinent feminist literature as well as research, surveys, and clinical articles. She concludes that long-term, insight-oriented treatment is less often affected by the therapist's gender than by the therapist's experience, personality, and self-awareness. The course of the treatment, however, may be influenced in a variety of ways. With respect to less inclusive treatments, she reviews a variety of ways in which the gender of the therapist may facilitate either the unfolding or the suppression of certain conflicts.

Person, Ethel (1983). Women in therapy: Therapist gender as a variable. *Int. Rev. Psycho-Anal.*, 10:193-204. Also in: *Between Analyst and Patient*, ed. H. Meyers. Hillsdale, NJ: The Analytic Press, 1986, pp. 193-212.

Person uses her experience in conducting analysis, therapy, and supervision to delineate some of the reasons for women's choosing female analysts more frequently in recent years. She outlines some of the difficulties that may arise in the female patient/male analyst dyad. These include value judgments by the male analyst that impede the treatment and countertransference difficulties in dealing with erotic transferences. She describes several common concerns of female patients about seeing a male analyst, such as worry that they will be able to "fake it" with the analyst, concerns about sexism, and fears about their ability to seduce the analyst. Person discusses several theoretical issues, including the transference and nontransference meanings of dissembling or "faking it," which may involve deference to the male, need for his approval, and shame at sexual inadequacy. This article contributes to our clinical data concerning female patients' conscious and unconscious motivations in choosing an analyst.

Bernstein, Anne and Warner, Gloria (1984). Treatment of women by women, pp. 181-276. In: *Women Treating Women*, ed. A. Bernstein and G. Warner. New York: International Universities Press, pp. 181-276.

Bernstein and Warner address the common errors and countertransferences of both male and female analysts. Common errors for male analysts are equating ambition with penis envy, infantilizing women, concentrating too exclusively on oedipal issues, failing to recognize the maternal transference, becoming entrapped by seductive female patients, and having problems with "phallic" female patients. Common errors for female analysts are resisting being seen in masculine roles, failing to recognize transferences to the rival oedipal mother, and tending to be too "maternal" and overprotective. The authors argue that female analysts are less resistant than male analysts to supervisory interpretation of such countertransferences. Ten case summaries demonstrate, among other issues, how maternal and paternal transferences and conflicts from different levels of development can emerge with female analysts or under female supervision. This chapter may be helpful in alerting the clinician to special problems in the transference-countertransference interplay related to gender.

Chasseguet-Smirgel, Janine (1984). The femininity of the analyst in professional practice. *Int. J. Psycho-Anal.*, 65:169-178.

The author posits a basic wish to destroy obstacles or rivals in the way of a return to the mother's womb as an earlier underpinning of the Oedipus complex. Because women possess a capacity for motherhood, they can more readily recover the state of union with a primary object and symbolically retain the father's penis. The "maternal" mode of relating occurs by way of the analyst's unconscious communicating with the unconscious of the analysand, like the mother-child union. Male and female analysts alike, possess this indispensable analytic maternal attitude. According to Chasseguet-Smirgel, the essence of feminine psychosexual development is postponement, and thus she feels that the analytic posture of patiently waiting for material comes more naturally to female analysts. She also states that male analysts may be prone to struggle against symbiosis and a maternal attitude because of their fears about femininity. She concludes that analysts' bisexuality must be well integrated for a successful, creative analytic outcome. This article enriches our understanding of the differences in psychosexual development that can result in differing attitudes and countertransference tendencies of the male and female analyst.

Kulish, Nancy (1984). The effect of the sex of the analyst on transference: A review of the literature. *Bull. Menn. Clin.*, 48:95-110.

In this critical review of the literature, Kulish focuses on the effect of the gender of the analyst or therapist on the process of treatment and on the transference in the psychotherapy and psychoanalysis of adults. The article is organized into the following sections: Selection of the Analyst (i.e., Would one gender be more suitable than another for a particular patient?); Patient's Choice of Analyst (i.e., Why does a patient opt for an analyst of a particular gender?); Attitudes Toward Sex Roles in the Therapeutic Relationship; and Effects of Gender on Transference. With respect to choice of analyst, Kulish concludes that while there are an abundance of clinical rules, no substantial body of research exists to buttress these clinical guidelines. She points to the large number of variables involved in studying the influence of gender on the analytic process and suggests that methodological difficulties and artificially simplified problems characterize many of the articles. This article is particularly useful in demonstrating what is absent from the literature.

Smith, Sydney (1984). The sexually abused patient and the abusing therapist: A study in sadomasochistic relationships. *Psychoanal. Psychol.*, 1:89-98.

[See Chapter 24 for annotation.]

Stern, Gloria and Auchincloss, Elizabeth (1984). Reporters, Symposium: The public and private woman. *Bull. Assoc. Psychoanal. Med.*, 24:1-19.

The authors report on a series of presentations at a symposium that addressed many issues concerning transference and countertransference with female patients and female therapists. Kestenbaum addresses the issue of how certain female patients may need permission from their mothers to succeed sexually and intellectually and thus may make more progress with female therapists. Notman describes certain dangers inherent in the transference and countertransference with female patients who choose female therapists. Strouse discusses a particular kind of morality characteristic of women with examples from 19th century literature. Person, speaking on "love," addresses the question of why erotic transference may be more prevalent with the female patient-male analyst dyad. Liebert, a male analyst, considers specific countertransferences in the treatment of females by a male analyst. Meyers discusses referral patterns to female therapists and common clinical errors by female analysts with their female patients. This group of papers gives a varied look at the gender related issues in treatment.

Goldberger, Marianne and Evans, Dorothy (1985). On transference manifestations in patients with female analysts. *Int. J. Psycho-Anal.*, 66:295-309.

On the basis of clinical data from the psychoanalyses of five patients, the authors assert that male patients display a full range of erotic transference phenomena with female analysts and that they also regularly manifest paternal transferences. The paternal transferences may be difficult to elucidate until the later stages of analysis. In some cases it was only after considerable analysis of defenses against aggression that the erotic transference manifestations emerged fully. The clinical material also illustrates the importance of the feared loss of maleness that accompanies male patients' identification with their female analysts. This identification with the female analyst is one way in which male homosexual transferences can be observed more directly. The authors disagree with Karme (1969) on the erotic transference in the male patient/female analyst dyads, and they also differentiate erotic from erotized transferences. Erotized transference also occur with male patients and female analysts but are better characterized as instinctualized transferences in patients who have difficulty with control of both aggressive and sexual impulses.

Kaplan, Alexandra (1985). Female or male therapists for women patients: New formulations. *Psychiat.*, 48:111-121.

Kaplan primarily addresses the effects of gender in psychotherapy, but also includes a brief review of the analytic literature. Although there is not yet demonstrable evidence from psychotherapeutic or analytic research of a strong specific gender effect, Kaplan argues that there is enough evidence to consider gender as a significant variable. She bases her argument on the research finding that female therapists are often more successful than men with female patients early in the training process. The gender difference tends to diminish with experience. She argues for the importance of open discussion and the teaching of female psychology early in training, particularly for male therapists.

Kulish, Nancy (1985). The effect of the therapist's gender on the transference. *The Yearbook of the Society for Psychoanalytic Psychotherapy,* 2:411-431. Emerson, NJ: New Concept Press.

Kulish uses as a basis for discussion the case of a man with homosexual problems and confusion around sexual identity. The man consciously sought out a female therapist after two previous therapies with male therapists. The dynamics and defensive meanings of this choice, and the possible influences of the therapist's gender in the subsequent unfolding of the transference, are discussed. Kulish speculates that her gender shaped the contents of the transference and was the focal point of the patient's resistance. She suggests that for other patients with problems of sexual identity or homosexuality, the gender of the therapist might also be of central concern and have an organizing influence on the transference. She concludes that further research on the question is needed. This paper raises valuable questions.

Lester, Eva (1985). The female analyst and the erotized transference. *Int. J. Psycho-Anal.,* 66:283-293.

Lester first reviews the literature on the concept of the erotized transference and then tries to account for the absence of reports of male patients developing erotized transferences to their female analysts. She describes two cases, one male and one female. The female patient developed an openly erotized transference, whereas, in the male patient, defenses against the erotic transference predominated. She does not, however, differentiate between erotic and erotized transferences. Lester's thesis is that the expression of strong erotic urges toward the female analyst by the male patient is inhibited by the fantasy of the overwhelming preoedipal mother, whereas these urges are more freely expressed, as well as utilized defensively, by the female patient. Although the cases presented are informative, and Lester's thesis seems to fit these patients to some extent, her assumption that it can be generalized to indicate more universal differences in the way male and female patients relate to female analysts has been subsequently challenged by Goldberger and Evans (1985) and Meyers (1986).

Person, Ethel (1985). The erotic transference in women and men: Differences and consequences. *J. Amer. Acad. Psychoanal.*, 13:159-180.

Person describes case material that illustrates aspects of the unfolding erotic transference in all four gender combinations, that is, female patient/male analyst, female patient/female analyst, male patient/female analyst, and male patient/male analyst. She concludes that the erotic transference used as a resistance is more common among female patients, whereas resistance to the awareness of the erotic transference is more common among male patients. Both types of resistances can cause their own set of problems. In women, the erotic transference may obscure other important dynamics and conflicts. In men, particularly when in treatment with women, the danger is greater that the erotic transference will fail to develop, owing to the intensity of defenses against it. She emphasizes the importance of analyzing defenses so that the erotic transference can be experienced directly. She also offers some theoretical formulations for her clinical observations of differences in transference patterns.

Kumin, Ivri (1985/86). Erotic horror: Desire and resistance in the psycho-analytic situation. *Int. J. Psychoanal. Psychother.*, 11:3-20.

Kumin discusses sexualized transference from the male analyst's point of view. He uses the phrase "erotic horror" to describe the unpleasurable affects most patients experience with this transference. He hypothesizes that the erotized transference reflects negative feelings under the influence of the aggressive drive and is derived from past relationships with exciting but frustrating objects. He points out that, similarly, the patient can be an exciting but frustrating object to the analyst. Kumin further asserts that the factor limiting the elucidation of the patient's erotic transference is the desire of the analyst, not the desire of the patient, and that only correct interpretation, spoken or silently understood, mitigates the resistance of the patient. Clear clinical examples with candid accounts of his erotic counter-transference reactions are given. This article is useful both in its elucidation of the dynamic meanings of erotic and erotized transference in general and in how erotized countertransference by the analyst is a powerful, but overlooked, phenomenon.

Lester, Eva (1985/86). On erotized transference and resistance. *Int. J. Psychoanal. Psychother.*, 11:21-25.

In this discussion of Kumin's (1985/1986) article, Lester points out that Kumin's experiences reflect a male analyst's point of view. She suggests that gender of the analyst and the homosexual or heterosexual character of the analyst-analysand dyad determine the unfolding of the transference, especially the erotic transference. Lester asserts that with the male patient/female analyst, the pregenital transference with the phallic mother inhibits the emergence of erotic material. She proposes that an erotized homosexual transference is common with the female patient/female analyst. This brief discussion is noteworthy for its particular focus on how gender shapes transference.

Tyson, Phyllis (1985). Discussion: Theoretical and technical considerations of cross-gender transferences with male patients. In: *The Yearbook of Psychoanalysis and Psychotherapy*, ed. R. Langs, 1:63-75. Emerson, NJ: New Concept Press,

In contrast to Kulish's (1984) paper contending that the reality of the therapist's gender influences the transference, Tyson emphasizes the conditions under which the therapist's gender recedes into the background. These conditions include the nature of the treatment (psychoanalysis versus psychotherapy), the level of psychopathology, the analyst's techniques, and countertransference phenomena. In psychoanalysis, the ability of the male patient to form an erotic transference or to elaborate a paternal transference will be determined more by the developmental level of the patient rather than by the gender of the analyst. The analyst needs to analyze the countertransferences and have free-floating attention, so as to not impede transference elaborations. A case history of a male analysand illustrates Tyson's views.

Gornick, Lisa (1986). Developing a new narrative: The woman therapist and the male patient. In: *Psychoanalysis and Women: Contemporary Reappraisals*, ed. J. Alpert. Hillsdale, NJ: The Analytic Press, 1986, pp. 257-286. Also in: *Psychoanal. Psychol.*, 3:299-325.

Gornick addresses a deficiency in the literature by examining the distinctive aspects of the therapeutic interaction between female therapist and male patient. She gathered data from in-depth interviews with 13 female therapists, including psychoanalysts, about their work with male patients. She argues that the different meanings of power and sexuality for men and for women are critical to the theoretical understanding of the interaction in this dyad. When a woman is the therapist, Gornick asserts, she steps out of the usual feminine role. This reversal of power has several implications for the transference: Her new authority may signal that she is not to be approached sexually; or she may be experienced as threatening or belittling to the patient's masculinity, which may lead to his erotizing the interaction. In the countertransference, the female therapist may feel threatened or guilty in response to the erotic transference; she may feel a lack of intuitive understanding for the male or frustrated at being cast as the bad mother. Gornick's theoretical discussion of the transference and countertransference in terms of the shifting balance of power between female therapist and male patient is illuminating, but more detailed clinical data and more interviews with therapists would have been useful.

**Kulish, Nancy (1986). Gender and transference: The screen of the phallic mother. *Int. Rev. Psycho-Anal.*, 13:393-404.**

Kulish focuses on the construct of the "phallic mother" to demonstrate how the analyst's gender may influence and organize both transference and countertransference. The concept of the phallic mother has been offered in the literature as a theoretical explanation for gender-related differences in the transference, i.e., for the purported lack of paternal transferences with female analysts and for a lack of strong erotic transferences by male patients to female analysts. Kulish argues that paternal transferences can be confused with and obscured by images of the phallic mother, but, she proposes that it is possible and useful to make such a distinction. In contrast to the formulation that male patients' images of the phallic mother inhibit their sexual impulses toward female analysts, Kulish suggests that inhibitions of sexual material may frequently come from the analyst's side in this dyad. From her clinical material, Kulish concludes that theoretical constructs such as the phallic mother may contribute to gender-related blind spots and may prevent therapists from perceiving themselves in the opposite-sex roles within the transference.

**Liebert, Robert (1986). Transference and countertransference issues in the treatment of women by a male analyst. In: *Between Analyst and Patient*, ed. H. Meyers. Hillsdale, NJ: The Analytic Press, pp. 229-236.**

On the basis of his own experience conducting analyses and supervision, Liebert contends that neither the process nor the outcome of an analysis is the same for male and for female analysts. He feels that many women may choose to see male analysts because they fear the unfolding of a maternal transference. Such women, who may enjoy warm relationships with other women, have split off a harsh, unnurturing imago of the mother. With male analysts, female patients may make use of their "dissembling" and seductive abilities to spare their analyst from this development. Such female patients develop an idealized erotic transference, an enactment of how they tried to win the father. A clinical case illustrates these points and shows how Liebert had difficulty seeing himself as the "bad mother" in an analytic narrative. The clinical material in this paper is especially helpful and candid in showing how the gender of a male analyst affects the countertransference-transference with a female patient.

McDougall, Joyce (1986). Eve's reflection: On the homosexual components of female sexuality. In: *Between Analyst and Patient*, ed. H. Meyers. Hillsdale, NJ: The Analytic Press, pp. 213-228.

McDougall focuses on a theoretical discussion of homosexual components of female sexuality by presenting a clinical case which illuminates the relationship between the analyst's gender and the transference-countertransference. The patient, a young phobic woman, had an overprotective, possessive mother. After months of interpreting the patient's anger toward the mother and the heterosexual oedipal implications of the patient's rageful fantasies, McDougall herself had a dream with homosexual content. In analyzing her own dream, McDougall realized that she had been colluding with the patient in defending against the homosexual meanings of the patient's fantasies in her symptoms and in the transference. In the theoretical section of the chapter, McDougall mentions some of her disagreements with Freud's concepts of female sexuality. She discusses how sublimated homosexual libido enriches a woman's life. Clinically, the paper highlights an infrequently described but important issue—a homosexual countertransference between the female analyst and the female analysand. Developmental levels of homosexual transferences are not differentiated. [See also Chapters 18 and 19.]

Meyers, Helen (1986). How do women treat men? In: *The Psychology of Men*, ed. G. Fogel, F. Lane, and R. Liebert. New York: Basic Books, pp. 262-276.

Giving many brief clinical illustrations, Meyers discusses theoretical and clinical aspects of the interaction between male patients and female analysts. She asserts that gender does effect the transference, but only in terms of the sequence, intensity, and inescapability of certain transference paradigms in both therapy and analysis. Myers believes that theoretically, in a well conducted analysis with a suitable patient, "actual gender should make less of a difference in the long run, as all transference paradigms will be worked through." Gender may be more of a factor in psychotherapy and in incomplete analyses. Much of the chapter focuses on particular countertransference pitfalls in the different dyads. These pitfalls include 1) in the male therapist/female patient dyad, the erotic countertransference and fear of the mother; 2) in the female therapist/male patient dyad, penis envy and difficulty in perceiving oneself as the paternal imago; and 3) in the female therapist/female patient dyad, the difficulty in perceiving oneself as the oedipal father or the split-off bad mother. She does not agree that the erotic transference is less apparent in the male patient/female analyst pair and gives examples to support her view. She provides a lucid review and reexamination of the complex issues concerning the male patient and female analyst.

Moldawsky, Stanley (1986). When men are therapists to women: Beyond the oedipal pale. In: *The Psychology of Today's Woman*, ed. T. Bernay and D. Cantor. Hillsdale, NJ: The Analytic Press, pp. 291-303.

Moldawsky presents clinical anecdotes that show how the conscious objections women give for preferring female over male analysts can be overcome by a male analyst. From his clinical experience, he concludes that maternal transferences to him are always preoedipal. He suggests that all conflicts will be experienced eventually with analysts of either sex, but he wonders if the nature of the experiences will be different. Valuable questions needing more research are raised by the author.

Ruderman, Ellen (1986). Creative and reparative uses of countertransference by women psychotherapists treating women patients: A clinical research study. In: *The Psychology of Today's Woman*, ed. T. Bernay and D. Cantor. Hillsdale, NJ: The Analytic Press, pp. 339-363.

This research study consists of in-depth interviews with 20 psychoanalytically oriented women psychotherapists, exploring their conscious feelings of countertransference with their women patients. The findings are derived from the subjects' perceptions, as well as the author's interpretations of them. Five common and major countertransference themes emerged: 1) the therapists' relationships with their mothers, especially with respect to separation-individuation, 2) the therapists' identifications with the patients' inhibitions about ambition and fears of success, 3) role conflicts around needs for the family and social relationships versus career pursuits, 4) envy related to reactivation of dependency wishes and mourning for lost opportunities, and 5) issues related to the life stage of the therapists. Ruderman observes that the therapists experienced profound resonance with their female patients, which suggested a specific, gender-linked component in countertransference. Although the data were limited to psychotherapy, not analysis, and the definition of countertransference is broad, this chapter is one of the few attempts at research on countertransference and gender. In addition, it is unusual in its demonstration of the positive and adaptive, as well as the negative, effects of countertransference.

Schactel, Zeborah (1986). The "Impossible profession" considered from a gender perspective. In: *Psychoanalysis and Women: Contemporary Reappraisals*, ed. J. Alpert, Hillsdale, NJ: The Analytic Press, pp. 237-256.

Using a social system model with attention to role/person boundary, Schactel hypothesizes that women have more permeable boundaries than males and that gender roles supersede work roles for self and others—for psychotherapists and patients alike. Women therapists evoke early, primitive selfobject internalizations for persons of both genders. Though the psychoanalytic work system uses collaborative efforts to resolve unconscious conflicts between levels of experience, these efforts may go awry and become collusive. Three clinical examples of countertransference illustrate how the gender role of "maternality" in the female analyst may lead to 1) collusion with the patient's anger and resistance, thus encouraging regression; 2) empathy, getting in the way of formulation; or 3) inadequate exploration of male patients' conflicts in acknowledging that their female analysts have a greater status and power than they do.

Torras de Bea, Eulalia (1987). Contribution to the papers by Eva Lester and Marianne Goldberger and Dorothy Evans. *Int. J. Psycho-Anal.*, 68:63-67.

This article discusses three points raised in the title papers and contributes further clinical material and insight toward theoretical understanding of the interactions between male patients and female analysts. First, Torras de Bea considers the erotized transference to be a disguise for hate and aggression as compared with the erotic transference, which concerns itself with transference love. Second, she disagrees with Goldberger and Evans (1985), who suggest that male patients have only limited opportunity to experience their passive homosexual conflicts with female analysts and she illustrates her point with clinical material. Third, she provides evidence from the same case to support her view that identification with the female analyst is most difficult when a debasing transference underlies the manifest one. The difficulty disappears once this transference is worked through.

Bernstein, Isidor and Glenn, Jules (1988). The child and adolescent analyst's emotional reactions to his patients and their parents. *Int. Rev. Psycho-Anal.*, 15:225-241.

This article differentiates countertransferences from other types of emotional reactions, such as transferences to patients and their parents, identification, empathy, and signal responses to behavior of the patients and their parents. Countertransference, the authors assert, is the analyst's response to a patient's transference with a transference of his own. In the section devoted to the personality of the child analyst, Bernstein and Glenn pay attention to gender issues. Analysts of both genders use their sublimated feminine and maternal identifications as well as their wishes to be both a father and a mother. The intricate web of wishes and identifications may evoke anxiety. A male analyst may become too active because of his female identification. If the wish to care for, nurture, or rescue patients is too intense in either a male or female therapist, he or she may abandon a neutral analytic stance. Quoting Tyson (1980), the authors assert that female analysts are more likely than males to take a maternal role when their patients engage in transferential preoedipal struggles, because they are more likely to have had the same difficulties with their own mothers. Analysts of both genders may develop blind spots, overlooking the fact that the patient views them in the transference as a person of the opposite sex.

Mann, Carola (1988). Male and female in a changing analytic world. *Contemp. Psychoanal.*, 24:676-684.

Mann reviews 35 of her supervisory evaluations of male and female candidates and concludes that there are gender-linked differences in cognitive style in analytic work. Women analysts tend to pay more attention to affects and nonverbal communications and use more open-ended interventions; men are more incisive and pay more attention to theory. She links these differences to Chodorow's theories about relational differences. Mann cautions that more detailed investigations of the impact of gender on the analytic interaction are needed. The study suggests a possibly fruitful approach to research on the effect of gender on the analytic process.

O'Leary, John (1988). Unacknowledged gender effects: Analyst and patient in collusion. *Contemp. Psychoanal.*, 24:668-675.

This brief paper is part of a panel on the gender of the analyst. O'Leary asserts that gender related, unconscious collusions between analysts and patients are seldom predictable at the beginning of treatment. He suggests that monitoring the affect of shame in both patient and analyst can provide a means for uncovering the transference-countertransference matrix of such collusions. Unacknowledged shame can cover resistance to the awareness of the erotic transferences in the female analyst/male patient dyad. Three brief vignettes illustrate O'Leary's points.

Ortmeyer, Dale (1988). Reporter, Panel: Gender of the psychoanalyst: Central or peripheral. *Contemp. Psychoanal.*, 24: 667-692

Members of this panel agree that gender is a central issue in psychoanalytic treatment. Papers by O'Leary and Mann are annotated separately. Katz cautions against attempting to apply insights from such discussions to a given idiosyncratic therapeutic dyad. She warns that predictions as to the direction of gender-linked countertransferences cannot be made and that cultural stereotypes should not be applied at the expense of individual psychodynamics.

Raphling, David and Chused, Judith (1988). Transference across gender lines. *J. Amer. Psychoanal. Assn.*, 36:77-104.

Raphling and Chused present four clinical examples of oedipally-based transference in which the parental object is the opposite sex from that of the analyst. Oedipal transferences that cross gender lines, while expectable theoretically, have seldom been reported. In general, the authors argue that the analyst's gender does bias the development of transference by serving an organizing and resistive function. With cross-gender oedipal transferences, desires aimed at the analyst may be attenuated and overlooked. The authors suggest that patients who best tolerate their own bisexual identifications are most capable of cross-gender transferences. Analysts also vary in their tolerance of, cognitive receptivity toward, and empathic responsiveness to cross-gender transferences. The clinical cases illustrate the complex defensive functions for which cross-gender transferences are used. This article contributes to the understanding of clinical complexities of oedipal transferences.

Roth, Sheldon (1988). A woman's homosexual transference with a male analyst. *Psychoanal. Q.*, 57:28-55.

Roth examines a female patient's homosexual transference, which he believes is derived from the negative oedipal phase. He argues that male analysts frequently conceptualize this material incorrectly as a primary pregenital dyadic maternal transference or as a regressive defense from the positive oedipal transference. Roth feels that the gender of the analyst influences the expression of the sexual element of such a homosexual transference. With a female analyst, a highly intense erotic homosexual transference usually emerges. With a male analyst, the homosexual transference is experienced in dreams, in fantasies, and in displacement to other figures. The homosexual transference to the male analyst (who would be perceived as a sexual woman) is only directly experienced fleetingly. A clinical case is presented. In elucidating this material, Roth distinguishes between girls' preoedipal phase and the negative oedipal phase. He believes that the negative oedipal phase is a distinct, normal, developmental stage that reemerges in the transference. The negative oedipal phase is characterized by clear self-object differentiation, an active orientation toward the mother, a desire to have a child by the mother, genital arousal, and triangularity. This article presents valuable clinical material and an interesting discussion of a neglected area, a homosexual transference to an opposite-sexed analyst.

Siegel, Elaine (1988). *Female Homosexuality: Choice Without Volition.* Hillsdale, NJ: The Analytic Press.

Siegel maintains that analysts of either gender can analyze female homosexuals because analysands project the kind of object they need. [See Chapter 19 for annotation.]

Balsam, Rosemary (1989). The paternal possibility: The father's contribution to the adolescent daughter when the mother is disturbed and a denigrated figure. In: *Fathers and Their Families*, ed. S. Cath, A. Gurwitt, and L. Gunsburg. Hillsdale, NJ: The Analytic Press, pp. 245-263.

The importance of the analyst's gender and her role as an ego ideal are discussed. [See Chapter 22 for annotation.]

Chertoff, Judith (1989). Negative oedipal transference of a male patient to his female analyst during the termination phase. *J. Amer. Psychoanal. Assn.*, 37:687-713.

Chertoff summarizes the debate in the literature about male patients' capacity to experience a paternal transference toward female analysts. She agrees with the more recent literature that such paternal transferences are common and ubiquitous. She then reports in depth her work with a male patient whose paternal transference toward her was evident throughout the analysis. Process material from the termination phase illustrates that the even more elusive negative oedipal paternal transference can be experienced directly with a female analyst by a male patient. Chertoff discusses various ways of understanding the material and speculates about the influence of her gender on the unfolding of the paternal transference.

Gabbard, Glen and Gabbard, Krin (1989). The female psychoanalyst in the movies. *J. Amer. Psychoanal. Assn.*, 37:1031-1050.

The author traces the stereotypical depiction of the female analyst in cinema from the 1940s to the present. The female analyst is viewed as lacking a stable relationship with a man and normal domesticity, using obsessive-compulsive defenses to guard against emotional or sexual expressiveness, devoted to her career as a pathological substitute for marriage and children, and dependent on a male mentor. The cure for this disorder is to fall in love with a male patient who proves himself more powerful than his female analyst and seduces her (happily) into a more traditional female role.

The Gabbards' search for an explanation for this stereotyped phenomenon, for it is opposite to clinical reality; sexual acting out by female analysts is rare, and the erotic transference of male patients to female analysts is heavily defended against and emerges with difficulty. The authors theorize that the stereotypical depiction of the female analyst is an attempt to cope with the universal male fear of the powerful preoedipal mother. This mother's potentially potent role is always reversed so that the male becomes the more powerful one.

Kulish, Nancy (1989). Gender and transference: Conversations with female analysts. *Psychoanal. Psychol.*, 6:59-71.

The author summarizes findings from interviews with 17 senior female analysts about the possible influence of analysts' gender on the transference. The following questions were posed: Does the analyst's gender affect the transference? What is the effect on sequence? What is the effect on assignment or choice of analyst and referrals? Are there differences between maternal and paternal transferences? What is the effect on erotic and erotized transferences and on oedipal transferences? Finally, how might these issues best be studied? In general, the responses of this group of women suggested that analysts' gender does influence the transference as well as the countertransference.

Lasky, Richard (1989). Some determinants of the male analyst's capacity to identify with female patients. *Int. J. Psycho-Anal.*, 70:405-418.

The author focuses on the impact of gender on the male analyst/female patient dyad. Beginning with the assumption that male analysts use maternal and feminine identifications in their work, Lasky examines the organization and employment of these identifications. To the extent that male analysts have overcome their castration anxiety and fears of penetration, they can use their maternal identifications to understand their female patients. Clinical material demonstrates how male analysts can preserve regressive fantasies and identifications concerning the preoedipal mother as a defense against oedipal associations from their patients. Candid clinical illustrations address a valuable but ignored area in the psychoanalytic literature.

Lester, Eva, Jodoin, Rose-Marie, and Robertson, Brian (1989). Counter-transference dreams reconsidered: A survey. *Int. Rev. Psychoanal.*, 16:305-314.

A questionnaire survey of psychoanalysts about countertransference dreams where patients appear undisguised revealed unexpectedly significant gender differences. Male analysts reported a high number of dreams in which the manifest content was erotic/sexual, whereas female analysts had a higher frequency of dreams in which the manifest content involved the analysand's intruding on the analyst's private space. The authors propose that an intense revival of the mother-infant dyadic relationship occurs in analyses when the analysand experiences oral and fusional longings that are sometimes erotized. Wishes for maternal gratification may evoke in the male analyst defenses against the wish to be a woman and defensive affirmation of phallic potency to ward off castration anxiety and depression. Erotic countertransference dreams may thus signal countertransference resistance defending against oral needs and fears. Female analysts experiencing similar pressures for maternal gratification from analysands respond with wishes to mother the analysand and with anxieties related to threats to body boundaries, signaled by dreams in which the analysand invades their home or bedroom. Women analysts' wish to mother their analysands, reverberating with wishes for reparative fusion with their own mother, threatens to invade and disorganize the analytic situation.

Wrye, Harriet and Wells, Judith (1989). The maternal erotic transference. *Int. J. Psycho-Anal.*, 70: 673-684.

The authors contend that early erotic maternal transferences in patients are often incompletely explored, despite increased knowledge of early mother-child relationships. Many analysts see these early transferences (often known as erotized transferences) only as defending against oedipal transferences. Wrye and Wells do not distinguish between erotic and erotized transferences but consider them to be analyzable transferences that occur on a developmental continuum. They focus on three aspects of maternal erotic transferences: the sensual reciprocity between baby and mother, with special attention to the anal period; maternal transferences that bridge the transition from dyadic to triadic relations; and the child/patient's attempt to establish an integrated view of the mother/therapist as a living, whole object. The authors support their thesis with a clinical description of the maternal erotic transference manifestations that emerged in the analysis of a 55-year-old woman. They conclude that the working through of this transference, including aspects of the analyst's countertransference, was necessary for the patient to move forward into a period of more deeply experienced heterosexual interests.

Bigras, Julien (1990). Psychoanalysis as incestuous repetiton: Some technical considerations. *Analysis and Childhood Sexual Abuse*, ed. H. Levine. Hillsdale, NJ: The Analytic Press, pp. 175-196.

Bigras discusses the incestuous negative maternal transference and suggests that it is difficult for analysts of both genders. [See Chapter 24 for annotation.]

Eber, Milton (1990). Erotized transference reconsidered: Expanding the countertransference dimension. *Psychoanal. Rev.*, 77:25-40.

Eber reconsiders the erotized transference by presenting the intersubjective viewpoint that the analyst is a coparticipant whose personality has a major impact on transference behaviors. He argues further that the erotized transference in the interaction between male analyst and female patient is partly a manifestation of traditional roles assumed in situations involving a male authority figure in close interaction with a female who perceives herself as powerless.

Eber reexamines Stoller's (1979) detailed material on the case of Belle in *Sexual Excitement: Dynamics of Erotic Life*. [See Chapter 18.] This erotized transference is reinterpreted as arising in a specific intersubjective context. Either analyst or patient may serve as an erotized selfobject for the other. The details of patients' fantasy life should be viewed as codetermined, including patients' subjective experience of the psychoanalytic interaction. Belle's erotized transference is viewed as expressing a conflict between her wish for a sustaining selfobject tie and her fear of being traumatized by repetition of the original selfobject failure with a distant and overstimulating mother. Her motivation included a wish to maintain the analyst's interest; the erotization was a manifestation of a protracted sadomasochistic transference-countertransference impasse, in which Belle believed that offering herself as a sexual object was the only means of preserving the relationship. The Dora case is also discussed.

Horner, Althea (1990). From idealization to ideal—from attachment to identification: The female analyst and the female patient. *J. Amer. Acad. Psychoanal.*, 18:223-232.

Horner discusses the female therapist's role in facilitating positive feminine identifications in nonborderline patients with oedipal and postoedipal identificatory conflicts with a devalued mother. [See Chapter 22 for annotation.]

Kaplan, Donald (1990). Some theoretical and technical aspects of gender and social reality in clinical psychoanalysis. *The Psychoanalytic Study of the Child*, 45:3-24. New Haven, CT: Yale University Press.

[See Chapter 4 for annotation.]

Lester, Eva (1990). Gender and identity issues in the analytic process. *Int. J. Psycho-Anal.*, 71:435-444.

Lester discusses the influence of the gender of both the analyst and the analysand on the unfolding analytic process. Selectively reviewing the analytic literature, she highlights the ways in which the influences of gender in the four gender-related dyads have been denied and neglected. She uses this literature and her own clinical experience to propose two common developments in the transference of female patients to female analysts: 1) the regression to the preoedipal, sadomasochistic relationship with the analyst (mother) and 2) the erotization of the transference. The meaning and optimal handling of these transference configurations are considered. The existing literature contradicting her point of view is not explored.

Liss-Levinson, Nechama (1990). Money matters and the woman analyst: In a different voice. *Psychoanal. Psychol.* (Suppl.), 7:119-130.

The author discusses a neglected area, the impact of gender on money matters. She suggests that women analysts may charge lower fees and have different fee policies than male analysts, and that patients have different expectations, related to gender-linked differences in the use of money as a means of interpersonal power and communication. Women therapists may experience moneyblindedness, or a devaluing of the value and place of money. Their self-esteem may come from a sense of caring for others, with financial success viewed as endangering personal connection, and with a desire for money viewed as unfeminine. Charging lower fees may reflect "pseudoempathy," or the therapist's need for excessive caretaking or the need to treat the patient as an extension of oneself. Clinical vignettes are provided.

Raphling, David (1990). Technical issues of the opening phase. *Adult Analysis and Childhood Sexual Abuse*, ed. H. Levine. Hillsdale, NJ: The Analytic Press, pp. 45-64.

Raphling discusses erotic transferences, erotization as a defense against aggression, and the gender of the analyst in relation to the gender of the abusing parent. [See Chapter 24 for annotation.]

Renik, Owen (1990). Analysis of a woman's homosexual strivings by a male analyst. *Psychoanal. Q.*, 59:41-53.

Renik reviews recent papers describing ways in which a female patient's homosexual transference unfolds with a male analyst. He agrees with authors who state that such transferences are ubiquitous but disagrees with those who contend that negative oedipal transferences in this dyad are most often displaced and only transiently experienced directly. He asserts that a female patient can experience a male analyst as a mother whom she wishes to penetrate and whose rivals she wants to destroy, for a sustained period of time. To support this view, Renik provides detailed clinical material from a period in the analysis of his female patient. He also describes the obstacles a male analyst needs to overcome within himself to allow such transference manifestations to emerge.

Bernstein, Doris (1991b). Gender specific dangers in the female/female dyad in treatment. *Psychoanal. Rev.*, 78.

Bernstein discusses the dangers inherent in analytic treatment for the female patient/female analyst dyad. These dangers include 1) countertransference overidentification with a patient's strivings for independence and career success and with her complaints against men, while these may be serving defensive functions, 2) the analyst's difficulty in experiencing herself as a penetrating person, 3) competitiveness with a female patient and the patient's mother, 4) defenses against homosexuality, and 5) prolonged, and perhaps resistive, regression to the original mother-child relationship. Bernstein illustrates these issues with case material and also discusses the influences of cultural values and theoretical biases in treatment. Three clusters of anxieties characteristic of female development illuminate transference/countertransference difficulties in the female analyst/female patient dyad: the genital anxieties—access, penetration, and diffusivity. Bernstein contends that female analysts must extricate themselves from regressive and sexual aspects of their relationship with mother, now represented in the female/female dyad. The article is a valuable presentation of specific countertransferences and biases for female analysts with female patients.

# Chapter 26

# The Pregnant Analyst: Clinical Issues

Diane Hoye Campbell

The topic of the pregnant analyst is relatively new in the psychoanalytic literature. Nothing appears to have been written on this topic during the lifetime of Freud. The contributions to date, though few in number, are rich in their understanding of female psychology, adult development, the vicissitudes of the transference-countertransference, and the effects on psychoanalytic technique within this complex specialized situation. The pregnant analyst is challenged to integrate a number of variables in a relatively short time. Profound feelings and reactions may be evoked in herself and in her patients. The analyst faces the practical demands imposed on her by the pregnancy, the intrapsychic changes of her own developmental crisis, the intrusion of a "real event" into the analysis, and the presence of the fetus as a third person in the analytic treatment room. Most complex may be the heightened transference-countertransference themes, new dimensions of which are experienced at each stage of pregnancy. The current literature provides many views on the central task of facilitating the process of interpretation of the patient's intrapsychic world, while simultaneously attending to the practical and developmental challenges imposed by this special event in the psychoanalytic situation.

Hannett, Frances (1949). Transference reactions to an event in the life of the analyst. *Psychoanal. Rev.*, 36:69-81.

This article is the first in the literature to mention the pregnant analyst. Because of a miscarriage, Hannett was suddenly absent from her practice for two weeks, before the pregnancy had been consciously acknowledged by any of her six analysands. After the event, five of the six patients developed fantasies approximating their analyst's actual situation. Hannett considers her analysands' responses to be a repetition compulsion in the transference that reactivated early conflicts. Common themes included a loss of fantasized omnipotence, the fear of being supplanted by a sibling, and the dread of mother's death. Hostile demands, avoidance of associations, and some acting out occurred. Case illustrations of the six analysands link the nature and degree of pathology to each transference response and offer ideas about the varieties of integration achieved by each patient.

Van Leeuwen, Kato (1966). Pregnancy envy in the male. *Int. J. Psycho-Anal.*, 47:319-324.

Drawing on her analytic experience while pregnant, Van Leeuwen discusses male envy of the female and her child-bearing functions. This envy, which received scant attention in the earlier psychoanalytic literature, is considered by Van Leeuwen to be a central dynamic for understanding the psychology of the male. Complex preoedipal and oedipal origins of this form of envy, and its influences and consequences for character pathology and neurotic symptom formation are reviewed. A male analytic case is described who intensely envied his pregnant analyst. Some of the developmental antecedents of his envy included excessive narcissism and overgratification of early dependency needs. Analytic working-through of specific pathological consequences of his pregnancy envy are summarized. Van Leeuwen explains his envy as a major transference manifestation based on his identification with women.

Lax, Ruth (1969). Some considerations about transference and countertransference manifestations evoked by the analyst's pregnancy. *Int. J. Psycho-Anal.*, 50:363-371.

In this article describing the reactions of six patients to her pregnancy, Lax adds a great deal to our theoretical and clinical understanding of the transference and countertransference issues pertaining to the analyst's pregnancy. She demonstrates how each patient's most significant infantile conflict was reactivated by her pregnancy. Borderline patients became aware of her pregnancy much sooner, reacted with greater intensity, and were more likely to act out their conflicts than did neurotic patients. Female patients used the predominant defense of identification to deal with their feelings, whereas male patients resorted most often to avoidance and isolation of affect. After exploring her own reactions and after discussions with colleagues who have been pregnant, Lax concludes that the most significant countertransference problems also derive from the analyst's childhood conflicts. In particular, she theorizes that analysts who hide the pregnancy, and attempt to deny their patients' awareness of it, are dealing with concerns about being robbed. Lax emphasizes the importance of the analyst's working out her own infantile conflicts sufficiently so that she can serve as the optimal screen for the working through of those conflicts reactivated in patients by the reality of her pregnancy.

Browning, Diane (1974). Patients' reactions to their therapist's pregnancies. *J. Amer. Acad. Child Psychiat.*, 13:468-482.

Although not based on analytic data, this article offers the reader valuable glimpses into the intrapsychic world of children involved in transference relationships with a pregnant therapist. The author was pregnant three times during a part-time child psychiatry residency. Two pregnancies led to childbirth: one ended with a second-trimester miscarriage. The author relates some ways in which her pregnancies were experienced by three young children and one borderline adolescent girl who were in psychotherapy. The children initially denied the pregnancy, then used displacement and other defenses on the way to eventual acknowledgment, which was characterized by transient regressions, anger, and fear of abandonment, followed by some developmental integration. Separation issues, sibling rivalry, heightened sexual concerns, and questions about the therapist's personal life were common clinical manifestations in response to the therapist's pregnancy. Some useful technical interventions are described.

Nadelson, Carol, Notman, Malkah, Arons, Elissa, and Feldman, Judith (1974). The pregnant therapist. *Amer. J. Psychiat.*, 131:1107-1111.

This article addresses psychodynamic issues pertaining to the therapist's pregnancy. The authors use examples from psychiatric training and dynamic psychotherapy to illustrate the transference and countertransference problems that arise among patients, staff members, and therapists in reaction to the therapist's pregnancy. They outline the pregnant therapist's physical and emotional vulnerabilities. Common fantasies of needing to leave the office abruptly, because of having labor pains begin or the membranes rupture during a session, are explored. The authors point out that recognition of physical limitations and mood swings caused by the pregnancy may challenge the therapist's fantasies of personal omnipotence. In male patients, the authors find reactivation of and defenses against fears of sexual competence, competitive strivings with the therapist's husband, and increased sexuality in the transference. Female patients frequently manifest envy, sadness, and revival of oedipal rivalry with the mother. Some patients also become pregnant as an expression of hostility and a wish to replace the therapist, or as a positive identification with her. Denial, projection, isolation, and reaction formation are commonly employed defense mechanisms. Threats to terminate treatment in response to the revival of infantile fears of abandonment, sibling rivalry, identification with the baby, and hostility are briefly discussed. The authors advocate that pregnant therapists deal with the pregnancy openly and realistically so that working through the reactions of therapist, staff, and patients can be facilitated. A review of the literature includes articles on the pregnancy of the psychoanalyst, but the clinical examples are taken primarily from cases of psychotherapy. Psychoanalytic theory is used to clarify transference and countertransference issues that arise.

Fenster, Sheri, Phillips, Suzanne, and Rapoport, Estelle (1986). *The Therapist's Pregnancy: Intrusion in the Analytic Space.* Hillsdale, NJ: The Analytic Press.

This book on the pregnant therapist extensively reviews the available literature, outlines the research study done by Fenster, and discusses technical recommendations for maintaining an analytic process and managing transference, countertransference, and resistance. Practical issues that inevitably arise during the therapist's pregnancy are also considered. The authors contend that the therapist's pregnancy is an intrusion by the therapist into the analytic setting. She is challenged to facilitate and maintain the analytic dyad and to further the analysis of transference and resistance, while simultaneously being intrapsychically preoccupied with her own physical and emotional changes. The chapter on supervision comments on the multiple relationships among therapist, fetus, patient, and supervisor. Intrapsychic and personal issues for male and female supervisors are discussed. Increased dependency needs in the analyst; denial of the significance of the pregnancy by the analyst, patient or supervisor; regression; and other potential problems are explored. Special situations, including the treatment of groups, adolescents, and homosexual patients are reviewed.

Penn, Linda (1986). The pregnant therapist: Transference and counter-transference issues. In: *Psychoanalysis and Women: Contemporary Reappraisals,* ed. J. Alpert. Hillsdale, NJ: The Analytic Press, pp. 287-316.

Penn explores the major transference and countertransference themes that emerge when the therapist is pregnant and discusses their psychoanalytic management. She reviews and integrates the analytic and developmental literature and provides case studies from her clinical work. The analyst's pregnancy is viewed as a powerful stimulus for both the patient and the analyst. The patient is often forced to experience and defend against the perception of the pregnant analyst as a maternal caretaking, abandoning, or sexual object (or all of these), with dramatic associations and reenactments of the early attachment process, of primitive separation fears, of sibling rivalry, and of oedipal exclusion. For some patients, the therapist who was previously experienced as a neutral and safe object for sexual fantasies may during her pregnancy be viewed as a taboo sexual object, dangerously real in her feminine sexuality. Role reversals can occur during pregnancy, particularly in the final months when patients may experience the therapist as vulnerable; sometimes patients wish to care for their therapist as a defense against dependency needs and envy. Varieties of rage against the pregnant therapist and death wishes toward the baby, and the possible countertransference responses to these powerful themes, are a brief but important section of this article. Penn views the patient's transference responses as interdigitating with the therapist's current developmental issues and intrapsychic conflicts, including her physiological changes, emotional and physical needs, maternal preoccupation, and guilt at viewing herself as an abandoning object. Finally, Penn describes useful technical guidelines in working with the transference, in facilitating exploration of the patient's conflicts, and in acknowledging nontransferential reactions. Practical considerations, including initial discussion of the pregnancy, scheduling the break, and contact during the maternity leave, are reviewed. Utilization of countertransference responses and reactions of supervisors are explored in depth.

Fuller, Ruth (1987). The impact of the therapist's pregnancy on the dynamics of the therapeutic process. *J. Amer. Acad. Psychoanal.*, 15:9-28.

The author presents her concept of five stages of pregnancy, beginning with a prepregnant phase of anticipation or planning, and culminating in a postpartum phase of consolidation.

For each stage she outlines practical and intrapsychic challenges for the therapist and a variety of responses by patients. She makes extensive use of lively vignettes from many women therapists' clinical work with adult individuals, groups, and children. This article focuses particularly on the unborn baby as a third person in the analytic room: competitor, eavesdropper, intruder, a focus for multiple affects and conflicts. Birth and the postpartum return of the therapist to the patient involves a new adjustment wherein the baby is now cared for elsewhere during the hours but remains a major influence in the ongoing intrapsychic work for patient and therapist.

Bassen, Cecile (1988). The impact of the analyst's pregnancy on the course of analysis. *Psychoanal. Inq.*, 2:280-298.

Bassen reports on a retrospective study of 13 analysts including herself, who as a group completed 18 pregnancies while analyzing adult patients either as candidates or graduate analysts. They each treated one to ten analytic patients. All the analysts reported an intensification of both transference and resistance in response to their pregnancies. The author proposes that the analyzability of the resistance is correlated with the level of psychopathology of the patient and that psychopathology determines either the facilitative, disruptive, or minimal effect on the analytic process. She discusses other factors influencing the range of responses by patients and their analyzability. They include the phase of the analysis, the skill of the analyst, and the analyst's ability to recognize and use countertransference reactions. Several analysts in the study noted that alternating or coexisting with the maternal transference, paternal transferences had persisted during their pregnancies. Productive responses to the analyst's pregnancy included the recall of previously repressed material, often related to the pregnancies of the patients' own mothers. Emergence of that material facilitated compelling genetic reconstructions. An inhibiting or disruptive effect on treatment occurred in patients with severe character pathology, whose basic analyzability was already in question prior to the pregnancy. One female analysand became persistently enraged, experiencing the pregnancy as an irreparable narcissistic injury until after the pregnancy. Some patients, who had been in treatment for less than a year, dropped out of analysis. Countertransference phenomena include reactivation of feelings of oedipal triumph, fears of retaliation, and ambivalent feelings for the analyst's own mother and for the fetus. Several analysts felt protective of their female patients who were childless and had difficulty interpreting their patients' envy and rage. The last section discusses the interweaving of the transference-countertransference issues with "real" and practical considerations such as disclosure and maternity leave.

McGarty, Maureen (1988). The analyst's pregnancy. *Contemp. Psychoanal.*, 24:684-692.

The analyst's pregnancy can intensify the transference and can provide new therapeutic opportunities. Historically, women analysts have felt guilty or deviant because they were interfering with analysis by no longer being a blank screen. McGarty differentiates analytic neutrality and an atmosphere of safety from appropriate self-revelation about the reality of the analyst's pregnancy. Analysts who are fearful or unwilling to discuss the pregnancy defensively collude with the patient's defenses and promote acting out. Personal vignettes illustrate typical patients' conflicts about separation, loss, early mother-child relations, sibling rivalry, and sexuality.

Fuerstein, Laura (1989). Some hypotheses about gender differences in coping with oral dependency conflicts. *Psychoanal. Rev.*, 76:163-184.

[See Chapter 23 for annotation.]

Imber, Ruth (1990). The avoidance of countertransference awareness in a pregnant analyst. *Contemp. Psychoanal.*, 26:223-236.

This article focuses on countertransference during the analyst's pregnancy. Case material is presented to highlight the particular resistance to the awareness of aggression in the transference-countertransference interaction. Pregnancy is viewed as a maturational crisis during which the analyst may experience a heightened sense of physical and emotional vulnerability. The pregnant analyst must also adapt to new psychological roles and environmental demands that can affect her clinical work. Parallels with illness in the analyst are drawn.

Lazar, Susan (1990). Patients' responses to pregnancy and miscarriage in the analyst. In: *Illness in the Analyst*, ed. H. Schwartz and A. Silver. New York: International Universities Press, pp. 1-2.

Lazar reports the experiences of an analyst who had multiple pregnancies, including several late miscarriages. Intense transference reactions were stimulated in patients of both sexes. The analyst also experienced a growth in her nurturing attitude toward her patients as she worked through countertransference reactions to negative transferences. Two male and one female patient are presented in considerable detail. Both male patients showed early recognition of their analyst's pregnancy, in the first trimester. In one man's analysis, the material showed an early identification with the preoedipal mother. The second man's heightened transference reactions reflected both his identification with his mother and his envy of women and their female procreative functioning. The woman patient responded with veiled envy and competitiveness to the analyst's first pregnancy and had intense and ambivalent reactions to the analyst's late miscarriage. Both pregnancies elicited preoedipal and oedipal themes, involving envy, rivalry, and identification with the procreative mother. Lazar found that premature termination may occur if an analysand's affects become intense without a stable alliance. Lazar asserts that a pregnancy or miscarriage differs from illness or threatened death of the analyst, because ongoing treatment can continue and thus facilitate working through.

# Section V

# Reading Lists

# Chapter 27

# Reading List: Feminist/Academic Writings

Nancy Chodorow, with Nadine Levinson
and Eleanor Schuker

This chapter is a partial list of feminist/academic writings on female psychology. Much of this literature has influenced and been influenced by psychoanalytic theory and thought, particularly as related to gender differences and gender relationships. This is a beginning reference list for any analyst interested in learning more about this area.

Abel, Elizabeth (1989). *Virginia Woolf and the Fictions of Psychoanalysis.* Chicago, IL: University of Chicago Press.

Abel, Elizabeth, Hirsch, Marianne, and Langland, Elizabeth (ed.)(1983). *The Voyage In: Fictions of Female Development.* Hanover, NH: University Press of New England.

Adelman, Janet (1991). *Suffocating Mothers: Fantasies of Maternal Origin in Shakespeare, Hamlet to the Tempest.* New York and London: Routledge.

Benjamin, Jessica (1980). The bonds of love: Rational violence and erotic domination. *Feminist Studies,* 6:144-175. Also in: *The Future of Difference,* ed. H. Eisenstein and A. Jardine. Boston, MA: G. K. Hall, 1980, pp. 41-70. [See Chapter 21 for annotation.]

Benjamin, Jessica (1988). *The Bonds of Love: Psychoanalysis, Feminism, and the Problem of Domination.* New York: Pantheon. [See Chapter 4 for annotation.]

Bernheimer, Charles and Kahane, Claire (ed.) (1985). *In Dora's Case: Freud-Hysteria-Feminism.* New York: Columbia University Press. [See Chapter 3 for annotation.]

Chodorow, Nancy (1978). *The Reproduction of Mothering: Psychoanalysis and the Sociology of Gender.* Berkeley, CA: University of California Press. [See Chapters 4, 5, 6, 7, 12, 14, 18 for annotations.]

Chodorow, Nancy (1981). Reply. Contribution to J. Lorber, R. Coser, A. Rossi, and N. Chodorow, On *The Reproduction of Mothering*: A methodological debate. *Signs,* 6:500-514.

Chodorow, Nancy (1986). Varieties of leadership among early women psychoanalysts. In: *Women Physicians in Leadership Roles*, ed. L. Dickstein and C. Nadelson. Washington, DC: American Psychiatric Press, pp. 45-54.

Chodorow, Nancy (1986b). Divorce, oedipal asymmetries and the marital age gap. *Psychoanal. Rev.*, 73:606-610. [See Chapter 13 for annotation.]

Chodorow, Nancy (1989a). *Feminism and Psychoanalytic Theory*. New Haven, CT: Yale University Press. [See Chapters 3B and 4 for individually annotated chapters.]

Dinnerstein, Dorothy (1976). *The Mermaid and the Minotaur*. New York: Harper. [See Chapters 5 and 13 for annotations.]

Eisenbud, Ruth Jean (1986). Woman feminist patients and a feminist woman analyst. In: *The Psychology of Today's Woman*, ed. T. Bernay and D. Cantor. Hillsdale, NJ: The Analytic Press, pp. 273-290. [See Chapter 25 for annotation.]

Eisenstein, Hester and Jardine, Alice (ed.) (1980). *The Future of Difference*, esp. Part I: Differentiation and the sexual politics of gender, pp. 1-70, and Part II: Contemporary feminist thought in France, pp. 71-122. Boston, MA: G. K. Hall.

Flax, Jane (1980). Mother-daughter relationships: Psychodynamics, politics, and philosophy. In: *The Future of Difference*, ed. H. Eisenstein and A. Jardine. Boston, MA: G. Hall, pp. 20-40.

Flax, Jane (1990). *Thinking Fragments: Psychoanalysis, Feminism and Post-modernism in the Contemporary West*. Berkeley: University of California Press.

Gallop, Jane (1982). *The Daughter's Seduction*. Ithaca, NY: Cornell University Press.

Garner, Shirley, Kahane, Claire, and Sprengnether, Madelon (1985). *The (M)other Tongue: Essays in Feminist Psychoanalytic Interpretation*. Ithaca, NY: Cornell University Press.

Gilligan, Carol (1982). *In a Different Voice: Women's Conceptions of the Self and Morality*, Cambridge, MA: Harvard University Press. [See Chapters 4 and 7 for annotations.]

Irigary, Luce (1974). This sex which is not one. In: *New French Feminisms*, ed. E. Marks and I. de Courtivron. Amherst: University of Massachusetts Press, 1980. [See Chapter 18 for annotation.]

Johnson, Miriam (1988). *Strong Mothers, Weak Wives: The Search for Gender Equality*. Berkeley: University of California Press.

Keller, Evelyn Fox (1985). The inner world of subjects and objects. In: *Reflections on Gender and Science*. New Haven, CT: Yale University Press, pp. 67-126.

Kristeva, Julia (1974). *Revolution in Poetic Language*. New York: Columbia University Press, 1984.

Lacan, Jacques and the École Freudienne (1982). *Feminine Sexuality*, ed. J. Mitchell and J. Rose (Trans. J. Rose). New York: Norton, 1985. [See Chapter 4 for annotation.]

Mitchell, Juliet (1974b). *Psychoanalysis and Feminism*. New York: Vintage Books, 1975. [See Chapter 4 for annotation.]

Mitchell, Juliet (1984). The question of femininity and the theory of psychoanalysis. In: *The British School of Psychoanalysis: The Independent Tradition*, ed. G. Kohon. New Haven, CT: Yale University Press, 1986, pp. 381-398. Also in: *Women: The Longest Revolution*. London: Virago Press, 1984, pp. 295-315. [See Chapter 3B for annotation.]

Montrelay, Michele (1974). Inquiry into femininity. *m/f*, 1:83-101, 1978.

Moustafa, Safouan (1976). Feminine sexuality in psychoanalytic doctrine. In: *Feminine Sexuality*, ed. J. Mitchell and J. Rose. New York: Pantheon Books, pp. 123-136.

Rose, Jacqueline (1983). Femininity and its discontents. In: *Sexuality in the Field of Vision*. London: Verso, 1986, pp. 83-103.

Rubin, Gayle (1975). The traffic in women: Notes on the "political economy" of sex. In: *Toward an Anthropology of Women*, ed. R. Reiter. New York: Monthly Review Press, pp. 157-210.

Turkle, Sherry (1978). *Psychoanalytic Politics—Freud's French Revolution*. New York: Basic Books.

Young-Bruehl, Elisabeth (1990). *Freud on Women*. New Haven, CT: Yale University Press. [See Chapter 4 for annotation.]

Zanardi, Claudia (ed.) (1990). *Essential Papers on Psychology of Women*. New York: New York University Press. [See Chapter 4 for annotation.]

# Chapter 28

# Suggested Readings: A Psychoanalytic Perspective on Female Psychology

Eleanor Schuker and Nadine Levinson

We have constructed four outlines for courses suitable for various academic levels. Each is designed to meet particular time constraints and interests. There exists an abundance of excellent books and papers from which to choose. Although we concentrated primarily on resources from the psychoanalytic literature, we also included relevant articles from related disciplines. For some seminars, more papers are listed than any individual student may find convenient to read. However, these readings can serve as a guide for instructors and may be modified to suit personal preferences.

The purpose of each course is to offer a comprehensive view of female psychology and feminine development for the appropriate academic level. Vicissitudes of female development in the life cycle are emphasized and integrated into a model for psychic structure. Clinical material can be employed throughout the respective courses to convey a sense of how work with patients is influenced by existing theories; the material serves, in turn, as a basis for new theories. For study at the college level, where instructors may not have clinical material available, Freud's (1905a) case history of Dora, "Fragment of an Analysis of a Case of Hysteria," is appropriate reading to highlight theoretical principles. **Course I** is designed for psychoanalytic candidates and advanced psychiatric residents and psychologists and offers a strong developmental orientation. **Course II** is recommended for advanced undergraduate study. It can be modified for graduate-level work. The course includes a general overview of female psychology as well as some basic papers on psychoanalysis. Specific areas of female psychology are investigated, and connections are drawn to the feminist literature. **Course III** is a two-day sequential course for general psychiatrists, psychologists, social workers, and other mental health professionals in clinical practice. Case material from participants could supplement the readings. **Course IV** is suitable for advanced psychoanalytic candidates and graduates of analytic institutes who are interested in matters of current controversy relating to female psychology. Each seminar is designed around a particular question or issue.

## COURSE I: FOR PSYCHOANALYTIC CANDIDATES AND ADVANCED PSYCHIATRIC RESIDENTS AND PSYCHOLOGISTS

### Seminar I: Historical Overview of Theories of Female Development

Freud, Sigmund (1925). Some psychical consequences of the anatomical distinction between the sexes. *Standard Edition*, 19:243-258. London: Hogarth Press, 1953.

Horney, Karen (1926). The flight from womanhood. *Int. J. Psycho-Anal.*, 12:360-374. Also in: *Feminine Psychology*, ed. H. Kelman. New York: Norton, 1967, pp. 54-70.

Freud, Sigmund (1931a). Female sexuality. *Standard Edition*, 21:223-243. London: Hogarth Press, 1953.

Fliegel, Zenia (1973). Feminine psychosexual development in Freudian theory. *Psychoanal. Q.*, 42:385-409.

### Seminar II: Early Gender Differentiation/Primary Femininity

Stoller, Robert (1976a). Primary femininity. *J. Amer Psychoanal. Assn.* (Suppl.), 24:59-78.

Galenson, Eleanor and Roiphe, Herman (1976). Some suggested revisions concerning early female development. *J. Amer. Psychoanal. Assn.* (Suppl.), 24:29-57.

Kleeman, James (1976). Freud's views on early female sexuality in the light of direct child observation. *J. Amer. Psychoanal. Assn.* (Suppl.), 24:3-27.

Fast, Irene (1979). Developments in gender identity: Gender differentiation in girls. *Int. J. Psycho-Anal.*, 60:443-453.

Person, Ethel and Ovesey, Lionel (1983). Psychoanalytic theories of gender identity. *J. Amer. Acad. Psychoanal.*, 11:203-226.

### Seminar III: Preoedipal Development I: Overview

Tyson, Phyllis and Tyson, Robert (1990). Gender development: Girls. In: *Psychoanalytic Theories of Development: An Integration*. New Haven, CT: Yale University Press, pp. 258-276.

Chehrazi, Shalah (1986). Female psychology: A review. *J. Amer. Psychoanal. Assn.*, 34:141-162.

Edgcumbe, Rose and Burgner, Marion (1975). The phallic-narcissistic phase: A differentiation between preoedipal and oedipal aspects of phallic development. *The Psychoanalytic Study of the Child*, 30:161-180. New Haven, CT: Yale University Press.

Silverman, Doris (1987b). What are little girls made of? *Psychoanal. Psychol.*, 4:315-334.

## Seminar IV: Preoedipal Development II: Body Image

Grossman, William and Stewart, Walter (1976). Penis envy: From childhood wish to developmental metaphor. *J. Amer. Psychoanal. Assn.* (Suppl.), 24:193-213.

Lerner, Harriet (1976). Parental mislabeling of female genitals as a determinant of penis envy and learning inhibitions in women. *J. Amer. Psychoanal. Assn.* (Suppl.), 24:269-283. Also in: *Women in Therapy.* Northvale, NJ: Aronson, 1988, pp. 25-41.

Bernstein, Doris (1990). Female genital anxieties, conflicts, and typical mastery modes. *Int. J. Psycho-Anal.*, 71:151-165.

Mayer, Elizabeth (1985). Everybody must be just like me: Observations on female castration anxiety. *Int. J. Psycho-Anal.*, 66:331-348.

Silverman, Martin (1981). Cognitive development and female psychology. *J. Amer. Psychoanal. Assn.*, 29:581-605.

## Seminar V: Oedipal Considerations and Development of Superego

Tyson, Phyllis (1989). Infantile sexuality, gender identity, and obstacles to oedipal progression. *J. Amer. Psychoanal. Assn.* 37:1051-1069.

Parens, Henri, Pollock, Leafy, Stern, Joan, and Kramer, Selma (1976). On the girl's entry into the Oedipus complex. *J. Amer Psychoanal. Assn.* (Suppl.), 24:79-108.

Bernstein, Doris (1983). The female superego: A different perspective. *Int. J. Psycho-Anal.*, 64:187-202.

Gilligan, Carol (1977). In a different voice: Women's concepts of self and morality. *Harvard Educational Review*, 47:481-517. Also in: *In A Different Voice.* Cambridge, MA: Harvard University Press, 1982.

## Seminar VI: Latency and Adolescence

Clower, Virginia (1976). Theoretical implications in current views of masturbation in latency girls. *J. Amer. Psychoanal. Assn.* (Suppl.), 24:109-125.

Silverman, Martin (1982). The latency period. In: *Early Female Development, Current Psychoanalytic Views*, ed. D. Mendell. Jamaica, NY: S. P. Medical and Scientific Books, pp. 203-226.

Blos, Peter (1980). Modification in the traditional theory of female adolescent development. In: *Adolescent Psychiatry: Developmental and Clinical Studies*, Vol. 8, ed. S. Feinstein, P. Giovacchini, and A. Miller. Chicago: University of Chicago Press, pp. 8-24.

Esman, Aaron (1979). Adolescence and the "new sexuality." In: *On Sexuality: Psychoanalytic Observations*, ed. B. Karasu and C. Socarides. New York: International Universities Press, pp. 19-28.

Rosenbaum, Maj-Britt (1979). The changing body image of the adolescent girl. In: *Female Adolescent Development*, ed. M. Sugar. New York: Brunner/Mazel, pp. 234-251.

Whisnant, Lynn, Brett, Elizabeth, and Zegans, Leonard (1979). Adolescent girls and menstruation. *Adol. Psychiat.*, 7:157-170.

### Seminar VII: Adult Development I: Identity Conflicts

Person, Ethel (1982). Women working: Fears of failure, deviance and success. *J. Amer. Acad. Psychoanal.*, 10:67-84.

Moulton, Ruth (1986). Professional success: A conflict for women. In: *Psychoanalysis and Women: Contemporary Reappraisals*, ed. J. Alpert. Hillsdale, NJ: The Analytic Press, pp. 161-181.

Bernstein, Doris (1979). Female identity synthesis. In: *Career and Motherhood, Struggles for a New Society*, ed. A. Roland and B. Harris. New York: Human Science Press, pp. 103-123.

Schecter, Doreen (1979). Fear of success in women: A psychodynamic reconstruction. *J. Amer Acad. Psychoanal.*, 7:33-43.

### Seminar VIII: Adult Development II: Pregnancy and the Pregnant Analyst.

Lester, Eva and Notman, Malkah (1986). Pregnancy, developmental crises and object relations. *Int. J. Psycho-Anal.*, 67:357-366.

Benedek, Therese (1970c). Parenthood during the life cycle. In: *Parenthood: Its Psychology and Psychopathology*, ed. E. J. Anthony and T. Benedek. Boston, MA: Little, Brown, pp. 185-206.

Penn, Linda (1986). The pregnant therapist: Transference and countertransference issues. In: *Psychoanalysis and Women: Contemporary Reappraisals*, ed. J. Alpert. Hillsdale, NJ: The Analytic Press, pp. 287-316.

## Seminar IX: Female Sexuality and Sexual Inhibition

Person, Ethel (1980). Sexuality as the mainstay of identity: Psychoanalytic perspectives. *Signs,* 5:605-630. Also in: *Women: Sex and Sexuality,* ed. C. Stimpson and E. Person. Chicago, IL: University of Chicago, 1980, pp/ 31-61.

Montgrain, Noel (1983). On the vicissitudes of female sexuality: The difficult path from "anatomical destiny" to psychic representation. *Int. J. Psycho-Anal.,* 64:169-186.

Kulish, Nancy (1991). The mental representation of the clitoris. *Psychoanal. Inq.*

Masters, William and Johnson, Virginia (1966). *Human Sexual Response.* London: J. and A. Churchill.

## Seminar X: Gender Identity Disorders

Freud, Sigmund (1920). The psychogenesis of a case of homosexuality in a woman. *Standard Edition,* 18:146-172. London: Hogarth Press, 1955.

Deutsch, Helene (1932). On female homosexuality. *Psychoanal. Q.,* 1:484-510.

McDougall, Joyce (1970). Homosexuality in women. In: *Female Sexuality: New Psychoanalytic Views,* ed. J. Chasseguet-Smirgel. Ann Arbor: University of Michigan Press, pp. 171-212.

Eisenbud, Ruth-Jean (1982). Early and later determinants of lesbian choice. *Psychoanal. Rev.,* 69:85-109.

Wolfson, Abby (1987). Reporter, Panel: Toward the further understanding of homosexual women. *J. Amer. Psychoanal. Assn.,* 35:165-173.

Raphling, David (1989). Fetishism in a woman. *J. Amer. Psychoanal. Assn.,* 37:465-491.

## Seminar XI: Masochism and Narcissism in Women

Simons, Richard (1987). Psychoanalytic contributions to nosology: Forms of masochistic behavior. *J. Amer. Psychoanal. Assn.,* 35:583-608.

Meyers, Helen (1988). A consideration of treatment techniques in relation to the functions of masochism. In: *Masochism: Current Analytic Perspectives,* ed. R. Glick and D. Meyers. Hillsdale, NJ: The Analytic Press, pp. 175-188.

Novick, Kerry and Novick, Jack (1987). The essence of masochism. *The Psychoanalytic Study of the Child,* 42:353-384. New Haven, CT: Yale University Press.

Reich, Annie (1940). A contribution to the psychoanalysis of extreme submissiveness in women. *Psychoanal. Q.,* 9:470-480. Also in: *Psychoana-*

*lytic Contributions*. New York: International Universities Press, 1973, pp. 85-120.

Lachmann, Frank (1982b). Narcissistic Development. In: *Early Female Development*, ed. D. Mendell. New York: S.P. Medical and Scientific Books, pp. 227-248.

Lang, Joan (1984). Notes toward a psychology of the feminine self. In: *Kohut's Legacy*, ed. P. Stepansky and A. Goldberg. Hillsdale, NJ: The Analytic Press, pp. 51-70.

Freyberg, Joan (1984). The psychoanalytic treatment of narcissism. *Psychoanal. Psychol.*, 1:99-112.

### Seminar XII: Transference and Countertransference

Freud, Sigmund (1915c). Observations on transference-love. *Standard Edition*, 12:158-171. London: Hogarth Press, 1953.

Person, Ethel (1985). The erotic transference in women and men: Differences and consequences. *J. Amer. Acad. Psychoanal.*, 13:159-180.

Liebert, Robert (1986). Transference and countertransference issues in the treatment of women by a male analyst. In: *Between Analyst and Patient*, ed. H. Meyers. Hillsdale, NJ: The Analytic Press, pp. 229-236.

Meyers, Helen (1986). How do women treat men? In: *The Psychology of Men*, ed. G. Fogel, F. Lane, and R. Liebert. New York: Basic Books, pp. 262-276.

Kulish, Nancy (1984). The effect of the sex of the analyst on transference: A review of the literature. *Bull. Menn. Clin.*, 48:95-110.

## COURSE II: FOR UNDERGRADUATE STUDY

### Seminar I: Early Contributions

Freud, Sigmund (1925). Some psychical consequences of the anatomical distinction between the sexes. *Standard Edition*, 19:243-258. London: Hogarth Press, 1953.

Horney, Karen (1926). The flight from womanhood. *Int. J. Psycho-Anal.*, 12:360-374. Also in: *Feminine Psychology*, ed. H. Kelman. New York: Norton, 1967, pp. 54-70.

Freud, Sigmund (1931a). Female sexuality. *Standard Edition*, 21:223-243. London: Hogarth Press, 1953.

Thompson, Clara (1942). Cultural pressures on the psychology of women. *Psychiat.*, 5:331-339. Also in: *Psychoanalysis and Women*, ed. J. B. Miller. New York: Brunner/Mazel, 1973, pp. 49-64.

### Seminar II: Critique of Classical Psychoanalytic Theory

Levinson, Nadine, Schuker, Eleanor, Tyson, Phyllis, and Fischer, Ruth (1991). Sigmund Freud and the psychology of women. In: *Female Psychology: An Annotated Psychoanalytic Bibliography*, ed. E. Schuker and N. Levinson. Hillsdale, NJ: The Analytic Press, pp. 3-9.

Fliegel, Zenia (1986). Women's development in analytic theory: Six decades of controversy. In: *Psychoanalysis and Women: Contemporary Reappraisals*, ed. J. Alpert. Hillsdale, NJ: The Analytic Press, pp. 3-31.

Gay, Peter (1988). Woman, the dark continent. In: *Freud: A Life for Our Time*. New York: Norton, pp. 501-522.

Miller, Jean Baker and Mothres, Ira (1971). Psychological consequences of sexual inequality. *Amer. J. Orthopsychiat.*, 41:767-775.

### Seminar III: Feminist Critique of Psychoanalytic Theory

Chodorow, Nancy (1986a). Feminism, femininity, and Freud. In: *Advances in Psychoanalytic Sociology*, ed. J. Rabow, G. Platt, and M. Goldman. Malabar, FL: Robert E. Krieger. Also in: *Feminism and Psychoanalytic Theory*, ed. N. Chodorow. New Haven, CT: Yale University Press, 1989a, pp. 166-177.

Mitchell, Juliet (1974a). On Freud and the distinction between the sexes. In: *Women and Analysis*, ed. J. Strouse. New York: Grossman/Viking Press, pp. 27-36.

Flax, Jane (1980). Mother-daughter relationships: Psychodynamics, politics, and philosophy. In: *The Future of Difference*, ed. H. Eisenstein and A. Jardine. Boston, MA: G. K. Hall, pp. 20-40.

Chodorow, Nancy (1991). Freud on women. In: *Cambridge Companion to Freud*, ed. J. Neu. New York: Cambridge University Press.

### Seminar IV: Basic Psychoanalytic Concepts of Development

Mahler, Margaret, Pine, Fred, and Bergman, Anni (1975). *The Psychological Birth of the Human Infant*. New York: Basic Books (esp. pp. 104-106, 109-116, 210-224).

Stoller, Robert (1976a). Primary femininity. *J. Amer Psychoanal. Assn.* (Suppl.), 24:59-78.

Tyson, Phyllis and Tyson, Robert (1990). *Psychoanalytic Theories of Development: An Integration*. New Haven, CT: Yale University Press (esp. pp. 41-65).

Tyson, Phyllis (1986). Female psychological development. *The Annual of Psychoanalysis*, 4:357-373. New York: International Universities Press.

## Seminar V: Biological Aspects of Gender Differences

Money, John and Ehrhardt, Anke (1972). *Man and Woman, Boy and Girl.* Baltimore, MD: Johns Hopkins University Press.

Baker, Susan (1980). Biological influences in human sex and gender. *Signs,* 6:80-96.

Notman, Malkah (1991). Gender development. In: *Women and Men: New Perspectives on Gender Differences,* ed. M. Notman and C. Nadelson. Washington, DC: American Psychiatric Press, pp. 117-127.

Silverman, Doris (1987b). What are little girls made of? *Psychoanal. Psychol.,* 4:315-334.

## Seminar VI: Social/Cultural Views

Mead, Margaret (1974). On Freud's view of female psychology. In: *Women and Analysis,* ed. J. Strouse. New York: Viking, pp. 95-106.

Chodorow, Nancy (1980). Difference, relation and gender in psychoanalytic perspective. In: *The Future of Difference,* ed. H. Eisenstein and A. Jardine. Boston, MA: G. K. Hall, pp. 3-19. Also in: *Feminism and Psychoanalytic Theory.* New Haven, CT: Yale University Press, 1989, pp. 99-113.

Moulton, Ruth (1972). The fear of female power. *J. Amer. Acad. Psychoanal.,* 5:499-519.

Lerner, Harriet (1978). Adaptive and pathogenic aspects of sex-role stereotypes. *Amer. J. Psychiat.,* 1:48-52. Also in: *Women in Therapy.* Northvale, NJ: Aronson, 1988, pp. 79-92.

## Seminar VII: Current Psychoanalytic Views

Chehrazi, Shalah (1986). Female psychology: A review. *J. Amer. Psychoanal. Assn.,* 34:141-162.

Tyson, Phyllis and Tyson, Robert (1990). Gender development: Girls. In: *Psychoanalytic Theories of Development: An Integration.* New Haven, CT: Yale University Press, pp. 258-276.

Mendell, Dale (1988). Early female development: From birth through latency. In: *Critical Psychophysical Passages in the Life of a Woman,* ed. J. Offerman-Zuckerberg. New York: Plenum, pp. 17-36.

Person, Ethel (1991). The "construction" of femininity: Its influence throughout the life cycle. In: *The Course of Life,* Vol. 4, ed. S. Greenspan and G. Pollock. Madison, CT: International Universities Press.

## Seminar VIII: Female Adolescence

Dalsimer, Katherine (1986). *Female Adolescence: Psychoanalytic Reflections on Literature.* New Haven, CT: Yale University Press.

Person, Ethel (1985). Female sexual identity: The impact of the adolescent experience. In: *Sexuality: New Perspectives*, ed. Z. DeFries, R. Friedman, and R. Corn. Westport, CT: Greenwood Press, pp. 71-88.

Shopper, Moisy (1979). The (re)discovery of the vagina and the importance of the menstrual tampon. In: *Female Adolescent Development*, ed. M. Sugar. New York: Brunner/Mazel, pp. 214-233.

Rosenbaum, Maj-Britt (1979). The changing body image of the adolescent girl. In: *Female Adolescent Development*, ed. M. Sugar. New York: Brunner/Mazel, pp. 234-251.

### Seminar IX: Eating Disorders

Reiser, Lynn Whisnant (1988a). Love, work, and bulimia. In: *Bulimia: Psychoanalytic Treatment and Theory*, ed. H. Schwartz. Madison, CT: International Universities Press, pp. 373-398.

Bruch, Hilde (1978). *The Golden Cage: The Enigma of Anorexia Nervosa.* Cambridge, MA: Harvard University Press.

Ritvo, Samuel (1984). The image and uses of the body in psychic conflict with special reference to eating disorders. *The Psychoanalytic Study of the Child*, 39:449-469. New Haven, CT: Yale University Press.

### Seminar X: Adulthood

Colarusso, Calvin and Nemiroff, Robert (1981). *Adult Development.* New York: Plenum Press (esp. pp. 59-81.)

Giele, Janet (1982a) Women in adulthood: Unanswered questions. In: *Women in the Middle Years*, ed. J. Giele. New York: Wiley, pp. 1-35.

Nadelson, Carol, Notman, Malkah, Miller, Jean Baker, and Zilbach, Joan (1982). Aggression in women: Conceptual issues and clinical implications. In: *The Woman Patient: Aggression, Adaptations and Psychotherapy*, Vol. 3, ed. M. Notman and C. Nadelson. New York: Plenum Press, pp. 17-28.

Notman, Malkah (1982a). Feminine development: Changes in psychoanalytic theory. In: *The Woman Patient: Concepts of Femininity and the Life Cycle*, Vol. 2, ed. C. Nadelson and M. Notman. New York: Plenum Press, pp. 3-29.

Clower, Virginia (1990). The acquisition of mature femininity. In: *Women and Men: New Perspectives on Gender Differences*, ed. M. Notman and C. Nadelson. Washington, DC: American Psychiatric Press, pp. 75-88.

### Seminar XI: Love, Pregnancy, Childrearing, and Gender

Dinnerstein, Dorothy (1976). *The Mermaid and the Minotaur.* New York: Harper and Row, 1977.

Kernberg, Otto (1977). Boundaries and structure in love relationships. *J. Amer. Psychoanal. Assn.*, 25:81-114.

Nadelson, Carol and Notman, Malkah (1981). To marry or not to marry. *Amer. J. Psychiat.*, 138:352-356. Also in: *The Woman Patient: Concepts of Femininity and the Life Cycle*, Vol. 2, ed. C. Nadelson and M. Notman. New York: Plenum Press, 1982b, pp. 111-120.

Lester, Eva and Notman, Malkah (1986). Pregnancy, developmental crises and object relations. *Int. J. Psycho-Anal.*, 67:357-366.

Benedek, Therese (1970c). Parenthood during the life cycle. In: *Parenthood: Its Psychology and Psychopathology*, ed. E. J. Anthony and T. Benedek. Boston, MA: Little, Brown, pp. 185-206.

Person, Ethel (1986). Working mothers: Impact on the self, the couple and the children. In: *The Psychology of Today's Woman: New Psychoanalytic Visions*, ed. T. Bernay and D. Cantor. Hillsdale, NJ: The Analytic Press, pp. 121-138.

### Seminar XII: Sexual Identity and Sexuality

Person, Ethel (1980). Sexuality as the mainstay of identity: psychoanalytic perspectives. *Signs*, 5:605-630. Also in: *Women: Sex and Sexuality*, ed. C. Stimpson and E. Person. Chicago: University of Chicago, pp. 33-61.

Masters, William and Johnson, Virginia (1966). *Human Sexual Response.* London: J. and A. Churchill.

Sherfey, Mary Jane (1966). The evolution and nature of female sexuality in relation to psychoanalytic theory. *J. Amer. Psychoanal. Assn.*, 14:28-128.

Benjamin, Jessica (1986b). A desire of one's own: Psychoanalytic feminism and intersubjective space. In: *Feminist Studies/Critical Studies*, ed. T. De Lauretis. Bloomington: Indiana University Press, pp. 78-101.

### Seminar XIII: Female Values

Gilligan, Carol (1977). In a different voice: Women's concepts of self and morality. *Harvard Educational Review*, 47:481-517.

Schafer, Roy (1974). Problems in Freud's psychology of women. *J. Amer. Psychoanal. Assn.*, 22:459-485. Also in: *J. Amer. Psychoanal. Assn.* (Suppl.), 24:331-360, 1976.

Kirkpatrick, Martha (1989b). Women in love in the 80s. *J. Amer. Acad. Psychoanal.*, 17:535-542.

## COURSE III: TWO-DAY COURSE
### First Day: Overview of Early and Contemporary Theories of Female Development

(Participants are asked to bring in their own clinical material for discussion.)

Freud, Sigmund (1931a). Female sexuality. *Standard Edition*, 21:223-243. London: Hogarth Press, 1953.

Chehrazi, Shalah (1986). Female psychology: A review. *J. Amer. Psychoanal. Assn.*, 34:141-162.

Tyson, Phyllis (1986). Female psychological development. *The Annual of Psychoanalysis*, 4:357-373. New York: International Universities Press.

Person, Ethel (1985). The erotic transference in women and men: Differences and consequences. *J. Amer. Acad. Psychoanal.*, 13:159-180.

### Second Day: Adult Female Development: The Third Individuation—Contemporary Clinical and Theoretical Issues

Colarusso, Calvin (1990). The third individuation: The effect of biological parenthood on separation-individuation processes in adulthood. *The Psychoanalytic Study of the Child*, 45:179-194. New Haven, CT: Yale University Press.

Notman, Malkah, Zilbach, Joan, Miller, Jean B., and Nadelson, Carol (1986). Themes in psychoanalytic understanding of women: Some reconsiderations of autonomy and affiliation. *J. Amer. Acad. Psychoanal.*, 14:241-253.

Bernstein, Anne and Warner, Gloria (1984). What does a woman want? Other opportunities for women to rework separation-individuation and the oedipal conflict. In: *Women Treating Women*. New York: International Universities Press, pp. 143-160.

Lerner, Harriet (1980b). Internal prohibitions against female anger. *Am. J. Psychoanal.*, 40:137-148. Also in: *Women in Therapy*. Northvale, NJ: Aronson, 1988, pp. 57-75.

Person, Ethel (1982). Women working: Fears of failure, deviance and success. *J. Amer. Acad. Psychoanal.*, 10:67-84.

Moulton, Ruth (1986). Professional success: A conflict for women. In: *Psychoanalysis and Women: Contemporary Reappraisals*, ed. J. Alpert. Hillsdale, NJ: The Analytic Press, pp. 161-181.

Riviere, Joan (1929). Womanliness as a masquerade. *Int. J. Psycho-Anal.*, 10:303-313. Also in: *Psychoanalysis and Female Sexuality*, ed. H. Ruitenbeek. New Haven, CT: College and University Press, 1966, pp. 209-220.

## COURSE IV: ADVANCED STUDY OF FEMALE PSYCHOLOGY—SELECTED CURRENT CONTROVERSIES

### 1. What did Freud misunderstand about women?

Schafer, Roy (1974). Problems in Freud's psychology of women. *J. Amer. Psychoanal. Assn.*, 22:459-485. Also in: *J. Amer. Psychoanal. Assn.* (Suppl.), 24:331-360, 1976.

Person, Ethel and Ovesey, Lionel (1983). Psychoanalytic theories of gender identity. *J. Amer. Acad. Psychoanal.*, 11:203-226.

Person, Ethel (1983). The influence of values in psychoanalysis: The case of female psychology. *Psychiatry Update*, ed. L. Grinspoon. Washington, DC: American Psychiatric Press, Vol. 2, pp. 36-50.

Grossman, William and Kaplan, Donald (1989). Three commentaries on gender in Freud's thought: A prologue on the psychoanalytic theory of sexuality. In: *Fantasy, Myth, and Reality: Essays in Honor of Jacob A. Arlow*, ed. H. Blum, Y. Kramer, A. K. Richards, and A. D. Richards. Madison, CT: International Universities Press, pp. 339-370.

Kaplan, Donald (1990). Some theoretical and technical aspects of gender and social reality in clinical psychoanalysis. *The Psychoanalytic Study of the Child*, 45:3-24. New Haven, CT: Yale University Press.

### II. Which neglected historical papers foreshadowed contemporary formulations?

Lynn Whisnant Reiser, with Nadine Levinson (1991). Early psychoanalytic views. In: *Female Psychology: An Annotated Psychoanalytic Bibliography*, ed. E. Schuker and N. Levinson. Hillsdale, NJ: The Analytic Press, pp. 22-40.

Horney, Karen (1926). The flight from womanhood. *Int. J. Psycho-Anal.*, 12:360-374. Also in: *Feminine Psychology*, ed. H. Kelman. New York: Norton, 1967, pp. 54-70.

Klein, Melanie (1928). Early stages of the Oedipus conflict. In: *Love, Guilt and Reparation and Other Works: The Writings of Melanie Klein*, Vol. 1. London: Hogarth Press, 1975, pp. 186-198.

Fenichel, Otto (1934). Further light upon the preoedipal phase in girls. In: *The Collected Papers of Otto Fenichel*. New York: Norton, 1953, pp. 241-288. First published in *Int. Z. Psa.*, 20:151-190, 134.

Jones, Ernest (1935). Early female sexuality. *Int. J. Psycho-Anal.*, 16:263-273.

Brierley, Marjorie (1936). Specific determinants in feminine development. *Int. J. Psycho-Anal.*, 17:163-180.

### III. What is the role of infant observational studies and their contribution to psychoanalytic knowledge about female development?

Klein, Melanie (1932). *The Psychoanalysis of Children*. New York: Norton.
Kleeman, James (1971a,b). The establishment of core gender identity in normal girls. Parts I and II. *Arch. Sex. Behav.*, 1:103-129.
Roiphe, Herman and Galenson, Eleanor (1981). *Infantile Origins of Sexual Identity*, New York: International Universities Press.
Silverman, Doris (1987a). Female bonding: Some supportive findings for Melanie Klein's views. *Psychoanal. Rev.*, 74:201-215.

### IV. What is the nature of female genital representation, and how is this related to female sexuality?

Bernstein, Doris (1990). Female genital anxieties, conflicts, and typical mastery modes. *Int. J. Psycho-Anal.*, 71:151-165.
Kulish, Nancy (1991). The mental representation of the clitoris. *Psychoanal. Inq.*
Montgrain, Noel (1983). On the vicissitudes of female sexuality: The difficult path from "anatomical destiny" to psychic representation. *Int. J. Psycho-Anal.*, 64:169-186.
Mayer, Elizabeth (1985). Everybody must be just like me: Observations on female castration anxiety. *Int. J. Psycho-Anal.*, 66:331-348.
Shopper, Moisy (1979). The (re)discovery of the vagina and the importance of the menstrual tampon. In: *Female Adolescent Development*, ed. M. Sugar. New York: Brunner/Mazel, pp. 214-233.

### V. What are the preoedipal and oedipal contributions to core female neuroses?

Tyson, Phyllis (1991). Some nuclear conflicts of the infantile neurosis in female development. *Psychoanal. Inq.*
Edgcumbe, Rose and Burgner, Marion (1975). The phallic-narcissistic phase: A differentiation between preoedipal and oedipal aspects of phallic development. *The Psychoanalytic Study of the Child*, 30:161-180. New Haven, CT: Yale University Press.
Dahl, Kirsten (1983). First class or nothing at all? Aspects of early feminine development. *The Psychoanalytic Study of the Child*, 38:405-428. New Haven, CT: Yale University Press.
Tyson, Phyllis (1989). Infantile sexuality, gender identity, and obstacles to oedipal progression. *J. Amer. Psychoanal. Assn.*, 37:1051-1069.

### VI. Is there a negative oedipal phase? How is it revived in the transference with analysts of either gender?

Lampl-de Groot, Jeanne (1927). The evolution of the Oedipus complex in women. *Int. J. Psycho-Anal.* 9:332-345. Also in: *The Psychoanalytic Reader*, ed. R. Fliess. New York: International Universities Press, 1948, pp. 180-194.

Edgcumbe, Rose, Lunberg, Sara, Markowitz, Randi, and Salo, Frances (1976). Some comments on the concept of the negative oedipal phase in girls. *The Psychoanalytic Study of the Child*, 31:35-61. New Haven, CT: Yale University Press.

Roth, Sheldon (1988). A woman's homosexual transference with a male analyst. *Psychoanal. Q.*, 57:28-55.

Tyson, Phyllis (1980). The gender of the analyst in relation to transference and countertransference manifestations in prelatency children. *The Psychoanalytic Study of the Child*, 35:321-338. New Haven, CT: Yale University Press.

Renik, Owen (1990). Analysis of a woman's homosexual strivings by a male analyst. *Psychoanal. Q.*, 59:41-53.

### VII. How is the superego different in women?

Greenacre, Phyllis (1948). Anatomical structure and superego development. *Amer. J. Orthopsychiat.*, 18:636-648. Also in: *Trauma, Growth, and Personality*, New York: Norton, 1952, pp. 149-164.

Chasseguet-Smirgel, Janine (1970b). Feminine guilt and the Oedipus complex. In: *Female Sexuality: New Psychoanalytic Views*, ed. J. Chasseguet-Smirgel. Ann Arbor: University of Michigan Press, pp. 94-134.

Gilligan, Carol (1977). In a different voice: Women's concepts of self and morality. *Harvard Educational Review*, 47:481-517.

Bernstein, Doris (1983). The female superego: A different perspective. *Int. J. Psycho-Anal.*, 64:187-202.

Alpert, Judith and Spencer, Jody (1986). Morality, gender, and analysis. In: *Psychoanalysis and Women: Contemporary Reappraisals*, ed. J. Alpert, Hillsdale, NJ: The Analytic Press, pp. 83-111.

Tyson, Phyllis and Tyson, Robert (1990). Gender differences in superego development. In: *Psychoanalytic Theories of Development: An Integration*. New Haven, CT: Yale University Press, pp. 228-245.

## VIII. What is a father's influence on the development of his daughter?

Forrest, Tess (1966). Paternal roots of female character development. *Contemp. Psychoanal.*, 3:21-38.

Abelin, Ernest (1980). Rapprochement and developmental issues. In: *Rapprochement*, ed. R. Lax, S. Bach, and J. Burland. New York: Aronson, pp. 151-169.

Herzog, James (1984). Fathers and young children: Fathering daughters and fathering sons. In: *Frontiers of Infant Psychiatry*, Vol. 2, ed. J. Call, E. Galenson, and R. Tyson. New York: Basic Books, pp. 335-342.

Spieler, Susan (1984). Preoedipal girls need fathers. *Psychoanal. Rev.*, 71:63-68

Pruett, Kyle (1985). Oedipal configurations in young father-raised children. *The Psychoanalytic Study of the Child*, 40:435-455. New Haven, CT: Yale University Press.

Chused, Judith (1986). Consequences of paternal nurturing. *The Psychoanalytic Study of the Child*, 41:419-438. New Haven, CT: Yale University Press.

## IX. How does an understanding of object relations enhance our theories of female sexuality and feminine identity?

Person, Ethel (1980). Sexuality as the mainstay of identity: psychoanalytic perspectives. *Signs*, 5:605-630. Also in: *Women: Sex and Sexuality*, ed. C. Stimpson and E. Person. Chicago: University of Chicago, pp. 33-61.

Kirkpatrick, Martha (1989b). Women in love in the 80s. *J. Amer. Acad. Psychoanal.*, 17:535-542.

Clower, Virginia (1990). The acquisition of mature femininity. In: *Women and Men: New Perspectives on Gender Differences*, ed. M. Notman and C. Nadelson. Washington, DC: American Psychiatric Press, pp. 75-88.

Person, Ethel (1985). Female sexual identity: The impact of the adolescent experience. In: *Sexuality: New Perspectives*, ed. Z. DeFries, R. Friedman, and R. Corn. Westport, CT: Greenwood Press, pp. 71-88.

## X. How does the menstrual cycle influence the transference?

Benedek, Therese and Rubenstein, Boris (1939a). The Correlations between ovarian activity and psychodynamic processes I: The ovulative phase. *Psychosom. Med.*, 1:245-270.

Benedek, Therese and Rubenstein, Boris (1939b). The correlations between ovarian activity and psychodynamic processes II: The menstrual phase. *Psychosom. Med.*, 1:461-485.

Whisnant, Lynn, Brett, Elizabeth, and Zegans, Leonard (1979). Adolescent girls and menstruation. *Adol. Psychiat.*, 7:157-170.

Renik, Owen (1984). An example of disavowal involving the menstrual cycle. *Psychoanal. Q.*, 53:523-532.

Severino, Sally, Bucci, Wilma, and Creelman, Monica (1989). Cyclical changes in emotional information processing in sleep and dreams. *J. Amer. Acad. Psychoanal.*, 17:555-577.

## XI. What is the role of aggression in female psychology?

Lerner, Harriet (1980b). Internal prohibitions against female anger. *Am. J. Psychoanal.*, 40:137-148. Also in: *Women in Therapy*. Northvale, NJ: Aronson, 1988, pp. 57-75.

Mahler, Margaret (1981). Aggression in the service of separation-individuation: Case study of a mother-daughter relationship. *Psychoanal. Q.*, 50:625-638.

Person, Ethel (1982). Women working: Fears of failure, deviance and success. *J. Amer. Acad. Psychoanal.*, 10:67-84.

Bernay, Toni (1986). Reconciling nurturance and aggression: A new feminine identity. In: *The Psychology of Today's Woman*, ed. T. Bernay and D. Cantor. Hillsdale, NJ: The Analytic Press, pp. 51-80.

Tyson, Phyllis (1989). Infantile sexuality, gender identity, and obstacles to oedipal progression. *J. Amer. Psychoanal. Assn.*, 37:1051-1069.

## XII. What is the impact of female reproductive experience on adult female development?

Deutsch, Helene (1925a). The psychology of women in relation to the function of reproduction. *Int. J. Psycho-Anal.*, 6:405-418. Also in: *The Psychoanalytic Reader*, ed. R. Fliess. New York: International Universities Press, 1948, pp. 165-179.

Pines, Dinora (1982). The relevance of early psychic development to pregnancy and abortion. *Int. J. Psycho-Anal.*, 63:311-319.

Lester, Eva and Notman, Malkah (1986). Pregnancy, developmental crises and object relations. *Int. J. Psycho-Anal.*, 67:357-366.

Schuker, Eleanor (1988). Psychological effects of the new reproductive technologies. In: *Embryos, Ethics and Women's Rights*, ed. E. Baruch and A. D'Adamo. Haworth Press, New York, pp. 141-147. Also in: *Women and Health* 13, 1/2 (1987).

Leon, Irving (1990). *When a Baby Dies: Psychotherapy for Pregnancy and Newborn Loss.* New Haven, CT: Yale University Press.

### XIII. Are perversions less common in women? Are they rare or merely masked?

Zavitzianos, George (1982). The perversion of fetishism in women. *Psychoanal. Q.*, 51:405-425.

Person, Ethel and Ovesey, Lionel (1983). Psychoanalytic theories of gender identity. *J. Amer. Acad. Psychoanal.*, 11:203-226.

Raphling, David (1989). Fetishism in a woman. *J. Amer. Psychoanal. Assn.*, 37:465-491.

Richards, Arlene (1990). Female fetishes and female perversions: Hermine Hug-Hellmuth's "A Case of Female Foot or More Properly Boot Fetishism" reconsidered. *Psychoanal. Rev.*, 77:11-23.

Kaplan, Louise (1991). Women masquerading as women. In: *The Perversions and Near Perversions in Clinical Practice: New Psychoanalytic Perspectives,* ed. G. Fogel and W. Myers, New Haven, CT: Yale University Press, pp. 127-152.

### XIV. Female homosexualities: Pathological symptoms or normal variants?

Deutsch, Helene (1932). On female homosexuality. *Psychoanal. Q.*, 1:484-510.

Kirkpatrick, Martha and Morgan, Carole (1980). Psychodynamic psychotherapy of female homosexuality. In: *Homosexual Behavior,* ed. J. Marmor. New York: Basic Books, pp. 357-375.

McDougall, Joyce (1980). *Plea for A Measure of Abnormality.* New York: International Universities Press.

Eisenbud, Ruth-Jean (1982). Early and later determinants of lesbian choice. *Psychoanal. Rev.*, 69:85-109.

Wolfson, Abby (1987). Reporter, Panel: Toward the further understanding of homosexual women. *J. Amer. Psychoanal. Assn.*, 35:165-173.

Siegel, Elaine (1988). *Female Homosexuality: Choice Without Volition.* Hillsdale, NJ: The Analytic Press.

### XV. How do women and men treat female analysands?

Viederman, Milton (1976). The influence of the person of the analyst. *Psychoanal. Q.*, 45:231-249.

Person, Ethel (1983). Women in therapy: Therapist gender as a variable. *Int. Rev. Psycho-Anal.*, 10:193-204. Also in: *Between Analyst and Patient*, ed. H. Meyers. Hillsdale, NJ: The Analytic Press, 1986, pp. 193-212.

Liebert, Robert (1986). Transference and countertransference issues in the treatment of women by a male analyst. In: *Between Analyst and Patient*, ed. H. Meyers. Hillsdale, NJ: The Analytic Press, pp. 229-236.

Raphling, David and Chused, Judith (1988). Transference across gender lines. *J. Amer. Psychoanal. Assn.*, 36:77-104.

### XVI. The pregnant analyst: How are transference and countertransference affected?

Penn, Linda (1986). The pregnant therapist: Transference and counter-transference issues. In: *Psychoanalysis and Women: Contemporary Reappraisals*, ed. J. Alpert. Hillsdale, NJ: The Analytic Press, pp. 287-316.

Fenster, Sheri, Phillips, Suzanne, and Rapoport, Estelle (1986). *The Therapist's Pregnancy: Intrusion in the Analytic Space*. Hillsdale, NJ: The Analytic Press.

Lax, Ruth (1969). Some considerations about transference and counter-transference manifestations evoked by the analyst's pregnancy. *Int. J. Psycho-Anal.*, 50:363-371.

Imber, Ruth (1990). The avoidance of countertransference awareness in a pregnant analyst. *Contemp. Psychoanal.*, 26:223-236.

### XVII. What are the issues in treatment of patients who have experienced sexual assault, abuse, or incest?

Schuker, Eleanor (1979). Psychodynamics and treatment of sexual assault victims. *J. Amer. Acad. Psychoanal. Assn.*, 7:553-573.

Nadelson, Carol and Notman, Malkah (1979). Psychoanalytic considerations of the response to rape. *Int. Rev. Psycho-Anal.*, 6:97-103.

Shengold, Leonard (1979). Child abuse and deprivation: Soul murder. *J. Amer. Psychoanal. Assn.*, 27:533-559.

Ganzarain, Ramon and Buchele, Bonnie (1988). *Fugitives of Incest: A Perspective from Psychoanalysis and Groups*. New York: International Universities Press.

Levine, Howard (ed.)(1990a). *Adult Analysis and Childhood Sexual Abuse*. Hillsdale, NJ: The Analytic Press.

## XVIII. What is the relationship of feminism to psychoanalysis?

Chodorow, Nancy (1989). *Feminism and Psychoanalytic Theory*, New Haven, CT: Yale University Press.

Benjamin, Jessica (1986b). A desire of one's own: Psychoanalytic feminism and intersubjective space. In: *Feminist Studies/Critical Studies*, ed. T. De Lauretis. Bloomington: Indiana University Press, pp. 78-101.

Mitchell, Juliet (1974b). *Psychoanalysis and Feminism*. New York: Pantheon.

Kristeva, Julia (1974). *Revolution in Poetic Language*. New York: Columbia University Press, 1984.

# Author Index

Aaron, Ruth (1974). The analyst's emotional life during work. 573

Abarbanel, Janice (1983). The revival of the sibling experience during the mother's second pregnancy. 323

Abelin, Ernest (1971). The role of the father in the separation-individuation process. 103, 308

Abelin, Ernest (1980). Triangulation, the role of the father, and the origins of core gender identity during the rapprochement subphase. 113, 310

Abend, Sander (1984). Sibling love and object choice. 325

Abraham, Hilda (1956). A contribution to the problem of female sexuality. 348

Abraham, Hilda (1969). New aspects of the psychopathology of patients presenting for termination of pregnancy and abortion on psychoanalytic grounds. 248

Abraham, Karl (1916). The first pregenital stage of the libido. 22, 515

Abraham, Karl (1919). The applicability of psycho-analytic treatment to patients at an advanced age. 276

Abraham, Karl (1922). Manifestations of the female castration complex. 23, 400

Abraham, Karl (1923). An infantile theory of the origin of the female sex. 24

Abraham, Karl (1924). A short study of the development of the libido, viewed in the light of mental disorders. 24, 225, 333, 516

Abrams, Samuel and Shengold, Leonard (1974). The meaning of "nothing." 369

Adams-Silvan, Abby (1986). The active and passive fantasy of rape as a specific determinant in a case of acrophobia. 550

Agger, Eloise (1988). Psychoanalytic perspectives on sibling relationships. 325

Agoston, Tibor (1945). Some psychological aspects of prostitution: The pseudo-personality. 341

Alonso, Anne (1982). Leftover life to live: Issues of entitlement, power, and generativity. 286

Alpert, Judith (ed.) (1986). *Psychoanalysis and Women: Contemporary Reappraisals.* 68

Alpert, Judith and Spencer, Jody (1986). Morality, gender, and analysis. 68, 149

Altman, Leon (1977). Some vicissitudes of love. 231

Andreas-Salomé, Lou (1916). "Anal" und "Sexual." 22

Andreas-Salomé, Lou (1921). The dual orientation of narcissism. 23, 496

Anthony, E. James (1970). The reactions of parents to the oedipal child. 249

Anthony, E. James (1981). Shame, guilt, and the feminine self in psychoanalysis. 458

Anthony, E. James and Benedek, Therese (ed.) (1970). *Parenthood, Its Psychology and Psychopathology.* 249

Anthony, E. James and Kreitman, Norman (1970). Murderous obsessions in mothers toward their children. 250

Appelbaum, Ann (1988). Psychoanalysis during pregnancy: The effect of sibling constellation. 268, 326

Applegarth, Adrienne (1976). Some observations on work inhibitions in women. 142, 209

Applegarth, Adrienne (1986). Women and work. 216

Applegarth, Adrienne (1988). Origins of femininity and the wish for a child. 268

Arden, Margaret (1987). "A concept of femininity": Sylvia Payne's 1935 paper reassessed. 55

Auchincloss, Elizabeth and Michels, Robert (1989). The impact of middle age on ambitions and ideals. 296, 468

Bak, Robert (1968). The phallic woman: The ubiquitous fantasy in perversions. 405

Bak, Robert (1973). Being in love and object loss. 229

Baker, Susan (1980). Biological influences in human sex and gender. 87

Balint, Enid (1973). Technical problems in the analysis of women by a woman analyst: A contribution to the question "What does a woman want?" 572

Balint, Michael (1937). A contribution to the psychology of menstruation. 185

Balint, Michael (1947). On genital love. 226

Balint, Michael (1963). The younger sister and Prince Charming. 323, 442

Balsam, Rosemary (1989). The paternal possibility: The father's contribution to the adolescent daughter when the mother is disturbed and a denigrated figure. 182, 318, 590

Bank, Stephen and Kahn, Michael (1982). The Sibling Bond. 323, 545

Barglow, Peter and Schaefer, Margret (1976). A new female psychology? 61

Barglow, Peter and Schaefer, Margret (1979). The fate of the feminine self in normative adolescent regression. 172

Barker, Warren (1968). Reporter, Panel: Female sexuality. 357

Barnett, Marjorie (1966) Vaginal awareness in the infancy and childhood of girls. 101, 355

Barnett, Marjorie (1968). I can't versus he won't. 139, 358

Barnett, Rosalind (1984). The anxiety of the unknown—Choice, risk, responsibility: Therapeutic issues for today's adult women. 290

Barnett, Rosalind and Baruch, Grace (1978). Women in the middle years: Conceptions and misconceptions. 284

Barrett, Carol (1977). Women in widowhood. 283

Barrett, William (1939). Penis envy, urinary control, pregnancy fantasies, constipation. 97, 338

Bartemeier, Leo (1954). A psychoanalytic study of pregnancy in an 'as if' personality. 244

Baruch, Grace (1984). The psychological well-being of women in the middle years. 290

Baruch, Grace and Brooks-Gunn, Jeanne (ed.) (1984). Women in Midlife. 291

Bassen, Cecile (1988). The impact of the analyst's pregnancy on the course of analysis. 600

Bassin, Donna (1982). Woman's images of inner space: Data for expanded interpretative categories. 383, 460

Baudry, Francis (1983). The evolution of the concept of character in Freud's writings. 462

Baudry, Francis (1984). Character: A concept in search of an identity. 463

Becker, Ted (1974). On latency. 159

Beiser, Helen (1982). Styles of supervision related to child-analysis training and the gender of the supervisor. 576

Bell, Susan (1990). The medicalization of menopause. 299

Benedek, Therese (1950). Climacterium: A developmental phase. 277

Benedek, Therese (1952a). Studies in Psychosomatic Medicine. 188

Benedek, Therese (1952b). Infertility as a psychosomatic defense. 243

Benedek, Therese (1959). Parenthood as a developmental phase. 195, 245

Benedek, Therese (1960). The organization of the reproductive drive. 245, 350

Benedek, Therese (1970a). Fatherhood and providing. 307

Benedek, Therese (1970b). Motherhood and nurturing. 250

Benedek, Therese (1970c). Parenthood during the life cycle. 250

Benedek, Therese (1970d). The psychobiology of pregnancy. 251

Benedek, Therese (1973). Psychoanalytic Investigations: Selected Papers. 281

Benedek, Therese (1977). Ambivalence, passion and love. 231

Benedek, Elissa, Poznanski, Elva, and Mason, Sheila (1979). A note on the female adolescent's psychological reactions to breast development. 173

Benedek, Therese and Rubenstein, Boris (1939a,b). The Correlations between ovarian activity and psychodynamic processes. 185

Benjamin, Jessica (1980). The bonds of love: Rational violence and erotic domination. 483

Benjamin, Jessica (1986a). The alienation of desire: Women's masochism and ideal love. 316, 487

Benjamin, Jessica (1986b). A desire of one's own: Psychoanalytic feminism and intersubjective space. 388, 465,488

Benjamin, Jessica (1987). The decline of the Oedipus complex. 151, 508

Benjamin, Jessica (1988). *The Bonds of Love: Psychoanalysis, Feminism, and the Problem of Domination.* 71, 466, 490

Berezin, Martin (1969). Reporter, Panel: The theory of genital primacy in the light of ego psychology. 227

Berezin, Martin and Cath, Stanley (ed.) (1965). *Geriatric Psychiatry: Grief, Loss, and Emotional Disorders in the Aging Process.* 280

Bergler, Edmund (1951). Neurotic counterfeit sex. 344, 403

Bergman, Anni (1982). Considerations about the development of the girl during the separation-individuation process. 116

Bergman, Anni (1987). On the development of female identity: Issues of mother-daughter interaction during the separation-individuation process. 124, 465

Bergmann, Maria (1982). The female Oedipus complex. 147

Bergmann, Maria (1985). The effect of role reversal on delayed marriage and maternity. 215, 292

Bergmann, Maria (1988). On eating disorders and work inhibition. 219, 529

Bergmann, Martin (1971). Psychoanalytic observations on the capacity to love. 228

Bergmann, Martin (1980). On the intrapsychic function of falling in love. 233

Bergmann, Martin (1988). Freud's three theories of love in the light of later developments. 235

Berliner, Bernhard (1947). On some psychodynamics of masochism. 476

Bernay, Toni and Cantor, Dorothy (ed.) (1986). *The Psychology of Today's Woman: New Psychoanalytic Visions.* 69, 202

Bernay, Toni (1986). Reconciling nurturance and aggression: A new feminine identity. 202, 465

Bernheimer, Charles and Kahane, Claire (ed.) (1985) *In Dora's Case: Freud-Hysteria-Feminism.* 49

Bernstein, Anne (1989). Analysis of two adult female patients who had been victims of incest in childhood. 556

Bernstein, Anne (1990). The impact of incest trauma on ego development. 559

Bernstein, Anne and Warner, Gloria (1984). *Women Treating Women.* 68, 463

Bernstein, Anne and Warner, Gloria (1984). Treatment of women by women. 578

Bernstein, Doris (1979). Female identity synthesis. 146, 211, 455

Bernstein, Doris (1983). The female superego: A different perspective. 148

Bernstein, Doris (1990). Female genital anxieties, conflicts, and typical mastery modes. 127, 393, 469

Bernstein, Doris (1991a). The female Oedipal complex. 153, 320

Bernstein, Doris (1991b). Gender specific dangers in the female/female dyad in treatment. 595

Bernstein, Isidor (1976). Masochistic reactions in a latency-age girl. 160, 481

Bernstein, Isidor (1983). Masochistic pathology and feminine development. 485

Bernstein, Isidor (1988). A woman's fantasy of being unfinished: Its relation to Pygmalion, Pandora, and other myths. 390, 509

Colarusso, Calvin, Nemiroff, Robert, and Zuckerman, Susan (1981). Female midlife issues in prose and poetry. 286, 505

Colonna, Alice and Newman, Lottie (1983). The psychoanalytic literature on siblings. 324

Cooper, Arnold (1988). The narcissistic-masochistic character. 490

Corby, Nan and Zarit, Judy (1983). Old and alone: The unmarried in later life. 289

Dahl, Kirsten (1983). First class or nothing at all? Aspects of early feminine development. 120, 385

Dahl, Kirsten (1988). Fantasies of gender. 390

Dahl, Kirsten (1989.) Daughters and mothers: Oedipal aspects of the witch-mother. 152

Dalsimer, Katherine (1979). From preadolescent tomboy to early adolescent girl: An analysis of Carson McCullers's "The Member of the Wedding." 173

Dalsimer, Katherine (1982). Female adolescent development: A study of "The Diary of Anne Frank." 178

Dalsimer, Katherine (1986a). Early adolescence: The Prime of Miss Jean Brodie. 180

Dalsimer, Katherine (1986b). *Female Adolescence: Psychoanalytic Reflections on Literature.* 180, 508

Dalsimer, Katherine (1986c). Late adolescence: Persuasion. 181

Dalsimer, Katherine (1986d). Middle adolescence: Romeo and Juliet. 181

Daly, Claude (1935). The menstruation complex in literature. 185

Daly, Claude (1943). The role of menstruation in human phylogenesis and ontogenesis. 186

Datan, Nancy (1990). Aging into transitions: Cross-cultural perspectives on women at midlife. 300

De Cereijido, Fanny Blanck (1983). A study on feminine sexuality. 386

Decker, Hannah (1990). *Freud, Dora and Vienna 1900.* 52

De Folch, T. Eskelinen, Adroer, S., Oliva, M, and Tous, J. (1984). Hysteric's use and misuse of observation. 464

DeFries, Zira (1978). Political lesbianism and sexual politics. 411

DeFries, Zira (1979). A comparison of political and apolitical lesbians. 412

De Goldstein, Raquel Zak (1984). The dark continent and its enigmas. 387

Delaney, Janice, Lupton, Mary, and Toth, Emily (1988). *The Curse: A Cultural History of Menstruation.* 192

De Monchy, Rene (1952). Oral components of the castration complex. 99, 346

Deutsch, Helene (1925a). The psychology of women in relation to the function of reproduction. 26, 95, 240, 333

Deutsch, Helene (1925b). The menopause: Psychoanalysis of the sexual functions of women. 26, 276, 334

Deutsch, Helene (1930). The significance of masochism in the mental life of women. 30, 335, 473

Deutsch, Helene (1932). On female homosexuality. 31, 401

Deutsch, Helene (1944, 1945). *The Psychology of Women: A Psychoanalytic Interpretation,* Vol. 1 and 2. 39, 98, 164, 243, 497, 157, 187

Deutsch, Helene (1944a). Eroticism: The feminine woman. 340, 437

Deutsch, Helene (1944b). Feminine masochism. 475

Deutsch, Helene (1944c). Feminine passivity. 341, 438

Deutsch, Helene (1944d). Homosexuality. 402

Deutsch, Helene (1944e). The "active" woman: The masculinity complex. 340, 438

Deutsch, Helene (1945a). Epilogue: The climacterium. 277

Deutsch, Helene (1945b). The psychology of the sex act. 341

Deutsch, Helene (1960). Frigidity in women. 350

Deutsch, Helene (1967). *Selected Problems of Adolescence: With Special Emphasis on Group Formation.* 168

Sours, John (1980). *Starving to Death in a Sea of Objects: The Anorexia Nervosa Syndrome.* 524

Sperling, Melitta (1949). The role of the mother in psychosomatic disorders in children. 519

Sperling, Melitta (1968). Trichotillomania, trichophagy, and cyclic vomiting: A contribution to the psychopathology of female sexuality. 361, 406, 520

Sperling, Melitta (1970). The clinical effects of parental neurosis on the child. 253

Sperling, Melitta (1973). Conversion hysteria, conversion symptoms: Revision of concepts. 449, 521

Spiegel, Nancy (1967). An infantile fetish and its persistence into young womanhood: Maturational stages of a fetish. 405

Spiegel, Rose (1966). The role of father-daughter relationships in depressive women. 168, 307

Spieler, Susan (1984). Preoedipal girls need fathers. 315

Spieler, Susan (1986). The gendered self: A lost maternal legacy. 123

Spitz, Rene (1952). Authority and masturbation: Some remarks on a bibliographical investigation. 346

Spitz, Rene and Wolf, Katherine (1949). Autoerotism. 98, 342

Sprince, Marjorie (1962). The development of a preoedipal partnership between an adolescent girl and her mother. 101, 167

Spruiell, Vann (1979). Alterations in the ego-ideal in girls in mid-adolescence. 175

Steele, Brandt (1990). Some sequelae of the sexual maltreatment of children. 564

Stein, Martin (1969). The problem of character theory. 446

Stein, Yehoyakim (1988). Some reflections on the inner space and its contents. 271, 391

Stekel, Wilhelm (1926). *Frigidity in Woman in Relation to Her Love Life.* 334

Sterba, Edith (1941). An important factor in eating disturbances of childhood. 517

Stern, Gloria and Auchincloss, Elizabeth (1984). Reporters, Symposium: The public and private woman. 579

Sternschein, Irving (1973). Reporter, Panel: The experience of separation-individuation in infancy and its reverberation through the course of life: Maturity, senescence, and sociological implications. 282 , 502

Stoller, Robert (1968a). *Sex and Gender: On the Development of Masculinity and Femininity.* 60, 81

Stoller, Robert (1968b). The sense of femaleness. 102, 361

Stoller, Robert (1972). The "bedrock" of masculinity and femininity: Bisexuality. 367

Stoller, Robert (1973a). The impact of new advances in sex research on psychoanalytic theory. 369

Stoller, Robert (1973b). *Splitting.* 408

Stoller, Robert (1974). Facts and fancies: An examination of Freud's concept of bisexuality (1973). 46, 371, 409

Stoller, Robert (1975a). *Perversion: The Erotic Form of Hatred.* 410

Stoller, Robert (1975b). *Sex and Gender: The Transsexual Experiment.* 85, 410

Stoller, Robert (1976a). Primary femininity. 64, 86, 110, 378

Stoller, Robert (1976b). Sexual excitement. 378

Stoller, Robert (1979). *Sexual Excitement: Dynamics of Erotic Life.* 380

Stoller, Robert (1985). *Observing the Erotic Imagination.* 420

Stolorow, Robert and Frank Lachmann (1980). *Psychoanalysis of Development Arrests: Theory and Treatment.* 415, 504, 544

Stolorow, Robert and Lachmann, Frank (1982). Early loss of the father: A clinical case. 313

Stone, Michael (1980). Traditional psychoanalytic characterology reexamined in the light of constitutional and cognitive differences between the sexes. 88, 458

Strouse, Jean (1974). *Women and Analysis.* 57, 61

Stueve, Ann and O'Donnell, Lydia (1984). The daughter of aging parents. 292

Sugar, Max (1979a). Developmental issues in adolescent motherhood. 176

# Subject Index

462, 477

**E**

Eating disorders 513-534
    aggression and 518, 520, 530, 533
    ambivalence and 520, 534
    anxiety and 523, 533
    autonomy and 522, 524
    compromise formation in 516-517,
        528-529
    conflict in 532, 534
    cultural factors in 518, 521, 526, 533
    defense in 512-513, 518, 524-525,
        529, 531-533
    depression and 518, 521-522
    guilt and 525, 532
    masochism and 519, 532
    object relations in 522, 526-528, 532
    regression in 517-519, 521-524, 529,
        532
    technical issues of 279, 518-519,
        521-522, 524-525, 528, 532-533
    *See also* Anorexia; Bulimia
Ego
    boundary 65, 111, 374, 526
    integration 167, 211, 337
    *See also sub* Instinct; Splitting
Ego development 37, 46, 67, 74-75, 92,
        96, 105, 111, 124, 129, 140-141,
        161-168, 189, 205, 227-228, 245,
        250, 252, 315, 325, 345, 405-406,
        412, 434-435, 447, 466, 483, 515,
        537, 561
    gender differences in 36, 167, 201,
        375, 383
Ego functions 45, 48, 73, 126, 196, 219,
        233, 248, 279, 314, 341, 348,
        353, 365, 390, 414, 418, 421,
        426, 437, 439, 449, 462, 474,
        476-477, 497, 507, 526, 530-532,
        542, 547, 556, 559, 570-573
    differentiating 104-106, 113, 119,
        366, 377, 391, 393-395, 480, 499
    integrating 560
    reality testing 377, 544, 549, 553,
        563, 569, 572
    *See also* Symbolization
Ego-ideal
    conflict 216-217, 232, 256, 278

feminine 129, 137-138, 142, 210,
    268, 318, 528
maternal 126, 139, 260, 485, 505,
    511
Ego psychology 120, 215, 217, 228, 236,
    299, 301, 364, 403, 404, 424,
    492, 499, 507
Empathy 151, 168, 177, 230, 302, 463,
    464, 469, 509, 549, 574
    analytic 587, 589, 594
    bisexual 207
    failure of 123, 502, 507, 563
Empty-nest syndrome 291, 295
Envy *See* Penis envy; *sub* Childbirth;
        Father; Motherhood
Erotism 26, 96, 126, 354
    anal 11, 13, 55, 145, 154, 240, 246,
        493-494
    defensive use of 416, 419-420, 423,
        445, 536, 539, 563
    oral 28, 36, 229, 400
    *See also* Autoerotism; *sub* Fantasy
Exhibitionism 106, 112, 114, 124, 320,
    405, 408, 417, 573
Externalization 48, 171, 207, 254, 394,
    404, 454, 527

**F**

Fantasy
    beating 14, 322, 358, 405, 472, 474,
        478-480, 483, 484, 486, 487, 489,
        493, 546
    development of 13, 47, 54, 106, 161,
        369, 449, 543, 550
    erotic 340-342, 359, 367, 372-374,
        380, 392, 437, 523-524, 541,
        556-557
    family romance 162
    function of 12, 60, 173, 237, 332,
        369, 415-417, 459, 554, 556, 587
    masochistic 127, 142, 337, 370, 392,
        412, 451, 472, 474, 478-479,
        481-482, 484-485
    merger 235, 418, 534
    oedipal 31, 133, 152, 215, 255, 305,
        370, 482, 544, 551, 573
    oral 265, 366, 447, 520, 532, 534
    phallic 394, 426
    phallic woman 11-12, 39, 405, 425,

243, 253, 265, 273, 449, 521,
528, 532 *See also sub* Object
relations

R

Rage 114, 255, 265, 531, 543, 551, 561,
600, 601
at mother 65, 107, 120, 154, 154,
211, 215, 412, 474, 493
narcissistic 504, 507
Rape 59, 410, 538-539, 541-542, 549-550,
554-556
fantasy 504, 549, 553
*See also* Sexual abuse
Rapprochement phase 116, 126, 129, 323,
482, 563
conflict 124, 130-131, 153, 270-273,
389, 392, 470, 488
crisis 115, 119, 127, 205
Reaction formation 134, 401, 433, 435,
462, 477, 533, 539, 599
Reality
adaptation to 23, 80, 150, 164, 179,
198, 279, 285, 443, 476, 499
and fantasy, confusion of 192, 542,
558, 563-564, 573
contact in therapy 570
sense of 227, 248, 344, 364, 418,
551, 559, 562
Reality principle 351, 478
Reality testing *See sub* Ego functions
Receptivity 28, 36, 118, 141, 172, 186,
244-245, 251, 262, 439, 462, 482
Regression 24, 99, 184, 203, 210, 218,
222, 341, 352, 365, 443, 479,
493, 522, 526
technical issues of 587, 589, 594-595,
599 *See also sub* Transference
*See also sub* Adolescence; Eating
disorders; Pregnancy; Sexual
abuse
Repression 11, 17-18, 30, 33, 48, 65, 75,
115, 135, 155, 158, 171-172, 175,
181, 187, 231-232, 262, 276, 296,
310, 317, 355, 362, 374, 396,
433, 440, 450, 452, 472, 479,
526, 533, 540, 544, 548, 552, 556
Reproduction
female capacity for 26, 84, 161, 189,

374
functions of 36, 39, 89, 164,
186, 225, 245, 255, 262, 352-354,
360, 383, 416, 476, 498
hormones in 243, 245-246, 257
motivation for 68-69, 265, 267,
270-271
social 258
*See also* Fertility; Menopause; Motherhood; Pregnancy; Sterility
Resistance 73, 167, 192, 279, 296, 401,
462, 556-561, 572, 576-577,
581-582, 587-589, 595, 599,
601-602
countertransference 592
transference 374, 511, 533, 568-570
Role *See* Feminine role; Gender role;
Gender role identity; Role
reversal; *sub* Conflict;
Parenthood; Work(ing)
Role reversal 215, 600

S

Sadism 28, 186, 405, 432, 472-473, 519,
531
oral 36, 336, 354-355, 400, 402, 527
Sadomasochism 50, 164, 406, 426, 482,
489, 545-546, 558-559 *See also*
*sub* Fantasy; Mother-daughter
relation; Transference
Schizophrenia 218, 418, 439, 455, 495,
499, 546
Screen memory 538, 551
Secondary process 55, 116-117
Seduction 348, 402, 419-420, 441, 504,
537, 539, 543, 550, 556, 559, 562
theory 453, 536-537, 548, 554, 556
*See also* Rape; Sexual abuse
Self
-assertion 448, 457, 466, 501
-awareness 178, 203, 529, 577
cohesion of 125, 180, 500, 504,
506-507, 511
-concept *See* Self-image
-confidence *See* Self-esteem
-constancy 215, 418
-control 126, 150, 161, 364, 559
-definition 80, 116, 121, 310, 490,
492, 553